Design & Analysis of Algorithms

Fifth Edition

DR. GAJENDRA SHARMA

KHANNA BOOK PUBLISHING CO. (P) LTD.

Publisher of Engineering and Computer Books

4C/4344, Ansari Road, Darya Ganj, New Delhi-110002

Phone : 011-23244447-48 **Mobile:** +91-9910909320

E-mail : contact@khannabooks.com

Website : www.khannabooks.com

Dear Readers,

To prevent the piracy, this book is secured with HIGH SECURITY HOLOGRAM on the front title cover. In case you don't find the hologram on the front cover title, please write us to at contact@khannabooks.com or whatsapp us at +91-99109 09320 and avail special gift voucher for yourself.

Specimen of Hologram on front Cover title:

Moreover, there is a SPECIAL DISCOUNT COUPON for you with EVERY HOLOGRAM.

How to avail this SPECIAL DISCOUNT:

Step 1: Scratch the hologram
Step 2: Under the scratch area, your "coupon code" is available
Step 3: Logon to www.khannabooks.com
Step 4: Use your "coupon code" in the shopping cart and get your copy at a special discount
Step 5: Enjoy your reading!

ISBN: 978-93-82609-43-8

Design & Analysis of Algorithms
yb Gajendra Sharma

First Edition: 2003
Third Edition: 2008
Fourth Edition: 2016
Fifth Edition: 2023
Reprint Edition: 2026

To view complete list of books, Please scan the QR Code:

Published by:
Khanna Book Publishing Co. (P) Ltd.
CIN: U22110DL1998PTC095547

Visit us at: **www.khannabooks.com**
Write us at: **contact@khannabooks.com**

Printed in Bharat.

Dedicated to

My wife Shruti
&
Two Lovely Daughters
Khushi (Urvi) & Prisha

PREFACE

The study of algorithms is at the very heart of computer science. In recent years numerous advancements have been made in the field of algorithms, which includes development of faster algorithms like Fast Fourier Transform, to starting discoveries of natural number problems for which algorithms are inefficient. These results have kindled considerable interest in the study of algorithms. The intent of this book is to bring together the results and applications of design and analysis of algorithms in the easiest form.

THE SCOPE OF THE BOOK

The book covers all aspects of algorithm design in wide range of chapters. Topics are concise and constains lot of solved numericals in each chapter elaborating the concepts. Chapter 2 gives initial introduction for analysis design of algorithms. Chapter 2 which is core of all chapters having more than 50 solved examples describes the asymptotic function and their growth in great details, Chapter 3 gives some summation formulas and Chapter 4 again discusses the method for solving recurrences. Chapter 5-6 gives some mathematical foundations which is very much needed to study the algorithms. Chapter 7-9 gives detailed description of heaps and quicksort and linear time sorting algorithms. Chapter 10 gives medians and order statistics.

Chapter 11 introduces basic data structures like Stacks, Queues, Linked List, Doubly linked list, Circular linked list, Priority Queues, Post fix evaluation etc.

Chapter 12 covers different Hashing techniques, Chapter 13 is of utmost importance with BS Tree and 2, 4 Trees covered in detail. Chapter 14, 15, 16 covers advanced trees like Optimal Binary Search Tree, AVL Trees and RB-Trees respectively. Chapter 17 gives Augmenting Data Structures, Chapter 18-19 emphasizes on practical problems of Dynamic Programming and greedy algorithms. Chapter 20 gives Amortized analysis.

Chapter 21-23 gives B-Trees, B* Tree B^+ tree, Binomial Trees, Fibonacci Heaps, Binomial Heaps etc.

Chapter 24-30 introduces data structures for disjoint sets, Graph algorithms like BFS/DFS, topological sorting, strongly connected components, Transpose of graph, Back Tracking, Minimum Spanning Tree, Dijkstras algorithm, Bellman Ford, DAG, Floyd Warshall, Johnson's algorithm. Maximum flow, Cuts, Augmented paths and many more related graph algorithms and concepts in broader way with lot of numerical problems based on their concepts have been solved.

Chapter 32-36 introduces arithmetic circuits, parallel algorithms, Straseen's matrix multiplication algorithms, FFT, DFT, GCD, Extended Euclid's algorithm, chinese remainder theorem. RSA public key cryptographic concepts and algorithms. Chapter 37 discusses string matching algorithm like Rabin Karp, Knuth Morris Pratt, Bin Packing and simpler algorithms in greater detail.

Chapter 38 introduces Convex Hull, Graham Scan's algorithm. Chapter 39-42 emphasizes on NP-completeness and Approximation algorithms, Non Deterministic algorithms.

THE USE OF THE BOOK

This book is intended as a first course in the design and analysis of algorithms. The emphasis is on ideas and ease of understanding. The book contains lot of solved numericals based on concepts and algorithms to give students a good hands on experience. The book is self contained and require no specific background in mathematics or programming languages.

This book is of great use to **graduate and post graduate students in computer science at M. Tech, B. Tech and MCA level**. It is normally taught as one semester course but may be stretched to two semesters in few universities.

Numerous exercises are provided at the end of each chapter to provide students and instructors with wide range of homework problems.

ACKNOWLEDGEMENTS

This book has been written after lot of dedication and hardwork through several years. This book was my obsession, since I was a student. Motivation and contribution of many people while writing this book cannot be left unnoticed.

I would like to thank many people who inspired me to write this book. First I am thankful to Prof. S.B. Singh (G.B. Pant Agriculture and Technical University, Pantnagar) who inspired me to write the book, then I am thankful to Prof. Rajeev Wankar (Hyderabad Central University) who with lot of his experience on this topic boosted my morale to write this book. I am also thankful to Prof. S.K. Samdarshi (Jharkhand Central University) who has given me several tips and guidance, then I am also thankful to Dr. Ashok Kumar (Scientist Harvard University, U.S.A.) for his suggestions.

I am also thankful to my students of B. Tech and MCA, who worked with me while solving few problems included in this book.

Not to forget, this book has been possible with great sacrifice of my wife and loving daughters whose time I stole for writing this book.

I am also thankful to Khanna Book Publishying Co. (P) Ltd. for showing keen interest in publishing the third edition of the book. I am also thankful to Stride Computers for the typing work and making this book more presentable.

CONTENTS

CONTENTS

1

INTRODUCTION

The word algorithm comes from the name of Persian author, Abu Jafar Mohammed Bin Musa al Khowarizmi (c. 625 A.D.), who wrote a text book on Mathematics. This word is of special significance in computer science., where "*algorithm*" refers to a word which can be used by computer for the solution of problem.

Algorithms are the ideas behind computer programs.

An algorithm is the thing which stays the same whether the program is in Pascal running on a Cray in New York or in BASIC running on a Macintosh in Kathmandu.

To be interesting, an algorithm has to solve a general, specified problem. An algorithmic problem is specified by describing the set of instances it must work on and what desired properties the output must have.

1.1 Algorithm

An algorithm is a finite set of instructions that if followed accomplishes a particular task.

Algorithm *(Euclids algorithm)*. Given two positive integers m and n find their greatest common divisor, that is, the largest positive integer that evenly divides both m and n.

E_1 [Find remainder]. Divide m by n and let r be the remainder, [where $0 \le r \le n$]

E_2 [Is it zero] if $r = 0$, the algorithm terminates; n is answer.

E_3 [Reduce]. Set $m \leftarrow n$, $n \leftarrow r$ and go back to step E_1.

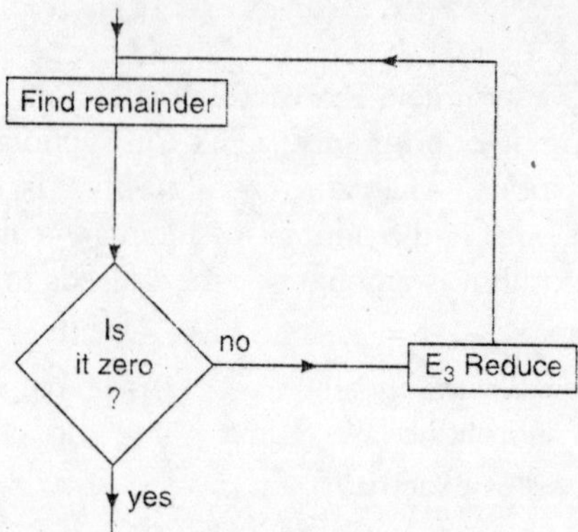

Fig. 1.1. Flowchart for algorithm E.

1.2 Pseudo Code Conventions

For writing any algorithm following pseudo codes have been used through out this book :

1. Proper identification should be followed
2. Looping constructs while, for, repeat-until if-then-else
3. The symbol ∇ and // indicates comment.
4. Left Arrow, ← is assignment operator.
5. Length [*A*] is length of Array.
6. *A*[*i* .. *j*] indicates array from *i* to *j*.
7. Arithmetic operators +, −, *, / are used.
8. ↔ for swapping.

Let us consider few simple algorithms.

1.2.1 Searching Problem

Input : A sequence of n numbers $A = < a_1, a_2, ..., a_n >$ and a value v.

Output : An index i such that $v = A[i]$ or NIL if v does not exist.

```
for i ← 1 to n
      if v = A[i] then
            return i
      else
            return NIL
```

1.3 Analyzing-Algorithms

For analyzing algorithm we assume a RAM model (Random Access Machine) and algorithm will be implemented as computer programs. In this, instructions are executed one after another, with no concurrent operations. Analyzing an algorithm is concerned of **space and time complexity.** Space complexity is the amount of memory it needs to run to completion. The time complexity of an algorithm is amount of time it needs to run to completion.

- Each "simple" operation (+, –, =, if, call) takes exactly 1 step.
- Loops and subroutine calls are *not* simple operations, but depend upon the size of the data and the contents of a subroutine. We do not want "sort" to be a single step operation.
- Each memory access takes exactly 1 step.

```
Sum (A, n)
    S ← 0
    for i ← 1 to n
    S ← S + A[i]
    return S
```

iterative algorithm for sum

```
RecSum (A, n)
    if (n ≤ 0) then return 0
    else return RecSum (A, n – 1) + A[n]
```

Space requirement

$$S_{sum} \le n + 3 \quad (\ n \text{ for } A[\ ],\ i,\ s,\ n)$$

So space requirements depends upon the number and size of input. Here length of Array is n, so total space taken is n and also three variables takes three space. Hence, $S_{sum} \le n + 3$.

Time Complexity

Total Running time of an algorithm depends upon the compilation and running time of algorithm but once compiled program can be run several times. So we are concerned only with the run time of algorithm, we can obtain some general formula for all arithmetic operations performed at run time given by

$$T_P(n) = C_1 \text{ Add } (n) + C_2 \text{ SUB } (n) + C_3 \text{ MULT } (n) + C_4 \text{ DIV } (n) + \ldots$$

where C_i's are cost and ADD(n), SUB(n) etc. are coresponding number of operations for respective operations.

1.3.1 Analysis of Insertion Sort

INSERTION-SORT (A){	COST	Times
for $j \leftarrow 2$ to length $[A]$	C_1	n
do key $\leftarrow A[j]$	C_2	$n-1$
$i \leftarrow j-1$	C_3	$n-1$
While ($i > 0$ and $A[i] >$ key){	C_4	$\Sigma_{j=2}^{n} k$
do $A[i+1] \leftarrow A[i]$	C_5	$\Sigma_{j=2}^{n} k-1$
$i \leftarrow i-1$}	C_6	$\Sigma_{j=2}^{n} k-1$
$A[i+1] \leftarrow$ key}	C_7	$n-1$

Total running time is given by,

$$T(n) = C_1 n + C_2(n-1) + C_3(n-1) + C_4 \sum_{j=2}^{n} k + C_5 \sum_{j=2}^{n} (k) - 1$$

$$+ C_6 \sum_{j=2}^{n} (k) - 1 + C_7(n-1) \qquad \ldots(1)$$

Here while loop runs k times for each j, where k is number of comparisons performed before the number is inserted at appropriate position.

We have $\displaystyle\sum_{j=2}^{n} k = \frac{n(n+1)}{2} - 1$

Therefore,

$$T(n) = C_1 n + C_2(n-1) + C_3(n-1) + C_4\left(\frac{n(n+1)}{2} - 1\right)$$

$$C_5\left(\left(\frac{n(n+1)}{2} - 1\right) - 1\right) + C_6\left(\left(\frac{n(n+1)}{2} - 1\right) - 1\right) + C_7(n-1)$$

Solving this we get

$$\left(\frac{C_4}{2} + \frac{C_5}{2} + \frac{C_6}{2}\right)n^2 + \left(C_1 + C_2 + C_3 + \frac{C_4}{2} - \frac{C_5}{2} - \frac{C_6}{2} + C_7\right)n - (C_2 + C_3 + C_4 + C_7)$$

This worst case running time can be expressed as $an^2 + bn + c$ which is quadratic order. Equation (1) is obtained by multiplying **each step** with its cost of single execution multiplied to number of times that step is executed e.g., in previous example, $C_1 ADD(n)$, C_1 is cost of doing one addition and ADD(n) is no. of additions performed.

Bestcase. Can be obtained **when array is sorted,** such that $k = 1$ and no comparisons are performed.

Therefore, $\displaystyle\sum_{n=2}^{n} 1 = n - 1$, for $k = 1$.

$\therefore$ $T(n)$ is of the form $an + b$ which is linear order.

1.3.2 Insertion Sort

This algorithm is like bunch of cards in hand kept in sequential order we insert new card by comparing with each card and put it at correct position.

e.g.,

7	6	5	1	2
6	7	5	1	2
5	6	7	1	2
1	5	6	7	2
1	2	5	6	7

Fig. 1.2 Operation of insertion sort on the array A = [7 6 5 1 2] position of index j is indicated by square.

Look at example in Fig. 1.2. Every time elements are compared to its previous elements and inserted at sorted position.

EXAMPLE 1.1 Recursive Algorithm Finds

```
          Rcount (A, n)
1.        count ← count + 1
2.        if (n ≤ 0) then
3.                count ← count + 1 :
4                 return 0
5.        else
6.                count ← count + 1
7.                return Rcount (A, n − 1) + A[n]
```

If $n = 0$ then step 1 and step 3 gets executed once,

If $n \neq 0$ then step 1 and step 2 gets executed once and step 6, 7 gets executed $n - 1$ times so recursive time complexity is given by relation,

$$T(n) = \begin{cases} 2 & \text{if} \quad n = 0 \\ 2 + T(n-1) & \text{if} \quad n > 0 \end{cases}$$

This can be solved as

$$\begin{aligned} T(n) &= 2 + T(n-1) \\ &= 2 + 2 + T(n-2) \\ &= 2(1 + 1 + \ldots n \text{ times}) + T(0) \end{aligned}$$

$$T(n) = 2n + 2$$

Similarly we calculate the time complexity for sum algorithm given in section 1.3 as below:

		Cost	Times
1.	$S \leftarrow 0$	C_1	1
2.	for $i \leftarrow 1$ to n do	C_2	$n + 1$
3.	$S \leftarrow S + A[i]$	C_3	$.n$
4.	return S	C_4	1

$$T(n) = C_1 . 1 + C_2 . (n+1) + C_3 . n + C_4 . 1$$
$$= (C_1 + C_2 + C_4) + (C_2 + C_3)n.$$
$$= (C_2 + C_3)n + (C_1 + C_2 + C_4)$$

This is of the form $an + b$, linear order.

1.4 Designing Algorithms

Rules for Algorithm Design

The secret to successful algorithm design, and problem solving in general, is to make sure you ask the right questions. Below, I give a possible series of questions for you to ask yourself as you try to solve difficult algorithm design problems:

1. Do I really understand the problem?
   (a) What exactly does the input consist of?
   (b) What exactly are the desired results or output?
   (c) Can I construct some examples small enough to solve by hand? What happens when I solve them?
   (d) Are you trying to solve a numerical problem? A graph algorithm problem? A geometric problem? A string problem? A set problem? Might your problem be formulated in more than one way? Which formulation seems easiest?
2. Can I find a simple algorithm for the problem?
   (a) Can I solve my problem exactly by searching all subsets or arrangements and picking the best one?
      (i) If so, why am I sure that this algorithm always gives the correct answer?
      (ii) How do I measure the quality of a solution once I construct it?
      (iii) Does this simple, slow solution run in polynomial or exponential time?
      (iv) If I can't find a slow, *guaranteed* correct algorithm, am I sure that my problem is well defined enough to permit a solution?
   (b) Can I solve my problem by repeatedly trying some heuristic rule, like picking the biggest item first? The smallest item first? A random item first?
      (i) If so, on what types of inputs does this heuristic rule work well? Do these correspond to the types of inputs that might arise in the application?
      (ii) On what types of inputs does this heuristic rule work badly ? If no such examples can be found, can I show that in fact it always works well?
      (iii) How fast does my heuristic rule come up with an answer ?

(a) Are there special cases of this problem I know how to solve exactly ?
   (i) Can I solve it efficiently when I ignore some of the input parameters ?
   (ii) What happens when I set some of the input parameters to trivial values, such as 0 or 1 ?
   (iii) Can I simplify the problem to create a problem I can solve efficiently? How simple do I have to make it?

(d) If I can solve a certain special case, why can't this be generalised to a wider class of inputs?

4. Which of the standard algorithm design paradigms seem most relevant to the problem?
   (a) Is there a set of items which can be sorted by size or some key? Does this sorted order make it easier to find what might be the answer?
   (b) Is there a way to split the problem in two smaller problems, perhaps by doing a binary search, or a partition of the elements into big and small, or left and right? If so, does this suggest a divide-and-conquer algorithm?
   (c) Are there certain operations being repeatedly done on the same data, such as searching it for some element, or finding the largest/smallest remaining element? If so, can I use a data structure of speed up these queries, like hash tables or a heap/priority queue?
5. Am I still stumped?
   (a) Why don't I go back to the beginning of the list and work through the questions again? Do any of my answers from the first trip change on the second?

Based on these queries, let us discuss two approaches :

1. Incremental Approach. In this approach every time we increase the index to insert the element in proper place, e.g., selection sort.

2. Divide And conquer Approach

Divide the problem into a number of subproblems.

Conquer the subproblems by solving them recursively, if the subproblem sizes are small enough, however, just solve the subproblems in a straight forward manner.

Combine the solutions to the subproblems into the solution for the original approach.

e.g., merge sort uses this approach.

1.4.1 Incremental Approach Example

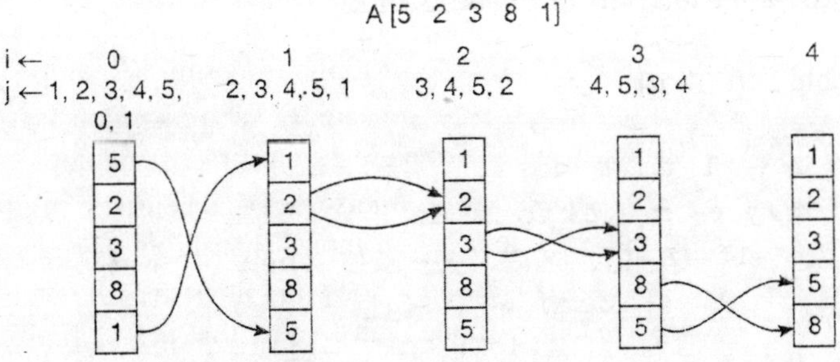

Fig. 1.3. Selection sort illustration on A [5 2 3 8 1].

Selection Sort

Selection Sort (A, n)	Cost	Time
For $i \leftarrow 1$ to n do	C_1	$n+1$
$j \leftarrow i$	C_2	n
for $k \leftarrow i+1$ to n do	C_3	$\sum_{j=1}^{n} k$
If $A[k] < A[j]$ then	C_4	$\sum_{j=1}^{n} k$
$j \leftarrow k$	C_5	$\sum_{j=2}^{n} k-1$
temp $\leftarrow A[i]$	C_6	$\sum_{j=2}^{n} k-1$
$A[i] \leftarrow A[j]$	C_7	$\sum_{j=2}^{n} k-1$
$A[j] \leftarrow$ temp		

Time complexity is given by

$$T(n) = C_1(n+1) + C_2 n + C_3 \sum_{j=1}^{n} k + C_4 \sum_{j=1}^{n} k + C_5 \sum_{j=2}^{n} (k-1)$$

$$+ C_6 \sum_{j=1}^{n} (k-1) + C_7 \sum_{j=2}^{n} (k-1)$$

Taking help of previous example of section 1.3.1 this can be solved.

EXAMPLE 1.1 *Give the analysis of Bubble Sort algorithm.*

SOLUTION. Bubble Sort (A, n)

```
for i ← 1 to n do {
   for j ← n - 1 to i do {
         If (A [j] > A [j - 1]) then
              { temp ← A [j]
                    A[j] ← A[j - 1]
                    A[j - 1] ← temp
              }
         }
}
```

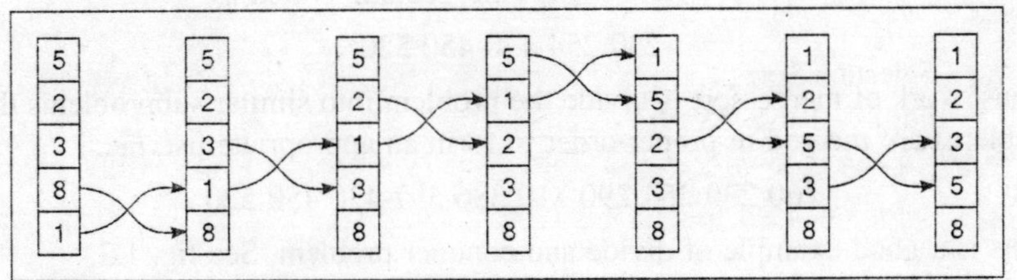

Fig. 1.4. Illustration of Bubble Sort on array A [5, 2, 3, 8, 1].

The number of comparisons is same in each case (best, average, worst)

$$\sum_{i=0}^{n-2} (n-1-i) = \frac{n(n-1)}{2} = O(n^2)$$

1.4.2 Divide and Conquer Example

EXAMPLE 1.2 Merge Sort

```
MERGE-SORT (A, P, r)
1.   if P < r
     then q ← ⌊(P + r)/2⌋
          MERGE-SORT (A, p, q)
          MERGE-SORT (A, q + 1, r)
          MERGE (A, p, q, r)
```

Here we have not defined MERGE, which merges the subproblem. If we have array

$A[1..10]$ = [310, 397, 386, 290, 160, 430, 230, 450, 520, 254].

Pictorially it can be viewed as follows :

Array is split into $A[1, .. 5]$ and $A[6..10]$

310 | 397 | 386 | 390 | 160, 430, 230. 450, 520, 254

↑ ↑

$A[1..5]$ Splitting

$A[1..5]$ can be sorted as,

310 397 | 386 | 290 | 160 |

↑ ↑

merged and sorted

310 386 397 | 290 | 160

↑ ↑

290 310 386 397 | 160

↑ ↑

160 290 310 386 397

↑ ↑

merged and sorted

Similarly, Array $A[6..10]$ can be split, merged and sorted as

230 254 430 450 520

Thus, work of merge-sort is divide the problem into similar subproblems then the smaller subproblems are merged in proper order to form an appropriate list, *i.e.*,

160 230 254 290 310 386 397 430 450 520

This is a good example of divide and conquer problem. See fig. 1.3.

Array spliting of merge sort (1, 10) can be given as

The node containing 1, 2, 3 represents merging of $A[1..2]$ and $A[3]$

If the time for merging operation is proportional to n then the computing time for merge sort is described by the recurrence relation

$$T(n) = \begin{cases} a & n = 1, \quad a \text{ is constant} \\ 2T(n/2) + cn & n > 1, \quad c \text{ is constant} \end{cases} \qquad ...(1.41)$$

This can be solved later on in chapter 4.

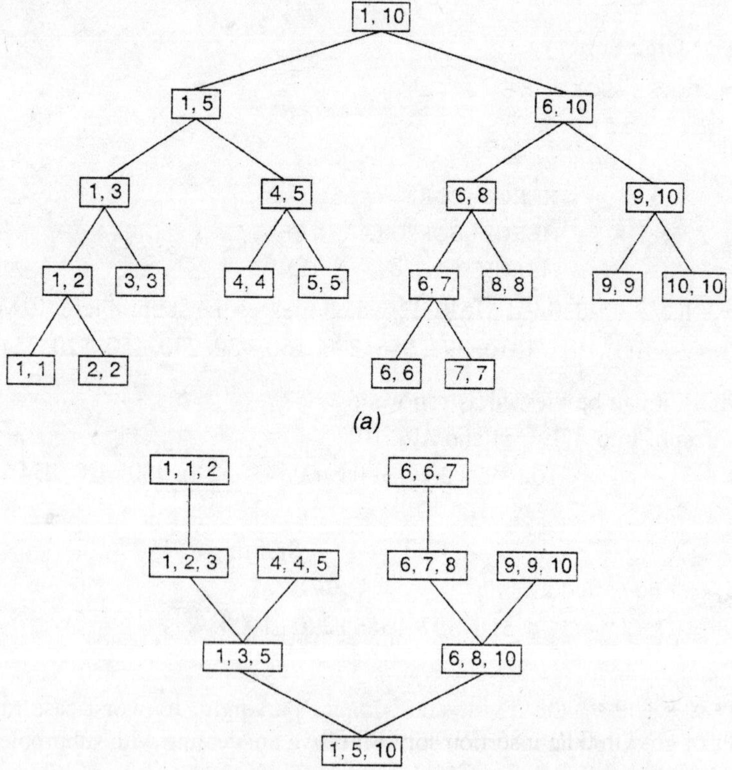

Fig. 1.5. (a) Partitioning (b). Tree Calls of Merge.

DEFINITION. Worst case complexity : Let D_n be the set of inputs of size n for the problem under considertion and I be an element of D_n. Let $t(I)$ be the no. of basic operation performed by the algorithm on input I. We define the function W by

$$W(n) = \max \{t(I) + I \varepsilon Dn\}$$

The function $W(n)$ is called the worst-case complexity of the algorithm. $W(n)$ is the maximum no. of basic operations performed by the algorithm on any input of size n.

DEFINITION. Average case complexity : Let $Pr(I)$ be the probability that I input occurs. Then the average behaviour of the algorithm is defined as

$$A(n) = \sum_{I \in Dn} Pr(I)\, t(I).$$

where $t(I)$ is defined as above.

Best, Worst, and Average-Case

The *worst case complexity* of the algorithm is the function defined by the maximum number of steps taken on any instance of size n.

The *best case complexity* of the algorithm is the function defined by the minimum number of steps taken on any instance of size n.

The *average-case complexity* of the algorithm is the function defined by an average number of steps taken on any instance of size n.

Each of these complexities defines a numerical function—time vs. size! as shown in Fig. 1.6.

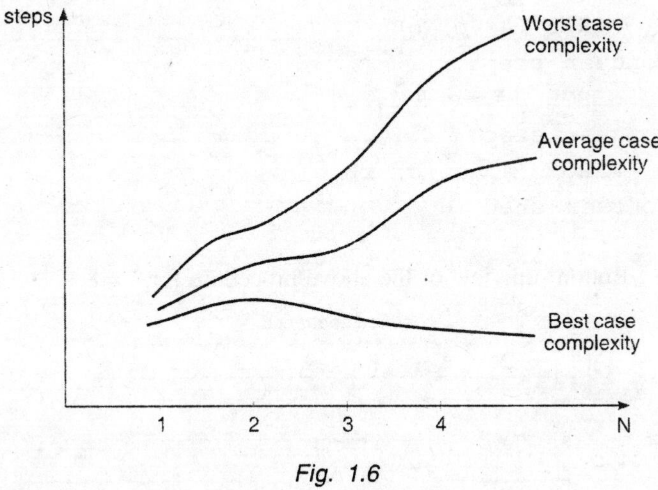

Fig. 1.6

1.4.3 Merge Sort

Merge sort is based on the divide-and-conquer paradigm. Its worst-case running time has a lower order of growth than insertion sort. Since we are dealing with subproblems, we state each subproblem as sorting a subarray $A[p \ldots r]$. Initially, $p = 1$ and $r = n$, but these values change as we recurse through subproblems.

To sort $A[p \ldots r]$:

1. **Divide Step :** If a given array A has zero or one element, simply return; it is already sorted. Otherwise, split $A[p \ldots r]$ into two subarrays $A[p \ldots q]$ and $A[q + 1 \ldots r]$, each containing about half of the elements of $A[p \ldots r]$. That is, q is the halfway point of $A[p \ldots r]$.

2. **Conquer Step :** Conquer by recursively sorting the two subarrays $A[p \ldots q]$ and $A[q + 1 \ldots r]$.
3. **Combine Step :** Combine the elements back in $A[p \ldots r]$ by merging the two sorted subarrays $A[p \ldots q]$ and $A[q + 1 \ldots r]$ into a sorted sequence. To accomplish this step, we will define a procedure MERGE (A, p, q, r).

Note that the recursion bottoms out when the subarray has just one element, so that it is trivially sorted.

Algorithm : Merge Sort

To sort the entire sequence $A[1 \ldots n]$, make the initial call to the procedure MERGE-SORT $(A, 1, n)$.

```
Merge-Sort (A, p, r)
  1. IF p < r                                              //
  Check for base case
  2. THEN q = FLOOR [(p + r) / 2]                          //
  Divide step
  3. MERGE (A, p, q)                                       //
  Conquer step
  4. MERGE (A, q + 1, r)                                   //
  Conquer step
  5. MERGE (A, p, q, r)                                    //
  Conquer step
```

Example : Bottom-up view of the above procedure for $n = 8$.

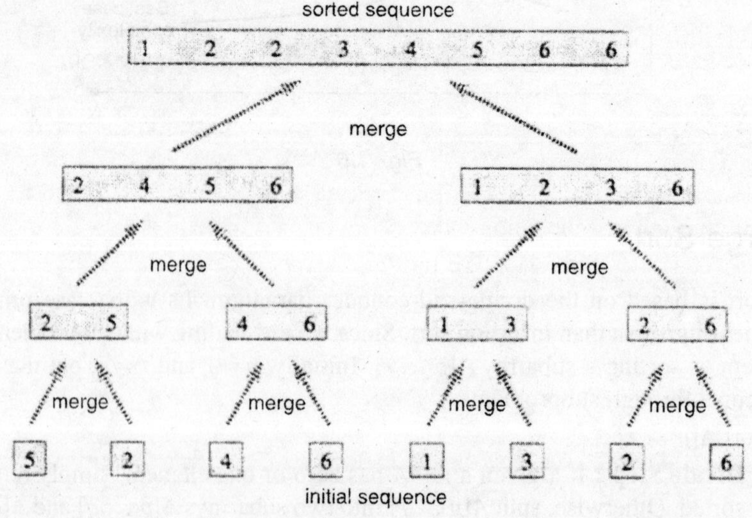

Fig. 1.7

Merging

What remains is the MERGE procedure. The following is the input and output of the MERGE procedure.

- **Input :** Array A and indices p, q, r such that $p \leq q \leq r$ and subarray $A[p \ldots q]$ is sorted and subarray $A[q + 1 \ldots r]$ is sorted. By restrictions on p, q, r, neither subarray is empty.
- **Output :** The two subarrays are merged into a single sorted subarray in $A[p \ldots r]$.

We implement it so that it takes $\Theta(n)$ time, where $n = r - p + 1$, which is the number of elements being merged.

Idea Behind Linear Time Merging

Think of two piles of cards, each pile is sorted and placed face-up on a table with the smallest cards on top. We will merge these into a single sorted pile, face-down on the table.

A basic step :

- Choose the smaller of the two top cards.
- Remove it from its pile, thereby exposing a new top card.
- Place the chosen card face-down onto the output pile.
- Repeatedly perform basic steps until one input pile is empty.
- Once one input pile empties, just take the remaining input pile and place it face-down onto the output pile.

Each basic step should take constant time, since we check just the two top cards. There are at most n basic step,s since each basic step removes one card from the input piles, and we started with n cards in the input piles. Therefore, this procedure should take $\Theta(n)$ time.

Now the question is do we actually need to check whether a pile is empty before each basic step?

The answer is no, we do not. Put on the bottom of each input pile a special sentinel card. It contains a special value that we use to simplify the code. We use ∞, since thawt's guaranteed to lose to any other value. The only way that ∞ cannot lose is when both piles have ∞ exposed as their top cards. But when that happens, all the nonsentinel cards have already been placed into the output pile. We know in advance that there are exactly $r - p + 1$ nonsentinel cards so stop once we have performaed $r - p + 1$ basic steps. Never a need to check for sentinels, since they will always lose. Rather than even counting basic steps, just fill up the output array from index p up through and including index r.

The pseudocode of the MERGE procedure is as follows :

```
MERGE
n1 ← q - p + 1
n2 ← r - q
Create arrays L[1 ... n1 + 1] and R[1 ... n2 + 1]
FOR i ← 1 TO n1
    DO L[i] ← A[p + i - 1]
FOR j ← 1 TO n2
```

```
    DO R[j] ← A[q + j]
L[n1 + 1] ← ∞
R[n2 + 1] ← ∞
i ← 1
j ← 1
FOR k ← p TO r
```

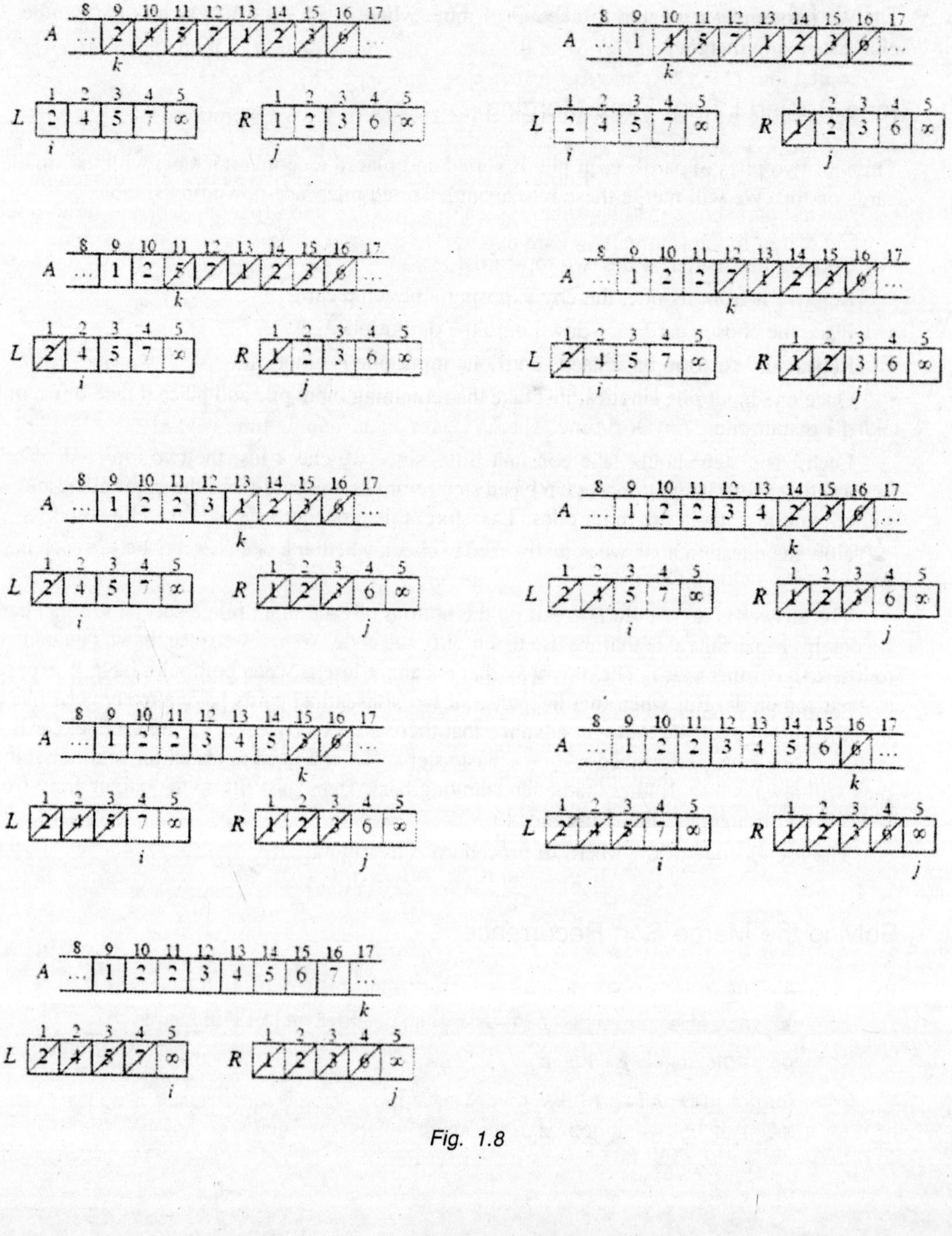

A (8–17): ... 2 4 5 7 1 2 3 6 ... (k at 9); L: 2 4 5 7 ∞ (i at 1); R: 1 2 3 6 ∞ (j at 1)

A (8–17): ... 1 4 5 7 1 2 3 6 ... (k at 10); L: 2 4 5 7 ∞ (i at 1); R: 1 2 3 6 ∞ (j at 2)

A (8–17): ... 1 2 5 7 1 2 3 6 ... (k at 11); L: 2 4 5 7 ∞ (i at 2); R: 1 2 3 6 ∞ (j at 2)

A (8–17): ... 1 2 2 7 1 2 3 6 ... (k at 12); L: 2 4 5 7 ∞ (i at 2); R: 1 2 3 6 ∞ (j at 3)

A (8–17): ... 1 2 2 3 1 2 3 6 ... (k at 13); L: 2 4 5 7 ∞ (i at 2); R: 1 2 3 6 ∞ (j at 4)

A (8–17): ... 1 2 2 3 4 2 3 6 ... (k at 14); L: 2 4 5 7 ∞ (i at 3); R: 1 2 3 6 ∞ (j at 4)

A (8–17): ... 1 2 2 3 4 5 3 6 ... (k at 15); L: 2 4 5 7 ∞ (i at 4); R: 1 2 3 6 ∞ (j at 4)

A (8–17): ... 1 2 2 3 4 5 6 6 ... (k at 16); L: 2 4 5 7 ∞ (i at 4); R: 1 2 3 6 ∞ (j at 5)

A (8–17): ... 1 2 2 3 4 5 6 7 ... (k at 17); L: 2 4 5 7 ∞ (i at 5); R: 1 2 3 6 ∞ (j at 5)

Fig. 1.8

```
13.        DO IF L[i] ≤ R[j]
14.              THEN A[k] ← L[i]
15.                    i ← i + 1
16.              ELSE A[k] ← R[j]
17.                    j ← j + 1
```

Example : A call of MERGE (*A*, 9. 12, 16). Read the following figure 1.8 row by row. That is how we have done in the class.

- The first part shows the arrays at the start of the "for $k \leftarrow p$ to r" loop, where $A[p \ldots q]$ is copied into $L[1 \ldots n_1]$ and $A[q+1 \ldots r]$ is copied into $R[1 \ldots n_2]$.
- Succeeding parts show the situation at the start of successive iterations.
- Entries in *A* with slashes have had their values copied to either *L* and *R* and have not had a value copied back in yet. Entries in *L* and *R* with slashes have been copied back into *A*.
- The last part shows that the subarrays are merged back into $A[p \ldots r]$, which is now sorted, and that only the sentinels (∞) are exposed in the arrays *L* and *R*.

Running Time

The first two for loops (that is, the loop in line 4 and the loop in line 6) take $\Theta(n_1 + n_2) = \Theta(n)$ time. The last for loop (that is, the loop in line 12) makes *n* iterations, each taking constant time, for $\Theta(n)$ time. Therefore, the total running time is $\Theta(n)$.

Analyzing Merge Sort

For simplicity, assume that *n* is a power of 2 so that each divide step yields two subproblems, both of size exactly $n/2$.

The base case occurs when $n = 1$.

When $n \geq 2$, time for merge sort steps :

- **Divide :** Just compute *q* as the average of *p* and *r*, which takes constant time, *i.e.*, $\Theta(1)$.
- **Conquer :** Recursively solve 2 subproblems, each of size $n/2$, which is $2T(n/2)$.
- **Combine :** MERGE on an *n*-element subarray takes $\Theta(n)$ time.

Summed together they give a function that is linear in *n*, which is $\Theta(n)$. Therefore, the recurrence for merge sort running time is

$$T(n) = \begin{cases} \Theta(1) & \text{if } n = 1, \\ 2T(n/2) + \Theta(n) & \text{if } n > 1. \end{cases}$$

Solving the Merge Sort Recurrence

By the master theorem, we can show that this recurrence has the solution

$$T(n) = \Theta(n \lg n)$$

Reminder : $\lg n$ stands for $\log_2 n$.

Compared to insertion sort [$\Theta(n^2)$ worst-case time], merge sort is faster. Trading a factor of *n* for a factor of $\lg n$ is a good deal. On small inputs, insertion sort may be faster. But for large enough inputs, merge sort will always be faster, because its running time grows more slowly than insertion sorts.

Recursion Tree

We can understand how to solve the merge-sort recurrence without the master theorem. There is a drawing of recursion tree, which shows successive expansions of the recurrence.

The following figure shows that for the original problem, we have a cost of cn, plus the two subproblems, each costing $T(n/2)$.

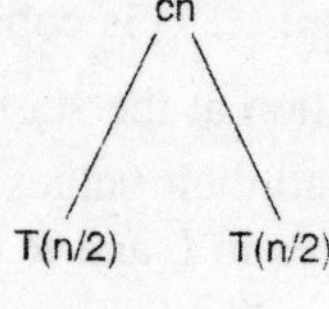

Fig. 1.9

The following figure shows that for each of the size $n/2$ subproblems, we have a cost of $cn/2$, plus two subproblems, each costing $T(n/4)$.

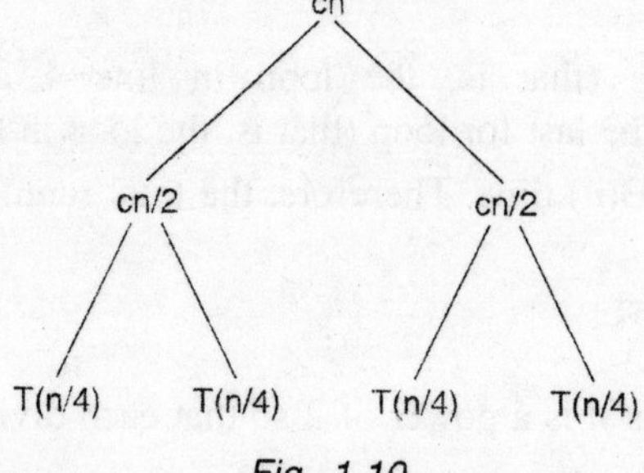

Fig. 1.10

The following figure tells to continue expanding until the problem sizes get down to 1.

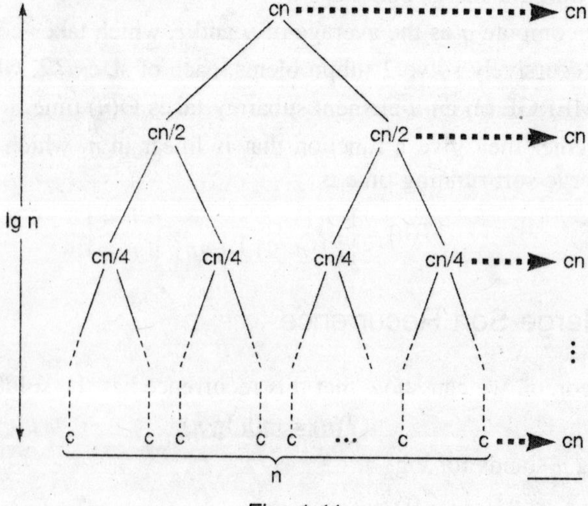

Fig. 1.11

In the above recursion tree, each level has cost cn.

- The top level has cost cn.
- The next level down has 2 subproblems, each contributing cost $cn/2$.
- The next level has 4 subproblems, each contributing cost $cn/4$.
- Each time we go down one level, the number of subproblems doubles but the cost per subproblem halves. Therefore, cost per level stays the same.

The height of this recursion tree is $\lg n$ and there are $\lg n + 1$ levels.

Mathematical Induction

We use induction on the size of a given subproblem n.

Base case : $n = 1$.

Implies that there is 1 level, and $\lg 1 + 1 = 0 + 1 = 1$.

Inductive Step : Our inductive hypothesis is that a tree for a problem size of 2^i has $\lg 2^i + 1 = i + 1$ levels. Because we assume that the problem size is a power of 2, the next problem size up after 2^i is $2^i + 1$. A tree for a problem size of $2^i + 1$ has one more level than the size-2^i tree implying $i + 2$ levels. Since $\lg 2^i + 1 = i + 2$, we are done with the inductive argument.

Total cost is sum of costs at each level of the tree. Since we have $\lg n + 1$ levels, each costing cn, the total cost is

$$cn \lg n + cn$$

Ignore low-order term of cn and constant coefficient c, and we have

$$\Theta(n \lg n)$$

which is the desired result.

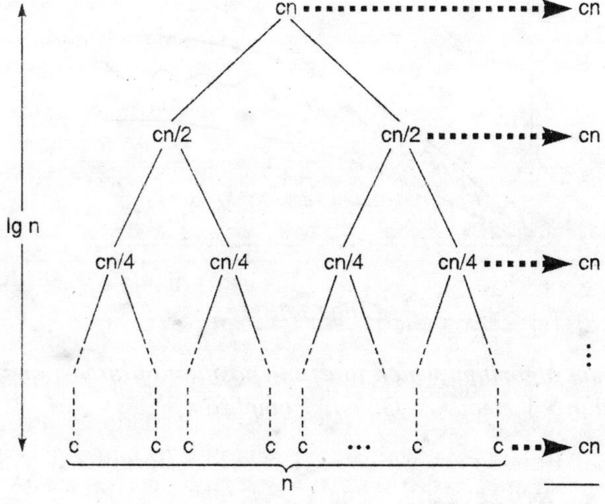

Fig. 1.12

EXAMPLE 1.2. *How can we modify almost any algorithm to have a good best-case running time ?*

SOLUTION. To improve the best case, all we have to do it to be able to solve one instance of each size efficiently. We could modify our algorithm to first test whether the input is the special instance we know how to solve, and then output the canned answer. For sorting, we can check if the values are already ordered, and if so output them. For the travelling salesman, we can check if the points lie on a line, and if so output the points in that order. The supercomputer people pull this trick on the linpack benchmarks.

Because it is so easy to cheat with the best case running time, we usually don't rely too much about it.

Because it is usually very hard to compute the average running time, since we must somehow average over all the instances, we usually strive to analyze the worst case running time.

The worst case is usually fairly easy to analyze and often close to the average or real running time.

Exact Analysis is Hard!

We have agreed that the best, worst and average case complexity of an algorithm is a numerical function of the size of the instances.

However, it is difficult to work with exactly because it is typically very complicated!

Thus it is usually cleaner and easier to talk about *upper and lower bounds* of the function. This is where the dreaded big O notation discussed in chapter 2 comes in!

Since running our algorithm on a machine which is twice as fast will effect the running times by a multiplicative constant of 2 - we are going to have to ignore constant factors anyway.

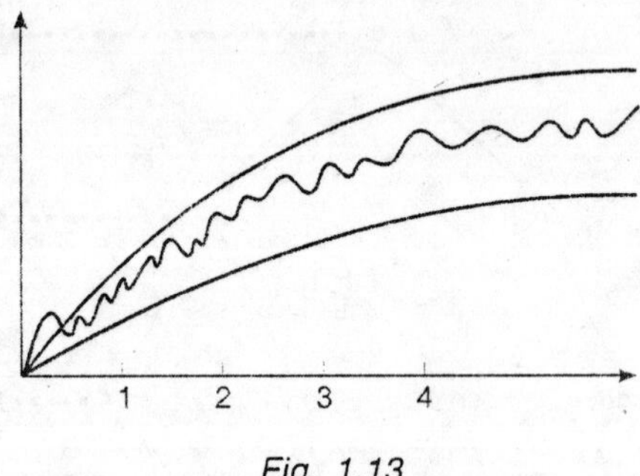

Fig. 1.13

EXAMPLE 1.3. *Write an algorithm which finds the position of largest and second largest element in an array A with $n > 1$ elements. Give its complexity.*

SOLUTION.

```
Find (A, N, l1 l2)
{ First ← A[1]
  Second ← A[2]
  l1 ← 1, l2 ← 2
  if (first < second) then
```

```
            first ↔ second
            l1 ← 2, l2 ← 1
      For k ← 3 to N do
      { if (First < A[k]) then
            {     second ← first
                  first ← A[k]
                  l2 ← l1, l1 ← k
            }
            else
                  if (second < A[k]) then
                  { second ← A[k]
                        l2 ← k
                  }
            }
            print l1, l2
      }
Complexity is O(n).
```

EXAMPLE 1.4. *Write an algorithm which finds the number of non-zero elements in an array A and give its complexity.*

SOLUTION.

```
k ← 0
for i ← 1 to n do
   for j ← 1 to n do
         if (A[i] [j] ≠ 0) then
               k ← k + 1
Complexity is O(n²)
```

EXAMPLE 1.5. *Write a recursive algorithm for finding factorial of n.*

SOLUTION.

```
Factorial (Fact, n)
   if n = 0 then
         fact ← 1, return
   Factorial (fact, n − 1)
         fact ← n * fact
         return fact.
```

EXAMPLE 1.6. *Write a recursive algorithm for Fibonacci Series.*

SOLUTION.

```
Fibonacci (FIB, n)
   if (n = 0 or n = 1) then
```

```
        FIB ← N, return FIB
    Fibonacci (FIBA, n – 2)
    Fibonacci (FIbB, n – 1)
    FIB ← FIBA + FIBB
    return FIB.
```

Towers of Hanoi

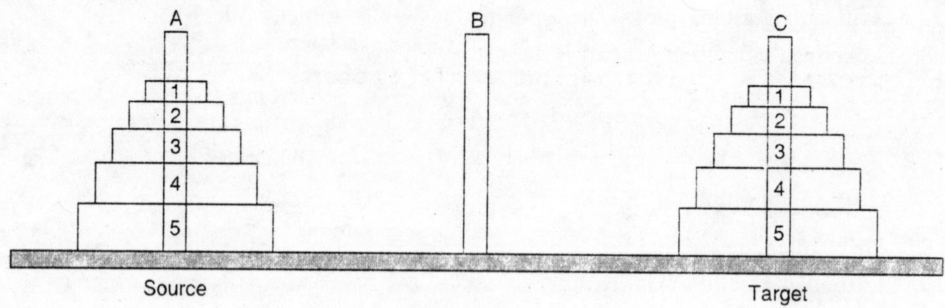

Fig. 1.14

- Only one disk moved at a time.
- At no time larger disk be placed on a smaller disk.

Problem is to move all disks from peg A to peg C, peg B may be used as intermediate vertex.

```
Tower (n, Beg, Aux, End)
  if (n = 1) then
      Beg ← End
      return
Tower (n – 1, Beg, End, Aux)
  Beg ← End
Tower (n – 1, Aux, Beg, End)
Return.
```

with $n = 4$ following shifting of disks takes place from pegs A, B, C in the direction of arrow.

$$A \to B, A \to C, B \to C, A \to B, C \to A, C \to B, A \to B, A \to C, B \to C, B \to A,$$
$$C \to A, B \to C, A \to B, A \to C, B \to C.$$

$T(n) = 2^n - 1$ moves are required

$\therefore\ T(n) = \theta(2^n)$.

EXERCISE

1. How can we modify an algorithm to have a good best-case running time?
2. Write an algorithm for matrix multiplication and find its running time.
3. Write an algorithm for towers of Honoi problem.
4. Devise an algorithm that inputs three integers and outputs them in non decreasing order?

5. Write an algorithm for factorial of a number?
6. Write an algorithm for fibonacci series.
7. Horner's rule is a means for evalulating a polynomial at a point x_0 using a minimum no of multiplications. If the polynomial is $P(x)$ where

$$P(x) = a_n x^n + a_{n-1} x^{n-1} + \ldots a_1 x + a_0.$$

Horner's rule is

$$P(x_0) = (\ldots(a_n x_0 + a_{n-1})x_0 + \ldots + a_1)x_0 + a_0$$

write an algorithm to evaluate a polynomial using Horner's rule.

8. Ackerman's function $A(m, n)$ is defined as follows :

$$A(m, n) = \begin{cases} n+1 & \text{if } m = 0 \\ A(m-1, 1) & \text{if } n = 0 \\ A(m-1, A(m, n-1)) & \text{otherwise} \end{cases}$$

write an algorithm for this.

9. Prove by induction that if $n \geq 10$, then $2^n > n^3$.
10. **Extended Euclid's Algorhthm** Given two positive integers m and n, compute their $gcd\ d$ and two integers a and b such that $am + bn = d$
11. Express $\frac{n^3}{1000} - 100n^2 - 100n + 3$ in terms of Θ-notation.
12. Write pseudocode for MERGE.
13. What is smallest value of n such that an algorithm whose running time is $100n^2$ runs faster than an algorithm whose running time 2^n on the same machine.
14. Show that $\frac{n}{k}$ sublists, each of length k, can be sorted by insertion sort in $\Theta(nk)$ worst case time.
15. Show that sublists can be merged in $\Theta(nlg\ (n/k))$ worst-case time.
16. Consider a function $f(x)$ that is defined by "if x is even, then $f(x) = \frac{x}{2}$; else $f(x) = f(f(3x + 1))$. Prove that $f(x)$ terminates for all integers x.
17. Discuss the effect on the running time of algorithm with input size.
18. What are the factors which affect the running time of an algorithm?
19. What are the different methodologies involved in the design of an algorithm?
20. Write an algorithm for declaring three points to be collinear.

❑❑❑

2

GROWTH OF FUNCTIONS

Asymptotic Notations is used to describe the running time of an algorithm. This shows the order of growth of function. We can map the time taken by an algorithm in terms of mathematical function. For example an algorithm taking n^2 *microseconds* can be thought of "of the order of n^2", as unit is constant. Asymptotic notations are mathematical way of representing "order of". We have many asymptotic notations like θ, O, Ω, ω, o described in coming sections.

2.1 Asymptotic Notations

θ-notation

For a *given* function $g(n)$, we denote $\theta(g(n))$, the set of functions as

$$\theta(g(n)) = \{ f(n) \text{ there exists the constants } C_1, C_2 \text{ and } n_0 \text{ such that}$$
$$0 \leq C_1 g(n) \leq f(n) \leq C_2 g(n) \ \forall\ n > n_0 \}$$

i.e., a function $f(n)$ is sandwitched between $C_1 g(n)$ and $C_2 g(n)$. See Fig. 2.1(a). Since $\theta(g(n))$ is a set and $f(n)\ \varepsilon\ \theta g(n)$ we can write,

$$f(n) = \theta(g(n)) \ \forall\ n > n_0,$$

where $f(n)$ and $\theta(g(n))$ are positive asymptotically,

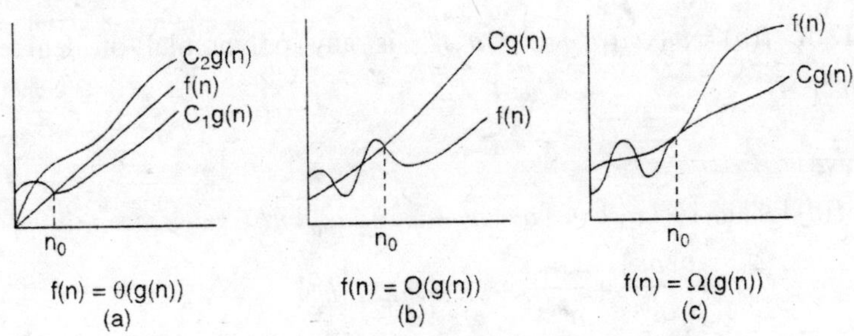

Fig. 2.1. Asymptotic function graph.

It is useful to think of g as some *given* function, and f as the function we are analyzing. Generally we choose $g(n)$ as highest degree term of $f(n)$, e.g. If $f(n) = 3n^2 + 2$ then $g(n) = n^2$.

Note : $g(n)$ is highest order term in $f(n)$

EXAMPLE 2.1. $f(n) = \frac{1}{2}n^2 - 3n$ *find* θ *notation.*

SOLUTION : Since $\theta(g(n))$ is a set and $f(n)$ is its member by definition.

We can assume $g(n) = n^2$

$$C_1n^2 \leq \frac{1}{2}n^2 - 3n \leq C_2n^2$$

$$\Rightarrow \qquad C_1 \leq \frac{1}{2} - \frac{3}{n} \leq C_2$$

$$C_2 \geq \frac{1}{2} - \frac{3}{n}$$

Since C_2 is +ve constant, C_2 can have maximum value $\frac{1}{2}$ as –ve term is subtracted,

$$\therefore \qquad C_2 \geq \frac{1}{2}$$

and
$$C_1 \leq \frac{1}{2} - \frac{3}{n}$$

for $n = 7$ C_1 is +ve so

$$C_1 = \frac{1}{2} - \frac{3}{7} = \frac{1}{14}$$

$$\therefore \qquad C_1 \leq \frac{1}{14}$$

Hence, lowest value of n for which $f(n)$ lies between $C_1g(n)$ and $C_2(g(n))$ is $n_0 = 7$.

∴ Order of $\theta(n^2)$

THEOREM 2.1. If $f(n) = a_0 + a_1 n + \ldots + a_m n^m$ is any polynomial of degree m or less, then $f(n) = \Theta(n^m)$

PROOF : We have

$$|f(n)| \leq |a_0| + |a_1| n + |a_2| n^2 + \ldots + |a_m| n^m$$

$$= \left(\frac{|a_0|}{n^m} + \frac{|a_1|}{n^{m-1}} + \ldots + |a_m|\right) n^m$$

$$\leq (|a_0| + |a_1| + \ldots |a_m|) n^m, \; n \geq 1$$

when $n = 1$,

$$C_2 = |a_0| + |a_1| + \ldots + |a_m|$$

$\therefore$ $f(n) \leq C_2 g(n)$ where $g(n) = n^m$.

Similarly we can check for lower bound.

i.e., $C_1 g(n) \leq f(n)$

thus, $C_1 g(n) \leq f(n) \leq C_2 g(n)$

thus $f(n) = \Theta(n^m)$, where $g(n) = n^m$.

EXAMPLE 2.2. *Find* Θ*-notation for* $\frac{1}{3} n^3 + \frac{1}{2} n^2 + \frac{1}{6} n$.

SOLUTION : Let

$$f(n) = \frac{1}{3} n^3 + \frac{1}{2} n^2 + \frac{1}{6} n.$$

$$= \left(\frac{1}{3} + \frac{1}{2n} + \frac{1}{6n^2}\right) n^3.$$

$$\leq \left(\frac{1}{3} + \frac{1}{2} + \frac{1}{6}\right) n^3 \; ; \; n \geq 1$$

$$\leq C_2 n^3$$

Let $g(n) = n^3$.

$f(n) \leq C_2 g(n)$

$\therefore$ $f(n) = \Theta(n^3)$

We can write $2n^2 + 3n + 1 = 2n^2 + f(n)$

$$= 2n^2 + \Theta(n)$$

$$= \Theta(n^2)$$

O-notation (Big-oh)

Θ-notation asymptotically bounds a function from upper and lower bound but if a function is only having its upper bound then it is denoted by Θ-notation. As shown in Fig. 2.1b, above.

$$O(g(n)) = \begin{cases} f(n) : \text{there exists +ve constant } c \text{ and } n_0 \\ s.t.\ 0 \le f(n) \le cg(n)\ \forall\ n \ge n_0 \end{cases}$$

If a function $f(n) = \Theta(g(n))$ then it must be $O(g(n))$ as Θ-notation is stronger notation than O-notation. Thus any polynomial function $\Theta(n^m)$ also means that it is $O(n^m)$, for quadratic $an^2 + bn + c$ it is $O(n^2)$ and for linear, $an + b$ it is $O(n)$. Doubly nested loops are $O(n^2)$, above Ex. 2.2 is $O(n^3)$. Consider the following discussion :

Let $f : N \rightarrow R^{\le 0}$ be an arbitrary function from the natural numbers to the non-negative reals, such as $f(n) = 27n^2 + \frac{355}{113}n + 12$.

Now, consider another function $g : N \rightarrow R^{\le 0}$ such as $g(n) = n^2$. We say that $f(n)$ is *in the order of* $g(n)$ if $f(n)$ is bounded above by a positive real multiple of $g(n)$ for all sufficiently large n. Mathematically, this means that there exist a positive real constant c and an integer *threshold* n_0 such that $f(n) \le cg(n)$ whenever $n \ge n_0$.

For instance, consider the functions $f(n)$ and $g(n)$ defined above. It is clear that both $n \le n^2$ and $1 \le n^2$ whenever $n \ge 1$. Therefore, provided $n \ge 1$.

$$\begin{aligned} f(n) &= 27n^2 + \frac{355}{113}n + 12 \\ &\le 27n^2 + \frac{355}{113}n^2 + 12n^2 \\ &= 42\frac{16}{113}n^2 = 42\frac{16}{113}g(n). \end{aligned}$$

Taking $c = 42\frac{16}{113}$ (or anything larger) and $n_0 = 1$, we therefore conclude that $f(n)$ is in the order of $g(n)$ since $f(n) \le cg(n)$ whenever $n \ge n_0$. It is easy to see that we could just as well have chosen $c = 28$ and $n_0 = 6$. Such a tradeoff between the smallest possible value for n_0 and that for c is common.

Thus, if an implementation of an algorithm takes in the worst case $27n^2 + \frac{355}{113}n + 12$ microseconds to solve instance of size n, we may simplify by saying that the time is in the order of n^2.

It is allowable to talk about the order of $n/\log n$, even though this function is not defined when $n = 0$ or $n = 1$, and it is correct to write $n^3 - 3n^2 - n - 8 \in O(n^3)$ even though $n^3 - 3n^2 - n - 8 < 0$ when $n \le 3$.

The **threshold rule** states that $f(n) \in O(g(n))$ if and only if there exists a positive real constant c such that $f(n) \le cg(n)$ for *each* natural number n.

When we say $f(n) = O(n^2)$ we mean the **worst case running time**.

Ω-notation

As O-notation provides upper bound Ω-notation provides the lower bound of asymptote see fig 2.1(c).

$$\Omega(g(n)) = \begin{Bmatrix} f(n) : \text{there exists +ve constants } c \text{ and } n_0 \text{ s.t.} \\ 0 \le cg(n) \le f(n) \ \forall \ n \ge n_0 \end{Bmatrix}$$

We saw that most obvious algorithms such as insertion sorting and selection sorting take a time in $O(n^2)$, whereas more sophisticated algorithms such as *heapsort* are more efficient since they do in time $O(n \log n)$. But it is easy to show that $n \log n \in O(n^2)$. As a result, *it is correct* to say that *heapsort* takes a time in $O(n^2)$, or even in $O(n^3)$ for that matter! This is confusing at first, but it is the unavoidable consequence of the fact that the O notation is designed solely to give *upper bounds* on the amount of resources required. Clearly. we need a dual notation for *lower* bounds. This is the Ω notation.

It is easy to see the **duality rule :** $f(n) \in \Omega(g(n))$ if and only if $g(n) \in O(f(n))$ because $f(n) \ge cg(n)$ if and only if $g(n) \le \frac{1}{c} f(n)$. You may therefore question the usefulness of introducing a notation for Ω when the O notation seems to have the same expressive power. The reason is that it is more natural to say that a given algorithm takes a time in $\Omega(n^2)$ than to say the mathematically equivalent but clumsy "n^2 is in O of the time taken by the algorithm".

THEOREM 2.2. For any two functions $f(n)$ and $g(n)$ $f(n) = \Theta(g(n))$ Iff $f(n) = 0(g(n))$ and $f(n) = \Omega(g(n))$.

o-notation

Asymptotic upper bound provided by θ-notation may not be asymptotically tight. So 0-notation is used to denote an upper bound that is asymptotically tight.

$o(g(n)) = \{f(n) :$ for any +ve constant $c > 0$, if a constant

$n_0 > 0$, s.t., $0 \le f(n) < cg(n) \ \forall \ n \ge n_0\}$.

note that right side has no equality i.e. $f(n) < g(n)$.

e.g., $3n^2 = O(n^2)$

but $3n \ne O(n^2)$

So, $3n = o(n^2)$, but $3n^2 \ne o(n^2)$

The relation $0 \le f(n) \le cg(n)$ holds for some +ve constant c in Big-Oh notation but it holds for all the constant in small-Oh notation. The function $f(n)$ becomes insignificant relative to $g(n)$ as n approaches infinity.

Thus $$\lim_{n \to \infty} \frac{f(n)}{g(n)} = 0 \qquad ...(2.1)$$

e.g. $\lim_{n \to \infty} \frac{3n}{n^2} = 0$ thus $0(n^2)$ for $f(n) = 3n$.

ω-notation

As o-notation is to O-notation, similarly we have ω-notation as Ω-notation. To denote lower bound that is not asymptoticaly tight. (little omega)

$\omega(g(n)) = \{f(n) : \text{for any +ve constant } c > 0, \exists \text{ a constant } n_0 > 0, \text{ s.t. } 0 \le c(g(n)) < f(n)\}$.

Here also equality from big-omega. is eliminated.

Here we have

$$\underset{n \to \infty}{\text{Lt}} \frac{g(n)}{f(n)} = 0. \qquad \text{...(2.2)}$$

$$\frac{n^2}{2} = \omega(n) \text{ but } \frac{n^2}{2} \ne \omega(n^2)$$

One way to define it by $f(n)\ \varepsilon\ \omega\ g(n)$ if $g(n)\ \varepsilon\ 0\ (f(n))$.

2.2 Some Operations On *O*-notation

$$f(n) = O(f(n))$$
$$C.O(f(n)) = O(f(n)). \ C \text{ is a constant.}$$
$$O(f(n)) + O(f(n)) = O(f(n))$$
$$O(O(f(n))) = O(f(n))$$
$$O(f(n))\ O(g(n)) = O(f(n)\ .\ g(n))$$
$$O(f(n)\ .\ g(n)) = f(n)\ .\ O(g(n))$$

EXAMPLE 2.3. $C_1 n^2 + C_2 n \le C_3 n$

if $C_1 = 1$, $C_2 = 2$, $C_3 = 1000$

$\Rightarrow$ $$n^2 + 2n \le 1000n.$$

$$n^2 \le 998n \qquad n \le 998$$

No matter what the value C_1, C_2, C_3 takes, there will be n beyond which the algorithm with complexity $C_3 n$ will be faster than the one with $C_1 n^2 + C_2 n$. This value of n is called the **break-even point.** If break even point is zero, then the algorithm with complexity $C_3 n$ will always be faster (or atleast as fast)

EXAMPLE 2.4 (i) *If $3n + 2 = O(n)$ find $g(n)$.*

We have $3n + 2 \le 4n \ \forall \ n \ge 2$, thus $g(n) = 4n$

(ii) If $f(n) = 10n^2 + 4n + 2 = O(n^2)$ find $g(n)$

We have $f(n) \le 11n^2$

for $n \ge 5$, thus $g(n) = 11n^2$

(iii) If $f(n) = 6 \,.\, 2^n + n^2 = O(2^n)$ find $g(n)$

We have $f(n) \le 7.2^n \ \forall \ n \ge 4$ thus $g(n) = 7.2^n$

For above examples it is clear that $g(n)$ is not always equal to highest degree term. e.g. in (i) $10n^2$ in $f(n)$ and $11n^2$ in $g(n)$, coefficients are not same.

Running time of an algorithm in general can be in following order,

$$\boldsymbol{O(1) < O(\log_2 n) < O(n) < O(n \lg n) < O(n^2) < O(n^2) < O(2^n)}$$

We can see the growth of various functions with n in fig. 2.2.

Function Values

$lg\ n$	n	$n\ lg\ n$	n^2	n^3	2^n
0	1	0	1	1	2
1	2	2	4	8	4
2	4	8	16	64	16
3	8	24	64	512	256
4	16	64	256	4096	65, 536
5	32	160	1024	32768	4, 294, 967, 296

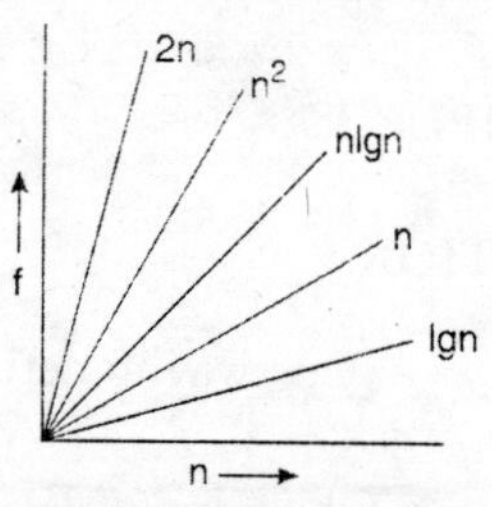

Fig. 2.2. Shows approximate plot of functions.

2^n grows very rapidly. See fig. 2.2.

Note : In these type of problems choose n as power of 2.

THEOREM 2.3. If $f(n) = a_m n^m + \ldots + a_1 n + a_o$, then $f(n) = O(n^m)$.

PROOF :

$$f(n) \le \sum_{i=0}^{m} |a_i| n^i$$

$$\le n^m \sum_{i=0}^{m} |a_i| n^{i-m}$$

$$\le n^m \sum_{i=0}^{m} |a_i| \ \forall\ n > 1$$

So, $\quad f(n) = O(n^m)$

EXAMPLE. 2.5 (i) Prove $\quad 3n + 2 = o(n^2)$.

SOLUTION : $\displaystyle \mathop{\text{Lt}}_{n \to \infty} \frac{3n+2}{n^2} = \mathop{\text{Lt}}_{n \to \infty} \frac{3}{n} + \frac{2}{n^2} = 0.$

Thus, $O(n^2)$ holds.

THEOREM. 2.4. Two functions $f_1(n)$ and $f_2(n)$ are polynomially related if there are polynomials $P_1(x)$ and $P_2(x)$ s.t.

$$\forall\ n, f_1(n) \le P_1(f_2(n)) \text{ and } f_2(n) \le P_2(f_1(n))$$

EXAMPLE. 2.6. $f_1(n) = 2n^2$, $f_2(n) = n^5$, $P_1(x) = 2x, P_2(x) = x^3$, *show whether* f_1 and f_2 *are polynomially related.*

SOLUTION : Case I.

$$f_1(n) \le P_1(f_2(n))$$

$$\le P_1(n^5)$$

$$2n^2 \le 2n^5$$

Case II. $n^5 \leq (2n^2)^3$. Hence f_1, f_2 are polynomially related.

However n^2 and 2^n are not polynomially related, since there is no polynomial $P(x)$ s.t. $P(n^2) \geq 2^n$.

EXAMPLE 2.7. *Prove that $lg(n\,!) = O(n \; lg \; n)$*

SOLUTION :

$$n\,! = n(n-1)(n-2) \ldots 3.2.1.$$
$$\geq \left(\frac{n}{2}\right)^{n/2}$$

Taking log of both sides, (To the base 2)

$$lg\; n\,! \geq \frac{n}{2}\, lg \,\frac{n}{2}$$
$$= \frac{n}{2}\,(lg\; n - lg_2\, 2)$$
$$= \frac{n}{2}\,(lgn - 1) = \frac{n}{2} \log n - \frac{n}{2}$$
$$\leq n\; lgn.$$
$$= O(nlg\; n)$$

EXAMPLE 2.8. *Is $2^{n+1} = O(2^n)$?*

SOLUTION : $2^n \,.\, 2 \leq cg(n)$

$$2^n.\, 2 \leq 2^n.$$
$$\Rightarrow \quad c \geq 2$$
$$\therefore \quad 2^{n+1} = O(2^n)$$

EXAMPLE 2.9. $2^{2n} = O(2^n)$

SOLUTION :

$$2^{2n} \leq c\,.\,2^n.$$
$$c \leq \frac{2^{2n}}{2^n} = 2^{2n-n}$$
$$c \geq 2^n$$

This shows c does not have any fixed value. Therefore above does not hold.

Formula If $$\underset{n \to \infty}{Lt} \frac{f(n)}{g(n)} = \text{constant} \qquad \ldots(2.3)$$

then $$f(n) = O(g(n))$$

EXAMPLE 2.10. *Prove $2^{n+1} = 0(2^n)$*

by formula $$\lim_{n \to \infty} \frac{2^{n+1}}{2^n} = 2$$

$$\therefore \quad f(n) = O(2^n)$$

EXAMPLE 2.11. $(n+a)^b = \theta(n^b)$, $b > 0$, *a and b are real constants.*

$$f(n) = n^b\left(1+\frac{a}{n}\right)^b$$

$$g(n) = n^b$$

$$\underset{n\to\infty}{\text{Lt}} \frac{n_b\left(1+\dfrac{a}{n}\right)^b}{n^b} = 1 = \text{consant}$$

$\therefore$ **$\theta(n^b)$ holds.**

EXAMPLE 2.12. *Prove that $o(g(n)) \cap \omega(g(n))$ is empty set.*

We have form definition.

Let $A = \{x \mid x\varepsilon\, o(g(n))$, where $0 \le f(n) < cg(n)\}$

$B = \{y \mid y\varepsilon\, \omega(g(n))$, where $0 \le cg(n) < f(n)\}$

Clearly,

$A \cap B = \phi$ as o defines the loosely upper asymptotic bound while ω defines the loosely lower asymptotic bound.

Stirling's Approximation

$$n\,! = \sqrt{2\pi n}\left(\frac{n}{e}\right)^n\left(1+\theta\left(\frac{1}{n}\right)\right)$$

$$n! \approx \left(\frac{n}{e}\right)^n \qquad ...(2.4)$$

EXAMPLE 2.13. Prove $lg\, n! = \theta\,(nlgn)$

SOLUTION : We have $lgn\,! = n\, lg\left(\frac{n}{e}\right)$, from stirling's approximation

$$= n\, lgn - n\, lg_2\, e$$

$$\underset{n\to\infty}{Lt}\frac{f(n)}{g(n)} = \frac{n\, lg\, n - n\, lg\, e}{\underset{n\to\infty}{Lt}\; n\, lg\, n}$$

$$= 1 - \frac{lg\, e}{lg\, n} = 1$$

$\therefore \qquad lg\, n\,! \approx \theta(n\, lg\, n) \qquad\qquad \underset{n\to\infty}{Lt}$ (as $\log\infty = \infty$)

EXAMPLE 2.14. *Prove $n\,! = o(n^n)$*

SOLUTION : We have $\qquad n\,! = n(n-1)\, \ldots\, 3.2.1.$

$$= n^n\left(1-\frac{1}{n}\right)\ldots\frac{3}{n}.\frac{2}{n}.\frac{1}{n}.$$

$$\underset{n \to \infty}{\text{Lt}} \frac{f(n)}{g(n)} = \frac{n^n \left(1 - \frac{1}{n}\right) \ldots \frac{3}{n} \cdot \frac{2}{n} \cdot \frac{1}{n}}{\underset{n \to \infty}{\text{Lt}} \quad n^n} = 0$$

$$\therefore \qquad n\,! = o(n^n)$$

F2.1 Exponentials Formula

For all real $a > 0$, m and n we have

$$a^0 = 1$$
$$a^1 = 1$$
$$a^{-1} = 1/a$$
$$(a^m)^n = a^{mn}$$
$$a^m \cdot a^n = a^{m+n}$$
$$0^0 = 1, \text{ assumed}$$
$$\underset{n^{\prime\prime} \to \infty}{\text{Lt}} \frac{n^b}{a^n} = 0$$

thus $\qquad n^b = O(a^n)$

for all real constants a and b s.t. $a > 1$.

EXAMPLE 2.15. Prove $n\,! = \omega(2^n)$

SOLUTION : We have $\underset{n \to \infty}{\text{Lt}} \frac{f(n)}{g(n)} = \infty$ for $f(n) = \omega(g(n))$

$\Rightarrow$ We can write,

$$n! \approx n^n$$

Applying $\qquad \underset{n \to \infty}{Lt} \frac{f(n)}{g(n)} = \frac{n^n}{2^n} \approx \left(\frac{n}{2}\right)^n$

$$\approx n^n$$

Using L' Hospitals Rule

$$\underset{n \to \infty}{Lt} \frac{f(n)}{g(n)} = \frac{n^n}{1} = \frac{nn^{n-1}}{0}$$
$$= \infty$$

Thus $\qquad n! = \omega(2^n)$

Note : Here we can't apply F2.1 as in the formula $\underset{n \to \infty}{Lt} \frac{n^b}{a^n} = 0$, where b and a must be constant, but here, in $\frac{n^n}{2^n}$, b is not constant.

Hence it holds.

Fibonacci Numbers

$$F_0 = 0$$
$$F_1 = 1$$
$$F_j = F_{i-1} + F_{i-2}, \text{ for } i \geq 2$$

Numbers are, 0 1 1 2 3 5 8 13 21 ...

Golden Ratio

$$\phi = \frac{1+\sqrt{5}}{2} = 1.61803\ldots, \quad \hat{\phi} = \frac{1-\sqrt{5}}{2} = -0.61803\ldots$$

We can express ϕ as

$$F_i = \frac{\phi^i - \hat{\phi}^i}{\sqrt{5}}$$

F2.2 Iterated Logarithm Function

$$lg^{(i)}(n) = \begin{cases} n & \text{if } \quad i = 0 \\ lg(lg^{i-1} n) & \text{if } \quad i > 0 \text{ and } lg^{(i-1)} n > 0 \\ \text{undefined} & \text{otherwise} \end{cases}$$

$$lg^* n = \min\{i \geq 0 : lg^{(i)} n \leq 1\}$$

e.g. $\log^3 n = \log^2 \log n$

THEOREM 2.5. A function $f(n) \in O(g(n))$ if $\underset{n \to \infty}{Lt} \frac{f(n)}{g(n)} = c < \infty$, including the case in which the limit is 0. (*i.e.*, $c = 0$)

EXAMPLE 2.16. *Let* $f(n) = \frac{n^3}{2}$ *and* $g(n) = 37n^2 + 12n + 17$, *show that* $g(n) \in O(f(n))$ *but* $f(n) \notin O(g(n))$

SOLUTION :

$$\underset{n \to \infty}{\text{Lt}} \frac{g(n)}{f(n)} = \underset{n \to \infty}{\text{Lt}} \frac{37n^2 + 120n + 17}{\frac{n^3}{2}} = 0$$

Thus $g(n) \in O(f(n))$.

We can show that $f(n) \notin O(g(n))$

for $f(n) \in O(g(n))$

we have $\frac{f(n)}{\underset{n \to \infty}{\text{Lt}}\ g(n)} = c$

i.e.,

$$\underset{n \to \infty}{\text{Lt}} \frac{\frac{n^3}{2}}{37n^2 + 120n + 17} = \infty$$

Thus $f(n) \notin O(g(n))$ by theorem 2.5 above.

THEOREM 2.6. (*L'Hospital Rule*) Let $f(n)$and $g(n)$ be differentiable functions with derivatives $f'(n)$ and $g'(n)$ respectively, such that

$$\operatorname*{Lt}_{n \to \infty} f(n) = \operatorname*{Lt}_{n \to \infty} g(n) = \infty.$$

then
$$\operatorname*{Lt}_{n \to \infty} \frac{f(n)}{g(n)} = \operatorname*{Lt}_{n \to \infty} \frac{f'(n)}{g'(n)}$$

EXAMPLE 2.17. *Use of L' Hospital Rule.*

Let $f(n) = n^2$, $g(n) = n \lg n$, show that $f \notin O(g)$, but $g \in O(f)$

SOLUTION : $\operatorname*{Lt}_{n \to \infty} \frac{f(n)}{g(n)} = \operatorname*{Lt}_{n \to \infty} \frac{n^2}{n \lg n} = \operatorname*{Lt}_{n \to \infty} \frac{n}{\lg n}$

We have
$$\lg n = \frac{\log_e n}{\log_e 2} = \frac{\ln n}{\ln 2} \text{ (changed to natural log)}$$

So, applying the *L'* Hospital's Rule.

$$\operatorname*{Lt}_{n \to \infty} \frac{n \ln (2)}{\ln n} = \operatorname*{Lt}_{n \to \infty} \frac{\ln (2)}{\frac{1}{n}} \quad \operatorname*{Lt}_{n \to \infty} n \ln (2) = \infty.$$

$\therefore f \notin O(g)$, However $g \in O(f)$, since inverse ratio goes to 0.

LEMMA 2.1. Function $f \in \Omega(g)$ if $\operatorname*{Lt}_{n \to \infty} \frac{f(n)}{g(n)} > 0$, including the case in which the limit is ∞.

LEMMA 2.2. Function $f \in \theta(g)$ if $\frac{f(n)}{g(n)} = c$ for some constant such that $0 < c < \infty$ i.e., *O* and ∞ not transitive.

LEMMA 2.3. If $f \in O(g)$ and $g \in O(h)$, then $f \in O(h)$; that is O is transitive, also Ω, θ, o, and ω are transitive.

PROOF : Let c_1 and n_1 be s.t. $f(n) \le c_1 g(n)$ $\forall$ $n \ge n_1$ and let c_2 and n_2 be s.t. $g(n) \le c_2 h(n)$ $\forall$ $n \ge n_2$. Then for all $n \ge \max(n_1, n_2)$, $f(n) = c_1 c_2 h(n)$. So, $f \in O(h)$. The proofs for others are same.

LEMMA 2.4. 1. $f \in O(g)$ iff $g \in \Omega(f)$

2. If $f \in \theta(g)$, then $g \in \theta(f)$

3. θ defines an equivalence relation on the functions. Each set $\theta(f)$ is an equivalence class, which we call a complexity class.

4. $O(f + g) = O(\max(f, g))$. Similar equations hold for Ω and θ.

EXAMPLE 2.18. *Prove that $f(n) = lgn$ is $O(n^{\alpha})$, for any $\alpha > 0$*

SOLUTION : By definition, $f \varepsilon O(n)$ if

$$\operatorname*{Lt}_{n \to \infty} \frac{f(n)}{g(n)} = 0$$

$$\frac{f(n)}{g(n)} = \frac{lgn}{n^{\alpha}} = \operatorname*{Lt}_{n \to \infty} \frac{\ln n}{\ln 2 \cdot n^{\alpha}}$$

$$\frac{f'(n)}{g'(n)} = \frac{\frac{1}{n}}{\ln 2 \cdot \alpha \cdot n^{\alpha - 1}} = \frac{n}{n \, \alpha \ln 2 \, n^{\alpha}} = \frac{1}{\alpha \ln 2 \cdot n^{\alpha}}$$

By L' Hospital Rule

$$\lim_{n \to \infty} \frac{f(n)}{g(n)} = \operatorname*{Lt}_{n \to \infty} \frac{f'(n)}{g'(n)} = \operatorname*{Lt}_{n \to \infty} \frac{1}{(\alpha \ln 2) \cdot n^{\alpha}} = \frac{1}{\alpha \ln 2 \cdot \infty} = 0$$

$\therefore$ $f \varepsilon O(g)$ proved.

EXAMPLE 2.19. *Prove that* $\sum_{i=1}^{n} \log(i)$ *is* $\theta(n \log n)$

SOLUTION : Let

$$f(n) = \sum_{i=1}^{n} \log i$$

$$= \log 1 + \log 2 + \log 3 + \log 4 + \ldots + \log n$$

$$= \log 2 \cdot 3 \cdot 4 \ldots n, \text{ as } \log 1 = 0.$$

$$= \log (n-1)\,!$$

$$\leq \log n\,!$$

But $\log n\,! = \theta(n \, lg \, n)$

$\therefore$ $f(n) \, \varepsilon \, \theta(n \, lg \, n)$ proved

Note : log 1 is zero to any base.

EXAMPLE 2.20. *Compute x^n, write an algorithm and improve its running time.*

SOLUTION :

```
Power ← x
For  i ← 1 to n − 1 do
Power ←  Power × x.
```

This algo takes $\theta(n)$ time.

We can modify this algo to reduce the runtime, Let $2^K = n$, s.t. $K = lgn$,

then,

```
Power ← x.
for   i ← 1 to k do
Power = Power²
```

This algo excutes in $\theta(\log n)$ time this is significant improvement over the previous algorithm.

EXAMPLE 2.21. *What does all this mean?*

$$3n^2 - 100n + 6 = O(n^2) \text{ because } 3n^2 > 3n^2 - 100n + 6$$
$$3n^2 - 100n + 6 = O(n^3) \text{ because } .01n^3 > 3n^2 - 100n + 6$$
$$3n^2 - 100n + 6 \neq O(n) \text{ because } c \cdot n < 3n^2 \text{ when } n > c$$
$$3n^2 - 100n + 6 = \Omega(n^2) \text{ because } 2.99n^2 < 3n^2 - 100n + 6$$
$$3n^2 - 100n + 6 \neq \Omega(n^3) \text{ because } 3n^2 - 100n + 6 < n^3$$
$$3n^2 - 100n + 6 = \Omega(n) \text{ because } 10^{10^{10}} n < 3n^2 - 100 + 6$$
$$3n^2 - 100n + 6 = \theta(n^2) \text{ because } O \text{ and } \Omega$$
$$3n^2 - 100n + 6 \neq \theta(n^3) \text{ because } O \text{ only}$$
$$3n^2 - 100n + 6 \neq \theta(n) \text{ because } \Omega \text{ only}$$

Note that

$$\log (n^{473} + n^2 + n + 96) = O(\log n)$$
$$n^{473} + n^2 + n + 96 = O(n^{473}), \text{ and}$$

Since $\log n^{473} = 473 \cdot \log n$

Any exponential dominates *every* polynomial. This is why we will seek to avoid exponential time algorithms.

EXAMPLE 2.22. *Suppose $f(n) = O(n^2)$ and $g(n) = O(n^2)$*

What do we know about $g'(n) = f(n) + g(n)$ where g' is some other function ? Adding the bounding constants shows $g'(n) = O(n^2)$

What do we know about $g''(n) = f(n) - g(n)$? Since the bounding constants don't necessary cancel, $g''(n) = O(n^2)$. Here g'' is some other function, not second derivative.

SOLUTION : We know nothing about the lower bounds on $g' + g''$ because we know nothing about lower bounds on f, g.

Suppose $f(n) = \Omega(n^2)$ and $g(n) = \Omega(n^2)$

What do we know about $g(n) = f(n) + g(n)$? Adding the lower bounding constants shows $g''(n) = \Omega(n^2)$

What do we know about $g''(n) = f(n) - g(n)$? We know nothing about the lower bound of this.

EXAMPLE 2.23. The k Days of Christmas

To reduce $S(n)$, we must structure the song differently.

Consider "The k Days of Christmas". All one must memorize is:

On the kth Day of Christmas, my true love gave to me, $gift_k$

⋮

On the First Day of Christmas, my true love gave to me, a partridge in a pear tree But the time it takes to sing it is

$$\sum_{i=1}^{k} i = k(k+1)/2 = \theta(k^2)$$

If $n = O(k^2)$, then $k = O(\sqrt{n})$, so $S(n) = O(\sqrt{n})$

EXAMPLE 2.24. *100 Bottles of Beer*

What do kids sing on really long car trips?

n bottles of beer on the wall,

n bottles of beer.

You take one down and pass it around

$n - 1$ bottles of beer on the ball.

All you must remember in this song is this template of size $\theta(1)$, and the current value of n. The storage size for n depends on its value, but $\log_2 n$ bits suffice.

This for this song, $S(n) = O(\log n)$.

EXAMPLE 2.25. *Find the asymptotic notation for the given function $f(n)$ and $g(n)$.*

$$f(n) = n^{3/2},\ g(n) = n \log^2 (n)$$

SOLUTION : Finding
$$\frac{f(n)}{g(n)} = \frac{n^{3/2}}{n \log^2 (n)}$$

$$= \frac{n^{3/2}}{n \log\log (n)} \qquad \text{Using F2.2, logarithmic iterative function}$$

$$= \frac{n^{1/2}}{\log\log (n)}$$

Using L' Hospital's Rule

$$\underset{n\to\infty}{Lt} \frac{f(n)}{g(n)} = \frac{f'(n)}{g'(n)} = \frac{\frac{1}{2} n - 1/2}{\frac{1}{\log n} \cdot \frac{1}{n}}$$

$$\underset{n\to\infty}{Lt} = \frac{1}{2} n^{1/2} \log (n) = \infty$$

$\therefore$
$$f(n) = \omega\, g(n)$$

i.e.
$$n^{3/2} = \omega\, (n \log^2 (n)).$$

THEOREM 2.6(a). Prove that if $f(x) = O(g(x))$, and $g(x) = O(f(x))$, then $f(x) = \Theta(g(x))$.

PROOF : If $f(x) = O(g(x))$, then there are positive constants c_2 and n_0' such that

$$0 \le f(n) \le c_2\, g(n) \text{ for all } n \ge n_0'$$

Similarly, if $g(x) = O(f(x))$, then there are positive constants c_1' and n_0'' such that

$$0 \le g(n) \le c_1' f(n) \text{ for all } n \ge n_0''$$

We can divide this by c_1' to obtain

$$0 \le \frac{1}{c_1'} g(n) \le f(n) \text{ for all } n \ge n_0''$$

Setting $c_1 = 1/c_1'$ and $n_0 = \max(n_0', n_0'')$, we have

$$0 \le c_1 g(n) \le f(n) \le c_2\, g(n) \text{ for all } n \ge n_0$$

Thus, $f(x) = \Theta(g(x))$.

THEOREM 2.6(b). Let $f(x) = O(g(x))$ and $g(x) = O(h(x))$. Show that $f(x) = O(h(x))$.

PROOF : If $f(x) = O(g(x))$, then there are positive constants c_1 and n_0' such that

$$0 \le f(n) \le c_1 g(n) \text{ for all } n \ge n_0'$$

and if $g(x) = O(h(x))$, then there are positive constants c_2 and n_0'' such that

$$0 \le g(n) \le c_2 h(n) \text{ for all } n \ge n_0''$$

Set $n_0 = \max(n_0', n_0'')$ and $c_3 = c_1\, c_2$. Then

$$0 \le f(n) \le c_1 g(n) \le c_1 c_2 h(n) = c_3 h(n) \text{ for all } n \ge n_0$$

Thus, $f(x) = O(h(x))$.

EXAMPLE 2.25(a). *Find a tight bound on* $f(x) = x^8 + 7x^7 - 10x^5 - 2x^4 + 3x^2 - 17$.

SOLUTION (1) : We will prove that $f(x) = \Theta(x^8)$. First, we will prove an upper bound for $f(x)$. It is clear that when $x > 0$,

$$x^8 + 7x^7 - 10x^5 - 2x^4 + 3x^2 - 17 \le x^8 + 7x^7 + 3x^2.$$

- We can upper bound any function by removing the lower order terms with negative coefficients, as long as $x \ge 0$.

Next, it is not hard to see that when $x \ge 1$,

$$x^8 + 7x^7 + 3x^2 \le x^8 + 7x^8 + 3x^8 = 11x^8$$

- We can upper bound any function by replacing lower order terms with positive coefficients by the dominating term with the same coefficients. Here, we must make sure that the dominating term is larger than the given term for all values of x larger than some threshold x_0 and we must make note of the threshold value x_0.

Thus, we have

$$f(x) = x^8 + 7x^7 - 10x^5 - 2x^4 + 3x^2 - 17 \le 11x^8 \text{ for all } x \ge 1,$$

and we have proved that $f(x) = O(x^8)$.

Now, we will get a lower bound for $f(x)$. It is not hard to see that when $x \ge 0$,

$$x^8 + 7x^7 - 10x^5 - 2x^4 + 3x^2 - 17 \ge x^8 - 10x^5 - 2x^4 - 17.$$

- We can lower bound any function by removing the lower order terms with positive coefficients, as long as $x > 0$.

Next, we can see that when $x \ge 1$,

$$x^8 - 10x^5 - 2x^4 - 17 \ge x^8 - 10x^7 - 2x^7 - 17x^7 = x^8 - 29x^7.$$

- We can lower bound any function by replacing lower order terms with negative coefficients by a sub-dominating term with the same coefficients. (By sub-dominating, I mean one which dominates all but the dominating term). Here, we must make sure that the sub-dominating term is larger than the given term for all values of x larger than some threshold x_0, and we must make note of the threshold value x_0. Making a wise choice for which sub-dominating term to use is crucial in finishing the proof.

Next, we need to find a value $c > 0$ such that $x^8 - 29x^7 \geq cx^8$. Doing a little arithmetic, we see that this is equivalent to $(1 - c)x^8 \geq 29x^7$. When $x \geq 1$, we can divide by x^7 and obtain $(1 - c)x \geq 29$. Solving for c, we obtain

$$c \geq 1 - \frac{29}{x}$$

If $x \geq 58$, then $c = 1/2$ suffices. We have just shown that if $x \geq 58$, then

$$f(x) = x^8 + 7x^7 - 10x^5 - 2x^4 + 3x^2 - 17 \geq \frac{1}{2}x^8$$

Thus, $f(x) = \Omega(x^8)$. Since we have shown that $f(x) = \Omega(x^8)$ and that $f(x) = O(x^8)$, we have shown that $f(x) = \Theta(x^8)$.

SOLUTION (2) : We guess (or know, if we read Solution (1)) that $f(x) = \Theta(x^8)$. To prove this, notice that

$$\begin{aligned}
\lim_{x \to \infty} \frac{x^8 + 7x^7 - 10x^5 - 2x^4 + 3x^2 - 17}{x^8} &= \lim_{x \to \infty} \frac{x^8}{x^8} + \frac{7x^7}{x^8} - \frac{10x^5}{x^8} - \frac{2x^4}{x^8} + \frac{3x^2}{x^8} - \frac{17}{x^8} \\
&= \lim_{x \to \infty} 1 + \frac{7}{x} - \frac{10}{x^3} - \frac{2}{x^4} + \frac{3}{x^6} - \frac{17}{x^8} \\
&= \lim_{x \to \infty} 1 + 0 - 0 - 0 + 0 - 0 = 1
\end{aligned}$$

Thus, $f(x) = \Theta(x^8)$ by the Theorem.

EXAMPLE 2.25(b). *Find a tight bound on $f(x) = x^4 - 23x^3 + 12x^2 + 15x - 21$.*

SOLUTION (1) : It is clear that when $x \geq 1$,

$$x^4 - 23x^3 + 12x^2 + 15x - 21 \leq x^4 + 12x^2 + 15x \leq x^4 + 12x^4 + 15x^4 = 28x^4$$

Also, $x^4 - 23x^3 + 12x^2 + 15x - 21 \geq x^4 - 23x^3 - 21 \geq x^4 - 23x^3 - 21x^3 = x^4 - 44x^3 \geq \frac{1}{2}x^4$

whenever $$\frac{1}{2}x^4 \geq 44x^3 \Leftrightarrow x \geq 88$$

Thus, $$\frac{1}{2}x^4 \leq x^4 - 23x^3 + 12x^2 + 15x - 21 \leq 28x^4, \text{ for all } x \geq 88.$$

We have shown that $f(x) = x^4 - 23x^3 + 12x^2 + 15x - 21 = \Theta(x^4)$.

SOLUTION (2) : From Solution (1) we already know that $f(x) = \Theta(x^4)$. We verify this by noticing that

$$\lim_{x \to \infty} x^4 - 23x^3 + 12x^2 + 15x - 21 = \lim_{x \to \infty} \frac{x^4}{x^4} - \frac{23x^3}{x^4} + \frac{12x^2}{x^4} + \frac{15x}{x^4} - \frac{21}{x^4}$$

$$= \lim_{x \to \infty} 1 - \frac{23}{x} + \frac{12}{x^2} + \frac{15}{x^3} - \frac{21}{x^4}$$

$$= \lim_{x \to \infty} 1 - 0 + 0 + 0 - 0 = 1$$

EXAMPLE 2.25(c). *Show that* $\log x = O(x)$.

SOLUTION :

$$\lim_{x \to \infty} \frac{\log x}{x} = \lim_{x \to \infty} \frac{1/x}{1} = \lim_{x \to \infty} \frac{1}{x} = 0$$

Therefore, $\log n = O(n)$.

EXAMPLE 2.25(d). *Show that* $n! = O(n^n)$.

SOLUTION : Notice that when $n \geq 1, 0 \leq n! = 1 . 2 . 3 \ldots n \leq n . n \ldots n = n^n$. Therefore $n! = O(n^n)$ (Here $n_0 = 1$, and $c = 1$).

EXAMPLE 2.25(e). *Show that* $\log n! = O(n \log n)$.

SOLUTION : In the previous problem, we showed that when $n \geq 1$, $n! \leq n^n$. Notice that $n! \geq 1$, so taking logs of both sides, we obtain $0 \leq \log n! \leq \log n^n = n \log n$ for all $n \geq 1$. Therefore $\log n! = O(n \log n)$. (Here, $n_0 = 1$, and $c = 1$).

EXAMPLE 2.25(f). *Find a good upper bound on* $n \log (n^2 + 1) + n^2 \log n$.

SOLUTION : If $n > 1$,

$$\log (n^2 + 1) \leq \log (n^2 + n^2) = \log (2n^2) = (\log 2 + \log n^2) \leq (\log n + 2 \log n) = 3 \log n$$

Thus when $n > 1$,

$$0 \leq n \log (n^2 + 1) + n^2 \log n \leq n^3 \log n + n^2 \log n \leq 3n^2 \log n + n^2 \log n \leq 4n^2 \log n$$

Thus, $n \log (n^2 + 1) + n^2 \log n = O(n^2 \log n)$.

EXAMPLE 2.25(g). *Show that* $(\sqrt{2})^{\log n} = O(\sqrt{n})$, *where log means* $\log_2$.

SOLUTION : It is not too hard to see that

$$(\sqrt{2})^{\log n} = n^{\log \sqrt{2}} = n^{\log 2^{1/2}} = n^{1/2 \log 2} = n^{1/2} = \sqrt{n}$$

Thus it is clear that $(\sqrt{2})^{\log n} = O(\sqrt{n})$.

EXAMPLE 2.25(h). *Show that* $2^x = O(3x^x)$.

SOLUTION (1) : This is easy to see since $\lim_{x\to\infty} \frac{2^x}{3^x} = \lim_{x\to\infty} \left(\frac{2}{3}\right)^x = \lim_{x\to\infty} 0.$

SOLUTION (2) : If $x \geq 1$, then clearly $(3/2)^x \geq 1$, so

$$2^x \leq 2^x \left(\frac{3}{2}\right)^x = \left(\frac{2\times 3}{2}\right)^x = 3^x.$$

2.3 Maximum Rule

A useful tool for proving that one function is in the order of another is the **maximum rule**. Let $f, g : N \to R^{\geq 0}$ be two arbitrary functions from the natural numbers to the non negative reals. The maximum rule says that $O(f(n) + g(n)) = O$ (max $(f(n), g(n))$). More specifically, let $p, q : N \to R^{\geq 0}$ be defined for each natural number n by $p(n) = f(n) + g(n)$ and $q(n) =$ max $(f(n), g(n))$ and consider an arbitrary function $t : N \to R^{\geq 0}$. The maximum rule says that $t(n) \in O(p(n))$ if and only if $t(n) \in O(q(n))$. This rule generalizes to any finite constant number of functions. Before proving it, we illustrate a natural interpretation of this rule. Consider an algorithm that proceeds in three steps; initialization, processing and finalization. Assume for the sake of argument that these steps take, time in $O(n^2)$, $O(n^3)$ and $O(n \log n)$, respectively. It is therefore clear that the complete algorithm takes a time in $O(n^2 + n^3 + n \log n)$. Although it would not be hard to prove directly that this is the same as $O(n^3)$, it is immediate from the maximum rule.

$$\begin{aligned} O(n^2 + n^3 + n \log n) &= O(\max (n^2, n^3, n \log n)) \\ &= O(n^3) \end{aligned}$$

In other words, even though the time taken by an algorithm is logically the sum of the times taken by its disjoints parts, it is in the order of the time taken by its most time-consuming part, provided the number of parts is a constant, independent of input size.

We now prove the maximum rule for the case of two functions. The general case of any fixed number of functions is left as an exercise. Observe that

$$f(n) + g(n) = \min (f(n), g(n)) + \max (f(n), g(n))$$

and

$$0 \leq \min (f(n), g(n)) \leq \max (f(n), g(n))$$

If follows that

$$\max (f(n), g(n)) \leq f(n) + g(n) \leq 2 \max (f(n), g(n)) \qquad \ldots(2.5)$$

Now consider any $t(n) \in O(f(n) + g(n))$. Let c be an appropriate constant such that $t(n) \leq c((n) + g(n))$ for all sufficiently large n. By equation 2.5, it follows that $t(n) \leq 2c \max (f(n), g(n))$. Therefore $t(n)$ is bounded above by a positive real multiple—namely $2c$—of max $(f(n), g(n))$ for all sufficiently large n, which proves that $t(n) \in O(\max (f(n), g(n)))$. For the other direction, consider any $t(n) \in O(\max (f(n), g(n)))$. Let $\hat{c}$ be an appropriate new constant such that $t(n) \leq \hat{c} \max (f(n), g(n))$ for all sufficiently large n. By equation 2.5 again, it follows that $t(n) \geq \hat{c}\,(f(n) + g(n))$. By definition of the O notation, this implies directly that $t(n) \in O(f(n) + g(n))$, which completes the proof of the maximum rule. In accordance with our allowed occasional misuse of the notation, we are entitled to invoke the maximum rule even if the function concerned are negative or undefined on a finite set of values. Be careful however not to use the rule if some of the functions are negative infinitely often; otherwise you risk reasoning as follows :

$$O(n) = O(n + n^2 - n^2) = O(\max(n, n^2, -n^2)) = O(n^2),$$

where the middle equality is obtained by incorrect use of the maximum rule.

The maximum rule tells us that if $t(n)$ is a complicated function such as $t(n) = 12n^3 \log n - 5n^2 + \log^2 n + 36$ and if $f(n)$ is the most significant term of $t(n)$ with its coefficient discarded, here $f(n) = n^3 \log n$, then $O(t(n)) = O(f(n))$, which allows for dramatic yet automatic simplifications in asymptotic notation. In other words, lower-order terms can be ignored because they are negligible compared to the higher order term for n sufficiently large. Note in this case that one should *not* prove $O(t(n)) = O(f(n))$ by reasoning along the lines of

$$O(t(n)) = O(\max(12n^3 \log n, -5n^2, \log^2 n, 36))$$
$$= O(12n^3 \log n) = O(n^3 \log n)$$

where the second line is obtained from the maximum rule. This does not use the maximum rule properly since the function $-5n^2$ negative. Nevertheless, the following reasoning is correct :

$$O(t(n)) = O(11n^3 \log n + n^3 \log n - 5n^2 + \log^2 n + 36)$$
$$= O(\max(11n^3 \log n, n^3 \log n - 5n^2, \log^2 n, 36))$$
$$= O(11n^3 \log n) = O(n^3 \log n).$$

Even though $n^3 \log n - 5n^2$ is negative and 36 is larger than $11n^3 \log n$ for small values of n, all is well since this does not occur whenever n is sufficiently large.

EXAMPLE 2.26. *Solve the following using asymptotic definition*

$$(f(n) + g(n)) = \max(\theta(f(n)), \theta(g(n)))$$

SOLUTION : Using asymptotic definition we have

if $\quad f(n) = \theta g(n)$ then

$$0 \le c_1\, g(n) \le f(n) \le c_2\, g(n) \qquad \ldots(1)$$

if $\quad g(n) = \theta(f(n))$

$$0 \le c' f(n) \le g(n) \le c_2' f(n) \qquad \ldots(2)$$

Therefore, summing eqn. (1) and (2), we get

$$f(n) + g(n) = \theta(g(n)) + \theta(f(n)) \qquad \ldots(3)$$

$$0 \le c_1 g(n) + c_1' g(n) \le f(n) + g(n) \le c_2 g(n) + c_2' f(n) \qquad \ldots(4)$$

We can rewrite the above eqn. (3), as below

$$f(n) + g(n) = \max(\theta f(n), \theta(g(n)))$$

using maximum rule.

For example, let

$$f(n) = n^2 + 2 = \theta(n^2)$$
$$g(n) = n^3 + n^2 = \theta(n^3)$$
$$f(n) + g(n) = n^3 + 2n^2 + 2$$

$$= \Theta(n^3)$$
$$= \max(\Theta(n^2), \Theta(n^3))$$
$$= \max(\Theta(f(n)), \Theta(g(n)))$$ **Proved**

The Theta Notation

When we analyse the behaviour of an algorithm, we are happiest if its execution time is bounded simultaneously both above and below by possibly different positive real multiples of the same function. For this reason, we introduce the Θ notation. We say that $t(n)$ is in Theta of $f(n)$, or equivalently that $t(n)$ is in the *exact order* of $f(n)$, denoted $t(n) \in \Theta(f(n))$, if $t(n)$ belongs to both $O(f(n))$ and $\Omega(f(n))$. The formal definition of Θ is

$$\Theta(f(n)) = O(f(n)) \cap \Omega(f(n)) \qquad \ldots(2.6)$$

EXAMPLE 2.27. $\sum_{i=1}^{n} i^k \in \Theta(n^{k+1})$, *for any fixed integer $k \geq 0$, where the left-hand side summation is considered as a function of n.*

SOLUTION : The "O" direction is easy to prove. For this, simply notice that $i^k \leq n^k$ whenever $1 \leq i \leq n$. Therefore $\sum_{i=1}^{n} i^k \leq \sum_{i=1}^{n} n^k = n^{k+1}$ for all $n \geq 1$, which proves $\sum_{i=1}^{n} i^k \in O(n^{k+1})$ using 1 as the multiplicative constant.

To prove the "Ω" direction, notice that $i^k \geq (n/2)^k$ whenever $i \geq [n/2]$ and that the number of integers between $[n/2]$ and n inclusive is greater than $n/2$. Therefore, provided $n \geq 1$ (which implies that $[n/2] \geq 1$),

$$\sum_{i=1}^{n} i^k \geq \sum_{i=\left[\frac{n}{2}\right]}^{n} i^k \geq \sum_{i=\left[\frac{n}{2}\right]}^{n} \left(\frac{n}{2}\right)^k \geq \frac{n}{2} \times \left(\frac{n}{2}\right)^k = \frac{n^{k+1}}{2^{k+1}}$$

This proves $\sum_{i=1}^{n} i^k \in \Omega(n^{k+1})$ using $1/2^{k+1}$ as the multiplicative constant.

EXAMPLE 2.28. *$7n - 2$ is $O(n)$.*

SOLUTION : By the big-Oh definition., we need to find a real constant $c > 0$ and an integer constant $n_0 > 1$ such that $7n - 2 \leq c_n$ for every integer $n \geq n_0$. It is easy to see that a possible choice is $c = 7$ and $n_0 = 1$. Indeed, this is one of ir.finitely many choices available because any real number greater than or equal to 7 will work for c and any integer greater than or equal to 1 will work for n_0.

THEOREM 2.7. The running time of algorithm *arrayMax* for computing the maximum element in an array of n integers is $O(n)$.

PROOF : The number of primitive operations executed by algorithm *arrayMax* is at most $7n - 2$ (How?). We may therefore apply the big-Oh definition with $c = 7$ and $n_0 = 1$ and conclude that the running time of algorithm arrayMax is $O(n)$.

EXAMPLE 2.29. $20n^3 + 10n \log n + 5$ *is* $O(n^3)$.

SOLUTION : $20n^3 + 10n \log n + 5 \leq 35n^3$, for $n \geq 1$.

In fact, any polynomial $a_k n^k + a_{k-1} n^{k-1} + \ldots + a_0$ will always be $O(n^k)$.

EXAMPLE 2.30. $3 \log n + \log \log n$ *is* $O(\log n)$.

SOLUTION : $3 \log n + \log \log n \leq 4 \log n$, for $n \geq 2$. Note that $\log \log n$ is not even defined for $n = 1$. That is why we use $n \geq 2$. Hence $O(\log n)$.

EXAMPLE 2.31. 2^{100} *is* $O(1)$.

SOLUTION : $2^{100} \leq 2^{100} \cdot 1$, for $n \geq 1$. Note that variable n does not appear in the inequality, since we are dealing with constant-valued functions.

EXAMPLE 2.32. $5/n$ *is* $O(1/n)$.

SOLUTION : $5/n \leq 5(1/n)$, for $n \geq 1$ (even though this is actually a decreasing function).

In general, we should use the big-Oh notation to characterize a function as closely as possible. While it is true that $f(n) = 4n^3 + 4n^{4/3}$ is $O(n^5)$, it is more accurate to say that $f(n)$ is $O(n^3)$. Instead of always applying the big-Oh definition directly to obtain a big-Oh characterization, we can use the following rules to simplify notation.

THEOREM 2.8. Let $d(n)$, $e(n)$, $f(n)$, and $g(n)$ be function mapping non-negative integers to non-negative reals. Then

1. If $d(n)$ is $O(f(n))$, then $ad(n)$ is $O(f(n))$, for any constant $a > 0$.
2. If $d(n)$ is $O(f(n))$ and $e(n)$ is $O(g(n))$, then $d(n) + e(n)$ is $O(f(n) + g(n))$.
3. If $d(n)$ is $O(f(n))$ and $e(n)$ is $O(g(n))$, then $d(n)\, e(n)$ is $O(f(n)\, g(n))$.
4. If $d(n)$ is $O(f(n))$ and $f(n)$ is $O(g(n))$, then $d(n)$ is $O(g(n))$.
5. If $f(n)$ is a polynomial of degree d (that is, $f(n) + a_0 - a_1 n + \ldots + a_d n^d$), then $f(n)$ is $O(n^d)$.
6. n^x is $O(a^n)$ for any fixed $x > 0$ and $a > 1$.
7. $\log n^x$ is $O(\log n)$ for any fixed $x > 0$.
8. If $\log^x n$ is $O(n^y)$ for any fixed constants $x > 0$ and $y > 0$.

It is considered poor taste to include constant factors and lower order terms in the big-Oh notation. For example, it is not fashionable to say that the function $2n^2$ is $O(4n^2 + 6n \log n)$, although this is completely correct. We should strive instead to describe the function in the big-Oh in *simplest terms*.

EXAMPLE 2.33. *$2n^3 + 4n^2 \log n$ is $O(n^3)$.*

SOLUTION : We can apply the rules of Theorem 2.8 as follows :

$\log n$ is $O(n)$	(Rule 8)
$4n^2 \log n$ is $O(4n^3)$	(Rule 3)
$2n^3 + 4n^2 \log n$ is $O(2n^3 + 4n^3)$	(Rule 2)
$2n^3 + 4n^3$ is $O(n^3)$	(Rule 5 or Rule 1)
$2n^3 + 4n^2 \log n$ is $O(n^3)$	(Rule 4)

Some functions appear often in the analysis of algorithms and data structures, and we often use special terms to refer to them.

EXAMPLE 2.34. *$3 \log n + \log\log n$ is $\Omega(\log n)$.*

SOLUTION : $3 \log n + \log\log n \geq 3 \log n$, for $n \geq 2$.

This example shows that lower order terms are not dominant is establishing lower bounds with the big-Omega notation. Thus, as the next example sums up, lower order terms are not dominant in the big-Theta notation either.

EXAMPLE 2.35. *$3 \log n + \log\log n$ is $\Theta(\log n)$.*

SOLUTION : This follows from Examples 2.28 and 2.32.

EXAMPLE 2.36. *Order the following list of functions by the big-Oh notation. Group together (for example, by underlining) those functions that are big-Theta of one another.*

$6n \log n$	2^{100}	$\log\log n$	$\log^2 n$	$2^{\log n}$
2^{2^n}	$[\sqrt{n}]$	$n^{0.01}$	$1/n$	$4n^{3/2}$
$3n^{0.5}$	$5n$	$[2n \log^2 n]$	2^n	$n \log_4 n$
4^n	n^3	$n^2 \log n$	$4^{\log n}$	$\sqrt{\log n}$

[**Hint :** When in doubt about two functions $f(n)$ and $g(n)$, consider $\log f(n)$ and $\log g(n)$ or $2^{f(n)}$ and $2^{g(n)}$].

SOLUTION : $1/n$, 2^{100}, $\log\log n$, $\sqrt{\log n}$, $\log^2 n$, $n^{0.01}$, $[\sqrt{n}]$, $3n^{0.5}$, $2^{\log n}$, $5n$, $n \log_4 n$, $6n \log n$, $\lfloor 2n \log^2 n \rfloor$, $4n^{3/2}$, $4^{\log n}$.

EXAMPLE 2.37. *For each function $f(n)$ and time t in the following table, determine the largest size n of a problem that can be solved in time t assuming that the algorithm to solve the problem takes $f(n)$ microseconds. Recall that $\log n$ denotes the logarithm in base 2 of n. Some entries have already been completed to get you started.*

SOLUTION : The numbers in the first row are quite large. The table below calculates it approximately in powers of 10. People might also choose to use powers of 2. Being close to the answer is enough for the big numbers (within a few factors of 10 from the answers shown).

	1 Second	1 Hour	1 Month	1 Century
$\log n$	$2^{10^6} \approx 10^{300000}$	$2^{3.6\times10^9} \approx 10^{10^9}$	$2^{2.6\times10^{12}} \approx 10^{0.8\times10^{12}}$	$2^{3.1\times10^{15}} = 10^{10^{15}}$
$\sqrt{n}$	$\approx 10^{12}$	$\approx 1.3\times10^{19}$	$\approx 6.8\times10^{24}$	$\approx 9.7\times10^{30}$
n	10^6	3.6×10^9	$\approx 2.6\times10^{12}$	$\approx 3.12\times10^{15}$
$n\log n$	$\approx 10^5$	$\approx 10^9$	$\approx 10^1\ 1$	$\approx 10^{14}$
n^2	1000	6×10^4	$\approx 1.6\times10^6$	$\approx 5.6\times10^7$
n^3	100	≈ 1500	≈ 14000	≈ 1500000
2^n	19	31	41	51
$n!$	9	12	15	17

EXAMPLE 2.38. *Bill has an algorithm, find 2D, to find an element x in an $n\times n$ array A. The algorithm find 2D iterates over the rows of A and calls the algorithm arrayFind, until x is found or it has searched all rows of A. What is the worst-case running time of find2D in terms of n ? Is this a linear-time algorithm ? Why or why not ?*

SOLUTION : The worst case running time of find2D is $O(n^2)$. This is seen by examining the worst case where the element x is the very last item in the $n\times n$ array to be examined. In this case, find2d calls the algoritm arrayFind n times, arrayFind will then have to search all n elements for each call until the final call when x is found. Therefore, n comparisons are done for each arrayFind call. Since arrayFind is called n times, we have $n * n$ operations, or an $O(n^2)$ running time. This is not a linear time algorithm; it is quadratic. If this were a linear time algorithm, the running time would be proportional to its input size.

```
Algorithm Loop1(n):
        s ← 0
for i ← 1 to n do

Algorithm Loop2(n):
        p ← 1
for i ← 1 to 2n do
        p ← p * i

Algorithm Loop3(n):
        p ← 1
for i ← 1 to n² do
        p ← p * i

Algorithm Loop4(n):
        s ← 0
for i ← 1 to 2n do
```

```
for j ← 1 to i do
        s ← s + i

Algorithm Loop5(n):
        s ← 0
for i ← 1 to n² do
for j ← 1 to i do
    s ← s + i
```

ALGORITHM. E-2.1.

EXAMPLE 2.39. *Perform a analysis for method Loop1 shown in Algorithm E-2.1.*

SOLUTION : The Loop1 method runs in $O(n)$ time.

EXAMPLE 2.40. *Perform a similar analysis for method Loop2 shown in Algorithm E-2.1.*

SOLUTION : The Loop2 method runs in $O(n)$ time.

EXAMPLE 2.41. *Perform a similar analysis for method Loop3 shown in Algorithm E-2.1.*

SOLUTION : The Loop3 method runs in $O(n^2)$ time.

EXAMPLE 2.42. *Perform a similar analysis for method Loop4 shown in Algorithm E-2.1.*

SOLUTION : The Loop4 method runs in $O(n^2)$ time.

EXAMPLE 2.43. *Perform a similar analysis for method Loop5 shown in Algorithm E-2.1.*

SOLUTION : The Loop5 method runs in $O(n^4)$ time.

EXAMPLE 2.44. *Show that $(n+1)^n$ is $O(n^5)$.*

SOLUTION : By the definition of big-Oh, we need to find a real constant $c > 0$ and an integer constant $n_0 \geq 1$ such that $(n+1)^5 \leq c(n^5)$ for every integer $n \geq n_0$. Since $(n+1)^5 = n^5 + 5n^4 + 10n^3 + 10n^2 + 5n + 1$, $(n+1)^5 \leq c(n^5)$ for $c = 8$ and $n \geq n_0 = 2$.

EXAMPLE 2.45. *Show that $n^3 \log n$ is $\Omega(n^3)$.*

SOLUTION : By the definition of big-Omega, we need to find a real constant $c > 0$ and an integer constant $n_0 \geq 1$ such that $n^3 \log n \geq cn^3$ for $n \geq n_0$. Choosing $c = 1$ and $n_0 = 2$, shows $n^3 \log n \geq cn^3$ for $n \geq n_0$, since $\log n \geq 1$ in this range.

EXAMPLE 2.46. *A1 and B1 are arguing about the performance of their sorting algorithms. A1 claims that his $O(n \log n)$-time algorithm is always faster than B1's $O(n^2)$-time algorithm. To settle the issue, they implement and run the two algorithms on many randomly generated data sets. To A1's dismay, they find that if $n < 100$, the $O(n^2)$-time algorithm actually runs faster, and only when $n \geq 100$ is the $O(n \log n)$-time algorithm better. Explain why this scenario is possible. You may give numerical examples.*

SOLUTION : To say that A1's algorithm is "big-oh" of B1's algorithm implies that A1's is algorithm will run faster than B1's for all input greater than someone-zero positive integer n_0. In this case, $n_0 = 100$.

EXAMPLE 2.47. *Show that* $\sum_{i=1}^{n} i^2$ *is* $O(n^3)$.

SOLUTION : $\sum_{i=1}^{n} i^2 < \int_0^{n+1} x^2\,dx < \frac{(n+1)^3}{3} = O(n^3)$

EXAMPLE 2.48. *An array A contains $n - 1$ unique integers in the range $[0, n-1]$, that is, there is one number from this range that is not in A. Design an $O(n)$-time algorithm for finding that number. You are allowed to use only $O(1)$ additional space besides the array A itself.*

SOLUTION : First calculate the sum $\sum_{i=1}^{n-1} = \frac{n(n-1)}{2}$. Then calculate the sum of all values in the array A. The missing elements is the difference between these two numbers.

EXAMPLE 2.49. *Give a recursive algorithm to compute the product of two positive integers m and n using only addition.*

SOLUTION : We use the recursion : Multiply $(m, k) = m +$ Multiply $(m, k-1)$, for $2 \leq k \leq n$ and Multiply $(m, 1) = m$ (base of recursion). We start with the call Multiply (m, n).

EXAMPLE 2.50. *Show that the summation* $\sum_{i=1}^{n} \lceil \log_2 i \rceil$ *is* $O(n \log n)$.

SOLUTION : $\sum_{i=1}^{n} \log_2 i < \sum_{i=1}^{n} \log_2 n = n \log_2 n$, hence $O(n \log n)$.

EXAMPLE 2.51. *Characterize each of the following recurrence equations using the master method (assuming that $T(n) = c$ for $n < d$, for constants $c > 0$ and $d \geq 1$).*

(a) $T(n) = 2T(n/2) + \log n$

(b) $T(n) = 8T(n/2) + n^2$

(c) $T(n) = 16T(n/2) + (n \log n)^4$

(d) $T(n) = 7T(n/3) + n$

(e) $T(n) = 9T(n/3) + n^3 \log n$

SOLUTION : 1. $T(n)$ is $O(n)$ (case 1).

2. $T(n)$ is $O(n^3)$ (case 1).
3. $T(n)$ is $O(n^4 \log^5 n)$ (case 2).
4. $T(n)$ is $O(n^{\log_3 7})$ (case 1).
5. $T(n)$ is $O(n^3 \log n)$ (case 3).

EXAMPLE 2.52. *Show that the summation* $\sum_{i=1}^{n} \lceil \log_2 i \rceil$ *is* $\Omega(n \log n)$.

SOLUTION : For convenience assume that n is even. Then

$$\sum_{i=1}^{n} \log_2 i \geq \sum_{i=\frac{n}{2}+1}^{n} \log_2 \frac{n}{2} = \frac{n}{2} \log_2 \frac{n}{2}.$$

which is Ω ($n \log n$).

EXAMPLE 2.53. *An evil king has a cellar containing n bottles expensive wine, and his guards have just caught a spy trying to poison the king's wine. Fortunately, the guards caught the spy after he succeeded in poisoning only one bottle. Unfortunately, they don't know which one. To make matters worse, the poison the spy used was very deadly; just one drop diluted even a billion to one will still kill someone. Even so, the poison works slowly; it takes a full month for the person so die. Design a scheme that allows the evil king to determine exactly which one of his wine bottles was poisoned in just one month's time while expending at most O(log n) of his taste testers.*

SOLUTION : Let $B_{n-1}, B_{n-2}, \ldots, B_1, B_0$ be the n bottles of wine. Consider any binary string $\mathbf{b} = b_{n-1}\, b_{n-2} \ldots b_1 b_0$ of length n. A string b corresponds to a test as follows. If b has k 1's, we give a taste tester to drink a simple that consists of exactly k drops; a drop of bottle B_i is included to the sample only if $b_i = 1$. The idea is to have that sufficient collection of tests $\mathbf{b_1}, \mathbf{b_2}, \ldots, \mathbf{b_T}$ running in parallel, so that, when (after a month) their outcome is known, we can deterministically identify the poisoned bottle.

There are several ways for someone to construct the tests. A naive solution uses n tests, each of them having a drop from only one distinct bottle. We can do much better. An efficient construction of the tests will be in such a way so that a binary search is performed in the sequence of the bottles.

For simplicity assume that n is a power of 2, *i.e.*, $n = 2^k$ for some integer k. We define $\mathbf{B}(t)$ to be the binary string of length t that consists of $\frac{t}{2}$ consecutive 0's and followed by $\frac{t}{2}$ 1's. Let the first test be $\mathbf{b_1} = \mathbf{B}(n)$. Given the output of this test, our search space is reduced by half; if $\mathbf{b_1}$ is positive then we know that the poisoned bottle is one of $B_{\frac{n}{2}-1}, \ldots, B_1, B_0$, otherwise one of $B_{n-1}, B_{n-2}, \ldots, B_{\frac{n}{2}}$. Let now the second test be $\mathbf{b_2} = \mathbf{B}\left(\frac{n}{2}\right) \| \mathbf{B}\left(\frac{n}{2}\right)$, where $\|$ denotes string concatenation. Clearly tests $\mathbf{b_1}$ and $\mathbf{b_2}$ reduce the search space to one forth of the initial. We proceed in the same way : $\mathbf{b_3} = B\left(\frac{n}{4}\right) \| \mathbf{B}\left(\frac{n}{4}\right) \| \mathbf{B}\left(\frac{n}{4}\right) \mathbf{B}\left(\frac{n}{4}\right)$ and, generally, $\mathbf{b_i} = \mathbf{B}\left(\frac{n}{i+1}\right) \| \mathbf{B}\left(\frac{n}{i+1}\right) \| \mathbf{B}\left(\frac{n}{i+1}\right) \| \mathbf{B}\left(\frac{n}{i+1}\right)$, for $1 \le i \le k$, where $k = \log n$. Combining all k tests $\mathbf{b_1}, \mathbf{b_2}, \ldots, \mathbf{b_k}$ the search space is finally reduced to only one bottle. A similar reasoning can be followed in the case that n is not an exact power of 2; in that case, the number of tests are $[n]$.

We give an example for $n = 13$. The tests could be :

test 1 : $\mathbf{b_1} = 1111110000000$

test 2 : $\mathbf{b_2} = 1110001110000$

test 3 : $\mathbf{b_3} = 1001001001100$

test 4 : $\mathbf{b_4} = 1101101101010$.

that is, we use 4 taste testers. Suppose that only test 2 is positive. Given the structure of the tests, we can infer that the 5th bottle B_4 is the poisoned one.

When n is not a power of 2, there are generally more than one possible test structures. They all can determine the poisoned bottle, but the king should choose that collection of tests that have the least number of 1's (why ?) ...

Why is the king not similing ? No, it's not because the rumour about the queen-everybody believes she organized this!... The king is unhappy because all the bottles of wine (some of them were really old) had to be opened.

EXAMPLE 2.54. *Suppose that each row of an $n \times n$ array A consists of 1's and 0's such that, in any row i of A, all the 1's come before any 0's in that row. Assuming A is already in memory, describe a method running in $O(n)$ time (not $O(n^2)$ time) for finding the row of A that contains the most 1's.*

SOLUTION : Start at the upper left of the matrix. Walk across the matrix until a 0 is found. Then walk down the matrix until a 1 is found. This is repeated until the last row or column is encountered. The row with the most 1's is the last row which was walked across.

Clearly this is an $O(n)$-time algorithm since at most $2{\cdot}n$ comparisons are made.

EXAMPLE 2.55. *Suppose that each row of an $n \times n$ array A consists of 1's and 0's such that, in any row i of A, all the 1's come before any 0's in that row. Suppose further that the number of 1's in row i is at least the number in row i + 1, for i = 0, 1, ..., n – 2. Assuming A is already in memory, describe a method running in O(n) time (not O(n^2) time) for counting the number of 1's in the array A.*

SOLUTION : Using the two properties of the array, the method is described as follows :

Starting from element $A[n-1, 0]$, we scan A moving only to the right and upwards.

If the number at $A[i, j]$ is 1, then we add the number of 1s in that column $(i+1)$ to the current total of 1s.

Otherwise we move up one position until we reach another 1.

An example of the traversal of the array is shown in the figure 2.3.

1	1	1	1	1	1	1	1
1	1	1	1	1	1	0	0
1	1	1	1	1	1	0	0
1	1	1	1	1	0	0	0
1	1	1	1	0	0	0	0
1	1	1	1	0	0	0	0
1	1	0	0	0	0	0	0
0	0	0	0	0	0	0	0

Fig. 2.3. The traversal of the Array.

The pseudo-code of the algorithm is shown below.

The running time is $O(n)$. In the worst case, you will visit at most $2n-1$ places in the array. In the case that the diagram has all 0s in rows 2 through n and 1s in the first row, then there will be $n-1$ iterations of the **for** loop at constant time (since it will never enter the **while** loop) and 1 iteration of the **while** loop which has n iterations of constant time.

```
NumberOfOnes (A)
N ← 0
j ← 0
for i ← n - 1 to 0 do
while j ≤ n - 1 and A[i, j] = 1 do
  N ← N + i + 1
  j ← j + 1
return N
```

EXERCISE

1. Arrange the following functions into increasing order, of their running time.

(i) 1000000 (ii) $(lgn)^3$ (iii) 2^n (iv) $nlgn$

(v) $n^3 - 100n^2$ (vi) $n + lgn$ (vii) $lg(lgn)$ (viii) $n^{0.1}$

(ix) n^2 (x) 100 $nlgn$ (xi) $\left(\frac{3}{2}\right)^n$ (xii) $(2/3)^n$

(xiv) e^n (xv) 2^{2n} (xvi) $2n$!

2. Let α and β be real number such that $0 < \alpha < \beta$. Show that n^α is in $O(n^\beta)$ but n^β is not in $O(n^\alpha)$.

3. Prove or give a counter example : For every +ve constant c and every function f from non-negative integers into non- negative reals, $f(cn)\ \varepsilon\ \theta(f(n))$.

4. Let x and y be real numbers with $0 < x < y$. Prove that n^x is $O(n^y)$ but n^y is not $O(n^x)$?

5. Prove that $\sum_{i=1}^{n} i^d \log(i)$ is in $O(n^{d+1} \log(n))$

6. Prove or disprove $\sum_{i=1}^{n} i\ \varepsilon\ \theta(n^2)$

7. Prove that running time of an algorithm is $\theta(g(n))$, iff the worst case running time is $\Omega(g(n))$.

8. Write an algorithm for selection sort and give the best and worst case running time.

9. Why do we use asymptotic notation in study of algorithm? Describe various asymptotic notations and give their significance?

10. If $f(n)$ and are $g(n)$ asymptotically non negative functions then using the definition of θ-notation prove that

$$\max(f(n), g(n)) = \theta(f(n) + g(n))$$

11. Let $f(n)$ and $g(n)$ be asymptotically non negative functions. If $f(n) = \theta(g(n))$, then $g(n) = \theta(f(n))$, prove or disprove.

12. Prove or Disprove :

(i) $O(2^{\log_b n}) = O(2^{\log_a n})$

(ii) If $a < b$ then $n^a/2^n\ \varepsilon\ o(n^b)$

13. Suppose we have n total elements divided into m sorted lists. Explain how to produce a single sorted list of all n elements in time $O(nlgn)$.

14. A computer performs 10^9 operations per second, what is the largest problem you can solve in an hour if your algorithm takes 3^n operations on problems of size n?

15. Show that the following equalities are correct

(a) $5n^2 - 6n = \theta(n^2)$

(b) $2n^2\ 2^n + nlgn = \theta(n^2\ 2n)$

(c) $\sum_{l=0}^{n} l^2 = O(n^3)$

(d) $n^3 + 10^6 n^2 = \theta(n^{2n})$

(e) $n^{k+\varepsilon} + n^k \lg n = \theta(n^{k+\varepsilon}),\ k \geq 0,\ \varepsilon > 0.$

16. Prove or Disprove

(a) $10n^2 + 9 = O(n)$

(b) $n^2 \lg n = \theta(n^2)$

(c) $\dfrac{n^2}{\log n} = \theta(n^2)$

(d) $n^3 2^n + 6n^2 3^n = O(n^3 2^n)$

17. Prove $\sum_{i=1}^{n} \dfrac{i}{2^i} = O(n)$

18. Prove $f(n) + g(n) = \theta(\min(f(n), g(n)))$

19. Prove if $f(n) = O(g(n))$ then $1g\,(f(n)) = O(1g(g(n)))$ where $1g(g(n)) > 0$ and $f(n) \geq 1$ for sufficiently larger n.

20. Is the function $\lceil lgn \rceil!$ polynomially bounded? Is the function $\lceil lglgn \rceil!$ polynnomially bounded ?

21. Which is asymptotically larger $lg\,(1g*\,n)$ or $lg*\,(lgn)$?

22. Prove $\sum_{i=2}^{n} \left(\dfrac{1}{2} i + O(1)\right) = O(n^2)$.

23. Prove that n^K is in $o(2^n)$, for any $K > 0$.

24. Graph the functions $12n$, $6n \log n$, n^2, n^3 and 2^n using a logarithmic scale for the x-and y-axes; that is, if the function value $f(n)$ is y, plot this as a point with x-coordinate at $\log n$ and y-coordinate at $\log y$.

25. Algorithm A uses $10n \log n$ operations, while algorithm B uses n^2 operations. Determine the value n_0 such that A is better than B for $n \geq n_0$.

26. Repeat the previous problem assuming B uses $n\sqrt{n}$ operations.

27. Show that $\log^3 n$ is $o(n^{1/3})$.

28. Show that the following two statements are equivalent :

(a) The running time of algorithm A is $O(f(n))$.

(b) In the worst case, the running time of algorithm A is $O(f(n))$.

29. Give a big-oH characterization, in terms of n, of the running time of the Loop1 method shown in Algorithm 1.22.

30. Show that 2^{n+1} is $O(2^n)$.

31. Show that $n^3 \log n$ is $\Omega(n^3)$.

32. Show that $\lceil f(n) \rceil$ is $O(f(n))$ is $f(n)$ is a positive nondecreasing function that is always greater than 1.

33. Justify the fact that if $d(n)$ is $O(f(n))$ and $e(n)$ is $O(g(n))$, then the product $d(n)\,e(n)$ is $O(f(n)\,g(n))$.

34. What is the total running time of counting from 1 to n in binary if the time needed to add 1 to the current number i is proportional to the number of bits in the binary expansion of i that must change in going from i to $i + 1$?

35. Consider the following recurrence equation, defining a function $T(n)$:

$$T(n) = \begin{cases} 1 & \text{if } n = 1 \\ T(n-1) + n & \text{otherwise.} \end{cases}$$

Show, by induction, that $T(n) = n(n + 1)/2$.

36. Consider the following recurrence equation, defining a function $T(n)$:

$$T(n) = \begin{cases} 1 & \text{if } n = 0 \\ T(n-1) + 2^n & \text{otherwise.} \end{cases}$$

Show, by induction, that $T(n) = 2^{n+1} - 1$.

37. Consider the following recurrence equation, defining a function $T(n)$:

$$T(n) = \begin{cases} 1 & \text{if } n = 0 \\ 2T(n-1) & \text{otherwise.} \end{cases}$$

Show, by induction, that $T(n) = 2^n$.

38. Communication security is extremely important in computer networks, and one way many network protocols achieve security is to encrypt messages. Typical *cryptographic* schemes for the secure transmission or messages over such networks are based on the fact that no efficient algorithms are known for factoring large integers. Hence, if we can represent a secret message by a large prime number p, we can transmit over the network the number $r = p \cdot q$, where $q > p$ is another large prime number that acts as the *encryption key*. An eavesdropper who obtains the transmitted number r on the network would have to factor r in order to figure out the secret message p.

Using factoring to figure out a message is very difficult without knowing the encryption key q. To understand why, consider the following naive factoring algorithm :

For every integer p such that $1 < p < r$, check if p divides r. If so, print "The secret message is p!" and stop; if not, continue.

(a) Suppose that the eavesdropper uses the above algorithm and has a computer that can carry out in 1 microseconds (1 millionth of a second) a division between two integers of up to 100 bits each. Give an estimate of the time that it will take in the worst case to decipher the secret message if r has 100 bits.

(b) What is the worst-case time complexity of the above algorithm ? Since the input to the algorithm is just one larger number r, assume that the input size n is the number of bytes needed to store r, that is, $n = (\log_2 r)/8$, and that each division takes time $O(n)$.

39. What is the amortized running time of an operation in a series of n add operations on an initially empty extendable table implemented with an array such that the capacity Increment parameter is always maintained to be $\lceil \log(m + 1) \rceil$, where m is the number of elements of the stack? That is, each time the table is expanded by $\lceil \log(m + 1) \rceil$ cells, its capacity Increments is reset to $\lceil \log(m' + 1) \rceil$ cells, where m is the old size of the table and m' is the new size (in terms of actual elements present).

40. Describe a recursive algorithm for finding both the minimum and the maximum elements in an array A of n elements. Your method should return a pair (a, b), where a is the minimum element and b is the maximum. What is the running time of your method?

41. Give an example of a positive function $f(n)$ such that $f(n)$ is neither $O(n)$ nor $\Omega(n)$.

42. Show that $\sum_{i=1}^{n} i/2^i < 2$.

Hint : Try to bound this sum term by term with a geometric progression.

43. Show that $\log_b f(n)$ is $\Theta(\log f(n))$ if $b > 1$ is a constant.

❑❑❑

3

SUMMATIONS

Given a finite sequence $a_1, a_2, \ldots, a_n$ of n numbers, it can be represented as,

$$\sum_{k=1}^{k} a_k = a_1 + a_2 + a_3 + \ldots + a_k$$

The value of finite series is always well defined.

Also, $$\sum_{k=1}^{n} (c_1 a_k + b_k) = c_1 \sum_{k=1}^{n} a_k + \sum_{k=1}^{n} b_k$$

Arithmetic Series

$$\sum_{k=1}^{n} k = 1 + 2 + \ldots. + n.$$

Common difference, $d = 1$

$$a_n = a + (n-1)d.$$

Here, $$a_n = 1 + (n-1) \,.\, 1 = n$$

$$a_0 = 1$$

$$S_n = \frac{n}{2}(2a + (n-1)d) = \frac{n}{2}(a_0 + a_n)$$

$$= \frac{n}{2}(1+n) = \frac{n(n+1)}{2}$$

$$= \frac{n^2}{2} + n.$$

$$= \theta(n^2)$$

Geometric Series

$$\sum_{k=0}^{n} x^k = 1 + x + x^2 + \ldots + x^n, x \neq 1$$

$$\frac{a(r^n - 1)}{r - 1}$$

when $|r| > 1$ and series is infinite.

we have, $S_\infty = \frac{1}{1-r}$

Harmonic Series

$$H_n = 1 + \frac{1}{2} + \frac{1}{3} + \frac{1}{4} + \ldots + \frac{1}{n}.$$

$$= \sum_{k=1}^{n} \frac{1}{k} = \ln n + O(1)$$

Telescopic Series

$$\sum_{k=1}^{n} (a_k - a_{k-1}) = a_n - a_0$$

Since each of the terms $a_1, a_2, ..., a_{n-1}$ is added exactly once.

Products

$$a_1 . a_2 . a_3, ... a_k = \prod_{k=1}^{n} a_k$$

Logarithms

For all real $a > 0$, $b > 0$, $c > 0$ and n.

(i) $a = b^{\log_b a}$

(ii) $\log_e(ab) = \log_e a + \log_e b$

(iii) $\log_b a^n = n \log_b a$

(iv) $\log_b a = \dfrac{\log_e a}{\log_e b}$, **base changed**

(v) $\log_b\left(\dfrac{1}{a}\right) = -\log_b a$

(vi) $\log_b a = \dfrac{1}{\log_a b}$

(vii) $lg\, n = \log_2 n$

(viii) $\ln n = \log_e n$

(ix) $lg^k\, n = (lg\, n)^k$

(x) $lg\, lgn = lg(lgn)$

EXAMPLE. 3.1. *Prove that* $a^{\log_b n} = n^{\log_b a}$

SOLUTION :

$$a^{\left(\frac{\log n}{\log b}\right)} = a^{\left(\frac{\log_a n}{\log_a b}\right)}$$

$$= (a^{\log_a n})^{\frac{1}{\log_a b}}$$

as, $\quad a = b^{\log_b a}$, from rule (i)

$$= n^{\frac{1}{\log_a b}}$$

also, $\quad \dfrac{1}{\log_a b} = \log_b a$

$$= n^{\log_b a},$$ **Proved**

Formulae

$$\ln(1+x) = x - \frac{x^2}{2} + \frac{x^3}{3} - \frac{x^4}{4} + \frac{x^5}{5} + \ldots$$

$$e^x = 1 + x + \frac{x^2}{2\,!} + \frac{x^3}{3\,!} + \ldots$$

$$= \sum_{i=0}^{n} \frac{x^i}{i\,!}$$

EXAMPLE. 3.2. *Prove that*

$$lg\left(\prod_{k=1}^{n} a_k\right) = \sum_{k=1}^{n} lg\, a_k.$$

SOLUTION : **L.H.S.** $= \log(a_1 . a_2 . a_3 \ldots a_n)$

$$= \sum_{k=1}^{n} \log a_k = \text{R.H.S.}$$

EXAMPLE. 3.3. *Find the summation of*

$$\sum_{k=1}^{n} (2k-1)$$

SOLUTION : $\sum_{k=1}^{n} 2k - \sum_{k=1}^{n} 1$

$$2 . \sum_{k=1}^{n} k - \sum_{k=1}^{n} 1$$

$$2 . \frac{n(n+1)}{2} - n$$

$$n(n+1) - n = n^2$$

$$= \theta(n^2).$$

EXAMPLE. 3.4. *Show that* $\sum_{k=1}^{n} \frac{1}{(2k-1)} = \ln(\sqrt{n}) + O(1)$

$$\sum_{k=1}^{n} \left(\frac{1}{2k-1}\right) = 1 + \frac{1}{3} + \frac{1}{5} + \frac{1}{7} + \frac{1}{9} + \ldots$$

SOLUTION : We have $\sum_{k=1}^{n} \frac{1}{n} = \ln n + O(1).$

$$\sum_{k=1}^{n} \frac{1}{n} = 1 + \frac{1}{2} + \frac{1}{3} + \frac{1}{4} + \frac{1}{5} + \ldots$$

$$= \left(1 + \frac{1}{3} + \frac{1}{5} + \ldots\right) + \left(\frac{1}{2} + \frac{1}{4} + \ldots\right)$$

$$= \ln n^{1/2} + \ln n^{1/2} + O(1)$$

$$= \ln n + O(1)$$

$$\therefore \quad \sum_{k=1}^{n} \frac{1}{2k-1} = \ln(\sqrt{n}) + O(1)$$

Mathematical Induction

Prove that $\Sigma k = \frac{1}{2} n(n+1)$

$$P(1): \sum_{k=1}^{n} 1 = 1$$

$$\text{R.H.S.} = \frac{1}{2} . 1(1+1)+1$$

Thus $P(1)$ holds

Let $\quad P(n) : \sum_{k=1}^{n} k = \frac{1}{2} n(n+1)$ be to true.

$$\therefore \quad P(n+1) \sum_{k=1}^{n+1} k = \sum_{k=1}^{n} k + (n+1)$$

$$= \frac{1}{2} n(n+1) + n + 1$$

$$= \frac{1}{2} (n+1)(n+2)$$

$\therefore$ $P(n+1)$ holds.

EXAMPLE 3.5. *Prove that* $\sum_{k=0}^{n} 3^k$ *is of the order.* $O(3^n)$ *by induction.*

SOLUTION : By Definition,

$$\sum_{k=0}^{n} 3^k \le c3^n.$$

for $n = 0$

$$3^{\circ} = 1 < c . 3^{\circ}$$

$$\Rightarrow \quad c \ge 1$$

Let it holds for n, Now prove that

$$\sum_{k=0}^{n+1} 3^k \le c3^{n+1}$$

$$\text{L.H.S.} = \sum_{k=0}^{n} 3^k + 3^{k+1}$$

$$\le c . 3^n + 3^{n+1} = \left(\frac{1}{3} + \frac{1}{c}\right) c3^{n+1}$$

$$\le c3^{n+1} , \frac{1}{3} + \frac{1}{C} \le 1$$

$$\Rightarrow \quad c \ge \frac{3}{2}$$

$$\therefore \quad O(3^n). \quad \textbf{Proved.}$$

EXAMPLE 3.6. *Find the asymptotic upper bound of* $\sum_{k=0}^{\infty} \frac{k^2}{2^k}$

SOLUTION : Ratio of two consecutive terms

$$\frac{\dfrac{(k+1)^2}{2^{k+1}}}{\dfrac{K^2}{2^k}} = \frac{(k+1)^2}{2k^2}$$

$$\leq \frac{8}{9} \text{ if } k \geq 3$$

Thus, splitting the summation; we get

$$\sum_{k=0}^{\infty} \frac{k^2}{2^k} = \sum_{k=0}^{2} \frac{k^2}{2^k} + \sum_{k=3}^{\infty} \frac{k^2}{2^k}$$

$$\leq O(1) + \frac{9}{8} \sum_{k=0}^{\infty} \left(\frac{8}{9}\right)^k$$

$= O(1)$ as second term is decreasing geometric series.

EXERCISE

1. Show that $\sum_{K=0}^{\infty} (K-1)/2^K = 0$.
2. Evaluate the sum $\sum_{K=1}^{\infty} (2K+1)x^{2K}$.
3. Prove that $\sum_{K=1}^{\infty} O(f_K(n)) = O\left(\sum_{K=1}^{n} f_K(n)\right)$.
4. Prove that $\sum_{K=1}^{\infty} \Omega(f(K)) = \Omega\left(\sum_{K=1}^{\infty} f(K)\right)$.
5. Evaluate the product $\Pi_{K=2}^{n} (1 - 1/K^2)$.
6. Find an asymptotic upper bound on the summation.

$$\sum_{K=0}^{\lfloor lgn \rfloor} \lceil n/2^k \rceil .$$

□□□

4

RECURRENCES

4.1 Recurrence

It is an equation or inequality that describes a function in terms of its value on smaller inputs. For example merge-sort procedure is described by the recurrence

$$T(n) = \begin{cases} \theta(1) & \text{if } n = 1 \\ 2T(n/2) + \theta(n) & \text{if } n > 1 \end{cases} \qquad \ldots(4.1)$$

there are three methods for solving this : **Substitution method,** we guess a bound and then use mathematical induction to prove our guess correct **iteration method,** converts the recurrence into summation an then relies on techniques for bounding summations to solve the recurrence. The **master method** provides bounds for recurrence of the form.

$$T(n) = a\,T\left(\frac{n}{b}\right) + f(n), \qquad \ldots(4.2)$$

where $a \geq 1$, $b > 1$ and $f(n)$ is given function.

While solving the recurrence if we have $T(n) = \theta(1)$ for small n, then we can omit such condition, *i.e.*, we can omit the boundary conditions as it will change the running time by a constant factor only. We can also omit floor and ceilings.

4.1.1 Substitution Method

Let us guess a solution $O(ngln)$ to recurence 4.1, thus we have to prove $T(n) \le cnlgn$ for some constant $c > 0$. We assume that this holds for $T(\lfloor n/2 \rfloor) \le c \lfloor n/2 \rfloor\, lg(\lfloor n/2 \rfloor)$. Substituting in 4.1, we get

$$\begin{aligned} T(n) &\le 2(c\lfloor n/2 \rfloor)\, lg(\lfloor n/2 \rfloor) + n \\ &\le cn\ lg\frac{n}{2} + n \\ &= cn\ lgn - cn\ lg\ 2 + n \\ &= cnlgn - cn + n \\ T(n) &\le cnlgn,\ c \ge 1 \end{aligned}$$

by mathematical induction, we require to show that our solution holds for the boundary conditions

$T(1) \le c\ 1\ lg\ 1 = 0$, thus for any value of c, this will not hold, so by asymptotic definition we need to prove $T(n) \le cnlgn$, for $n > n_0$,

$$T(2) \le c2lg2,\ T(3) \le c3lg3$$

as n can not be 1, this relation holds for $c \ge 2$, thus $T(n) \le cnlgn$ holds.

Hence our guess $T(n) = O(ngln)$ is true.

BAD-GUESS

1. Let us guess $O(n)$ for the recurrence

$$T(n) = 2T(\lfloor n/2 \rfloor) + 1$$

thus we need to prove $T(n) \le cn$, substituting this we get

$$\begin{aligned} T(n) &\le 2c\ [\lfloor n/2 \rfloor] + 1 \\ &\le \frac{cn}{2} + 1 \\ &= cn + 1 \end{aligned}$$

for any value of c, $T(n)$ is not less than cn, because of 1. hence it is a bad guess

2. We make a larger guess $T(n) = O(n^2)$, thus.

$$\begin{aligned} T(n) &\le 2c\frac{n^2}{2} + 1 \\ &= cn^2 + 1 \\ &= cn^2 \end{aligned}$$

if $c \ge 1$, for large values of n this relation will hold as n grows much faster than 1, so we can ignore this value. $T(n) = O(n^2)$ will hold.

3. Now we make an intermediae guess such that $O(n)$ should hold. Let $T(n) \le cn - b$, where $b \ge 0$ then

$$T(n) \leq 2\left(\frac{cn}{2} - b\right) + 1$$
$$= cn - 2b + 1 \leq cn - b,$$

for $b \geq 1$ (if $b = 1$, b cancels out with 1). Since b is constant this of order $O(n)$.

4. Let us guess $O(n)$ in the recurrence

$$T(n) = 2T(\lfloor n/2 \rfloor) + n$$

Thus we need to prove $T(n) \leq cn_1$ substituting,

$$T(n) \leq 2c\left(\frac{n}{2}\right) + n = cn + n$$

$\neq cn$ as addition term is a variable

hence $T(n) \neq O(n)$ in this recurrence

5. Changing Variables

We have $T(n) = 2T(\lfloor \sqrt{n} \rfloor) + lgn$

here we can choose another variable, say

$$m = lgn \;\Rightarrow n = 2^m,\; n^{1/2} = 2^{m/2}$$

thus,

$$T(2^m) = 2T(2^{m/2}) + m$$

we rename $T(2^m) = S(m)$,

$$S\left(\frac{m}{2}\right) = T(2^{m/2})$$

hence new recurrence is

$$S(m) = 2S\left(\frac{m}{2}\right) + m$$

as 2^m is written as m in new notation S, hence we can write $T(2^{m/2})$ as $S\left(\frac{m}{2}\right)$, but above recurrence has solution $O(mlgm)$. Substituting for m we get $O(lgn \,.\, lg\, lgn)$.

EXAMPLE 4.1. *Show that solution of $T(n) = T(\lfloor n/2 \rfloor) + 1$ is $O(lgn)$*

SOLUTION : Let us guess that solution is $O(lgn)$, thus we need to prove $T(n) \leq clgn$. Substituting this we get,

$$T(n) \leq c \log \frac{n}{2} + 1$$
$$= c\, lg\, n - c\, lg\, 2 + 1$$
$$= c\, lgn - c + 1$$
$$\leq clgn \text{ for } c \geq 1$$

Hence, $T(n) = O(lgn)$

EXAMPLE 4.2. *Show that solution of $T(n) = 2T(\lfloor n/2 \rfloor) + n$ is $\Omega(nlgn)$. Conclude that the solution is $\theta(nlgn)$.*

SOLUTION : Let the solution to $T(n)$ is $\Omega(nlgn)$ then we need to prove $T(n) \geq cnlgn$.

$$
\begin{aligned}
T(n) &\geq 2\left(c\frac{n}{2}\frac{lgn}{2}\right)+n \\
&\geq cn\frac{lgn}{2}+n \\
&= cnlgn - cnlg2 + n \\
&= cnlgn - cn + n \\
&\geq cnlgn \text{ for } c \geq 1
\end{aligned}
$$

therefore $T(n) = \Omega(nlgn)$, for $c \leq 1$ but for large values of n, and c $T(n) \leq cnlgn$ also holds hence $T(n) = \theta(n)$

EXAMPLE 4.3. *Show that solution to* $T(n) = 2T(\lfloor\frac{n}{2}\rfloor + 17) + n$ *is* $O(nlgn)$.

SOLUTION : Let us guess solution is $O(nlgn)$ then we have to prove $T(n) \leq cnlgn$, substituting this we get

$$
\begin{aligned}
T(n) &\leq 2\left(\frac{cn}{2}lg\left(\frac{n}{2}\right)+17\right)+n \\
&= cn\ lg\left(\frac{n}{2}\right)+34+n. \\
&= cnlgn - cnlg\ 2 + 34 + n \\
&= cnlgn - cn + 34 + n \\
&= cnlgn - (c-1)n + 34 \\
&= cnlgn - bn + 34 \leq cnlgn
\end{aligned}
$$

if $c \geq 1$, where b is constant.

Hence $T(n) = O(nlgn)$

EXAMPLE 4.4. *Solve* $T(n) = 2T(\sqrt{n}) + 1$

SOLUTION : Let $m = lgn$, s.t. $n = 2^m$, $n^{1/2} = 2^{m/2}$

Thus $T(2^m) = 2T(2^{m/2}) + 1$

Changing the recurrence to $S(m) = T(2^m)$, we get

$$S(m) = 2S\left(\frac{m}{2}\right)+1$$

Solution to this $O(lgm)$

Therefore $T(n) = O(lg\ lgn)$

4.1.2 Iteration Method

In this method recurrence is expanded as summation of terms, then summation provides the solution.

$$
\begin{aligned}
T(n) &= 3T(\lfloor n/4 \rfloor) + n = n + 3T(\lfloor n/4 \rfloor) \\
&= n + 3(\lfloor n/4 \rfloor + 3T(\lfloor n/16 \rfloor))
\end{aligned}
$$

$$= n + 3(\lfloor n/4 \rfloor) + 3T((\lfloor n/16 \rfloor) + 3T(\lfloor n/64 \rfloor)))$$

$$= n + \frac{3n}{4} + \frac{9n}{16} + 27T\,(\lfloor n/64 \rfloor) + 3^i\, T\,(n/4i)$$

ith term in this series is $3^i\, T\left(\frac{n}{4^i}\right)$ and since it is a decreasing series, $T(1) = 1$ when $\lfloor n/4^i \rfloor = 1$

$$\frac{n}{4^i} = 1 \Rightarrow n = 4^i,\ i = \log_4 n$$

thus $$T(n) \le n + \frac{3n}{4} + \frac{9n}{16} + \frac{27n}{64} + \ldots\ 3^{\log_4 n}\, T(1)$$

$$\le n \sum_{i=0}^{\infty} \left(\frac{3}{4}\right)^i + \theta(n^{\log_4 3}),\ \text{as } 3^{\log_4 n} = n^{\log_4 3}$$

$$\le n \frac{(3/4)^{\circ}}{1 - \frac{3}{4}} + \theta(n^{\log_4 3})$$

$$\le 4n + o(n),\ \text{as } \log_4 3 < 1$$

$$= O(n),\ [O(n) + O(n) = O(n)]$$

4.1.2.1 Recursion Trees

We can visualise iteration method as recursion tree in which at each level nodes are expanded. We consider second term in recurrence as root. It is useful when divide-and-conquer algorithm is used.

$$T(n) = 2T\left(\frac{n}{2}\right) + n^2$$

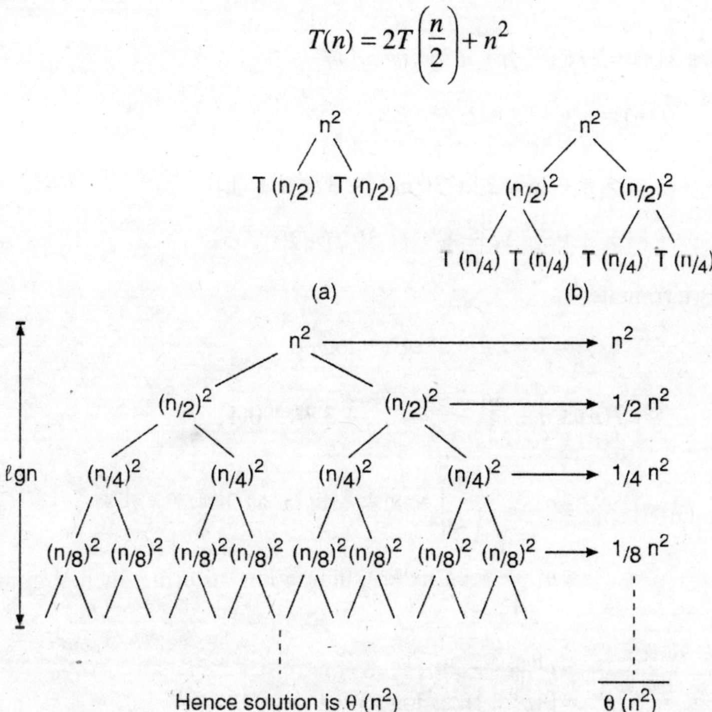

Fig. 4.1. Recursion tree.

Summing the values at each level, we get

$$n^2 + \frac{n^2}{2} + \frac{n^2}{4} + \ldots = n^2\left(1 + \frac{1}{2} + \frac{1}{4} + \ldots\right)$$

Hence solution is $\theta(n^2)$.

EXAMPLE 4.5. *Solve the recurrence* $T(n) = T\left(\frac{n}{3}\right) + T\left(\frac{2n}{3}\right) + n$ *by recursion trees.*

SOLUTION :

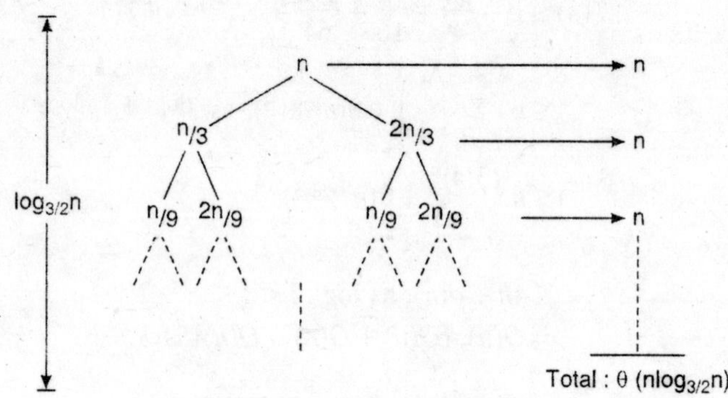

$$T(n) = n + n + \ldots \log_{3/2} n \text{ times}$$
$$= \theta(n\ lgn)$$

Here, recurrence with $T\left(\frac{2n}{3}\right)$ terminates later, therefore height must be taken of the longer tree.

EXAMPLE. 4.6. *Solve* $T(n) = 3T(\lfloor n/2 \rfloor) + n$ *by iteration.*

SOLUTION :

$$T(n) = n + 3T(\lfloor n/2 \rfloor)$$
$$= n + 3(\lfloor n/2 \rfloor + 3.T(\lfloor n/4 \rfloor))$$
$$= n + 3(\lfloor n/2 \rfloor + 3(\lfloor n/4 \rfloor + 3T(\lfloor n/16 \rfloor)))$$
$$= n + \frac{3n}{2} + \frac{9n}{4} + \ldots + 3^i.\ T(n/2^i)$$

When series terminates

$$\frac{n}{2^i} = 1 \Rightarrow n = 2^i \text{ or } i = \log_2 n$$

Hence,
$$T(n) \le n + \frac{3n}{2} + \frac{9n}{4} + \ldots + 3^{\log_2 n}\,\theta(1)$$
$$\le n \sum_{i=0}^{\infty} \left(\frac{3}{2}\right)^i + n^{\log_2 3}.\ \theta(1), \text{ as } 3^{\log_2 n} = n^{\log_2 3}$$
$$\le n . \frac{1}{1 - \frac{3}{2}} + n^{\log_2 3},\ \theta(1) = 1$$
$$\le n^{\log_2 3} - 2n.$$
$$= \theta(n^{\log 3}), \text{ as } \log_2 3 > 1$$

EXAMPLE. 4.7. *Draw the recursion tree for $T(n) = 4T(\lfloor n/2 \rfloor) + n$ and provide light asymptotic bounds*

SOLUTION :

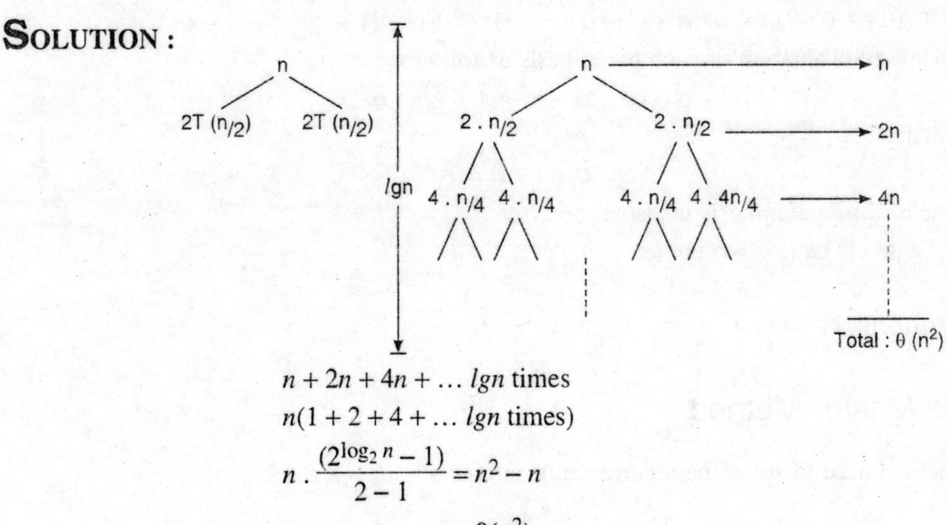

$n + 2n + 4n + \ldots\ lgn$ times

$n(1 + 2 + 4 + \ldots\ lgn$ times)

$$n \cdot \frac{(2^{\log_2 n} - 1)}{2 - 1} = n^2 - n$$

$$= \theta(n^2)$$

Note : Height of tree with n nodes is $\log n$.

EXAMPLE 4.8. *Solve the following recurrence*

$$T(n) = T(\alpha n) + T[(1 - \alpha)n] + n$$

SOLUTION : Using Recursion Tree Method

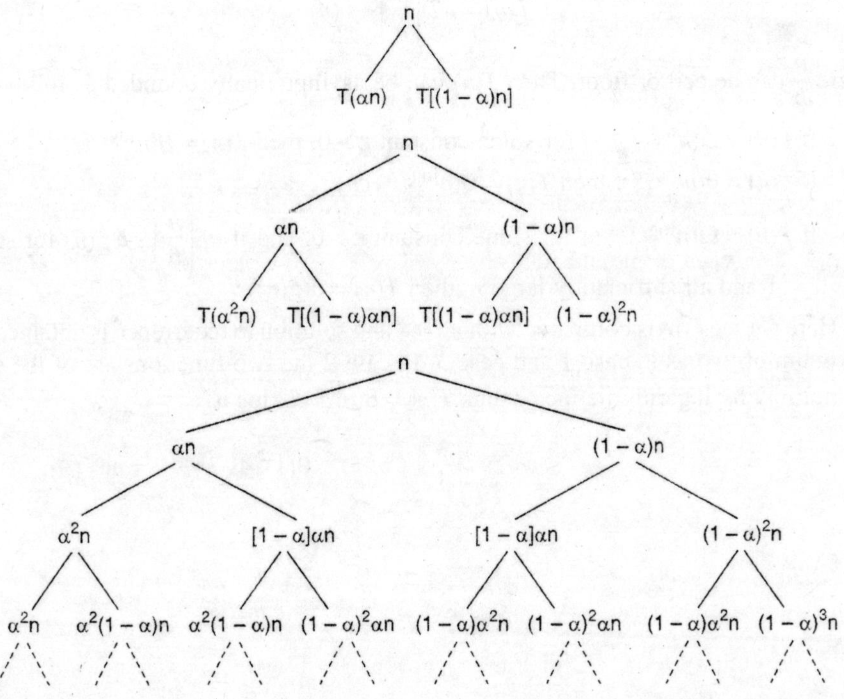

Summing the values at each level of node.

$$n[1 + (\alpha + 1 - \alpha) + (\alpha^2 + (1 - \alpha)\alpha + (1 - \alpha)\alpha + (1 - \alpha)^2) + (\alpha^3 + \alpha^2(1 - \alpha) + \alpha^2(1 - \alpha) + (1 - \alpha)^2\alpha + (1 - \alpha)\alpha^2 + (1 - \alpha)^2\alpha + (1 - \alpha)^2\alpha + (1 - \alpha)^3) + \ldots] \quad \ldots(1)$$

We can see evaluation of each parenthesis as follows

$$\alpha^2 + \alpha - \alpha^2 + \alpha - \alpha^2 + 1 - 2\alpha + \alpha^2 = 1$$

Similarly,

$$\alpha + 1 - \alpha = 1$$

also value of third parenthesis is also 1.

Thus eqn. (1) can be written as

$$n\,[1 + 1 + \ldots + 1] = n^2$$

$\therefore\ T(n) = \theta(n^2)$.

4.1.3 The Master Method

It is a method used to solve the recurrence of the form

$$T(n) = aT\left(\frac{n}{b}\right) + f(n)$$

where $a \geq 1$, $b > 1$ are constants and $f(x)$ is an asymptotically positive function.

THEOREM 4.1 (Master Theorem)

Let $a \geq 1$ and $b > 1$ be constants. let $f(n)$ be a function, and let $T(n)$ be defined on the non negative integers by recurrence

$$T(n) = aT\left(\frac{n}{b}\right) + f(n),$$

where $\frac{n}{b}$ can be ceil or floor. Then $T(n)$ can be asymptotically bounded as follows.

1. If $f(n) = O(n^{\log_b a - \varepsilon})$ for some constant $\varepsilon > 0$, then $T(n) = \theta(n^{\log_b a})$
2. If $f(n) = \theta(n^{\log_b a})$, then $T(n) = \theta(n^{\log_b a}\, lgn)$
3. If $f(n) = \Omega(n^{\log_b a + \varepsilon})$ for some constant $\varepsilon > 0$, and if $af\left(\frac{n}{b}\right) \leq c\, f(n)$ for some constant $c < 1$ and all sufficiently large n, then $T(n) = \theta(f(n))$.

Here we see $f(n)$ is compared with $n^{\log_b a}$ and solution to recurrence is obtained by selecting maximum of two as in case 1 and case 3. In case 2 the two functions are of the same size, so we multiply by logarithmic factor thus $T(n) = \theta(n^{\log_b a} . \log n)$.

EXAMPLE. 4.9. *Solve the recurrence using Master Method.*

$$T(n) = 9T\left(\frac{n}{3}\right) + n$$

SOLUTION : Here $a = 9$, $b = 3$, $f(n) = n$

$$n^{\log_b a} = n^{\log_3 9} = \theta(n^2)$$

writting $f(n)$ in appropriate form.

$$f(n) = O(n^{\log_3 9 - 1}) = O(n)$$

hence we can apply case 1.

So the solution is $\theta(n^{\log_b a})$ by case 1, *i.e.*,

$$\theta(n^{\log_3 9}) = \theta(n^2)$$

EXAMPLE. 4.10. *Solve the recurrence by master method.*

$$T(n) = T\left(\frac{2n}{3}\right) + 1$$

SOLUTION : Here $a = 1$, $b = 3/2$, $f(n) = 1$

$$n^{\log_b a} = n^{\log_{3/2} 1} = n^0 = 1$$

which is equal to $f(n)$, hence case 2 applies. Thus solution is

$$T(n) = \theta(n^{\log_b a}.\ lgn) = \theta(1\ lgn)$$
$$= \theta(lgn)$$

EXAMPLE. 4.11. *Solve the recurrence by master method.*

$$T(n) = 3T\left(\frac{n}{4}\right) + nlgn$$

SOLUTION : Here, $a = 3$, $b = 4$, $f(n) = nlgn$

$$n^{\log_b a} = n^{\log_4 3} = O(n^{0.793})$$

$$f(n) = \Omega(n^{(\log_4 3 + \varepsilon)}), \text{ where } \varepsilon \simeq 0.2, \text{ case 3 applies}$$

Here we can see that **regularity condition** of case 3 holds,

i.e., $$af\left(\frac{n}{b}\right) \leq cf(n)$$

$$3\left(\frac{n}{4}\right)\log\left(\frac{n}{4}\right) \leq \left(\frac{3}{4}\right)nlgn = cf(n) \text{ for } c = \frac{3}{4}$$

therefore solution to the recurrence is $T(n) = \theta(nlgn) = \theta(f(n))$

Analysis of Master Theorem

As we are selecting the maximum of the two in case 1 and case 3 we can see that not only the $f(n)$ is smaller than $n^{\log_b a}$, it must be *polynomially* smaller. That is $f(n)$ must be asymptotically smaller than $n^{\log_b a}$ by a factor of n^{ε} for some constant $\varepsilon > O$ and in third case it must be *polynomially* larger and satisfy the "regularity" condition that $af(n) \leq cf(n)$.

One more thing to be noted that there is a gap between case 1 and case 2, when $f(n)$ is smaller than $n^{\log_b a}$ (*i.e.*, $O(f(n) < O(n^{\log_b a}))$) but not polynomially smaller (*i.e.*, $f(n) \neq n^{\log_b a - \varepsilon}$ by any permutation of ε subtracted- from $n^{\log_b a}$). Similarly if $f(n)$ is larger than $n^{\log_b a}$ but it is not polynomially larger (*i.e.*, $f(n) > n^{\log_b a}$, but $f(n) \neq n^{\log_b a + \varepsilon}$) and if regularity condition is not satisfied then master theorem can't be applied for solving the recurrence. See the following example.

EXAMPLE. 4.12. $T(n) = 2T\left(\frac{n}{2}\right) + nlgn$

SOLUTION : $a = 2, b = 2, f(n) = nlgn$

We have $$n^{\log_b a} = n^{\log_2 2} = n$$

thus $f(n) = nlgn$ is asymptotically larger than $n^{\log_b a}$, *i.e.*, n but it is not polynomially greater as the ratio of $\frac{f(n)}{n^{\log_b a}} = lgn$ is asymptotically less than n^{ε} for any positive value of ε. Hence, Master theorem can not be applied.

More Recurrence Examples

EXAMPLE 4.13. *Solve* $T(n) = 2T\left(\frac{n}{2}\right) + n^3$ *by master method*

SOLUTION : We have $a = 2,\ b = 2, f(n) = n^3$

$$n^{\log_b a} = n^{\log_2 2} = n$$

Case III, $$f(n) = \Omega(n^{\log_b a + \varepsilon}) = \Omega(n^{1+2}), \text{ here } \varepsilon = 2$$

and also, $2f\left(\frac{n^3}{2^3}\right) < cf(n^3)$, is true for $c = \frac{1}{4}$

hence regularity condition holds, therefore

$$T(n) = \Theta(n^3)$$

EXAMPLE 4.14. *Solve* $T(n) = T(9n/10) + n$ *by master method, if possible*

SOLUTION : Here $a = 1, b = \frac{10}{9}, f(n) = n$.

$$n^{\log_b a} = n^{\log_{10/9} 1} = n^0 = 1$$

we can write $f(n) = n = \Theta(n) = \Theta(n^{\log_b a + \varepsilon})$

$= \Theta(n^{0+1})$, where $\varepsilon = 1$, so case III applies

also, $af\left(\frac{n}{b}\right) \leq cn$, as

$$f\left(\frac{9n}{10}\right) = \frac{9n}{10} \le cn, \text{ for } c = \frac{9}{10}$$

hence regularity condition is also satisfied.

therefore $\quad T(n) = \theta\,(f\,(n))$

$\qquad\qquad\quad = \theta(n)$

EXAMPLE 4.15. *Solve,* $T(n) = 16T\left(\frac{n}{4}\right) + n^3$

SOLUTION : By master theorem,

$$a = 16,\ b = 4,\ f\,(n) = n^3$$

$$n^{\log_b a} = n^{\log_4 16} = n^2 = 0(n^2)$$

$$f\,(n) = n^3 = (n^{\log_b a + \varepsilon}) = (n^{2+1}) = \Omega(n^3)$$

and $\qquad \varepsilon = 1$

also, $\qquad 16f\left(\frac{n^3}{4^3}\right) \le cf\,(n^3)$

$$16 \,.\, \frac{n^3}{64} \le cn^3, \text{ for } c = \frac{1}{4}$$, it is true so regularity condition holds.

Hence by case III, $T(n) = \theta(f\,(n)) = \theta(n^3)$

EXAMPLE 4.16. *Solve* $T(n) = 3T\left(\frac{n}{2}\right) + n \log n$

SOLUTION : By master method,

$$a = 3,\ b = 2,\ f\,(n) = n \log n$$

$$n^{\log_b a} = n^{\log_2 3} = O(n^{1.58})$$

$$f\,(n) = \Omega(n^{\log_2 3 - \varepsilon}), \text{ where } \varepsilon = 0.58$$

We are not sure whether we can apply the master method.

As we have $f\,(n) = n\ lg\ n$, and $n^{\log_b a} = n^{1.58}$, and also it is in proper form, *i.e.*, $a = 3$, $b = 2, f\,(n) = n\ lg\ n$,

but $f\,(n)$ is asymptotically smaller than $n^{\log_b a} = n^{1.58}$ *i.e.*, $O(n^{1.58}) > O(n\log n)$.

but is not polynomially smaller than $n^{\log_b a}$. *i.e.*, $n\log n > n^{1.58 - 0.58}$. The ratio $\frac{f\,(n)}{n^{\log_b a}}$ is asymptotically greater than n^{ε} for some +ve constant ε. So the recurrence falls in the gap of case 1 and case 2.

Master Theorem

THEOREM 4.2. Let $a \ge 1$ and $b > 1$ be constants, left $f\,(n)$ be a non-negative function defined on exact power of b by the recurrence

$$T(n) = \begin{cases} \Theta(1) & \text{if } n = 1 \\ aT(n/b) + f(n) & \text{if } n = b^2 \end{cases}$$

where i is a positive integer. Then

$$T(n) = \Theta(n^{\log_b a}) + \sum_{i=0}^{\log n - 1} a^i f\left(\frac{n}{b^i}\right)$$

PROOF : Iterating the recurrence yields

$$T(n) = f(n) + aT\left(\frac{n}{b}\right)$$

$$= f(n) + af\left(\frac{n}{b}\right) + a^2 T\left(\frac{n}{b^2}\right)$$

$$\leq f(n) + af\left(\frac{n}{b}\right) + a^2 f\left(\frac{n}{b^2}\right) + a^{\log_b n - 1} f\left(\frac{n}{b^{\log_b n - 1}}\right) + a^{\log_b n}\, T(1)$$

as it is a decreasing geometric series, ith terms in series is $a^i f\left(\frac{n}{b^i}\right)$ for this to terminate at nth term it should be $a^i.\, T(1)$

for this, $\frac{n}{b^i} = 1 \Rightarrow n = b^i$ or $i = \log_b n$

i.e., last term must be $a^{\log_b n}\, T(1)$

Since $\quad a^{\log_b n} = n^{\log_b a}$

$$a^{\log_b n}\, T(1) = \Theta(n^{\log_b a})$$

using boundary conditions, $T(1) = \Theta(1)$, the remaining term can be expressed as the sum,

$$\sum_{j=0}^{\log_b n - 1} a^j f\left(\frac{n}{b^j}\right)$$

Thus,

$$T(n) = \Theta(n^{\log_b a}) + \sum_{j=0}^{\log_b n - 1} a^j f\left(\frac{n}{b^j}\right)$$

THEOREM 4.3. Let $a \geq 1$ and $b > 1$ be constants, let $f(n)$ be a non-negative function defined on exact powers of b. A function defined over exact powers of b by

$$g(n) = \sum_{j=0}^{\log_n - 1} a^j f\left(\frac{n}{b^j}\right)$$

can then be bounded asymptotically for exact powers of b as follows.

1. If $f(n) = O(n^{\log_b a - \varepsilon})$ for some constants $\varepsilon > 0$, then $g(n) = O(n^{\log_b a})$
2. If $f(n) = \Theta(n^{\log_b a})$, then $g(n) = \Theta\,(n^{\log_b a} \log n)$
3. If $af\left(\frac{n}{b}\right) \leq cf(n)$ for some constant $c < 1$ and all $n \geq b$, then $g(n) = \Theta(f(n))$.

PROOF : For case 1, we have $f(n) = O(n^{\log_b a - \varepsilon})$, impyling that

$f\left(\frac{n}{b^j}\right) = O\left[\left(\frac{n}{b^j}\right)^{\log_b a - \varepsilon}\right]$. Substituting into equation (1) yields

$$g(n) = O\left[\sum_{j=0}^{\log_b n - 1} a^j \left(\frac{n}{b^j}\right)^{\log_b a - \varepsilon}\right] \qquad \ldots(2)$$

We bound the summation within the O-notation by factoring out terms and simplifying, which leaves an increasing geometric series :

$$\sum_{j=0}^{\log_b n - 1} a^j \left(\frac{n}{b^j}\right)^{\log_b a - \varepsilon} = n^{\log_b a - \varepsilon} \cdot \sum_{j=0}^{lob_b n - 1} \left(\frac{ab^\varepsilon}{b^{\log_b a}}\right)^j$$

$$= n^{\log_b a - \varepsilon} \sum_{j=0}^{\log_b n - 1} (b^\varepsilon)^j$$

$$= n^{\log_b a - \varepsilon}\left(\frac{b^{\varepsilon \log_b n} - 1}{b^\varepsilon - 1}\right)$$

$$= n^{\log_b a - \varepsilon}\left(\frac{n^\varepsilon - 1}{b^\varepsilon - 1}\right)$$

Since b an ε are constants, the last expression reduces to $n^{\log_b a - \varepsilon} O(n^\varepsilon) = O(n^{\log_b a})$. Substituting this expession for the summation in equation (2),

we get $\quad g(n) = O(n^{\log_b a})$, hence case 1 is proved.

for case 2 we have $f(n) = \Theta(n^{\log_b a})$

thus $\quad f\left(\frac{n}{b^j}\right) = \Theta\left[\left(\frac{n}{b^j}\right)^{\log_b a}\right]$, Substituting this in (1), we get

$$g(n) = \Theta\left(\sum_{j=0}^{\log_b n - 1} a^j \left(\frac{n}{b^j}\right)^{\log_b a}\right) \qquad \ldots(3)$$

We have,

$$\sum_{j=0}^{\log_b n - 1} a^j \left(\frac{u}{b^j}\right)^{\log_b a} = n^{\log_b a} \sum_{j=0}^{\log_b n - 1} \left(\frac{a}{b^{\log_b a}}\right)^j$$

$$= n^{\log_b a} \sum_{j=0}^{\log_b n - 1} 1$$

$$= n^{\log_b a} \log_b n$$

Substituting this in eqn. (3), we get

$$g(n) = \Theta(n^{\log_b a} \log_b n)$$

$$\log_b n = \frac{\log_2 n}{\log_2 b}, \text{where } \log_2 b \text{ is constant}$$

thus, $g(n) = \Theta(n^{\log_b a}\, lg\, n)$, hence case 2 proved.

For case 3, we have

$a^j f\left(\frac{n}{b^j}\right) \le c^j f(n)$, substituting this in eqn. (1), we get

$$g(n) \le \sum_{j=0}^{\log_b n-1} a^j f\left(\frac{n}{b^j}\right)$$

$$\le \sum_{j=0}^{\log_b n-1} c^j f(n)$$

$$\le f(n) \sum_{j=0}^{\infty} c^j$$

$$= f(n)\left(\frac{1}{1-c}\right)$$

$$= O[f(n)]$$

as c is constant. Thus we conclude that $g(n) = \Theta(f(n))$ for exact powers of b. Hence case 3 is proved.

THEOREM 4.4. Let $a \ge 1$ and $b > 1$ be constants, and let $f(n)$ be a non-negative function defined an exact powers of b. Define $T(n)$ on exact powers of b by the recurrence.

SOLUTION :

$$T(n) = \begin{cases} \Theta(1) & \text{if } n = 1 \\ aT(n/b) + f(n) & \text{if } n = b^i, \end{cases}$$

where i is a positive integer. Then $T(n)$ can be bounded asymptotically for exact powers of b as follows.

1. If $f(n) = 0(n^{\log_b a - \varepsilon})$ for some constant $\varepsilon > 0$, then $T(n) = \Theta(n^{\log_b a})$
2. If $f(n) = \Theta(n^{\log_b a})$, then $T(n) = \Theta(n^{\log_b a} . \lg n)$
3. If $f(n) = \Omega(n^{\log_b a + \varepsilon})$ for some constant $\varepsilon > 0$, and if $af\left(\frac{n}{b}\right) \le cf(n)$ for some constant $c < 1$ and all sufficiently large n, then $T(n) = \Theta(f(n))$.

PROOF : Using the bounds proved in theorem 4.2 to evaluate the summation

Case 1, $T(n) = \Theta(n^{\log_b a}) + O(n^{\log_b a})$

$= \Theta(n^{\log_b a})$

Case 2, $T(n) = \Theta(n^{\log_b a}) + \Theta(n^{\log_b a} \lg n)$

$= \Theta(n^{\log_b a} \lg n)$

for case 3, the condition $af\left(\frac{n}{b}\right) \le cf(n)$ implies.

$f(n) = \Omega(n^{\log_b a + \varepsilon})$,

thus, $T(n) = \Theta(n^{\log_b a}) + \Theta(f(n))$

$= \Theta(f(n))$

EXAMPLE 4.17. *Solve the recurrence,* $T(n) = 7T\left(\frac{n}{2}\right) + n^2$

SOLUTION : By master theorem,

$$a = 7,\ b = 2,\ f(n) = n^2$$
$$n^{\log_b a} = n^{\log_2 7} = O(n^{2.81})$$
$$f(n) = O(n^{\log_b a - \varepsilon}) = O(n^{2.81 - 0.81}) = O(n^2)$$

there by case 1, we have

$$T(n) = O(n^{\log_b a}) = O(n^{2.81})$$

EXAMPLE 4.18. *Solve the recurrence,* $T(n) = 7T\left(\frac{n}{3}\right) + n^2$

SOLUTION : Applying Master theorem

$$a = 7,\ b = 3,\ f(n) = n^2$$
$$n^{\log_b a} = n^{\log_3 7} = O(n^{1.77})$$
$$f(n) = \Omega(n^{\log_b a + \varepsilon}) \text{ to match with } n^2$$
$$\Omega(n^{1.77 + 0.23}),\ \varepsilon = 0.23$$

So case 3 can be applied, check for regularity condition,

$$af\left(\frac{n}{b}\right) \le cf(n)$$
$$7f\left(\frac{n^2}{3^2}\right) \le cf(n^2), \text{ is true for } c = \frac{7}{9}$$

hence case 3 holds

thus, $T(n) = \theta(f(n)) = \theta(n^2)$

EXAMPLE 4.19. $T(n) = T(\sqrt{n}) + 1$, *solve this recurrence*

SOLUTION : Let $m = lg\ n$, $n = 2^m$

$\Rightarrow$ $T(2^m) = T(2^{m/2}) + 1,$

Renaming, $S(m) = S\left(\frac{m}{2}\right) + 1$ $[\because\ T(2^m) = S(m)]$

Here $a = 1,\ b = 2,\ f(m) = 1$

$$m^{\log_b a} = m^{\log_2 1} = 1 \qquad (\because\ \log_2 1 = 0)$$
$$= \theta(1)$$

by case 2

$$S(m) = \theta(m^{\log_b a}.\ lg\ m)$$
$$S(m) = \theta(1.l\ gm)$$
$$S(m) = \theta(lg\ lgn)$$

thus, $T(n) = T(2^m) = S(m) = \theta(lg\ lgn)$

EXAMPLE 4.20. *Solve the recurrence by iteration and draw its recursion tree if possible.*

SOLUTION : $T(n) = T(n-1) + n$, by Iteration method,

$$= n + T(n-1)$$
$$= n + (n - 1 + T(n-2))$$
$$= n + (n - 1 + (n - 2 + T(n-3)))$$
$$= n + n - 1 + n - 2 + n - 3 + \ldots + T(1)$$

we have $T(1) = \theta(1)$

$$= (n + n + n + \ldots n \text{ times}) - (1 + 2 + 3 + \ldots n) + \theta(1)$$
$$= n^2 - n + \theta(1)$$
$$= \Omega(n^2)$$

$$\begin{array}{l|l}
\uparrow & n \rightarrow n \\
 & \quad | \\
n & n-1 \rightarrow n-1 \\
 & \quad | \\
 & n-2 \rightarrow n-2 \\
 & \quad \vdots \qquad \vdots
\end{array}$$

Total : $\Omega(n^2)$

EXAMPLE 4.21. *Solve the recurrence,* $T(n) = 2T\left(\frac{n}{4}\right) + \sqrt{n}$

SOLUTION : By master method,

$$a = 2,\ b = 4,\ f(n) = n^{1/2}$$

$$n^{\log_b a} = n^{\log_4 2} = n^{0.5} = O(n^{1/2}) \qquad \left[\log_4 2 = \frac{\log_{10} 2}{\log_{10} 4}\right]$$

By case 2, $f(n) = \theta(n^{\log_b a}\, lg\, n) = \theta(n^{1/2}\, lgn)$

therefore, $T(n) = \theta(\sqrt{n}\, lg\, n)$

EXAMPLE 4.22. $T(n) = T(n-1) + \frac{1}{n}$

SOLUTION : By iteration method

$$T(n) = \frac{1}{n} + T(n-1)$$
$$= \frac{1}{n} + \left(\frac{1}{n-1} + T(n-2)\right)$$
$$= \frac{1}{n} + \frac{1}{n-1} + \left(\frac{1}{n-2} + T(n-3)\right)$$
$$= \frac{1}{n} + \frac{1}{n-1} + \frac{1}{n-2} + \frac{1}{n-3} + \ldots T(1)$$
$$= \sum_{i=0}^{n-2} \frac{1}{n-i} + T(1) \le \sum_{i=0}^{n} \frac{1}{n-i} + \theta(1)$$

Let $n - i = x, - di = dx, di = - dx$

thus, it can be transformed into an integral $\sum_{i=0}^{n} \frac{1}{n-i} = -\int_{n}^{0} \frac{dx}{x} = \ln n$

thus
$$T(n) = \theta(\ln n) + \theta(1)$$
$$= \theta(lgn)$$

EXAMPLE 4.23. $T(n) = 2T\left(\frac{n}{2}\right) + \frac{n}{lg\, n}$, *solve this recurrence*

SOLUTION :
$$T(n) = 2T\left(\frac{n}{2}\right) + \frac{n}{lg\, n}$$
$$\leq 2T\left(\frac{n}{2}\right) - n\, lg\, n = 2T\left(\frac{n}{2}\right) - \theta(n\, lg\, n)$$

this can't be solved by master method, so using the iteration method we have the summation

$$2T\left(\frac{n}{2}\right) = \left(\sum_{i=0}^{k-1} 2^i\, 2^{k-i} \log(2^{k-i})\right)$$
$$= 2^k \sum_{i=0}^{k-1} (k-i)$$
$$= 2^{k-1} k(k+1) = O(n \log^2 n)$$

as $k = \log n$

and this term is greater than $\theta(n\, lg\, n)$

therefore solution to recurrence is $T(n) = O(n \log^2 n)$

EXAMPLE 4.24. *Solve the recurrence*

$$T(1) = 1$$
$$T(n) = 3T\left(\frac{n}{2}\right) + 2n^{1.5}$$

SOLUTION : We have
$$T(n) = 3T\left(\frac{n}{2}\right) + 2n^{1.5} \quad \text{...(1)}$$

For converting it to proper form divide both sides by 2

$$\frac{T(n)}{2} = \frac{3}{2} T\left(\frac{n}{2}\right) + n^{1.5} \quad \text{...(2)}$$

Let $\frac{T(n)}{2} = U(n)$

$\Rightarrow$ $U\left(\frac{n}{2}\right) = \frac{1}{2} T\left(\frac{n}{2}\right)$

Substituting in (2), we get

$$U(n) = 3U\left(\frac{n}{2}\right) + n^{1.5} \quad \text{...(3)}$$

and also, $$U(1) = \frac{1}{2} = 0.5$$

Now, we can solve the recurrence eqn. (3) by master method

here $a = 3,\ b = 2,\ f(n) = n^{1.5}$

$$n^{\log_b a} = n^{\log_2 3} \approx n^{1.585} \approx n^{1.59}$$

By case 1, $f(n) = \theta(n^{\log_b a - \varepsilon}) = \theta(n^{1.59 - 0.09})$, where $\varepsilon = 0.09$

$= \theta(n^{1.59})$

Hence $U(n) = O(n^{1.59}) = O(n^{\log_2 3})$

Since $T(n) = 2.U(n)$

$T(n) = O(n^{\log_2 3})$

EXAMPLE 4.25. *Solve the following recurrence.*

$$T(n) = 4T\left(\frac{n}{2}\right) + n^3$$

SOLUTION : By master method,

$$a = 4,\ b = 2,\ f(n) = n^3$$

$$n^{\log_b a} = n^2 = O(n^2)$$

By case 3, $f(n) = \Omega(n^{\log_b a + \varepsilon}) = \Omega(n^{2+1}),\ \varepsilon = 1$

thus case 3 can be applied, now check for the regularity condition $4f\left(\frac{n^3}{2^3}\right) \le c\,f(n^3)$, this is true for $c = \frac{1}{2}$

hence solution to this recurrence is $\theta(f(n))$

i.e., $T(n) = \theta(n^3)$

EXAMPLE 4.26. *Solve the recurrence,* $T(n) = 4T\left(\frac{n}{2}\right) + n^2$

SOLUTION : By master theorem,

$$a = 4,\ b = 2,\ f(n) = n^2$$

$$n^{\log_b a} = n^{\log_2 4} = n^2 = O(n^2)$$

hence case 2 can be applied.

$$f(n) = \theta(n^{\log_b a}) = \theta(n^2)$$

thus solution to recurrence is,

$$T(n) = \theta(n^{\log_b a}\ lgn) = \theta(n^2\ lgn).$$

EXAMPLE 4.27. *Give a recursive algorithm to compute the product of two positive integers m and n using only addition.*

SOLUTION : We use the recursion : Multiply $(m, k) = m +$ Multiply $(m, k-1)$, for $2 \le k \le n$, and Multiply $(m, 1) = m$ (base of recursion). We start with the call Multiply (m, n).

EXAMPLE 4.28. *Characterize each of the following recurrence equations using the master method (assuming that $T(n) = c$ for $n < d$, for constants $c > 0$ and $d \ge 1$).*

(a) $T(n) = 2T(n/2) + \log n$

(b) $T(n) = 8T(n/2) + n^2$

(c) $T(n) = 16T(n/2) + (n \log n)^4$

(d) $T(n) = 7T(n/3) + n$

(e) $T(n) = 9T(n/3) + n^3 \log n$

SOLUTION : (a) $T(n)$ is $O(n)$ (case 1).

(b) $T(n)$ is $O(n^3)$ (case 1).

(c) $T(n)$ is $O(n^4 \log^5 n)$ (case 2).

(d) $T(n)$ is $O(n^{\log_3 7})$ (case 1).

(e) $T(n)$ is $O(n^3 \log n)$ (case 3).

EXAMPLE 4.29. $f(n) = n^3 > (n/3)^3 + (n/3)^3$. *In fact this holds unless* $a \ge 27$!

In case 3 of the Master Theorem, the additive term dominates.

In case 2, both parts contribute equally, which is why the log pops up. It is (usually) what we want to have happen in a divide and conquer algorithm.

EXAMPLE 4.30.

Matrix Multiplication

The standard matrix multiplication algorithm for $n \times n$ matrices is $O(n^3)$.

$$\begin{bmatrix} 2 & 3 \\ 3 & 4 \\ 4 & 5 \end{bmatrix} \begin{bmatrix} 2 & 3 & 4 \\ 3 & 4 & 5 \end{bmatrix} \begin{bmatrix} 13 & 18 & 23 \\ 18 & 25 & 32 \\ 23 & 32 & 41 \end{bmatrix}$$

Strassen discovered a divide-and-conquer algorithm which takes $T(n) = 7T(n/2) + O(n^2)$ time. Find the complexity of algorithm.

SOLUTION :

$$a = 7, b = 2, f(n) = O(n^2)$$

$$n^{\log_b a} = n^{\log_2 7} = n^{2.81}$$

$$f(n) = O(n^{2.81 - 0.81}). \text{ So by Case I}$$

$$T(n) = O(n^{2.81})$$

EXAMPLE 4.31. Polygon Triangulation

Given a polygon in the plane, add diagonals so that each face is a triangle None of the diagonals are allowed to cross.

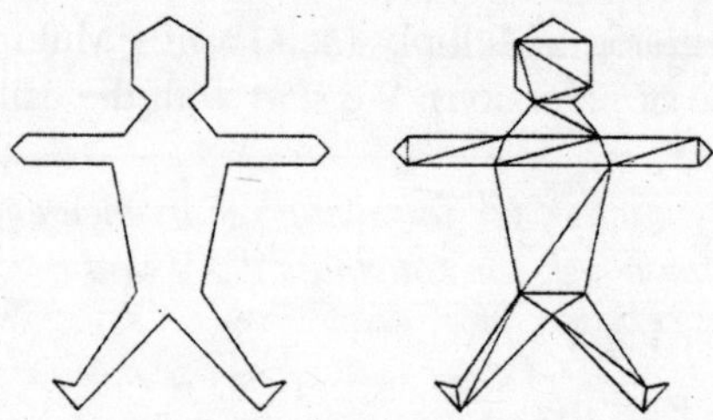

Triangulation is an important first step in many geometric algorithms.

SOLUTION : The simlest algorithm might be to try each pair of points and check if they see each other. If so, add the diagonal and recur on both halves, for a total of $O(n^3)$.

However, Chazelle gave an algorithm which runs in $T(n) = 2n(n/2) + O(\sqrt{(n)})$ time.

Since $n^{1/2} = O(n^{1-\varepsilon})$, by case 1 of the Master Theorem, Chazelle's algorithm is linear, i.e. $T(n) = O(n)$.

EXAMPLE 4.32. *Use iteration to solve $T(n) = T(n-a) + T(a) + n$, where $a \geq 1$ is a constant.*

SOLUTION :

$$\begin{aligned}
T(n) &= T(n-a) + T(a) + n \\
&= (T(n-2a) + T(a) + n - a) + T(a) + n \\
&= (T(n-3a) + T(a) + n - 2a) + 2T(a) + 2n - 3 \\
&= \sum_{i=0}^{n/a} T(a) + \sum_{i=0}^{n/a} n - ia \\
&= (n/a)\, T(a) + \sum_{i=0}^{n/a} n - a \sum_{i=0}^{n/a} i \\
&= (n/a)\, T(a) + n \sum_{i=0}^{n/a} 1 - a \sum_{i=0}^{n/a} i \\
&= (n/a)\, T(a) + n(n/a) - a(n/a^2)/2.
\end{aligned}$$

EXERCISE

1. Solve the recurrence exactly for n a power of 2.

$$T(n) = \begin{cases} 1 & \text{if } n = 1 \\ 5T(n/2) + (n \lg n)^2 & \text{otherwise.} \end{cases}$$

2. Solve the following recurrence exactly for n a power of 2.

$$T(n) = \begin{cases} 1 & \text{if } n = 1 \\ 3/2 & \text{if } n = 2 \\ 3/2T(n/2) - 1/2\, T(n/4) & \text{otherwise.} \end{cases}$$

3. Solve the following recurrence exactly

$$T(n) = \begin{cases} n & \text{if } n = 0 \text{ or } n = 1 \\ \sqrt{\frac{1}{2}T^2(n-1) + \frac{1}{2}T^2(n-2) + n} & \text{otherwise.} \end{cases}$$

4. Solve the following recurrence for n of the form 2^{2^k}

$$T(n) = \begin{cases} 1 & \text{if } n = 2 \\ 2T(\sqrt{n}) + lg\, n & \text{otherwise} \end{cases}$$

5. Solve the following reucrrence exactly as a function of initial conditions a and b.

$$T(b) = \begin{cases} a & \text{if } n = 0 \\ b & \text{if } n = 1 \\ (1 + T(n-1))/T(n-2) & \text{otherwise} \end{cases}$$

6. Solve the following recurrences, where $T(1) = 1$ and $T(n)$ for $n \geq 2$ satisfies.

(a) $T(n) = 3T(n/2) + n$

(b) $T(n) = 3T(n/2) + n^2$

(c) $T(n) = 8T(n/2) + n^3$

(d) $T(n) = 8T(n/3) + n$

(e) $T(n) = 4T(n/3) + n^2$

(f) $T(n) = 9T(n/3) + n^3$

7. Give tight big-oh and big-omega bounds on $T(n)$ defined by the following recurrences. Assume $T(1) = 1$.

(a) $T(n) = T(n/2) + 1$

(b) $T(n) = 2T(n/2) + lgn$

(c) $T(n) = 2T(n/2) + n$

(d) $T(n) = 2T(n/2) + n^2$

8. Solve for $T(n)$:

$$T(1) = 1$$
$$T(n) = \sqrt{n}\,T(\sqrt{n}) + n \text{ for } n \geq 2$$

9. Solve the following recurrence

$$T(1) = 0$$
$$T(n) = T(\lfloor \tfrac{n}{2} \rfloor) + T(\lfloor \tfrac{n}{2} \rfloor) + n - 1$$

10. Find the closed form expression and their asymptotic notations

(a) $\sum_{i=0}^{n} i$ (b) $\sum_{i=0}^{n} i^k$ (c) $\sum_{i=0}^{n} 2^i$ (d) $\sum_{i=0}^{n} [\binom{n}{i}]$

11. Find the asymptotic order of the solutions for following recurrences, where $T(1) = 1$, c is any positive constant.

(a) $T(n) = T(n/2) + c\, lg\, n$.

(b) $T(n) = T(n/2) + cn$

(c) $T(n) = 2T(n/2) + cn$

(d) $T(n) = 2T(n/2) + cn\, lg\, n$

(e) $T(n) = 2T(n/2) + cn^2$

12. Use recursion tree to solve the recurrence $T(n) = T(\alpha n) + T[(1 - \alpha)n] + n$, where α is constant in the range $0 < \alpha < 1$.

13. Use iteration to solve

$$T(n) = T(n - a) + T(a) + n, \text{ where } a \geq 1 \text{ is a constant.}$$

14. Solve the recurrence. $T(n) = 3T(n/3 + 5) + n/2$.

15. Show that if $f(n) = \theta(n^{\log_b a} + lg^k n)$, where $k \geq 0$, then the master recurrence has solution $T(n) = \theta(n^{\log_b a}. lg^{k+1} n)$. For simplicity confine your analysis to exact power of b.

16. Solve the recurrence $T(n) = T(n - 1) + lgn$

17. **Fibonacci numbers.** In this problem we will use the technique of generating functions to solve the fibnacci recurrence. Define the **generating function** (or formal power series) F as

$$F(z) = \sum_{i=0}^{\infty} F_i Z^i$$

$$= 0 + Z + Z^2 + 3Z^3 + 3Z^4 + 5Z^5 + 8Z^6 + 13Z^7 + 21Z^8 + \ldots$$

(a) Show that $F(Z) = Z + ZF(Z) + Z^2F(Z)$

(b) Show that $F(Z) = \dfrac{Z}{1 - Z - Z^2} = \dfrac{Z}{(1 - \phi Z)(1 - \hat{\phi} Z)}$

$$= \frac{1}{\sqrt{5}}\left(\frac{1}{(1 - \phi Z)} - \frac{1}{(1 - \hat{\phi} Z)}\right)$$

where $\phi = \dfrac{1 + \sqrt{5}}{2} = 1.61803 \ldots$

and $\hat{\phi} = \dfrac{1 - \sqrt{5}}{2} = -0.61803 \ldots$

(c) Show that

$$F(Z) = \sum_{i=0}^{\infty} \frac{1}{\sqrt{5}} (\phi^i - \hat{\phi}^i) Z^i.$$

(d) Prove that

$$F_i = \frac{\phi^i}{\sqrt{5}} \text{ for } i > 0, \text{ rounded to nearest integer}$$

[Hint : $|\hat{\phi}| < 1$**]**

(e) Prove that

$$F_{i+2} \geq \phi^i \quad \text{of} \quad i \geq 0.$$

□□□

5

SETS RELATION AND FUNCTIONS

5.1 Sets

Set is a collection of distinguishable objects, these objects are called members or elements

if $S = \{x_1, x_2, ..., x_n\}$

$x_i \in S$ (x_i is element of S)

$\phi = \{ \}$ is empty set

Z denotes integers

R denotes real number

N Natural numbers.

Subset

If all the elements of set A is contained in set B, *i.e.*, $x \in A$ and $x \in B$, then we write $A \subseteq B$

e.g., $A = \{1, 2, 3, 4, 5\}$

$B = \{1, 2, 3, 4, 5, 6, 7, 8\}$

$C = \{1, 2, 3, 4, 5\}$.

$A \subseteq C$

but $A \subset B$ is called the proper set, means there are few elements in B which are not a member of A.

Intersection

$$A \cap B = \{x : x \in A \text{ and } x \in B\}$$

e.g. in above example, $A \cap B = \{1, 2, 3, 4, 5\}$

$$A \cup B = \{x : x \in A \text{ or } x \in B\}$$

$$A - B = \{x : x \in A \text{ and } x \notin B\}.$$

Properties

1. $A \cap \phi = \phi$

2. $A \cup \phi = A$

3. Idempotent law.

$$A \cap A = A$$
$$A \cup A = A.$$

4. Commutative

$$A \cap B = B \cap A$$
$$A \cup B = B \cup A$$

5. Associative laws.

$$A \cap (B \cap C) = (A \cap B) \cap C$$
$$A \cup (B \cup C) = (A \cup B) \cup C$$

6. Distributive law.

$$A \cap (B \cup C) = (A \cap B) \cup (A \cap C)$$
$$A \cup (B \cap C) = (A \cup B) \cap (A \cup C)$$

7. Absorption Law.

$$A \cap (A \cup B) = A$$
$$A \cup (A \cap B) = A$$

8. De Morgan's Law

$$A - (B \cap C) = (A - B) \cup (A - C)$$
$$A - (B \cup C) = (A - B) \cap (A - C)$$

9. Complements

$$\overline{\overline{A}} = A$$
$$A \cup \overline{A} = \phi$$
$$A \cup \overline{A} = U$$

10.

$$\overline{A \cap B} = \overline{A} \cup \overline{B}$$
$$\overline{A \cup B} = \overline{A} \cap \overline{B}$$

Venn Diagram

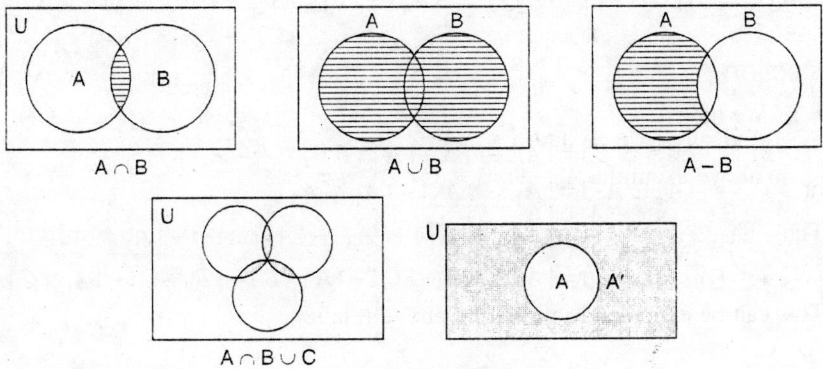

Fig. 5.1. Venn diagram.

We have

$$|A \cup B| = |A| + |B| - |A \cap B|$$

Powerset

The set of all subsets of S is called power set

$$S = \{1, 2, 3\}.$$
$$= \{\phi, \{1\}, \{2\}, \{3\}, \{1, 2\}, \{1, 3\}, \{2, 3\}, \{1, 2, 3\}\}$$

Total number of elements in power set of S are 2^k where k is the number of element in set S.

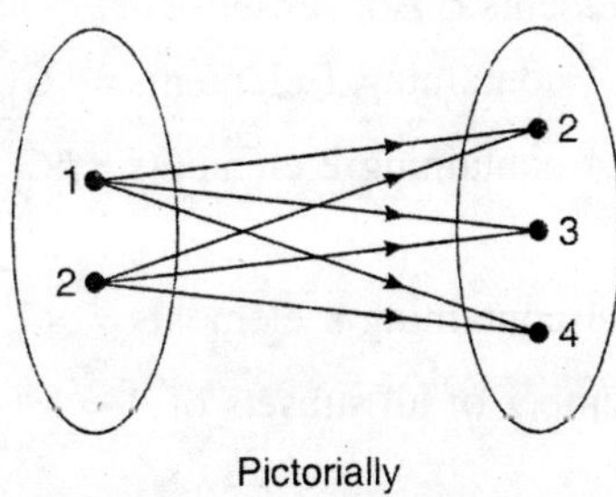

Pictorially

Fig. 5.2. Powerset.

Cartesian Product

$$A \times B = \{(a, b) : a \in A \text{ and } b \in B\}$$

e.g.,
$$A = \{1, 2\}.$$
$$B = \{2, 3, 4\}.$$
$$A \times B = \{(1, 2), (1, 3), (1, 4), (2, 2), (2, 3), (2, 4)\}.$$

also, $|A \times B| = |A| . |B|$, is called cardianality.

EXAMPLE 5.1. *Prove that*

$$|A_1 \cup A_2 \cup \ldots A_1| = |A_1| + |A_2| + \ldots |A_n| - |A_1 \cap A_2| - |A_1 \cap A_3| + |A_1 \cap A_2 \cap A_3| + \ldots + (-1)^{n-1} |A_1 \cap A_2 \cap \ldots \cap A_n|$$

SOLUTION : We have,

$$|A \cup B| = |A| + |B| - |A \cap B|$$

or, $$|A_1 \cup A_2| = |A_1| + |A_2| - |A_1 \cap A_2|$$

Thus, $|A_1 \cup A_2 \cup A_3| = |A_1| + |A_2| + |A_3| - |A_1 \cap A_2| - |A_1 \cap A_3|$

$$|A \cup B \cup C| = |A| + |B| + |C| - |A \cap B| - |B \cap C| - |A \cap C| + |A \cap B \cap C|$$

This can be extended to prove the above relation.

EXAMPLE 5.2. *Prove the following generalization.*

$$\overline{A_1 \cap A_2 \cap \ldots \cap A_9} = \overline{A}_1 \cup \overline{A}_2 \cup \ldots \cup \overline{A}_n$$

$$\overline{A_1 \cup A_2 \cup \ldots \cup A_n} = \overline{A}_1 \cap \overline{A}_2 \cap \ldots \cap \overline{A}_n$$

SOLUTION : We have $\overline{A \cap B} = \overline{A} \cup \overline{B}$

and $\overline{A \cup B} = \overline{A} \cap \overline{B}$

which can be extended to prove the generalisation.

EXAMPLE 5.3. *Show that power set of set A contains at most 2^n elements, where there are n elements in set A.*

PROOF : Let A be a set of n elements ϕ is a subset of A.

Number of subsets of A containing 1 elements $= {}^nC_1$

Number of subsets of A containing 2 elements $= {}^nC_2$

⋮

Number of subsets of A containing n elements $= {}^nC_n$

∴ Total number of all subsets of $A = 1 + {}^nC_1 + {}^nC_2 + \ldots {}^nC_n = 2^n$

Hence proved.

EXAMPLE 5.4. *Prove that $A + (B \cap C) = (A \times B) \cap (A \times C)$*

PROOF : $(x, y)\ \varepsilon\ A \times (B \cap C) \Leftrightarrow x\ \varepsilon\ A$ and $y\ \varepsilon\ B \cap C$

$\Leftrightarrow x\ \varepsilon\ A$ and $(y\ \varepsilon\ B$ and $y\ \varepsilon\ C)$

$\Leftrightarrow (x\ \varepsilon\ A$ and $y\ \varepsilon\ B)$ and $(x\ \varepsilon\ A$ and $y\ \varepsilon\ C)$

$\Leftrightarrow (x, y)\ \varepsilon\ (A \times B)$ and $(x, y)\ \varepsilon\ (A \times C)$

$\Leftrightarrow (x, y)\ \varepsilon\ (A \times B) \cap (A \times C)$

∴ $A \times (B \cap C) = (A \times B) \cap (A \times C)$

EXAMPLE 5.5. *Prove that $(A \times B) \cap (C \times D) = (A \cap C) \times (B \cap D)$*

PROOF : $(x, y) \varepsilon (A \times B) \cap (C \times D)$

$\Leftrightarrow (x, y) \varepsilon (A \times B)$ and $(x, y) \varepsilon (C \times D)$

$\Leftrightarrow (x \varepsilon A$ and $y \varepsilon B)$ and $(x \varepsilon C$ and $y \varepsilon D)$

$\Leftrightarrow (x \varepsilon A$ and $x \varepsilon C)$ and $(y \varepsilon B$ and $y \varepsilon D)$

$x \varepsilon (A \cap C)$ and $y \varepsilon (B \cap D)$

$\Rightarrow (x, y) \varepsilon (A \cap C) \times (B \cap D)$

RELATION DEFINITION. A relation R from a set A to set B is a subset of $A \times B$.

Thus $R \subset (A \times B)$. The sets A and B are respectively called the sets of departure and the set of destination of R.

If $(a, b) \varepsilon R$, then we write it as $a R b$ and read it as 'a is in relation R to b' or 'a is R-related to b'.

The domain of a relation R is the first element of ordered pairs in R and is denoted by $D(R)$,

Thus domain $R = \{a \mid (a, b) \varepsilon R$, for some $b \varepsilon B\}$.

range, $R = \{b \mid (a, b) \varepsilon R$, for some $a \varepsilon A\}$

Inverse of a relation. The inverse of a relation R is

$$R^{-1} = \{(b, a) \mid (a, b) \varepsilon R\}$$

Reflexive relation. A relation R in a set A is said to be reflexive of aRa, *i.e.* if $(a, a) \varepsilon R$ $\forall a \varepsilon A\}$

Symmetric relation. A relation R in a set A is said to be symmetric if $aRb \Leftrightarrow bRa$,

Transitive relation. A relation R in a set A is said to be transitive if aRb and $bRc \Rightarrow aRc$

Equivalence Relation. A relation R in a set A is said to be an equivalence relation (or an RST) if R is reflexive, symmetric and transitive.

EXAMPLE 5.6. *Determine whether the relation*

$R = \{(1, 1), (2, 2), (3, 3), (4, 4), (1, 3), (3, 1), (1, 4), (4, 1)\}$ *is an equivalence relation in* $\{1, 2, 3, 4\}$

SOLUTION : $\because (1, 1) \varepsilon R, (2, 2) \varepsilon R, (3, 3) \varepsilon R, (4, 4) \varepsilon R$

$\therefore$ R is relflexive (1, 3) and (3, 1) belong to R and (1, 4) and (4, 1) belong to R

$\therefore$ R is symmetrie (1, 3), (3, 1) and (1, 1) belong to R

$\therefore$ R is transitive

$\therefore$ R is an equivalence Relation.

EXAMPLE 5.7. *If* $R = \{(1, 2), (2, 4), (3, 6), (4, 8)\}$ *find* R^{-1}, *Domain and Range*

SOLUTION : $R^{-1} = \{(2, 1), (4, 2), (6, 3), (8, 9)\}$.

Domain $= \{1, 2, 3, 4\}$. (first element of ordered pair (a, b) in relation R)

Range $= \{2, 4, 6, 8\}$ (2nd element of ordered pair in relation R.)

EXAMPLE 5.8. *Determine the domain and the range of each of the following relations.*

(i) $R = \{(x, y) \mid x$ *is a multiple of 3 and* y *is a multiple of* $5\}$

(ii) $R = \left\{\left(x, \frac{1}{x}\right) \mid 0 < x \le 12\right\}$

(iii) $R = \{(x, y) \mid x^2 + y^2 = 25$, *x and y are integers}.*

SOLUTION : (i) Domain $R = \{x \mid x$ is a multiple of $3\}$
$= \{3, 6, 9, 12, ...\}$

Range $R = \{y \mid y$ is multiple of $5\}$
$= \{5, 10, 15, ...,\}$

(ii) Domain $R = \{x \mid 0 < x \le 12\} = \{1, 2, 3, ..., 12\}$

Range $R = \left\{\frac{1}{x} \mid 0 < x \le 12\right\} = \left\{1, \frac{1}{2}, \frac{1}{3}, ..., \frac{1}{12}\right\}$

(iii) Domain $R = \{3, -3, 4, -4, 5, 0, -5, 0\}$

Range $R = \{4, -4, 3, -3, 0, 5, -5, 0\}$

as, $3^2 + 4^2 = 25$, $5^2 + 0 = 25$ etc.

General Relation. The relation $A \times A$ is called the universal relation in the set A
For each ordered pair (a, b) with $a \varepsilon A$ and $b \varepsilon A$, we have aRb, *i.e.*, $(a, b) \varepsilon R$
For example, if $A = \{1, 2\}$ then

$$R = A \times A = \{(1, 1), (1, 2), (2, 1), (2, 2)\}$$

is the universal relation in A.

Void Relation. The realtion $\phi \subset A \times A$ is called the void relation in A

Anti Symmetric Relation. A relation R in a set A is said to be antisymmetric if for every pair of distinct elements a and b belonging to A, atmost one of aRb and bRa holds.

EXAMPLE 5.9. *Let R be the relation "divides" in the set natural numbers. Then R is an antisymmetric relation.*

$$2R4,\ 4 \not{R}\ 2 \text{ and } 2 \not{R}\ 5,\ 5 \not{R}\ 2.$$

i.e., at the most one of aRb and bRa holds.

EXAMPLE 5.10. · *Let R be the relation "is congruent to" in the set of triangles. Then R is not an antisymmetric relation,* **because** $\Delta ABC \cong \Delta DEF$ **and** $\Delta DEF \cong \Delta ABC$,

i.e., $\Delta ABC\ R\ \Delta DEF$ *and* $\Delta DEF\ \mathbf{R}\ \Delta RBC$,

i.e., *both aRb and bRa hold, hence R is symmetric*

Order Relation. A relation R in a set A is said to be an order relation if it is antisymmetric and transitive.

EXAMPLE 5.11. *Let R be the relation "divides" in the set of natural numbers. Then R is an order relation.*

$2R4$, $4 \not{R}\ 2$, $2 \not{R}\ 5$, $5 \not{R}\ 2$, *i.e., at the most one of aRb and bRa holds.*

$2R4$, $4R8$, $2R8$, *i.e., aRb and bRc* $\Rightarrow$ *aRc.*

EXAMPLE 5.12. *The relation 'is congruent to' in the set of tri is not an order relation, because it is not antisymmetric.*

Linear Order Relation. An order relation in a set A is said to be a linear order relation if for every pair of distinct elements a and b belonging to A, exactly one of aRb and bRa holds.

EXAMPLE 5.13. *Let R be the relation "is less than" in the set of natural numbers. Then R is a linear order relation.*

$2R3$, $3\not R 2$; *i.e., exactly one of aRb and bRa holds.*

$2R3$, $3R4$, *and* $2R4$, *i.e.,* aRb *and* $bRc \Rightarrow aRc$.

EXAMPLE 5.14. *Let R be the relation "divides" in the set of natural numbers. Then R is not a linear order relation, because none of 2R5 and 5R2 holds, i.e.,* $2\not R5$, $5\not R2$, *It may be noted that R is an order relation.*

EXAMPLE 5.15. *Let R be the relation "is a subset of"* $\rho(A)$. *Then R is not a linear order relation.*

Let $A = \{1, 2, 3\}$. Then

$\rho(A) = \{\phi, \{1\}, \{2\}, \{3\}, \{1, 2\}, \{2, 3\}, \{3, 1\}, \{1, 2, 3\}\}$.

$\{\{2, 3\} \not R \{1, 2\}, \{1, 2\} \not R \{2, 3\}, \{1, 2\} R \{1, 2, 3\}$, *i.e.*, at the most one of aRb and bRa holds

$\{1\} R\{1, 2\}, \{1, 2\} R\{1, 2, 3\}, \{1\} R\{1, 2, 3\}$, *i.e.*, aRb and $bRc \Rightarrow aRc$.

5.2 Function

A function or mapping f from a set A to a set B is a correspondence which associates to each element x of A, a unique elements y of B and written as

$$f: A \rightarrow B$$

and is read as "f is a function from A to B or f maps A into B".

y is called the image of x under f and is denoted by

$$f(x), \text{ i.e., } y = f(x).$$

x is called the pre-image by y.

The set A is called the domain of the function f, and is denoted by dom f.

The set B is called the co-domain of the function f, and is denoted by codom f.

The set of all images of all the elemetns of A under f is called the range of the function f and is denoted by $f(A)$ or *ran* f or Rf. Thus, $f(A) = \{f(x) : x \in A\}$ and $f(A) \subset B$.

EXAMPLE 5.16. *Several ways of picturing a function are given below.*

(i)

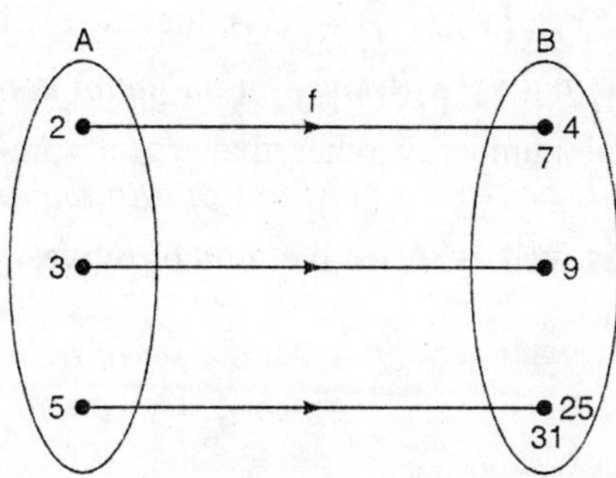

(ii) $f: A \to B$ where $A = \{2, 3, 5\}, B = \{4, 7, 9, 25, 31\}$, $2 \to 4$, $3 \to 9$, $5 \to 25$.

(iii) $f: x \to x^2$, where domain of $f = \{2, 3, 5\}$, co-domain of $f = \{4, 7, 9, 25, 31\}$

Thus, $2 \to 2^2 = 4$, $3 \to 3^2 = 9$, $5 \to 5^2 = 25$.

(iv) $f(x) = x^2$ where domain of $f = \{2, 3, 5\}$, codomain of $f = \{1, 7, 9, 25, 31\}$.

Thus, $f(2) = 2^2 = 4, f(3) = 3^2 = 9, f(5) = 5^2 = 25$.

(v) $f = \{(2, 4), (3, 9), (5, 25)\}$

Note : In the above ex., range of function

$$f = f(A) = \{4, 9, 25\} \subset B.$$

But $f(A) \neq B$. Thus, $f(A)$ is a proper subset of B. domain $f = \{2, 3, 5\}$, co-domain $f = \{4, 7, 9, 25, 31\}$

Equality of Functions

Two functions $f: A \to B$ and $g: A \to B$ are said to be equal (or the same) if and only if

$$f(a) = g(a) \ \forall \ a \in A.$$

Types of Function or Surjection onto Function

If the function $f: A \to B$ is such that each element of B is the f-image of at least one element of A, *i.e.*, $f(A) = B$, then f is called a surjection or onto function.

EXAMPLE 5.17. *Let* $A = \{-1, 1, 2, 3\}$, $B = \{1, 4, 9\}$.

$$f: A \to B, f(x) = x^2.$$

Then $f(-1) = (-1)^2 = 1$, $\quad f(1) = 1^2 = 1$,

$f(2) = 2^4 = 4$, $\quad f(3) = 3^2 = 9$.

$\therefore f(A) = \{1, 4, 9\} = B$. Hence f is a surjection.

Injection function or injection or one-one function or $1 - 1$ *function.* If the function $f: A \to B$ is such that distinct elements of A have distinct f-images in B, then f is called an injective function or injection function or 1-1 function.

Thus, in the case of one-one function, if $x_1 \neq x_2$, then $f(x_1) \neq f(x_2)$.

EXAMPLE 5.18. (i) *Let the function f be given as*

$$f: f(x) = x^5 \ \forall \ x \in R, \text{ the set of real numbers.}$$

If $x_1 \neq x_2$, then $x_1{}^5 \neq x_1{}^5$, *i.e.*, $f(x_1) \neq f(x_2)$, therefore, f is one-one function.

(ii) Let $A = \{1, 2, 3\}$, $B = \{1, 4, 5, 9\}$, $f: A \to B, f(x) = x^2$.

Therefore every real number y other than f, has pre image, hence consequently f is surjective.

Since f is injective as well as surjective, it is bijective.

Product or Composition of Functions

Let $f: A \to B$ and $g: B \to C$ be two functions. Then the product or composition of functions f and g denoted by gof, is a mapping of A into C given by $gof: A \to C$, such that,

$$(gof)(x) = g(f(x)),\ \forall\, x \in A.$$

EXAMPLE 5.19. *Does the table bleow give a commutative binary operation on the set $\{a, b, c\}$?*

0	a	b	c
a	b	c	a
b	c	a	b
c	a	b	c

SOLUTION : From the table we get

$$aob = boa = c$$
$$boc = cob = b$$
$$coa = aoc = a, \text{ and}$$
$$aoa = b,\ bob = a,\ coc = c.$$

Hence, $xoy \in \{a, b, c\}$ and $xoy = yox\ \forall\ x, y \in \{a, b, c\}$. Hence, the table gives a commutative binary operation on the set $\{a, b, c\}$.

EXAMPLE 5.20.

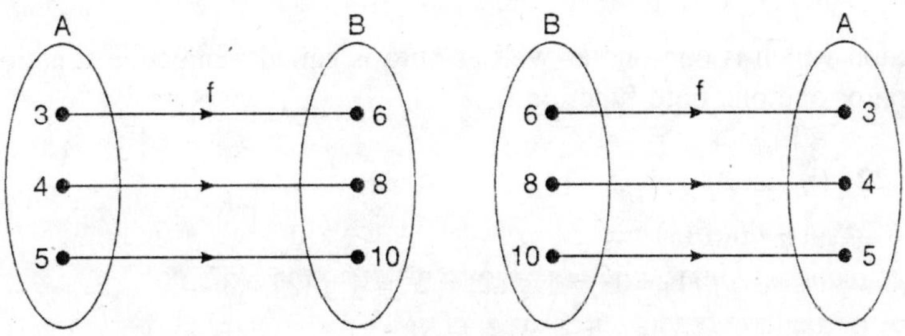

$A = \{3, 4, 5\}$, $B = \{6, 8, 10\}$, $f: A \to B$, $f(x) = 2x$, *find f and f^{-1}*

SOLUTION : $f: A \to B, f(x) = 2x, f(3) = 6, f(4) = 8, f(5) = 10.$

$$f^{-1}: B \to A, f^{-1}(x) = \frac{x}{2}, f^{-1}(6) = 3, f^{-1}(8) = 4, f^{-1}(10) = 5$$

$$f = \{(3, 6), (4, 8), (5, 10)\}$$
$$f^{-1} = \{(6, 3), (8, 4), (10, 5)\}$$

The function $f^{-1}: B \to A$ is also one-one onto function.

EXAMPLE 5.21. *Let $A = R - \{3\}$, $B = R - \{1\}$. R being the set of real numbers.*

Let the function $f : A \rightarrow B$ be defined by $f(x) = \dfrac{x-2}{x-3}$. In this function bijective? Give reasons.

SOLUTION : *Let*
$$y = \frac{x-2}{x-3}$$

Then
$$y(x-3) = x-2$$
$$\Rightarrow \quad x(y-1) = 3y-2$$
$$\Rightarrow \quad x = \frac{3y-2}{y-1}$$

Since
$$f(x) = \frac{x-2}{x-3}$$

Therefore,
$$f(x_1) \neq f(x_2) \text{ if } x_1 \neq x_2 \qquad \left(\because \frac{x_1-2}{x_1-3} \neq \frac{x_2-2}{x_2-3}\right)$$

$\therefore$ f is injective.

Since
$$x = \frac{3y-2}{y-1}$$
$$f(1) = 1^2 = 1, f(2) = 2^2 = 4, f(3) = 3^2 = 9$$

$\because$ Distinct elements of A have distinct f-image in B,

$\therefore$ f is one-one function.

Bijective Function or Bijection or one-one onto Function

A function which is one-one as well as onto is called a bijection function or bijective map or bijection or one-one onto function.

EXAMPLE 5.22. (i) Let $A = \{1, 2, 3\}$, $B = \{1, 4, 9\}$,

$f : A \rightarrow B, f(x) = x^2.$
$$f(1) = 1^2 = 1, f(2) = 2^2 = 4, f(3) = 3^2 = 9.$$
$$\therefore \quad f(A) = \{1, 4, 9\} = f(B),$$

Therefore f is a surjection.

$\because$ Distinct elements of A have distinct f-images in B,

$\therefore$ f is an injection.

$\because$ f is surjection as well as injection.

$\therefore$ f is bijection or one-one onto function.

EXAMPLE 5.23. *Let the function f be given as $f : f(x) = x^3 \ \forall \ x \in R$, R being the set of real numbers. Prove that f is bijection.*

PROOF : $f(x_1) = x^3, f(x_2) = {x_2}^3.$

If $x_1 \neq x_2$, then ${x_1}^3 \neq {x_2}^3$, *i.e.*, $f(x_1) \neq f(x_2)$.

$\therefore$ f is one-one function.

Any element y of the co-domain of f is the f-image of $y^{1/3}$ belonging to the domain of f, because $f(y^{1/3}) = y$.

$\therefore$ f is onto function.

Hence, f is one-one onto function or bijection.

Inverse Image of a Subset

If $A \to B$ is a function and $D \subset B$, then the inverse image of D, under f, denoted by $f^{-1}(D)$, is the set of those elements of A f-image belong to D.

Symbolically $f^{-1}(D) = \{x \mid x \in A \text{ and } f(x) \in D\}$

EXAMPLE 5.24. *Let $A = \{a, b, c, d, e\}$, $B = \{x, y, z\}$.*

Let the function $f : A \to B$ be defined by

$$f = \{(a, x), (b, x), (c, y), (d, x), (c, z)\}.$$

Then
$$f^{-1}(x, y\}) = \{a, b, c, d, e\},$$
$$f^{-1}\{(x, y, z) = \{a, b, c, d, e\}$$
$$f^{-1}(\{x\}) = \{a, b, d\}, f^{-1}(\{z\}) = \phi.$$

EXAMPLE. 5.25. *Let the function $f : R \to R$ be defined by $f(x) = [x]$ where R is the set of real numbers, and $[x]$ is the largest integer less than or equal to $x \in R$,*

and
$$D = \left\{\frac{1}{4}, \frac{1}{2}, \frac{3}{4}\right\}.$$

Since all the f-images of the elements of the domain of f are integers, therefore there is no element of the domain of f whose f–image belongs to D. Hence $f^{-1}(D) = \phi$.

Inverse function : Let $f : A \to B$ be a one-one onto function, then the function $f^{-1} : B \to A$ which associates to each elment $y \in B$, the element $x \in A$, such that $f(x) = y$, is called the inverse function of the function $f : A \to B$. Domain of $f^{-1} = B$, and range of $f^{-1} = A$.

It is easy to see that $f^{-1} : B \to A$ is also one-one onto function.

5.3 Sets with One Binary Operation

A binary opertion on a set A is a rule which assigns to every ordered pair (a, b) of elements from A, a unique element denoted by $a * b$ we give below five postulates on binary operated.

P_1 : **Closure**. If a and b are in S then $a * b$ is in A.

P_2 : **Associalitivity.** If a, b, c are in A then

$$(a * b) * c = a * (b * c)$$

P_3 : **Identity element.** There exists a unique element e in A s.t. for any element x in A,

$$x * e = e * x = x$$

P_4 : **Inverse** for every element x in A there exists a unique element x^1 in A s.t. $x * x' = x' * x = e$. The element x' is called the inverse of x w.r.t $*$.

P_5 : **Commutativity :** If $a, b \in S$ then $a * b = b * a$

DEFINITIONS

(i) A set A with binary operation * is called a semigroup if postulates P_1 and P_2 are satisfied.

(ii) A set A with * is called a gp. if postulates P_1 to P_4 are satisfied.

(iii) $P_1 - P_3$ monoid

(iv) A semigroup (monoid or gp) is called commutative or abelian semi gp. (Monoid or gp.) if P_5 is satisfied. See Fig. 5.3.

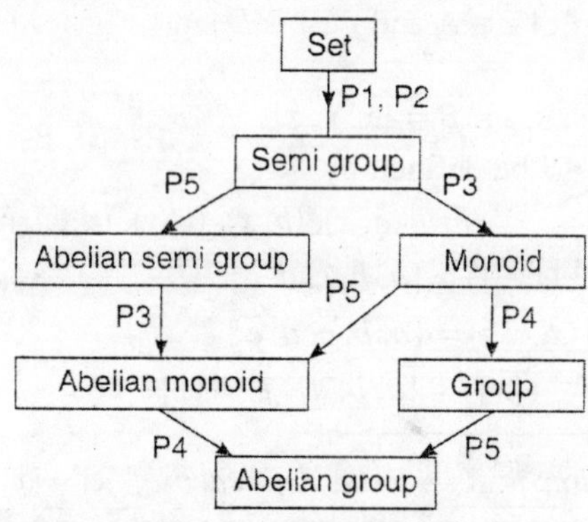

Fig. 5.3

EXAMPLE 5.26. *If A is set of integers then,*

(i) A with addition is an abelian gp.

(ii) A with multiplication is an abelian monoid (It is not a gp. since if does not satisfy P_4)

(iii) $\{1, 2, 3, \ldots\}$ with addition is a commutative semigroup but not a monoid. (The identify element can be only 0, but 0 is not in the set)

(iv) The power set 2^A of A $(A \neq \phi)$ with union is commutative monoid. (The identify element in ϕ)

(v) The set of all 2×2 matrices under multiplication is a monoid but not an abelian monoid.

Sets with Two Binary Operations

Let A be a set with two binary operations $*$ and O. Then we have some additional postulates.

(i) postulate $P_1 - P_5$ refers to $*$ postulates.

(ii) postulate $P_6 - P_{10}$ are simply postulates $P_1 - P_5$ for the binary operations O.

(iii) P_9 : If A under $*$ satisfies $P_1 - P_5$ then for every x in A, with $x \neq e$, there exists a unique element x' in S s.t., $x'ox = xox' = e'$, where e' is identify coresponding to o.

(iv) P_{11} : Distributivity : for a, b, c in S

$$ao(b * c) = (a \; o \; b) * (a \; o \; c)$$

A set with one or more binary operations is called algebraic system, *e.g.*, groups, monoids, semigroups are algebraic system with one binary operation.

Let us consider, some algebraic systems with two binary operations.

(i) A set with two binary operations * and o is called ring. if (a) it is an abelian gp. w.r.t. * and (b) o satisfies closure, associativity and distributivity postulate $(P_6 - P_{11})$

(ii) A ring is called commutative ring if the commutativity postulate is satisfied for o

(iii) A commutative ring with unity is a commutative ring that satisfies the identify postulate (P_8) for o.

(iv) A field is a set with too binary operations * and o if it satisfies $P_1 - P_{11}$

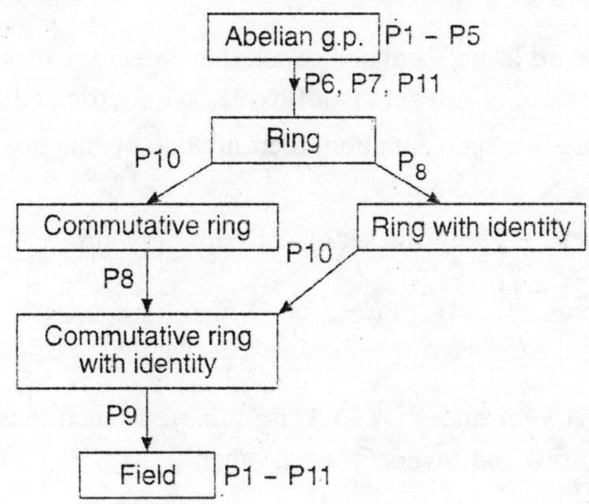

Fig. 5.4. Sets with two binary operations.

EXAMPLE 5.27. $R = [(1, 2), (2, 3), (2, 4)]\}$ *be a relation in* $\{1, 2, 3, 4\}$ *find* R^+

SOLUTION : $R^2 = \{(1, 2), (2, 3), (2, 4)\}\ o\{(1, 2), (2, 3), (2, 4)\}.$

$= \{(1, 3), (1, 4)\}$

We combine (a, b) and (b, c) in R to get (a, c) in R^2

$$R^3 = R^2\ oR = \{(1, 3), (1, 4)\}\ o\{(1, 2), (2, 3), (2, 4)\} = \phi$$

Here no pair (a, b) in R^2 can be combined with any pair in R)

$\therefore \quad R^4 = R^5 = \ldots = \phi$

$\therefore \quad R^1 = R \cup R^2 = \{(1, 2), (2, 3), (2, 4), (2, 4), (1, 3), (1, 4)\}.$

EXERCISE

1. Prove that for every function f from non-negative integers into non-negative reals, $o(f) = O(f) - \theta(f)$, where (–) (minus) denotes set difference.
2. Prove that for every function f from non-negative integers into non-negative reals, no function g is in both $\theta(f)$ and $o(f)$ that $\theta(f) \cap o(f) = \phi$.

3. Give an example of two functions $f_1 g : N \rightarrow R*$, such that $f \notin O(g)$ and $g \in O(f)$.
4. Let A and B be finite sets and $f: A \rightarrow B$ be function, show that:
(a) f is injective then $|A| <= |B|$
(b) f is surjective then $|A| >= |B|$
5. Is the function $f(x) = x + 1$ is bijective when the domain and codomain are N or Z where Z is set of natural no. and Z is set of integers.
6. Prove that for any integer n the relation "Equivalent modulo n" is an equivalences relation on the integer.
7. Give a bijection from Z to $Z \times Z$.
8. Prove that $f(n) = (-1)^n \left\lceil \frac{n}{2} \right\rceil$ is objection from N to Z. and find f^{-1}.
9. An integer m is said to be R-related to another integer n if m is multiple of n. Check if the relation R in the set Z of integers is reflexive, symmetric and transitive.
10. If $f: A \rightarrow B$ is one-one onto function, then inverse of function f is unique.
11. Let the function f be given as
$f: f(x) = x^3 \; \forall \; x \, \varepsilon \, R$, R being the set of real numbers, prove that f is bijection.
12. Let $f(x) = \frac{x^2 + 2x - 11}{x - 3}$. If $f: R - \{3\} \rightarrow R - \{x : a < x < b, \; x \, \varepsilon \, R\}$ in surjective, find a and b.
13. Prove that if $f = A \rightarrow A$ and $g : A \rightarrow A$ are functions such that $fog = gof = I_A$ (idnetify), then f and g are bijections and inverse if each other.
14. The binary operation 'o' in the set $\{a, b\}$ is defined by $aoa = a$, $bob = b$, $aob = b$, $boa = a$. Verify that the operation 'o' is associative.
15. If $f: A \rightarrow B$, $g : B \rightarrow C$ are one-to-one injecive function show that gof is also one-to-one.
16. If R is the relation in $N \times N$ defined by $(a, b) \, R(c, d)$ iff $a + d = b + c$, show that R is an equivalence relation.
17. If f, $g : R \rightarrow R$ are defined respectively by

$$f(x) = x^3 + 3x + 1, \; g(x) = 2x - 3$$

find formula for (i) fog (ii) gof (iii) fof (iv) gog.
18. If $f: A \rightarrow B, f(x) = x^2$, $A = \{1, 3, 5, 7\}$, $B = \{1, 9, 25, 49, 64\}$ find whether it is invertible or not.
19. Out of 880 boys in a school, 224 played cricket, 240 played hockey and 336 played basket ball, 64 played basket ball and hockey, 80 played cricket and basket ball, and 40 played cricket and hockey. 24 played all three games. How many boys did not play any game?
(**Ans.** 240 boys)
20. Let $R = \{(a, b), (b, c), (c, a)$. Find R^+.

❑❑❑

6

PROBABILITY

6.1 Basic Definitions of Probability

Event

A sub collection of a number of sample points under a definite rule or law is called an event e.g., let us take a die. Let its faces 1, 2, 3, 4, 5, 6 be represented by events $E_1, E_2, ..., E_6$ respectively. Then all $E_i s$ are sample points.

Null Event

An event having no sample point is called a null event and is denoted by ϕ.

Discrete Sample Points

A sample space whose elements are finite or infinite but countable is called discrete sample space, e.g., if we toss a coin as many times as we require for turning up one head then the sequence of points $S_1 = (1)$, $S_2 = (0, 1)$, $S_3 = (1, 0, 1)$, $S_4 = (0, 0, 0, 1)$ etc. is a discrete sample space.

Continuous Sample Space

A sample space whose elements are infinite and uncountable or assume all the values on a real line R is called continuous sample space. e.g., all points on a line or plane.

Exhaustive Cases or Events

It is the total number of all the possible outcomes of an experiment e.g., six faces of dice can be obtained in a throw. So all of them form exhaustive cases.

Mutually Exclusive Events

If in an experiment the occurrence of an event prevents or rules out the happening of all other event then events are said to be mutually exclusive e.g., in tossing a coin. if head occurs, occurence of tail is ruled out.

Equally Likely

Events are said to be equally likely if-there is no reason to expect any one in preference to other, e.g., in throwing a dice all the six faces are equally likely.

Favourable Cases

The cases which ensure the occurence of an event are said to be favourable events.

Independent and Dependent Events

When the experiments are conducted in such a way that occurence of an event in one trial does not have any effect on occurence of this or other events at a subsequent experiment then the events are said to be independent otherwise dependent e.g., in picking up the second card from a pack of well shuffled cards, it is dependent on the first pick.

6.1.1 Definition of Probability

CLASSICAL DEFINITION. If an experiment has n mutually exclusive equally likely and exhaustive cases out of which m are favourable to the happening of an event A then, probability $Pr(A)$ of happening of A is given by

$$Pr(A) = \frac{m}{n} = \frac{\text{No. of cases favourable to } A}{\text{Total no. of cases}}$$

EXAMPLE 6.1. *What is the probability of getting an even no. in a single throw with a dice.*

SOLUTION : Favourable cases = 2, 4, 6, *i.e.*, $m = 3$

Exhaustive cases = 1, 2, 3, 4, 5, 6, *i.e.*, $n = 6$

$$\therefore \qquad Pr(A) = \frac{3}{6} = \frac{1}{2}.$$

EXAMPLE 6.2. *What is the probabilities of getting a tail in single throw with a dice.*

SOLUTION : Favourable cases = $\{T\}$ *i.e.*, $m = 1$

Exhaustive cases = $\{H, T\}$ *i.e.*, $n = 2$

$$\therefore \qquad Pr(A) = \frac{m}{n} = \frac{1}{2}$$

EXAMPLE 6.3. *A bag contains 6 white balls, 9 black balls. What is the probability of drawing a black ball?*

SOLUTION : The total no. of equally likely and exhaustive cases = 6 + 9 = 15.

No. of favouralbe cases = $m = {}^9C_1 = 9$. ($\because$ no of black balls = 9)

Probability of drawing a black ball $= \frac{9}{15} = \frac{3}{5}$.

EXAMPLE 6.4. *What is the probability that if a card is drawn at random from an ordinary pack of cards, it is (i) a red card, (ii) a club, (iii) one of the court cards (Jack or queen or king).*

SOLUTION : Number of exhaustive cases = 52.

(i) There are 26 red cards and 26 black cards in an ordinary pack.

$\therefore$ Favourable cases = n = 26 (no. of red cards)

$\therefore$ Probability of getting a red card $= \frac{26}{52} = \frac{1}{2}$.

(ii) Number of clubs in a pack = 13

$\therefore$ Favourable cases = 13.

$\therefore$ Probability of getting a club $= \frac{13}{52} = \frac{1}{4}$.

(iii) There are $4 \times 3 = 12$ court cards in a pack of cards

$\therefore$ Number of favourable cases = m = 12.

Number of exhaustive cases = n = 52.

$\therefore$ Probability of getting a court card $= \frac{12}{52} = \frac{3}{13}$.

EXAMPLE 6.5. *What is the probability that a leap year, selected at random, will have 53 sunday?*

SOLUTION : There are 366 days in a leap year and it has 52 complete weeks and 2 days over. These two extra days can occur in following possible ways.

(i) Sunday and monday;

(ii) Monday and Tuesday;

(iii) Tuesday and Wednesday;

(iv) Wednesday and Thursday;

(v) Thursday and Friday;

(vi) Friday and Saturday;

(vii) Saturday and Sunday;

$\therefore$ Number of exhaustive case = 7

Number of favourable cases = 2

($\because$ There are 2 cases which have sunday [(i) and (vii)]).

$$\therefore \quad \text{Probability} = \frac{2}{7}.$$

EXAMPLE 6.6. *A card is drawn from an ordinary pack of playing cards and a person bets that it is a spade or an ace. What are odds against his winning this bet?*

SOLUTION : *In a pack of 52 cards, 1 card can be drawn in 52 ways. Since there are 13 spades and 3 aces (one ace is also present in spades)*

$\therefore$ The favourable cases = $m = 13 + 3 = 16$.

Number of exhaustive cases $n = 52$.

$$\text{Probability of getting a spade or an ace} = \frac{16}{52} = \frac{4}{13}$$

$$= \frac{4}{9+4}$$

$\therefore$ Odds against winning the bet are 9 to 4.

6.2 Theorems on Probability

(i) Addition theorem or the theorem on total probability : If the events are mutually exclusive, then the probability of hapenning of any one of them is equal to the sum of probabilities of the happening of the separate events, *i.e.*, in other words if $E_1, E_2, E_3, ..., E_n$ be n events and $Pr(E_1)$, $Pr(E_2)$, ..., $Pr(E_n)$, be their respective probabilities, then

$$Pr(E_1 + E_2 + E_3 + \ldots + E_n) = Pr(E_1) + Pr(E_2) + ... + Pr(E_4)$$

EXAMPLE 6.7. *A dice is rolled. What is the probability that number 1 or 6 may appear on the upper face.*

SOLUTION : The probability of appearing the no. 1 on the upper face $= \frac{1}{6}$

The probability of appearing the no. 6 on the upper face $= \frac{1}{6}$.

$\therefore$ The probability 1 or 6 may appear on the face $= \frac{1}{6} + \frac{1}{6} = \frac{1}{3}$

EXAMPLE 6.8. *If the probability of the horse A winning at the race is* $\frac{1}{5}$ *and the probability of the horse B winning the same race is* $\frac{1}{6}$. *What is the probability that one of the horses will win the race?*

SOLUTION : Probability of the winning of the horse

$A = \frac{1}{5}$. Probability of the winning of the horse

$B = \frac{1}{6}$.

$$\therefore \qquad Pr(A + B) = Pr(A) + Pr(B) = \frac{1}{5} + \frac{1}{6} = \frac{11}{30}.$$

EXAMPLE 6.9. *In a horse race the odds in favour of four horses.* H_1, H_2, H_3, H_4 *are* $1:3$; $1:4$; $1:5$; $1:6$ *respectively not more than one wins at the time. Find the chance that one of them will win the race.*

SOLUTION : Since the dead heat is not possible, therefore, the events are exclusive.

Now odds in favour of horse H_1 is $\frac{1}{3}$.

$$\therefore \qquad Pr(H_1) = \frac{1}{1+3} = \frac{1}{4}$$

Similarly, $$Pr(H_2) = \frac{1}{1+4} = \frac{1}{5}, \; Pr(H_3) = \frac{1}{1+5} = \frac{1}{6},$$

and $$Pr(H_4) = \frac{1}{1+6} = \frac{1}{7}$$

We know that

$$Pr(H_1 + H_2 + H_3 + H_4) = Pr(H_1) + Pr(H_2) + Pr(H_3) + Pr(H_4)$$

$$= \frac{1}{4} + \frac{1}{5} + \frac{1}{6} + \frac{1}{7} = \frac{319}{420}$$

6.3 Multiplicative Theorem or Theorem on Compound Probability

Compound Events : When 2 or more than 2 simple events occur in connection with each other then their simultaneous occurence is called compound event.

Conditional Probability : The probability of the happening of the event *A* when it is known that when *B* has already happened is called conditional probabilities and is denoted by $Pr\,(A/B)$.

Theorem on Compound Probability : The probability of the simultaneous occurence of the two events A and B is equal to the probability of one of the events multiplied by the conditional probability of other, given the occurence of the first, *i.e.*,

$$Pr(AB) = Pr(A) \,.\, Pr\,(B/A) = Pr(B) \,.\, Pr\,(A/B)\,.$$

EXAMPLE 6.10. *A card is drawn from a pack of 52 cards and then a second is drawn. What is the probability that both the cards drawn are queens?*

SOLUTION : First draw probability of getting a queen

$$= \frac{4}{52} = \frac{1}{13}\,.$$

Second draw, After drawing the first queen, we are left with 51 Cards having 3 queen.

$\therefore$ Probability of getting a queen in second draw $= \frac{3}{51} = \frac{1}{17}$

$\therefore$ Probability that both the cards are queen $= \frac{1}{13} \times \frac{1}{17} = \frac{1}{221}\,.$

EXAMPLE 6.11. *A bag contains 5 white and 3 black balls. Two balls are drawn at random one after the other without replacement. Find the probability that both the balls drawn are black.*

SOLUTION : Let $Pr(A)$, $Pr\,(B/A)$ denote the probability of drawing a black ball in the first and second attempt respectively.

$\therefore$ Probability of drawing a black ball in the first attempt is $Pr(A)$

where $$Pr(A) = \frac{\text{favourable cases}}{\text{Total exhaustive cases}} = \frac{3}{5+3} = \frac{3}{8}\,.$$

Probability of drawing the second black ball given the first ball drawn in black is

$$Pr\,(B/A) = \frac{\text{favourable cases}}{\text{Total no. of exhaustive cases}} = \frac{2}{5+2} = \frac{2}{7}$$

Probabilty that both the balls drawn are black is

$$Pr(AB) = Pr(A)\, Pr\,(B/A) = \frac{3}{8} \times \frac{2}{7} = \frac{3}{28}$$

Addition theorem for compatible events : The probability of the occurence of at least one of the events A and B is given by

$$Pr(A + B) = Pr(A) + Pr(B) - Pr(AB).$$

Happening of at least one event : Let A and B be 2 independent events and P_1 and P_2 be the probabilities of their happening, then the chance that both A and B happen is $Pr_1 \times Pr_2$. Also the probabilities of not happening of A and B are $1 - Pr_1$, $1 - Pr_2$ respectively. The probability that both do not happen is

$$(1 - Pr_1) \times (1 - Pr_2).$$

Now the chance that at least one of them happens :

$$Pr_1\, Pr_2 + Pr_1(1 - Pr_2) + Pr_2(1 - Pr_1) = 1 - (1 - Pr_1)(1 - Pr_2)$$

EXAMPLE 6.12. *4 coins are tossed. Find the probability that at least one head turns up.*

SOLUTION : Probability of getting a head in a toss of a coin $= \frac{1}{2}$.

Probability of getting tail in each case $= \frac{1}{2}$.

Probability of getting a tail in all the 4 cases $= \frac{1}{2} \times \frac{1}{2} \times \frac{1}{2} \times \frac{1}{2} = \frac{1}{16}$.

$\therefore$ Probability of getting at least one head $1 - \frac{1}{16} = \frac{15}{16}$.

EXAMPLE 6.13. *A problem in Mathematics is given to 3 students Daya, Ramesh and Naresh whose chances of solving it are $\frac{1}{2}, \frac{1}{3}, \frac{1}{4}$ respectively what is the probability that the problem will be solved.*

SOLUTION : The probabilities of Daya, Ramesh and Naresh solving the problem are $\frac{1}{2}, \frac{1}{3}, \frac{1}{4}$ respectively.

$\therefore$ The probabilities of Daya, Ramesh, Naresh not solving the problem are

$$1 - \frac{1}{2} = \frac{1}{2};\ 1 - \frac{1}{3} = \frac{2}{3};\ 1 - \frac{1}{4} = \frac{3}{4} \text{ respectively.}$$

$\therefore$ The probability that the problem is not solved by any one of them is $\frac{1}{2} \times \frac{2}{3} \times \frac{3}{4} = \frac{1}{4}$.

The probability that the problem will be solved by at least one of them $= 1 - \frac{1}{4} = \frac{3}{4}$.

EXAMPLE 6.14. *A card is drawn at random from a well shuffled pack of 52 cards. Find the probability of getting a two of heart or diamond.*

SOLUTION : Since there is only one two of hearts and only one two of diamonds, therefore, the probability of getting a two of hearts $= \frac{1}{52}$ and the probability of getting *a* 2 of diamonds $= \frac{1}{52}$.

Since these are mutually exclusive cases, therefore, the probability of getting a two of heart or a two of diamond

$$= \frac{1}{52} + \frac{1}{52} = \frac{2}{52} = \frac{1}{26}$$

EXAMPLE 6.15. *Three groups of children contain 3 girls 1 boy, 2 girls and 2 boys, 1 girl and 3 boys respectively. One child is slected at random from each group. Find the chance that the three selected comprise 1 girl and 2 boys.*

SOLUTION : The event may happen in any one of the following three mutually exclusive ways.

1. Girl from first group, boy from the second group and boy from third group.

The probability of this happening is

$$\frac{3}{4}\cdot\frac{1}{2}\cdot\frac{3}{4}=\frac{9}{32}.$$

2. Boy from the first group, girl from the second group and boy from the third group. The probability of this happening is

$$\frac{1}{4}\cdot\frac{1}{2}\cdot\frac{3}{4}=\frac{3}{32}$$

3. Boy from the first group, boy from 2nd group and girl from the 3rd group. The probability of this happening is

$$\frac{1}{4}\cdot\frac{1}{2}\cdot\frac{1}{4}=\frac{1}{32}$$

∴ By the theorem of total probability, the required probability is

$$\frac{9}{32}+\frac{3}{32}+\frac{1}{32}=\frac{13}{32}.$$

EXAMPLE 6.16. *A speaks truth in 75% and B in 80% of the cases. In what percentage of cases are they likely to contradict each other narrating the same incident?*

SOLUTION : Let $Pr(A)$, $Pr(B)$ be the porbability of A and B speaking the truths, then

$$Pr(A)=\frac{75}{100}=\frac{3}{4},\ Pr(B)=\frac{80}{100}=\frac{4}{5}.$$

$$Pr(\overline{A})=Pr(A \text{ tells a lie})=1-Pr(A)=1-\frac{3}{4}=\frac{1}{4}$$

$$Pr(\overline{B})=Pr(B \text{ tells a lie})=1-Pr(B)=1-\frac{4}{5}=\frac{1}{5}.$$

Now A and B will contradict as,

$$Pr(A)\,Pr(\overline{B})+Pr(B)\,Pr(\overline{A})=\frac{3}{4}\times\frac{1}{5}+\frac{4}{5}\times\frac{1}{4}=\frac{7}{20}=351.$$

EXAMPLE 6.17. *A man has 5 one rupees coins and one of them is known to have two heads. He takes out a coin at random and tosses it 5 times, it always falls head upwards. What is the probability that it is a coin with two heads?*

SOLUTION : Probability of getting a head with a rupee $=\frac{1}{2}$

Probability of selecting 2-head rupee $=\frac{1}{5}$

Probability that the rupee with two heads is taken out and it falls head upward all the 5 time $=\left(\frac{1}{5}\right)\times 1\times 1\times 1\times 1=\frac{1}{5}.$

Probability that a rupee with one head, head is taken out and it falls head all the 5 times

$$=\left(\frac{4}{5}\right)\times\left(\frac{1}{2}\right)\times\frac{1}{2}\times\frac{1}{2}\times\frac{1}{2}\times\frac{1}{2}=\frac{1}{40}$$

Probability of the rupee with 2 heads $= \dfrac{\frac{1}{5}}{\frac{1}{5}+\frac{1}{40}} = \frac{1}{5} \times \frac{40}{9} = \frac{8}{9}$.

6.4 Random Variable and Mathematical Expectation

Random Variable : A random variable x is a real valued function defined on a sample space S of an experiment. In other word to each outcomes of an experiment E_i of S, there corresponds a unique real no. x_i known as the value of the random variable x, *e.g.*,

(i) No. of sixes in a toss of two dice

(ii) The no. of two tails in a toss of 3 coins

(iii) No. of queens in a draw of two cards from a well shuffled deck.

A random variable is also called a stochastic variable or simply a variable. It is written as $x(E_i) = x_i$ which implies that the random variable x takes the value x_i corresponding to the outcome x_i corresponding to the outcome E_i.

Discrete Random Variable. A random variable is said to be discrete if it takes only a finite or an infinite but countable no. of values.

Continuous Random Variable. A random variable is said to be continuous if it takes a continuum of values, *i.e.*, if takes any value in an interval.

Mathematical Expectation. Let x be a discrete random variable which takes $x_1, x_2, x_3, \ldots, x_n$ mutually exclusive values with respective probability $P_1, P_2, P_3, \ldots, P_n$ then the expectation of x is

$$E(x) = P_1x_1 + P_2x_2 + P_3x_3 + \ldots + P_nx_n$$

$$\sum_{i=1}^{n} P_i x_i, \qquad \text{where } \Sigma P_i = 1$$

Mean

$E(x)$ is also called the mean or expected value of the discrete random variable x provided the series $\Sigma x_i P_i$ is convergent. It is denoted by μ.

Variance

The quantity $E(x - \bar{x})^2$ is called the variance, where

$$E(x_i - \bar{x})^2 = \sum_{i=1}^{n} P_i (x - \bar{x}_i)^2$$

$$= E(x)^2 - [E(x)]^2$$

$$\sigma^2 = \Sigma P_i x_i^2 - \mu^2$$

Theorems or Mathematical Expectation

THEOREM 6.1. The expectation of a sum of two random variables is equal to the sum of their expectations, *i.e.*,

$$E(x+y) = E(x) + E(y)$$

where x and y are two discrete random variables.

THEOREM 6.2. The expectation of the product of two independent random variables is equal to the product of their expectations.

$$E(xy) = E(x) \, . \, E(y)$$

EXAMPLE 6.18. *What is the expectation of the sum of points on a dice.*

SOLUTION : Here the random variable x is the no. of points on the dice which takes up the values 1, 2, 3, 4, 5, 6. These are equiprobable with probability 1/6.

$$E(x) = P_1x_1 + P_2x_2 + P_3x_3 + P_4x_4 + P_5x_5 + P_6x_6.$$

$$= \frac{1}{6} \, . \, 1 + \frac{1}{6} \, . \, 2 + \frac{1}{6} \, . \, 3 + \frac{1}{6} \, . \, 4 + \frac{1}{6} \, . \, 5 + \frac{1}{6} \, . \, 6$$

$$= \frac{1}{6}(1+2+3+4+5+6) = \frac{21}{6} = \frac{7}{2}$$

EXAMPLE 6.19. *Thirteen cards are drawn simultaneously from a pack of 52 cards. If aces counts 1, face cards, 10 and others according to denominations, find the expectation of the total score on the 13 cards.*

SOLUTION : Let x be the random variable which takes up the values 1, 2, 3, 4, 5, 6, 7, 8, 9, 10, 10, 10, 10 with equal probability each equal to 1/13.

$$\therefore \quad E(x) = \frac{1}{13} \, . \, 1 + \frac{1}{13} \, . \, 2 + \frac{1}{13} \, . \, 3 + \frac{1}{13} \, . \, 10 + \frac{1}{13} \, . \, 10 + \frac{1}{13} \, . \, 10 + \frac{1}{13} \, . \, 10$$

$$= \frac{1}{13}(1+2+3+4+5+6+7+8+9+10+10+10+10)$$

$$= \frac{85}{13}$$

6.5 Probability Distribution

The random variable X taking the values $x_1, x_2, x_3, \ldots, x_n$ with probabilities $P_1, P_2, \ldots, P_n$ respectively where $P_i = Pr(X = x_i)$ s.t.

(i) every probability is non negative no. not greater than 1

$$P_i > 0, \; i = 1, 2, 3, \ldots, n, \; 0 \le P_i \le 1$$

(ii) the sum of all the probability is always unity

$$P_1 + P_2 + \ldots + P_n = 1$$

is said to possess the probability distribution. It is represented in a tabular form as given below:

X	x_1	x_2	x_3	...	x_r	...	x_n
$Pr(X)$	P_1	P_2	P_3	...	P_r	...	P_n

Also random variable X will have mean, $\mu = \sum_{i=1}^{n} P_i x_i$ variance

$$\sigma^2 = \sum_{i=1}^{n} P_i x_i^2 - \mu^2$$

EXAMPLE 6.20. *Find the probability distribution of the no. of heads in two tosses of a coin.*

SOLUTION : When we toss a coin twice, we get the four outcomes viz. *HH, HT, TH, TT* (head is 0, 1 or 2)

$$\therefore \quad Pr\text{ (zero head)} = \frac{1}{9}.$$

$$Pr\text{ (one head)} = \frac{2}{4}, \; Pr\text{ (two head)} = \frac{1}{4}$$

Thus, X takes the values 0, 1, 2 with probabilities $\frac{1}{4}, \frac{1}{2}, \frac{1}{4}$ respectively. Hence we have the probability distribution.

X :	0	1	2
$Pr(X)$:	$\frac{1}{4}$	$\frac{1}{2}$	$\frac{1}{4}$

EXAMPLE 6.21. *Two cards are drawn successively, with replacement from a well shuffled deck of 52 cards. Find the probability distribution of the no. of kings.*

SOLUTION : Let X denote the no. of kings. Here X can takes the values 0, 1, or 2, Now

$$Pr\text{ (kings)} = \frac{4}{52} = \frac{1}{13}$$

$$Pr\text{ (not kings)} = 1 - \frac{1}{13} = \frac{12}{13}$$

$$Pr(X = 0) = Pr\text{ (not king and not king)} = Pr\text{(not king)} \,.\, Pr\text{ (not king)}$$

$$= \frac{12}{13} \times \frac{12}{13} = \frac{144}{169}$$

$$Pr(X = 1) = Pr\text{(king and not king)} + Pr\text{(not king and king)}$$

$$= \frac{1}{13} \times \frac{12}{13} + \frac{12}{13} \times \frac{1}{13} = \frac{24}{169}$$

$$Pr(X = 2) = Pr\text{ (king and king)} = Pr\text{ (king)} \,.\, Pr\text{ (King)}$$

$$= \frac{1}{13} \times \frac{1}{13} = \frac{1}{169}$$

∴ We have the following probability distribution.

X :	0	1	2
$Pr(X)$:	$\frac{144}{169}$	$\frac{24}{169}$	$\frac{1}{169}$

6.6 Binomial Distribution

It is a probability distribution which is obtained when the probability of the happening of an event is same in all the trials and there are only two events in each trial e.g., probability of getting a head, when a coin is tossed number of times, must remain same in each toss, *i.e.*, $\frac{1}{2}$

Let us consider an experiment of n trials in which p is the probability of success and q be be the probability of failure thus probability of happening of an event r times is p^r (by multiplicative theorem) and not happening is q^{n-r}. But the total no. of ways in which the event can happen r times exactly in n trials is ${}^nC_r$. These ${}^nC_r$ ways are equally likely, mutualy exclusive and exhaustive.

Therefore, the probability of r success and $(n - r)$ failure in n trials in any order, what so ever is ${}^nC_r\, p^r\, q^{n-r}$.

It can also be expressed as

$$P(r) = {}^nC_r\, p^r\, q^{n-r},\ r = 0, 1, 2, ..., n$$

it is called **Binomial distribution.**

frequency function of the Binomial distribution is given by

$$f(r) = NPr(r) = N\, {}^nC_r\, p^r\, q^{n-r}$$

where n-trials are repeated N times.

Mean

$$P(r) = {}^nC_r\, q^{n-r}\, p^r.$$

$$\text{Mean} = \mu = E(x) = \sum_{i=0}^{n} x_i P_{r_i} = np$$

$$\text{Variance} = \sigma^2 = \sum_{r=0}^{n} (x_r^2 P_r) - \mu^2$$

$$P_r = P_r(r)$$

$$x_r^2 = r^2 = r + r(r - 1),\ r = 0, 1, ..., n$$

6.7 Randomized Algorithms

A randomized algorithm is one that makes use of a randomizer (such as random no generator) some of the Decision made in algorithm depend on the output of the randomizer since the output of any randomizer might differ in an unpredictable way from run to run, the output of a randomized algorithm could also differ from run to run for the same input and so varies the execution time.

Randomized algorithm — → Las Vegas
→ Monte Carlo

Las Vagas

Execution time of Las Vegas algorithms depends upon the output of the randomizer. It may terminate fast or may run for a long.

Monte Carlo

Its output depends upon run to run.

Typically, for a fixed input, a monte carlo algorithm does not display much variation in excution time between runs, where as in case of LAS VEGAS, algo this variation is significant.

DEFINITION. We say that the following definition holds for randomized algorithm $O(g(n))$, $f(n) \le c\,\alpha gn$ with probability $Pr \ge 1 - \frac{1}{n^{\alpha}}$, this is called high probablity bound, where α is probability parameter.

[Markovs inequality] If X is any non negative random variable whose mean is μ, then

$$Pr[X \ge x] \le \frac{\mu}{x}.$$

EXAMPLE 6.22. *If a coin a tossed 1000 times, what is the probability that the no. of head is* ≥ 600

SOLUTION : We have expected value of X, $E(X) = Px$

$$E(x) = \frac{1}{2} \times 1000 = 500.$$

but mean $\mu = 500$

and $x = 600$

$$P(X \ge 600) \le \frac{500}{600} = \frac{5}{6}.$$

[Chernoff bounds] If X is a binomial with parameter (n, p) and $m > np$ is an integer.

$$Pr(X \ge m) \le \left(\frac{np}{m}\right)^{m} e^{m - np}$$

also $Pr(X \le \lfloor (1 - \varepsilon)\, pn \rfloor) \le e^{(-\varepsilon^2 np/2)}$

and $PR(x \le \lfloor (1 + \varepsilon)\, np \rfloor) \le e(-\varepsilon^2 np/3)$

$$0 < \varepsilon < 1$$

For above bounds

Let $\varepsilon = 0.2$, $n = 1000$, $P = \frac{1}{2}$

$$P[x \le 600] \le e^{[-(0.2)^2(500/3)}$$
$$= e^{-20/3} \le 0.001273.$$

EXAMPLE 6.23. *There are 64 beds in a garden and 3 seeds of a particular type of flower are sawn in each bed. The probability of a flower being white is $\frac{1}{4}$. Find the no. of beds with 3, 2, 1, and 0 white flowers.*

SOLUTION : The probability P of a white flower $= \frac{1}{4}$

$$q = 1 - p = 1 = \frac{1}{4} = \frac{3}{4}$$

Here, $n = 3$, $N = 64$

$$f(r) = {}^3C_r \left(\frac{1}{4}\right)^r \left(\frac{3}{4}\right)^{3-r}$$

Number of beds with zero flower $Nf(0) = 64 \times {}^3C_0 \left(\frac{1}{4}\right)^0 \left(\frac{3}{4}\right)^3 = 64 \times \frac{27}{64} = 27.$

$$\text{Beds with 1 white flower} = 64\,f(1) = 64 \times {}^3C_1 \left(\frac{1}{4}\right)^1 \times \left(\frac{3}{4}\right)^2$$
$$= 64 \times 3 \times \frac{1}{4} \times \frac{9}{16} = 27$$

$$\text{Beds with 2 white flowers} = 64 \times {}^2C_2 \left(\frac{1}{4}\right)^2 \left(\frac{3}{4}\right) = 9.$$

$$\text{Beds with 3 white flowers} = 64 \times {}^3C_3 \left(\frac{1}{4}\right)^3 \left(\frac{3}{4}\right)^0 = 1$$

EXAMPLE 6.24. *Eight coins are thrown simultaneously. Find the probability of getting at least 6 heads.*

SOLUTION : Here $P = \frac{1}{2}$, $q = \frac{1}{2}$

Probability of getting 6 heads, when either 6, 7 or 8 coins show heads is

$$= Pr(6) + P_r(7) + P_r(8)$$
$$= {}^8C_6 \left(\frac{1}{2}\right)^6 \left(\frac{1}{2}\right)^2 + {}^8C_7 \left(\frac{1}{2}\right)^7 \left(\frac{1}{2}\right) + {}^8C_8 \left(\frac{1}{2}\right)^8$$
$$= \left(\frac{1}{2}\right)^8 ({}^8C_6 + {}^8C_7 + {}^8C_8) = \frac{1}{256}(28 + 8 + 1) = \frac{37}{256}.$$

$$\sigma^2 = \sum_{r=0}^{n} r^2 P_r(r) - n^2 p^2$$

$$= \Sigma[r(r-1)+r]\,{}^nC_r\, q^{n-r} p^r - n^2p^2$$

$$= \sum_{r=0}^{n} r\,(r-1)\,{}^nC_r\, q^{n-r}\, p^2 + \sum_{r=0}^{n} r\,{}^nC_r\, q^{n-r} p^r - n^2p^2$$

$$= \Sigma\, r(r-1)\frac{n\,!}{r\,!\,(n-r)\,!}\, q^{n-r}\, p^2 + np - n^2p^2$$

$$= np(1-p) = npq$$

$$\therefore \quad \sigma^2 = npq$$

$$S.D. = \sqrt{npq}$$

Recursion formula of Recurrence Relation for Binomial Distribution.

$$P(r) = {}^nC_r\, p^r\, q^{n-r}$$

$$P(r+1) = {}^nC_{r+1}\, p^{r+1}\, q^{n-r-1}$$

Solving this, we get

$$P(r+1) = \frac{n\,.\,r}{r+1}\,.\,\frac{p}{q}\,.\,P(r)$$

EXAMPLE 6.25. *If 10 coins are tossed 100 times, how many times would you expect 7 coins to fall head upward.*

SOLUTION : $Pr(\text{head}) = \frac{1}{2}$.

$\therefore\ P = \frac{1}{2},\ q = 1 - p = \frac{1}{2}.\ n = 10,\ N = 100,\ r = 7.$

We have $\quad f(r) = N\,.\,Pr(r) = N\,{}^nC_r\, q^{n-r}\, p^r$

$$= 100 \times {}^{10}C_7 \left(\frac{1}{2}\right)^3 \left(\frac{1}{2}\right)^7$$

$$= \frac{375}{32} = 11.7 \approx 12$$

6.7.1 Advantages and Disadvantages of Randomized Algorithm

Two of the most important advantages of using randomized algorithms are their simplicity and efficiency. A majority of randomized algorithms found are simpler than the best deterministic algorithms for the same problems. Randomized algorithms have also been shown to yield better complexity bounds. e,g.,

Find-match takes $\theta(n)$ whereas **randomized. Find match** takes θ (log n)

```
find-match (A, n)

    for i ← 1 to n do
    If i ≠ j and (A[i] = A[j]) then
        return i
```

```
Randomize-find-match (A, n)
    while (true)
        {
        i ← Random( ) mod n + 1;
        j ← Random( ) mod n + 1;
        If i ≠ j and (A[i] = A[j]) then
    return i
        }
```

Above Algorithm finds two matching element in an array which contains $\frac{n}{2}$ distinct elements and rest $\frac{n}{2}$ are repeated copies. The problem is to identify the repeated element.

Any deterministic algorithm for solving algo 1 take $\Theta(n)$ time.
In algo 2, sampling performed is with repeations, that is first and second elements are randomly picked from out of n elements (each is equally likely to be picked). Thus there is a probability (equal to $\frac{1}{n}$) that the same array element is picked each time. If we just check for the equality of the 2 elements picked, our answer might be incorrect (in case the algorithm picked the same array index each time) therefore, it is essential to make sure that the 2 indices picked are different and the 2 array cells contain the same value. Any iteration of while loop (in randomized find match) will be successful in identifying the repeated number if i is any one of $\frac{n}{2}$ array indices and j is from other $\frac{n}{2}$ indices other then i

$\therefore$ Probability that match is found and algo terminates

$$Pr = \frac{\frac{n}{2}}{n} \cdot \frac{\left(\frac{n}{2} - 1\right)}{n}$$

i.e., $$Pr = \frac{1}{2n}\left(\frac{n}{2} - 1\right) = \frac{1}{4} - \frac{1}{2n} \geq \frac{1}{5} \ \forall \ n \geq 10$$

Let $n = 13$

We have $$Pr = \frac{1}{4} - \frac{1}{2n}$$

$\therefore$ $$Pr = \frac{1}{4} - \frac{1}{26} = \frac{13 - 2}{\cdot 52} = \frac{11}{52} = \frac{1}{4.727} > 0.2$$

This implies that the probability that the algorithm does not quit in a given iteration is $< \left(\frac{4}{5}\right)$.

For 10 iterations, if coins quit in.

$$< \left(\frac{4}{5}\right)^{10} = 0.1074.$$

For 100 iteration if

$$\left(\frac{4}{5}\right)^{100} < 2.04 \times 10^{-10}.$$

In general. the algorithm does not quit in

$$< \left(\frac{4}{5}\right)^{c\,\alpha\, lg\, n} = n^{-c\,\alpha \log (5/4)}$$

Which will be $< n^{-\alpha}$, if $c \geq \frac{1}{\log\left(\frac{5}{4}\right)}$

Thus, the algorithm terminates in $\frac{1}{\log\left(\frac{5}{4}\right)} \alpha \log n$ iterations or less with probability $\geq 1 - n^{-\alpha}$. Since each iteration take $O(1)$ time, run time of algorithm is $O(lgn)$.

There are critical applications where small probability of error cannot be tolerated (*e.g.*, nuclear reactors). So the use of randomizer does not always give a better performance.

EXERCISE

1. A carnival game consists of three dice in a cage. A player can bet a rupee on any of the numbers 1 through 6. The cage is shaken and the pay off is as follows :
   If the player no. doesn't appear on any of the dice he loses his rupee, otherwise if the player no. appears on exactly K dice he keeps his rupee and wins K more what is expected gain from playing the carnival game once ?
2. Describe Baye's Theorem for computing conditional probabilities.

7

HEAPS AND HEAPSORT

7.1 Heaps

It is a complete binary tree with some of the rightmost leaves removed. It provides an efficient implementation of the *priority queue*. In a heap the elements of highest priority are kept in the root of a binary tree. Depending on the notion of priority this might be the minimum key (for a minimizing heap) or the maximum key (for a maximizing heap). For heapsort to sort in ascending order, a maximizing heap is used otherwise minimizing heap is used.

DEFINITION. A binary tree T is a heap structure iff it satisfies following condition :

1. T is complete at least through depth $h - 1$
2. All leaves are at depth h or $h - 1$.
3. All paths to a leaf at depth h are to the left of all paths to a leaf of depth $h - 1$.

Another name for a heap structure is a *left-complete binary tree.*

If an Array A contains key values of nodes in a heap, *length*[A] is total number of elements.

$$\text{heap-size } [A] = \text{length } [A] = n \ (n \text{ is no. of elements})$$

Root of tree is $A[i]$, Parent (i), Left (i), Right (i) return index of Parent, Left child and Right child respectively as below :

```
PARENT (i)
        return ⌊i / 2⌋
LEFT (i)
        return 2i
RIGHT (i)
        return (2i + 1)
```

7.1.1 Heap Property

For every node i other than root $A[\text{PARENT}(i)] \geq A[i]$ i.e., value of any node is less than or equal to its parent.

Consider forming a heap from an Array {40, 80, 90, 35, 60, 70, 50, 45}

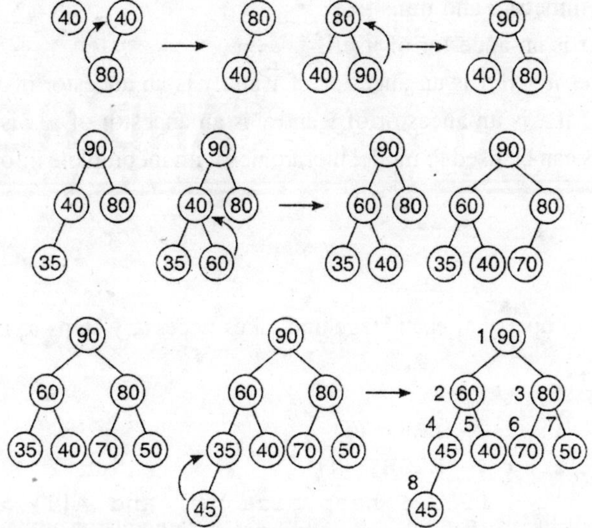

Fig. 7.1. Heap construction with given array A.

Thus we can see that at each stage *heap property* is checked, that child key value should not be greater than its parent, if it is so child key is promoted as parent node and parent as child.

The array value after satisfying the heap property are

index →	1	2	3	4	5	6	7	8
$A \leftrightarrow$	90	60	80	45	40	70	50	35

```
e.g.,       if i = 4.
         Parent (i)
```

$$\text{return } \left\lfloor \frac{4}{2} \right\rfloor$$

```
        i.e., at 2 position parent lies.
    thus
```

or left child or for index $i = 2$ lies at,

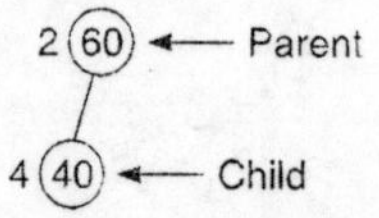

2 (60) ← Parent

4 (40) ← Child

```
    left (i)
    return 2i i.e., 4
```

The ancestor relation in a heap defines a *partial order* on its elements, which means it is reflexive, anti-symmetric, and transitive.

1. *Reflexive* : x is an ancestor of itself.
2. *Anti-symmetric* : if x is an ancestor of y and y is an ancestor of x, then $x = y$.
3. *Transitive* : if x is an ancestor of y and y is an ancestor of z, x is an ancestor of z.

Partial orders can be used to model hierarchies with incomplete information or equal-valued elements.

Algorithm

It checks of heap property at each stage and takes necessary steps to maintain it

```
Heapify (A, i)
    1. l ← LEFT (i)
    2. r ← RIGHT (i)
        If l ≤ heap-size [A] and A[l] > A[i]
            then largest ← l
            else largest ← i
        If r ≤ heap-size [A] and A[r] > A[largest]
            then largest ← r
        If largest  ≠ i
            then exchange A[i] ↔ A[largest]
                HEAPIFY (A, largest)
```

In this algorithm at each stage $A[i]$,A[LEFT(i)], and A[RIGHT(i)] is determined and its index is stored in largest. If $A[i]$ is largest then subtree rooted at node i is a heap and procedure terminates otherwise one of two children has largest value, so $A[i]$ is swapped with A[largest]. This process is repeated recursively. This can be seen clearly in fig. 7.2 shown below.

It is clear form the figure that heapify procedure works in **top down** fashion for every index passed to heapify procedure (here $i = 2$). Here gray shades shows the movement of index starting from $i = 2$ to $i = 9$ (in (c)). One thing to be noted that, **through the use of heapify**

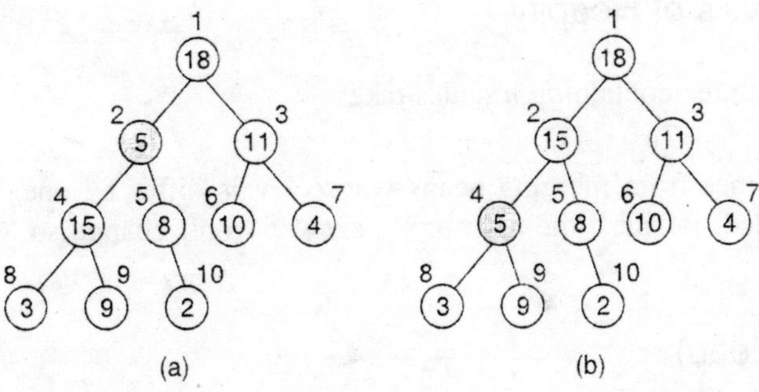

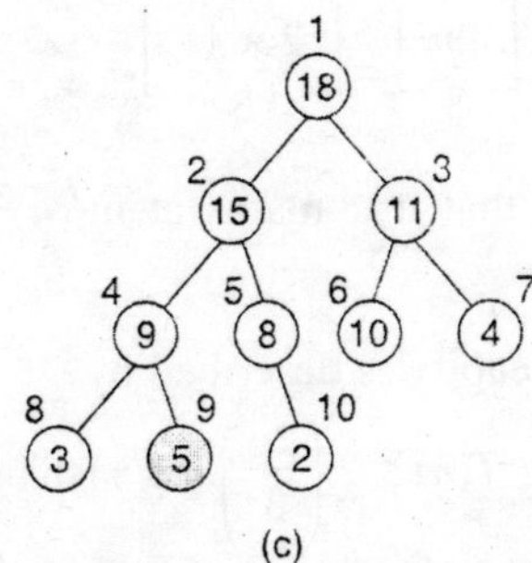

Fig. 7.2. Steps (a)-(c) shows heapify (A. 2).

algorithm, it is not necessary that we always get a heap. We can also note that in this algorithm while comparision of key value of child with parent, we do not directly move the key value of child, if it is greater than its parent, rather we store the *index* of bigger key value between parent and left child in largest and then we again compare the key of right child with A[largest], after finding the appropriate largest we swap the values *i.e.*, **swapping is done only in the end. It is also not necessary that key value of left child is always greater than key value of right child in case of heap formation.**

The running time of Heapify on a subtree of size n rooted at a given node i is the $\theta(1)$ time to fix up the relationships among the elements subtree rooted at one of the children of node i. In a complete binary tree if last row is exactly half full (*i.e.*, forms a left complete binary tree) then children subtree can have at most size $\frac{2n}{3}$ as illustrated below in fig. 7.3.

Let an array A contains 11 elements.

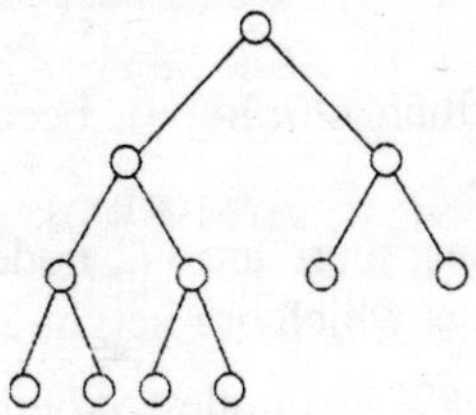

Fig. 7.3

Rough Analysis of Heapify

Heapify on a subtree containing n nodes takes

$$T(n) \leq T(2n/3) + O(1)$$

The 2/3 comes from merging heaps whose levels differ by one. The last row could be exactly half filled. Besides, the asymptotic answer won't change so long the fraction is less than one.

Half full (a Heap)

Maximum no. of elements in Left subtree is

$$\left\lfloor \frac{2n}{3} \right\rfloor = \left\lfloor \frac{2 \times 11}{3} \right\rfloor = 7$$

we can see from the Fig. 7.3 that it contains at most $\frac{2n}{3}$ elements. So at most this no. of comparisons are required.

So, running time time of heapify is described by

$$T(n) \leq T\left(\frac{2n}{3}\right) + \theta(1)$$

The solution of this recurrence by case 2 of master theorem is

$$T(n) = O(lgn) \quad \text{or} \quad O(h), \text{ as } h = lgn$$

only this much number of comparisions are required.

Constructing a Heap

Heapify is used in bottom up manner to construct heap for array A, starting with the leaves, since at $\left\lfloor \frac{n}{2} \right\rfloor + 1$, all are leaves we have algorithm as follows.

```
BUILD-HEAP (A)
For i ← ⌊length [A]/2⌋ down to 1
      do HEAPIFY (A, i)
```

Exact Analysis of Heapify

In fact, Heapify performs better than $O(n \log n)$, because most of the heaps we merge are extremely small.

In a full binary tree on n nodes, there are $n/2$ nodes which are leaves (i.e. height 0), $n/4$ nodes which are height 1, $n/8$ nodes which are height 2, ...

In general, there are at most $[n/2^{h+1}]$ nodes of height h, so the cost of building a heap is:

$$\sum_{h=0}^{[\log n]} [n/2^{h+1}]\, O(h) = O\left(n \sum_{h=0}^{[\log n]} h/2^h\right)$$

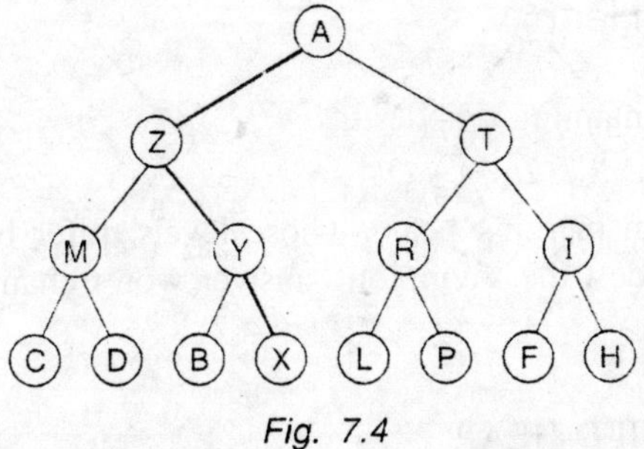

Fig. 7.4

Since this sum is not quite a geometric series, we can't apply the usual identity to get the sum. But it should be clear that the series converges.

In BUILD-HEAP algorithm, Heapify works in top down fashion for each call of BUILD-HEAP which works in, bottom-up fashion, thus we get a final Heap.

we can calculate this summation for infinity as

We have

$$\sum_{h=0}^{\infty} x^h = \frac{1}{1-x}$$

differentiating both sides, we get

$$\Sigma\, hx^{h-1} = \frac{1}{(1-x)^2}$$

$$\Sigma\, hx^h = \frac{x}{(1-x)^2},$$

if $x = \frac{1}{2}$, we have

$$\sum_{h=0}^{\infty} \frac{h}{2^h} = \frac{\frac{1}{2}}{\left(1-\frac{1}{2}\right)^2}$$

$$= 2$$

Thus, the running time of BUILD-HEAP is bounded us

$$O\left(n \sum_{h=0}^{\lfloor lgn \rfloor} \left(\frac{h}{2^h}\right)\right) = O\left(n \sum_{n=0}^{\infty} \frac{h}{2^h}\right)$$

$$= O(n)$$

Thus a heap can be created in linear time.

EXAMPLE 7.1. *Illustrate the operation of BUILD-HEAP on the array A = < 5, 3, 17, 10, 84, 19, 6, 22, 9>.*

SOLUTION :

Here $i = \left\lfloor \frac{n}{2} \right\rfloor = 4.$

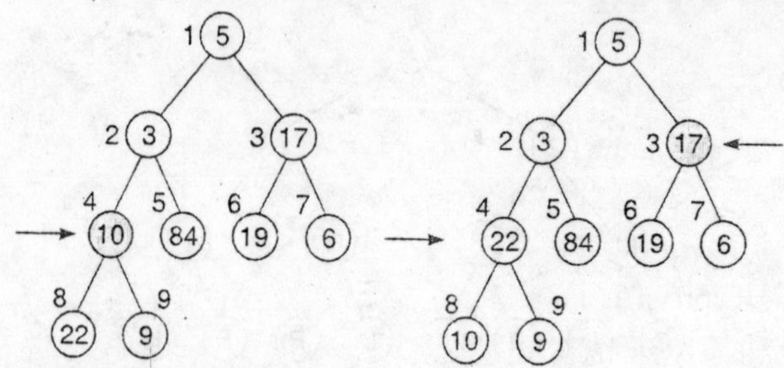

i.e., *i* points to 4, in BUILD-HEAP.

i.e., *A*(*i*), LEFT (*i*), RIGHT (*i*) are compared at node 4 so as to satisfy the heap-property now *i* becomes 2

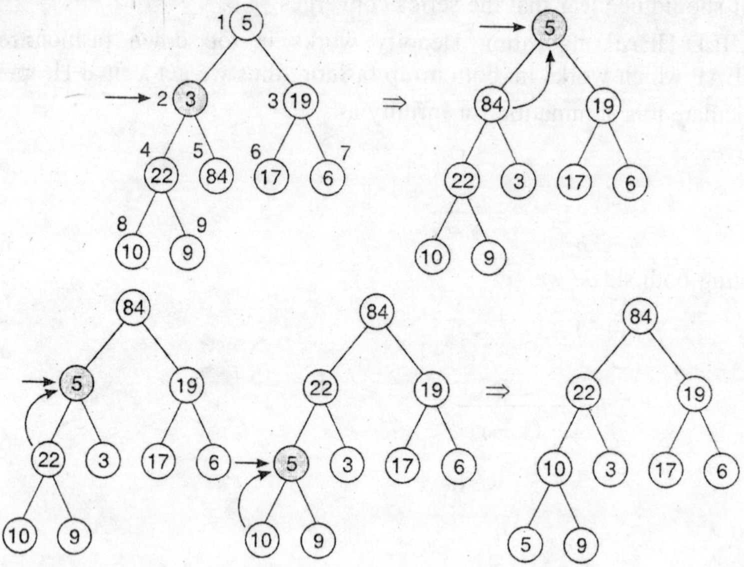

7.1.2 Heapsort Algorithm

Since in a heap (maximum heap) the largest element resides at the top, *i.e.*, root, if we delete this element and apply Heapify property then again largest element will come to top and we continue this process till we get last element. So in the end we will get the smallest element. the elements deleted can be stored in another array s.t. first element is stored at the last so that we get a list in ascending order. Heap size is reduced by 1 at each stage and we store the last element of root before reducing the size and calling heapify procedure.

B is the final sorted listed in ascending order.

Heapsort (*A*)

1. BUILD-HEAP(*A*) $O(n)$
2. $n \leftarrow$ length [*A*] 1

```
for i ← length [A] down to 2            n – 1
    B[n] ← A[1]                          1
    do exchange A[1] ↔ A[i]              1
    heap-size [A] ← heap-size – 1        1
    n ← n – 1                            1
    Heapify (A, 1)                       lgn
```

this algorithm is shown to work in Fig. 7.5 below.

Running time

Each of $n - 1$ calls to BUILD-HEAP takes $O(lgn)$ time so total time of Heapsort is $O(nlgn)$

We can see that BUILD-HEAP works in bottom UP manner as if we start from top every time down the tree process will be unnecessarily repeated for each node to check for heap-property.

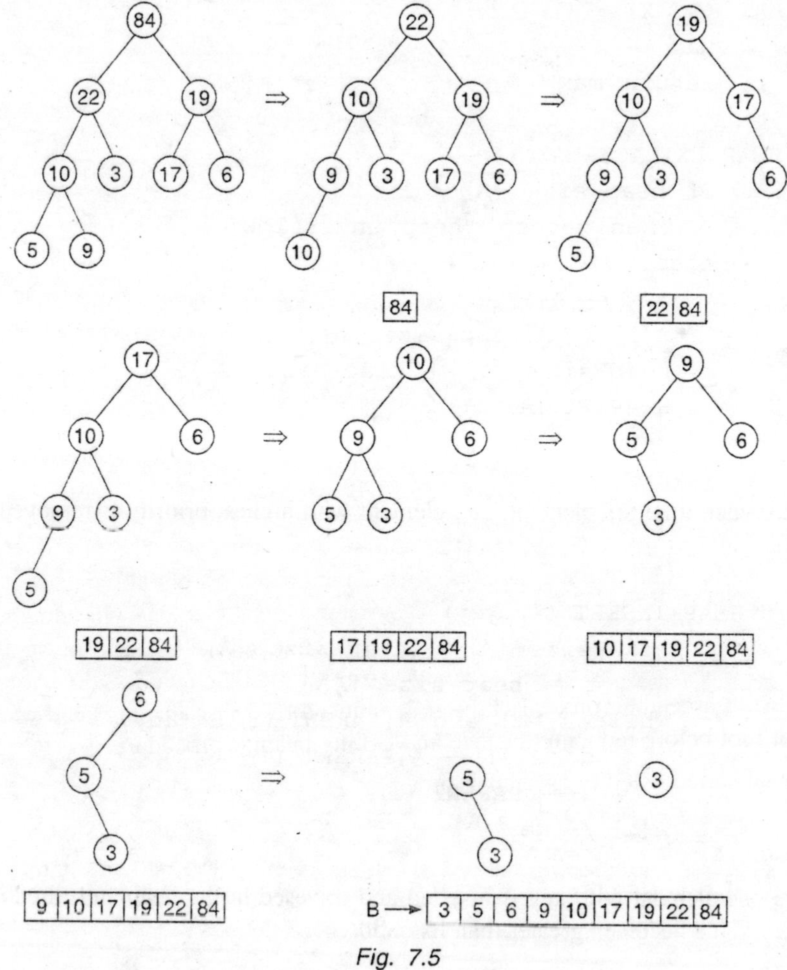

Fig. 7.5

7.2 Priority Queue

It consists of entries, each of which contains a key called the priority of the entry.

Application : In a time sharing system for example large number of tasks may be competing for CPU. The one with highest priority is given preference. For example simulations of time dependent system and solution of sparse system of linear equations by row reduction.

```
MAX (S, x) → finds maximum of S.
INSERT (S, x) →  inserts an element x into S.
MAXIMUM (S, x) returns the elements of S
          with largest key.

EXTRACT-MAX(S) remove and returns the elemtnt of S with
               largest key.
MAX (S, X)
    max ← A[1]
    return max

HEAP-EXTRACT-MAX (A)
    If heap-size [A] < 1
       Then return "heap underflow"
    else.
       max ← A[1]
       A[1] ← A[heap-size [A]]
       heap-size [A] ← heap-size [A] - 1
       HEAPIFY (A, 1)
       return max
```

In this each time top element, *i.e.*, element with highest priority is removed *running time is O(lgn)*

```
HEAP-INSERT (A, key)
    heap-size [A] ← heap-size [A] + 1
         i ← heap-size [A]
    while i > 1 and A[PARENT (i)] < key
         do A[i] ← A[PARENT (i)]
         i ← PARENT (i)
    A[i] ← key
```

Here one element with key is inserted and travesed in the heap and fitted at the position where key value becomes greater than its children.

Running time

$O(lgn)$, path traced from leaf to root is equal to ht, of tree.

EXAMPLE 7.2. *Illustrate the HEAP-INSERT (A, 3) on the heap*

$A = <15, 13, 9, 5, 12, 8, 7, 4, 0, 6, 2, 1>$

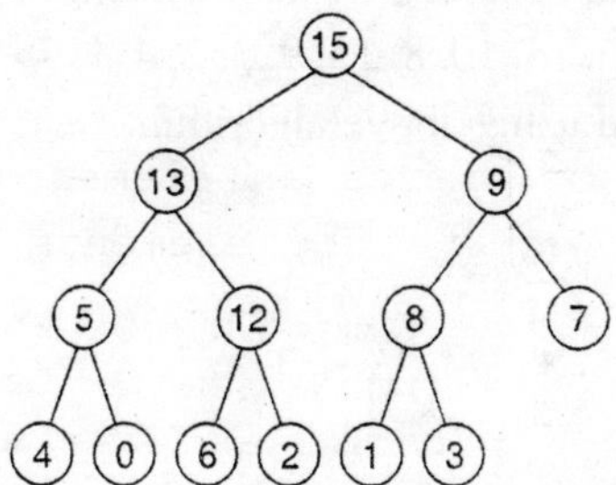

SOLUTION : Nothing will happen, as it is already a heap. Note that there is no relation between left child and right child key value, as heap is not a BST always.

EXAMPLE 7.3. $A = <16, 14, 10, 8, 7, 9, 3, 2, 4, 1>$, *perform HEAP- INSERT (A, 15).*

SOLUTION :

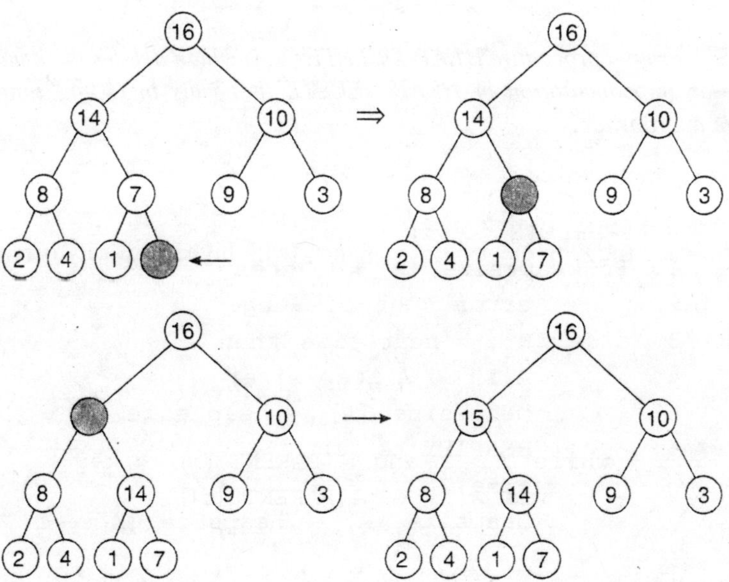

EXAMPLE 7.4. *Modify BUILD-HEAP(A) s.t. elements of heap are inserted using HEAP-INSERT procedure.*

SOLUTION :

```
BUILD-HEAP (A)
      heap-size[A] ← 1
For i ← 2 to length [A]
      do HEAP-INSERT (A, B[i])
```

Running time : $\theta(nlgn)$

e.g., *A* = <16, 14, 10, 8, 15, 9, 3, 2, 4, 1, 7>

this way heap can be created using above algorithm.

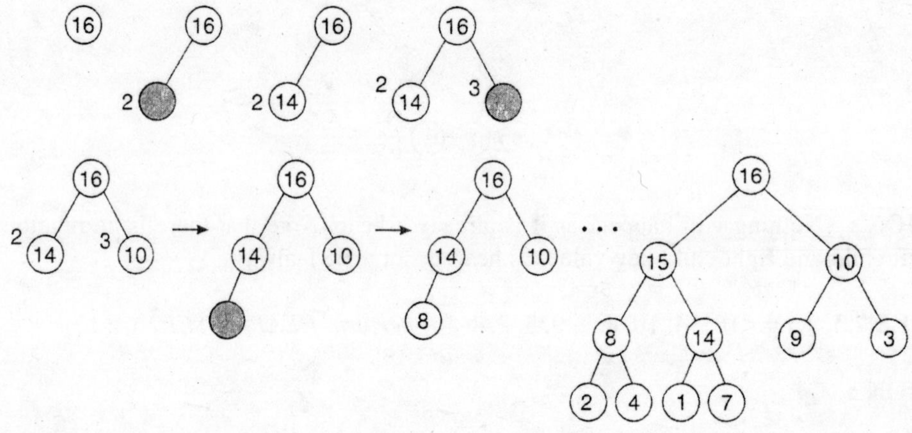

EXAMPLE 7.5. *From a procedure HEAP-DELETE (A, i) which deletes the item in node i from heap A. Give an impelmentation of HEAP-DELETE that runs in O(lgn) time and updates heap structure appropriately.*

SOLUTION :

```
HEAP-DELETE (A, i)
1. If heap-size [A] < i then
2.         error "Out of Range"
3. else IF i ≠ heap-size then
4.         A[i] ← A[heap-size]
5.         heap-size [A] ← heap size [A] - 1
6.         HEAPIFY (A, i)
           else
           heapsize [A] ← heapsize [A] - 1
```

Running time

Line 1–5 take $O(1)$ time and HEAPIFY take $O(lgn)$ time so HEAP-DELETE take $O(lgn)$ time.

EXAMPLE 7.6. *Illustrate HEAP-EXTRACT-MAX on heap A = <15, 13, 9, 5, 12, 8, 7, 4, 0, 6, 2, 1>*

SOLUTION : max $\leftarrow A(1)$

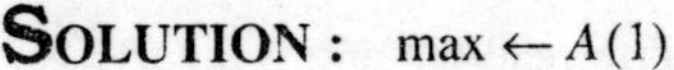

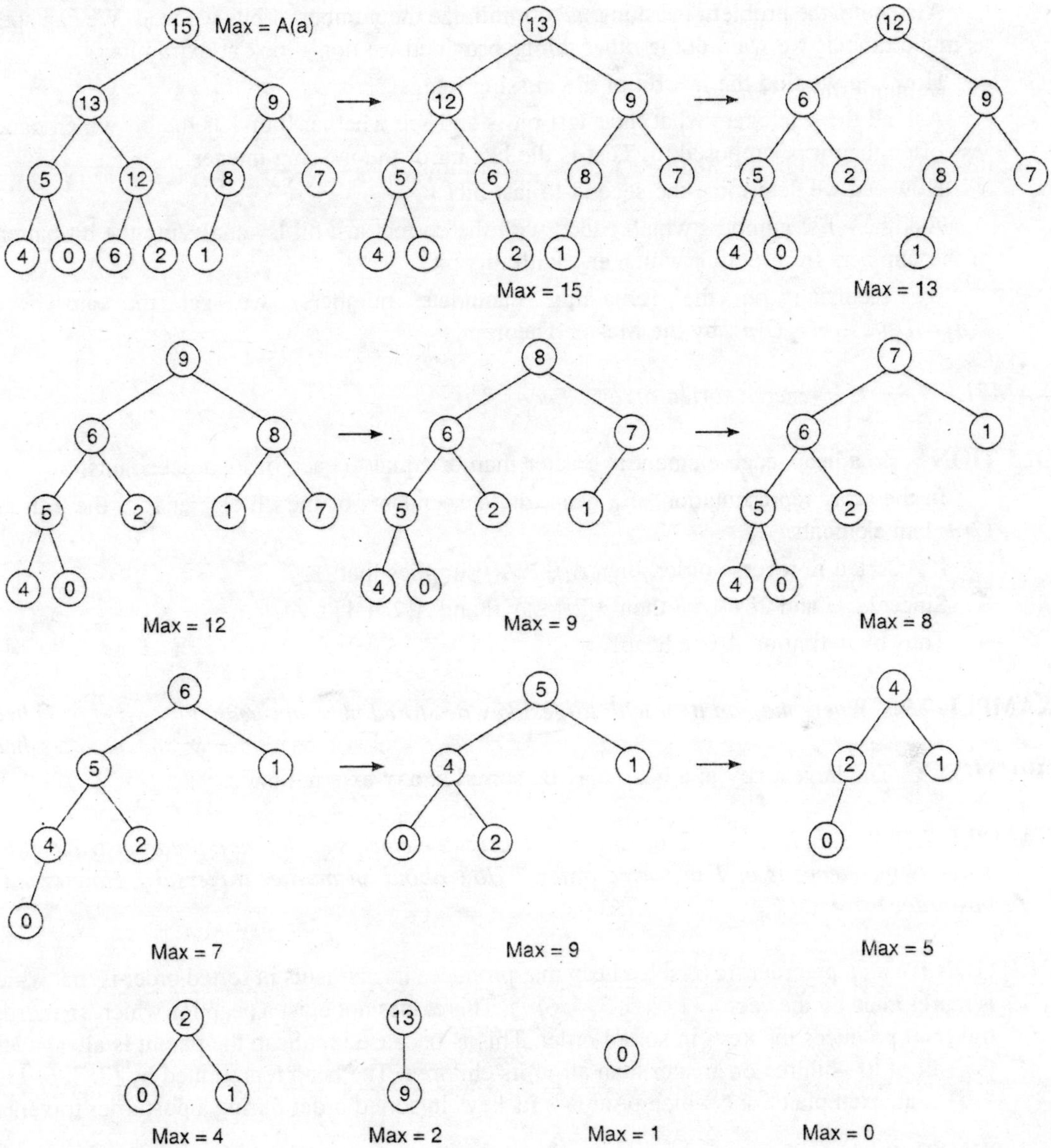

Max = A(a)

Max = 15

Max = 13

Max = 12

Max = 9

Max = 8

Max = 7

Max = 9

Max = 5

Max = 4

Max = 2

Max = 1

Max = 0

Thus at each stage we get the maximum of heap which is at root and then HEAPIFY procedure readjusts the heap.

EXAMPLE 7.7. *Find the missing integer from 0 to n using O(n) "is bit[j] in A[i]" queries.*

SOLUTION : There are a total of $n \log n$ bits, so we are not allowed to read the entire input!

Also note, the problem is asking us to minimize the number of bits we read. We can spend as much time as we want doing other things provided we don't look at extra bits.

How can we find the last bit of the missing integer?

Ask all the n integers what their last bit is and see whether 0 or 1 is the bit which occurs less often than it is supposed to. That is the last bit of the missing integer!

How can we determine the second-to-last bit?

Ask the $\approx n/2$ numbers which ended with the correct last bit By analyzing the bit patterns of the numbers from O to n which end with this bit.

By recurring on the remaining candidate numbers, we get the answer in $T(n) = T(n/2) + n = O(n)$, by the Master Theorem.

EXAMPLE 7.8. *Is a reverse sorted array a heap?*

SOLUTION : In a heap, each element is greater than or equal to each of its descendants.

In the array representation of a heap, the descendants of the ith element are the $2i$th and $(2i + 1)$th elements.

If A sorted in reverse order, then $A[i] \geq A[j]$ implies that $i \leq j$.

Since $2i > i$ and $2i + 1 > i$ then $A[2i] \leq A[i]$ and $A[2i + 1] \leq A[i]$

Thus by definition A is a heap!

EXAMPLE 7.9. *Where may an item with largest key be stored in a min-heap ?*

SOLUTION : The largest key in a heap may be sorted at any external node.

EXAMPLE 7.10. *Is there a heap T storing seven distinct elements such that a preorder traversal of T yields the elements of T in sorted order ? How about an inorder traversal ? How about a postorder traversal ?*

SOLUTION : With a preorder traversal, a heap that produces its elements in sorted order is that which is represented by the vector (1, 2, 5, 3, 4, 6, 7). There does not exist a heap for which an inorder traversal produces the keys in sorted order. This is because in a heap the parent is always less than all of its children or greater than all of its children. The heap represented by (7, 3, 6, 1, 2, 4, 5) is an example of one which produces its keys in sorted order during a postorder traversal.

EXAMPLE 7.11. *Show that the problem of finding the kth smallest element of a set of n distinct integers in $O(n + k \log n)$ time.*

SOLUTION : Construct a heap, which takes $O(n)$ time. Then call Extract-Min k times, which takes $O(k \log n)$ time.

EXAMPLE 7.12. *Let T be a heap storing n keys. Give an efficient algorithm for reporting all the keys in T that are smaller than or equal to a given query key x (which is not necessarily in T).*

Note that the keys do not need to be reported in sorted order. Ideally, your algorithm should run in O(k) time, where k is the number of keys reported.

SOLUTION : Starting at the root of the tree, recursively search the left and right subtrees if the root of the subtree has a key value less than x. This algorithm takes $O(k)$ time, because there is no node in T sorting a key larger than x that has a descendent storing a key less than x.

EXAMPLE 7.13. *Show that worst case time complexity of heapsort is Ω (nlogn)?*

SOLUTION : Since order of elements in a heap is always same i.e. we have either max-heap or min-heap. So maximum time taken to sort a heap in worst-case and best-case are same i.e. *nlogn*. Hence we can write Ω (*nlogn*) for worst case also (not O (*nlogn*)).

EXERCISE

1. Give on $O(lgn)$ time implementation of the procedure HEAP- INCREASE-KEY (A, j, k), which sets $A[i] \leftarrow \max(A(i), k)$ and updates the heap structure appropriately.
2. Show how to implement a FIFO queue with a priority queue and how to impement stack with p-queue.
3. Illustrate HEAPSORT on the array

   A <16, 14,10, 8, 7, 9, 3, 2, 4, 1>
4. Illustrate BUILD-HEAP on the array A = <4, 1, 3, 2, 16, 9, 19, 14, 8, 7>
5. Construct a heap with the following sequence <23, 17, 14, 6, 13, 10, 1, 5, 7, 12>
6. Is the array that is in reverse sorted order a heap?
7. Show that ht. of tree in a heap is $\lfloor lgn \rfloor$.
8. What are minimum and maximum no. of elements in a heap of ht. h.
9. What is the effect of calling HEAPIFY (A, i), for $i >$ heap-size $\frac{[A]}{2}$?
10. Impement a minimum heap?
11. Write an algo combine (A) that accepts an array A in which the subtrees rooted at $A[1]$ and $A[2]$ are heaps and that modifies the Array A so that if represents a single heap.
12. Define ternary heap (ternary tree is a tree in which each node have 3 children s.t. LEFT(i) returns $3i + 1$ and MIDDLE (i) returns $3i + 2$ and RIGHT (i) return $3i + 3$. Write a heap-sort algorithm for this. Similarly implement d-ary heap. heap with d no. of children.
13. Given $O(nlgk)$ time algorithm to merge k-sorted lists into one sorted list where n is total no. of elements in all input lists (Hint use a heap for k-way merging).
14. Illustrate the performance of the heap-sort algorithm on the following input sequence: (2, 5, 16, 4, 10, 23, 39, 18, 26, 15).
15. Show that the sum $\sum_{i=1}^{n} \log i$, which appears in the analysis of heap-sort, is Ω ($n \log n$).

❑❑❑

8

QUICKSORT

Quicksort or partition exchange sort works on divide and conquer method. Array $A[p..q]$ is partitioned into sub arrays, $A[p..q]$ and $A[q+1..r]$ s.t. each element in $A[p..q]$ is less than or equal to $A[q+1..r]$ index of q is found by partitioning method and each sub arrays are sorted through recursive calls. e.g.,

Let $x = A[0]$. Suppose that elements of A are partitioned so that x is a placed into position j and following condition hold.

(i) Each of the element in position 0 through $j - 1$ is less than or equal to x.

(ii) Each of the elements in position $j + 1$ through $n - 1$ is greater than or equal to x.

The two pointers (down) *dn* and up are moved towards each other in following manner.

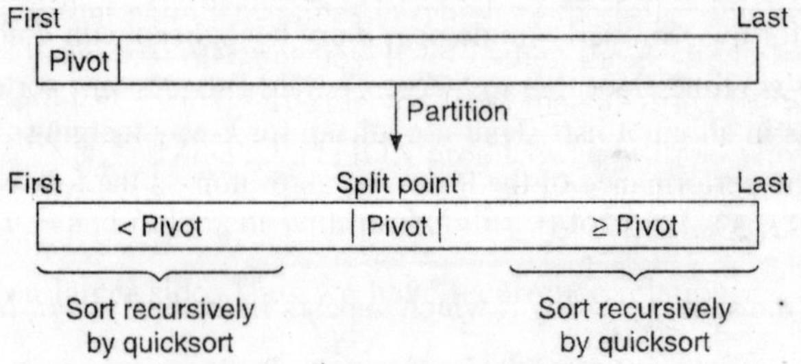

First | Last
Pivot
Partition
First | Split point | Last
< Pivot | Pivot | ≥ Pivot
Sort recursively by quicksort | Sort recursively by quicksort

Fig. 8.1. Shows partitioning point.

1. Repeatedly increase the pointer *dn* by one position until $A[dn] > x$ (till any element becomes greater than *x*)
2. Repeatedly decrease the pointer *up* by one position until $A[up] <= x$ (till any element becomes less than *x*)
3. If $up > dn$, interchange $A[dn]$ with $A[up]$, this, process is repeated till condition of step 3 fails (*i.e.*, $up <= dn$.) at which $A[up]$ is interchanged with *x*

Let $x = A[0] = 25$

Step 1

25	57	48	37	12	92	86	33

$\vec{dn}$ (under 25) *up.* (under 33)

25	57	48	37	12	92	86	33

$\vec{dn}$ (under 57) *up* (under 33)

Step 2

25	57	48	37	12	92	86	33

$\vec{dn}$ (under 57) $\overleftarrow{up}$ (under 12)

$up > dn$ interchange

Step 3

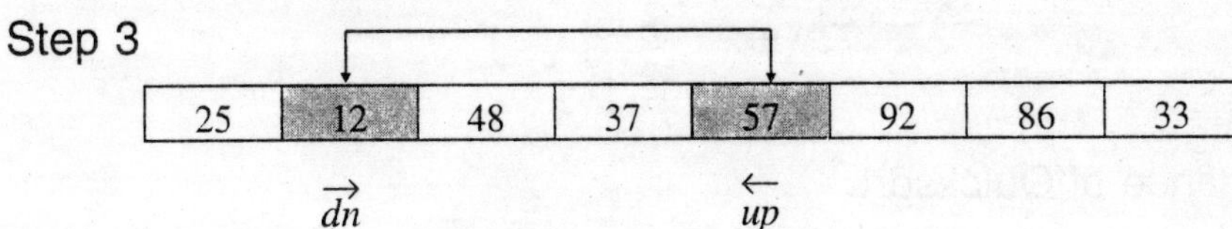

Step 1

25	12	48	37	57	92	86	33

$\vec{dn}$ (under 48) *up* (under 57)

Step 2

25	12	48	37	57	92	86	33

dn (under 48) *up* (under 37)

25	12	48	37	57	92	86	33

up (under 12) *dn* (under 48)

$up < dn$, condition 3 fails, interchange $A[up]$ with *x*

12	25	48	37	57	92	86	33

Fig. 8.2. Execution of quicksort on array [25, 57, 48, 37, 12, 92, 86, 33]

At this point 25 is in its proper position (pos 1) and every element to its left is-less than or equal to 25, and every element to its right is greater than or equal to 25. We could now proceed to sort the two subarrays (12) and (48 37 57 92 86 33) by applying the same method recursively,

The above procedure can be implemented using following procedure.

```
QUICKSORT (A, p, r)
    if p < r
    then q ← PARTITION (A, p, r)
    QUICKSORT (A, p, q)
    QUICKSORT (A, q + 1, r)

PARTITION (A, p, r)
    x ← A[p]
    dn ← p
    up ← r
    while     (dn < up)
        while     (A[dn] < = x)
                  dn ← dn + 1
        while     A[up] > x
                  up ← up − 1
        if (dn < up) then
            exchange A[dn] ←→ A[up]
        else return up.
```

Performance of Quicksort

Running time of quicksort is very much dependent an partitioning procedure. an array can be partitioned at the middle, one third etc.

Worst case : It occurs when partitioning is such that at every stage, one subarray contains $n - 1$ elements and another contains one element, since partitioning for n number of times costs $\theta(n)$ time and single element takes $T(1) = \theta(1)$, its recurrence relation is given by

$$T(n) = T(n-1) + \theta(n) \qquad \text{...(8.1)}$$

$$= \sum_{k=1}^{n} \theta(k)$$

$$= \theta\left(\sum_{k=1}^{n} (k)\right)$$

$$= \theta(n^2)$$

Its recurrsion tree is given by

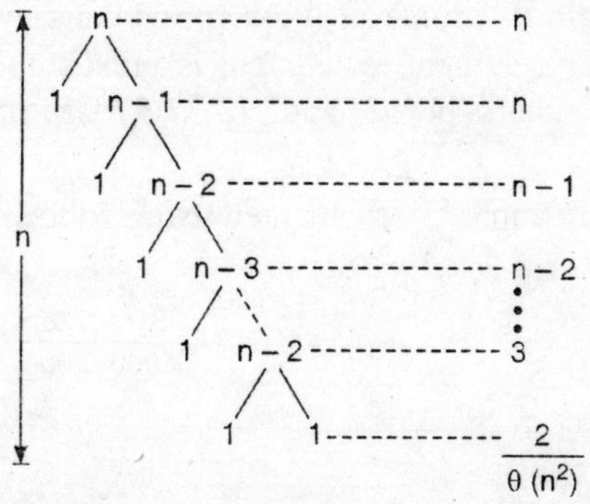

Fig. 8.3 Recursion tree for quick sort.

Best Case. ∴ If partitioning is done at the middle it will be fastest

$$T(n) = 2T(n/2) + \Theta(n) \qquad ...(8.2)$$

by case 2 of master theorem $T(n) = \Theta(nlgn)$

Average Case. When quicksort is performed on random input array it is unlikely that partitioning always happens in the same way at every level we expect some of the splits will be reasonably well balanced and that some will be fairly unbalanced. Let the split is of 9 to 1 then average case recurrence is given by

$$T(n) = T\left(\frac{9n}{10}\right) + T\left(\frac{n}{10}\right) + n \qquad ...(8.3)$$

during time is given by

Randomized Quick Sort : In Randomized versions all permutations of input numbers are not necessarily equally likely. This version will show worst case or average case depends upon

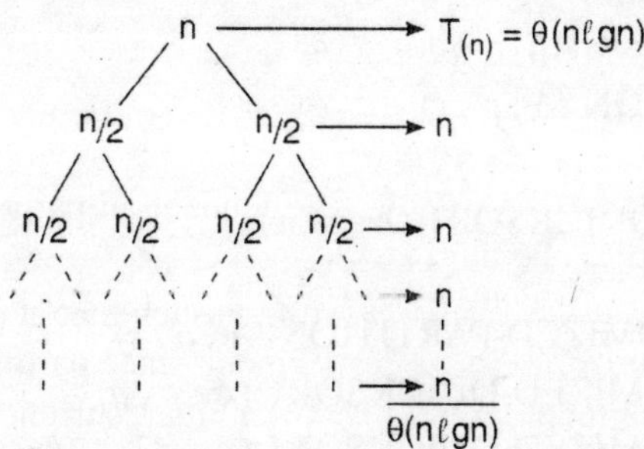

Fig. 8.4 (a) Shows recurrence 8.2

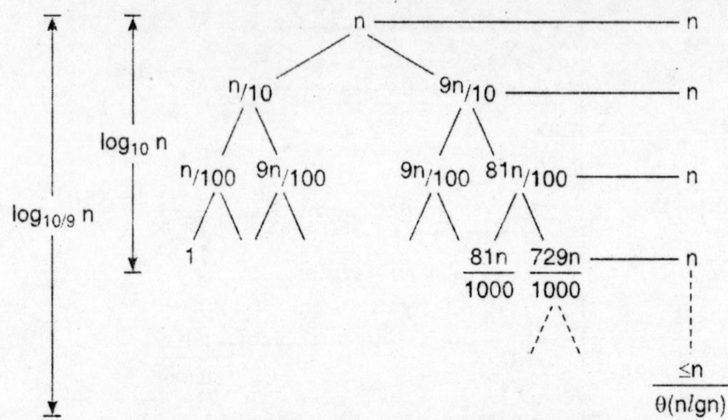

Fig. 8.4 (b) Shows recurrence on equation 8.3

the *random-number-generator.* The randomized algorithm performs badly only if the random-number-generator produces an unlucky permutation to be sorted. All permulation cause quick sort to perform nearly as the average case, there are very few permutations that cause near worst case behavior.

By modifying the PARTITION procedure we can design another randomized versions of quick sort that uses this random-choice strategy. At each step of quicksort algorithm, before the array is partitioned, we exchange element $A[p]$ with an element chosen at random from $A[p .. r]$. It means that pivot element is equally likely to be any of $r - p + 1$ elements. Thus we expect the split of the input array to be reasonably well balanced on average slight change to previous algorithm will result in

```
RANDOMIZED-PARTITION (A , p , r)
1. i ← RANDOM (p , r)
2. exchange A[p] <-> A[i]
3. return PARTITION (A , p , r)

RANDOMIZED-QUICKSORT (A , p , r)
if p < r
then q ← RANDOMIZED-PARTITION (A , p , r)
        RANDOMIZED-QUICKSORT (A , p , q)
        RANDOMIZED-QUICKSORT (A , q + 1 , r)
```

Worst-case analysis : Maximum of recurrence will produce the worst case running time. $\theta(n)$ is partitioning time thus if $T(n)$ is runtime then,

$$T(n) = \max_{1 \leq q < n-1} \left(T(q) + T(n - q) \right) + \theta(n)$$

where q is some partitioning point produced by random-no- generator, by substitution method, we make a guess $T(n) \leq cn^2$

Thus,

$$T(n) \le \max_{1 \le q \le n-1} \left(cq^2 + c(n-q)^2\right) + \Theta(n)$$

$$= c \, . \max_{1 \le q \le n-1} (q^2 + (n-q)^2) + \Theta(n) \qquad \text{...(1)}$$

Let

$$y = q^2 + (n-q)^2$$

$$\frac{dy}{dq} = 2q + -2(n-q) = 4q - 2n$$

$$= 2q - 2n + 2q = 4q - 2n$$

For maximum $\frac{dy}{dq} = 0$

$$\Rightarrow \qquad n = 2q \qquad \text{...(2)}$$

$$\frac{d^2y}{dq^2} = 4 \qquad \text{...(3)}$$

As second derivative is +ve, it produces minimum at intermediate points, so it can achieve maximum at one of the end points, *i.e.*, at $q = 1$ or $q = n - 1$, Let $q = 1$ then,

$$\max_{1 \le q \le n-1} \left(q^2 + (n-q)^2\right) = 1^2 = 1^2 + (n-1)^2 = n^2 - 2(n-1)$$

Continuing with equation (1) above, we get

$$T(n) \le cn^2 - 2c(n-1) + \Theta(n) \le cn^2$$

If c is large enough, $T(n) = \Theta(n^2)$

Average Case Analysis

From the Randomized-Quicksort, the value of a returned by PARTITION depends upon the rank of x (*i.e.*, no. of elements less than or equal to x). If $n = r - p + 1$ then swapping $A[p]$ with a random element from $A[p \,..\, r]$ yields probability $\frac{1}{n}$ that rank $(x) = i$, where $i = 1, 2, ..., n$.

We can see that that PARTITION procedure is also called recursively to produce index q, so that splitting produced is q and $n - q$, RANDOM function finds the split point in $\Theta(1)$ time and subarrays produced are 1 and $n - 1$, and swapping $A[p]$ with random element from $A[p \,..\, r]$ produces a probability $\frac{1}{n}$ so total running time is

$$T(n) = \frac{1}{n}\left[T(1) + T(n-1) + \sum_{q=1}^{n-1} (T(q) + T(n-q))\right] + \Theta(n)$$

but

$$\frac{1}{n}(T(1) + T(n-1)) = \frac{1}{n}(\Theta(1) + O(n^2))$$

$$= O(n)$$

The term $\Theta(n)$ in above expression contains $O(n)$ so,

$$T(n) = \frac{1}{n} \sum_{q=1}^{n-1} (T(q) + T(n-q)) + \Theta(n)$$

We can express the above term as $T(k)$, for $k = 1, 2, ..., n-1$ as each term $T(q)$ and $T(n-q)$ are repeated as

$$T(n) = \frac{2}{n} \sum_{k=1}^{n-1} T(k) + \Theta(n)$$

Since recursion tree has depth $\Theta(\log n)$ and $\Theta(n)$ work (partition) is performed at each of the levels we can assume the solution to above recurrence as $T(n) \leq anlgn + b$, where $a > 0$, $b > 0$, so by substitution.

$$T(n) = \frac{2}{n} \sum_{k=1}^{n-1} (aklg\,k + b) + \Theta(n)$$

$$= \frac{2a}{n} \sum_{k=1}^{n-1} klgk + \frac{2b}{n}(n-1) + \Theta(n) \qquad ...(1)$$

We can obtain the summation as,

$$\sum_{k=1}^{n-1} klgk = \sum_{k=1}^{\lceil n/2 \rceil - 1} klgk + \sum_{k=\lceil n/2 \rceil}^{n-1} k\,lg\,k \qquad ...(2)$$

But upper bound of first summation gives lgk as $lg\frac{n}{2} = lgn - lg2 = lgn - 1$ and second summation gives lgn, so (2) becomes

$$\leq (lgn - 1) \sum_{k=1}^{\lceil n/2 \rceil - 1} k + lgn \sum_{k=\lceil n/2 \rceil}^{n-1} k$$

$$= lgn \sum_{k=1}^{\lceil n/2 \rceil - 1} k + lgn \sum_{k=\lceil n/2 \rceil}^{n-1} k - \sum_{k=1}^{\lceil n/2 \rceil - 1} k$$

$$= lgn \sum_{k=1}^{n-1} k - \sum_{k=1}^{n/2-1} k, \qquad \left[\sum_{k=1}^{n} k = \frac{1}{2} . n(n-1) \right]$$

$$\leq lgn \frac{n(n-1)}{2} - \frac{1}{2}\left(\frac{n}{2} - 1\right)\frac{n}{2}$$

$$\leq \frac{1}{2} n^2\, lgn^2 - \frac{1}{8} n^2$$

Substituting this in (1), we get

$$T(n) \leq \frac{2a}{n}\left(\frac{1}{2} n^2\, lgn - \frac{1}{8} n^2\right) + \frac{2b}{n}(n-1) + \Theta(n)$$

$$\leq anlgn - \frac{an}{4} + 2b + \Theta(n)$$

$$= anlgn + b + \left(\Theta(n) + b - \frac{a}{4}n\right)$$

$$\leq anlgn$$

So, average case running time is $\Theta(nlgn)$

What *is* the Worst Case ?

The worst case for Quicksort depends upon how we select our partition or pivot element. If we always select either the first or last element of the subarray, the worst-case occurs when the input is already sorted!

A B D F H J K
B D F H J K
D F H J K
F H J K
H J K
J K
K

Having the worst case occur when they are sorted or almost sorted is *very bad*, since that is likely to be the case in certain applications.

To eliminate this problem, pick a better pivot:

1. Use the middle element of the subarray as pivot.
2. Use a *random* element of the array as the pivot.
3. Perhaps best of all, take the median of three elements (first, last, middle) as the pivot. Why should we use median instead of the mean?

Whichever of these three rules we use, the worst case remains $O(n^2)$. However, because the worst case is no longer a natural order it is much more difficult to occur.

Is Quicksort really faster than Heapsort?

Since Heapsort is $\Theta(n \log n)$ and selection sort is $\Theta(n^2)$, there is no debate about which will be better for decent-sized files.

But how can we compare two $\Theta(n \log n)$ algorithms to see which is faster ? Using the RAM model and the big Oh notation, we can't!

When Quicksort is implemented well, it is typically 2-3 times faster than mergesort or heapsort. The primary reason is that the operations in the innermost loop are simpler. The best way to see this is to implement both and experiment with different inputs.

Since the difference between the two programs will be limited to a multiplicative constant factor, the details of how you program each algorithm will make a big difference.

If you don't want to believe me when I say Quicksort is faster, I won't argue with you. It is a question whose solution lies outside the tools we are using.

Randomization

Suppose you are writing a sorting program, to run on data given to you by your worst enemy. Quicksort is good on average, but bad on certain worst-case instances.

If you used Quicksort, what kind of data would your enemy give you to run it on? Exactly the worst-case instance, to make you look bad.

But instead of picking the median of three or the first element as pivot, suppose you picked the pivot element at *random*.

Now your enemy cannot design a worst-case instance to give to you, because no matter which data they give you, you would have the same probability of picking a good pivot!

Randomization is a very important and useful idea. By either picking a random pivot or scrambling the permutation before sorting it, we can say:

"With high probability, randomized quicksort runs in $\Theta(n \log n)$ time."

Where before, all we could say is:

"If you give me random input data, quicksort runs in expected $\Theta(n \log n)$ time."

Since the time bound how does not depend upon your input distribution, this means that unless we are *extremely* unlucky (as opposed to ill prepared or unpopular) we will certainly get good performance.

Randomization is a general tool to improve algorithms with bad worst-case but good average-case complexity.

The worst-case is still there but we almost certainly won't see it.

EXAMPLE 8.1. *What value will PARTITION return when all the values in array are same? (e.g., 2, 2, 2, ...)*

	1	2	3	4	5	6	7	8
A	2	2	2	2	2	2	2	2

SOLUTION : According to algorithm

$$x = A[1] = 2$$

$dn \leftarrow 1$, $up \leftarrow 8$.

$$\left.\begin{array}{l} \text{while} \quad (1 < 8) \\ \text{while} \ (A[dn] <= x) \\ \qquad dn \leftarrow dn + 1 \end{array}\right\} \begin{array}{l} (i.e., x = 2) \\ \Rightarrow dn \text{ becomes } 8. \end{array}$$

$up = 8$ no. decrement

$\therefore$ $up = 8$, $dn = 8$.

return $up = 8$.

$\therefore$ Pivot $q = 8$

So, it will return $q = 8$, *i.e.*, last bound of array.

EXAMPLE 8.2. *Draw the recursion tree for 26, 33, 35, 29, 19, 12, 22 using quicksort partition method.*

SOLUTION : First pivot = 26

So sublists are (33 35 29) and (19 12 22) or (19 12 22) and (33 35 29)

In sublist 1 pivot = 19 so partition produces (12 22)

In sublist 2 pivot = 33 so parttion give (35 29) or (29 35)

Therefore recursion tree is

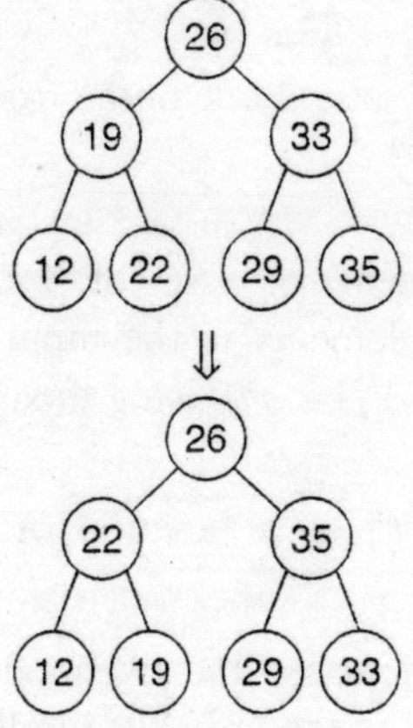

Fig. 8.5

So that sorted list is 12, 19, 22, 26, 29, 33, 35.

Lomuto Partitioning Algorithm

To partition $A[p .. r]$, this version grows into two regions $A[p .. i]$ and $A[i + 1 .. j]$, such that every element in the first region is less than or equal to $x = A[r]$ and every element in the second region is greater than x.

```
LOMUTO-PARTITION (A, P, r)
        x ← A[r]
        i ← p − 1
        for j → p to r
            do if A[j] ≤ x
                then i ← i + 1
                    exchange A[i] ↔ A[j]
        if i < r
            then return i
            else return i − 1
```

STOOGE-SORT

```
    STOOGE-SORT (A, i, j)
        if A[i] > A[ j ]
            then exchange A[i] ↔ A[j]
```

```
        if i + 1 ≥ j
            then return
        k ← ⌊(j - i + 1)/3⌋
    STOOGE-SORT (A, i, j - k)
    STOOGE-SORT (A, i + k, j)
    STOOGE-SORT (A, i, j - k)
```

Median of 3-partition

Choose x as median (middle element) of a set of 3 elements randomly selected from the subarray. Let us assume that the elements in the input Array $A[1 .. n]$ are distinct and that $n \geq 3$, we denote the sorted output. $A'[1 .. n]$. Using this method let the pivot element x, define $p_i = p_r\{x = A'[i]\}$

(i) Give an exact formula for P_i as a function of n and i for $i = 2, 3, \ldots n-1$ (Note $P_1 = P_n = 0$)

(ii) By what amount have we increased the likehood of choosing $x = A'[\lfloor (n+1)/2 \rfloor]$, the median if $A[1 .. n]$, compared to the ordinary implementation? Assume that $n \to \infty$, and give the limiting ratio of these probabilities.

(iii) If we define a "good" split to mean choosing $x = A'[i]$, where $\frac{n}{3} \leq i \leq \frac{2n}{3}$ by what amount have we increased. the likelihood of getting a good split compared to the ordinary implementation? (Hint : Approx the sum given by integral).

EXAMPLE 8.3. *Show that $q^2 + (n - q^2)$ achieves a maximum over $q = 1, 2, \ldots, n-1$ when $q = 1$ or $q = n - 1$*

SOLUTION : Let $y = q^2 + (n - q)^2 = 2q^2 - 2nq + n^2$

$$\frac{dy}{dq} = 4q - 2n$$

for max/min, $\frac{dy}{dq} = 0.$

$$\Rightarrow \quad 4q = 2n.$$

$$n = 2q$$

$$\Rightarrow \quad \frac{d^2y}{dq^2} = 4 > 0 \text{ so minimum.}$$

As second derivative is +ve the function is minimum but maximum can exist at boundary. *i.e.*, at $q = 1$ or $q = n - 1$.

EXAMPLE 8.4. *Draw recursion tree for*

Tim	Dot	Eva	Roy	Tom	Kim	Guy	Amy	Ann	Jim	Kay	Ron	Jan

SOLUTION :

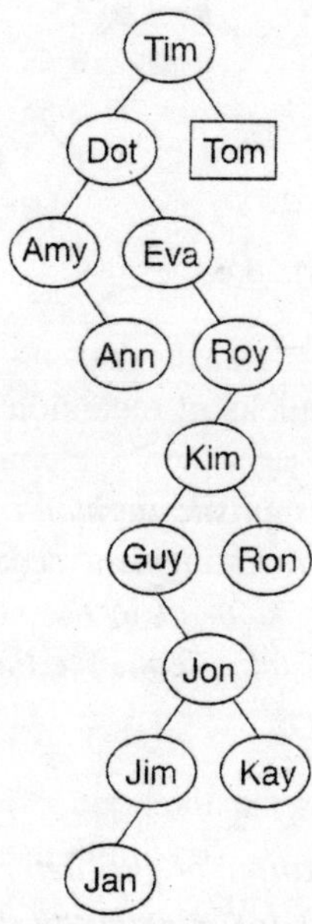

Argue that Insertion Sort is Better than Quicksort for Sorting Checks

In the best case, Quicksort takes $\Theta(n \log n)$. Although using median-of-three turns the sorted permutation into the best case, we lose if insertion sort is better on the given data.

In insertion sort, the cost of each insertion is the number of items which we have to jump over. In the check example, the expected number of moves per items is small, say c. We win if $c << \log n$.

Why do we analyze the average-case performance of a randomized algorithm, instead of the worst-case?

In a randomized algorithm, the worst case is not a matter of the input but only of luck. Thus we want to know what kind of luck to expect. Every input we see is drawn from the uniform distribution.

How many calls are made to Random in randomized quicksort in the best and worst cases?

Each call to random occurs once in each call to partition.

The number of partitions is $\Theta(n)$ in any run of quicksort!!

There is some potential variation depending upon what you do with intervals of size *1*-do you call partition on intervals of size one? However, there is no asymptotic difference between best and worst case.

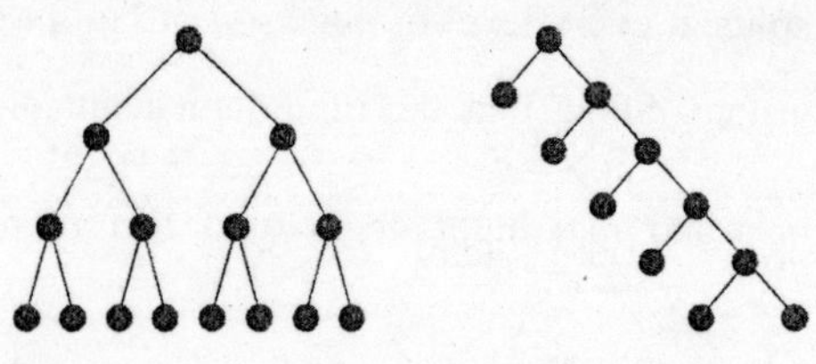

Fig. 8.6

The reason - any binary tree with n leaves has $n - 1$ internal nodes, each of which corresponds to a call to partition in the quicksort recursion tree.

EXAMPLE 8.4. *Suppose we modify the deterministic version of the quick-sort algorithm so that, instead of selecting the last element in an n-element sequence as the pivot, we choose the element at rank (index)* $\lfloor n/2 \rfloor$, *that is, an element in the middle of the sequence. What is the running time of this version of quick-sort on a sequence that is already sorted?*

SOLUTION : $O(n \log n)$ time.

EXAMPLE 8.5. *Consider again the modification of the deterministic version of the quick-sort algorithm so that, instead of selecting the last element in an n-element sequence as the pivot, we choose the element at rank* $\lfloor n/2 \rfloor$. *Describe the kind of sequence that would cause this version of quick-sort to run in* $\Theta(n^2)$ *time.*

SOLUTION : · The sequence should have the property that the selected pivot is the largest element in the subsequence. This is to say that if G contains no element, the worst case $\Theta(n^2)$ bound is obtained.

EXERCISE

1. Show how quicksort sort the following sequence of keys 1, 1, 1, 1, 1, 1, 1 and 5, 5, 8, 3, 4, 2, 2?
2. In function partition, discuss the merrits and demerrits of altering the statement if $(dn < up)$ to if $(dn \leq up)$. Simulate both the algorithms on data set (5,4, 3, 2, 5, 8, 9) to see the difference in how they work.
3. (a) On which input data does the algorithm *quick sort* exhibit its worst case behaviour.
   (b) Answer Part (a) for the case in which the partitioning element is selected according to the median of three-rule.
4. Why do we analyze the average-case behaviour of a Randomized algorithm and not its worst case?
5. Show that the running time of quicksort is $\theta(n^2)$ when the array A is sorted in descending order?

6. Suppose that the splits at every level of quicksort are in the proportion to $1-\alpha$ to α, where $0<\alpha\leq\frac{1}{2}$ is a constant. Show that the minimum depth of a leaf in the recursion tree is approximately $\frac{-lgn}{lg\alpha}$ and maximum depth of a leaf in recursion tree is approximately $\frac{-lgn}{lg(1-\alpha)}$.
7. Show that quicksort's best case running time is Ω (nlgn)
8. Show that RANDOMIZED-QUICKSORT'S expected running time is Ω (*nlgn*)
9. Modify partition such that middle value $\left(\frac{up+dn}{2}\right)$ is used each time at partioning index and find its efficiency?
10. **Odd even transposition sort** proceeds as follows. Pass through the data sets, on first pass, compare $A[i]$ with $A[i+1]$ for all odd i, on second pass perform the same for all even i. For each if $A[j] > A[i+1]$, interchange the two. Continue alternating in this fashion till the file is sorted. Find the run time of this sort?
11. Take iterative versions of merge sort and quicksort and compare them for same-size data sets.
12. Argue that LOMUTO-PARTITION is correct.
13. What are the maximum no. of times that an element is moved by partition and LOMUTO-PARTITION?
14. Prove that LOMUTO-PARTITION runs in $\theta(n)$ time on an n-element subarray.
15. How does replacing PARTITION by LOMUTO-PARTITION affect the running time of quicksort?
16. Argue about the correctness of STOOGE-SORT.
17. Give a recurrence for the worst cast running time of STOOGE-SORT and a tight asymptotic (θ-notation) bound on worst case running time.
18. Show that randomized quick-sort runs in $O(n \log n)$ time with probability $1 - 1/n^2$.
Hint : Use the *Chernoff bound* that states that if we flip a coin k times, then the probability that we get fewer than $k/16$ heads is less than $2^{-k/8}$.

9

SORTING IN LINEAR TIME

9.1 Radix Sort

We have different type of numbers like 2-digit (*e.g.* 12), 3-digit (123), 4-digit (1234) or a *d*-digit number which contains *d* number of digits.

1 2 3 4

Here number 1 2 3 4 has least significant digit (LSD) 4 and most significant digit (MSD) is 1 rest are intermediate digits.

Radix sort works on sorting a collection of *d*-digit numbers, where LSD is sorted first, then next digit and so on till it reaches MSD, e.g.,

		↓		↓		↓
329		190		121		121
768		121		423		190
423	⇒	423	⇒	329	⇒	329
121		768		768		423
190		329		190		768
		(a)		(b)		(c)

Fig. 9.1. Sorting with Radix-sort.

```
RADIX-SORT (A, d)
        for j ← 1 to d
        do use a stable sort to sort array A an digit i
```

EXAMPLE 9.1. *e.g.,*

	1	2	3	
$A[1]$	3	2	9	1
A	7	5	8	2
	4	2	3	3
	1	2	1	4
	1	9	0	5

5 × 3 Array
A [5][3]
For $j \leftarrow 3$ to 1 do
  For $i \leftarrow 1$ to 5 do
    If $(A[i][j] < A[i+1][j])$
      interchange $A[i][j]$
        $\leftrightarrow A[i+1][j]$

From above example if it clear that it takes 15 iteration to sort above numbers. Here $d = 3$, $n = 5$ so 15. Therefore running time is $\Theta(nd)$ or $\Theta(n)$ *i.e., linear time.* if another technique is used for sorting each digits of Radix Sort, like *counting sort* and numbers are in the range 1 to k then running time is $\Theta(nd + dk)$ but k is constant so running time is again *linear, i.e.,* $\Theta(n)$.

9.2 Bucket Sort

In bucket sort n-element array A satisfies $0 \leq A[i] < 1$, *i.e.,* each element lies between 0 and 1. These elements are mapped into array $B[0 .. n-1]$ which is an array of linked lists called buckets which holds the sorted values.

Let 0.78, 0.79, 0.83, 0.89, 0.92, 0.53, 0.23, 0.56 are input numbers of array A these can be sorted by bucket sort. See Fig. 9.2.

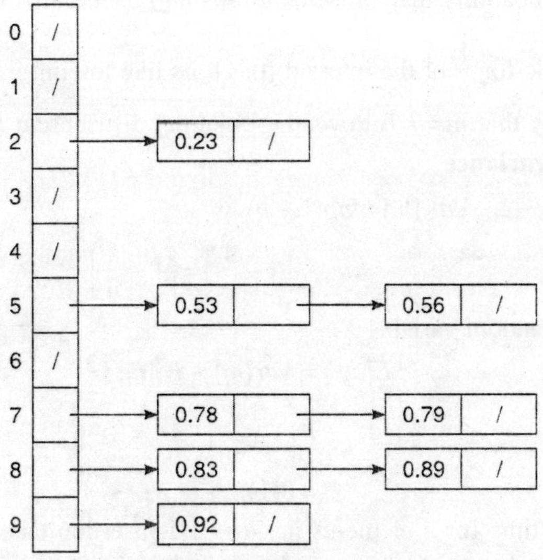

Fig. 9.2. Bucket sort.

Here index of i is calculated by multiplying each element of A by 10 and taking its floor value. If two elements have same index then in linked list they are sorted according to their value.

e.g, $0.73 \times 10 = \lfloor 7.3 \rfloor = 7$ so it will be mapped at $i = 7$

$0.78 \times 10 = \lfloor 7.8 \rfloor = 7$ so it will also be mapped at $i = 7$ but $0.73 < 0.78$ so 0.78 will appear next to 0.73, *i.e.*, each elements are sorted if they map into same index.

BUCKET-SORT (A)

```
n ← length [A]
for j ← 1 to n
      do insert A[i] into list B[⌊nA[j]⌋]
for i ← 0 to n − 1
      do sort list B[j] with insertion
                                  sort
Concatenate the list B[0], B[1], ...,
B[n − 1] together in order.
```

Run Time

Let n_i be a random variable denoting number of variable in Bucket $B[i]$ and since insertion sort takes $O(n^2)$ time so exepcted time to sort elements in Bucket $B[i]$ is $E[O(n_i^2)] = O(E(n_i^2))$. Therefore, total expected time to sort all the elements in all the buckets is therefore

$$\sum_{i=0}^{n-1} O(E(n_i^2)) = O\left(\sum_{i=0}^{n-1} E[n_i^2]\right)$$

But we should also calculate the distribution of random variable n_i. We have n elements and n buckets so probability that an element falls into bucket $B[i]$ is $\frac{1}{n}$, *i.e.*, $P = \frac{1}{n}$, since each bucket is responsible for $\frac{1}{n}$ of the interval [0, 1], its like tossing n balls falling into n buckets. Thus the probability that $n_i = k$ follows the binomial distribution $b(k : n, p)$, which has **mean** $E(n_i) = np = 1$ and **variance**

$$Var\,[n_i] = np(1-p)$$

$$= n \cdot \frac{1}{n}\left(1 - \frac{1}{n}\right) = \left(1 - \frac{1}{n}\right)$$

Thus, for any random variable X,

$$E[n_i^2] = Var[n_i] + E^2[n_i]$$

$$= \left(1 - \frac{1}{n}\right) + 1^2 = 2 - \frac{1}{n}$$

$$= \theta(1)$$

Thus expected time for n elements in $O(n)$ if 1-insertion takes $\theta(1)$ time. Since all other lines of bucket sort takes $\theta(n)$ time, so bucket sort running time is linear, *i.e.*, $\theta(n)$.

Analysis of Bucket Sort

Suppose we are sorting n numbers from 1 to m. where we know the numbers are approximately uniformly distributed.

We can set up n buckets, each responsible for an interval of mn numbers from *1* to m

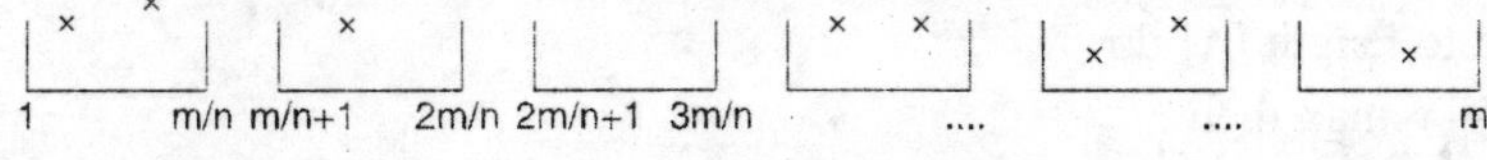

Fig. 9.3

Given an input number x, it belongs in bucket number $\lceil xn/m \rceil$

If we use an array of buckets, each items ges mapped to the right bucket in $O(1)$ time.

With uniformly distributed keys, the expected number of items per buckets is 1. Thus sorting each bucket takes $O(1)$ time!

The total effort of bucketing, sorting buckets, and concatenating the sorted buckets together is $O(n)$.

What happened to our $\Omega(n \log n)$ lower bound!

We can use bucketsort effectively whenever we understand the distribution of the data.

However, bad things happen when we assume the wrong distribution.

Suppose in the previous example all the keys happened to be 1. After the bucketing phase, we have, Fig. 9.4.

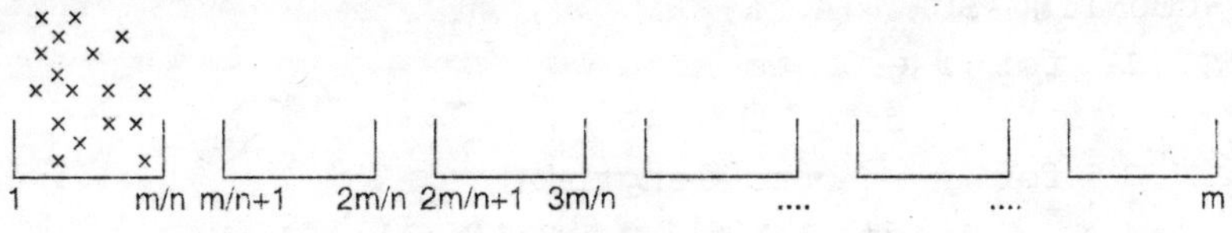

Fig. 9.4

We spent linear time distributing our items into buckets and learned *nothing*. Perhaps we could split the big bucket recursively, but it is not certain that we will ever win unless we understand the distribution.

Problems like this are why we worry about the worst-case performance of algorithms!

Such distribution techniques can be used on strings instead of just numbers. The buckets will corresond to letter ranges instead of just number ranges.

The worst case "shouldn't" happen if we understand the distribution of our data.

9.3 Counting Sort

This method is based on assigning the position to an element into an array equal to its value (*i.e.*, 18 goes to 18th position) but if the numbers have same value it may create a problem. So we slightly modify this procedure.

	1	2	3	4	5	6	7
A:	5	3	2	1	4	7	6

to sort this array of 7 elements required $O(n)$ time, if the elements are stored at the index equal to their value

	1	2	3	4	5	6	7
B:	1	2	3	4	5	6	7

```
max ← A[1]
for i ← 2 to length [A] do
    If A[i] > max then
      max ← A[i]
          for i ← 1 to max do
              k ← A[i]
          B[k] ← k
```

Complexity is : $O(n)$.

But this algorithm will not work if the values are duplicate in array A. Therefore this algorithm is modified to sort array with duplicate values.

Here input array $A[1 .. n]$ is sorted into $B[1 .. n]$ where $C[1 .. k]$ is a temporary array **where k is the highest number in array A.**

Algorithm

```
COUNTING-SORT (A, B, k)
for i ← 1 to k
        do c[i] ← 0
for j ← 1 to length[A]
        do C[A[j]] ← C [A[j]] + 1
for i ← 2 to k
        do C[i] ← C[i] + C[i − 1]
for j ← length[A] down to 1
        do   B[C[A[j]]] ← A[j]
             C[A[j]] ← C[A[j]] − 1
```

EXAMPLE 9.2.

	1	2	3	4	5	6	7	8	9	10	11
A	7	1	3	1	2	4	5	7	2	4	3

SOLUTION : Here k is maximum value in given array A. Array C is used to store the index for the elements of Array A, so that it can be used to store elements of Array A in B. Create Array C equal to size value of k. Here $k = 7$

	1	2	3	4	5	6	7	
C:	0	0	0	0	0	0	0	
for $j = 1$, $A[j]$ is 7	0	0	0	0	0	0	1	$C[A[j]] \leftarrow C[A[j]] + 1$

$j = 2, A[j] = 1$	1	0	0	0	0	0	1	Previous value plus 1
$j = 3, A[j] = 3$	1	0	1	0	0	0	1	
$j = 4, A[4] = 1$	2	0	1	0	0	0	1	
$j = 5, A[5] = 2$	2	1	1	0	0	0	1	
$j = 6, A[6] = 4$	2	1	1	1	0	0	1	
$j = 7, A[7] = 5$	2	1	1	1	1	0	1	
$j = 8, A[8] = 7$	2	1	1	1	1	0	2	
$j = 9, A[9] = 2$	2	2	1	1	1	0	2	
$j = 10, A[10] = 4$	2	2	1	1	1	0	2	
$j = 11, A[j] = 3$	2	2	2	2	1	0	2	

this whole step can be summarised in single step by looking at array A and find out the duplicate values in array A and store in C, the number of times that value gets repeated at the index in C equal to the value in A, e.g. 7 is repeated twice, there fore $C[7] = 2$, 1 is repeated twice, so $C[1] = 2$, 2 is repeated twice, so $C[2] = 2$, 3 is repeated twice, $C[3] = 2$, 4 repeated twice $C[4] = 2$, 5 appears once, $C[5] = 0$, 6 does not appear, so $C[6] = 0$, thus we get same array as above in single step.

After calculating C in single step we can solve further to get new value of C by summing to itself diagonally from index 2 on wards

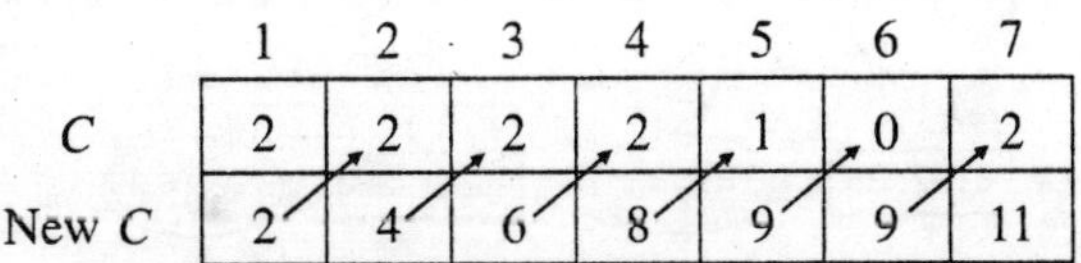

	1	2	3	4	5	6	7
C	2	2	2	2	1	0	2
New C	2	4	6	8	9	9	11

Now writing array A in reverse and also looking at C to calculate index for B

Index in C = value of A

Index in B = value at above index in C

Value at B = value at A

at index obtained in C

New C = old $C - 1$

	11	10	9	8	7	6	5	4	3	2	1
A:	3	4	2	7	5	4	2	1	3	1	7

1	2	3	4	5	6	7
2	4	6	8	9	9	11

		1	2	3	4	5	6	7	8	9	10	11
$A[11]=3$	B :						3					
$C[3]=6$	B :						3		4			
$B[6]=3$	B :				2		3		4			
	B :				2		3		4			7
	B :				2		3		4	5		7
	B :				2		3	4	4	5		7
	B :			2	2		3	4	4	5		7
	B :		1	2	2		3	4	4	5		7
	B :		1	2	2	3	3	4	4	5		7
	B :	1	1	2	2	3	3	4	4	5		7
Stored	B :	1	1	2	2	3	3	4	4	5	7	7

2	4	5	8	9	9	11
2	4	5	7	9	9	11
2	3	5	7	9	9	11
2	3	5	7	9	9	10
2	3	5	7	8	9	10
2	3	5	6	8	9	10
2	2	5	6	8	9	10
1	2	5	6	8	9	10
1	2	4	6	8	9	10
0	2	4	6	8	9	10
0	2	4	6	8	9	9

Above each row is current state of array B and C, so don't get confused with 2–D matrix and its complex looking picture. Each time it represents execution of algorithm steps 7-9.

Run time of this algo is $O(n + k)$.

9.4 Decision Tree

Comparision sorts can be viewed abstractly in terms of decision trees. In decision tree, each internal node is annotated by $a_i : a_j$ for some i and j in the range $1 \le i, j \le n$ where n is the no. of inputs. At each internal node a comparison between a_i and a_j is made.

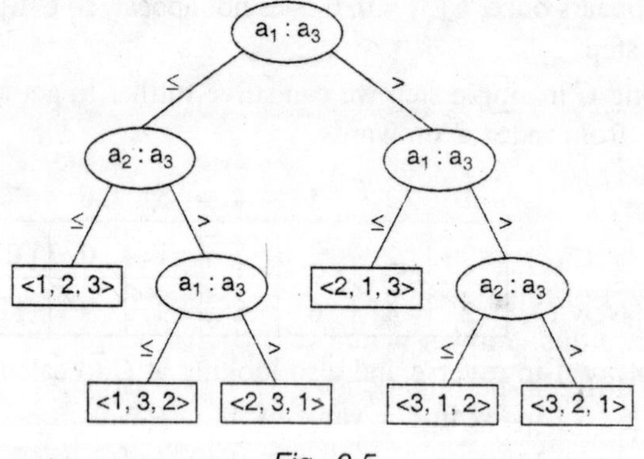

Fig. 9.5

There are six permutations of 3-digit number

123

132

312

231

321

213

Thus, there are n ! permutations of leaves that can be generated in a decision tree.

Can we sort in better than $n \log n$?

Any comparison-based sorting program can be thought of as defining a decision tree of possible executions.

Running the same program twice on the same permutation causes it to do exactly the same thing, but running it on different permutations of the same data causes a different sequence of comparisons to be made on each.

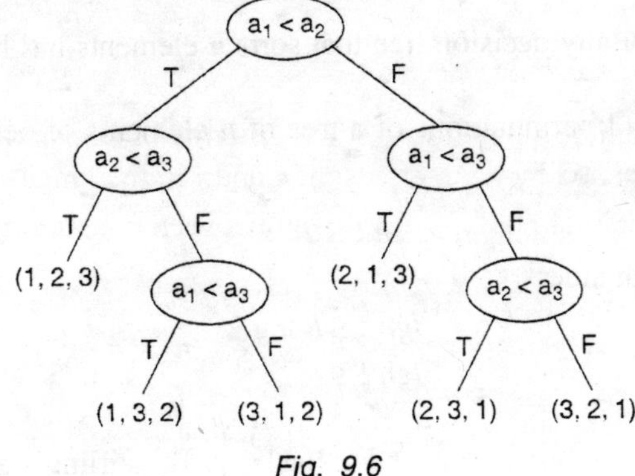

Fig. 9.6

Claim: the height of this decision tree is the worst-case complexity of sorting.

Once you believe this, a lower bound on the time complexity of sorting follows easily.

Since any two different permutations of n elements requires a different sequence of steps to sort, there must be at least $n!$ different paths from the root to leaves in the decision tree, i.e. at least $n!$ different leaves in the tree.

Since only binary comparisons (less than or greater than) are used, the decision tree is a binary tree.

Since a binary tree of height h has at most 2^h leaves, we know $n! \leq 2^h$, or $h \geq \log (n!)$. By inspection $n! > (n/)^{n/2}$, since the last $n/2$ terms of the product are each greater than $n/2$. By Stirling's approximation, a better bound is $n! > (n/e)^n$ where $e = 2.718$.

$$h \geq \log (n/e)^n = n \log n - n \log e = \Omega(n \log n)$$

Non-Comparison-Based Sorting

All the sorting algorithms we have seen assume binary comparisons as the basic primitive, questions of the form "is x before y?"

Suppose you were given a deck of playing cards to sort. Most likely you would set up 13 piles and put all cards with the same number in one pile.

A 2 3 4 5 6 7 8 9 10 J Q K
A 2 3 4 5 6 7 8 9 10 J Q K
A 2 3 4 5 6 7 8 9 10 J Q K
A 2 3 4 5 6 7 8 9 10 J Q K

With only a constant number of cards left in each pile, you can use insertion sort to order by suite and concatenate everything together.

If we could find the correct pile for each card in constant time, and each pile gets $O(1)$ cards, this algorithm takes $O(n)$ time.

THEOREM 9.1. Prove that any decision tree that sorts n elements has height $\Omega(nlgn)$

PROOF : Since there are n ! permutations of a tree of n elements of height h binary tree can have no more than 2^h leaves, so

$$n! \leq 2^h$$

Taking log of both sides

$$lgn! \leq h \log 2$$

$$lgn! \leq h$$

or $$h \geq \log\left(\frac{n}{e}\right)^n,$$ By stirling's approximation,

where $$e = 2.71828.$$

$$= nlgn - nlge$$

$$h = \Omega(nlgn)$$

COROLLARY : Heapsort and mergesort are asymptotically optimal comparision sorts.

PROOF : *The $O(nlgn)$ upper bounds on the running times for heapsort and merge sort matches the $\Omega(nlgn)$ worst case lower bound of above theorem.*

EXAMPLE 9.3. *Illustrate the operation of RADIX-SORT on the following list of English words COW, DOG, SEA, RUG, ROW, MOB, BOX, TAB, BAR, EAR, TAR, DIG, BIG, TEA, NOW, FOX*

SOLUTION :

		↓		↓		↓
COW		SEA		TAB		BAR
DOG		TEA		BAR		BIG
SEA		MOB		EAR		BOX
RUG		TAB		TAR		DIG
ROW		DOG		SEA		DOG
MOB		RUG		TEA		EAR
BOX		DIG		DIG		FOX
TAB		BIG		BIG		MOB
BAR	⇒	BAR	⇒	MOB	⇒	NOW
EAR		EAR		DOG		ROW
TAR		TAR		ROW		RUG
DIG		ROW		NOW		SEA
BIG		NOW		BOX		TAB
TEA		BOX		FOX		TAR
NOW		FOX		RUG		TEA
FOX						

EXAMPLE 9.4. *Illustrate the operation of BUCKET-SORT on the array*

$A = <0.79, 0.13, 0.16, 0.39, 0.20, 0.89, 0.53, 0.71, 0.42>$

SOLUTION :

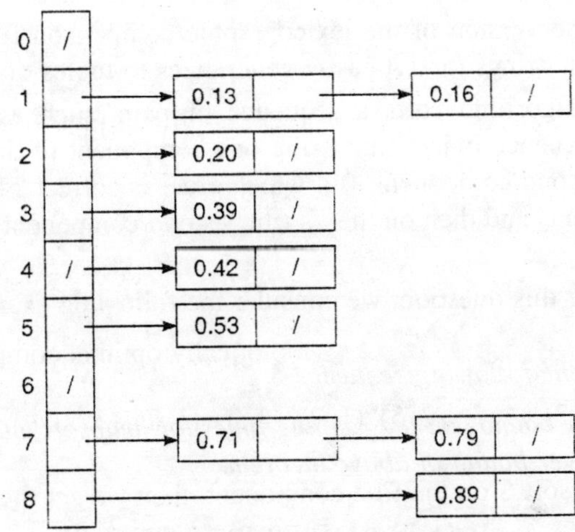

Above figure shows how the elements of array *A* are mapped to corresponding buckets.

Stable : A sorting algorithm is said to be stable if numbers with the same value appear in the output array in the same order as they do in the input array, *i.e.*, counting sort, Radix Sort, Bucket Sort are stable sort algorithms.

Stable Sorting

When sorting key-element items, an important issue is how equal keys are handled. Let $S = ((k_0, e_0), \ldots, (k_{n-1}, e_{n-1}))$ be a sequence of items. We say that a sorting algorithm is **stable** if, for any two items (k_i, e_i) and (k_j, e_j) of S, such that $k_i = k_j$ and (k_i, e_i) precedes (k_j, e_j) in S before sorting (that is, $i < j$), item (k_i, e_i) also precedes item (k_j, e_j) after sorting. Stabilty is important for a sorting algorithm because applications may want to preserve the initial ordering of element with the same key.

Our informal description of bucket-sort in Algorithm does not guarantee stability. This is not inherent in the bucket-sort method itself, however, for we can easily modfiy our description to make bucket-sort stable, while still preserving its $O(n + N)$ running time. Indeed, we can obtain a stable bucket-sort algorithm by always removing the **first** element from sequence S and from the sequences $B[i]$ during the execution of the algorithm.

One of the reasons that stable sorting is so important is that it allows the bucket-sort approach to be applied to more general contexts than to sort integers. Suppose, for example, that we want to sort items with keys that are pairs (k, l), where k and l are integers in the range $[0, N-1]$, for some integer $N \geq 2$. In a context such as this, it is natural to define an ordering on these items using the **lexicographical** (dictionary) convention, where $(k_1, l_1) < (k_2, l_2)$ if

$$k_1 < k_2$$

or

$$k_1 = k_2 \text{ and } l_1 < l_2.$$

This is a pair-wise version of the lexicographic comparison function, usually applied to equal-length character strings (and it easily generalizes to tuples of d numbers for $d > 2$).

The **radix-sort** algorithm sorts a sequence of pairs such as S, by applying a stable bucket-sort on the sequence twice; first using one component of the pair as the ordering key and then using the second component. But which order is correct ? Should we first sort on the k's (the first component) and then on the l's (the second component), or should it be the other way around?

Before we answer this question, we consider the following example.

EXAMPLE 9.5. *Consider the following sequence S :*

$$S = ((3, 3), (1, 5), (2, 5), (1, 2), (2, 3), (1, 7), (3, 2), (2, 2)).$$

SOLUTION : If we stably sort S on the first component, then we get the sequence

$$S_1 = ((1, 5), (1, 2), (1, 7), (2, 5), (2, 3), (2, 2), (3, 3), (3, 2)).$$

If we then stably sort this sequence S_1 using the second component, then we get the sequence

$$S_{1,2} = ((1, 2), (2, 2), (3, 2), (2, 3), (3, 3), (1, 5), (2, 5), (1, 7)),$$

which is not exactly a sorted sequence. On the other hand, if we first stably sort S using the second component, then we get the sequence

$$S_2 = (11, 2), (3, 2), '(2, 2), (3, 3), (2, 3), (1, 5), (2, 5), (1, 7)).$$

If we then stably sort sequence S_2 using the first component, then we get the sequence

$$S_{2,1} = ((1, 2), (1, 5), (1, 7), (2, 2), (2, 3), (2, 5), (3, 2), (3, 3)),$$

which is indeed sequence S lexicographically ordered.

So, from this example, we are led to believe that we should first sort using the second component and then again using the first component. This intuition is exactly right. By first stably sorting by the second component and then again by the first component, we guarantee that if two elements are equal in the second sort (by the first component), then their relative order in the starting sequence (which is sorted by the second component) is preserved. Thus, the resulting sequence is guaranteed to be sorted lexicographically every time. I leave the determination of how this approach can be extended to triples and other d-tuples of numbers to readers. We can summarize this section as follows:

THEOREM 9.2. Let S be a sequence of n key-element items, each of which has a key $(k_1, k_2, \ldots, k_d)$, where k_i is an integer in the range $[0, N-1]$ for some integer $n \geq 2$. We can sort S lexicographically in time $O(d(n+N))$ using radix-sort.

As important as it is, sorting is not the only interesting problem dealing with a total order relation on a set of elements. There are some applicatons, for example, that do not require an ordered listing of an entire set, but nevertheless call for some amount of ordering information about the set. Before we study such a problem (called "selection"), let us step back and briefly compare all of the sorting algorithms we have studied so far.

EXAMPLE 9.6. *Show that there is no sorting algorithm which sorts at least* $(1/2^n) \times n!$ *instances in O(n) time.*

SOLUTION : Think of the decision tree which can do this. What is the shortest tree with $(1/2^n) \times n!$ leaves ?

$$\begin{aligned} h > \log(n!/2^n) &= \log(n!) - \log(2^n) \\ &= \Theta(n \log n) - n \\ &= \Theta(n \log n) \end{aligned}$$

Moral: there cannot be too many good cases for any sorting algorithm!

EXAMPLE 9.7. *Show that the* $\Omega(n \log n)$ *lower bound for sorting still holds with ternary comparisons.*

The maximum number of leaves in a tree of height h is 3^h,

$$\log(n!) = \Theta(n \log n)$$

So it goes for any constant base.

EXAMPLE 9.8. *Illustrate the performance of the selection-sort algorithm on the following input sequence: (22, 15, 36, 44, 10, 3, 9, 13, 29, 25).*

SOLUTION :

22 15 36 44 10 3 9 13 29 25
3 15 36 44 10 22 9 13 29 25
3 9 36 44 10 22 15 13 29 25
3 9 10 44 36 22 15 13 29 25
3 9 10 13 36 22 15 44 29 25
3 9 10 13 15 22 36 44 29 25
3 9 10 13 15 22 36 44 29 25
3 9 10 13 15 22 25 44 29 36
3 9 10 13 15 22 25 29 44 36
3 9 10 13 15 22 25 29 36 44

EXAMPLE 9.9. *Illustrate the performance of the insertion-sort algorithm on the input sequence of the previous problem.*

SOLUTION :

22 15 36 44 10 3 9 13 29 25
15 22 36 44 10 3 9 13 29 25
15 22 36 44 10 3 9 13 29 25
10 15 22 36 44 3 9 13 29 25
3 10 15 22 36 44 9 13 29 25
3 9 10 15 22 36 44 13 29 25
3 9 10 13 15 22 29 36 44 25
3 9 10 13 15 22 25 29 36 44

EXAMPLE 9.10. *Give an example of a worst-case sequence with n element for insertion-sort, and show that insertion-sort runs in* $\Omega\ (n^2)$ *time on such a sequence.*

SOLUTION : A worst-case sequence for insertion sort would be one that is in descending order of keys, e.g., 44 36 29 25 22 15 13 10 9 3. With this sequence, each element will first be moved to the front and then moved back in the sequence incrementally, as every remaining is processed. Thus, each element will be moved n times. For n elements, this means at a total of n^2 times, which implies $\Omega(n^2)$ time overall.

EXAMPLE 9.11. *Suppose we are given two n-element sorted sequences A and B that should not be viewed as sets (that is, A and B may contain duplicate entires. Describe an* $O(n)$*-time method for computing a sequence representing the set* $A \cup B$ *(with no duplicates).*

SOLUTION : Merge sequence A and B into a new sequence C (i.e., call merge (A, B, C)). Do a linear scan through the sequence C removing all duplicate elements (i.e., if the next element is equal to the current element, remove it).

EXAMPLE 9.12. *Which, if any, of the algorithms bubble-sort, heap-sort, merge-sort, and quick-sort are stable?*

SOLUTION : The bubble-sort and merge-sort algorithms are stable.

EXERCISE

1. Show how to sort in integers in the range 1 to n^2 in $O(n)$ time?
2. Which of the following sorting algorithms are stable, insertion sort, merge sort, quick sort give a simple technique for stability.
3. Modify the bucket sort algorithm such that the key of each record has value 0 or 1.
4. Is it possible to implement (3) with radix sort for n record of b bits, If yes what will be its run time.
5. What is worst cases running time for the bucket sort algorithm?
6. Prove that conting sort is stable?
7. If loop of line 7 in COUNTING-SORT algorithm is forward what will be its effect?
8. Assuming the input to the sorting problem is given in an array A, describe how to implement the selection-sort algorithm using only the array A and at most six additional (base0type) variables.

10

MEDIANS AND ORDER STATISTICS

Order Statistics : ith order statistics of a set of n elements is ith smallest element.

Medians : It is the middle element in the set of n elements such that if n is odd median is $\left(\frac{n+1}{2}\right)^{\text{th}}$ element, otherwise if n is even then middle element lies at $i = \frac{n}{2}$ and $i = \frac{n}{2} + 1$.

EXAMPLE 10.1. *Write an algorithm MEDIAN (S) to get the median element from the sequence S of n elements.*

SOLUTION :

```
Median (S)
n ← length [S]
if (n % 2 = 0) then
        i ← ⌊(n + 1)/2⌋
        j ← ⌈(n + 1)/2⌉
else
        i ← ⌈(n + 1)/2⌉
```

Time complexity is $O(1)$, as middle element can be found in constant time.

EXAMPLE 10.2. *Find the median element in the following set S of elements : 1 9 3 3 4 5 6 7 7 8*

SOLUTION :

1	2	3	4	5	6	7	8	9	10
1	9	3	3	4	5	6	7	7	8

Here, $n = 10$, *i.e.*, even

So middle element lies at $\left\lfloor \frac{n+1}{2} \right\rfloor = \left\lfloor \frac{11}{2} \right\rfloor = 5$

and $\left\lceil \frac{n+1}{2} \right\rceil = \left\lceil \frac{11}{2} \right\rceil = 6.$

i.e., 5th and 6th elements are median

i.e., median is 4, 5

EXAMPLE 10.3. *Write an algorithm to find the minimum and max. of elements in an array A. [1 .. n].*

SOLUTION :

```
MINIMUM (A)
1.   min ← A(1)
2.   for i ← 2 to length [A]
3.        do if min > A[i]
4.             then min ← A[i]
5.   return min

MAXIMUM (A)
1.   max ← A(1)
2.   For i ← 2 to length [A]
3.        do if max < A[i]
4.             then max ← A[i]
5.   return max.
```

Running time of above algorithm is $\theta(n)$, as $n - 1$ comparisions are performed in worst case.

EXAMPLE 10.4. *Show that the expected running time of line 4, in above algorithm $\theta(lgn)$.*

SOLUTION : Assume that all numbers in A are randomly drawn from the interval [0, 1]. Let S_1 S_2, ..., S_n be n random variables where S_i represents the no. of items (0 or 1) that line 4 is executed during the ith iteration of the loop. where

$$S = S_1 + S_2 + S_3 + \ldots + S_n$$

We have

$$E[X] = \sum_{i=0}^{\infty} P_r\{X \geq i\}.$$

Probability that maximum is found out of n elements each time is $\frac{1}{n}$, for each random variable S_i since MAX or MIN algo runs in $O(n)$ time, total expected time is

$$E(O(n_i)) = O([E(n_i)])$$

$$\sum_{i=0}^{n-1} O[E(n_i)] = O\left(\sum_{i=0}^{n-1} E(n_i)\right)$$

from above formula.

$$= O\left(\sum_{i=0}^{n-1} P_r\{X \geq i\}\right)$$

$$= O\sum_{i=0}^{\infty}\left(\frac{1}{n}\right) = O(lgn)$$

Finding Maximum and Minimum

```
Algo Maxmin (A, n, max, min)
    max ← min ← A[1]
    for i ← 2 to n do
        if (A[i] > max) then max ← A [i]
        else if (A[i] < min) then min ← A[i]
```

Best case occurs when the elements are in the increasing order. The no. of element comparisions is $n - 1$. The worst case occurs when the element are in decreasing order. In this case the no. of element comparisions is $2(n - 1)$. The average no. if element comparisions is less than $2(n - 1)$, on the average, $A[i]$ is greater than max half the time, and so the average no. of comparisions is $\frac{3n}{2} - 1$.

EXAMPLE 10.5. *Show through a recursive MAXIMIN algo that* $\left\lfloor \frac{3n}{2} \right\rfloor - 2$ *comparisions are necessary in the worst case to find both the maximum and minimum of n numbers.*

SOLUTION :

```
MAXMIN2 (i, j, max, min)
if (i = j) then max ← min ← A[i]
else if (i = j - 1) then
    if (A[i] < A[j]) then
        max ← A[j]
        min ← A[i]
    else
```

```
            max ← A[i]
            min ← A[j]
    else mid = ⌊(i + j)/2⌋
        MaxMin2 (i, mid, max, min)
        MaxMin2 (mid + 1, j, max1, min1)
        if (max < max1) then max ← max1
        if (min > min1) then min ← min1
```

Let us simulate MaxMin2 on the following set of elements

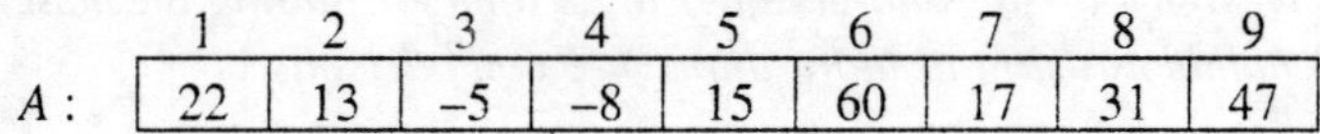

	1	2	3	4	5	6	7	8	9
A :	22	13	–5	–8	15	60	17	31	47

Here, $i = 1, j = 9$, max = 60, min = – 8

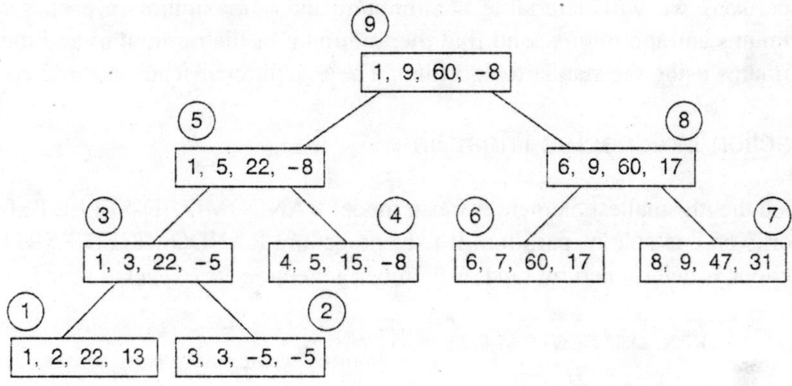

Fig. 10.1

The circled numbers in the upper left or right corner of each node represents the order in which max and min are assigned values.

Now the no. of elements comparisions in MaxMin2 is given by reecurrence relation $T(n)$,

$$T(n) = \begin{cases} T(\lceil n2 \rceil) + T(\lceil n/2 \rceil) + 2 & n > 2 \\ 1 & n = 2 \\ 0 & n = 1 \end{cases}$$

when n is a power of two, $n = 2^k$, for some +ve integer then,

$$\begin{aligned} T(n) &= 2T(n/2) + 2 \\ &= 2(2T(n/4) + 2) + 2 \\ &= 4T(n/4) + 4 + 2 \\ &\vdots \\ &= 2^{k-1}\, T(2) + \sum_{1}^{k-1} 2^i \end{aligned}$$

$$= 2^{k-1} + 2^k - 2 = 2^k\left(\frac{1}{2} + 1\right) - 2$$

$$= \frac{3}{2}2^k - 2$$

$$= \frac{3}{2}n - 2, \text{ as } 2^k = n$$

Note : that $\frac{3n}{2} - 2$ is best, average and worst case no. comparisions when n is a power of two.

EXAMPLE 10.6. *Design a divide-and-conquer algorithm for finding the minimum and the maximum element of n numbers using to more than 3n/2 comparisons.*

SOLUTION : Divide the set of numbers into $n/2$ groups of two elements each. With $n/2$ comparisons we will determine a minimum and a maximum in each group. Separate the maximums and minimums, and find the minimum of the minimums and the maximum of the maximums using the standard algorithm. These additional scans use $n/2$ comparisons each.

Selection in expected linear time

To find the ith smallest element, we can model RANDOMIZED-SELECT after quicksort algo. It works on one side of partition. It uses procedure RANDOMIZED PARTITION and whose behaviour is determined by random-number generator. Its expected time is $\theta(n)$

```
RANDOMIZED-SELECT (A, p, r, i)
    if p = r
        then return A[p]
    q ← RANDOMIZED-PARTITION (A, p, r)
        k ← q − p + 1
    if j ≤ k
        then return RANDOMIZED-SELECT (A, p, q, i)
        else return RANDOMIZED-SELECT (A, q+1, r, i-k)
```

After RANDOMIZED Partition is executed, the array $A[i .. r]$ is partitioned into two non-empty Subarray $A[p .. q]$ and $A[q + 1 \ldots r]$ such that each element of $A[p .. q]$ is less than each element of $A[q + 1 .. r]$. The algorithm computes the no. k of elements in the subarray $A[p .. q]$. The algorithm now determines in which of the following two subarrays $A[p .. q]$ and $A[q + 1 .. r]$ the ith smallest element lies. If $i \leq k$, then the desired element lies on the low side of the partition, and it is recursively selected from the subarray. If $i > k$ then it is on high side.

Algorithm RANDOMIZE-PARTITION produces a partition whose low side has 1 element with parobability $\frac{2}{n}$ and i element with probability $\frac{1}{n}$ for $i = 2, 3, \ldots n - 1$. If it is unlikely the ith element lies on larger side. Thus we have recurrence relation.

$$T(n) \le \frac{1}{n}\left(T(\max(1, n-1)) + \sum_{k=1}^{n-1} T(\max(k, n-k)) \right) + O(n)$$

$$\le \frac{1}{n}\left(T(n-1) + 2 \sum_{k=\lceil n/2 \rceil}^{n-1} T(k) \right) + O(n)$$

$$= \frac{2}{n} \sum_{\lceil n/2 \rceil}^{n-1} T(k) + O(n) \qquad \left[\max(k, n-k) = \begin{cases} k & \text{if } k \ge n/2 \\ n-k & \text{if } k < n/2 \end{cases} \right.$$

by induction,

$$T(n) \le \frac{2}{n} \sum_{k=\lceil n/2 \rceil}^{n-1} ck + O(n)$$

$$\le \frac{2c}{n}\left(\sum_{k=1}^{n-1} k - \sum_{k=1}^{\lceil n/2 \rceil - 1} k \right) + O(n)$$

$$= \frac{2c}{n}\left(\frac{1}{2}(n-1)n - \frac{1}{2}\left(\frac{n}{2}-1\right)\frac{n}{2} \right) + O(n)$$

$$= c(n-1) - \frac{c}{n}\left(\frac{n}{2}-1\right)\left(\frac{n}{2}\right) + O(n)$$

$$= c\left(\frac{3}{4}n - \frac{1}{2}\right) + O(n)$$

$$\le cn \quad \text{, thus } O(n).$$

Weighted Median

For n distinct elements $x_1, x_2, ..., x_n$ with positive weigths $w_1, w_2, ..., w_n$ such that $\sum_{i=1}^{n} w_i = 1$, the weighted median is the element x_k satisfying $\sum_{x_i < x_k} w_i \le \frac{1}{2}$ and $\sum_{x_i > x_k} w_i \le \frac{1}{2}$

Post office location Problem

We are given n points $P_1, P_2, ..., P_n$ with associated weights $w_1, w_2, ..., w_n$ wish to find on point P that minimises the sum $\sum_{i=1}^{n} w_i\, d(P, P_i)$ where $d(a, b)$ is distance between points a, b.

If it is a 2-dimensional problem the distance between point (a, b) where $a = (x_1, y_1)$ and $b = (x_2, y_2)$ is given by

$$d(a, b) = |x_1 - x_2| + |y_1 - y_2|$$

It is called **Manhattan distance.**

EXAMPLE 10.7. *Show that the running time of the merge-sort algorithm on an n-element sequence is O(n log n), even when n is not a power of 2.*

SOLUTION : For each element in a sequence of size n there is exactly one exterior node in the merge-sort tree associated with it. Since the merge-sort tree is binary with exactly n exterior nodes, we know it has height $\lceil \log n \rceil$.

EXAMPLE 10.8. *Show how to implement method equals (B) on a set A, which tests whether $A = B$, in $O(|A| + |B|)$ time by means of a variation of the generic merge algorithm, assuming A and B are implemented with sorted sequences.*

SOLUTION : This can be done by extending the Merger class to be an equalsMerger class. In the equalsMerger class, the methods firstLess and firstsGreater would be null methods. The method both are, equal would add a to the Sequence C. Then, after this is done, C could be checked against A and B to see that it is the same size.

EXAMPLE 10.9. *Let A be a collection of objects. Describe an efficient method for converting A into a set. That is, remove all duplicates from A. What is the running time of this method?*

SOLUTION : First we sort the objects of A. Then we can walk through the sorted sequence and remove all duplicates. This takes $O(n \log n)$ time to sort and n time to remove the duplicates. Overall, therefore, this is an $O(n \log n)$-time method.

EXAMPLE 10.10. *Suppose we are given a sequence S of n elements, each of which is coloured red or blue. Assuming S is representcd as an array, give an in-place method for ordering S so that all the blue elements are listed before all the red elements. Can you extend your approach to three colors ?*

SOLUTION : For the red and blue elements, we can order them by doing the following. Start with a marker at the beginning of the array and one at the end of the array. While the first marker is at a blue element, continue incrementing its index. Likewise, when the second marker is at a red element, continue decrementing its index. When the first marker has reached a red element and the second a blue element, swap the elements. Continue moving the markers and swapping until they meet. At this point, the sequence is ordered. With three colors in the sequence, we can order it by doing the above algorithm twice. In the first run, we will move one color to the front, swapping back elements of the other two colors. Then we can start at the end of the first run and swap the elements of the other two colors in exactly the same way as before. Only this time the first marker will begin where it stopped at the end of the first run.

EXAMPLE 10.11. *Suppose we are given an n-element sequence S such that each element in S represents a different vote in an election, where each vote is given as an integer representing the ID of the chosen candidate. Without making any assumptions about who is running or even how many candidates there are, design an $O(n \log n)$-time algorithm to see who wins the election S represents, assuming the candidate with the most votes wins.*

SOLUTION : First sort the sequence S by the candidate's ID. Then walk through the sorted sequence, storing the current max count and the count of the current candidate ID as you go. When you move on to a new ID, check it against the current max and replace the max if necessary.

EXAMPLE 10.12. *Consider the voting problem from the previous exercise, but now suppose that we know the number $k < n$ of candidates running. Describe an $O(n \log k)$-time algorithm for determining who wins the election.*

SOLUTION : In this case we can store candidate ID's in a balanced search tree, such as an AVL tree or red-black tree, where in addition to each ID we store in this tree the number of votes that ID has received. Initially, all such counts are 0. Then, we traverse the sequence of votes, incrementing the count for the appropriate ID with each vote. Since this data structure stored k elements, each such search and update takes $O(\log k)$ time. Thus, the total time is $O(n \log k)$.

EXAMPLE 10.13. *Suppose we are given a sequence S of n elements, each of which is an integer in the range $[0, n^2 - 1]$. Describe a simple method for sorting S in $O(n)$ time.*

Hint : Think of alternate ways of viewing the elements.

SOLUTION : To sort S, do a radix sort on the bits of each of the n elements, viewing them as pairs (i, j) such that i and j are integers in the range $[0, n - 1]$.

EXAMPLE 10.14. *Suppose we are given a sequence S of n elements, on which a total order relation is defined. Describe an efficient method for determining whether there are two equal elements in S. What is the running time of your method?*

SOLUTION : Sort the elements of S, which takes $O(n \log n)$ time. Then, step through the sequence looking for two consecutive elements that are equal, which takes an additional $O(n)$ time. Overall, this method takes $O(n \log n)$ time.

EXERCISE

1. Show that no algorithms based on comparisions uses less than $\frac{3n}{2} - 2$ comparisions *i.e.*, MaxMin2 is optimal?
2. Translate maxmin2 into a computationally equivalent procedure that uses no recursion.
3. Show that how quicksort can be made to run in $O(nlgn)$ time in worst case.
4. Analyze SELECT to show that the no. of element greater than the median-of-medians x and the no. of elements less than x is at least $\left\lceil \frac{n}{4} \right\rceil$ if $n \geq 38$.
5. Show how to compute weighted median of n elements in $O(nlgn)$ worst case time using sorting.
6. Let $X[1 .. n]$ and $Y[1 .. n]$ be two arrays, each containing n numbers already in sorted order. Give an $O(lgn)$ time algorithm to find median of all $2n$ elements in arrays X and Y.
7. Find the best solution for 1-dimensional post-office location problem, in which points are simply real numbers and the distance between points a and b is $d(a, b) = | a - b |$.

11

ELEMENTARY DATA STRUCTURES

11.1 Stack

Stack is an ordered collection of items into which new items may be inserted and from which items may be deleted at one end, called the **top** of stack, *i.e.*, **LIFO** method is followed.

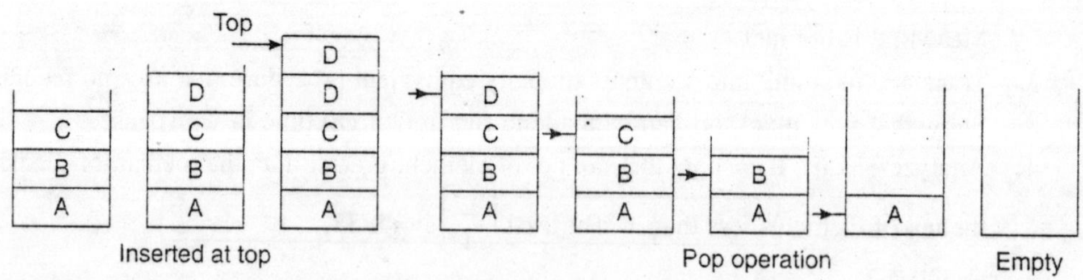

Fig. 11.1. Shows push and pop operation.

Primitive Operations

push (x) : Adds an item onto the top of stack

pop () : An item is removed from the top of stack.

```
STACK-EMPTY (S)
        If top = 0
        then return TRUE
        else return FALSE
   PUSH (S, x)
        if S[TOP] = MAX
              then error "stack overflow"
        else
              TOP ← TOP + 1
              S[TOP] ← x
   POP (S)
        if STACK-EMPTY (S)
              then error "Stack underflow"
        else
              TOP ← TOP - 1
        return S[TOP]
```

PUSH and POP operation takes $O(1)$ time.

11.2 Queue

Queue is a linear list of elements in which deletion can take place only at one end, called the front, and insertions can take place only at the other end, called the rear. It uses FIFO method. It's like *persons standing in queue at reservation counter* where the first person gets the ticket first and moves out and the new person stands at the last position of queue. If head and tail are two pointers which point to first and last element in the queue.

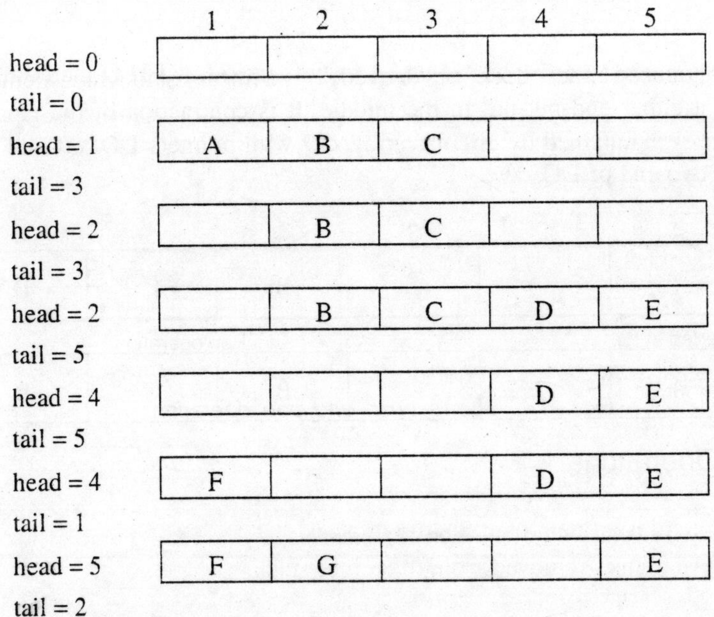

Fig. 11.2. Shows head and tail pointers

Algorithm for inserting elements in queue.

```
ENQUEUE (Q, x)
    Q[tail] ← x
    if tail = length[Q]
        then tail ← 1
    else tail ← tail + 1

DEQUEUE[Q]
    x ← Q[head]
    if head = length[Q]
        then head ← 1
    else head ← head + 1
    return x
```

In ENQUEUE and DEQUEUE operations, each operation takes $O(1)$ time. Note that the overflow conditions are not checked.

Sometimes, the order in which we retrieve data is independent of its content, being only a function of when it arrived.

A *stack* support last-in, first-out operations: push and pop.

A *queue* supports first-in, first-out operations: enqueue and dequeue.

A *deque* is a double ended queue and supports all four operations: push, pop, enqueue, dequeue.

Both can be used to traverse a tree, but the order is completely different.

11.3 Deque

A **deque** (pronounced either "deck" or "dequeue") is a linear list in which element can be added or removed at either end but not in the middle. It is contraction of the name *doubly-ended queue*. Deque is maintained by circular array *DQ* with pointers DQLeft and DQRight which points to the two end of DQ

	1	2	3	4	5	6	7
DQLeft : 3 DQRight : 6			A	B	C	D	

	1	2	3	4	5	6	7
DQLeft : 4 DQRight : 7				B	C	D	E

DQLeft : 5
DQRight : 6

				C	D	

DQLeft : 5
DQRight : 2

1	2	3	4	5	6	7
F	G			C	D	E

Fig. 11.3. Operation on deque.

You can assume that deque is like queue at reservation counter, except that in this case a person can leave the counter without ticket from last position also.

There are two variations of a deque-namely, an ***input restricted deque*** and ***output restricted deque***, input restricted deque is a deque which allows insertions at only one end of the list, but allows deletion at both ends and output restricted deque is a deque which allows deletions at only one end of the queue but allows insertions at both ends.

11.4 Priority Queues

A *priority queue* is a collection of elements such that each elements has been assigned a priority and such that the order in which the elements are deleted and processed according to the following rules.

(i) An element of higher priority is processed before any element of lower priority.

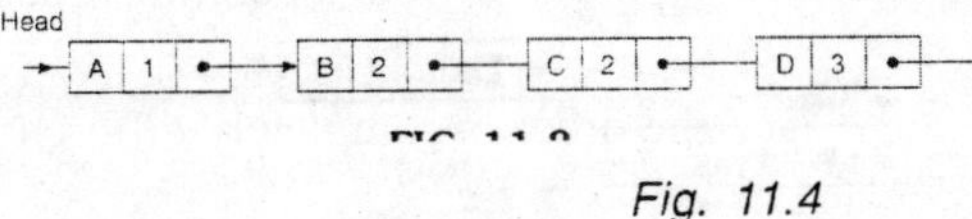

Fig. 11.4

(ii) Two elements with the same priority are processed according to the order in which they were added to queue. This can be implemented as linked list, or as two 2-D array.

Let us assume that a node in priority queue *PQ* contains following items.

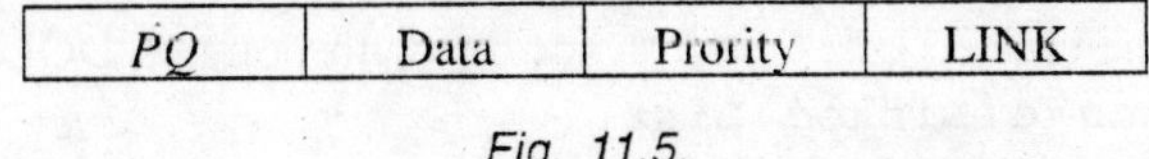

PQ	Data	Prority	LINK

Fig. 11.5.

It is assumed that we have two types of *PQ*'s, *ascending priority queue* and *descending priority queue* thus elements are stored in increasing or decreasing order of their priorities, *e.g., Fig.* 11.4 above shows ascending priority queue.

Elements can be deleted from priority queue as follows,

```
        PQDelete( )
        x ← PQ[Data]
        Delete first node from the list
    process x
        return.
```

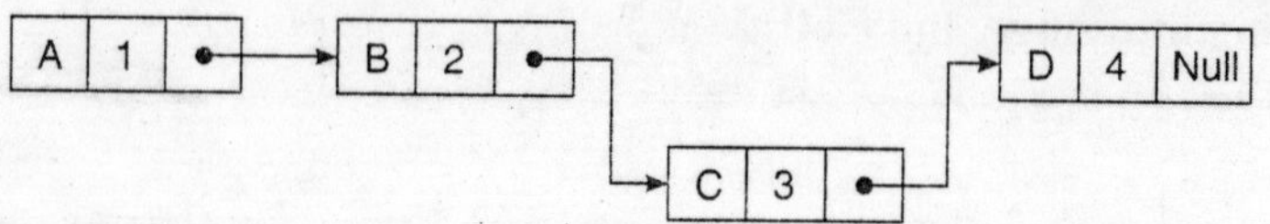

Fig. 11.6. Shows insertion.

Item with priority number m can be inserted by finding the appropriate position in the list s.t. after insertion all the element have less priority than this and all the elements beyond it have high priority.

```
PQ-Insert (P, Q, x, m)
while (PQ[priority]) <= m)
   Link ← link + 1
adjust pointers at this position
PQ[Data] ← x
PQ[Priority] ← m
return
```

11.5 Linked List

Its a data structure in which the objects are arranged in a linear order.

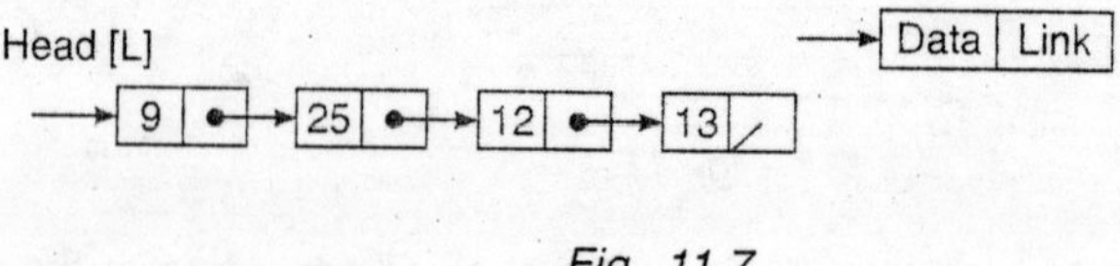

Fig. 11.7

above list contains data elements, 9, 25, 12, 13 and head $[L]$ points to first node. Link field points to next node.

```
Searching a Linked List.
        LIST-SEARCH (L, K)
        x ← Head[L]
        while x ≠ NIL  and  Key[x] ≠ k
                    do x ← Next[x]
        return x.
```

x contains the address of first node in the list L for the first time, so the list is traversed to find the correct match, *i.e.*, key $[x] = k$, where key $[x]$ gives data value of node. Next$[x]$ moves to new address each time.

To search for a list of n objects, the LIST-SEARCH procedure takes $\Theta(n)$ time in the worst case,. since it may have to search the entire list.

Inserting into singly linked list. (at the front)

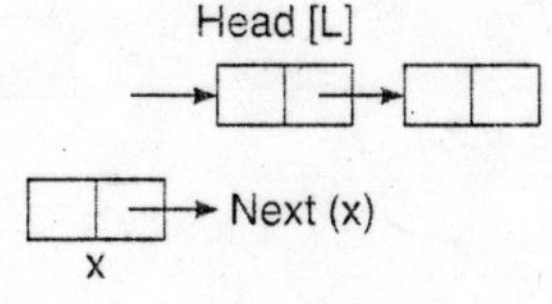


```
LIST-INSERT (L,x)
        next[x] ← Head[L]
Head[L] ← x.
```

Running time is $O(1)$ on a list of n elements.

Deleting from a singly linked List :

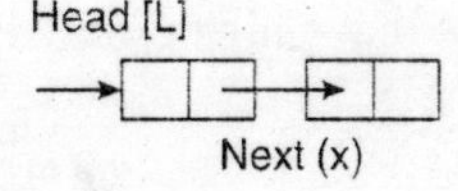


```
LIST-DELETE (L, x)
   if Head[L] ≠ NIL
        Head[L] ← Next[x]
   Running time is O(1)
```

Here we are inserting and the deleting at the first node, similarly, we have to traverse the list if we want to delete or insert the intermediate element and appropriate pointers need to be adjusted.

```
LIST-INSERT-MIDDLE (L, x, i)
x ← Head[L]
count ← 0
   While count <= i and x ≠ NIL
        do   x ← Next[x]
             count ← count + 1
Next[x] ← Next[y]
x ← y
y ← Next[x]
```

Fig. 11.8. shows one application of linked list.

Running time in worst case occurs when element is to be inserted at the last position, *i.e.*, $O(n)$. Similarly LIST-DELETE -MIDDLE can be implemented.

11.5.1 Doubly Linked List

In doubly linked list there are two pointers Prev, Next. Prev points to previous element and Next points to next element see Fig. 11.9. Following algorithm shows the element inserted at first position.

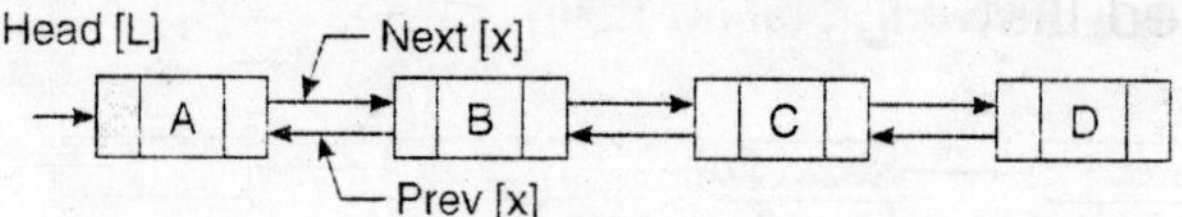

Fig. 11.9. Doubly linked list.

```
LIST-INSERT2 (L, x)
        Next[x] ← Head[L]
        if Head[L] ≠ NIL
            then Prev [Head[L]] ← x
        Head[L] ← x
        Prev[x] ← NIL
```

Running time is $O(1)$ on a list of n elements

Deleting from a doubly Linked List (First element)

```
LIST-DELETE2 (L, x)
        if Prev[x] ≠ NIL
            then Next[Prev[x]] ← Next[x]
            else Head[L] ← Next[x]
        if Next[x] ≠ NIL
            then Prev[Next[x]] ← Prev[x]
```

Running time is $O(1)$, in a list of n elements.

11.5.2 Header Linked Lists

A header linked list is a list which contains a special type of node, called **header** node, at the begining of the list

(i) *Grounded header* list is a header list where last node contains the null pointer.

(ii) *Circular header* list is a header list where the last node points back to the header node.

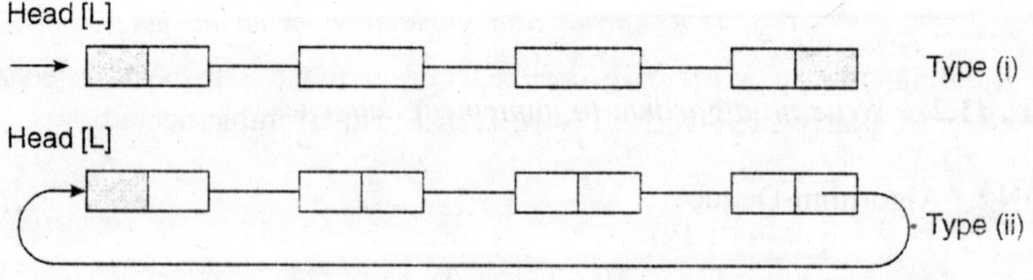

Fig. 11.10. Shows header linked list.

header node contains some special type of information.

11.5.3 Circular Linked List

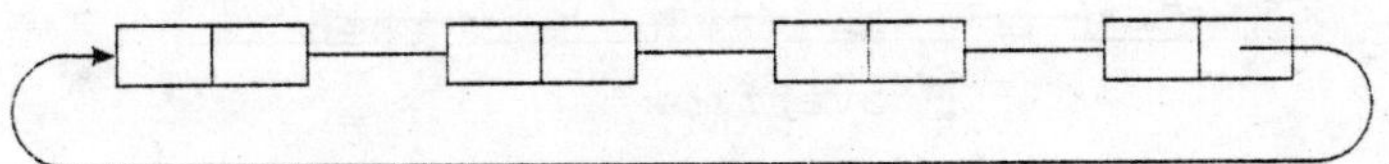

Fig. 11.11. Circular linked list.

Last node points back to first node.

11.5.4 Linked List with Header and Trailer Nodes

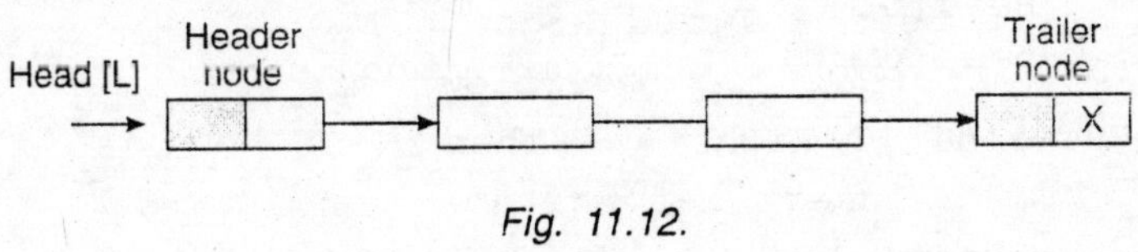

Fig. 11.12.

Two-way-Lists. A two way list is a collection of a elements, called nodes, which can be traversed from both sides, *i.e.*, it contains head [*L*] and tail [*L*] as forward and backward pointer.

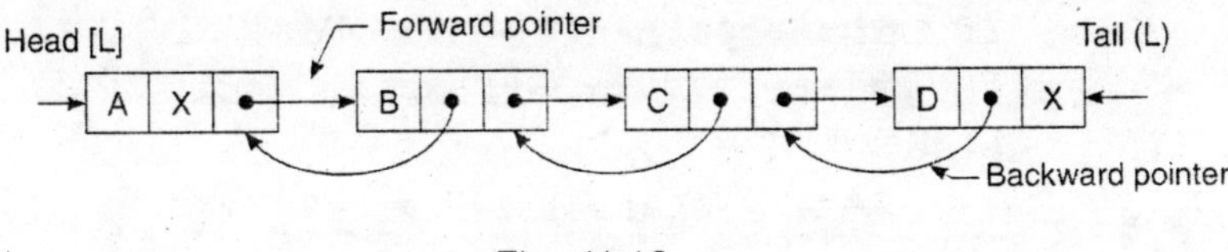

Fig. 11.13

EXAMPLE 11.1. *Represent* $P(x) = 2x^8 - 5x^7 - 3x^2 + 4$ *as a header list.*

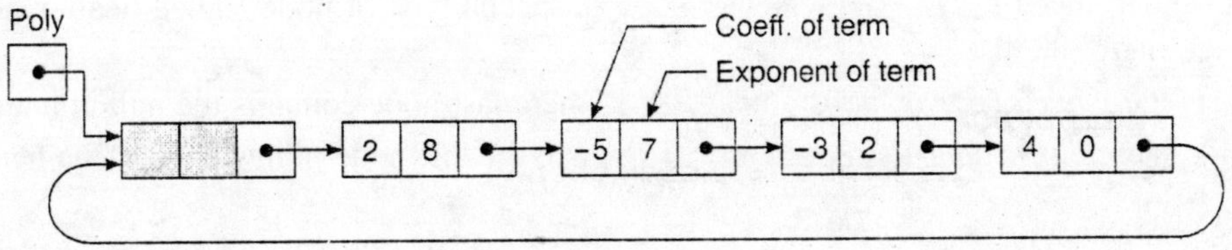

EXAMPLE. 11.2. *Write an algorithm to implement dequeue.*

SOLUTION : Algorithm Deque

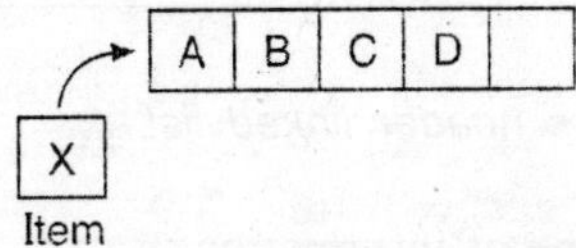

```
InsertLeft(item)

   if, Left = 1 and Right = N then
            "DQ overflow"
   else if Left = 1 then
   insertRight(item)
   else
   Left ← Left - 1
   DQ[Left] ← item

InsertRight(item)
         if Left = 1 and Right = N
              then "DQ" overflow,
         else if Right = N then
              Insert Left (item)
         else
              Right ← Right + 1
              DQ [Right] ← item
DeleteLeft( )
         If Left = 0 then
              error "DQ underflow"
         else
              Left ← Left + 1

DeleteRight( )
         if Right = 0 then
              error "DQ underflow"
         else
              Right ← Right - 1

EmptyDQ( )
         if Right < Left then
              Left ← 0
              Right ← 0
              return true
         else
              return false
```

EXAMPLE 11.3. *We have the following status of stack 3 which is obtained from stack 1 and 2 write the steps to perform the following operations.*

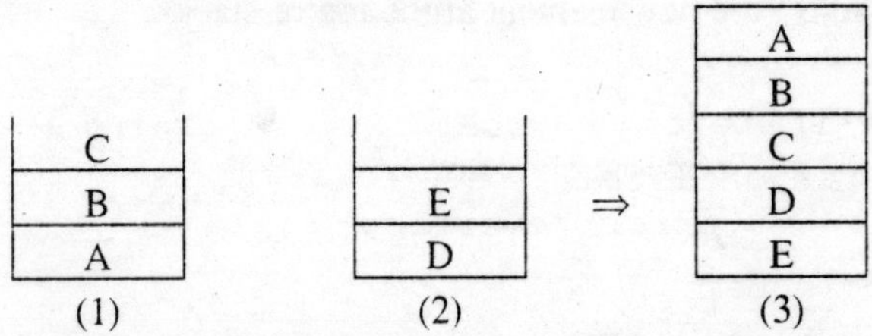

SOLUTION : Assuming that we can increase the size of stack and also we have some temporary stack. We can perform the following steps :

1. POP the elements from stack 2 and push it in temporary stack. S.T. Following picture is obtained

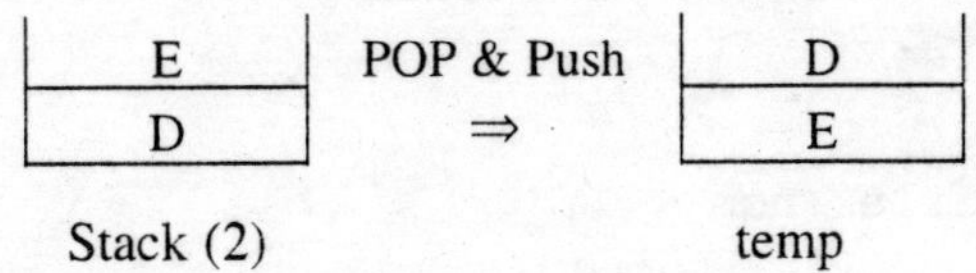

2. POP from temp. stack and push into stack 1

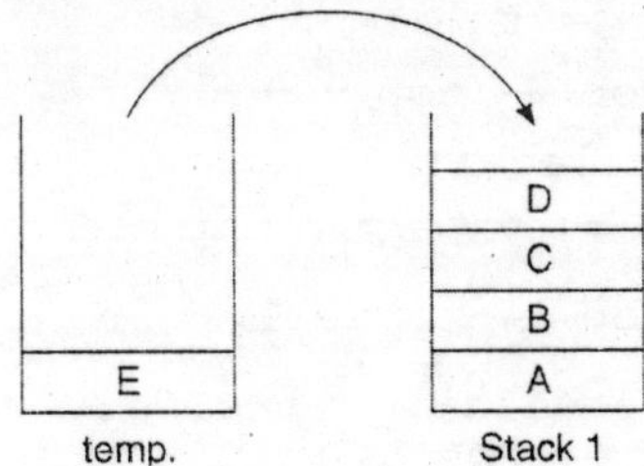

3. We obtain all the elemnts in stack1 as shown below :

E
D
C
B
A

4. Now POP the elements from stack 1 and push into the stack 3 to get the following picture.

A
B
C
D
E

EXAMPLE 11.4. *Write an algorithm to impelment a queue using two stacks.*

SOLUTION : Push into S1 the new element at the top of stack

```
Insert (x)
    If (top=max) then
        error "overflow"
else
S1 [top + 1] ← x
QDelete ( )
    if (top = 0) then
        error "stack underflow"
        Flag ← 0 return
    else
        t ← 0.
    While (top < 1)
        x ← POP(S1)
        push (S2, x)
        t ← t + 1
        top ← top - 1
    end while
        y ← POP (S1)
        top ← top - 1
    while (t ≠ 0)
        x ← POP (S2)
        push (S1, x)
        top ← top + 1
return y.
Running time is θ(n)
```

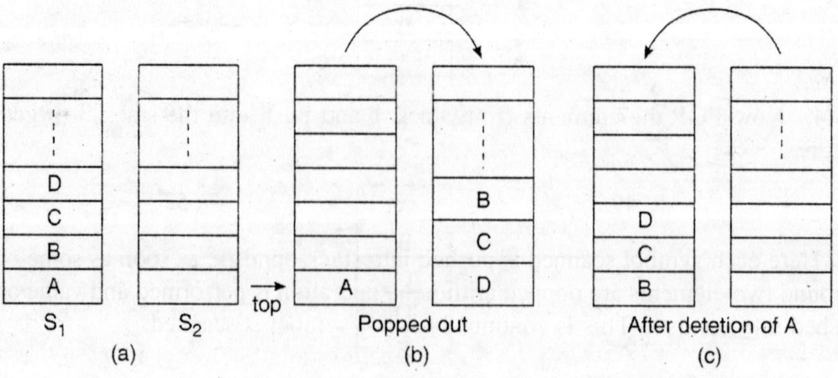

(a) (b) (c)

Queue can be implemented using two stacks as shown above the operations performed an stack S_1 and S_2 s.t. FIFO method is followed, is as follows :

Deletion

(1) POP all the elements from S_1 except the first bottom element and push each element into S_2 (Fig. (b)) above.

(2) Delete bottom element from S_1, it is the first element of queue in visulisation (FIFO).

(3) After deletion of all element from S_1 again pop element from S_2 push into S_1, one by one.

(4) Set flag = 1

(5) For each deletion follow step 1 to 3

11.6 Evaluating A Post Fix Notation

623 + – 382/+ * 2 $ 3 +

Symbol	opnd1	opnd2	Value	Opndstk
6				6
2				6, 2
3				6, 2, 3
+	2	3	5	6, 5
–	6	5	1	1
3				1, 3
8				1, 3, 8
2				1, 3, 8, 2
/	8	2	4	1, 3, 4
+	3	4	7	1, 7
*	1	7	7	7
2				7, 2
$	7	2	49	49
3				49, 3
+	49	3	52	52

Here each symbol scanned is pushed into stack opndstk, as soon as some operator symbol is found two elements are popped arithmetic operation is performed and value or result is again pushed into opndstk. This is continued till last symbol is scanned.

```
Evaluate PostFix( )
          Opndstk ← NULL
while (not end of input)
          Symb ← next input character.
if (symb is an operand)
          push (opndstk, symb)
else
          opnd2 ← pop (opndstk)
          opnd1 ← pop (opndstk)
          value ← opnd2 symb. opnd4
               (e.g. 2 + 3)
          push (opndstk, value)
     end while
return (pop (opndstk))
```

EXAMPLE 11.5. *Describe how to implement the queue ADT using two stacks, so that the amortized running time (See Chapter 20) for dequeue and enqueue is O(1), assuming that the stacks support constant time push, pop, and size methods. What is the running time of the enqueue() and dequeue() methods in this case?*

EXAMPLE : Name the two stacks as E and D, for we will enqueue into E and dequeue from D. To implement enqueue(e), simply call E.push (e). To implement dequeue(), simply call D.pop(), provided that D is not empty. If D is empty, iteratively pop every element from E and push it onto D, until E is empty, and then call D.pop(). For the amortized analysis, charge$1 to each enqueue, using $1 to do the push into E. Imagine that we store the extra cyber-dollar with the element just pushed. We use the cyber-dollar associated with an element when we move it from E to D. This is sufficient, since we never move elements back from D to E. Finally, we charge $1 for each dequeue to pay for the push from D (to remove the element returned). The total charges for n operations is $O(n)$; hence, each operation runs in $O(1)$ amortized time.

EXAMPLE 11.6. *Describe how to implement the stack ADT using two queues. What is running time of the push() and pop() methods in this case?*

SOLUTION : To implement the Stack ADT using two queues, $Q1$ and $Q2$, we can simply enqueue elements into $Q1$ whenever a push call is made. This takes $O(1)$ time to complete. For pop calls, we can dequeue all elements of $Q1$ and enqueue them into $Q2$ except for the last element which we set aside in a temp variable. We then return the elements to $Q1$ by dequeing from $Q2$ and enqueing into $Q1$. The last element that we set aside earlier is then returned as the result of the pop. Thus, performing a pop takes $O(n)$ time.

EXAMPLE 11.7. *Describe a recursive algorithm for enumerating all permutations of numbers* $\{1, 2, \ldots, n\}$. *What is the running time of your method ?*

SOLUTION : The number of permutations of n numbers in $n! = n(n-1)(n-2) \ldots 3 \cdot 2 \cdot 1$. The idea is to compute this product only with increments of a counter. We use a stack for that purpose. Starting with the call Enumerate (0, S), where S is a stack of n elements. The pseudo code should be like that:

```
Enumerate(t, S)
k = S.size() ; ;
while   (! S.isEmpty() )
        S.pop ();
        S ' : a new stack of size k - 1
        Enumerate(t, S ');
```

EXERCISE

1. Discuss the advantages, if any of a two-way list over a one-way list for each of the possible operations ?
2. Write an algorithm to convert infix expression to postfix expression.
3. Write a recursive algorithm to implement fibonacci series using recursion.
4. Write an algorithm to determine if an input string is of the form
$$x\,C\,y$$
where x is a string consisting of letters 'A' or 'B' and y is reverse of x (*i.e.*, if $x = ABABBA$ then $y = ABBABA$)
5. Write an algorithm to implement stacks and queues using linked list.
6. Design a method for keeping two stacks within a single linear array so that neither stack overflows until all memory is used and entire stack is never shifted to a different location within the array.
7. Write an algorithm to implement ascending and descending priority queue.
8. Write an algorithm to implement input and output restricted queue.
9. How will you implement a doubly linked list using multiple array representation.
10. Write an algorithm to implement Towers of Hanoi problem.
11. Evaluate the following arithmetic expressions
(a) $5 + 3 \uparrow 2 - 8/4 * 3 + 6$
(b) $6 + 2 \uparrow 3 + 9/3 - 4 * 5$
12. Evaluate the following post fix expression :
$$5\ 6\ 2\ +\ *\ 1\ 2\ /\ -$$
13. Evaluate the following infix expression :
$$A + (B * C - (D/E \uparrow F) * G) * H$$
14. Implement quicksort algo using stacks.
15. Write an algorithm to count the no. of elements in a singly linked list and give its running time.

16. Write an algorithm to sort the elements on its datafield in ascending order and give its running time.

17. Write an algorithm to swap two values in a singly linked list, give its running time.

18. Write an algorithm to find maximum value in a singly linked list, give its running time.

19. Write an algorithm to implement SUSTRING (string, *K*, *N*), such that it prints string from K^{th} to N^{th} position.

20. Write an algorithm to implement circular linked list, give its running time.

21. Describe, using pseudo-code, implementations of the methods insert Before (*p*, *e*), insert First (*e*), and insert Last (*e*) of the list ADT, assuming the list is implemented using a doubly linked list.

22. Describe, in pseudo-code, a link-hopping method for finding the mile node of a doubly linked list with header and trailer sentinels, and an odd number of real nodes between them. (Note: This method must only use link hopping it cannot use a counter.) What is the running time of this method?

12

HASHING

The search, insert or delete operation in an algorithm takes $\Theta(n)$ time if the data are searched linearly and there are n items stored in records. Hashing is a technique which directly refers to the memory location where the data is stored and data can be found in $O(1)$ time. The functions which calculate the position of records is called **hash function** and records are stored in hash tables. There is a key associated with each record.

1	100
2	200
3	300
4	400
5	500
	⋮
10	1000

Fig. 12.1. Shows hash table.

Consider the data stored as records in buckets in any order. Assuming that data stored are unique. Now suppose we want to find the key value 400. We can directly refer to it using some hash function that calculates its location.

$$h(400) = 400 \text{ DIV } 100 = 4$$

Thus data is located at 4th position. This take θ(1) time to find the key value. In this way there are many types of hash functions that calculates the index or location of the key.

12.1 Types of Hash Functions

Division Method

M is chosen as larger than n, the number of keys in K. Hash function is defined as

$$H(K) = K \bmod m \text{ or } H(k) = k \bmod m + 1$$

this can be explained as follows :

Let us consider that in an organization of 70 employees each employee is assigned a unique employee ID. But in data base it is required to store only two digit code. We can apply the above hash function to get 2-digit code for following employee numbers

3205, 7148, 2345

Let $m = 97$, chosen as greatest prime among 00 to 99

$H(3205) = 3205 \; mod \; 97 = 4$ or $4 + 1 = 5$

$H(7148) = 7148 \; mod \; 97 = 67$ or $67 + 1 = 68$

$H(2345) = 2345 \; mod \; 97 = 17$ or $17 + 1 = 18$

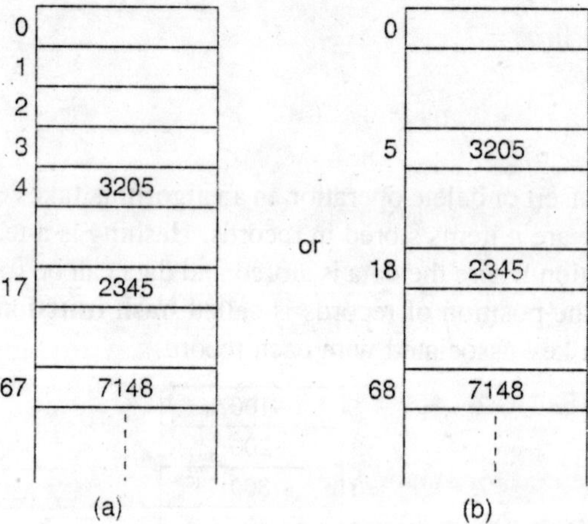

Fig. 12.2. Shows hash key calculated by Division Method.

Mid Square Method

Square key is found, then some of the digit from both ends are deleted then some mid value is considered for each key e.g.,

K	:	3205	7148	2345
K^2	:	10**27**2025	510**93**904	54**99**025
$H(K)$	:	72	93	99

Considering 4th and 5th digit from Right.

Folding Method

This method is applied when the key is very large. In this case we partition key k into $k_1, k_2, ..., k_n$ parts. Then hash function $H(k)$ can be calculated by either *shift folding* or *boundary folding*.

Shift Folding

Let $K = \mathbf{768932834567}$

$$\begin{aligned} k_1 &= 768 \\ k_2 &= 932 \\ k_3 &= 834 \\ k_4 &= 567 \\ \hline & 3101 \end{aligned}$$

$$H(K) = k_1 + k_2 + k_3 + k_4 = 3101$$

We can directly store data at key value 3101 or we can further reduce this to two digit applying some other hash function.

Boundary Folding

This is same as above except some of the K_i s are reversed and added to produce unique key

k_1 768

k_2 239 ← Reversed as above

k_3 834 $H(K) = k_1 + k_2 + k_3 + k_4 = 2408$

k_4 567

Multiplictive Method

Multiplicative method for creating hash functions operates in two steps. First we multiply key k by a constant A in the range $0 < A < 1$ and extract the fractional part of kA. Then multiply this value by m and take the floor of result hash function is

$$h(k) = \lfloor m(kA \ mod \ 1) \rfloor$$

$kA \ mod \ 1$ mean $kA - \lfloor kA \rfloor$, *i.e.*, fractional part value of A is calculated as golden ratio $\phi^{-1} = ((\sqrt{5} - 1)/2) \approx 0.6180339887$

EXAMPLE 12.1. *Let* $k = 123456$, $m = 10{,}000$, $A = 0.6180339887$

Then
$$\begin{aligned} h(k) &= \lfloor 10000 \times (123456 \times 0.6180339 \ldots \ mod \ 1) \rfloor \\ &= \lfloor 10000 \times (76300.0041151 \ldots \ mod \ 1) \rfloor \\ &= \lfloor 10000 \times (0.0041151 \ldots) \rfloor \\ &= 41 \end{aligned}$$

The multiplicative hash method calculates the successive values of hash $h(k)$, $h(k+1)$, $h(k+2)$, ..., they have essentially same bahaviour as hash values $h(0)$, $h(1)$, ...

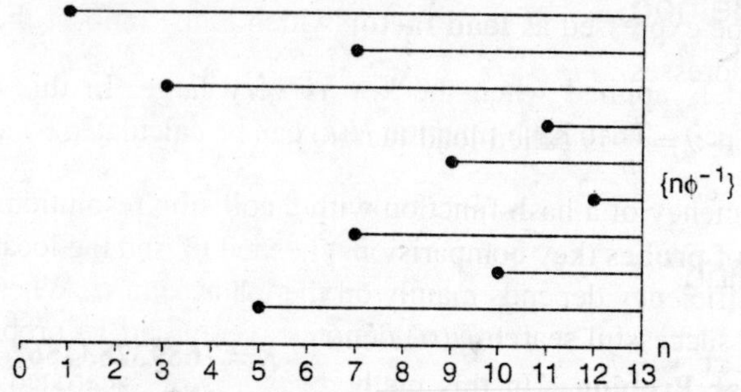

Fig. 12.3. Fibonacci Hashing.

We successively make off points $\{\phi^{-1}\}$, $\{2\phi^{-1}\}$, $\{3\phi^{-1}\}$, ... where $\{x\}$ denotes fractional part of x. ($h(x)$). These points are shown as Fibonacci hashing function above. Here each newly added point falls into one of the largest remaining intervals, and divides it into golden ratio.

The Birthday Paradox

No matter how good our hash function is, we had better be prepared for collisions, because of the birthday paradox.

The probability of there being *no* collisions after n insertions into an m-element table is

$$(m/m) \times ((m-1)/m) \times \ldots \times ((m-n+1)/m) = \Pi_{i=0}^{n-1} (m-1)/m$$

When $m = 366$, this probability sinks below 1/2 when $N = 23$ and to almost 0 when $n \geq 50$.

12.2 Collision and Collision Resolution

Suppose we want to add a new record R with key k to our file but if memory location address $H(k)$ is already occupied, the new key will not be mapped to exact location.

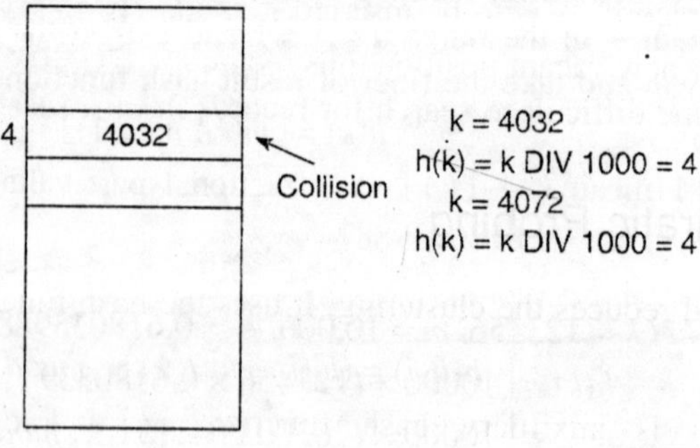

Fig. 12.4

So inorder to avoid the collision for different key mapping to same location we have different collision resolution technique but before that we calculate the **load density**, *i.e.*, what is the hash table size and how much records are to be inserted in this limited space. Thus, load density can be expressed as **load factor** which is the ratio of the no. n of keys in k to the no. m of hash addresses.

This ratio $\alpha = \frac{n}{m}$ is called load factor.

The efficiency of a hash function with a collision resolution procedure is measured by the average no. of **probes** (key comparisions) needed to find the location of the record with a given key k. The efficiency depends mainly on the load factor α. Where $S(\alpha)$ denotes average no. of probes for a successful search $U(\alpha)$ denotes average no. of probes for an unsuccessful search.

1. Linear Probing : In this method records are searched in sequential manner for the desired key or empty location. If record is obtained at the specified location its O.K. otherwise it will search for next location or vacant position in case of insertion. Linear probe for successful and unsuccessful search is given by

$$S(\alpha) = \frac{1}{2}\left(1 + \frac{1}{1-\alpha}\right) \text{ and } U(\alpha) = \frac{1}{2}\left(1 - \frac{1}{(1-\alpha)^2}\right)$$

2. Clustering : Suppose we have record $A, A_1, B, C, D, E, F, G, GA$. Then these records are inserted into hash table as show in Fig. 12.5

1	A
2	A_1
3	B
4	C
5	D
6	E
7	F
8	G
9	GA
	⋮

Fig. 12.5. Shows clustering.

If new record A_2 is to be inserted it should go to 10th position for new insertion again it will look for new vacant position thus records will tend to cluster after particular insertions and it will become difficult to search for records in this case.

12.2.1 Quadratic Probing

This method reduces the clustering. It uses the hash function of the form.

$$h(k, i) = (h'(k) + c_1 i + c_2 i^2) \; mod \; m.$$

where $h(k)$ is auxilliary hash function, c_1 and $c_2 \neq 0$ are auxillary constants and $i = 0, 1, ..., m-1$

12.2.2 Double Hashing

It is one of the best methods available for open addressing. It uses a hash function $h(k, i) = (h_1(k) + ih_2(k)) \bmod m$ where h_1 and h_2 are auxiliary hash functions.

Let us apply double hashing technique

$$h(k, i) = (h_1(k) + ih_2(k)) \ mod \ m$$

where $h_1(k) = k \ mod \ m$ and $h_2(k) = 1 + k \ \bmod \ m'$. Here $k = 123456$, $m = 701$, $m' = (m - 1 \text{ or } m - 2)$ then $h(k, i)$

$$h_1(k) = 123456 \ mod \ 701$$
$$= 80$$
$$h_2(k) = 123456 \ mod \ 679$$
$$= 257$$

Thus first probe is found at 80th position then record is searched at every 257th slot after that or each record is searched.

12.2.3 Key-Dependent Increments

We can have the hash function calculated on key e.g.,

$$\text{increment} = \text{increment} * \text{key}.$$

12.2.4 Random Probing

We can get the key value using the pseudo random no. generator.

$$h(k) = (\text{Random ( )})$$

12.2.5 Collision Resolution by Chaining

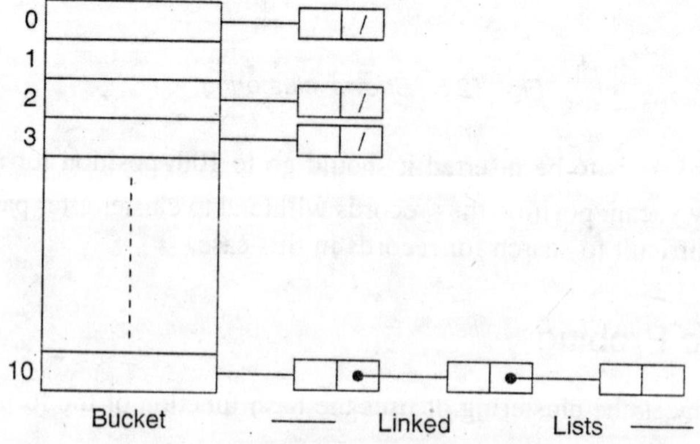

Fig. 12.6. Shows chaining method.

Up to now we have assumed that records are stored in contigous storage while working with hash tables. We can store records as linked lists and map them to bucket address which is calculated by hash function. This reduces collisions as records with same address are connected as chain. Then it avoids clustering, size of table is also not needed to be expanded with more insertions. Deletion is also quite easy in linked list. Memory is utilized properly.

The easiest approach is to let each element in the hash table be a pointer to a list of keys.

Insertion, deletion, and query reduce to the problem in linked lists. If the n keys are distributed uniformly in a table of size m/n, each operations takes $O(m/n)$ time.

Chaining is easy, but devotes a considerable amount of memory to pointers, which could be used to make the table larger. Still, it is my preferred method.

Performance on Set Operations

With either chaining or open addressing :

- Search—$O(1)$ expected, $O(n)$ worst case
- Insert—$O(1)$ expected, $O(n)$ worst case
- Delete—$O(1)$ expected, $O(n)$ worst case

Min, Max and Predecessor, Successor $\theta(n + m)$ expected and worst case

Pragmatically, a hash table is often the best data structure to maintain a dictionary. However, we will not use it much in proving the efficiency of our algorithms, since the worst-case time is unpredictable.

The best worst-case bounds come from balanced binary trees, such as red-black trees.

Let $h(k)$, the bucket address is calculated for one particular set of data 0.12, 0.13, 0.72, 0.83, 0.32, 0.69, 0.15 as $h(k) = \lfloor 10 * A[i] \rfloor$. Then we can picturize this data set as in following Fig. 12.7.

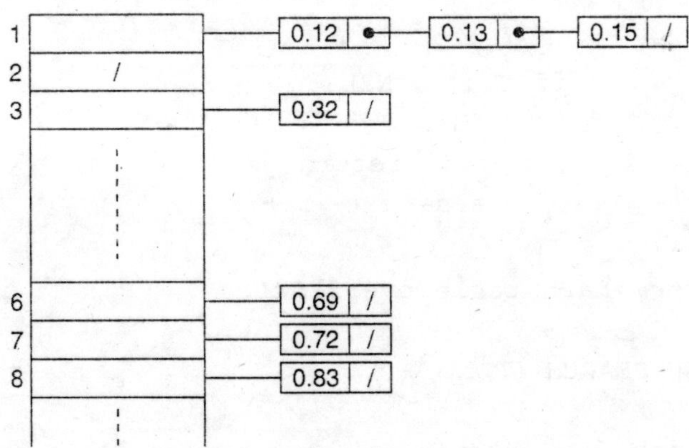

Fig. 12.7. Collision Resolution by chaining.

The average no. of probes using chaining is

$$S(\alpha) = 1 + \frac{\alpha}{2} \text{ and } U(\alpha) \approx e^{-\alpha} + \alpha$$

Here load factor $\alpha = \frac{n}{m}$ may be greater than 1, since no. of hash addresses or bucket address may be less than the no. of records, as records are stored in chain. Following flow chart depicts the chained hash table search and insertion.

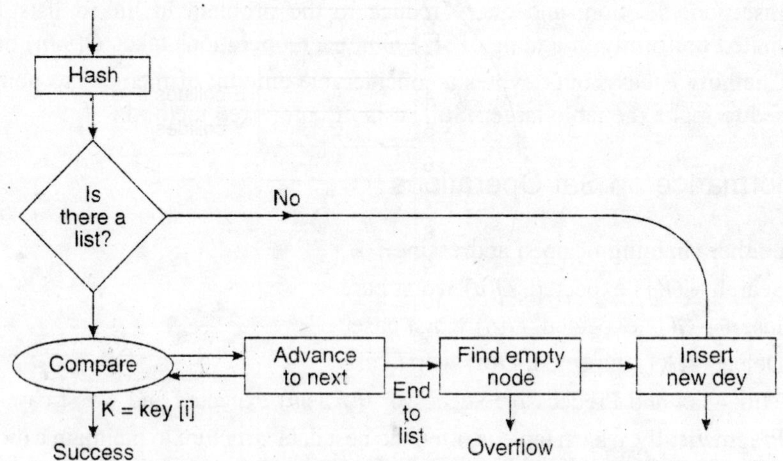

Fig. 12.8 : Chained hash table search and insertion.

EXAMPLE 12.2. *Write an algorithm for HASH-INSERT and HASH-SEARCH.*

SOLUTION :

```
HASH-INSERT (T, K)
i ← 0
repeat j ← h(k, i)
        if T[i] = NIL
            then T[j] ← k
                return j
            else i ← i + 1
until i = m
error "hash table overflow".

HASH-SEARCH (T, k)
i ← 0
repeat j ← h(k, i)
        if T[j] = k
            then return j
        i ← i + 1
until T[j] = NIL or i = m
return NIL
```

EXAMPLE 12.3. *Let the table T has 11 memory locations and suppose records, A, B, C, D, E, X, Y and Z are to be inserted with following hash address.*

Record :	A	B	C	D	E	X	Y	Z
	4	8	2	11	4	11	5	1

Find successful and unsuccessful probes (linear)

SOLUTION :

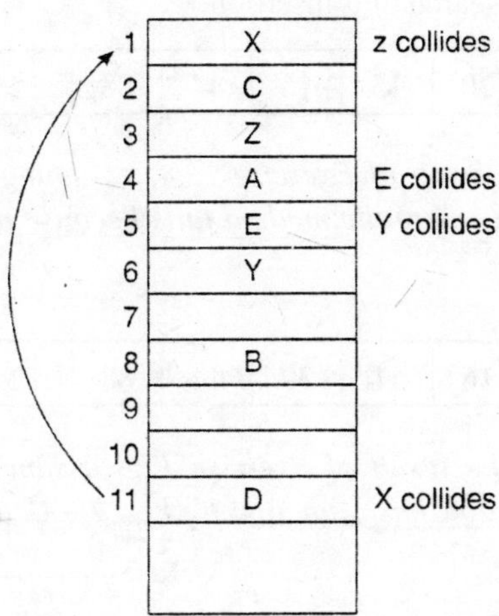

Here records are entered at given locations in order given if particular record collides it is entered at next vacant position.

Avg. no. of probe. $S = \frac{1+1+1+1+2+2+2+3}{8} = \frac{13}{8} = 1.6.$

Empty locations for each entry,

$$U = \frac{7+6+5+4+3+2+1+2+1+1+8}{11} = \frac{40}{11} = 3.6$$

EXAMPLE 12.4. *Draw the 11-item hash table resulting from hasing the keys 12, 4, 13, 88, 23, 94, 11, 39, 20, 16 and 5, using the hash function h(i) = (2i + 5) mod 11 and assuming collisions are handled by chaining.*

SOLUTION :

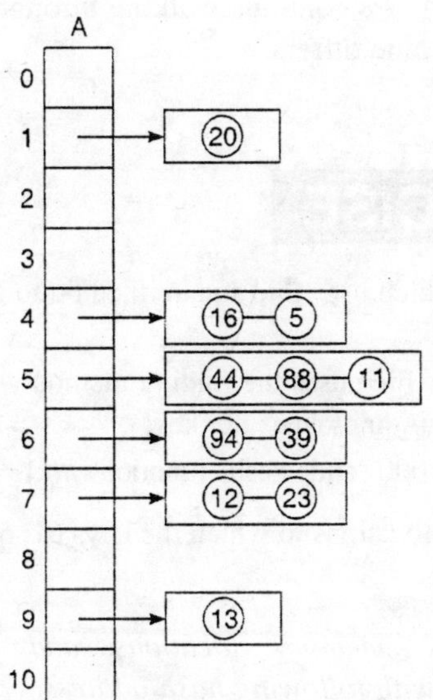

Let $i = 12$

$h(12) = (2 \times 12 + 5) \bmod 11$

$= 29 \bmod 11 = 7$

So key 12 will go to 7th pos.

if $i = 23$

$h(23) = 51 \bmod 11 = 7$

but $12 < 23$

Hence 23 will come after 12 as linked list. Similarly other key mapping are calculated.

EXAMPLE 12.5. *What is the result of the previous exercise, assuming collisions are handled by linear probing ?*

SOLUTION :

11	39	20	15	16	44	88	12	23	13	94

EXAMPLE 12.6. *Show the result of Exercise 12.4, assuming collisions are handled by quadratic probing, upto the point where the method fails because no empty slot is found.*

SOLUTION :

	20	16	11	39	44	88	12	23	13	94

EXAMPLE 12.7. *What is the result of Exercise 12.4 assuming collisions are handled by double hashing using a secondary hash function $h'(k) = 7 - (k \bmod 7)$?*

SOLUTION :

11	23	20	16	39	44	94	12	88	13	5

EXAMPLE 12.8. *Give the pseudo-code description for performing a removal from a hash table that uses linear probing to resolve collisions where we do not use a special marker to represent deleted elements. That is, we must rearrange the contents of the hash table so that it appears that the removed item was never inserted in the first place.*

SOLUTION : When we remove an item from a hash table that uses linear probing without using deleted element markers, we need to rearrange the hash table content so that it seems the removed item never existed. This action can be done by simple incrementally stepping forward through the table (much as we do when there are collisions) and moving back one spot each item k for which $h(k)$ equals $h(removeditem)$. We continue walking through the table until the encounter the first item for which the $h(k)$ value differs.

EXERCISE

1. Write an algorithm. MID (key, Hash) which uses mid square method to find the 2-digit hash address. Hash of a 4-digit employee code.
2. Write on algorithm FOLD (Key, Hash) which uses the folding method with reversing to find the 2-digit hash address Hash of a 4-digit employees no. key.
3. Consider a hash table of size $m = 1000$ and hash function $h(k) = \lfloor m[kA \bmod 1] \rfloor$ for $A = \frac{(\sqrt{5} - 1)}{2} \approx 0.61803$ ... compute the locations to which the keys 61, 62, 63, 64 and 65 are mapped.

4. Write an algorithm for HASH-SEARCH, HASH-INSERT and HASH-DELETE in case of open addressing method.
5. Write an algorithm to search a record in chained method.
6. Consider inserting the keys 10, 22, 31, 4, 15, 28, 17, 88, 59 into a hash table of length $m = 11$ using open addressing with hash function $h'(K) = k \bmod m$. Illustrate the result of inserting these keys using linear probing using quadratic probing with $c_1 = 1$ and $c_2 = 3$, and using double hashing with $h_2(k) = 1 + (k \bmod (m + 1))$.

13

BS TREES

13.1 Binary Trees

A binary Tree T is defined as a finite set of element, called nodes such that :

(a) T is empty (called the empty tree or null tree), or

(b) T contains distinguished node R called the root of T and the remaining nodes of T form an ordered pair of disjoint binary trees T_1 and T_2

If T_1 is non empty then its roots is called left successor, if T_2 is non empty then its root is called right successor.

If a node has no successor then it is called terminal node. We can also view R as parent

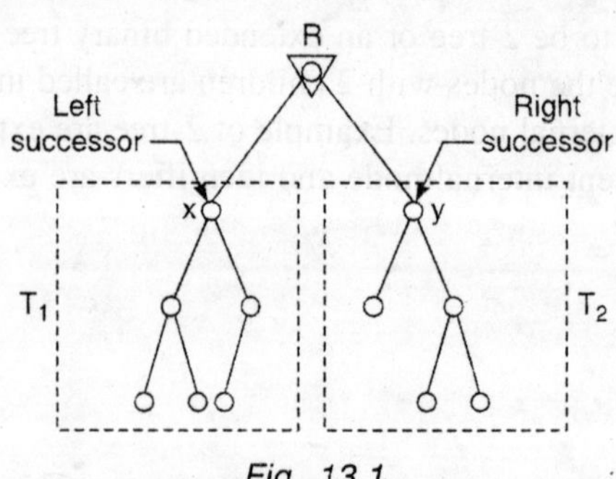

Fig. 13.1

and x and y as its Left and right child. R is also predecessor to x and y or x and y are successors to R.

Complete Binary Tree

A binary tree T is said to be complete binary tree if all its levels, except possibly the last level have maximum number of possible nodes, and if all the nodes at the last level appear as far left as possible.

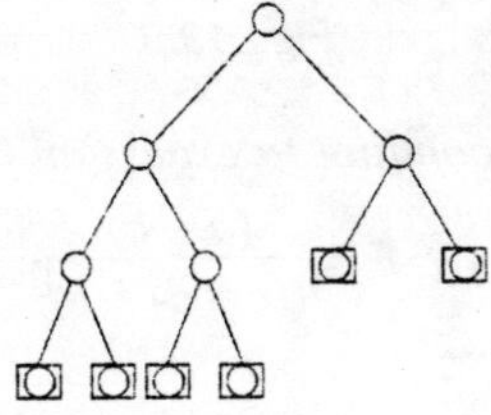

Fig. 13.2

EXAMPLE 13.1. *Show that there can be at most* $\lfloor \log_2 (n + 1) \rfloor$ *nodes in a complete binary tree.*

SOLUTION : We can have $2^0, 2^1, 2^2, 2^3, ..., 2^k$ nodes, in a k-level binary tree of n nodes, then

$$2^0 + 2^1 + 2^2 + 2^3 + 2^k \geq n$$

$$\frac{1 . (2^k - 1)}{2 - 1} \geq n.$$

$$2^k - 1 \geq n$$

$$2^k \geq n + 1$$

Taking the log to the base 2, on both sides

$$k \geq \log_2 (n + 1)$$

or $$k_{max} = \lfloor \log_2 (n + 1) \rfloor.$$

and, $$D_n = k + 1 \text{ (Depth of tree)}$$

$$\boxed{D_n = \log_2 (n + 1) + 1}$$

13.1.1 Extended Binary Trees (2 Trees)

A binary tree T is said to be 2-tree or an extended binary tree if each node N has either 0 or 2 children. In such a case the nodes with 2 children are called internal nodes, and the nodes with 0 children are called external nodes. Example of 2-tree are expressions with binary operations, where operators represent internal node and identifiers are external node.

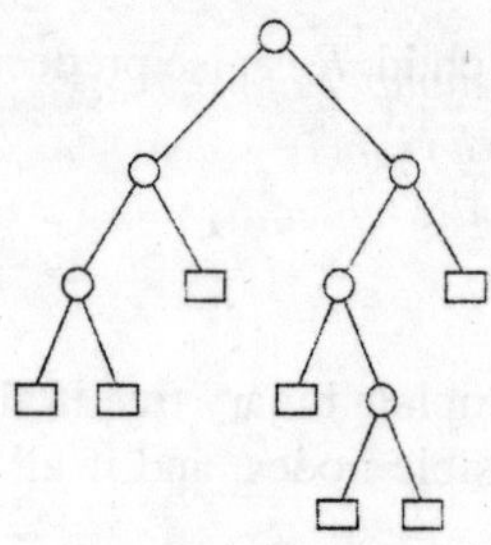

Fig. 13.3

EXAMPLE 13.2. *Find 2-tree corresponding to expession*

$$E = \frac{(a-b)}{((c*d)+e)}$$

SOLUTION : $E = \frac{(a-b)}{((c*d)+e)}$

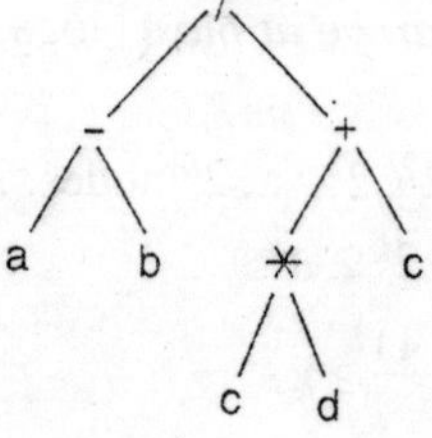

EXAMPLE 13.3. *Find the weighted length P of the given 2-tree.*

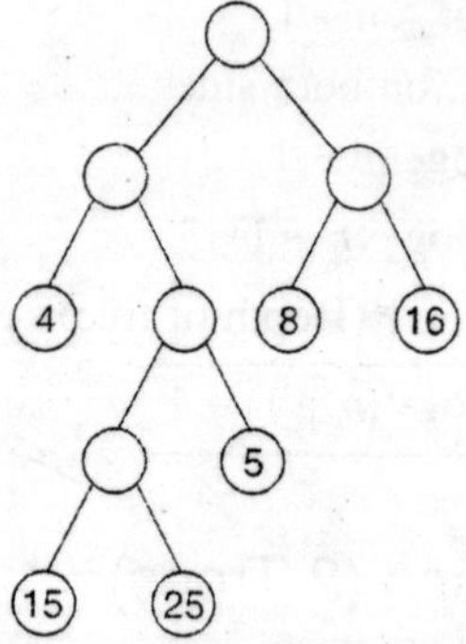

SOLUTION : Multiply each weight ω by the path length from root of *T*, to the node containing weight and then sum all these

$$P = 2.4 + 4.15 + 4.25 + 3.5 + 2.8 + 2.16$$
$$= 8 + 60 + 100 + 15 + 16 + 32$$
$$= 231.$$

Path length in extended binary tree :

External path length : It is path length from root to node having 0 children.

Internal path length : It is path length from root to a node having 2 children.

Note : In a 2-tree/extended tree node has either 0 or 2 children.

EXAMPLE 13.4. *If n(E) represents number of external nodes and n(I) represents number of internal nodes in a 2-tree prove that n(E) = n(I) + 1, if E and I and external and internal path lengths and n is number of internal nodes, then also prove that E = I + 2n.*

SOLUTION :

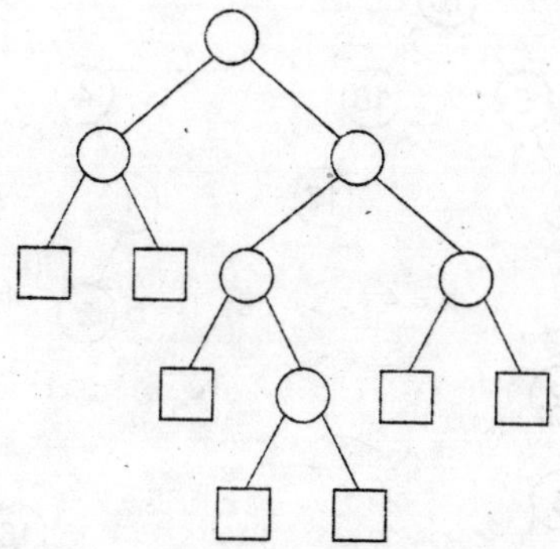

We can easily see that

$$n(E) = 7 \quad \text{and} \quad n(I) = 6$$

$\therefore$ $$n(E) = n(I) + 1 \qquad ...(1)$$

Also, $$E = 2 + 2 + 3 + 4 + 4 + 3 + 3 = 21$$

$$I = 0 + 1 + 1 + 2 + 2 + 3 = 9$$

and $$n = 6$$

therefore $$E = I + 2n$$

13.2 Binary Sequence Tree

It is a binary trees as shown below :

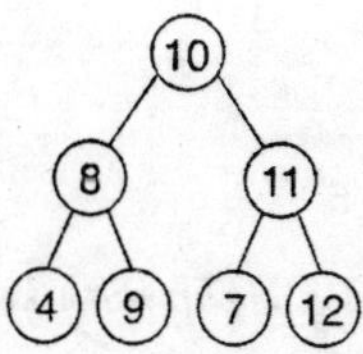

Fig. 13.4

Such a tree can be represented by a linked data structure in which each node is an object. In addition to the key field, each node contains field left, right, and P that most points to the nodes corresponding to its left child, right child and its parent respectively. If any of these is missing field contains the value NIL. Root node is the only node whose parent field is NIL.

The keys in a binary search tree is always stored statisfying the **binary-search-tree property.**

If x is any node in a tree and y is its left subtrees
then key $[x] \geq$ key $[y]$ and if z is right subtree
then key $[x] \leq$ key $[z]$

EXAMPLE 13.5. *Draw binary search trees of height 2, 3, 4, 5 and 6 on the set of keys 1, 4, 5, 10, 16, 17, 2.*

SOLUTION :

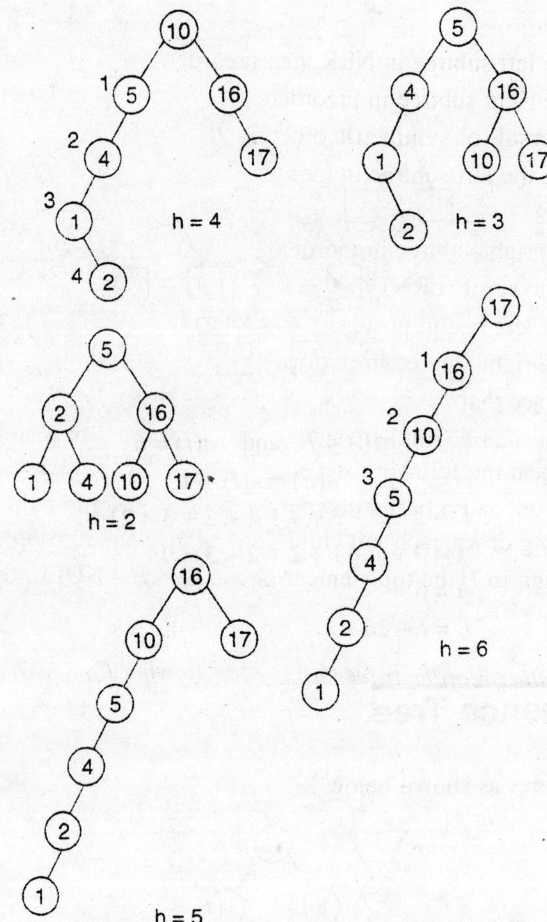

EXAMPLE 13.6. *Construct a BST and a Heap with keys 2, 3, 5, 6, 7, 8.*

SOLUTION : *Left* : A binary search tree. *Right* : A heap but not a binary search tree.

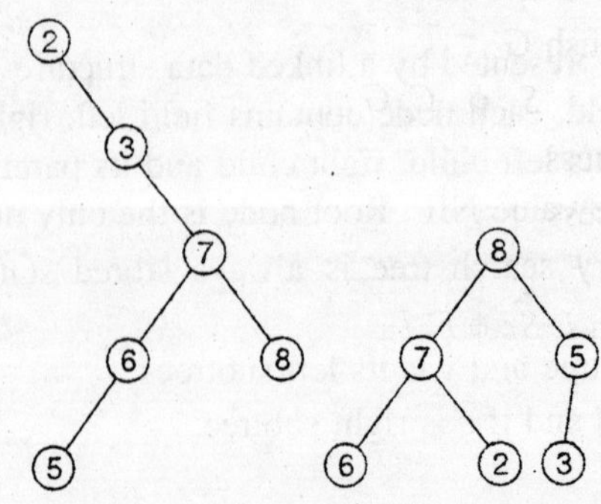

13.3 Tree Traversal

Traversing a binary tree means that passing through the tree, enumerating each of its node once *i.e.*, each node is visited exactly once.

Preorder (NLR or depth first order)

1. Visit the root
2. Traverse the left subtree in NLR, *i.e.*, preorder.
3. Traverse the right subtree in preorders.

Inorder Traversal (or symmetric order) LNR

1. Traverse the the left subtree in inorder.
2. Visit the root
3. Traverse the right subtree in inorder.

Post order Traversal (LRN)

1. Traverse the left tree in postorder
2. Traverse the right subtree in postorder
3. Visit the root

Preorder : This can be implemented using stack, Initially push NULL onto stack then set $P \leftarrow$ Root then repeat the folowing steps until $P \leftarrow$ NULL or while $P \neq$ NULL

1. Process the root and proceed down the left path, pushing right child Right [x] onto stack and processing down each left child, Left [x] Traversing stops when left [P] $\leftarrow$ NULL
2. Pop and assign to P the top element of stack. If $P \neq$ NULL, then goto step 1, otherwise exit.

EXAMPLE 13.7. *Give the preorder traversal of the following Binary tree.*

SOLUTION :

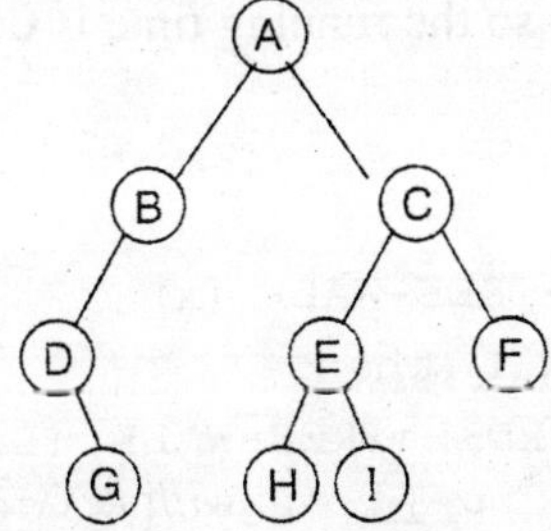

1. Push NULL to stack, S, ϕ
2. Process A, push C to S, $S : \phi, C$
3. Process B, D; push G

$$S : \phi, C, G$$

4. Pop G and process
5. Pop C and process
6. Push F, *i.e.*, ϕ, F
7. Process E, Push I, $S : \phi\, F, I$
8. Process H.

9. pop I and process
10. Pop F and process

This	ABDGCEHIF	← Preorder
	Inorder	: DGBAHEICF
	Postorder	: GDBHIEFCA

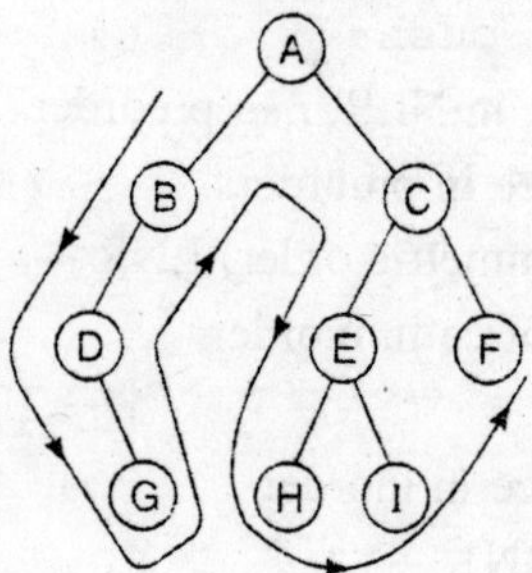

Fig. 13.5. Shows preorder traversal.

Preorder-Tree-Walk (x)

```
1. Push (S, ϕ)
2.   P ← x
3. while (Left [P] ≠ NULL)
4.    print (key (P))
5.        P ← Left [P]
6.        Push (S, Right [P])
7. P ← pop (S)
8. If P ≠ NULL goto step 3.
```

There are exactly n calls, so the running time is $\Theta(n)$.

Inorder Traversal

```
INORDER-TREE-WALK (x)
If x ≠ NIL then
      INORDER-TREE-WALK (Left [x])
            Print key [x]
      INORDER-TREE-WALK (Right [x])
```

Inorder Algo

Initially push NULL onto stack and then set $P \leftarrow$ root then repeat the following steps.

1. Proceed down the left-most path rooted at P, pushing each node onto stack and stopping when no left child is left to be pushed.
2. pop and process the nodes on stack. If NULL is popped then exit. If a node with right child is popped and processed set $P \leftarrow$ Right [P] and goto step 1.

EXAMPLE 13.8. *Give the stack implementation of Inorder traversal.*

SOLUTION :

```
INORDER (Key, Left, Right, x)
1.    top ← 1, push (S, NULL)
            p ← x
2.    While (P ≠ NULL)
            top ← top + 1
            S[top] ← key [P]
                  P ← Left [P]
      End while
3.    Key [P] ← S [top]
      top ← top - 1
4.    While (P ≠ NULL)
      print key [P]
            If Right [P] ≠ NULL
                  P ← Right [P]
                  goto step 2
            end if
      key [P] ← S [top]
            top ← top - 1
      end while
      return.
```

EXAMPLE 13.9. *Give the recursive postorder tree-walk LRN.*

SOLUTION :

```
POST-ORDER-TREE-WALK (x)
      if x ≠ NIL
            POST-ORDER-TREE-WALK (Left [x])
            POST-ORDER-TREE-WALK (Right [x])
            Print Key [x]
```

Running time is $\theta(n)$.

Post-Order Algo

1. Proceed down the left most path. At each node N push N onto stack and if N has right child, push – Right (N) onto stack.
2. Pop and process positive nodes. If –ve node N is popped set ptr = – N and repeat step 1.

EXAMPLE 13.10. *Let T be an ordered tree with more than one node. Is it possible that the preorder traversal of T visits the nodes in the same order as the postorder traversal of T? If so, give an example; otherwise, argue why this cannot occur. Likewise, is it possible that the preorder traversal of T visits the nodes in the reverse order of the postorder traversal of T? If so, give an example; otherwise, argue why this cannot occur.*

SOLUTION : It is not possible for the postorder and preorder travesal of a tree with more than one node to visit the nodes in the same order. A preorder traversal will always visit the root node first, while a postorder traversal node will always visit an external node first.

It is possible for a preorder and a postorder traversal to visit the nodes in the reverse order. Consider the case of a tree with only two nodes.

EXAMPLE 13.11. *The inorder and preorder traversals of tree T is given as below :*

Inorder : E A C K F H D B G

Preorder : F A E K C D H G B

Construct a binary tree.

SOLUTION :

(a) Root of tree is obtained by choosing first node in preorder. Here *F*.

(b) Left child of *F* is all nodes prior to *F* in inorder and all nodes to right of *F* forms right child.

Looking at inorder

(*E A C K*) *F* (*H D B G*)

F

EACK *HDBG*

In *EACK* *A* occurs as first node in preorder therefore *A* forms root.

and *E* occurs to left of *A* in inorder and *CK* to right of *A* in inorder.

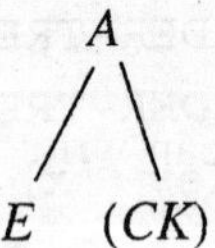

in *CK*, *K* occurs first in preorder,

C occurs to left of *K* in inorder

Thus

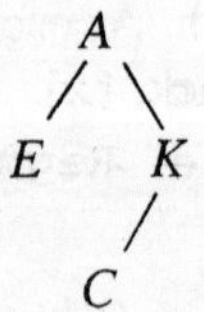

Thus we construct the tree as belows :

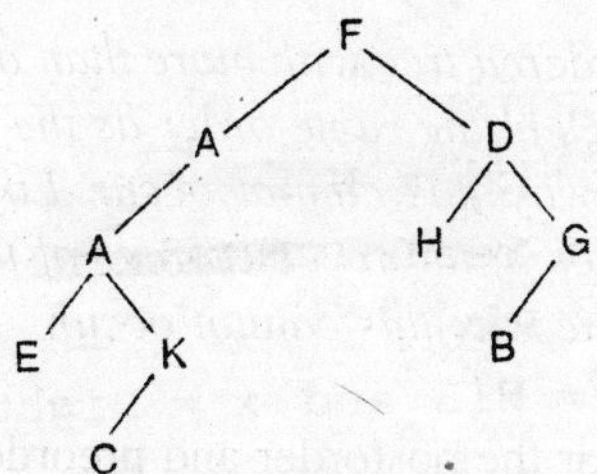

13.4 Querying a Binary Search Tree

Searching : finding a node with key value k in a binary tree

```
Tree-Search [x, k]
        If x = NIL or k = key [x]
                then return x
        If k < key [x]
                then return tree-search (Left [x], k)
                else return (Right [x], k).
```

running time $O(h)$ in a ht . h of a tree.

```
ITERATIVE-TREE-SEARCH (x, k)
while (x ≠ NIL and k ≠ key [x])
        do if k < key [x]
                then x ← Left [x]
                else x ← Right [x]
return x.
```

Minimum and Max

Using binary tree property we can write.

```
TREE-MINIMUM (x)
        While Left [x] ≠ NIL
                do x ← Left [x]
        return x
TREE-MAXIMUM (x)
        while Right [x] ≠ NIL
                do x ← Right [x]
        return x.
```

Both of these procedure run in $O(h)$ time.

Successor and Predecessor[1]

```
TREE-SUCCESSOR (x)
    If Right [x] ≠ NIL
        then return TREE-MINIMUM (Right [x])
        y ← P[x]
    while Y ≠ NIL and x = Right [Y]
        do x ← y
            y ← P(y)
    return y.
```

If right subtree of node x is nonempty, then the successor of x is just the left most node in the right subtree. Otherwise if right subtree is empty and x has a successor y, then y is lowest ancestor of x whose left child is also an ancestor of x.

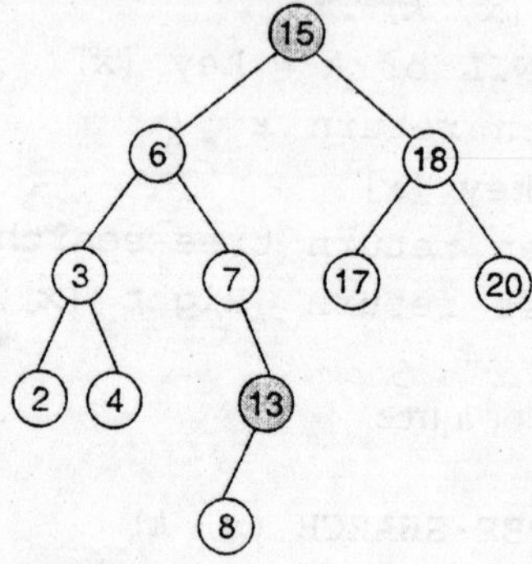

Fig. 13.6. Binary Tree.

As shown in Fig. 13.6 above successor of node with key 13 is the node with key 15. To find y, simply go up the tree from x until we encounter a node that is left child of its parent.

Running time of TREE-SUCCESSOR on a tree of *ht.* h is $O(h)$ Similarly we can have PREDECESSOR algorithm.

Insertion and Deletion

```
TREE-INSERT (T, Z)
    y ← NIL
    x ← Root [T]
while x ≠ NIL
    do y ← x
        if key [Z] < key[x]
            then x ← Left [x]
            else x ← Right [x]
P[z] ← y
```

1 Successor of a node x is the node with the smallest key greater than key $[x]$.

```
if y = NIL
      then Root [T] ← [Z]
      else if key [Z] < key [Y]
      then Left [y] ← Z
      else Right [Y] ← Z
```

Tree-Insert begins at the root of the tree and traces a path downward. The pointer x traces the path and pointer y is maintained as the parent of x. The two pointers move down comparing key [z] with key [x] until x is set to NIL. At this position Z is inserted.

```
key [z] = 13.
```

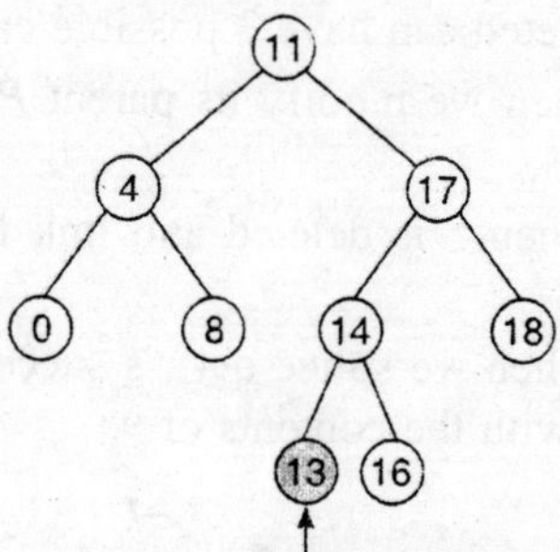

Fig. 13.7. Shows insertion.

```
      key [x] = 11.
      13 ≮ 11
∴     x ← Right [x]
   (i.e., at key [x] = 17)
      13 < 17.
∴     x ← left  [x]
   (i.e., key [x] = 14)
      13 ≮ 14.
∴     x ← left [x] = NIL
```

So key [z] is inserted at this position.

Running time is $O(h)$

```
Tree-Delete (T, Z)
        If Left [z] = NIL or Right [z] = NIL
            then y ← z
            else y ← TREE-SUCESSOR (Z)
        if Left [y] ≠ NIL
            then x ← Left [y]

            else x ← Right [y]
```

```
if x ≠ NIL
    then P(x) ← P(y)
if P[y] = NIL
    then Root [T] ← x
    else if y = left [P [y]]
    then Left [P(y)] ← x
    else Right [P(y)] ← x
if y ≠ z
    then key [z] ← key [y]
return y
```

A node z which is to be deleted can have 3 possible cases.

(i) Node have no children then we modify its parent $P[z]$ to replace z with its NIL as its child.

(ii) Node have single child then z is deleted and link is set between its parent and child directly.

(iii) Node have two children then we splice out z's successor y, which has no left child and replace the contents of z with the contents of y.

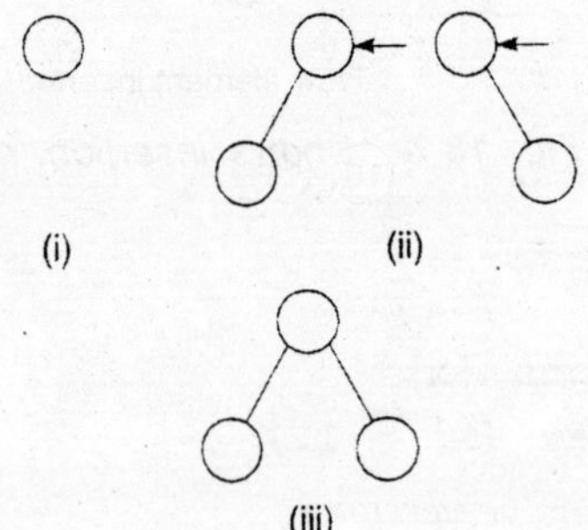

Fig. 13.8. Three cases for deletion.

Fig. 13.9 (a)–(c). Show BS tree deletion.

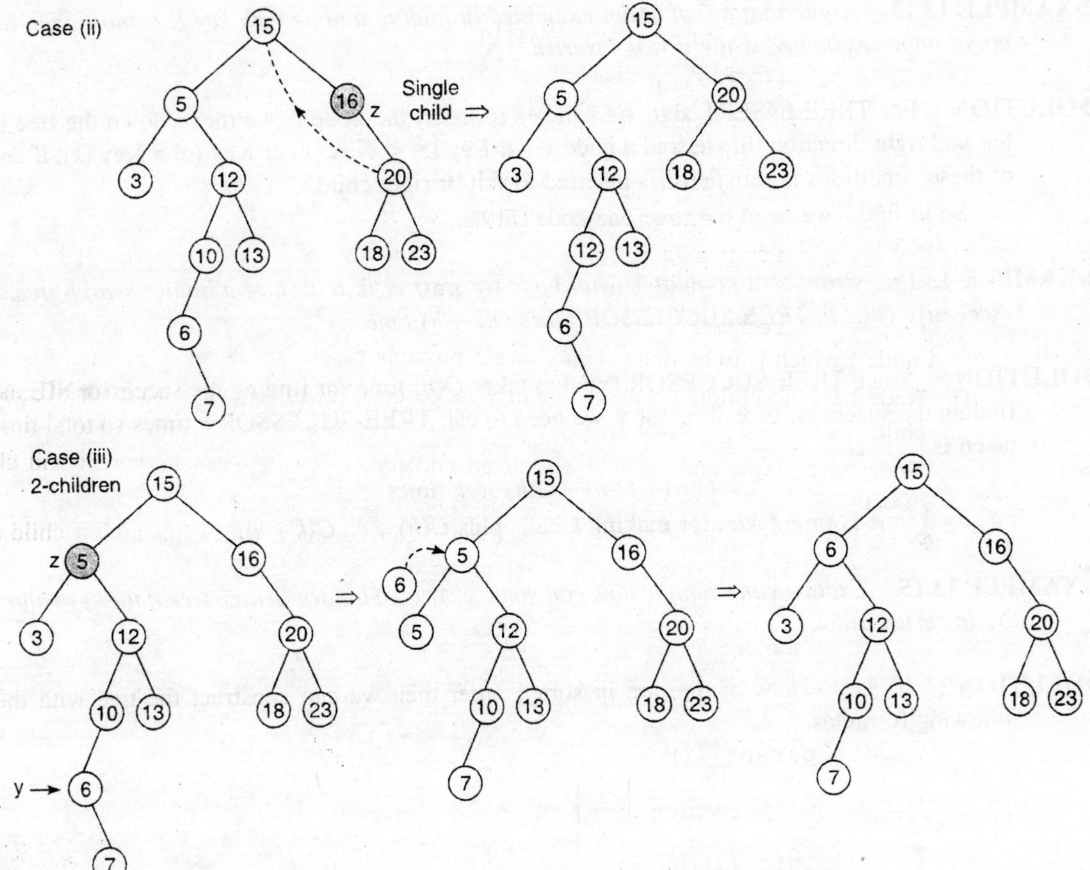

EXAMPLE 13.12. *Give a recursive version of the TREE-INSERT procedure.*

SOLUTION :

```
TREE-INSERT-REC (T, z, x)
        y ← x
        if (Key (z) < Key [x] and x ≠ NIL)
                TREE-INSERT-REC (T, z, Left [x])
        else    TREE-INSERT-REC (T, z, Right [x])
                P(z) ← y
                if y = NIL
                then root T ← z
                else if Key [z] < Key [y]
                then left [y] ← z
                else Right [y] ← z
```

EXAMPLE 13.13. *Argue that no. of nodes examined in finding a node with key K is more than the no. of nodes examined while it was inserted.*

SOLUTION : For TREE-INSERT algo we can see to insert the node z, we move down the tree in left and right direction till we find a node x, s.t. Key (z) < Key (x) or Key (z) > Key (x), if any of these conditions is satisfied z is inserted as left or right child.

So to find z we need to move one node further.

EXAMPLE 13.14. *Prove that no matter what node we start at in a ht. h of a binary search tree, k successive calls to TREE-SUCCESSOR takes O(k + h) time.*

SOLUTION : Since TREE-SUCCESOR (x) algo takes $O(h)$ time for finding the successor of x, so finding the successor of k different x, we need to call TREE-SUCESSOR k times so total time taken is

$$O(h) + O(h) + O(h) \ldots k \text{ times}$$

i.e., total time is time taken for making k calls plus $O(h)$, *i.e.*, $O(k + h)$.

EXAMPLE 13.15. *Explan with example how can you construct a binary-Search tree if the key values are in sorted order.*

SOLUTION : If key values of tree are in sorted order then we can construct the tree with the following formulas

```
parent (i)
        return ⌊i/2⌋
Left (i)
        return 2i
Right (i)
        return 2i + 1
```

e.g., take the input

	0	1	2	3	4	5	6	7	8	9	10	11	12	13	14	15	16	17	18
A	80	47	86	95	115	130	138	159	166	184	206	212	219	224	257	258	296	307	314

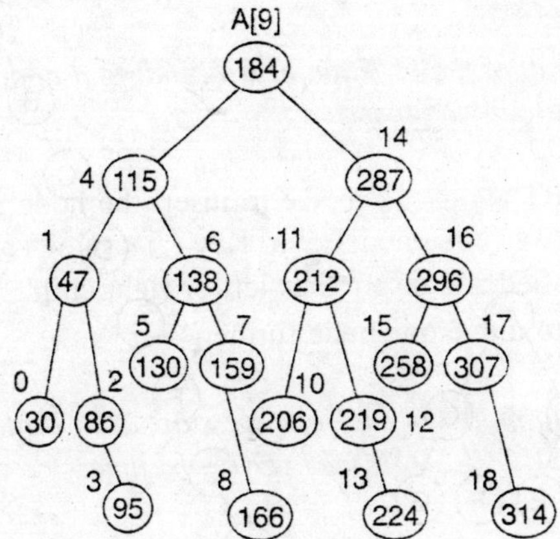

EXAMPLE 13.16. *From a binary search tree, taking the input as 30, 47, 86, 75, 115, 130, 135, 159, 160, 184 and starting with node 0 as the root construct a BS tree.*

SOLUTION :

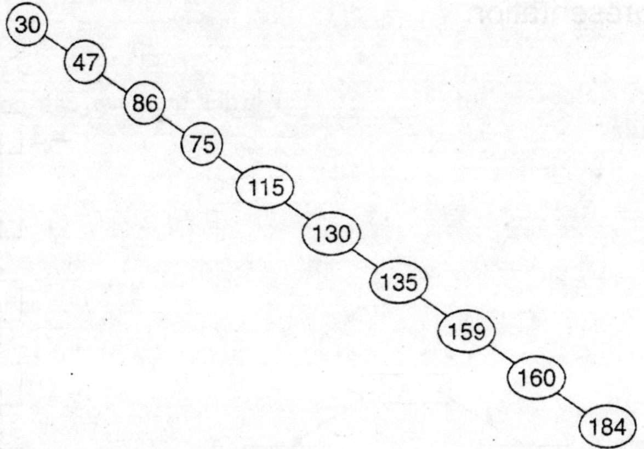

This is called **skewed** to right.

Sequential Representation of Trees

A	B	C	D	E	F	G	H	I
1	2	3	4	5	6	7	8	9

tree is given by

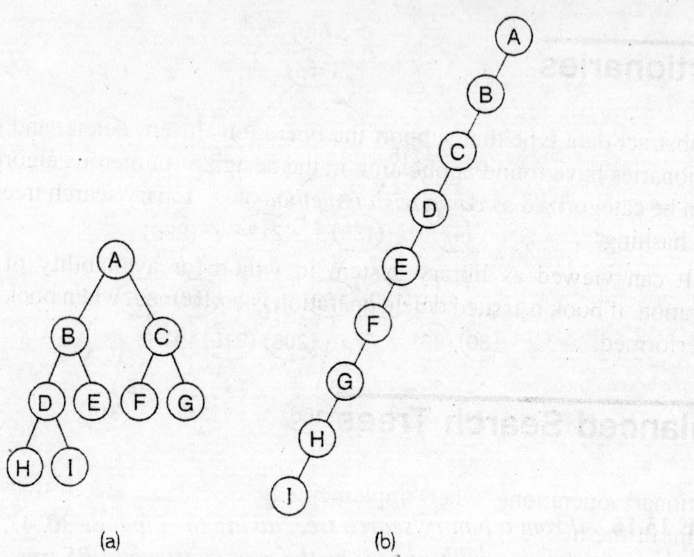

Fig. 13.10. Sequential representation of BS tree.

Linked Representation

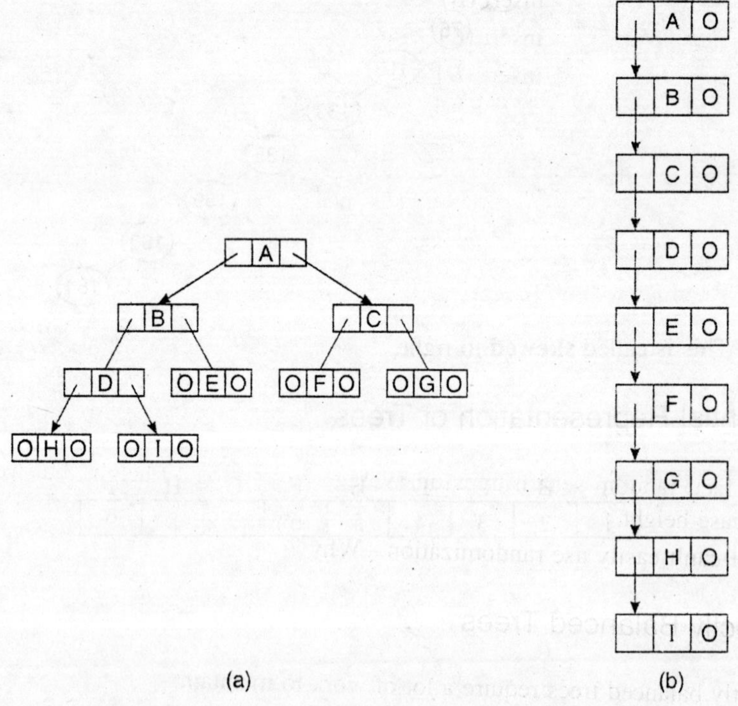

Fig. 13.11. Linked list representation of BS tree.

13.5 Dictionaries

An abstract data type that support the operations insert, delete, and search is called dictionary. Dictionaries have found application in the design of numerous algorithms. At a very high level it can be categorized as *comparision methods e.g.*, binary search tree and *direct access methods e.g.*, hashing.

It can viewed as library system in which for availability of book we perform search operation, if book is issued delete operation is performed, when book is returned insert operation is performed.

13.6 Balanced Search Trees

Dictionary operations, when implemented with binary search trees, take $O(h)$, where h is the height of the tree.

The best height we could hope to get is log n, if the tree was perfectly balanced, since

$$\sum_{i=0}^{[\log n]} 2^i = n$$

But if we get unlucky with our order of insertion or deletion, we could get linear height!

insert (A)
insert (B)
insert (C)
insert (D)
⋮

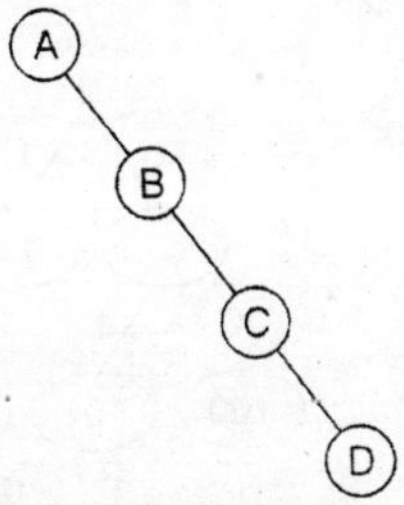

Fig. 13.12

In fact, random search trees on average have $\theta(\log N)$ height, but we are worried about worst case height.

We can't easily use randomization - Why ?

Perfectly Balanced Trees

Perfectly balanced trees require a lot of work to maintain:

If we insert the key, 1, we must move every single node in the tree to rebalance it, taking $\theta(n)$ time.

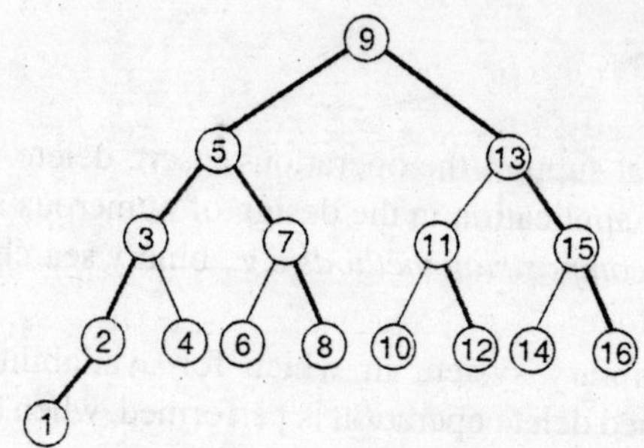

Fig. 13.13.

Therefore, when we talk about "balanced" trees, we mean trees whose height is $O(\log n)$. so all dictionary operations (insert, delete, search, min/max successor/predecessor) take $O(\log n)$ time.

Red-Black trees are binary search trees where each node is assigned a color, where the coloring schemes helps us maintain the height as $\Theta(\log n)$.

13.7 Radix Trees

It stores other bit strings 100, 101, 001, 11, 111, 1111, 1110. When searching for a key $a = a_0\, a_1, ..., a_p$ we go to left node of depth i if $a_i = 0$ and right. Otherwise, where $a_i = 0$ for left branch and $a_i = 1$ for right branch, level and key of node is concatenation of a_i's in its path. Let S be a set of distinct binary strings whose length sums to n.

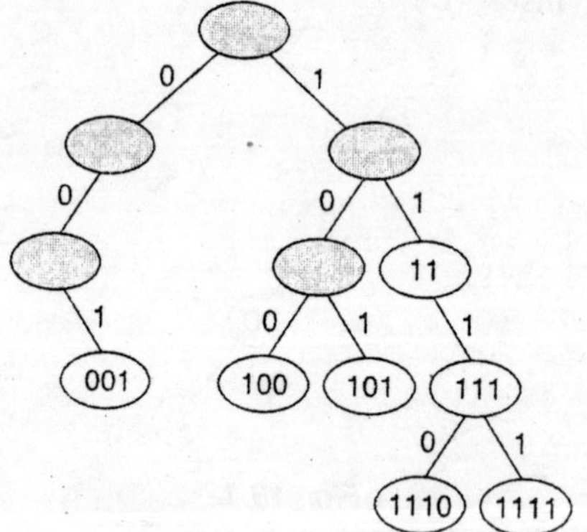

Fig. 13.14. Radix tree.

If $a = a_1\, a_2, ..., a_p$, $b = b_1 b_2 ..., b_q$ are two strings then

(i) if $p < q$ then $a < b$.

(ii) if for $j = 0$ to min (p, q), $a_j < b_j$ then $a < b$.

e.g., 10100 < 101000 by (i)

110100 < 111000 by (ii)

↑ ↑

above rules are called **lexico graphy.**

EXAMPLE 13.17. *Draw an expression tree that has four external nodes, storing the numbers 1, 5, 6 and 7 (with each number stored one per external node but not necessarily in this order), and has three internal nodes, each storing an operation from the set {+, −, ×,/} of binary arithmetic operators, so that the value of the root is 21. The operators are assumed to return rational numbers (not integers), and an operator may be used more than once (but we only store one operator per internal node).*

SOLUTION : The tree express the formula 6/(1–5/7).

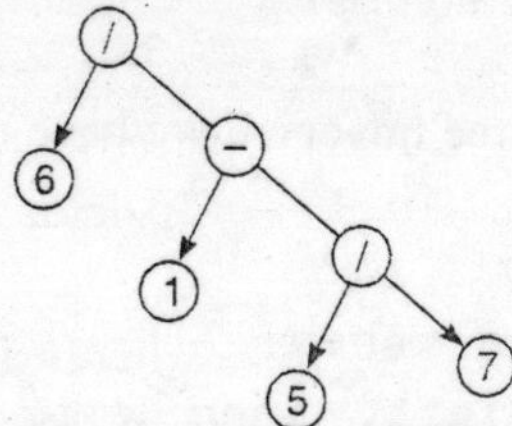

EXAMPLE 13.18. *Give an* $O(n)$*-time algorithm for computing the depth of all the nodes of a tree T, when n is the number of nodes of T.*

SOLUTION : The idea is to perform a preorder (or postorder) traversal of the tree, where the "visit" action is to report the depth of the node that is currently visited. This can be easily done by using a counter that keeps track of the current depth. Method PrintDepth (*v*, *d*) prints the depth *d* of the current node *v* and recursively traverses the subtrees defined by *v*. If *T* is the tree, then, initially, we call PrintDepth (*T*.root(), 0). Observe that we use only methods of the abstract tree ADT.

```
PrintDepth (v, d) :
        print (d)
        for each (w ∈ T.children (v) do)
              PrintDepth (w, d + 1)
```

EXAMPLE 13.19. *The balance factor of an internal node* v *of a binary tree is the difference between the heights of the right and left subtrees of* v*. Show how to specialize the Euler tour traversal to print the balance factors of all the nodes of a binary tree.*

SOLUTION : One way to do this is the following : in the external method, set height and balance to be zero. Then, alter the right method as follows :

```
right() :
   if visInternal (v) then
         if v.leftchild.height > v.rightchild.height then
               v.height = v. leftchild.height + 1;
         else
```

```
            v.height = v.rightchild.height + 1;
        v.balance = absval(v.rightchild.height -
                                v.leftchild.height);
    printBalanceFactor (v)
```

EXAMPLE 13.20. *Let a visit action in the Euler tour traversal be denoted by a pair (v, a), where v is the visited node and a is one of left, below, or right. Design an algorithm for performing operation tourNext (v, a), which returns the visit action (w, b) following (v, a). What is the worst-case running time of your algorithm ?*

SOLUTION : Examining the Euler tree traversal, we have the following method for finding

```
tourNext (v, α)
If v is a leaf, then:
        if α = left, then w is v and β = below,
        if α = below, then w is v and β = right,
        if α = right, then
            * if v is a left child, then w is v's parent
                                        and β = below,
            * if v is a right child, then w is v's parent
                                        and β = right.
```

If v is internal, then :

```
        if α = left, then β = left and w is v's
                                        left child,
        if α = below, then β = left and w is v's
                                        right child,
        if α = right, then
            * if v is a left child, then β = below and
                                        w is v's parent,
            * if v is a right child, then β = right and
                                        w is v's parent.
```

For every node v but the root, we can find whether v is a left or right child, by asking "$v = T$.leftChild(T.parent(v))". The complexity is always $O(1)$.

EXAMPLE 13.21. *Let T be a binary tree with n nodes (T may or may not be realized with a vector). Give a linear-time method that uses the methods of the Binary Tree interface to traverse the nodes of T by increasing values of the level numbering function p. This traversal is known as the level order traversal.*

SOLUTION :

```
levelOrder Traversal (Binary Tree T) :
        Queue Q = new Queue()
```

```
Q.enqueue (T.root())
while Q is not empty do
    Node V ← Q.dequeue()
    if T.isInternal (v) then
        Q.enqueue (v.leftchild)
        Q.enqueue (v.rightchild)
```

EXAMPLE 13.22. *Let T be a tree with n nodes, and, for any node v in T, let d_v denote the depth of v in T. The distance between two nodes v and w in T is $d_v + d_w - 2d_u$, where u is the LCA u of v and w (LCA is lowest common onces (or of two nodes θ and w and is lowest node in T-that has both v* and *w as descendents). The diameter of T is the maximum distance between two nodes in T. Describe an efficient algorithm for finding the diameter of T. What is the running time of your method ?*

SOLUTION : Let d_{uv} be the diameter of *T*. First observe that both *u* and *v* are tree leaves : if not, we can find a path of higher length, only by considering one of *u*'s or *v*'s children. Moreover, one of *u*, *v* has to be a leaf of highest depth. This can be proved by contradiction. Consider a tree and some leaf-to-leaf path *P* that does not include a leaf of highest depth. Then consider a leaf of greatest depth *v*; it is always possible to find a new path *P′* that starts at *v* and is longer than *P*. This yields the desired contradiction.

The main idea of the algorithm is to find a leaf *v* of highest depth and starting from this leaf to keep moving towards the tree's root. At each visited node *u* (including *v*, but excluding the tree's root), the height of *u*'s sibling is computed and the current length L_{max} of the longest path in which *v* belongs is updated accordingly. When we are at *T*'s root, L_{max} contains the diameter of *T*.

We give the pseudo-code for the above algorithm. We use methods depth (*T*, *v*) and height (*T*, *v*), and compute the depth and correspondingly the height of the subtree rooted at *v*. Method DeepestLeaf (*T*, *v*, *H*, *c*) returns the deepest node of *T* or NULL if it is not found in the subtree rooted at *v*. This is done by essentially performing a pre-order traversal that stops as soon as the deepest leaf is found. *H* is *T*'s height and *c* is a counter.

```
DeepestLeaf (T, v, H, d) :
Input : a tree T, a node v, the height H, and the
                                      current depth d
Output : The deepest node, or NULL if it is not found
if T.isExternal (v) then
    if d = H then {Base case : check for deepest node}
        return v
    return NULL
u ← NULL
{See if there is a deepest leaf in the left child}
u ← DeepestLeaf (T, T.leftChild (v), H, d + 1)
if u ≠ NULL then
```

```
        return u
    {See if there is a deepest leaf in the right child}
    u ← DeepestLeaf (T, T.rightChyild (v), H, d + 1)
    return u

findDiameter (T) :
Input : a tree T
Output : The diameter of T
H ← depth (T, T.root())
v ← Deepestleaf (T, v, H, 0)
if v = T.root() then
        return 0 {if deeps leaf is just the root node,
                                          diameter is 0}
Lmax ← 0
        x ← 1 {x : number of nodes visited}
        while v ≠ T.root() do
        {Assign y to be the length of the path going to
                                              the sibling}
        y ← height(T, T.sibling(v))
        {See if we have found a new longest path}
        if x + 1 + y > Lmax then
                Lmax ← x + 1 + y
        {Climb up the tree one step}
        x ← x + 1
        v ← T.parent(v)
return Lmax
```

The running time of the algorithm is linear. Both depth (T, v) and height (T, v) have complexity $O(S_v)$, where S_v is the size of the subtree rooted at v, depth (T, v) is called from the tree's root once, so its time complexity is $O(n)$, height (T, v) is called for each sibling on our way up to the root, so in total, it adds an $O(n)$ time complexity. DeepestLeaf also has linear worst case time complexity, for it is essentially a pre-order tree traversal. Finally, the leaf-to-root path traversal adds a linear time complexity.

We can improve on this algorithm, however. Note that the above algorithm can visit all the nodes in the tree twice, once to find the deepest node and once to find the height subtrees. We can combine these two operations into one algorithm with a little bit of ingenuity and recursion. We observe that given a binary tree T_v rooted at a node v, if we know the diameters and heights of the two subtrees, we know the diameter of T_v. Imagine we took a path from the deepest node of the left subtree to the deepest node of the other subtree, passing through v. This path would have length $= 2 +$ height $(T_v, T_v$.leftChild$(v))$ + height $(T_v, T_v$.rightChild$(v))$. Further, note that this is a longest path that runs through the root of T_v, since the height of the left and right subtrees is simply the longest path from their respective roots to any of their leafs. Therefore, the longest path in T_v is simply the maximum of longest path in the found in T_v's left and right subtrees and the longest path running through v. These observations give rise to the following algorithm. For convenience, we denote the return type of this algorithm to be in the form (h, d) where h and d represent height and diameter respectively, and the accessed using the $h()$ and $d()$ methods.

```
Diameter (T, v)
Input : a tree T and a node in that tree v
Output : a (h, d) pair
if T.is External (v) then {Base case}
      return (0, 0)
{Get the return pairs of the left and right subtrees}
L ← Diameter (T, T.leftChild(v))
R ← Diameter (T, T.rightChild(v))
{Find the height of this subtree}
H ← max(L . h(), R . H()) + 1
{Find the longest path length}
P ← L . h() + R . H() + 2
return (H.max(L.D(), R.d(), P))
```

Since this algorithm visits each node in the tree exactly once, and performs a constant amount of operations at each node, it follows that this algorithm runs in $O(n)$.

EXAMPLE 13.23. *We can represent a path from the root to a node of a binary tree by means of a binary string, where 0 means "go to the left child" and 1 means "go to the right child." Design a logarithmic-time algorithm for finding the last node of a heap holding n elements based on the this representation.*

SOLUTION : The path to the last node in the heap is given by the path represented by the binary expansion of n with the highest-order bit removed.

13.8 Binary Search

We consider three cases:

If k = key(mid), then we have found the item we were looking, for, and the search terminates successfully returning elem(mid).

If k < key(mid), then we recur on the first half of the vector, that is, on the range of ranks from low to mid—1.

If k > key(mid), we recur on the range of ranks from mid +1 to high.

```
BinarySearch (S, k, low, high):
if low > high then
```

```
return NO_SUCH_KEY
else
    mid ← [(log + high)/2]
    if k = key(mid) then
return elem(mid)
else if k < key(mid) then
return BinarySearch S, k, low, mid–1)
else
return BinarySearch (S, k, mid + 1, high)
```

We illustrate the binary search algorithm in Figure 13.15.

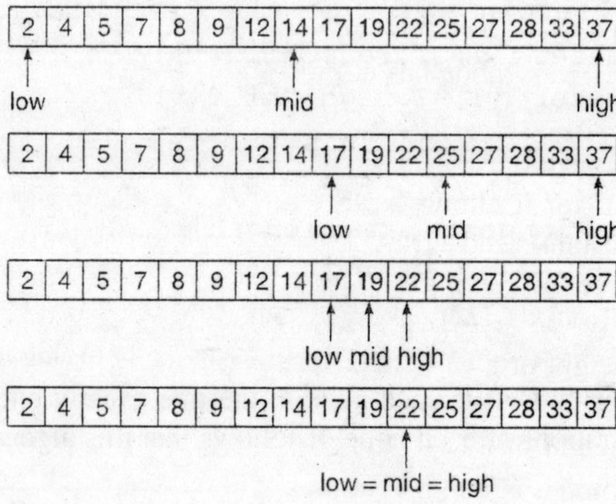

Fig. 13.15. Example of a binary search to perform operation find Element(22), in a dictionary with integer keys, implemented with an array-based ordered vector. For simplicity, we show the keys stored in the dictionary but not the elements.

Considering the running time of binary search, we observe that a constant number of operations are executed at each recursive call. Hence, the running time is proportional to the number of recursive calls performed. A crucial fact is that with each recursive call the number of candidate items still to be searched in the sequence S is given by the value high-low +1. Moreover, the number of remaining candidates is reduced by at least one half with each recursive call. Specifically, from the definition of mid the number of remaining candidates is either

$$(\text{mid} - 1) - \text{low} + 1 = \left\lfloor \frac{\text{low} + \text{high}}{2} \right\rfloor - \text{low} \leq \frac{\text{high} - \text{low} + 1}{2}$$

or

$$\text{high} - (\text{mid} + 1) + 1 = \text{high} - \left\lfloor \frac{\text{low} + \text{high}}{2} \right\rfloor \leq \frac{\text{high} - \text{low} + 1}{2}.$$

Initially, the number of candidate is n; after the first call to BinarySearch, it is at most $n/2$; after the second call, it is at most $n/4$; and so on. That is, if we let a function, $T(n)$, represent the running time of this method, then we can characterize the running time of the recursive binary search algorithm as follows:

$$T(n) \leq \begin{cases} b & \text{if } n < 2 \\ T(n/2) + b & \text{else,} \end{cases}$$

where b is a constant. In general, this recurrence equation shows that the number of candidate items remaining after each recursive call is at most $n/2^i$. In the worst case (unsuccessful search), the recursive calls stop when there are no more candidate items. Hence, the maximum number of recursive calls performed is the smallest integer m such that $n/2^m < 1$. In other words (recalling that we omit a logarithm's base when it is 2),$m > \log n$. Thus, we have $m = \lfloor \log n \rfloor + 1$; which implies that BinarySearch (S, k, 0. $n - 1$) runs in $O(\log n)$ time.

13.9 (2, 4) Trees

In using a multi-way search tree in practice, we desire that it be balanced, that is, have logarithmic height. The multi-way search tree we study next is fairly easy to keep balanced. It is the (2, 4) tree, which is sometimes also called the 2-4 tree or 2-3-4 tree. In fact, we can maintain balance in a (2, 4) tree by maintaining two simple properties (see Figure 3.18):

Size Property : Every node has at most four children.

Depth Property : All the external nodes have the same depth.

Enforcing the size property for (2, 4) trees keeps the size of the nodes in the multi-way search tree cosntant, for it allows us to represent the dictionary $D(v)$ stored at each internal node v using a constant-sized array. The depth property. On the other hand, maintains the balance in a (2.4) tree, by forcing it to be a bounded-depth structure.

THEOREM 13.1. The height of a (2.4) tree storing n items is Θ ($\log n$).

PROOF : Let h be the height of a (2.4) tree T storing n items. Note that, by the size property, we can have at most 4 nodes at depth 1, at most 4^2 nodes at depth 2, and so on. Thus, the number of external nodes in T is at most 4^h. Likewise, by the depth property and the definition of a (2, 4) tree, we must have at least 2 nodes at depth 1, at least 2^2 nodes at depth 2 and so on. Thus, the number of external nodes in T is at least 2^h. In addition, the number of external nodes in T is $n + 1$. Therefore, we obtain

$$2^h \leq n + 1 \text{ and } n + 1 \leq 4^h.$$

Taking the logarithm in base 2 of each of the above terms, we get that

$$h \leq \log (n + 1) \text{ and } \log (n + 1) \leq 2h,$$

which justifies our theorem.

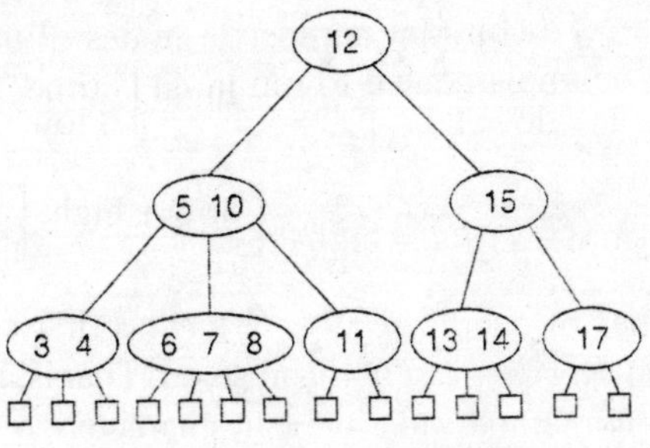

Fig. 13.16. A (2, 4) tree.

Insertion in a (2, 4) Tree

Theorem 13.1 states that the size and depth properties are sufficient for keeping a multi-way tree balanced. Maintaining these properties requires some effort after performing insertions and removals in a (2, 4) tree, however. In particular, to insert a new item (k, x), with key k, into a (2, 4) tree T, we first perform a search for k. Assuming that T has no element with key k, this search terminates unsuccessfully at an external node z. Let v be the parent of z. We insert the new item into node v and add a new child w (an external node) to v on the left of z. That is, we add item (k, x, w) to the dictionary $D(v)$.

Our insertion method preserves the depth property, since we add a new external node at the same level as existing external nodes. Nevertheless, it may violate the size property. Indeed, it a node v was previously a 4-node, then it may become a 5-node after the insertion, which causes the tree T to no longer be a (2, 4) tree. This type of violation of the size property is called an **overlow** at node v, and it must be resolved in order to restore the properties of a (2, 4) tree. Let $v_1, \ldots, v_5$ be the children of v, and let $k_1, \ldots, k_4$ be the keys stored at v. To remedy the overflow at node v, we perform a **split** operation on v as follows (see Figure 3.19):

Replace v with two nodes v' and v'', where

v' is a 3-node with children v_1, v_2, v_3 storing keys k_1 and k_2

v'' is a 2-node with children v_4, v_5 storing key k_4.

If v was the root of T, create a new root node u; else, let u be the parent of v.

Insert key k_3 into u and make v' and v'' children of u, so that if v was child i of u, then v' and v'' become children i and $i + 1$ of u, respectively.

We show a sequence of insertions in a (2, 4) tree in Figure 13.18.

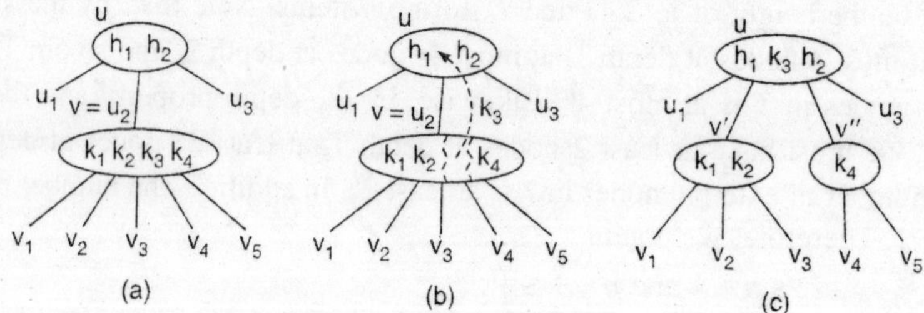

Fig. 13.17. A node split: (a) overflow at a 5-node v; (b) the third key of v inserted into the parent u of v; (c) node v replaced with a 3-node V′ and a 2-node V″.

A split operation affects a constant number of nodes of the tree and $O(1)$ items stored at such nodes. Thus, it can be implemented to run in $O(1)$ time.

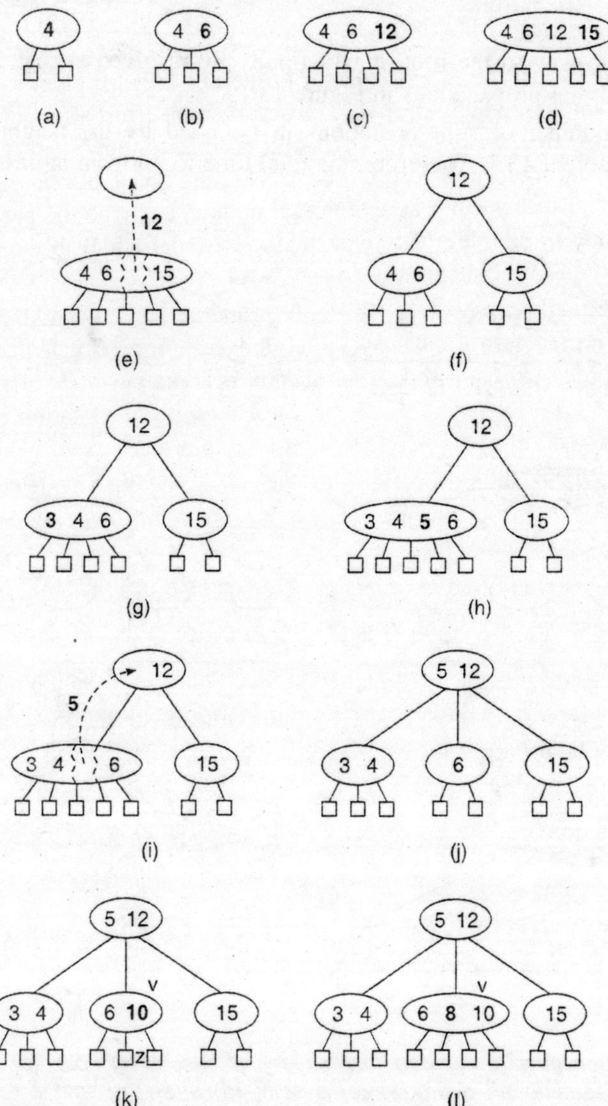

Fig. 13.18. A sequence of insertions into a (2, 4) tree: (a) initial tree with one item; (b) insertion of 6; (c) insertion of 12; (d) insertion of 15, which causes an overflow; (e) split, which causes the creation of a new root node; (f) after the split; (g) insertion of 3; (h) insertion of 5, which causes an overlow; (i) split; (j) after the split; (k) insertion of 10; (l) insertion of 8.

Performance of (2, 4) Tree Insertion

As a consequence of a split operation on node v, a new overflow may occur at the parent u of v. If such an overflow occurs, it triggers, in turn, a split at node u. (See Figure 13.19). A split operation either eliminates the overflow or propagates it into the parent of the current node. Indeed, this propagation can continue all the way up to the root of the search tree. But if it does propagate all the way to the root, it will finally by resolved at that point. We show such a sequence of splitting propagations in Figure 13.19.

Thus, the number of split operations in bounded by the height of the tree, which is $O(\log n)$ by Theorem 13.1. Therefore, the total time to perform an insertion in a (2, 4) tree is $O(\log n)$.

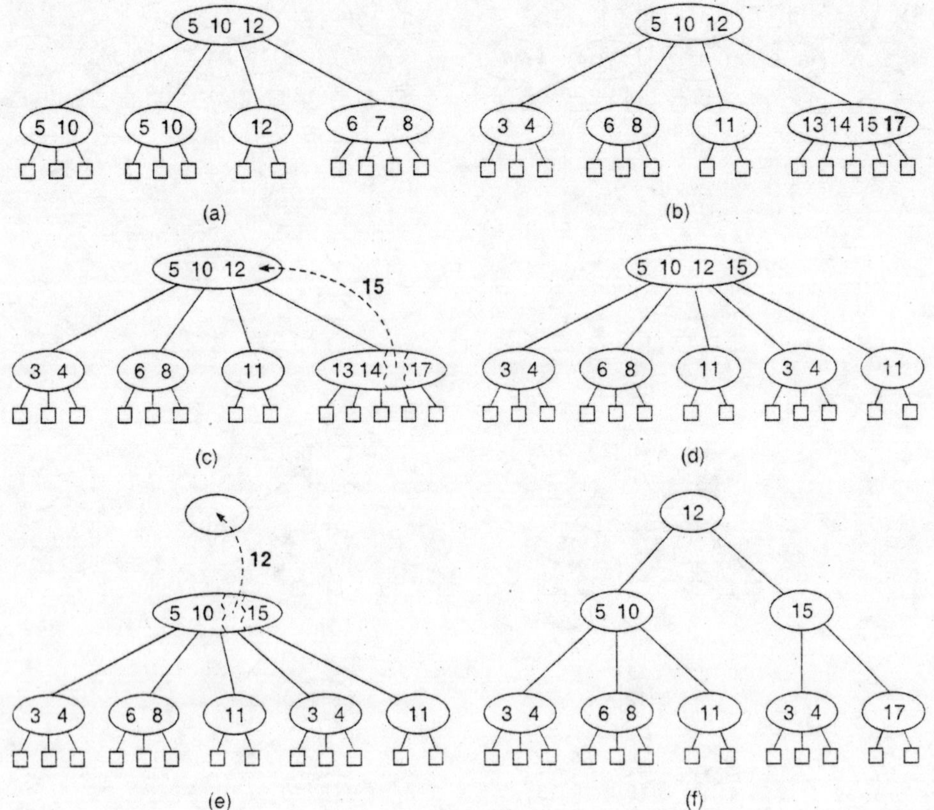

Fig. 13.19. An insertion in a (2, 4) tree that causes a cascading split: (a) before the insertion; (b) insertion of 17, causing an overflow; (c) a split; (d) after the split a new overflow occurs; (e) another split, creating a new root node; (f) final tree.

Removal in a (2, 4) Tree

Let us now consider the removal of an item when key k from a (2, 4) tree T. We begin such an operation by performing a search in T for an item with key k. Removing such an item from a (2, 4) tree can always be reduced to the case where the item to be removed is stored at a node v whose children are external nodes. Suppose, for instance, that the item with key k that we wish to remove is stored in the ith item (k_i, x_i) at a node z that has only internal-node children. In this case, we swap the item (k_i, x_i) with an appropriate item that is stored at a node v with external-node children as follows (Figure 13.20d) :

1. We find the right-most internal node v in the subtree rooted at the ith child of z, noting that the children of node v are all external nodes.
2. We swap the item (k_i, x_i) at z with the last item of v.

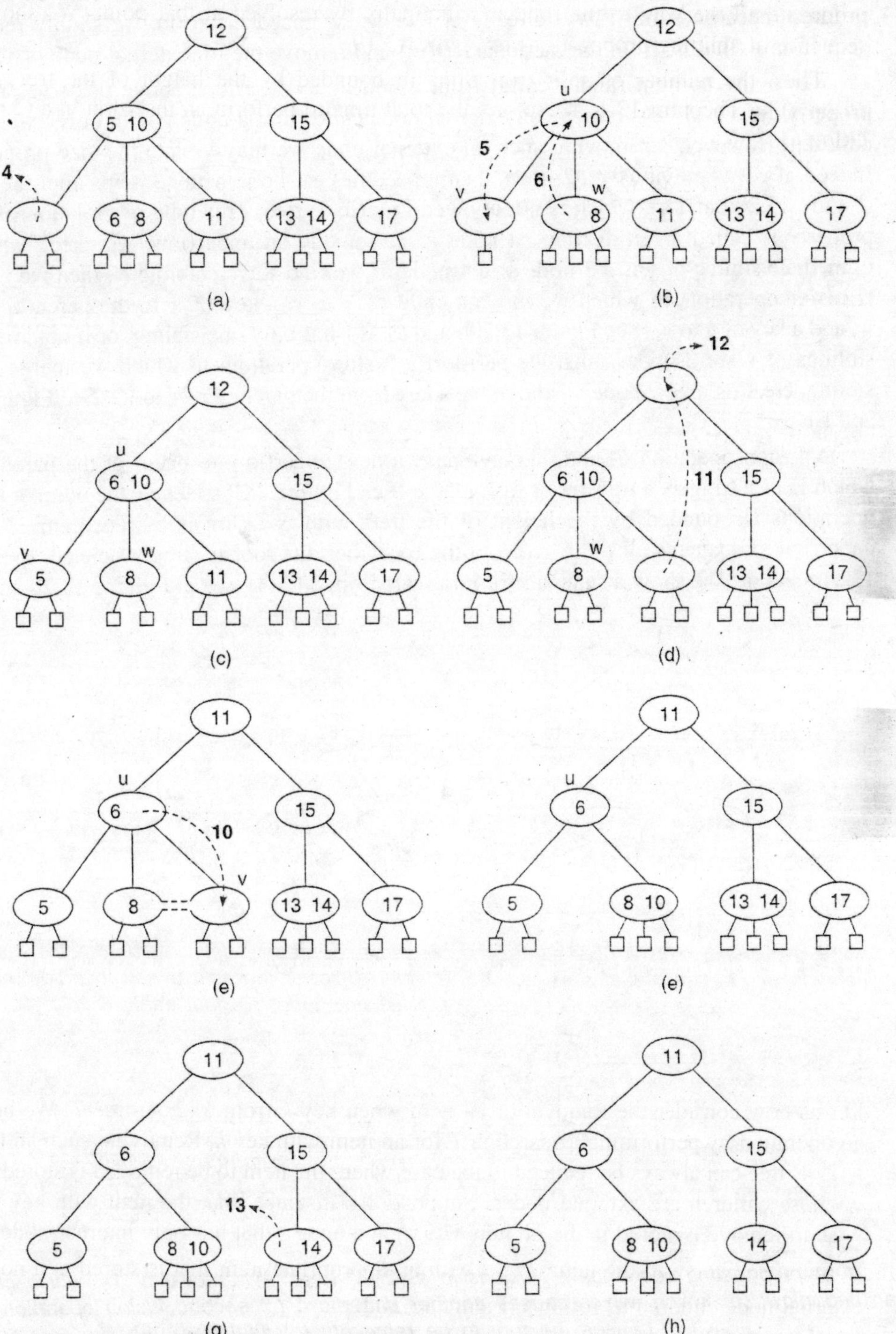

Fig. 13.20. A sequence of removals from a (2, 4) tree: (a) removal of 4, causing an underflow; (b) a transfer operation; (c) after the transfer operation; (d) removal of 12, causing an underflow; (e) a fusion operating; (f) after the fusion operation; (g) removal of 13; (h) after removing 13.

Once we ensure that the item to remove is stored at a node v with only external-node children (because either it was already at v or we swapped it into v), we simply remove the item from v (that is, from the dictionary $D(v)$) and remove the ith external node of v.

Removing an item (and a child) from a node v as described above preserves the depth property, for we always remove an external node child from a node v with only external-node children. However, a removing such an external node we may violate the size property at v. Indeed, if v was previously a 2-node, then it becomes a 1-node with no items after the removal (Figure 13.20d and e), which is not allowed in a (2, 4) tree. This type of violation of the size property is called an **underflow** at node v. To remedy an underflow, we check whether an immediate sibling of v is a 3-node or a 4-node. If we find such a sibling w, then we perform a **transfer** operation, in which we move a child of w to v, a key of w to the parent u of v and w, and a key of u to v. (See Figure 13.20b and c). If v has only one sibling, or if both immediate siblings of v are 2-nodes, then we perform a **fusion** operation, in which we merge v with a sibling, creating a new node v', and move a key from the parent u of v to v'. (See Figure 13.20e and f.)

A fusion operation at node v may cause a new underflow to occur at the parent u of v, which in turn triggers a transfer or fusion at u. (See Figure 13.21). Hence, the number of fusion operations is bounded by the height of the tree, with is $O(\log n)$ by Theorem 13.1. If an underflow propagates all the way up to the root, then the root is simply deleted. (See Figure 13.21c and d.) We show a sequence of removals from a (2, 4) tree in Fgiures 13.20 and 13.21.

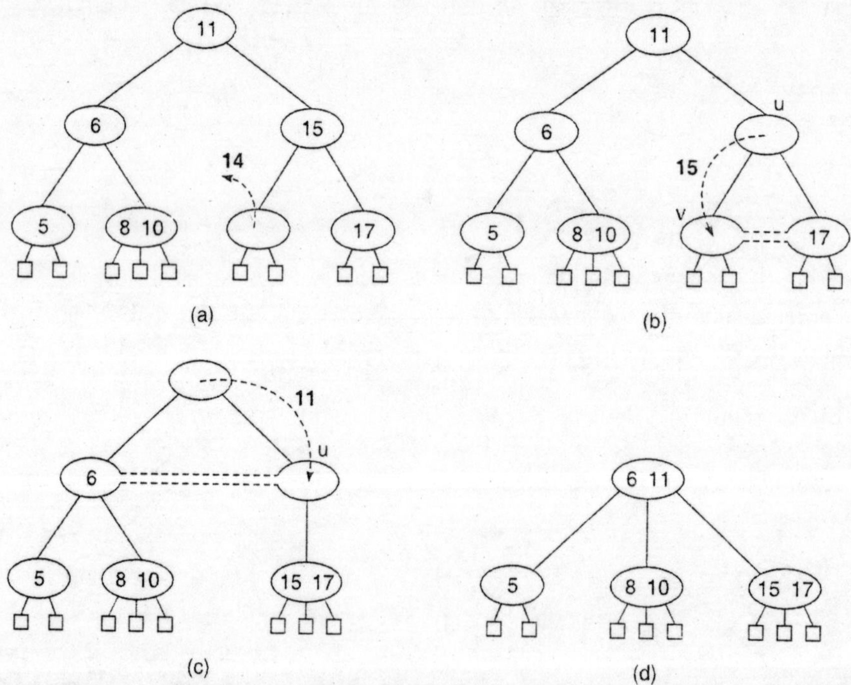

Fig. 13.21. A propagating sequence of fusions in a (2, 4) tree: (a) removal of 14, which causes an underflow; (b) fusion, which causes another underflow; (c) second fusion operation, which causes the root to be removed; (d) final tree.

Performance of a (2, 4) Tree

The time complexity analysis is based on the following:

The height of a (2, 4) tree storing n items is $O(\log n)$, by Theorem 13.1.

A split, transfer, or fusion operation takes $O(1)$ time.

A search, insertion, or removal of an item visit $O(\log n)$ nodes.

Thus, (2, 4) trees provide for fast dictionary search and update operations. (2, 4) trees also have an interesting relationship to the data structure.

EXAMPLE 13.24. *A certain Professor Amongus claims that the order in which a fixed set of elements is inserted into a binary tree does not matter—the same tree results every time. Give a small example that proves Professor Amongus wrong.*

SOLUTION : There are several solutions. One is to draw the binary search tree created by the input sequence : 9, 5, 12, 7, 13. Now draw the tree created when you switch the 5 and the 7 in the input sequence : 9, 7, 12, 5, 13.

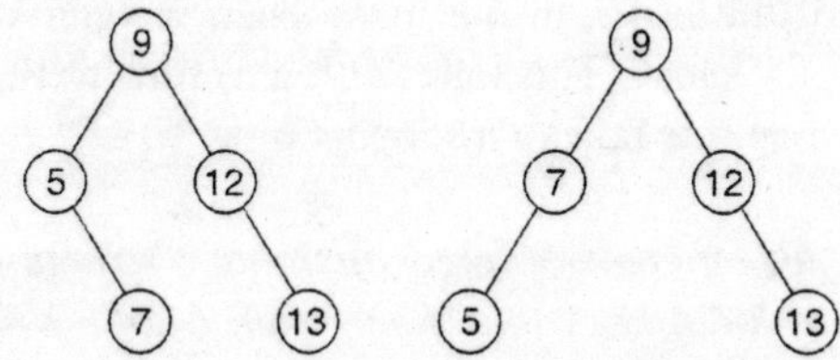

EXAMPLE 13.25. *An alternative way of performing a split at a node v in a (2, 4) tree is to partition v into v′ and v″, with v′ being a 2-node and v″ being a 3-node. Which of the keys k_1, k_2, k_3, or k_4 do we store at v's parent in this case ? Why ?*

SOLUTION : The key k_2 would be stored at v's parent in this case. This is done in order to maintain the ordering of the keys within the tree. By storing k_2 at v's parent, all of the children would still be ordered such that the children to the left of the key are less than the key and those to the right of the key are greater than the key.

EXAMPLE 13.26. *Describe how to perform the operation findAllElements(k) in an ordered dictionary implemented with a binary search tree T, and show that it runs in time $O(h + s)$, where h is the height of T and s is the number of items returned.*

SOLUTION :

```
FindAllElements (k, v, c) :
Input : The search key k, a node of the binary search
                                    tree v and a container c
Output : An insertion containing the found elements
if v is an external node then
       return c.elements()
  if k = key(v) then
       c.addElement (v)
```

```
        return findAllElements (k, T.rightChild (v), c)
        else if k < key (v) then
            return findAllElements (k, T.leftChild (v))
    else
    {we know k > key (v)}
    return findAllElements (k, T.rightChild (v))
```

Note that after finding *k*, if it occurs again, it will be in the left most internal node of the right subtree.

EXAMPLE 13.27. *Suppose that each row of an $n \times n$ array A consists of 1's and 0's such that, in any row of A, all the 1's come before any 0's in that row. Assuming A is already in memory, describe a method running in $O(n \log n)$ time (not $O(n^2)$ time!) for counting the number of 1's in A.*

SOLUTION : To count the number of '1's in *A*, we can do a binary search on each row of *A* to determine the position of the last 1 in that row. Then we can simply sum up these values to obtain the total number of 1's in *A*. This takes $O(\log n)$ time to find the last 1 in each row. Done for each of the *n* rows, then this takes $O(n \log n)$ time.

EXAMPLE 13.28. *Describe an efficient ordered dictionary structure for storing n elements that have an associated set of $k < n$ keys that come from a total order. That is, the set of keys is smaller than the number of elements. Your structure should perform all the ordered dictionary operations in $O(\log k + s)$ expected time, where s is the number of elements returned.*

SOLUTION : To implement an efficient ordered dictionary, we can use a hash table with separate chaining. By using this data structure, we will be able to group together all elements with the same key—they will all be chained together. The chains will also be sorted, so as to help with the ordered structure. In this system, all ordered dictionary operations can be handled in $O(\log k + s)$ expected time - a quick hash to the right spot in the table (constant time) plus a quick search through the chain to find the correct element (which takes $O(\log k)$ time).

EXERCISE

1. It is known that every comparison based algorithm to sort *n* element must make $O(nlgn)$ comparisions in the worst case. What implications does this have on the complexity of initializing a binary search tree with *n* elements?
2. Give the comparision if binary search tree with heap?
3. Give the algorithm for TREE-PREDECESSOR and give its running time.
4. An inorder tree walk of *n* nodes binary search tree can be implemented by finding the minimum element in the tree with TREE-MINIMUM and then making $n - 1$ calls to TREE-SUCCESSOR. Prove that this algo runs in $\Theta(n)$ time.

5. Prove that deletion of two nodes x and y in binary search tree is commutative.
6. Modify the TREE-DELETE algorithm using TREE PREDECESSOR, if possible and its running time.
7. Show that if a node in binary search tree has two children, then its successor has no left child and its predecessor has no right child.
8. What would be worst case time complexity if Inorder Tree walk is used with tree-Insert algo to sort the elements.
9. Implement an algorithm for radix tree and give its runing time.
10. Implement a binary Search tree for equal keys and modified tree-Insert and tree-Delete.

    [Hint : Keep a flag $b[x]$ at node x and based on tree insert at left and false insert at right for key $[z]$ = key $[x]$.
11. Insert items with the following keys (in the given order) into an initially empty binary search tree: 30, 40, 24, 58, 48, 26, 11, 13. Draw the tree after each insertion.

14

OPTIMAL BINARY SEARCH TREES

14.1 OBST

Optimal binary search tree is a tree with lowest expected search time. Let us illustrate this with examples.

Given a fixed set of identifiers, we wish to create a binary searrch tree organization. We may

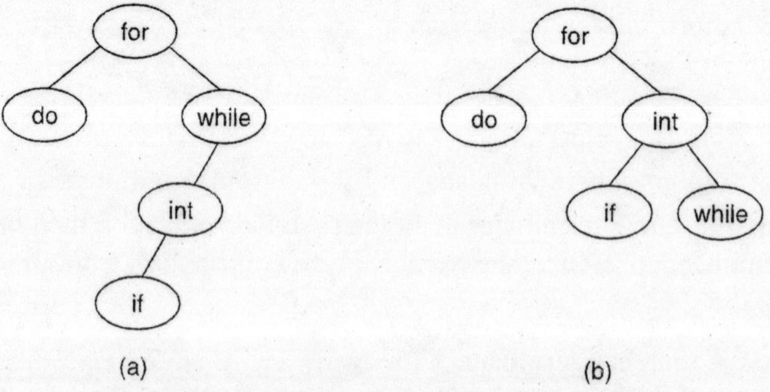

Fig. 14.1. Two possible binary search trees.

expect different binary search trees for the same identifier set to have different performance characteristics. The tree of Figure 14.1(a), in the worst case, requires four comparisons to find an identifier, whereas the tree of Figure 14.1(b) requires only three. On the average the two trees need 12/5 and 11/5 comparisons, respectively. For example, in the case of tree (a), it takes 1, 2, 2, 3, and 4 comparisons, respectively, to find the identifiers **for, do, while, int,** and **if.** Thus the average number of comparisons is $\frac{1+2+2+3+4}{5}=\frac{12}{5}$ and in tree (b) it requires 1, 2, 2, 3, 3 thus average number of comparisions is $\frac{11}{5}$. This calculation assumes that each identifier is searched for with equal probability and that no unsuccessful searches are made.

In a general situation, we can expect different identifiers to be searched for with different frequencies (or probabilities). In addition, we can expect unsuccessful searches also to be made. Let us assume that the given set of identifiers is $\{a_1, a_2, \ldots, a_n\}$ with $a_1 < a_2 < \ldots < a_n$. Let $p(i)$ be the probability with which we search for a_i. Let $q(i)$ be the probability that the identifier x being searched for is such that $a_i < x < a_{i+1}, 0 \le i \le n$ (assume $a_0 = -\infty$ and $a_{n+1} = +\infty$). Then, $\sum_{0 \le i \le n} q(i)$ is the probability of an unsuccessful search. Clearly, $\sum_{1 \le i \le n} p(i) + \sum_{0 \le i \le n} q(i) = 1$. Given this data, we wish to construct an optimal binary search tree for $\{a_1, a_2, \ldots, a_n\}$. First, of course, we must be precise about what we mean by an optimal binary search tree.

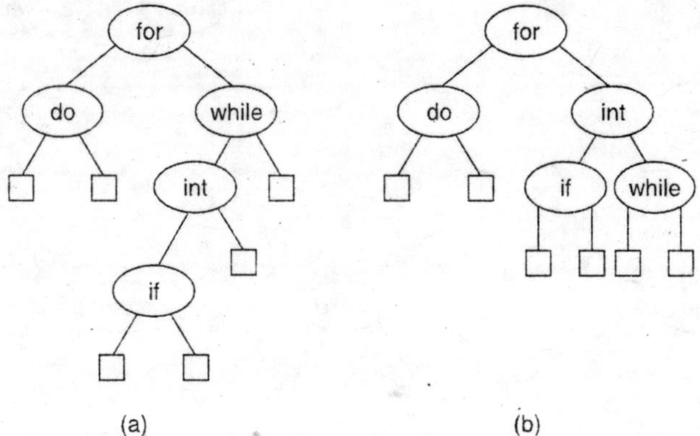

Fig. 14.2. Possible BST for identifier set ***{for, do, while, int, if}***

In obtaining a cost function for binary search trees, it is useful to add a fictitious node in place of every empty subtree in the search tree. Such nodes, called external nodes, are drawn square in Figure 14.2. All other nodes are internal nodes. If a binary search tree represents n identifiers, then there will be exactly n internal nodes and $n+1$ (fictitious) external nodes. Every internal node represents a point where a successful search may terminate. Every external node represents a point where an unsuccessful search may terminate.

If a successful search terminates at an internal node at level l, then l iterations of the **while** loop of BST are needed. Hence, the expected cost contribution from the internal node for a_i is $p(i)$ * level (a_i).

Unsuccessful searches terminate with $t = 0$ (i.e., at an external node) in algorithm. The identifiers not in the binary search tree can be partitioned into $n+1$ equivalence classes $E_i, 0 \le i \le n$. The classes E_0 contains all identifiers x such that $x < a_1$. The class E_i contains all identifiers x such that $a_i < x < a_{i+1}, 1 \le i < n$. The class E_n contains all identifiers $x, x > a_n$. It is easy to see that for all identifiers in the same class E_i, the search terminates at the same external node. For identifiers in different E_i the search terminates at different external nodes. If the failure node for E_i is at level l, then only $l - 1$ iterations of the **while** loop are made. Hence, the cost contribution of this node is $q(i) * (level\ (E_i) - 1)$.

The preceding discussions leads to the following formula for the expected cost of a binary search tree:

$$\sum_{1 \le i \le n} p(i) * level\ (a_i) + \sum_{0 \le i \le n} q(i) * (level\ (E_i) - 1) \qquad \ldots(14.1)$$

We define an optimal binary search tree for the identifier set $\{a_1, a_2, \ldots, a_n\}$ to be a binary search tree for which (14.1) is minimum.

EXAMPLE 14.1. *The possible binary search trees for the identifier set $(a_1, a_2, a_3) = (do, if, while)$ are given if Figure 14.3. With equal probabilities $p(i) = q(i) = 1/7$ for all i, we have*

cost(tree) a) = 15/7 *cost*(tree b) = 13/7

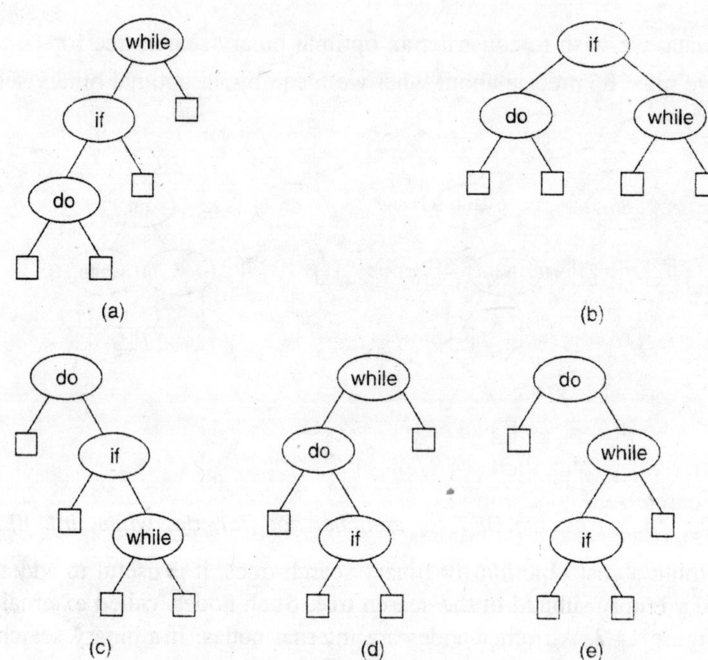

Fig. 14.3. Possible BST identifier set ***{do, if, while}***

cost(tree c) = 15/7 *cost*(tree d) = 15/7
cost(tree e) = 15/7

As expected, tree b is optimal. With $p(1) = .5$, $p(2) = .1$, $p(3) = .05$, $q(0) = .15$ $q(1) = .1$, $q(2) = .05$ and $q(3) = .05$ we have

cost(tree a) = 2.65 *cost*(tree b) = 1.9
cost(tree c) = 1.5 *cost*(tree d) = 2.05
cost (tree e) = 1.6

For instance, *cost*(tree a) can be computed as follows. The contribution from successful searches is $3 * 0.5 + 2 * 0.1 + 0.05 = 1.75$ and the contribution from unsuccessful searches is $3 * 0.15 + 3 * 0.1 + 2 * 0.05 + 0.05 = 0.90$. All the other costs can also be calculated in a similar manner. Tree c is optimal with this assignment of p's and q's.

To apply dynamic programming (see chapter 18) to the problem of obtaining an optimal binary search tree, we need to view the construction of such a tree as the result of a sequence of decisions and then observe that the principle of optimality holds when applied to the problem state resulting from a decision. A possible approach to this would be to make a decision as to which of the a_i's should be assigned to the root node of the tree. If we choose a_k, then it is clear that the internal nodes for $a_1, a_2, \ldots, a_{k-1}$ as well as the external nodes for the classes $E_0, E_1, \ldots, E_{k-1}$ will lie in the left subtree l of the root. The remaining nodes will be in the right subtree r. Define

$$cost\,(l) = \sum_{i \le i < k} p(i) * \text{level}\,(a_i) + \sum_{0 \le i < k} q(i) * (\text{level}\,(E_i) - 1)$$

and $$cost\,(r) = \sum_{k < i \le n} p(i) * \text{level}\,(a_i) + \sum_{k < i \le n} q(i) * (\text{level}\,(E_i) - 1)$$

In both cases the level is measured by regarding the root of the respective subtree to be at level 1.

Fig. 14.4. An optimal BST with root a_k.

Using $w(i, j)$ to represent the sum $q(i) + \sum_{l=i+1}^{j} (q(l) + p(l))$, we obtain the following as the expected cost of the search tree (Figure 14.4) :

$$p(k) = cost(l) + cost(r) + w(0, k-1) + w(k, n) \qquad \ldots(14.2)$$

If the tree is optimal, then (14.2) must be minimum. Hence $cost(l)$ must be minimum over all binary search trees containing $a_1, a_2, ,,,. a_{k-1}$ and $E_0, E_1, \ldots, E_{k-1}$. Similarly $cost\,(r)$ must be minimum. If we use $c(i, j)$ to represent the cost of an optimal binary search tree t_{ij} containing $a_{i+1}, \ldots, a_j$ and $E_i, \ldots, E_j$, then for the tree to be optimal, we must have $cost(l) = c(0, k-1)$ and $cost\,(r) = c(k, n)$. In addition, k must be chosen such that

$$p(k) = c(0, k-1) + c(k, n) + w(0, k-1) + w(k, n)$$

is minimum. Hence, for $c(0, n)$ we obtain

$$c(0, n) = \min_{1 \le k \le n} \{c(0, k-1) + c(k, n) + p(k) + w(0, k-1) + w(k, n)\} \qquad \ldots(14.3)$$

We can generalize (14.3) to obtain for any $c(i, j)$

$$c(i, j) = \min_{i < k \le j} \{c(i, k-1) + c(k, j) + p(k) + w(i, k-1) + w(k, j)\}$$

$$c(i, j) = \min_{i < k \le j} \{c(i, k-1) + c(k, j)\} + w(i, j) \qquad \ldots(14.4)$$

Equation 14.4 can be solved for $c(0, n)$ by first computing all $c(i, j)$ such that $j - 1 = 1$ (note $c(i, i) = 0$ and $w(i, i) = q(i)$, $0 \le i \le n$). Next we can compute all $c(i, j)$ such that $j - i = 2$, then all $c(i, j)$ with $j - i = 3$, and so on. If during this computation we record the root $r(i, j)$ of each tree t_{ij}, then an optimal binary search tree can be constructed from these $r(i, j)$. Note that $r(i, j)$ is the value of k that minimizes (14.4).

EXAMPLE 14.2. *Let $n = 4$ and $(a_1, a_2, a_3, a_4) =$ (do, if, int, while). Let $p(1 : 4) = (3, 3, 1, 1)$ and $q(0 : 4) = (2, 3, 1, 1, 1)$. The p's and q's have been multiplied by 16 for convenience. Initially, we have $w(i, i) = q(i)$, $c(i, i) = 0$ and $r(i, i) = 0$, $0 \le i \le 4$. Using Equation 14.4 and the observation $w(i, j) = p(j) + q(j) + w(i, j, -1)$, we get*

$$w(0, 1) = p(1) + q(1) + w(0, 0) = 8$$
$$c(0, 1) = w(0, 1) + \min\{c(0, 0) + c(1, 1)\} = 8$$
$$r(0, 1) = 1$$
$$w(1, 2) = p(2) + q(2) + w(1, 1) = 7$$
$$c(1, 2) = w(1, 2) + \min\{c(1, 1) + c(2, 2)\} = 7$$
$$r(0, 2) = 2$$
$$w(2, 3) = p(3) + q(3) + w(2, 2) = 3$$
$$c(2, 3) = w(2, 3) + \min\{c(2, 2) + c(3, 3)\} = 3$$
$$r(2, 3) = 3$$
$$w(3, 4) = p(4) + q(4) + w(3, 3) = 3$$
$$c(3, 4) = w(3, 4) + \min\{c(3, 3) + c(4, 3)\} = 3$$
$$r(3, 4) = 4$$

Knowing $w(i, i + 1)$ and $c(i, i + 1)$, $0 \le i < 4$, we can again use Equation 14.4 to compute $w(i, i + 2)$, $c(i, i + 2)$, and $r(i, i + 2)$, $0 \le i < 3$. This process can be repeated until $w(0, 4)$, $c(0, 4)$ and $r(0, 4)$ are obtained. The table of Figure 14.5 shows the results of this computation. The box in row i and column j shows the values of $w(j, j + i)$, $c(j, j + i)$ and $r(j, j + i)$ respectively. The computation is carried out by row from row 0 to row 4. From the table we see that $c(0, 4) = 32$ is the minimum cost of a binary search tree for (a_1, a_2, a_3, a_4). The root of tree t_{04} is a_2. Hence, the left subtree is t_{01} and the right subtree t_{24}. Tree t_{01} has root a_1 and subtree t_{00} and t_{11}. Tree t_{24} has root a_3; its left subtree is t_{22} and its right subtree t_{34}. Thus, with the data in the table it is possible to reconstruct t_{04}. Figure 14.6 shows t_{04}.

	0	1	2	3	4
0	$w_{00} = 2$ $c_{00} = 0$ $r_{00} = 0$	$w_{11} = 3$ $c_{11} = 0$ $r_{11} = 0$	$w_{22} = 1$ $c_{22} = 0$ $r_{22} = 0$	$w_{33} = 1$ $c_{33} = 0$ $r_{33} = 0$	$w_{44} = 1$ $c_{44} = 0$ $r_{44} = 0$
1	$w_{01} = 8$ $c_{01} = 8$ $r_{01} = 1$	$w_{12} = 7$ $c_{12} = 7$ $r_{12} = 2$	$w_{23} = 3$ $c_{23} = 3$ $r_{23} = 3$	$w_{34} = 3$ $c_{34} = 3$ $r_{34} = 4$	
2	$w_{02} = 12$ $c_{02} = 19$ $r_{02} = 1$	$w_{13} = 9$ $c_{13} = 12$ $r_{13} = 2$	$w_{24} = 5$ $c_{24} = 8$ $r_{24} = 3$		
3	$w_{03} = 14$ $c_{03} = 25$ $r_{03} = 2$	$w_{14} = 11$ $c_{14} = 19$ $r_{14} = 2$			
4	$w_{04} = 16$ $c_{04} = 32$ $r_{04} = 2$				

Fig. 14.5. Computation of c(0, 4), w(0, 4) and r(0, 4).

The above example illustrates how Equation 14.4 can be used to determine the c's and r's and also how to reconstruct t_{0n} knowing the r's. Let us examine the complexity of this procedure to evaluate the c's and r's. The evaluation procedure described in the above example requires us to compute $c(i, j)$ for $(j - i) = 1, 2, \ldots, n$ in that order. When $j - 1 = m$, there are $n - m + 1$ $c(i, j)$'s to compute. The computation of each of these $c(i, j)$'s requires us to find the minimum of m quantities (see Equation 14.4). Hence, each such $c(i, j)$ can be computed in time $O(m)$. The total time for all $c(i, j)$'s with $j - i = m$ is therefore $O(nm - m^2)$. The total time to evaluate all the $c(i, j)$'s and $r(i, j)$'s is therefore

$$\sum_{1 \le m \le n} (nm - m^2) = O(n^3)$$

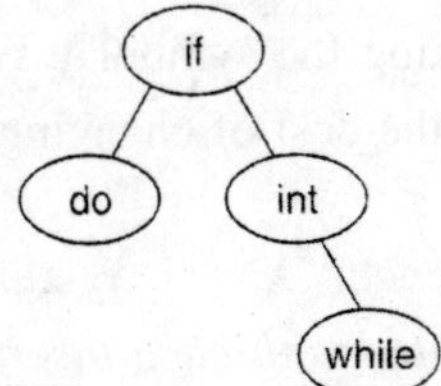

Fig. 14.6. Optimal search tree for Ex. 14.2.

```
OBST (p, q, n)
for i ← 0 to n - 1 do
    w[i, i] ← q[i]; r[i, i] ← 0; c[i, i] ← 0 . 0;
    w[i, i + 1] ← q[i] + q[i + 1] + p[i + 1];
```

```
    r[i, i + 1] ← i + 1;
    c[i, i + 1] ← q[i] + q[i + 1] + p[i + 1];
  w[n, n] ← q[n]; r[n, n] ← 0; c[n, n] ← 0 . 0;
  for m ← 2 to n do / / Find optimal trees with m nodes.
    for i ← 0 to n - m do
        j ← i + m;
        w[i, j] ← w[i, j - 1] + p[j] + q[j];
        k ← Find (c, r, i, j);
        c[i, j] ← w[i, j] + c[i, k - 1] + c[k, j];
        r[i, j] ← k;
  weire (c[0, n], w[0, n], r[0, n]);

  Algorithm Find (c, r, i, j)
  min ← ∞;
  for m ← r[i, j - 1] to r[i + 1, j] do
    if (c[i, m - 1] + c[m, j]) < min then
        min ← c[i, m - 1] + c[m, j]; 1 ← m;
  return 1;
```

This finds a minimum-cost binary search tree.

14.2 String Editing

We have two strings $X = x_1, x_2, \ldots, x_n$ and $Y = y_1, y_2, \ldots, y_m$, where x_i, $1 \le i \le n$, and y_j, $1 \le j \le m$, are members of a finite set of symbols known as the *alphabet.* We want to transform X into Y using a sequence of *edit operations* on X. The permissible edit operations are insert, delete, and change (a symbol of X into another), and there is a cost associated with performing each. The cost of a sequence of operations is the sum of the costs of the individual operations in the sequence. The problem of string editing is to identify a minimum-cost sequence of edit operations that will transform X into Y.

Let $D(x_i)$ be the cost of deleting the symbol x_i from X, $T(y_j)$ be the cost of inserting the symbol y_j into X, and $C(x_i, y_j)$ be the cost of changing the symbol x_i of X into y_j.

EXAMPLE 14.3. *Consider the sequences* $X = x_1, x_2, x_3, x_4, x_5 = a, a, b, a, b$ *and* $Y = y_1, y_2, y_3, y_4 = b, a, b, b$. *Let the cost associated with each insertion and deletion be 1 (for any symbol). Also let the cost of changing any symbol to any other symbol be 2. One possible way of transforming X into Y is delete each* x_i, $1 \le i \le 5$, *and insert each* y_j, $1 \le j \le 4$. *The total cost of this edit sequence is 9. Another possible edit sequence is delete* x_1 *and* x_2 *and insert* y_4 *at the end of string X. The total cost is only 3.*

SOLUTION : A solution to the string editing problem consists of a sequence of decisions, one for each edit operations. Let ε be a minimum-cost edit sequence for transforming X into Y. The first operation, O, in ε is delete, insert, or change. If $\varepsilon' = \varepsilon - \{O\}$ and X' is the result of applying O on X, then ε' should be a minimum-cost edit sequence that transforms X' into Y. Thus the principle of optimality holds for this problem. A dynamic programming solution for this problem can be obtained as follows. Define *cost* (i, j) to be the minimum cost of any edit sequence for transforming $x_1, x_2, \ldots, x_i$ into $y_1, y_2, \ldots, y_j$ (for $0 \le i \le n$ and $0 \le j \le m$). Compute *cost* (i, j) for each i and j. Then *cost* (n, m) is the cost of an optimal edit sequence.

For $i = j = 0$, *cost* $(i, j) = 0$, since the two sequences are identical (and empty). Also, if $j = 0$ and $i > 0$, we can transform X into Y by a sequence of deletes. Thus, $cost\ (i, 0) = cost\ (i-1, 0) + D\ (x_i)$. Similarly, if $i = 0$ and $j > 0$, we get $cost\ (0, j) = cost\ (0, j-1) + I(y_j)$. If $i \ne 0$, $x_1, x_2, \ldots, x_i$ can be transformed into $y_1, y_2, \ldots, y_j$ in one of three ways:

1. Transform $x_1, x_2, \ldots, x_{i-1}$ into $y_1, y_2, \ldots, y_j$ using a minimum-cost edit sequence and then delete x_i. The corresponding cost is $cost\ (i-1, j) + D\ (x_i)$.
2. Transform $x_1, x_2, \ldots, x_{i-1}$ into $y_1, y_2, \ldots, y_{j-1}$ using a minimum-cost edit sequence and then change the symbol x_i to y_j. The associated cost is $cost\ (i-1, j-1) + C\ (x_i, y_j)$.
3. Transform $x_1, x_2, \ldots, x_i$ into $y_1, y_2, \ldots, y_{j-1}$ using a minimum-cost edit sequence and then insert y_j. This corresponds to a cost of $cost\ (i, j-1) + I\ (y_j)$.

The minimum cost of any edit sequence that transform $x_1, x_2, \ldots, x_i$ into $y_1, y_2, \ldots, y_j$ (for $i > 0$ and $j > 0$) is the minimum of the above three costs, according to the principle of optimality. Therefore, we arrive at the following recurrence equation for *cost* (i, j) :

$$cost\ (i, j) = \begin{cases} 0 & i = j = 0 \\ cost(i-1, 0) + D\ (x_i) & j = 0, i > 0 \\ cost\ (0, j-1) + I\ (y_j) & i = 0, j > 0 \\ cost'\ (i, j) & i > 0, j > 0 \end{cases} \tag{5.13}$$

where $$cost'\ (i, j) = \min \begin{cases} cost\ (i-1, j) + D\ (x_i), \\ cost\ (i-1, j-1) + C\ (x_i, y_j), \\ cost\ (i, j-1) + I\ (y_j) \end{cases}$$

We have to compute *cost* (i, j) for all possible values of i and j $(0, \le i \le n$ and $0 \le j \le m)$. There are $(n + 1)\ (m + 1)$ such values. These values can be computed in the form of a table, M, where each row of M corresponds to a particular value of i and each column of M corresponds to a specific value of j. $M\ (i, j)$ stores the value *cost* (i, j). The zeroth row can be computed first since it correspnods to performing a series of insertions. Likewise the zeroth column can also be computed. After this, one could compute the entries of M in row-major order, starting from the first row. Rows should be processed in the order 1, 2, ... , n. Entries in any row are computed in increasing order of column number.

The entries of M can also be computed in column-major order, starting from the first column. Looking at Equations 14.5, we see that each entry of M takes only $O(1)$ time to compute. Therefore the whole algorithm takes $O\ (mn)$ time. The value *cost* (n, m) is the final answer we are interested in. Having computed all the entries of M, a minimum edit sequence can be obtained by a simple backward trace from *cost* (n, m). This backward trace is enabled by recording which of the three options for $i > 0, j > 0$ yielded the minimum cost for each i and j.

EXAMPLE 14.4. *Consider the string editing problem of Example 14.3. X = a, a, b, a, b and Y = b, a, b, b. Each insertion and deletion has a unit cost and a change costs 2 units. For the cases i = 0, j > 1 and j = 0, i > 1, cost (i, j) can be computed first (Figure 14.6). Let us compute the rest of the entries in row-major order. The next entry to be computed is cost* (1, 1).

SOLUTION : $cost\ (1, 1) = \min \{cost\ (0, 1) + D\ (x_1), cost\ (0, 0) + C\ (x_1, y_1), cost\ (1, 0) + I\ (y_1)\}$

$= \min \{2, 2, 2\} = 2$

Next is computed *cost* (1, 2).

$cost\ (1, 2) = \min \{cost\ (0, 2) + D\ (x_1), cost\ (0, 1) + C\ (x_1, y_2), cost\ (1, 1) + I\ (y_2)\}$

$= \min \{3, 1, 3\} = 1$

The rest of the entries are computed similarly. Figure 14.6 displays the whole table. The value *cost* (5, 4) = 3. One possible minimum-cost edit sequence is delete x_1, delete x_2, and insert y_4. Another possible minimum cost edit sequence is change x_1 to y_2 and delete x_4.

i ↓ *j* →	0	1	2	3	4
0	0	1	2	3	4
1	1	2	1	2	3
2	2	3	2	3	4
3	3	2	3	2	3
4	4	3	2	3	4
5	5	4	3	2	3

Fig. 14.7. Cost table of Ex. 14.4.

EXERCISE

1. Show that computing time of algorithm OBST is $O(n^2)$.
2. Write an algorithm to construct the OBST given the roots $r(i, j), 0 \le i < j \le n$. Show that this can be done in time $O(n)$.

❑❑❑

15

AVL TREES AND SPLAYING

15.1 AVL Trees

One classical method has been proposed by Adel'son-Vel'skii and Landis, which is commemorated in the name of the tree modified with this method: the AVL tree.

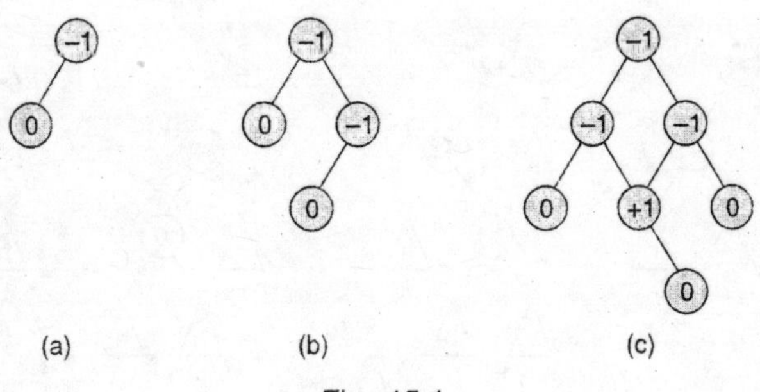

Fig. 15.1.

An *AVL tree* (originally called an *admissible tree*) is one in which the height of left and right subtrees of every node differ by at most one. For example, all the trees in figure 15.1 are AVL trees. Numbers in the nodes indicate the *balance factors* which are the differences between the heights of the left and right subtrees. A balance factor is the height of the right subtree minus the height of the left subtree. For an AVL tree, all balance factors should be + 1,0, or – 1. Notice that the definition of the AVL tree is the same as the definition of the balanced tree. However, the concept of the AVLtree always implicitly includes the techniques for balancing the tree. Moreover, the technique for balancing AVL trees does not guarantee that the resulting tree is perfectly balanced.

The definition of an AVL tree indicates that the minimum number of nodes in a tree is determined by the recurrence equation

$$AVL_h = AVL_{h-1} + AVL_{h-2} + 1$$

where $AVL_o = 0$ and $AVL_o = 1$ are the initial conditions[1]. As shown by Adel'son-Vel'skii and landis, this formula leads to the following bounds on the height h of an AVL tree depending on the number of nodes n.

$$lg(n+1) \leq h < 1.44lg\ (n+2) - 0.328$$

Therefore, h is bounded by $O\ (lg\ n)$; the worst case search requires $O\ (lg\ n)$ comparisons. For a perfectly balanced binary tree of the same height, $h = [lg(n+1)]$.

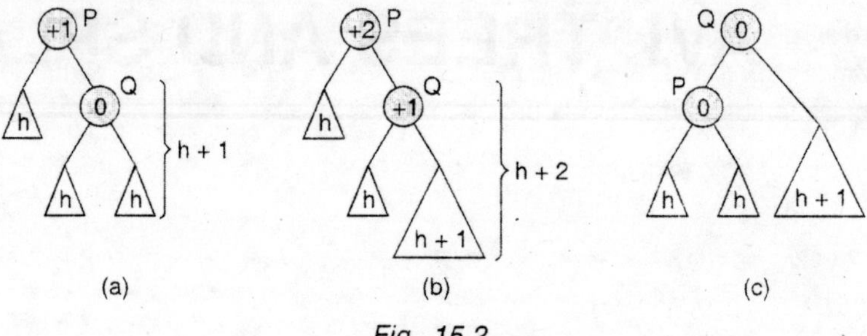

Fig. 15.2.

If the balance factor of any node in an AVL tree becomes less than – 1 or greater than 1, the tree has to be balanced. An AVL tree can become out of balance in four situations, but only two of them need to be analyzed ; the remaining two are symmetrical. The first case, the results of inserting a node in the right subtree of the right child, is illustrated in Figure 15.2. The heights

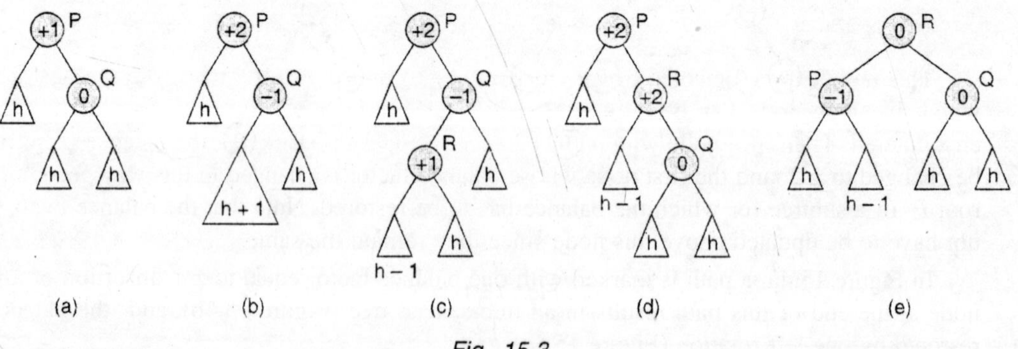

Fig. 15.3.

1 Numbers generated by this recurrence formula are called Leonardo numbers.

of the participating subtrees are indicated within these subtrees. In the AVL tree in Figure 15.2a, a node is inserted somewhere in the right subtree of Q (Figure 15.2b), which disturbs the balance of the trees P. In this case, the problem can be easily rectified by rotating node Q about its parent P(Figure 15.2c) so that the balance factor of both P and Q becomes zero, which is even better than at the outset.

The second case, the result of inserting a node in the left subtree of the right chlid, is more complex. A node is inserted into the tree in Figure 15.3a the resulting tree is shown in Figure 15.3b and in more detail in Figure 15.3c. To bring the tree back into balance, a double rotation is performed. The balance of the tree P is restored by rotating R about node Q (Figure 15.3b) and then by rotating R again, this time about node P (Figure 15.3d).

In these two cases, the tree P is considered a stand-alone tree. However, P can be part of a larger AVL tree; it can be a child of some other node in the tree. If a node is entered into the tree and the balance of P is disturbed and then restored, does extra work need to be done to the predecessor(s) of P? Fortunately not. Note that the heights of the trees in Figures 15.2c and 15.3e resulting from the rotations are the same as the heights of the trees before insertion (Figures 15.2a and 15.3a) and are equal to $h + 2$. This means that the balance factor of the parent of the new root (Q in Figure 15.2c and R in Figure 15.3e) remains the same as it was before the insertion.and the changes made to the subtree P are sufficient to restore the balance factor becomes entire AVL tree. The problem is finding a node P for which the balance factor becomes unacceptable after a node has been inserted into the tree.

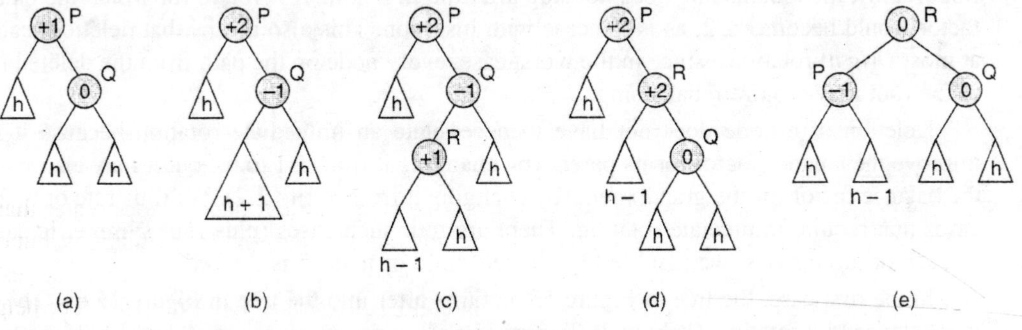

Fig. 15.4.

This node can be detected by moving up toward the root of the tree from the position in which the new node has been inserted and by updating the balance factors of the nodes encountered. Then, if a node with $a \pm 1$ balance factor is encountered, the balance factor may be changed to ± 2, and the first node whose balance factor is changed in this way becomes the root P of a subtree for which the balance has to be restored. Note that the balance factors do not have to be updated above this node since they remain the same.

In Figure 15.4a, a path is marked with one balance factor equal to ± 1. Insertion of a new node at the end of this path results in an unbalanced tree (Figure 15.4b), and the balance is restored by one left rotation (Figure 15.4c).

However, if the balance factors on the path from the newly inserted node to the root of the tree are all zero, all the them have to be updated, but no rotation is needed for any of the encountered nodes. In Figure 15.5a, the AVL tree has a path of all zero balance factors. After a node has been appended to the end of this path (Figure 15.5b), no changes are made in the tree except for updating the balance factors of all nodes along this path.

Deletion may be more time-consuming than insertion. First, we apply delete-ByCopying () to delete a node. This technique allows us to reduce the problem of deleting a node with two descendants to deleting a node with at most one descendant.

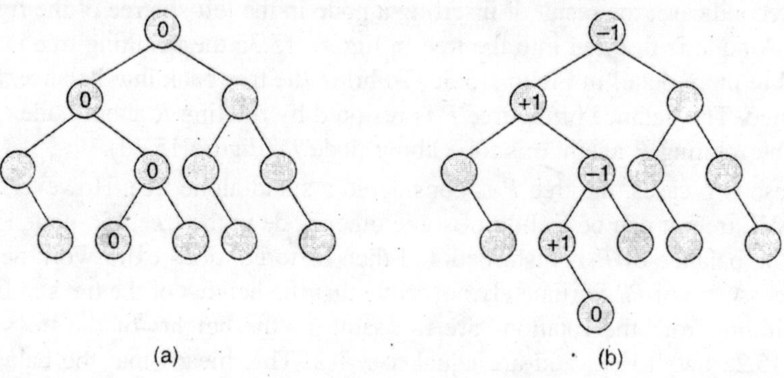

Fig. 15.5.

After a node has been deleted from the tree, balance factors are updated from the parent of the deleted node up to the root. For each node in this path whose balance factor becomes ± 2, a single or double rotation has to be performed to restore the balance of the tree. Importantly, the rebalancing does not stop after the first node P is found for which the balance factor would become ± 2, as is the case with insertion. This also means that deletion leads to at most $O(lg\ n)$ rotations, since in the worst case, every node on the path from the deleted node to the root may require rebalancing.

Deletion of a node does not have to necessitate an immediate rotation because it may improve the balance factor for its parent (by changing it from ± 1 to 0), but it may also worsen the balance factor for the grandparent (by changing it from ± 1 to ± 2). We illustrate only those cases that require immediate rotation. There are four such cases (plus four symmetric cases). In each of these cases, we assume that the left child of node P is deteted.

In the first case, the tree in Figure 15.6a turns after into the tree in Figure 15.6b. The tree is rebalanced by rotating Q about P (Figure 15.6c). In the second case, P has a balance factor equal to ± 1, and its right subtree Q has a balance factor equal to O (Figure 15.6d). After deleting a node in the left subtree of P (Figure 15.6e), the tree is rebalanced by the same rotation as in the first case (Figure 15.6f). In this way, cases one and two can be processed together in an implementation after checking that the balance factor of Q is + 1 or 0. If Q is – 1, we have two other cases, which are more complex. In the third case, the left subtree R of Q has a balance factor equal to – 1 (Figure 15.6g). To rebalance the tree, first R is rotated about Q and then about P (Figures 15.6h-i). The fourth case differs from the third in that R 's balance factor equals + 1, (Figure 15.6j), in which case the same two rotations are needed to restore the balance factor of P (Figures 15.6k-l). Cases three and four can be processed together in a program processing AVL trees.

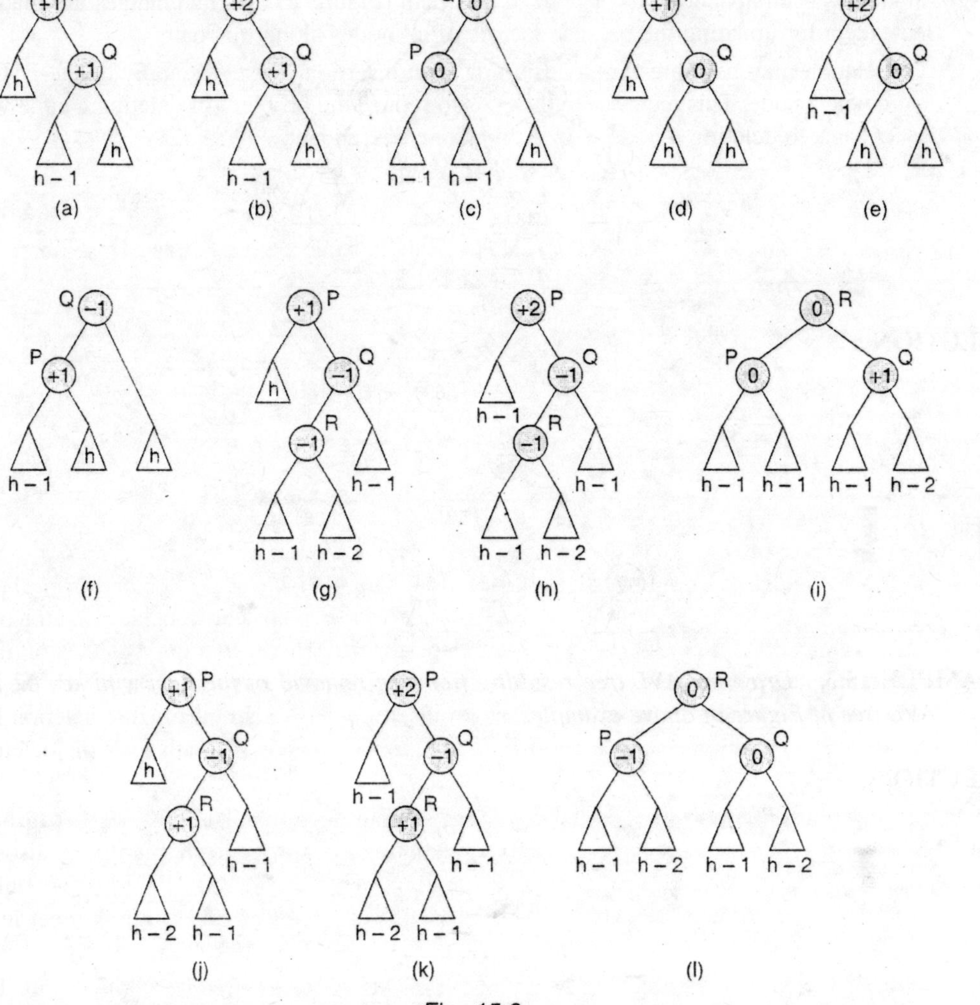

Fig. 15.6.

EXAMPLE 15.1. *Professor Amongus claims that the order in which a fixed set of elements is inserted into an AVL tree does not matter—the same AVL tree results every time. Give a small example that proves that Professor Amongus is still wrong.*

SOLUTION : There are several solutions. One is to draw the AVL tree created by the input sequence : 9, 5, 12, 7, 13. Now draw the tree created when you switch the 5 and the 7 in the input sequence 9, 7, 12, 5, 13.

EXAMPLE 15.2. *Draw the AVL tree resulting from the insertion of an item with key 52 into the AVL tree of Figure below.*

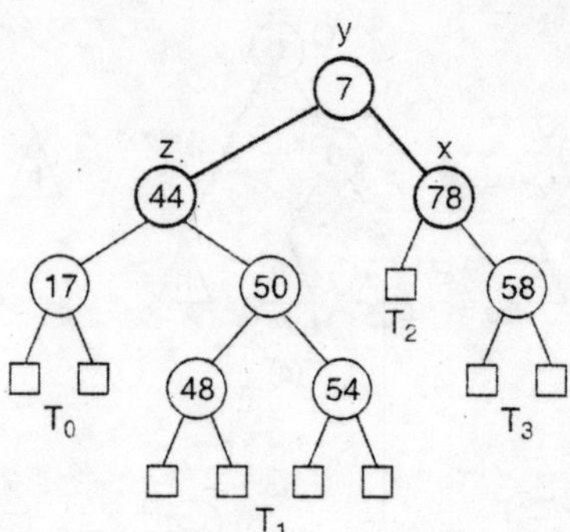

SOLUTION :

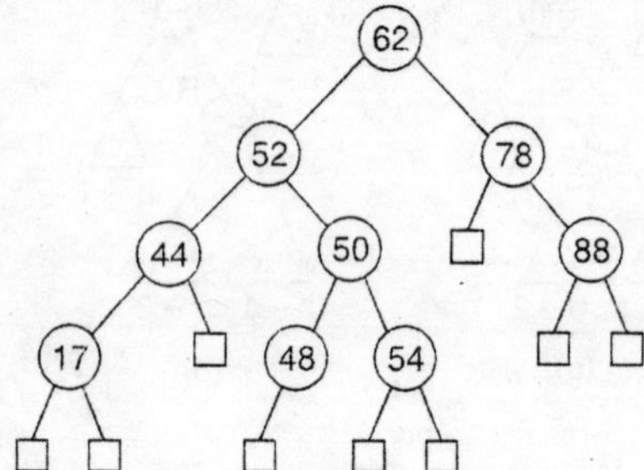

EXAMPLE 15.3. *Draw the AVL tree resulting from the removal of the item with key 62 from the AVL tree of Figure of above example.*

SOLUTION :

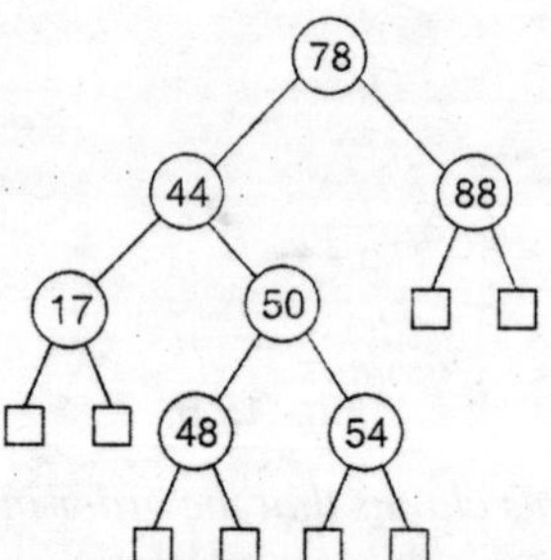

EXAMPLE 15.4. *Draw an example on an AVL tree such that a single removeElement operation could require* Θ (log *n*) *trinode restructurings (or rotations) from a leaf to the root in order to restore the height-balance property, (use triangles to represent subtrees that are not affected by this operation).*

SOLUTION :

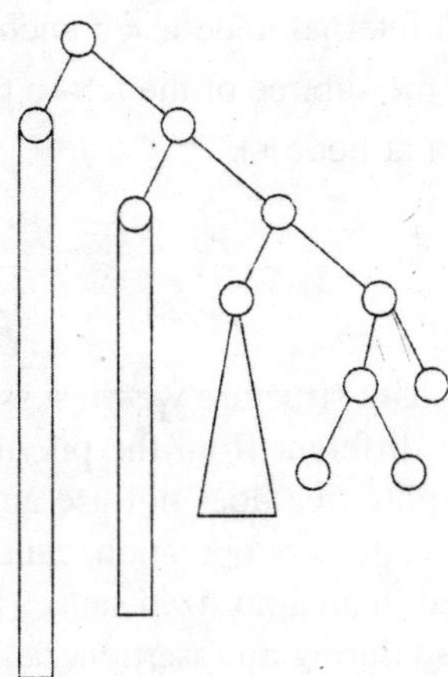

EXAMPLE 15.5. *Let D be an ordered dictionary with n items implemented by means of an AVL tree. Show how to implement the following operation on D in time O(log n + s), where s is the size of the iterator returned :*

FindAllInRange (k_1, k_2) *: Return an iterator of all the elements in D with key k such that* $k_1 \le k \le k_2$.

SOLUTION : Search for k_1 and then k_2, each while marking the path down to that node. Observe that all the nodes between the path towards k_1 and k_2 are within the specified range. A modified DFS can be performed, using the given paths as boundaries and starting at the intersection of the two paths, to enumerate all the elements inclusively between k_1 and k_2.

EXAMPLE 15.6. *Let D be an ordered dictionary with n items implemented with an AVL tree. Show how to implement the following method for D in time O (log n) :*

CountAllInRange (k_1, k_2) *: Compute and return the number of items in D with key k such that* $k_1 \le k \le k_2$.

Note that this method returns a single integer.

[**Hint :** You will need to extend the AVL tree becomes unbalanced after operation removeAboveExternal is performed within the execution of a removeElement dictionary operation.]

SOLUTION : For each node of the tree, maintain the size of the corresponding subtree, defined as the number of internal nodes in that subtree. While performing the search operation in both the insertion and deletion, the subtree sizes can be either incremented or decremented. During the rebalancing, care must be taken to update the subtree sizes of the three nodes involved (labeled *a*, *b* and *c* by the algorithm).

To calculate the number of nodes in a range (k_1, k_2), search for both k_1 and k_2, and let P_1 and P_2 be the associated search paths. Call v the last node common to the two paths. Tracerse path P_1 from v to k_1. For each internal node $w \ne v$ encountered, if the right child of w is in not in P_1, add one plus the size of the subtree of the child to the current sum. Similarly, traverse path P_2 from v to k_2. For each internal node $w \neq z$ encountered, if the left child of w is in not in P_2, add one plus the size of the subtree of the left to the current sum. Finally, add one to the current sum (for the key stored at node v).

15.2 Splay Trees

The final balanced search tree data structure we discuss in this chapter is the **splay tree.** This structure is conceptually quite different from the previously discussed balanced search trees (AVL and (2, 4) trees), for a splay tree does not use any explicit rules to enforce its balance. Instead, of applies a certain move-to-root operation, called **splaying** after every access, in order to keep the search tree balanced in an amortized sense. The splaying operation is performed at the bottom-most node x reached during an insertion, deletion, or even a search. The surprising thing about splaying is that it allows us to guarantee amortized running times for insertions, deletions, and searches that are logarithmic. The structure of a **splay tree** is simply a binary search tree T. In fact, there are no additional height, balance, or color labels that we associate with the nodes of this tree.

Splaying

Given an internal node x of a binary search tree T, we **splay** x by moving x to the root of T through a sequence of restructurings. The particular restructurings we perform are important, for it is not sufficient to move x to the root of T by just any sequence of restructurings. The specific operation we perform to move x up depends upon the relative positions of x, its parent y, and (if it exists) x's grandparent z. There are three cases that we consider.

SA : The node x and its parent y are both left or right children (see Fig. 15.7). We replace z by x, making y a child of x and z a child of y, while maintaining the inorder relationships of the nodes in T.

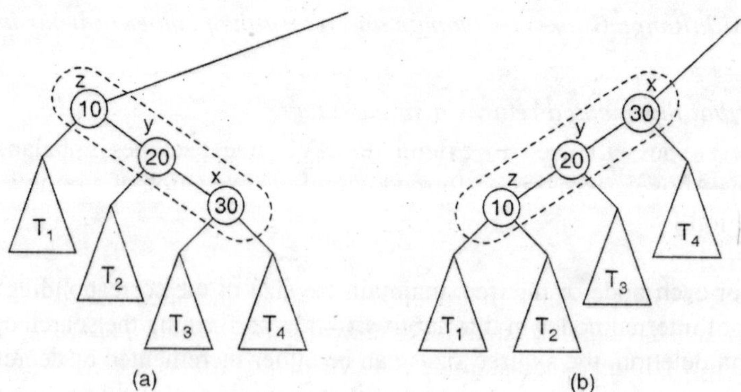

Fig. 15.7. SA : (a) before; (b) after. There is another symmetric configuration where x and y are left children.

SB : One of x and y is a left child and the other is a right child. (See Figure 15.8). In this case, we replace z by x and make x have as its children the nodes y and z, while maintaining the inorder relationships of the nodes in T.

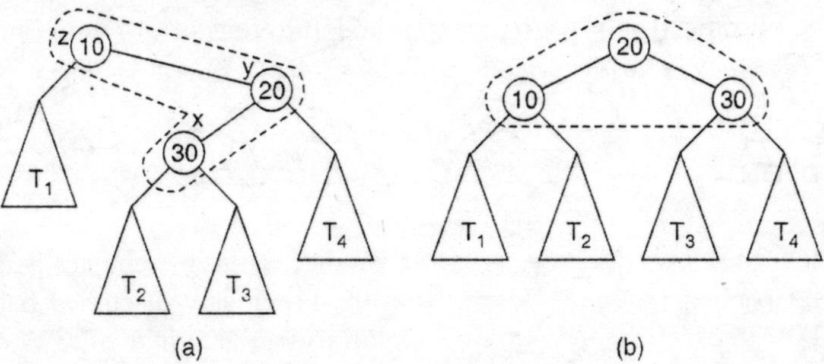

Fig. 15.8. SB : (a) before; (b) after. There is another symmetric configuration where x is a right child and y is a left child.

SC : x does not have a grandparent (or we are not considering x's grandparent for some reason). See (Figure 15.9). In this case, we rotate x over y, making x's children be the node y and one of x's former children w, so as to maintain the relative inorder relationships of the nodes in T.

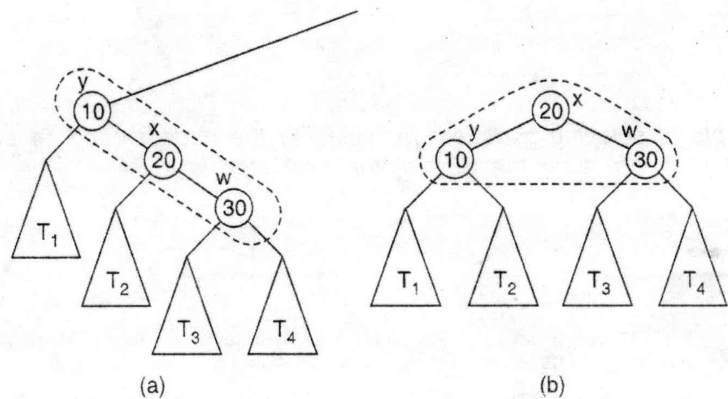

Fig. 15.9. SC : (a) before; (b) after. There is another symmetric configuration where x are left children.

We perform a SA or SB when x has a grandparent, and we perform a SC when x has a parent but not a grandparent. A **splaying** step consists of repeating these restructurings at x until x becomes the root of T. Note that this is not the same as a sequence of simple rotations that brings x to the root. An example of the splaying of a node is shown in Figure 15.10 and 15.11.

After a SA or SB, the depth of x decreases by two, and after a SC the depth of x decreases by one. Thus, if x has depth d, splaying x consists of a sequence of $\lfloor d/2 \rfloor$ Sa and/or SB, plus one final SC if d is odd. Since a single SA, SB or SC affects a constant number of nodes, it can be done in $O(1)$ time. Thus, splaying a node x in a binary search tree T takes time $O(d)$, where d is the depth of x in T. In other words, the time for performing a splaying step for a node x is asymptotically the same as the time needed just to reach that node in a top-down search from the root of T.

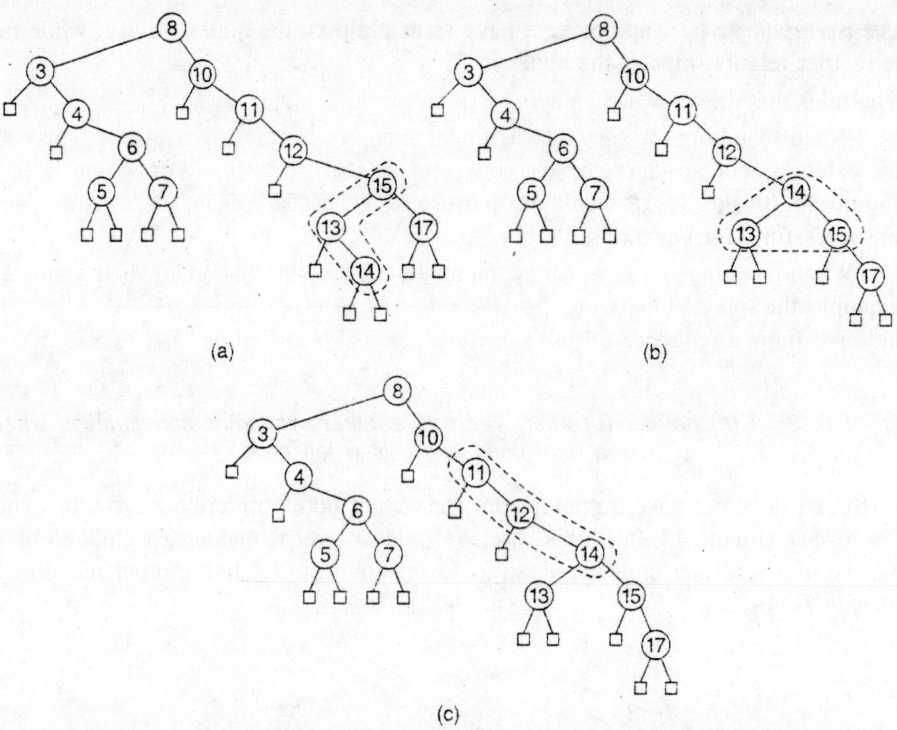

Fig. 15.10. Example of splaying a node : (a) splaying the node storing 14 starts with a SB; (b) after the SB; (c) the next step is a SA.

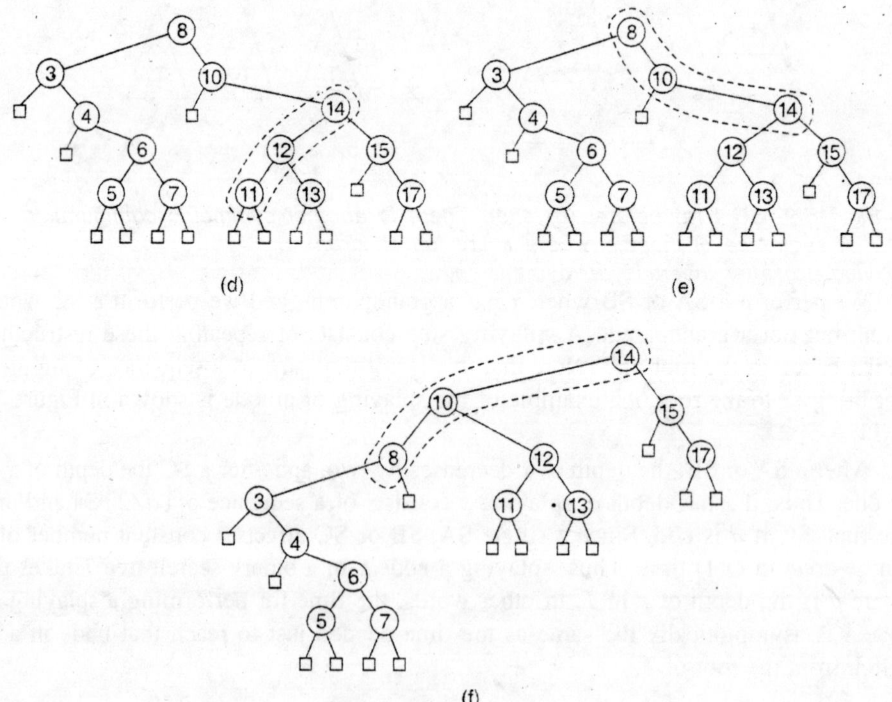

Fig. 15.11. Example of splaying a node (continued from Figure 15.10) : (d) after the SA; (e) the next step is again a SA; (f) after the SA.

When to Splay

The rules that dictate when splaying is performed are as follows :

When searching for key k, if k is found at a node x, we splay x else we splay the parent of the external node at which the search terminates unsuccessfully. For example, the splaying in Figure 15.10 and 15.11 would be performed after searchying successfully for key 14 or unsuccessfully for key 14.5.

When inserting key k, we splay the newly created internal node where k gets inserted. For example, the splaying in Figures 15.10–15.11 would be performed if 14 were the newly inserted key. We show a sequence of insertions in a splay tree in Figure 15.12.

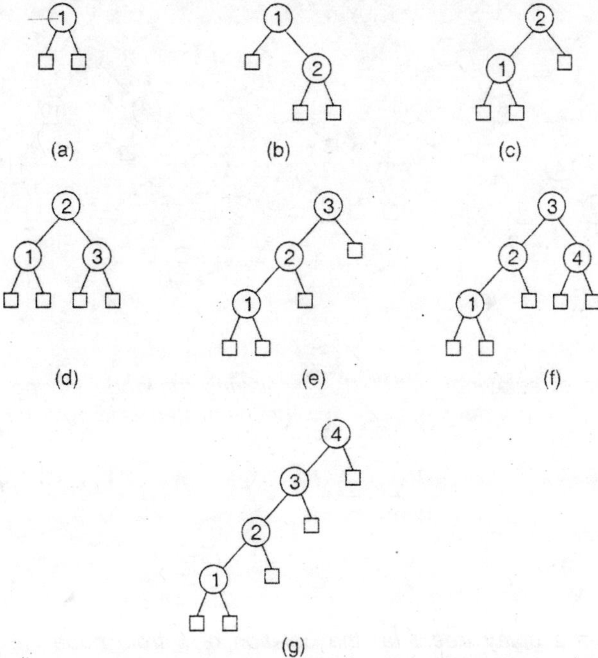

Fig. 15.12. A sequence of insertions in a splay tree : (a) initial tree; (b) after inserting 2; (c) after splaying; (d) after inserting 3; (e) after splaying; (f) after inserting 4; (g) after splaying.

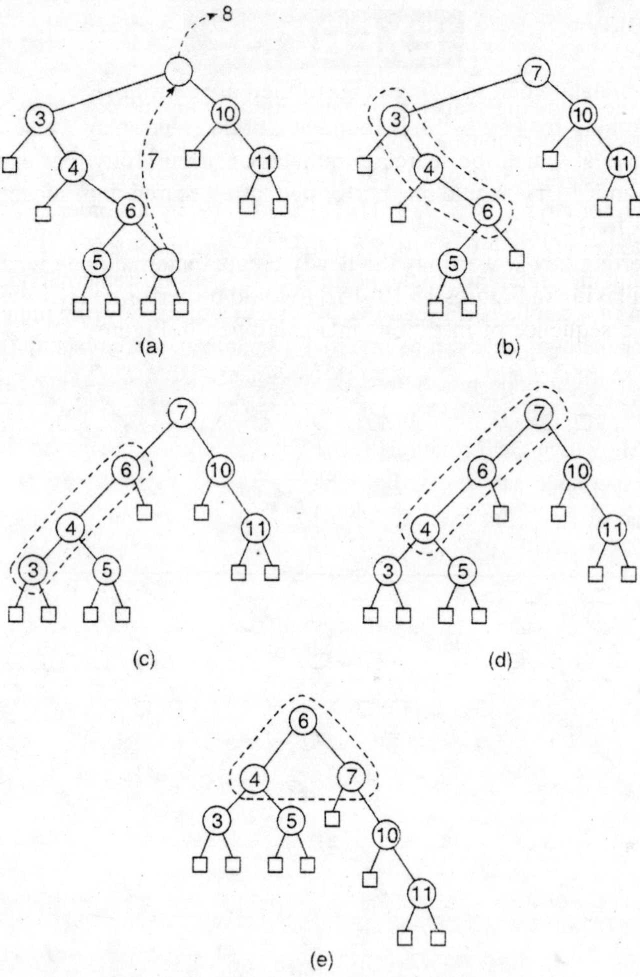

Fig. 15.13. Deletion from a splay tree : (a) the deletion of 8 from node r is performed by moving to r the key of the right-most internal node v, in the left subtree of r, deleting v, and splaying the parent u of v; (b) splaying u starts with a SA; (c) after the SA; (d) the next step is a SC; (e) after the SC.

When deleting a key k, we splay the parent of the node w that gets removed, that is, w is either the node storing k or one of its descendents. (Recall the deletion algorithm for binary search trees). An example of splaying following a deletion is shown in Figure 15.13.

In the worst case, the overall running time of a search, insertion, or deletion in a splay tree of height h is $O(h)$, since the node we splay might be the deepest node in the tree. Moreover, it is possible for h to be $\Omega(n)$, as shown in Figure 15.12. Thus, from a worst-case point of view, a splay tree is not an attractive data structure.

EXERCISE

1. Perform the following sequence of a operations in an initially empty splay tree and draw the tree after each operations.
   (a) Insert keys 0, 2, 4, 6, 8, 10, 12, 14, 16, 18, in this order.
   (b) Search for keys 1, 3, 5, 7, 9, 11, 13, 15, 17, 19, in this order.
   (c) Delete keys 0, 2, 4, 6, 8, 10, 12, 14, 16, 18, in this order.
2. If we maintain a reference to the position of the left-most internal node of an AVL tree, then operation first can be performed in $O(1)$ time. Describe how the implementation of the other dictionary methods needs to be modified to maintain a reference to the left-most position.
3. Show that any n-node binary tree can be converted to any other n-node binary tree using $O(n)$ rotations.
   [**Hint :** Show that $O(n)$ rotations suffice to convert any binary tree into a **left chain**, where each internal node has an external right child.]
4. Show that at most one trinode restructure operation (which corresponds to one single or double rotation) is needed to restore balance after any insertion in an AVL tree.

16

RB-TREES

16.1 About RB-Tree

DEFINITION. Let T be a binary search tree in which each node has a color, red or black, all external nodes are black. An edge to a black node is called *black edge*. The *black length* of a path is the no. of black edges on the path, *black depth* of a node is the black length of the path from the root of the tree to that node. A path from a specified node to an external node is called an external path for the specified node. Each node contains color, left, right, P field. A tree T is a *red black tree* iff

1. No red node has a red child
2. The black length of all external paths from a given node x is the same. This value is called **black height** of x, $bh[x]$
3. root is black, NIL
4. If a node is red then both its children are black.

A tree T is an almost-red-black tree (*ARB* tree) if the root is red, but other conditions above hold. see. Fig. 16.1

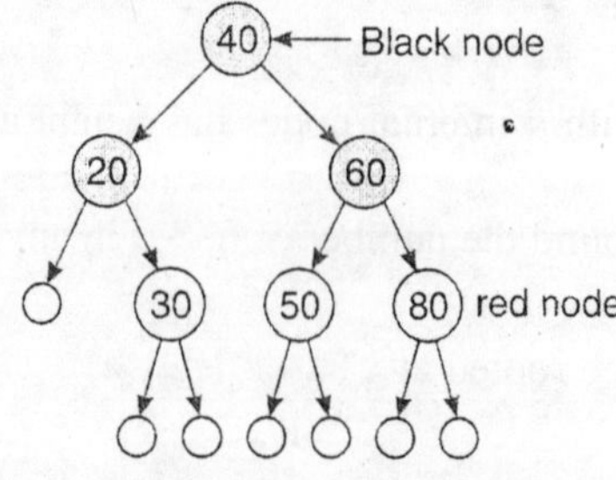

Fig. 16.1. Shows a RB-Tree.

What does the above definition mean?

If the root of a red-black tree is black can we just color it red?

No! For one of its children might be red.

If an arbitrary node is red can we color it black?

No! Because now all nodes may not have the same black height!

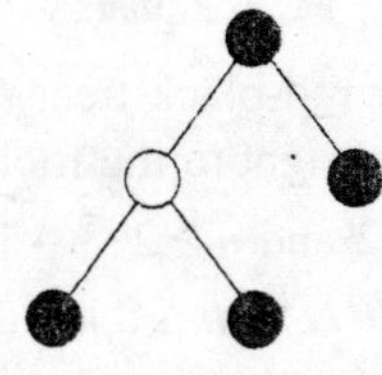

Fig. 16.2

What tree maximizes the number of nodes in a tree of black height h?

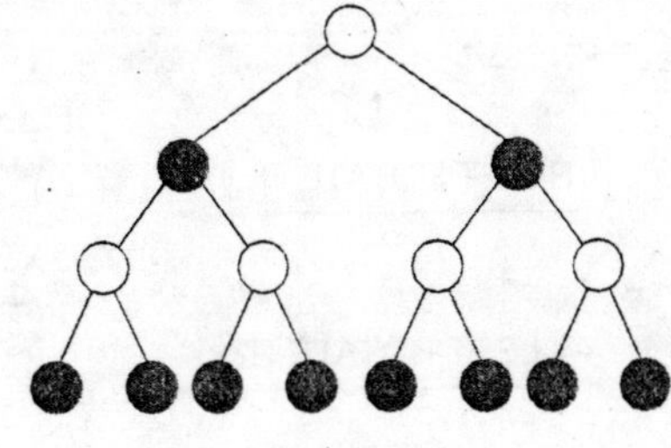

Fig. 16.3

What does a red-black tree with two real nodes look like?

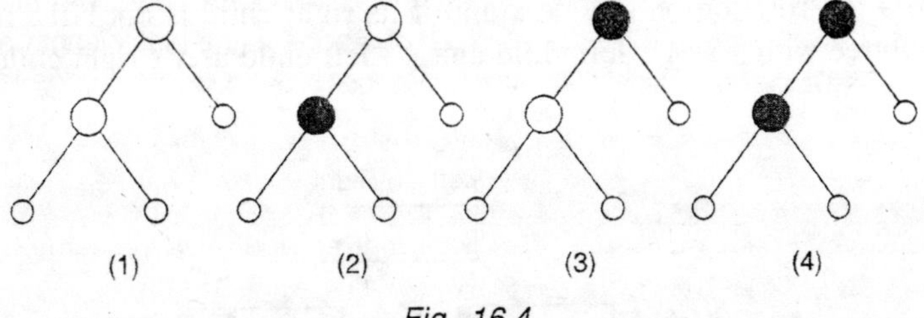

Fig. 16.4

Not (1) - consecutive reds Not (2), (4) - Non-Uniform black height

Red-Black Tree Height

LEMMA 16.1. A red-black tree with n internal nodes has height at most $2 \log (n + 1)$.

PROOF : Our strategy; first we bound the number of nodes in any subtree then we bound the height of any subtree.

We claim that any subtree rooted at x has at least $2^{bh(x)} - 1$ *intenral* nodes, where $bh(x)$ is the black height of node x.

Proof, by induction:

$$bh(x) = 0 \rightarrow x \text{ is a leaf} \rightarrow 2^0 - 1 = 0$$

Now assume it is true for all tree with black height $< bh(x)$.

If x is black, both subtrees have black height $bh(x) - 1$. If x is red, the subtrees have black height $bh(x)$.

Therefore, the number of internal nodes in any subtree is

$$n \geq 2^{bh(x) - 1} - 1 + 2^{bh(x) - 1} - 1 + 1 \geq 2^{bh(x)} - 1$$

Now, let h be the height of our red-black tree. At least half the nodes on any single path from root to leaf must be black if we ignore the root.

Thus $\qquad bh(x) \geq h/2$ and $n \geq 2^{h/2} - 1$, so $n + 1 \geq 2^{h/2}$

This implies that $\log (n + 1) \geq h/2$, so $h \leq 2 \log (n + 1)$, height 6 pt width 4 pt

Therefore red-black trees have height at most twice optimal. We have a balanced search tree if we can maintain the red-black tree structure under insertion and deletion.

16.1.1 Rotations

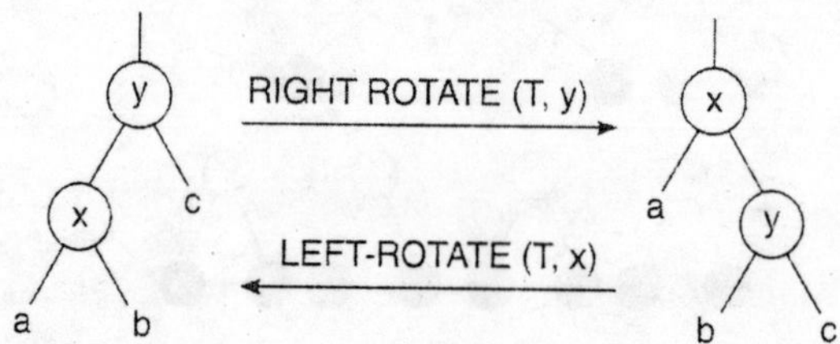

Fig. 16.5.

When we do a left rotation on a node x and if its right child is not NIL. It makes y the new root of the subtree with x as y's left child and y's left child as x's right child. Assuming Right $[x] \neq$ NIL

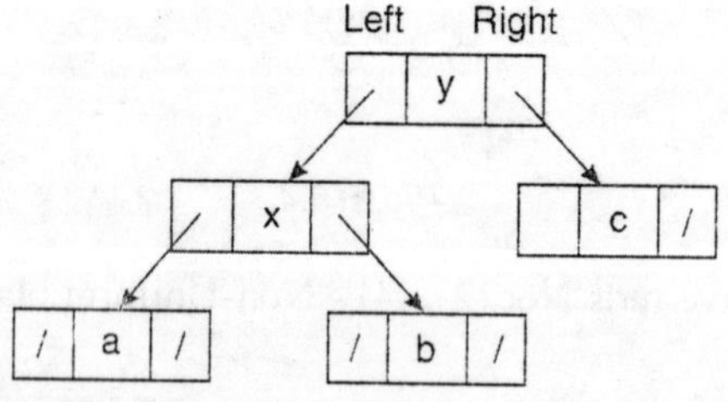

Fig. 16.6.

```
LEFT-ROTATE (T, x)
    y ← Right [x]
    Right [x] ← Left [y]
    If Left [y] ≠ NIL
```

```
        then P[Left[y]] ← x.
    P[Y] ← P[x].
    If P[x] = NIL
        then Root [T] ← y.
    else if x = Left[P[x]]
            then Left [P[x]] ← y
        else Right [P[x]] ← y
    Left [y] ← x.
    P[x] ← y.
```

Running time is $O(1)$, only pointers are adjusted.

To understand the rotation algorithm consider the following BST in fig. 16.7.

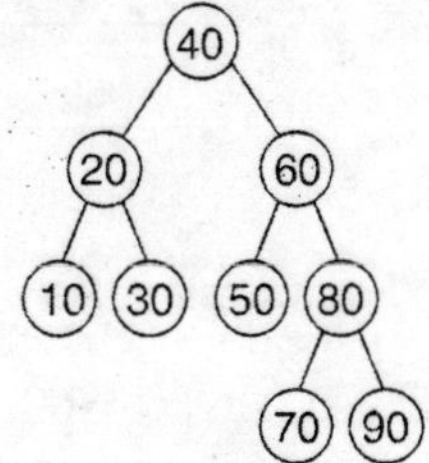

Fig. 16.7. Shows BST.

Linked list representation of this tree can be as shown below. This tree has four fields $P[x]$ which points to parent, key, left $[x]$, right $[x]$. If left $[x]$, right $[x]$ is NIL it means node x has no child, $p[x]$ is NIL for root $[T]$.

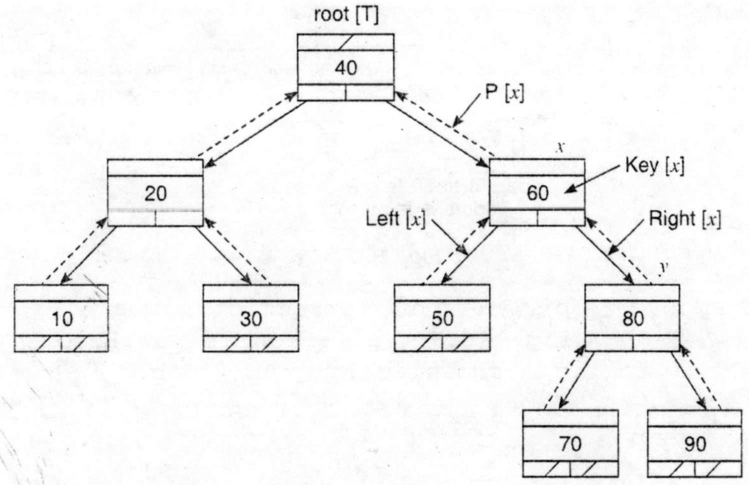

Fig. 16.7.1. Linked list representation of Fig. 16.7.

Let us perform a left rotation about node x with key $[x] = 60$ and key $[y] = 80$ then resultant tree is root $[T]$

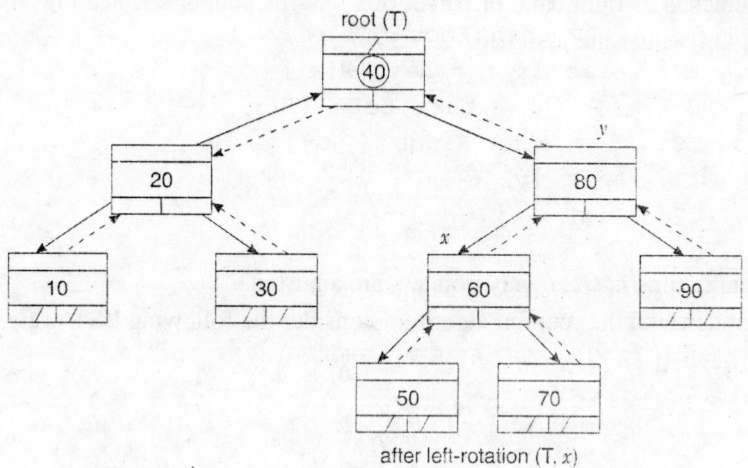

Fig. 16.7.2. Shows left rotation of fig. 16.7.1

Here x is the address of node, s.t. key$[x] = 60$, Y is Address of node s.t. key $[y] = 80$

```
Step 1.    y ← 80 (right [x] = 80)
Step 2.    right [x] ← 70 after rotation (left [y] = 70)
Step 3.    If left [y] ≠ NIL (70 ≠ NIL
Step 4.         then p[70] ← x
```

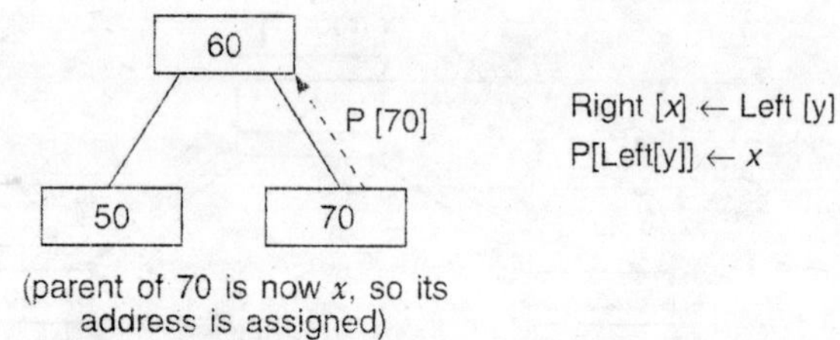

Fig. 16.7.3

```
Step 5.    p[y] ← p[x], parent of x was 40 as shown in
           Fig. 16.7.4(a) which is now becomes the parent
           y, shown in Fig. 16.7.4(b)
```

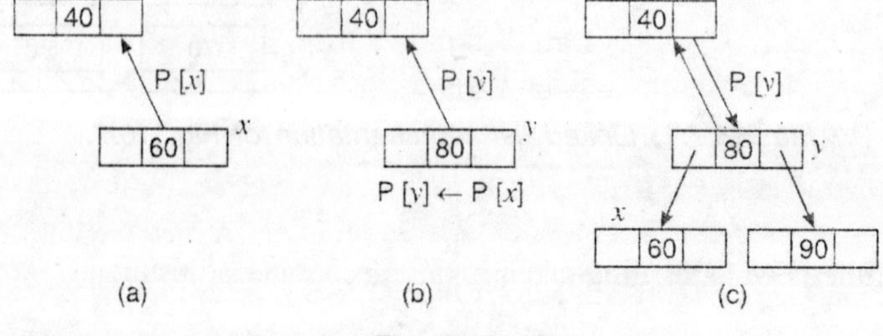

Fig. 16.7.4

Here $p[x] \neq$ NIL as it is not root $[T]$ then

Step 10. Right $[p[x]] \leftarrow y$,

i.e., y is attached as right child of parent of x with its pointer set. See Fig. 16.7.4(c).

Now, key values are assigned.

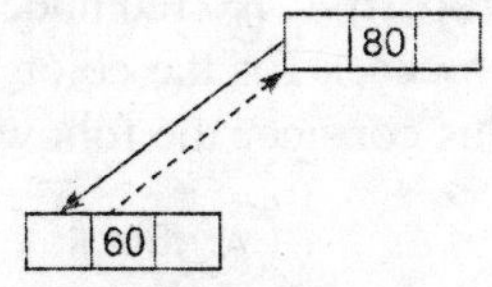

Fig. 16.7.5

Step 11. left $[y] \leftarrow x$, *i.e.*, x is made left child.

Right-Rotate [*T*, *Y*]

i.e., we again get the original tree of Fig. 16.7 after right rotation. See Fig. 16.8.

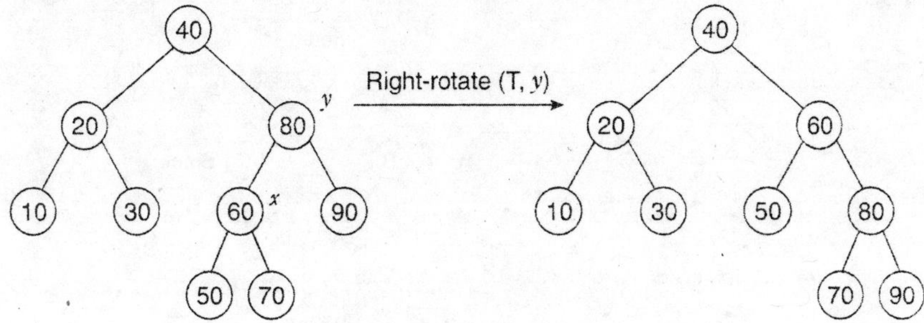

Fig. 16.8. Shows Right-Rotate (T, y).

```
RIGHT-ROTATE (T, y)
        x ← Left  [y]
        Left  [y] ← Right[x]
        if Right  [x] ≠ NIL
              then P[Right[x]] ← y
        P[x] ← P[y]
        if P[y] = NIL
              then root  [T] ← x
              else if y = Right[P[y]]
                    then Right  [P[y]] ← x
                    else Left  [P[y]] ← y
        Right  [x] ← y
        P[y] ← x
```

Running time is $O(1)$, as time taken is only in pointer adjustment.

16.1.2 Insertion

A node in RB tree is inserted just like binary search tree except color of the node are adjusted so as not to violate the RB-tree property and accordingly the rotations are performed.

In a R-B tree according to property 1, No red node has red child. Suppose we are inserting a node x at any position then we check for the color of uncle of this node whether it is red. *i.e.*, color of y is red or not. Let us consider the following cases :

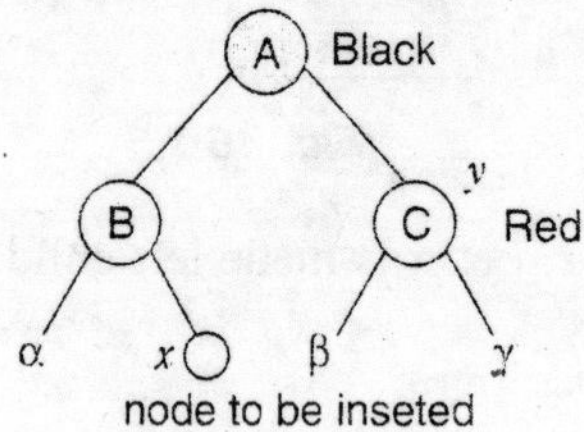

Fig. 16.9

Case I :

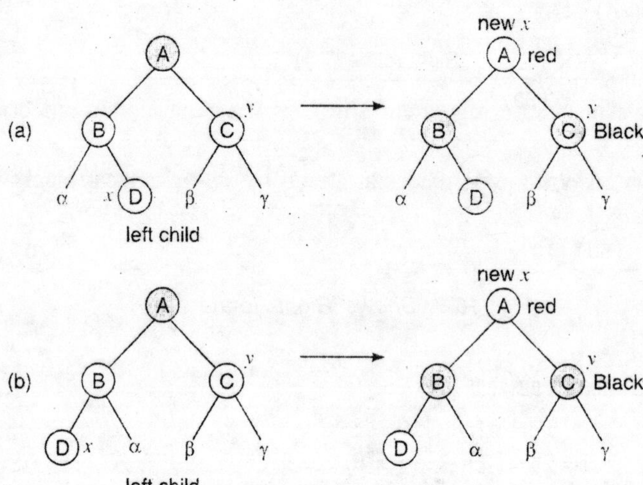

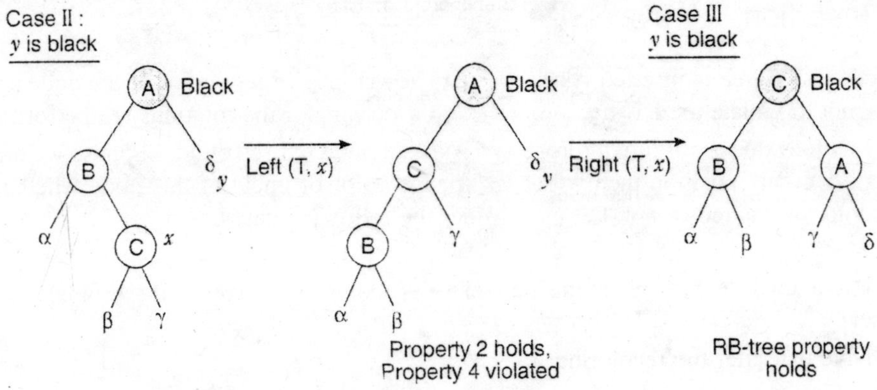

Fig. 16.10. Shows, case I, II and III for insertion.

More on Red-Black Insertion

Let us elaborate the previous cases for RB-tree insertion.

Since red-black trees have $\theta(\log n)$ height, if we can preserve all properties of such trees under insertion/deletion, we have a balanced tree!

Suppose we just did a regular insertion. Under what conditions does it stay a red-black tree?

Since every insertion take places at a leaf, we will change a black NIL pointer to a node with two black NIL pointers. See Fig. 16.11.

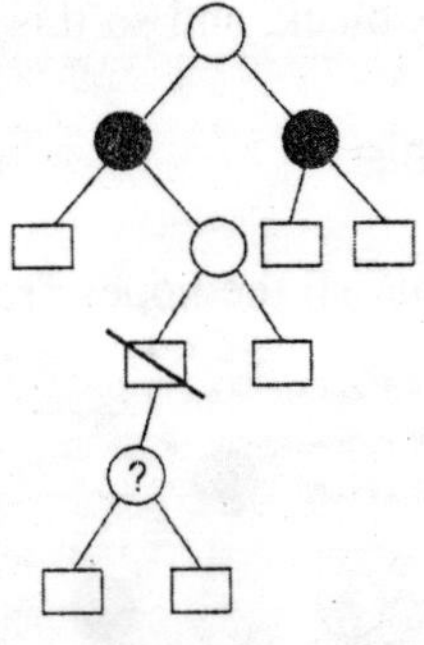

Fig. 16.11.

To preserve the black height of the tree, the new node must be *red*. If its *new* parent is black, we can stop, otherwise we must restructure!

How can we fix two reds in a row?

It depends upon our uncle's color:

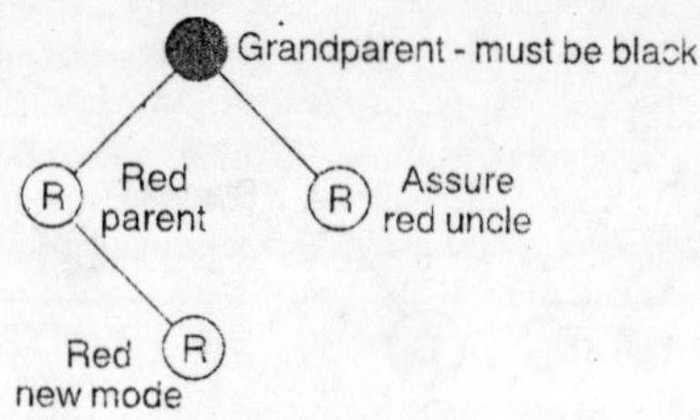

Fig. 16.12.

If our uncle is red, reversing our relatives' color either solves the problem or pushes it higher!

Note that after the recoloring:

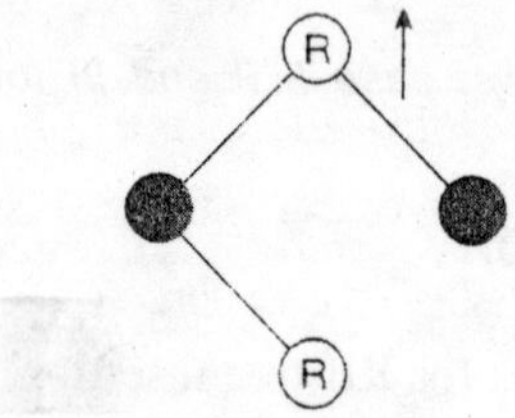

Fig. 16.13.

1. The black height is unchanged.
2. The shape of the tree is unchanged.
3. We are done if our great-grandparent is black.

If we get all the way to the root, recall we can always color a red-black tree's root black. We always will, so initially it *was* black, and so this process terminates.

The Case of the Black Uncle

If our uncle was black, observe that all the nodes around us have to be black:

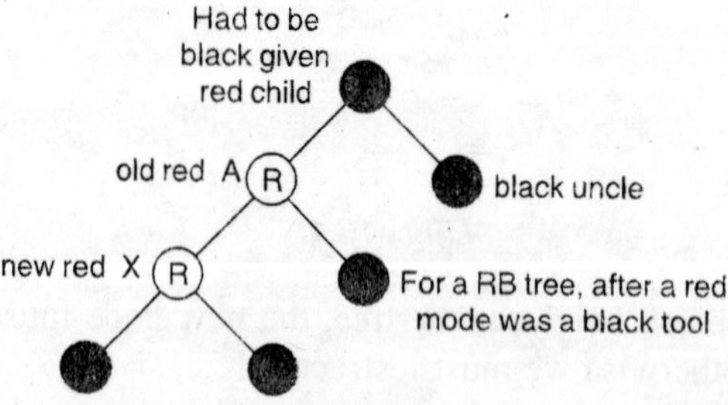

Fig. 16.14.

Solution - rotate right about B:

Since the root of the subtree is now black with the same black-height as before, we have restored the colors and can stop!

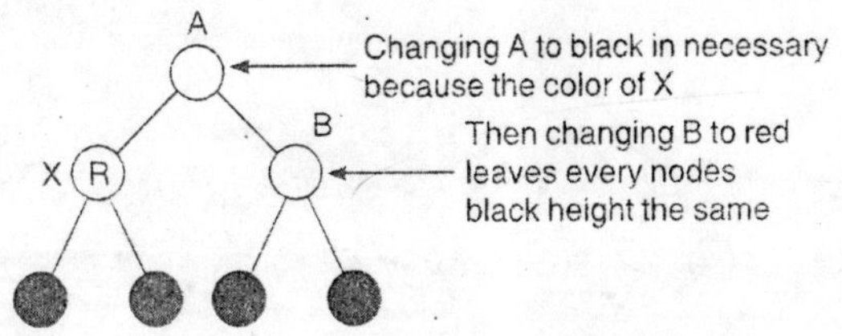

Fig. 16.15.

A double rotation can be required to set things up depending upon the left-right turn sequence, but the principle is the same.

Thus we have the following algorithm for RB-insert based on three cases discussed earlier.

```
RB-INSERT (T, x)
Color [x] ← Red
  while x ≠ Root [T]  and  Color [P[x]] = RED
      do if P[x] = Left[P[P[x]]
          then y ← Right[P[P[x]]]
              if Color [y] = RED
                  then Color [P[x]] ← BLACK
                      Color [y] ← BLACK                 Case-I
                      Color [P[P[x]]] ← RED
              else if x = Right[[P[x]]
                  then x ← p[x]                         Case-II
                  LEFT-ROTATE (T, x)
                  Color [P[x]] ← BLACK
                  Color [P[P[x]]] ← RED                Case-III
                  RIGHT-ROTATE (T, P(P[x]))
              else (same as then clause with "Right"
                  and "Left" exchanged)
Color [Root ·[T]] ← BLACK
```

Here key values are ignored and each node is referenced by index. Dark shade shows black color.

Since tree-insertion takes $\Theta(lgn)$ time equal to ht. of the tree RB-INSERT takesd $O(lgn)$ time. See Fig. 16.16 for illustration of RB-INSERT.

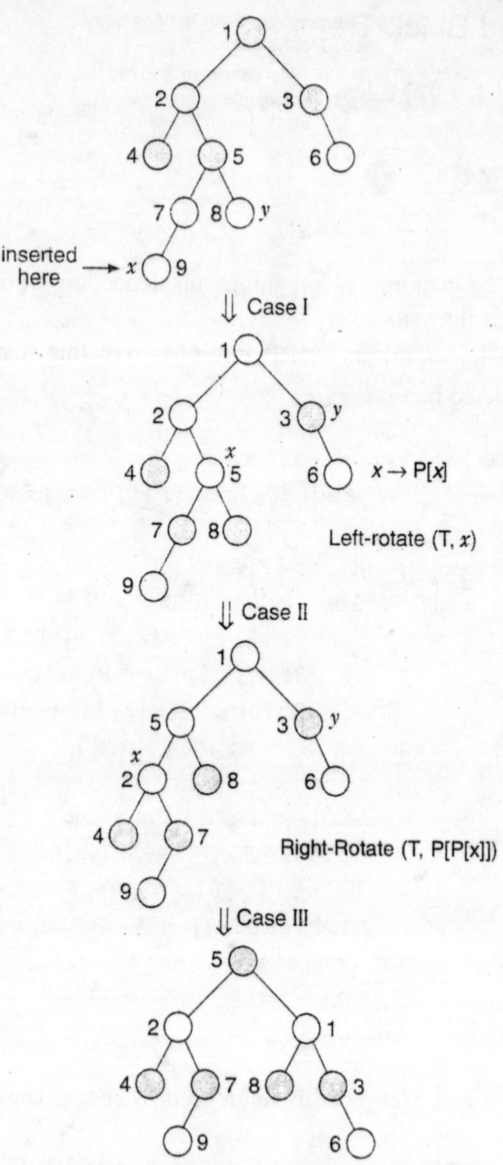

Fig. 16.16. Shows insertion in RB-Tree.

16.1.3 Deletion from Red Black Trees

Case (a) The node to be deleted was a leaf;

Possible color height change

Fig. 16.17.

Case (b) The node to be deleted had one child

Possible color height change

Fig. 16.18.

Case (c) relabel to node as its successor and delete the successor.

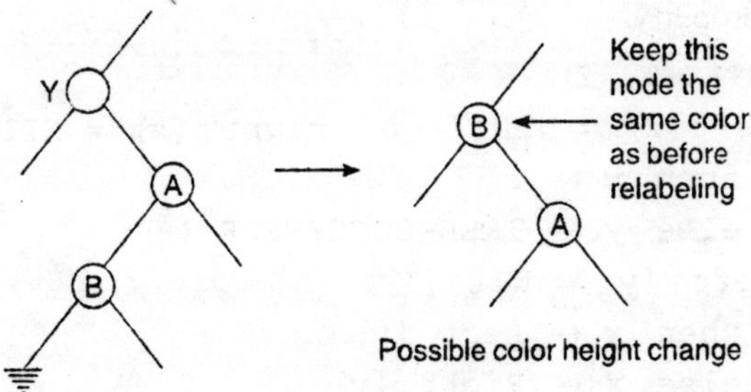

Fig. 16.19.

Deletion Color Cases

Suppose the node we remove was *red*, do we still have a red-black tree?

***Yes!* No two reds will be together, and the black height for each leaf stays the same.**

However, if the dead node *y* was black, we must give each of its decendants another black ancestor. If an appropriate node is red, we can simply color it black otherwise we must restructure.

Case (a) black NIL becomes "double black";

Case (b) red β becomes black and black β becomes "double black";-

Case (c) red β becomes black and black β becomes "double black".

Out goal will be to recolor and restructure the tree so as to get rid of the "double black" node.

In setting up any case analysis, we must be sure that:

1. All possible cases are covered.
2. No case is covered twice.

In the case analysis for red-black trees, the breakdown is:

Case 1: The double black node x has a red brother.

Case 2: x has a black brother and two black nephews.

Case 3: x has a black brother, and its left nephew is red and its right nephew is black.

Case 4: x has a black brother, and its right nephew is red (left nephew can be any color).

Conclusion

Red-Black trees let us implement all dictionary operations in $O(\log n)$. Further, in no case are more than 3 rotations done to rebalance. Certain very advanced data structures have data stored at nodes which requires a lot of work to adjust after a rotation—red-black trees ensure it won't happen often.

Procedure RB-Delete is minor modification of TREE-DELETE after deleting a node, it calls an auxillary procedure RB-DELETE-FIXUP which adjusts the color of nodes in order to hold the RB-tree property.

```
RB-DELETE (T, Z)
   if left[z] = NIL[T] or right [z] = NIL[T]
         then y ← z
         else y ← TREE-SUCCESSOR (z)
   if left [y] ≠ NIL [T]
         then x ← Left [y]
         else x ← Right [y]
   p[x] ← p[y]
   if p[y] = NIL[T]
         then root[T] ← x.
         else if y = left [p[y]]
               then left[p[y]] ← x
               else right[p[y]] ← x.
   If y ≠ z.
         then key[z] ← key[y]
         If color[y] = BLACK
               then RB-DELETE-FIXUP (T, x)
   return y.
```

```
RB-DELETE-FIXUP (T, x)
while x ≠ Root [T] and color[x] = BLACK
   do if x = left [P[x]]
         then w ← right[P[x]]
              if color[w] = RED.
                 then color[w] ← BLACK
                      color[P[x]] ← RED                    Case I

                      LEFT-ROTATE (T, p[x])
                      w ← Right[p[x]]
              if color[left [w]] = BLACK and
                 color[right [w]] = BLACK
                 then color[w] ← RED                       Case II

                      x ← p[x]
              else if color[right[w]] ← BLACK
                 then Color[left [w]] ← BLACK
                      Color[w] ←RED                        Case III

                      RIGHT-ROTATE (T, w)
                      w ← RIGHT[p[x]]
                      Color[w] ← Color[p[x]]
                      Color[p[x]] ← BLACK                  Case IV

                      Color[right [w]] ← BLACK
                      LEFT-ROTATE (T, p[x])
                      x ← root [T]
         else [same as then clause with "right" and
                                             "left" exchanged]
                      Color [x] ← BLACK
```

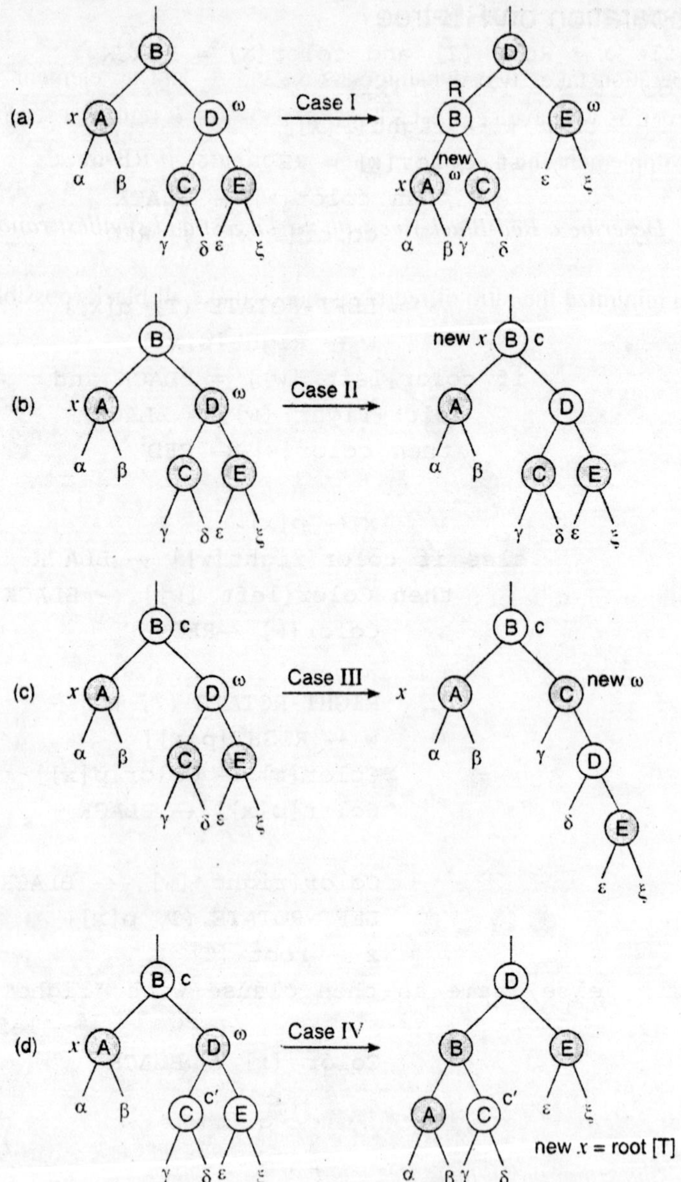

Fig. 16.20. Shows RB-Delete

Above Fig. 16.20 shows the 4 cases used in RB-DELETE-FIXUP algorithm, Running time for this algorithm is $O(lgn)$.

16.1.4 Join operation on RB-tree

The join operation takes two dynamic sets S_1 and S_2 and an element x such that for any $x_1 \in S_1$ and $x_2 \in S_2$ we have key $[x_1] \le$ key $[x] \le$ key $[x_2]$. It returns a set $S = S_1 \cup \{x\} \cup S_2$.

We can implement this keeping in mind of definition if RB-tree.

EXAMPLE 16.1. *Describe a Red-Black tree with the largest and smallest ratio of red nodes.*

SOLUTION : To minimize the ratio of red-black nodes make all black (possible for $n = 2^k - 1$)

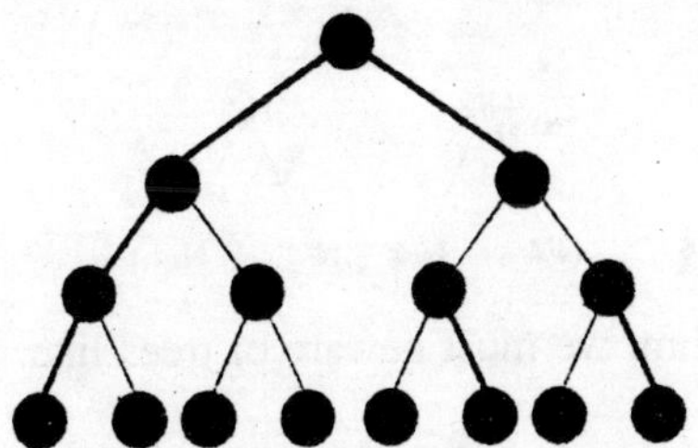

To maximize the ratio of red nodes, interleave with red nodes as *real* leaves

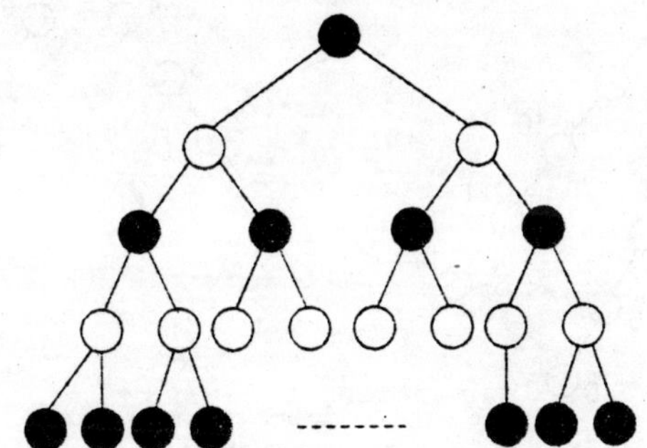

$$\#red/n \le n/2 + n/8 + n/32 = .656n$$

$$\#black/n \le n/4 + n/16 + n/64 = .328n$$

$$n - n \sum_{i=1}^{\max} (1/4)^i = 2n/3$$

EXAMPLE 16.2. *Show that any n-node tree can be transformed to any other using O(n) rotations (hint: convert to a right going chain).*

SOLUTION : I will start by showing weaker bounds - that $O(n^2)$ and $O(n \log n)$ rotations suffice - because that is how I proceeded when I first saw the problem.

First, observe that creating a right-going, for t_2 path from t_1 < and reversing the same construction gives a path from t_1 to t_2.

Note that it will take at most n notations to make the lowest valued key the root. Once it is root, all keys are to the right of it, so on more rotations need go through it to create a right-going chain. Repeating with the second lowest key, third, etc. gives that $O(n^2)$ rotations suffice.

Now that if we try to create a completely balanced tree instead. To get the $n/2$ key to the root takes at most n rotations. Now each subtree has half the nodes and we can recur...

N

N/2 N/2

N/4 N/4 N/4 N/4

To get a linear algorithm, we must beware of trees like:

The correct answer is that $n - 1$ rotations suffice to get to a rightmost chain.

By picking the lowest node on the rightmost chain which has a left ancestor, we can add one node *per* rotation to the right most chain!

Initially, the rightmost chain contained at least 1 node, so after *1* rotations it contains all n. Slick!

EXAMPLE 16.3. *The Boolean used to mark nodes in a red-black tree as being "red" or "black" is not strictly needed. Describe a scheme for implementating a red-black tree without adding any extra space to the binary search tree nodes. How does your scheme affect the running times for searching and updating a red-black tree ?*

SOLUTION : We give two possible solutions. Let v be a red node of a red-black tree T.

This solution assumes that keys in T are integers. We change keys stored in T using the following simple rule : if v is red, set new_key $(v) = 2\text{key}(v) + 1$, or if v is black. set new_key $(v) = 2\text{key}(v)$. Observe that this "mapping" function is 1-1 and strictly increasing; this property preserves the property of T of being a binary search tree and helps in uniquely identify a node's color. Namely, any node can be identified of being red or black, by simply checking whether new_key (v) is respectively odd or even.

This solution assumes that keys in T are unique. Because of the fact that v is red, it can not be a leaf. Let u and w be v's left and right child respectively. If both u and w are not place-holder nodes, we can represent the fact that v is red, implicitly, by exchanging the children of v i.e., by making u v's right child and w v's left child. This allows us to correctly identify if a node is red or black, only by checking the key values for nodes u, v and w. Node v is red, if and only if the property of T of being binary search is locally violated, i.e., if and only if $\text{key}(u) > \text{key}(v) > \text{key}(w)$. If one of v's children is a place holder node, then again a similar violation of T's property of being a binary tree can be used to identify v's color. Finally, if both children of v are place-holder nodes, then we can either store some fictitious element in one of them or remove v's right (or left) child.

EXERCISE

1. Implement the RB-Joint (T_1, x, T_2) where total no. of nodes in T_1 and T_2 is n and $T = T_1 \cup \{x\} \cup T_2$.
2. Show the red black trees that result after successively inserting keys 41, 38, 31, 12, 19, 8 into an initially empty red-black tree.
3. Consider a red-black tree formed by inserting n nodes with RB-INSERT. Argue that if $n > 1$, the tree has atleast one red node.
4. Show the successive deletion of keys 8, 12, 19, 31, 38, 41 in a tree constructed in question 2 above.
5. Does inserting a node into a red-black tree, then deleting it always result in the original tree? Prove it does or give a counter example where it does not and also prove the vice versa.
6. Find a RB-tree that is not AVL tree.
7. Prove that a RB tree with n internal nodes has height at most $2lg(n + 1)$
8. Draw the complete binary search tree of height 3 on the keys $\{1, 2, ..., 15\}$. Add the NIL leaves and color the nodes in three different ways such that the black heights of the resulting red-black trees are 2, 3 and 4.
9. What is the largest possible no. of internal nodes in a RB tree with black height k ? What is smallest m.

10. Suppose that the root of red-black tree is red. If we make it black, does the tree remain a red-black tree?

11. Consider the following sequence of keys:

(5, 16, 22, 45, 2, 10, 18, 30, 50, 12, 1).

Consider the insertion of items with this set of keys, in the order given, into:

(a) An initially empty (2, 4) tree T'.

(b) An initially empty red-black tree T''.

Draw T' and T'' after each insertion.

12. Draw four different red-back trees that correspond to the same (2, 4) tree using the correspondence rules described in earlier chapter.

13. Draw an example red-black tree that is not an AVL tree. Your tree should have at least 6 nodes, but no more than 16.

14. For each of the following statements about red-back trees, determine whether it is true or false. If you think it is true, provide a justification. If you think it is false, give a counterexample.

(a) A subtree of a red-black tree is itself a red-black tree.

(b) The sibling of an external node is either external or it is red.

(c) Given a red-black tree T, there is a unique (2, 4) tree T' associated with T.

(d) Given a (2, 4) tree T, there is a unique red-black tree T' associated with T.

17

AUGMENTING DATA STRUCTURE

17.1 Ordered-Static Tree

Is simply a red-black tree with additional information stored in each node, *i.e.*, SIZE [x] besides other information. Thus field contains the total no. of nodes (internal) including itself. Thus

$$\text{SIZE}[x] = \text{SIZE}\ [\text{LEFT}\ (x)] + \text{SIZE}\ [\text{RIGHT}\ [x]] + 1$$

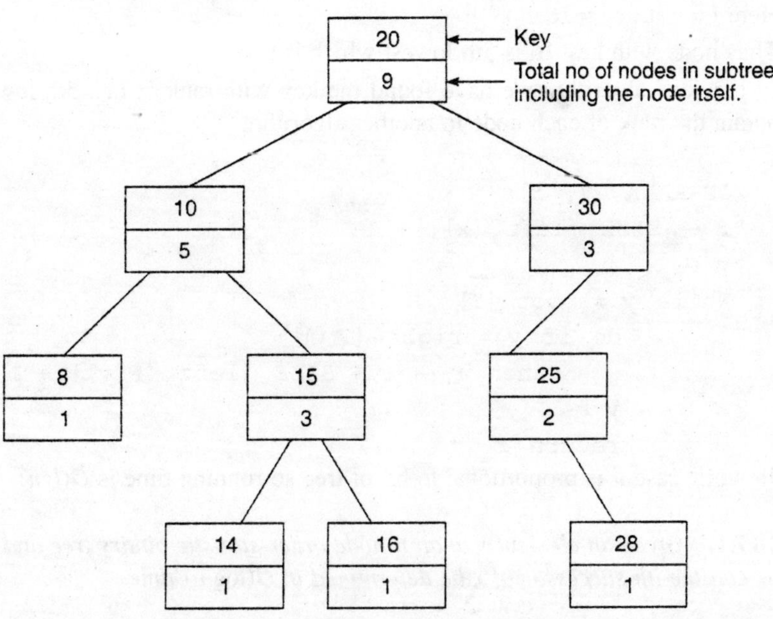

Fig. 17.1. Shows order-statistic tree.

17.1.1 Retrieving an element with a given rank

We define an algorithm,

OS-SELECT (x, i) which returns a pointer containing ith smallest key in subtree rooted at x.

```
OS-SELECT (x, i)
r ← SIZE [Left [x]] + 1
if i = r then return x.
else if i < r
        then return OS-SELECT (Left [x], i)
        else return OS-SELECT [Right [x], i − r]
```

Here r represent the rank, in this case it is of left subtree.

Running time is $O(lgn)$, proportional to ht. of Tree

To see how it works, consider Fig. 17.1 to find the 5th smallest element. Let us begin with x equal to root.

If $i < r$, $x = \text{Left}[x]$

$i \geq r$, $x = \text{Right}[x]$

$r = \text{SIZE [Left } [x]] + 1 = 6$

	x	i	r	
	20	5	6	
	10	5	2	
	15	3	2	
$i = r$	16	1	1	left $[x]$ = NIL

Here $i = r$ at key = 16.

Thus node with key 16 is 5th lowest which is true,

In previous algorithm we have found the key with rank 5, *i.e.*, 5th lowest, Similarly we can obtain the rank of each node in another algorithm.

```
OS-RANK [T, x]
r ← SIZE [left [x]] + 1
y ← x
While y ≠ root [T]
      do if y = right [P(y)]
            then r ← r + SIZE [left [P[y]] + 1
      y ← P[y]
      return r
```

In worst case it is proportional to ht. of tree so running time is $O(lgn)$.

EXAMPLE 17.1. *Given an element x in an n-node order-statistic binary tree and a natural number i, how can the ith successor of x be determined in O(log n) time.*

SOLUTION : This problem can be solved if our data structure supports two operations:

Rank (x) - what is the position of x in the total order of keys?

Get (i) - what is the key in the ith position of the total order of keys?

What we are interested in is $Get(Rank(x) + i)$.

In an order statistic tree, each node x is labeled with the number of nodes contained in the subtree rooted in x.

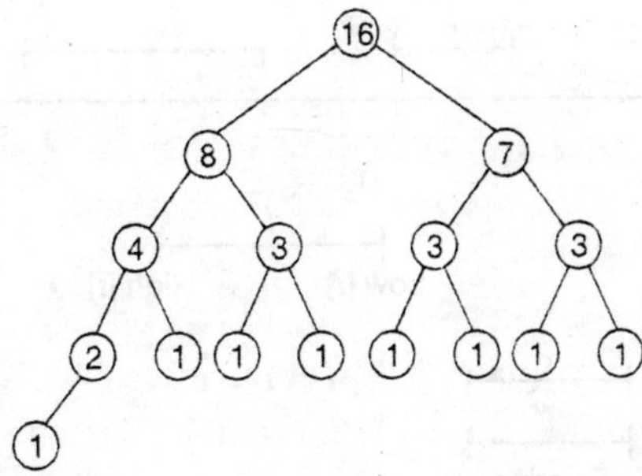

Implementing both operations involves keeping track of how many nodes lie to the left of our path.

17.1.2 How to augment a Data Structure

Augmenting a data structure can be broken into four steps

1. Choose an underlying data structure
2. Determine the underlying data structure,
3. Verify that the additional information can be maintained for the basic modifying operations on underlying data structure.
4. Developing new operations.

For example

Step 1. Choose *RB* tree, since it supports efficient operations like MAXIMUM, SUCCESSOR, PREDECESSOR.

Step 2. Provide the **size** field, which stores the size of subtree rooted as x. For example, we could have implemented OS-SELECT and OS-RANK using just the keys stored in the tree, but they would not have run in $O(lgn)$ time. Some times, the additional information is pointer rather than data.

Step 3. We ensure that insertion and deletion can maintain the size fields while still running in $O(lgn)$ time.

Step 4. We developed the operations OS-SELECT and OS-RANK that contains new information and speeds up the process.

17.2 Interval Trees

A red-black tree that maintains a dynamic set of elements, with each element x containing an interval int $[x]$.

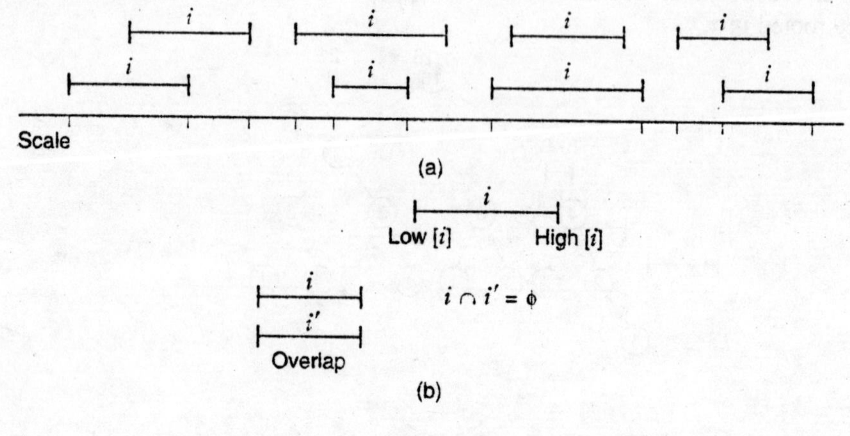

Fig. 17.2

15.2.1 Interval Trichotomy

Any two intervals i and i' is said to satisfy interval trichotomy if it satisfies any one of the following three properties.

(i) i and i' overlap

(ii) high $[i]$ < low $[i']$

(iii) high $[i']$ < low $[i]$

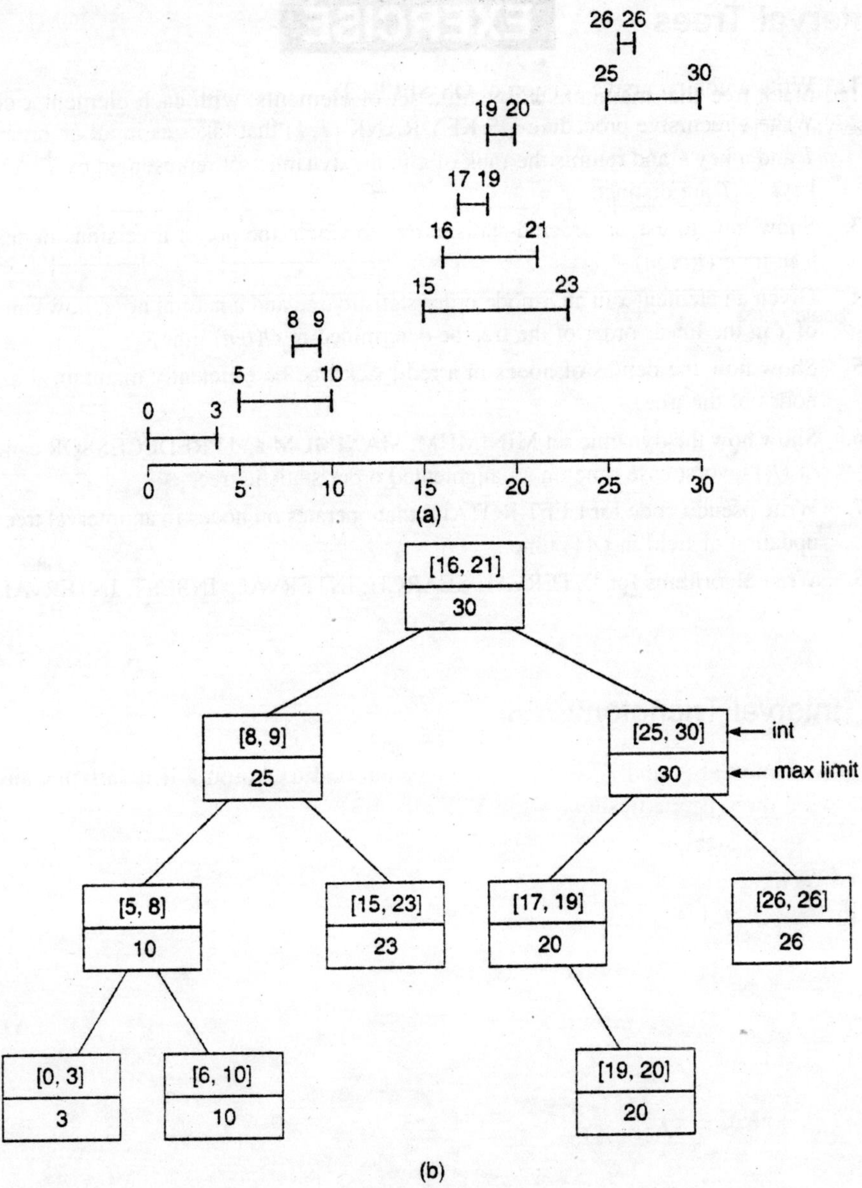

Fig. 17.3. Shows Interval Trichotomy.

An interval tree (a) A set of 10 intervals, shown sorted bottom to top by left end point (b) The interval tree that represents them. See Fig. 17.3.

EXERCISE

1. Write a non recursive version of OS-SELECT.
2. Write a recursive procedure OS-KEY-RANK (T, k) that takes as input an order statistic tree T and a key k and returns the rank of k in the dynamic set represented by T. Assume that the keys of T are distinct.
3. Show how to use an ordered-statistic tree to Count the no. of inversions in an array of size n in time $O(nlgn)$
4. Given an element x in an n-node order statistic tree and a natural no. i, how can ith successor of x in the linear order of the tree be determined in $O(lgn)$ time?
5. Show how the depths of nodes in a red-black tree be efficiently maintained as fields in the nodes of the tree?
6. Show how the dynamic set MINIMUM, MAXIMUM and PREDECESSOR can be supported in $O(1)$ worst case time on an augmented order statistic tree.
7. Write pseudo code for LEFT-ROTATE that operates on nodes in an interval tree and does the updation of field in $O(1)$ time.
8. Write algorithms for INTERVAL-SEARCH, INTERVAL- INSERT, INTERVAL-DELETE.

18

DYNAMIC PROGRAMMING

Dynamic programming is generally used with optimization problems, where sequence of solutions are available, each solutions has a value and we require to find the optimal (min or max) value such a solution is called an optimal solution. There are several solutions that attain optimal value at different stages but we select the best one and call it the optimal solution of the problem.

The development of a dynamic-programming algo can be broken into a sequence of four steps.

1. Characterize the structure of an optimal solution.
2. Recurisvely define the value of an optimal solution.
3. Compute the value of an optimal solution in a bottom-up fashion.
4. Construct an optimal solution from computed information.

Here are some examples of dynamic programming problems :

1. Knapsack problem.
2. Mathematical optimization problems.
3. Optimal merge patterns.
4. Shortest path problems.
5. Matrix chain multiplication.
6. LCS

18.1 Computing Fibonacci Numbers

$$F_n = F_{n-1} + F_{n-2}$$
$$F_n = 0, F_1 = 1$$

Implementing it as a recursive procedure is easy but slow!

We keep calculating the same value over and over!

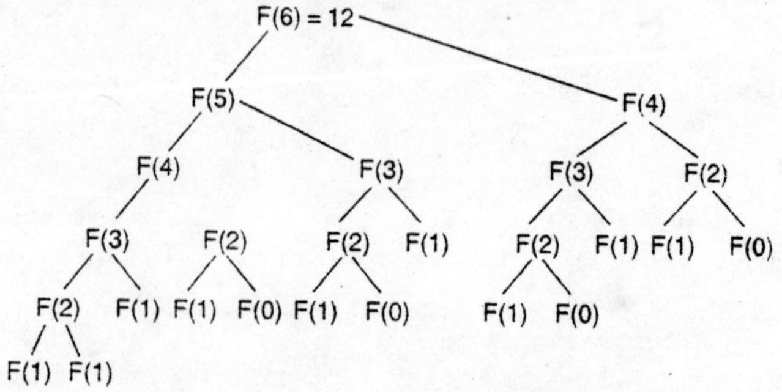

Fig. 18.1. Shows fibonacci number generation.

How slow is slow?

$$F_{n+1}/F_n \approx \phi = (1 + \sqrt{5})/2 \approx 1.61803$$

Thus $F_n \approx 1.6^n$, and since our recursion tree has *0* and *1* as leaves, means we have $\approx 1.6^n$ calls!

What about Dynamic Programming?

We can calculate F_n in linear time by storing small values:

$$F_0 = 0$$
$$F_1 = 1$$
For $i = 1$ to n
$$F_i = F_{i-1} + F_{i-2}$$

Moral: we traded space for time.

Dynamic programming is a technique for efficiently computing recurrences by storing partial results.

Once you understand dynamic programming, it is usually easier to reinvent certain algorithms than try to look them up!

Dynamic programming is best understood by looking at a bunch of different examples.

I have found dynamic programming to be one of the most useful algorithmic techniques in practice:

Morphing in Computer Graphics

Data Compression for High Density Bar Codes

Utilizing Grammatical Constraints for Telephone Keypads

18.2 Matrix Multiplication

Let us consider matrix multiplication problem where A is $m \times n$ and B is $n \times p$ then, matrix-multiply (A, B)

```
if col (A) ≠ row (B) then error "can't be multiplied"
else for i ← 1 to row [A]
      do for j ← 1 to col  [B]
           do c[i, j] ← 0
              for k ← 1 to col  [A]
              do c[i, j] ← c[i, j] + A(i, k) * B[k, j]
```

Total no. of iterations is $m \times n \times p$ and

If we have 3 matrices $A_1\, A_2\, A_3$ of 10×100, 100×5 and 5×50 respectively then $(A_1A_2)\, A_3$ gives $10 \times 100 \times 5 = (5000)$ scalar multiplications to multiply A_1A_2 and which will result in 10×5 matrix and $10 \times 5 \times 50 = 2500$ scalar multiplications are performed to multiply this with A_3 thus total scalar multiplication performed is 7500 but if A_2A_3 is multiplied first then $100 \times 5 \times 50 = 25000$ scalar multiplication is performed then A_1 is multiplied which requires $10 \times 100 \times 50 = 50000$ scalar multiplications thus total scalar multiplications performed are 75000 thus

$$n[(A_1A_2)A_3] \neq n[A_1(A_2A_3)]$$

$$\text{but, dim } [(A_1A_2)A_3] = \text{dim } [A_1(A_2A_3)] = 10 \times 50$$

i.e., order of multiplication changes the number of scalar multiplications and hence the speed of execution. Thus if we have four matrix $A_1A_2A_3A_4$ then how we should multiply to get the optimal solution. The multiplication can be parenthesized in following manner. (Assuming col of 1st equals row of next)

$$(A_1(A_2(A_3A_4)))$$
$$(A_1((A_2A_3)A_4))$$
$$((A_1A_2)(A_3A_4))$$
$$((A_1(A_2A_3))A_4)$$
$$(((A_1A_2)A_3)A_4)$$

Every parenthesisation will yield different number of scalar multiplication and one with lowest number will be optimal the order of matrix $A_1A_2A_3$ can be given as follows, $A_1(10 \times 100)$, and $A_2(100 \times 5)$ and $A_3(5 \times 50)$ then order is 10×50, *i.e.*, if $A_1 \times A_2$ are multiplied it is $\mathbf{10} \times \mathbf{5}$ and if it is multiplied to A_3 which has order 5×50 thus it is 10×5, if product P_1A_2 is P_{i-1} and A_3 is P_i then the final order of matrix is given by $P_{i-1} \times P_i$, *i.e.*, 10×50 in this case.

18.2.1 Multiplying a Sequence of Matrices

Suppose we want to multiply a long sequence of matrices $A \times B \times C \times D$ .... Multiplying an $X \times Y$ matrix by a $Y \times Z$ matrix (using the common algorithm) takes $X \times Y \times Z$ multiplications.

$$\begin{bmatrix} 2 & 3 \\ 3 & 4 \\ 4 & 5 \end{bmatrix} \begin{bmatrix} 2 & 3 & 4 \\ 3 & 4 & 5 \end{bmatrix} \begin{bmatrix} 13 & 18 & 23 \\ 18 & 25 & 32 \\ 23 & 32 & 41 \end{bmatrix}$$

We would like to avoid big intermediate matrices; and since matrix multiplication is *associative*, we can parenthesise however we want.

Matrix multiplication is *not commutative*, so we cannot permute the order of the matrices without changing the result.

18.2.2 Matrix-chain multiplication problem

Given a chain $<A_1A_2 \ldots A_n>$ of n matrix, where for $i = 1, 2, \ldots, n$ matrix A_i has dimension $P_{i-1} \times P_i$, fully parenthesize the product $A_1A_2, \ldots, A_n$ in a way that minimizes the number of scalar multiplications.

18.2.3 Recursive solution

In matrix chain multiplication problem we pick as our subproblems the problems of determining the minimum cost of a parenthesization of $A_i A_{i+1}, \ldots, A_j$ for $1 \le i \le j \le n$. Let $m[i, j]$ be the minimum no. of scalar multiplications needed to compute the matrix $A_{i..j}$ *e.g.*, the cost of a cheapest way to compute $A_{1..n}$ would 0.

If $i = j$ then $m[i, j] = 0$ as there is no cost of single matrix multiplication. To compute $m[i, j]$ when $i < j$, we take advantage of the structure of an optimal solution. Let us assume that the optimal parenthesization splits the product $A_i A_{i+1} \ldots, A_j$ between A_k and A_{k+1}, where $i \le k < j$, *i.e.*, $(A_i A_{i+1}, \ldots, A_k)(A_{k+1} \ldots A_j)$ then $m[i, j]$ is equal to the minimum cost for computing the subproducts $A_{i..k}$ and $A_{k+1..j}$ plus the cost of multiplying these two matrices together. Since computing the matrix process $A_{i..k} A_{k+1..j}$ takes $P_{i-1} P_k P_j$ scalar multiplication we obtain the formula for cost as,

$$\boldsymbol{m[i, j] = m[i, k] + m[k+1, j] + P_{i-1} P_k P_j} \quad \ldots(18.1)$$

Here k can have any value between $k = i, i + 1, \ldots, j - 1$ we need to check-them all and find the best thus minimum cost of product $A_j A_{j+1}, \ldots, A_j$ can be given by the equation

$$m[i, j] = \begin{cases} 0 & \text{if } i = j \\ \min\limits_{i \le k < j} \{m[i, k] + m[k+1, j] + P_{i-1} P_k P_j\} & \text{if } i < j \end{cases} \quad \ldots(18.2)$$

Note : P_i is column size of ith matrix. If there are only three matrices to be multiplied, assume that there is a A_0 matrix before A_1, therefore P_{i-1} which is column size of A_0 matrix is equal to row size of A_1 matrix.

EXAMPLE 18.1. *Consider the following matrix and its dimensions.*

matrix	dimension
A_1	30×35
A_2	35×15

A_3	15×5
A_4	5×10
A_5	10×20
A_6	20×25

Find optimal cost of multiplying $A_{2.5}$.

SOLUTION : Let us consider the different cost of multiplying matrix $A_2A_3A_4A_5$ which can be parenthesized in different manner.

$$m[2, 5] = \min \begin{cases} m[2, 2] + m[3, 5] + P_1P_2P_5 & \ldots(1) \\ m[2, 3] + m[4, 5] + P_1P_3P_5 & \ldots(2) \\ m[2, 4] + m[5, 5] + P_1P_4P_5 & \ldots(3) \end{cases}$$

Again dividing (1)

$$m[3, 5] = \min \begin{cases} m[3, 3] + m[4, 5] + P_2P_3P_5 & \ldots(4) \\ m[3, 4] + m[5. 5] + P_2P_4P_5 & \ldots(5) \end{cases}$$

$$m[4, 5] = \min m\{[4, 4] + m[5, 5] + P_3P_4P_5 \quad \ldots(6)$$

$$m[3, 4] = \min \{m[3, 3] + m[4, 4] + P_2P_3P_4 \quad \ldots(7)$$

Here we split each matrix till $m[i, i]$ is obtained.

Again dividing (2)

$$m[2, 3] = \{m[2, 2] + m[3, 3] + P_1P_2P_3 \quad \ldots(8)$$

we are not calculating $m[4, 5]$ as it is done in (6).

Now solving for eqn. (3)

$$m[2, 4] = \{m[2, 3] + m[3, 4] + P_1P_3P_4 \quad \ldots(9)$$

and here $m[2, 3]$ and $m[3, 4]$ obtained from eqn. (8) and (7) respectively.

Draw a matrix in pyramid graph form S.t. i is represented on R.H.S. and j in decreasing order on L.H.S.

e.g., for $m[2, 5]$ $i = 2, j = 5$

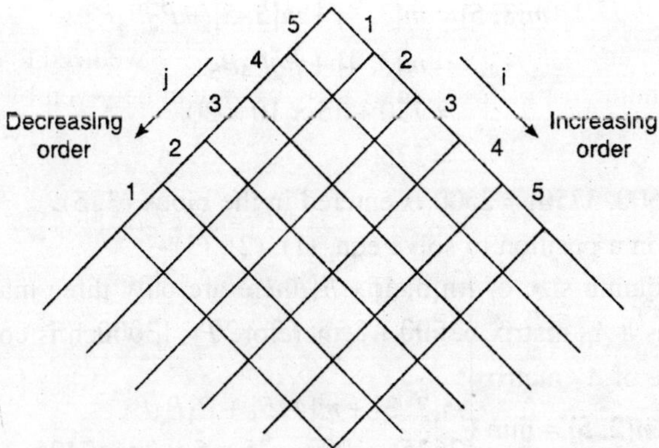

Now fill the entries which are easy to calculate in the corresponding (i, j) block from the equations derived using divide procedure.

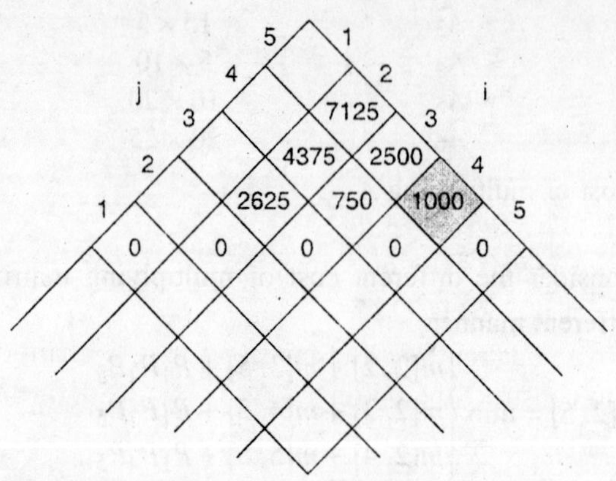

e.g., eqn. (6) is evaluated easily as

$$m[4, 4] = 0$$

$$m[5, 5] = 0$$

$$\therefore \quad m[4, 5] = P_3 P_4 P_5$$

$$= 5 \times 10 \times 20 = 1000$$

See figure above how the entries are made in $(i, j) = (4, 5)$.

In eqn. (7)

$$m[3, 4] = P_2 P_3 P_4 = 15 \times 5 \times 10 = 750$$

In eqn. (8)

$$m[2, 3] = P_1 P_2 P_3 = 35 \times 15 \times 5 = 2625$$

Now eqn. (4)

$$m[3, 5] = m[4, 5] + P_2 P_3 P_5$$

$$= 1000 + 15 \times 5 \times 20 \quad \text{Using (6)}$$

$$= 2500$$

Solving for eqn. (5)

$$m[3, 5] = m[3, 4] + m[5, 5] + P_2 P_4 P_5$$

$$= m[3, 4] + P_2 P_4 P_5$$

$$= 750 + 15 \times 10 \times 20$$

$$= 3750$$

Thus min (2500, 3750) = 2500 is entered in the block (3, 5).

Now we are in a position to solve eqn. (1), (2), (3)

$$\therefore \quad m[2, 5] = \min \begin{cases} m[3, 5] + P_1 P_2 P_5 \\ 2500 + 35 \times 15 \times 20 = 13000 \\ \\ m[2, 3] + m[4, 5] + P_1 P_3 P_5 \\ 2625 + 1000 + 35 \times 5 \times 20 = 7125 \\ \\ m[2, 4] + P_1 P_4 P_5 \\ 4375 + 35 \times 10 \times 20 = 11375 \end{cases}$$

$$m[2,4] = \min \begin{cases} m[2,2] + m[3,4] + P_1 P_2 P_4 \\ 0 + 750 + 35 \times 15 \times 10 = 6000 \\ m[2,3] + m[4,4] + P_1 P_3 P_4 \\ 2625 + 0 + 35 \times 5 \times 10 = 4375 \end{cases}$$

$$m[2,3] = \begin{cases} m[2,2] + m[3,3] + P_1 P_2 P_3 \\ 0 + 0 + 35 \times 15 \times 5 = 2625 \end{cases}$$

$\therefore$ optimal cost for $m[2, 5]$ is 7125.

Thus, from above equations we can construct matrix chain-order algorithm. To help us keep track of how to construct the optimal solution, let us define $\delta[i, j]$ to be a value equal to k at which we can split $A_i A_{i+1} \ldots A_k A_{k+1} \ldots A_j$.

```
MATRIX-CHAIN-ORDER (P)·
  n ← length [P] – 1
  for i ← 1 to n
      do m[i, i] ← 0
  for l ← 2 to n
      do for i ← 1 to n – l + 1
          do j ← i + l – 1
              m[i, j] ← ∞.
          for k ← i to j – 1
          do q ← m[i, k]+  m[k + 1, j] + p_{i-1} p_k p_j
              if q < m[i, j]
              then m[i,j] ← q
                  δ[i, j]← k
  return m and δ.
```

Here in this algorithm value of $m[i, j]$ is set to ∞ δ which is large quantity, so when we get a smaller value q than this it is replaced and stored in $m[i, j]$. This way optimal cost is calculated.

Running time of this algorithm is $\Theta(n^3)$.

18.2.4 Overlapping subproblems

Recursive algorithm for the problem solves the same subproblems over and over, rather than always generating new subproblems this is called overlapping subproblems. This is resolved in dynamic problem by storing the solution in some *look up table* where it can been seen when required *e.g.*, $m[3, 4]$ is referenced 4 times : during the computations of $m[2, 4]$, $m[1, 4]$, $m[3, 5]$ and $m[3, 6]$. This increases the running time and space. See the following algorithm :

```
Recursive-Matrix-Chain (p, i, j)
if i = j
then return 0
```

```
m[i, j] ← ∞.
for K ← i to  j − 1
do q ← Recursive-Matrix-chain (p, i, k) +
        Recursive-Matrix-chain (p, k + 1, j) + p_{i-1} p_k p_j
if q < m[i, j]
then m[i, j] ← q.
  return m[i, j]
```

Running Time :

$T(1) \geq 1$

$$T(n) \geq 1 + \sum_{k=1}^{n-1} (T(k) + T(n-k) + 1) \text{ for } n > 1$$

$$\geq 2 \sum_{i=1}^{n-1} T(i) + n = 2 \sum_{i=1}^{n-1} 2^{i-1} + n$$

as $T(1) \geq 1 = 2^{\circ}$ (*i.e.*, 2^{i-1})

$\therefore$ $T(n) \geq 2(2^{n-1} - 1) + n$

$= (2^n - 2) + n$

$\geq 2^{n-1}$

Thus, $T(n) = \Omega(2^n)$

EXAMPLE 18.2. *Boolean matrices are matrices such that each entry is 0 or 1, and matrix multiplication is performed by using AND for − and OR for +. Suppose we are given two $n \times n$ random Boolean matrices A and B, so that the probability that any entry in either is 1, is $1/k$. Show that if k is a constant, then there is an algorithm for multiplying A and B whose expected running time is $O(n^2)$. What if k is n?*

SOLUTION : Employ the trick used in Java, C, and C++, where we terminate an OR early if one its terms is 1. The probability that one of the terms in each row-column product is $1/k^2$; hence, the expected time for any row-column product is constant. Therefore, the expected running time of the entire product of A and B is $O(n^2)$. If k is n, on the other hand, then the probability than an entry in a row-column product is 1 is $1/n^2$; hence, the expected running time for a row-column product is $O(n)$ in this case. That is, in this case, the expected time to multiply A and B is $O(n^3)$.

18.2.5 Memoization

A memoized recursive algorithm maintains an entry in a table for the solution of each subproblem. Each table entry initially contains a special value to indicate that the entry has yet to be filled in when the subproblem is first encountered during execution of the recursive algorithms its solution is computed and then stored in the table. Each subsequent time the subproblem is encountered it is looked up in the table and simply returned.

```
MEMOIZED-MATRIX-CHAIN (P)
  n ← length[P] − 1
  for i ← 1 to n
      do for i ← i to n
          do m[i, j] ← ∞.
  return LOOK-UP-CHAIN (p, 1, n)

LOOKUP-CHAIN (p, i, j)
  if m[i, j] < ∞
      then return m[i, j]
  if i = j
      then m[i, i] ← 0
  else for k ← i to j − 1
      do q ← LOOKUP-CHAIN (p, i, k) +
          + LOOKUP-CHAIN (p, k + 1, j) + p_{i-1} p_k p_j
  if q < m[i, j]
      then m[i, j] ← q
  return m[i, j]
```

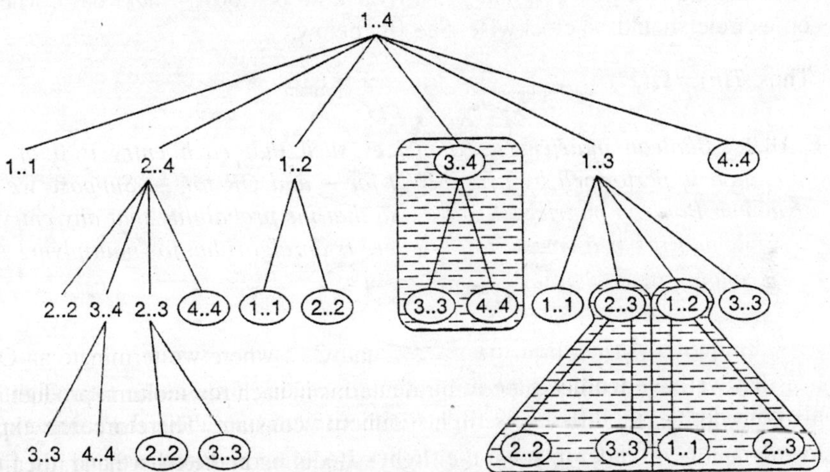

Fig. 18.2. Memorization.

Running time of MEMORIZED-MATRIX-CHAIN is $\theta(n^3)$ as for each $\theta(n^2)$ call LOOKUP-CHAIN takes $\theta(n)$ time.

EXAMPLE 18.3. *Suppose you are given a timetable, which consist of:*

A set A of n airports, and for each airport $a \in A$, a minimum connecting time $c(a)$

A set F of m flights, and the following, for each flight $f \in F$:

Origin airport $a_1(f) \in A$

Destination airport $a_2(f) \in A$

Departure time t_1 (f)

Arrival time t_2 (f).

Describe an efficient algorithm for the flight scheduling problem. In this problem, we are given airports a and b, and a time t, and we wish to compute a sequence of flights that allows one to arrive at the earliest possible time in b when departing from a at or after time t. Minimum connecting times at intermediate airports should be observed. What is the running time of your algorithm as a function of n and m?

SOLUTION : We will describe two solutions for the flight scheduling problem.

1. We will reduce the flight scheduling problem to the shortest paths problem. That means that we will construct an instance for the shortest paths problem, that when solved, gives us a solution for the flight scheduling problem. Given the set of airports A and the set of flights F, we consider a weighted directed graph $\vec{G}$ that is constructed as follows.

For each airport $a_i \in A$, draw a circle $circle_i$ to represent the time (24 hours).

For each flight $f_i \in F$, find the origin airport a_o, the destination airport a_d, the departure time t_d, and the arrival time t_a. Draw a vertex v_1 on $circle_o$ marked the time t_d and also draw a vertex v_2 on $circle_d$ marked the time $(t_a + c(a_d))$. Draw an directed edge from v_1 to v_2 with weight $t_a + c(a_d) - t_d$ (of course we must compute the correct weight (flight time) in case like the departure time is 10:00 PM and the arrival time is 1:00AM next day). The direction of edges on a circle should be clockwise. See fig. below.

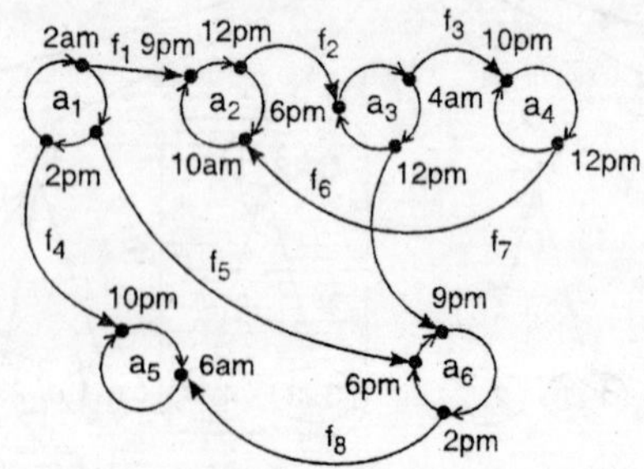

Note that we have included the minimum connecting time in the total flight time, so we can only consider the modified new flights without worrying about the connecting times.

Given graph $\vec{G}$, in order to solve the flight scheduling problem, we can just find a shortest path from the first vertex on *circle*(a) (origin airport a) representing time t or after t to one vertex on *circle* (b) (destination airport b) in the graph. The flights' sequence can be obtained from the shortest path from origin to destination.

We can use Dijkstra's algorithm to find the desired shortest path (observe that $\vec{G}$ has only positive weights), but we need to slightly modify the algorithm (as it is presented in the textbook), so that it is applicable to directed graphs. The modifications should be straightforward: in the relaxation step, we only consider edges with orientation from the previously selected vertex to some other vertex. Finally, we need keep track (mark) the shortest path, so we include a parent-child relationship to the visited nodes (value p).

```
FlightScheduling (a, b, t)
construct graph G⃗
v ← first vertex on circle(a) representing time t or
                                                   after t
D[v] ← 0
for each vertex u ≠ v of G⃗ do
      D[u] ← ∞
let a priority queue Q contain all the vertices of G⃗
                                       with D values as keys
while Q is not empty do
      u ← EXTRACT-MIN()
      for each vertex z such that
      (u⃗, z) ∈ E_G⃗ and z ≠ Q do
            if D[u] + w((u⃗, z)) < D[z] then
                  D[z] ← D[u] + w((u⃗, z))
                  change to D[z] they key of vertex z in Q
                  p[z] ← u
w ← vertex on circle(b) with minimum value D
return reversed path from w to v (using values p)
```

The time complexity of the algorithm essentially the time complexity of Dijkstra's algorithm (since the construction of the graph can be done in linear ($O(n+m)$) time). Using a heap as the priority queue, we achieve a total $O((N+M)\log N)$ time complexity, where N the number of vertices of $\vec{G}$ and M the number of edges of $\vec{G}$. Note that, generally, $M = O(m)$ and $N = O(m)$, so the running time of the algorithm is $O(m \log m)$.

The following algorithm finds the minimum travel time path from airport $a \in A$ to airport $b \in A$. Recall, we must depart from a at or after time t. Note, $\oplus$ and $\leq$ are operations which we must implement. We define these operations as follows: If $x \oplus y = z$, then z is the point in time (with date taken into consideration) which follows x by *by* time units. Also, if $a \leq b$, then a is a point in time which preceeds or equals b. These operations can be implemented in constant time.

```
FlightScheduling (a, b, t)
initialize a set P to a
initialize incoming_flight (x) to nil for each x ∈ A
earliest_arrival_time (a) ← t
for all x ∈ A such that x ≠ a do
      earliest_arrival_time (x) ← ∞
time_can_depart ← ∞
repeat
      remove from P airport x such that
                  earliest_arrival_time (x) is soonest
      if x ≠ b then
```

```
            if x = a then
                  time_can_depart ← t
            else
                  time_can_depart ←
                        earlist_arrival_time(x)  ⊕ c(x)
            for each flight f ∈ F such that a1(f) = x do
                  if time_can_depart ≤ t1 (f) and
                  t2 (f) ≤ earliest_arrival_time (a2 (f)) then
                        earliest-arrival_time (a2 (f)) ← t2 (f)
                        incoming_flight (a2 (f)) ← f
            add a2 (f) to P if it is not yet there
until x = b
initialize city to b
initialize flight_sequence to nil
while (city ≠ a) do
            append incoming_flight (city) to flight_sequence
            assign to city the departure city of
                                          incoming_flight (city)
reverse flight_sequence and output
```

The algorithm essentially performs Dijkstra's Shortest Path Algorithm (the cities are the vertices and the flights are the edges). The only small alternations are that we restrict edge traversals (an edge can only be traversed at a certain time) we stop at a certain goal, and we output the path (a sequence of flights) to this goal. The only change of possible consequence to the time complexity is the flight sequence computation (the last portion of the algorithm). A minimum time path will certainly never contain more that m flights (since there are only m total flights). Thus, we may discover the path (tracing from b back to a) in $O(m)$ time. Reversal of this path will require $O(m)$ time as well. Thus, since the time complexity of Dijkstra's algorithm is $O(m \log n)$, the time complexity of our algorithm is $O(m \log n)$.

Note: Prior to execution of this algorithm, we may (if not given to us) divide F into subsets $F_1, F_2, \ldots, F_N$, where F_i contains the flights which depart from airport i. Then when we say "for each flight $f \in F$ such that $a_1(f) = x$", we will not have to waste time looking through flights which do not depart from x (we will actually compute "for each flight $f \in F_x$"). This division of F will require $O(m)$ time (since there are m total flights), and thus will not slow down the computation of the minimum time path (which requires $O(m \log n)$ time).

18.3 Longest Common Subsequence

We given two subsequence $X = <x_1, x_2, \ldots, x_m>$ and $Y = <y_1, y_2, y_3, \ldots, y_n>$ and we wish to find a maximum length common subsequence of X and Y.

EXAMPLE 18.4. *Find the LCS of $X = <A, B, C, D, A, B>$ and $Y = <B, D, C, A, B, A>$*

SOLUTION : Here first element of *X* is matched with that *Y* for the first occurrence e.g., *A* in *X* matches in *Y* at 4th indices then *B* is matched but it should be beyond the 4th index not prior to it. *B* matches in *Y* at 5, then *C* is not found, *B* is not found finally *A* in *X* at index 6 is matched in *Y* at index 6 so subsequence obtained is ABA.

(1) ABA (Start in X at index 1)
(2) BCA (" " " " " 2)
(3) CBA (" " " " " 3)
(4) BDAB (" " " " " 4)
(5) DAB (" " " " " 5)
(6) AB (" " " " " 6)
(7) (B) (" " " " " 7)

We can see that (4) BDAB is longest common subsequence with length 4.

EXAMPLE 18.5. *Determine an LCS of* <1, 0, 0, 1, 0, 1, 0, 1> *and* <0, 1, 0, 1, 1, 0, 1, 1, 0>

SOLUTION : $X = <1, 0, 0, 1, 0, 1, 0, 1>$;
$Y = <0, 1, 0, 1, 1, 0, 1, 1, 0>$

(1) <1, 0, 0, 1, 0> index 1 in *X*
(2) <0, 0, 1, 0, 1, 0> index 2 in *X*
(3) <0, 1, 0, 1, 0, 1> index 3 in *X*
(4) <1, 0, 1, 0> index 4 in *X*

Here we obtain (2) and (3) as LCS as any other index beyond 4 in *X* will not yield any LCS greater than 6.

Applying Dynamic Programming to the LCS Problem

We can solve the LCS problem much faster than exponential time using dynamic programming. As mentioned earlier, one of the key components of the dynamic programming technique is the definition of simple subproblems that satisfy the subproblem optimization and subproblem overlap properties.

In LCS problem, we are given two character strings, *X* and *Y*, of length *n* and *m*, respectively, and are asked to find a longest string *S* that is a subsequence of both *X* and *Y*. Since *X* and *Y* are character strings, we have a natural set of indices with which to define subproblems—indices into the strings *X* and *Y*. Let us define a subproblem, therefore, as that of computing the length of the longest common subsequence of $X[0..i]$ and $Y[0..j]$, denoted $L[i, j]$.

This definition allows us to rewrite $L[i, j]$ in terms of optimal subproblem solutions. We consider the following two cases. (See Fig. 18.3).

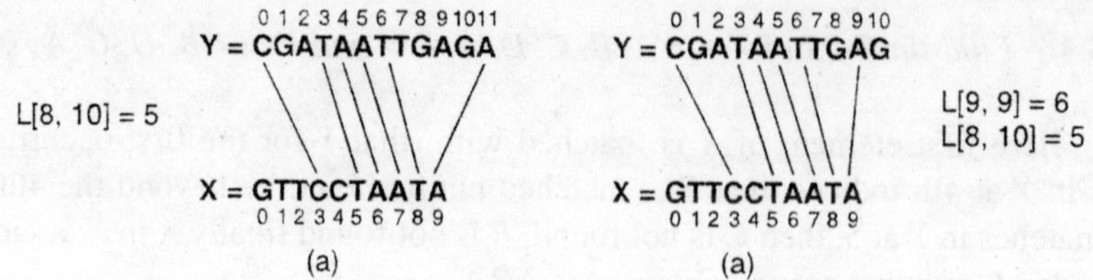

Fig. 18.3. The two cases in the definition of $L[i, j]$: (a) $X[i] = Y[j]$; (b) $X[i] \neq Y[j]$.

Case 1: $X[i] = Y[j]$

Let $c = X[i] = Y[j]$. We claim that a longest common subsequence of $X[0..i]$ and $Y[0..j]$ ends with c. To prove this claim, let us suppose it is not true. There has to be some longest common subsequence $X[i_1]\ X[i_2]\ \ldots\ X[i_k] = Y[j_1]\ Y[j_2]\ \ldots\ Y[j_k]$. If $X[i_k] = c$ or $Y[j_k] = c$, then we get the same sequence by setting $i_k = i$ and $j_k = j$. Alternately, if $X[j_k] \neq c$, then we can get an even longer common subsequence by adding c to the end. Thus, a longest common subsequence of $X[0..i]$ and $Y[0..j]$ ends with $c = X[i] = Y[j]$. Therefore, we set

$$L[i, j] = L[i-1, j-1] + 1 \text{ if } X[i] = Y[j]. \qquad \ldots(1)$$

Case 2: $X[i] \neq Y[j]$

In this case, we cannot have a common subsequence that includes both $X[i]$ and $Y[j]$. That is, a common subsequence can end with $X[i]$, $Y[j]$, or neither, but not both. Therefore, we set

$$L[i, j] = \max\{L[i-1, j], L[i, j-1]\} \text{ if } X[i] \neq Y[j]. \qquad \ldots(2)$$

In order to make Equations (1) and (2) make sense in the boundary cases when $i = 0$ or $j = 0$, we define $L[i, -1] = 0$ for $i = -1, 0, 1, \ldots, n-1$ and $L[-1, j] = 0$ for $j = -1, 0, 1, \ldots, m-1$.

The LCS Algorithm

The above definition of $L[i, j]$ satisfies subproblem optimization, for we cannot have a longest common subsequence without also having longest common subsequences for the subproblems. Also, it uses subproblem overlap, because a subproblem solution $L[i, j]$ can be used in several other problem (namely, the problem $L[i+1, j]$, $L[i, j+1]$, and $L[i+1, j+1]$).

Turning this definition of $L[i, j]$ into an algorithm is actually quite straightfordward. We initialize an $(n+1) \times (m+1)$ array, L, for the boundary cases when $i = 0$ or $j = 0$. Namely, we initialie $L[i, -1] = 0$ for $i = -1, 0, 1, \ldots, n-1$ and $L[-1, j] = 0$ for $j = -1, 0, 1, \ldots, m-1$. (This is a slight abuse of notation, since in reality, we would have to index the rows and columns of L starting with 0.) Then, we iteratively build up values in L until we have $L[n-1, m-1]$, the length of a longest common subsequence of X and Y. We give a pseudo-code description of how this approach results in a dynamic programming solution to the longest common subsequences (LCS) problem. Note that the algorithm stores only the $L[i, j]$ values, not the matches.

LCS (X, Y) :

```
for i ← -1 to n - 1 do
        L[i, -1] ← 0
for j ← 0 to m - 1 do
        L[-1, j] ← 0
```

```
for i ← 0 to n − 1 do
      for j ← 0 to m − 1 do
            if X[i] = Y[j] then
                  L[i, j] ← L[i − 1, j − 1] + 1
            else
                  L[i, j] ← max{L[i − 1, j], L[i, j − 1]}
return array L
```

Performance. The running time of Algorithm is easy to analyze, for it is dominated by two nested for-loops, with the outer one iterating n times and the inner one iterating m times. Since the if-statement and assignment inside the loop each requires $O(1)$ primitive operations, this algorithm runs in $O(nm)$ time. Thus, the dynamic programming technique can be applied to the longest common subsequence problem to improve significantly over the exponential-time brute-force solution to the LCS problem.

Algorithm LCS computes the length of the longest common subsequence (stored in $L[n-1, m-1]$), but not the subsequence itself. As shown in the following theorem, a simple postprocessing step can extract the longest common subsequence from the array L returned by the algorithm.

THEOREM 18.1. Given a string X of n characters and a string Y of m characters, we can find the longest common subsequence of X and Y in O (nm) time.

EXAMPLE 18.5. *Give dynamic programming version of fibonacci series.*

SOLUTION : Let us consider an object soln. Which creates the instance of some dictionary object DICT. The process of recording solutions of subproblems is called memoization operations available with DICT is **create, member, retrive, store.**

If A is normal algorithm then $DP(A)$ **is dynamic version of A.** Assuming that every call is stored in dictionary and every time is checked with new solution. whether it exists or not, if not it is stored

```
fibNew (n)
Soln ← create (n)
    return fibDP(Soln, n)
    fibDP(soln, k)
   if (k < 2)
          fib ← k
   else
          if Not (member (soln, k − 1))
                  f1 = fibDP (soln, k − 1)
   else
          f1 = retrive (soln, k − 1)
   if not (member (soln, k − 2))
```

```
            f2 = fibDP (soln, k - 2)
    else
            f2 = retrive (soln, k - 2)
    fib = f1 + f2
    store (soln, k, fib)
    return fib.
```

fib New does the initialization suitable for the top-level problem (*n* in this case), then calls fibDP (soln, *n*)

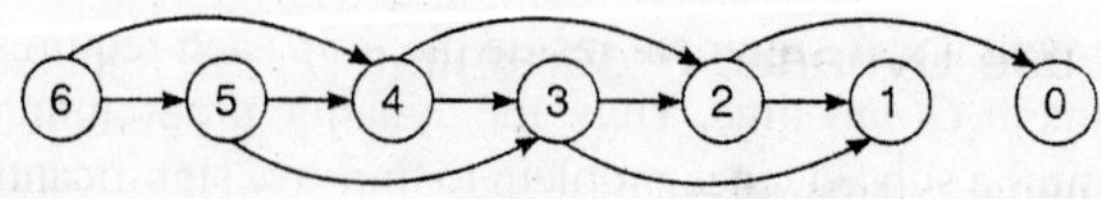

Fig. 18.4.

EXAMPLE 18.6. *Give an $O(n^2)$ algorithm to find the longest monotonically increasing sequence in a sequence of n numbers.*

SOLUTION : Build an example first: (5, 2, 8, 7, 1, 6, 4)

Ask yourself what would you like to know about the first $n - 1$ elements to tell you the answer for the entire sequence?

1. The length of the longest sequence in $S_1, S_2, \ldots S_{n-1}$. (seems obvious)
2. The length of the longest sequence S_n will extend! (not as obvious - this is the idea)

Let S_i be the length of the longest sequence ending with the *i*th character:

sequence 5 2 8 7 3 1 6 4

S_i 1 1 2 2 2 1 3 3

How do we compute *si* ?

$$s_i = \max_{0 < j < i,\ seq[j] < seq[i]} S_j + 1$$

$$s_0 = 0$$

To find the longest sequence - we know it ends somewhere, so length = $\max_{i=1}^{n} s_i$

The Principle of Optimality

To use dynamic programming, the problem must observe the *principle of optimality*, that whatever the initial state is, remaining decisions must be optimal with regard the state following from the first decision.

Combinational problems may have this property but may use too much memory/time to be efficient.

EXAMPLE 18.7. *The Traveling Salesman Problem*

SOLUTION : Let $T(i_1, j_1, j_2 \ldots, j_k))$ be the cost of the optimal tour for i to 1 that goes through each of the other cities once

$$T(i{:}\ i_1, j_2, \ldots, j_i) = Min_{1 \le m \le k}\ C\ [i, j_m] + T(j_m{:}\ j_1, j_2, \ldots, j_k)$$

$$T(i, j) = C(i, j) + C(j, 1)$$

Here there can be any subset of $j_1, j_2, \ldots, j_k$ instead of any subinterval - hence exponential.

Still, with other ideas (some type of pruning or best-first search) it can be effective for combinational search.

When can you use Dynamic Programming ?

Dynamic programming computers recurrences efficiently by storing partial results. Thus dynamic programming can only be efficient when there are not too many partial results to compute!

There are $n!$ permutations of an n-element set - we cannot use dynamic programming to store the best solution for each subpermutation. There are 2^n subsets of an n-element set - we cannot use dynamic programming to store the best solution for each.

However, there are only $n(n-1)/2$ continguous substrings of a string, each described by a starting and ending point, so we can use it for string problems (see chapter 14). There are only $n(n-1)/2$ possible subtrees of a binary search tree, each described by a maximum and minimum key, so we can use it for optimizing binary search trees (see chapter 14. OBST).

Dynamic programming works best on objects which are linearly ordered and cannot be rearranged - characters in a string, matrices in a chain, points around the boundary of a polygon, the left-to-right order of leaves in a search tree. Whenever your objects are ordered in a left-to-right way, you should smell dynamic programming!

18.4 Triangulation

Triangulation of a polygon is a set T of chords of the polygon that divides the polygon into disjoint triangles.

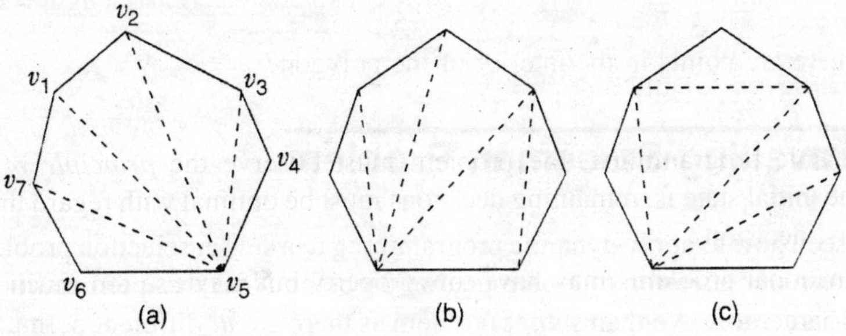

Fig. 18.5. Triangulation.

If we are given a convex polygon $P = <v_0, v_1, v_2, ..., v_{n-1}>$ and a ωt. Function ω defined on triangles formed by sides and chords of P. The problem is to minimize the sum of wts. of triangles in the triangulation.

$$\omega(\delta, v_i, v_j v_k) = | v_i v_j | + | v_j v_k | + | v_k v_i |, \ldots$$

where $| v_i v_j |$ is the *eucledian distance* from v_i to v_j.]

The length of a triangulation is the sum of the diagonal lengths.

We seek to find the minimum length triangulation. For a convex polygon, or part thereof:

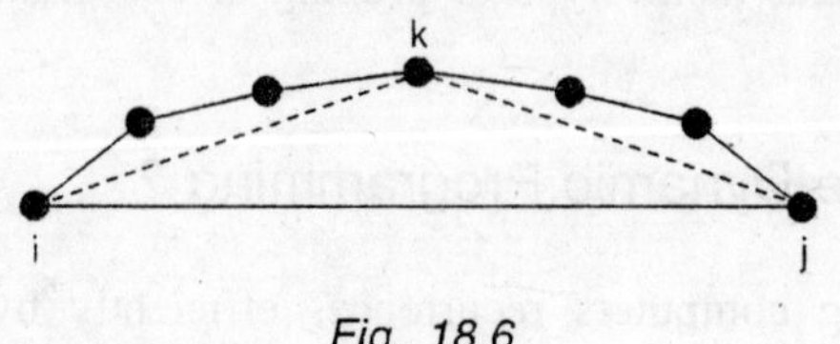

Fig. 18.6

Once we identify the correct connecting vertex, the polygon is partitioned into two smaller pieces, both of which must be triangulated optimally!

$$t[i, i+1] = 0$$

$$t[i, j] = \min_{k=1}^{j} [i, k] + i[k, j] + |ik| + |kj|$$

Evaluation proceeds as in the matrix multiplication example $\binom{n}{2}$ values of t, each of which takes $O(j - i)$ time if we evaluate the sections in order of increasing size.

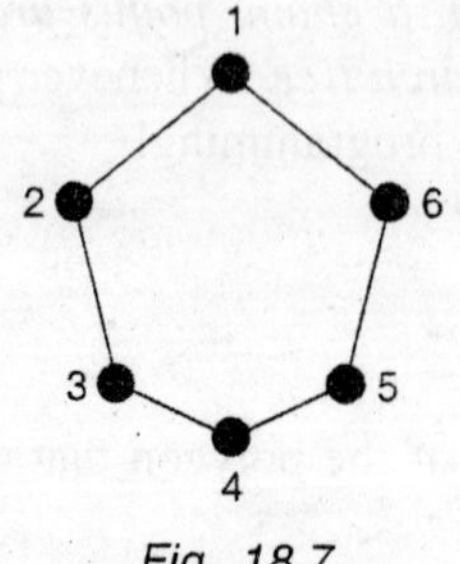

Fig. 18.7

$j - i = 2$

13, 24, 35, 46, 51, 62

$j - i = 3$

14, 25, 36, 41, 52, 63

$j - i = 4$

15, 26, 31, 42, 53, 64

Finish with 16

What if there are points in the interior of the polygon?

18.5 The Travelling-Salesman Problem

We have seen how to apply dynamic programming to a subset selection problem (0/1 knapsack). Now we turn our attention to a permutation problem. Note that permutation problems usually are much harder to solve than subset problem as there are $n!$ different permutations of n objects whereas there are only 2^n different subsets of n objects ($n! > 2^n$). Let $G = (V, E)$ be a directed graph with edge costs c_{ij}. The varibale c_{ij} is defined such that $c_{ij} > 0$ for all i and j and $c_{in} = \infty$ if $(i, j) \notin E$. Let $| V | = n$ and assume $n > 1$. A *tour* of G is a directed simple cycle that includes every vertex in V. The cost of a tour is the sum of the cost of the edges on the tour. The *travelling salesperson problem* is to find a tour of minimum cost.

The traveling salesperson problem finds application in a variety of situations. Suppose we have to route a postal van to pick up mail from mail boxes located at n different sites. An $n + 1$ vertex graph can be used to represent the situation. One vertex represents the post office from which the postal van starts and to which it must return. Edge (i, j) is assigned a cost equal to the distance from site i to site j. The route taken by the postal van is a tour and we are interested in finding a tour of minimum length.

As a second example, suppose we wish to use a robot arm to lighten the nuts on some piece of machinery on an assembly line. The arm will start from its initial position (which is over the first nut to be tightened), successively move to each of the remaining nuts, and return to the inittial position. The path of the arm is clearly a tour on a graph in which vertices represent the nuts. A minimum-cost tour will minimize the time needed for the arm to complete its task (note that only the total arm movement time is variable; the nut tightening time is independent of the tour).

Our final example is from a production environment in which several commodities are manufactured on the same set of machines. The manufacture proceeds in cycles. In each production cycle, n different commodities are produced. When the machine are changed from production of commodity i to commodity j, a change over cost c_{ij} is incurred. It is desired to find a sequence in which to manufacture these commodities. This sequence should minimize the sum of change over costs (the remaining production costs are sequence independent). Since the manufacture proceeds cyclically, it is necessary to include the cost of starting the next cycle. This is just the change over cost from the last to the first commodity. Hence, this problem can be regarded as a travelling salesperson problem on an n vertex graph with edge cost c_{ij}'s being the changeover cost from commodity i to commodity j.

In the following discussion we shall, without loss of generality, regard a tour to be a simple path that starts and ends at vertex 1. Every tour consists of an edge $(1, k)$ for some $k \in V - \{1\}$ and a path from vertex k to vertex 1. The path from vertex k to vertex 1 goes throught each vertex in $V - \{1, K\}$ exactly once. It is easy to see that if the tour is optimal, then the path from k to 1 must be shortest k to 1 path going through all vertices in $V - \{1, k\}$. Hence, the principle of optimality holds. Let $g(i, S)$ be the length of a shortest path starting at vertex i, going of an optimal salesperson tour. From the principal of optimality it follows that

$$g(1, V - \{1\}) = \min_{2 \le k \le n} \{c_{1k} + g(k, V - \{1, k\})\} \qquad \ldots(1)$$

Generalizing (1), we obtain (for $i \notin S$)

$$g(i, S) = \min_{j \in S} \{c_{ij} + g(j, S - \{j\})\} \qquad \ldots(2)$$

Equation (1) can be solved for $g(1, V - \{1\})$ if we know $g(k, V - \{1, k\})$ for all choices of k. The g values can be obtained by using (2). Clearly, $g(i, \phi) = c_{i1}$, $1 \le i \le n$. Hence, we can use (2) to obtain $g(i, S)$ for all S of size 1. Then we can obtain $g(i, S)$ for S with $|S| = 2$, and so on. When $|S| < n - 1$, the values of i and S for which $g(i, S)$ is needed are such that $i \ne 1$, $1 \notin S$ and $i \notin S$.

EXAMPLE 18.8. *Consider the directed graph of Figure 18.8(a). The edge lengths are given by matrix of Figure 18.8(b).*

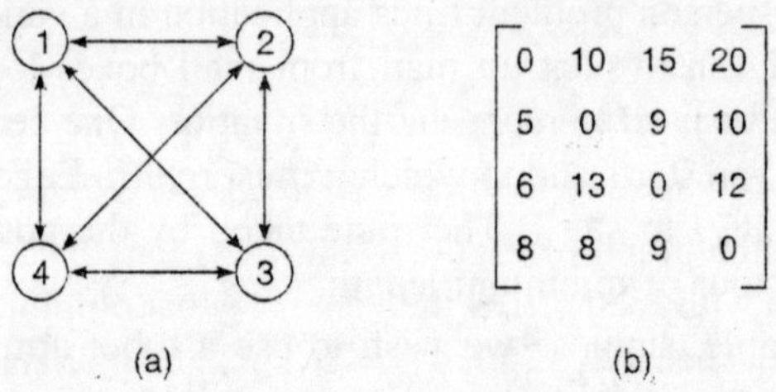

Fig. 18.8. Directed graph and edge length matrix C.

SOLUTION :

$$c = \begin{array}{c} \\ 1 \\ 2 \\ 3 \\ 4 \end{array}\begin{array}{c} \begin{array}{cccc} 1 & 2 & 3 & 4 \end{array} \\ \begin{bmatrix} 0 & 10 & 15 & 20 \\ 5 & 0 & 9 & 10 \\ 6 & 13 & 0 & 12 \\ 8 & 8 & 9 & 0 \end{bmatrix} \end{array}$$

$$g(1, \phi) = c_{11} = 0$$
$$g(2, \phi) = c_{21} = 5$$
$$g(3, \phi) = c_{31} = 6$$
$$g(4, \phi) = c_{41} = 8$$

We have $$g(i, S) = \min_{j \in S} \{c_{ij} + g(j\, S - \{j\})\}$$

Here in TSP we start from vertex 1 and move to next vertex, either one vertex, two vertex three vertex or n-vertex and measure distance from each vertex to start vertex and sum the minimum distance at each vertex to start vertex S contains number of vertex of a time going 1.

When $|S| = 1$,

$$g(2, \{3\}) = c_{23} + g(3, \{3\} - \{3\})$$
$$= c_{23} + g(3, \phi)$$
$$= 9 + 6 = 15$$
$$g(3, \{2\}) = c_{32} + g(2, \phi)$$
$$= 13 + 5 = 18$$

Since graph is bidirection, we calculate distance from (2, 3) as well as (3, 2)

$$g(4, \{2\}) = c_{42} + g(2, \phi) = 8 + 5 = 13$$
$$g(2, \{4\}) = c_{24} + g(4, \phi) = 10 + 8 = 18$$

Again calculating, (3, 4), (4, 3)

$$g(3, \{4\}) = c_{34} + g(4, \phi) = 12 + 8 = 20$$
$$g(4, \{3\}) = c_{43} + g(3, \phi) = 9 + 6 = 15$$

Next we compute $g(i, S)$ with $|S| = 2$, $i \neq 1$ where $1 \notin S$, $i \notin S$

$$g(2, \{3, 4\}) = \min \{c_{23} + g(3, \{4\}), c_{24} + g(4, \{3\})\}.$$
$$= \min (9 + 20, 10 + 15) = 25$$

$$g(3, \{2, 4\}) = \min \{c_{32} + g(2, \{4\}), c_{34} + g(4, \{2\}) = 25\}$$
$$g(4, \{2, 3\}) = \min \{c_{42} + g\{2, 3\}, c_{43} + g\{3, 2\} = 23\}$$

Finally, from (1) we obtain

$$g(1, \{2, 3, 4\}) = \min \{c_{12} + g(2, \{3, 4\}), c_{13} + g(3, \{2, 4\}), c_{14} + g(4, \{2, 3\})\}$$
$$= 35$$

An optimal tour o the graph of Figure 18.8(a) has length 35. A tour of this length can be constructed if we retain with each $g(i, S)$ the value of j that minimizes the right-hand side of (2). Let $J(i, S)$ be this value. Then $J(1, \{2, 3, 4\}) = 2$. Thus the tour starts from 1 and goes to 2. The remaining tour can be obtained from $g(2, \{3, 4\})$. So $J(2, \{3, 4\}) = 5$. Thus the next edge is (2, 4). The remaining tour is for $g(4, \{4\})$. So $J(4, \{3\}) = 3$. The optimal tour is 1, 2, 4, 3, 1.

Let N be the number of $g(i, S)$'s that have to the computed before (1) can be used to compute $g(1, V - \{1\})$. For each value of $|S|$ there are $n - 1$ choices for i. The number of distinct sets S of size k not including 1 and i is $\binom{n-2}{k}$. Hence

$$N = \sum_{k=0}^{n-2} (n-1)\binom{n-2}{k} = (n-1)\, 2^{n-2}$$

An algorithm that proceeds to find an optimal tour by using (1) and (2) will require $\Theta(n^2\, 2^n)$ time as the computation of $g(i, S)$ with $|S| = k$ required $k - 1$ comparisons when solving (2). This is better than enumerating all $n!$ different tours to find the best one. The most serious drawback of this dynamic programming solutions is the space needed, $O(n\, 2^n)$. This is too large even for modest values of n.

EXERCISE

1. Suppose that dimensions of matrices A, B, C, D are 20×2, 2×15, 15×40 and 40×4 respectively. what will be the optimal number of scalar multiplications?
2. Give a memoized version of LCS-LENGTH that runs in $O(mn)$ time.
3. Give an $O(n^2)$ time and $O(\text{nlgn})$ algorithm to find the longest monotonically increasing subsequence of n numbers.
4. Find an optimal triangulation of a regular octagon with unit length sides
$$\omega(\delta\, v_i\, v_j\, v_k) = |v_i\, v_j| + |v_j\, v_k| + |v_k\, v_i|, \ldots$$
5. Prove that every triangulation of an n-vertex convex polygon has $n - 3$ chords and divides the polygons into $n - 2$ triangles.
6. Explain why memoization is ineffective in speeding up a good divide and conquer algorithm such as *MERGE SORT.*

19

GREEDY ALGORITHMS

The difference between greedy and dynamic algorithm is that, greedy algorithms looks for locally optimal solution and assumes it as best but they do not always yield the optimal solution.

All of the greedy problems have n inputs and. require to obtain a subset that satisfies some constraints. Any subset that satisfies these constraints is called a *feasible* solution, we need to find a feasible Solution that either maximizes or minimises a given *objective function.*

Consider a greedy algorithm that selects an input (by Select) function) and check for its feasibility constraints. If it is feasible then it is added to solution.

```
Greedy (A, n)
Soln ← ϕ
For i ← 1 to n
     do x ← select (A)
          if feasible (soln., x) then
               soln. ← Union (soln, x)
return soln.
```

19.1 Knapsack Problem

A thief robbing a store finds n items, *ith* items is worth v_i dollars and weighs w_i pounds where- v_i and w_i are integers. He wants to take as valuable load as possible, but he can carry at most pounds in his knapsack (bag) for some integer w.

If a thief carries all or none of a goods in the store (e.g., some solid object) which can not be parted or broken then it is **0 – 1 knapsack problem.**

If a thief can carry fractional part then it is fractional knapsack problem (*i.e.*, powdered form of good)

If object i has *wt.* w_i and knapsack has a capacity m and if a fraction x_i, $0 \le x_i \le 1$ of object i is placed into the knapsack, then a profit of $P_i\, x_i$ is earned. The objective is to obtain the filling of knapsack that maximizes the total profit earned, thus,

$$\text{maximise} \quad \sum_{1 \le i \le n} P_i\, x_i \qquad \ldots\text{(i)}$$

$$\text{Subjet to} \quad \sum_{1 \le x \le n} w_i\, x_i \le m$$

and $0 \le x_i \le 1$, $1 \le \omega_i \le n$ profits and wts. are +ve quantity

EXAMPLE 19.1. *Consider the following instance of the knapsack problem* $n = 3$, $m = 20$, $(P_1, P_2, P_3) = (25, 24, 15)$ *and* $(w_1, w_2, w_3) = (18, 15, 10)$

SOLUTION : Here n is no of objects, m is capacity of bag, P_i is profit related to w_i.

	(x_1, x_2, x_3)	$\Sigma\, w_i\, x_i$	$\Sigma\, P_i\, x_i$
1.	$\left(\frac{1}{2}, \frac{1}{3}, \frac{1}{4}\right)$	16.5	24.25
2.	$\left(1, \frac{2}{15}, 0\right)$	20	28.2
3.	$\left(0, \frac{2}{3}, 1\right)$	20	31
4.	$\left(0, 1, \frac{1}{2}\right)$	20	**31.5**

Solution 4 yields the maximum profit. This is optimal soln.

EXAMPLE 19.2. *Find an optimal solution to the knapsack instance* $n = 7$, $m = 15$, $(P_1, P_2, \ldots, P_7) = (10, 5, 15, 7, 6, 18, 3)$ *and* $(w_1, w_2, w_3, \ldots, w_7) = (2\ 3, 5, 7, 1, 4, 1)$

SOLUTION :

	$x_1\ x_2\ x_3\ x_4\ x_5\ x_6\ x_7$	$\Sigma\ w_i\ x_i$	$\Sigma\ P_i\ p_i$
1.	(1, 1, 0, 1, 1, 0, 1)	14	31
2.	(1, 0, 1, 0, 1, 1, 0)	13	52
3.	(1 1, 1, 0, 1, 1, 0)	15	**54**
4.	(1, 1, 1, 0, 0, 1, 1)	15	51

Soln. 3 gives the optimal solution.

THEOREM 19.1. All optimal solutions will fill the knapsack exactly.

EXAMPLE 19.3. *Sally is hosting an Interest auction to sell n widgets. She receives m bids, each of the form "I want k_i widgets for d_i dollars," for $i = 1, 2, \ldots, m$. Characterize her optimization problem as a knapsack problem. Under what conditions is this a 0-1 versus fractional problem?*

SOLUTION : This is a knapsack problem, where the weight of the sack is n, and each bid i corresponds to an item of weight k_i and value d_i. If each bidder i is unwilling to accept fewer than k_i widgets, then this is a 0/1 problem. If bidders are willing to accept partial lots, on the other hand, then this is a fractional version of the knapsack problem.

19.2 Huffman Code Algorithm

Suppose we have alphabet of n symbols and a long message consisting of the symbols from this alphabet. We wish to encode the message as a long bit string by assigning a bit string code to each symbol of the alphabet and concatenating the individual codes of the symbols making up the message to produce an encoding for the message.

e.g., Table 1

Symbols	Code	Frequency
A	010	3
B	100	1
C	000	2
D	111	1

Table—1 (T–1)

The message ABACCDA could then be encoded as 010100010 000000111010. This is very long. If we are we are using 2-bit encoding then we can shorten the message. In this message letter A appears thrice where as B and D appears only once. So in order to shorten the message length we can choose shorter bit string for symbols with more number of occurence (higher frequency of occurrence) *e.g.*, Here for A we can use 1-bit string code.

Symbols	Code	Frequency
A	0	3
B	110	1
C	10	2
D	111	1

Table—2 (T–2)

Then ABACCDA is encoded as 0110010101110 which requires only 13 bits Table-1 $(T-1)$ e.g.-1 shows **fixed length** (Here 3 bits) coding Table-2 $(T-2)$ shows **variable length coding.**

The codes in which no code word is prefix of some other code word is called **prefix codes,** we can construct a tree corresponding to T-1 and T-2 keeping in mind that left branch represents 0 and right branch represents 1

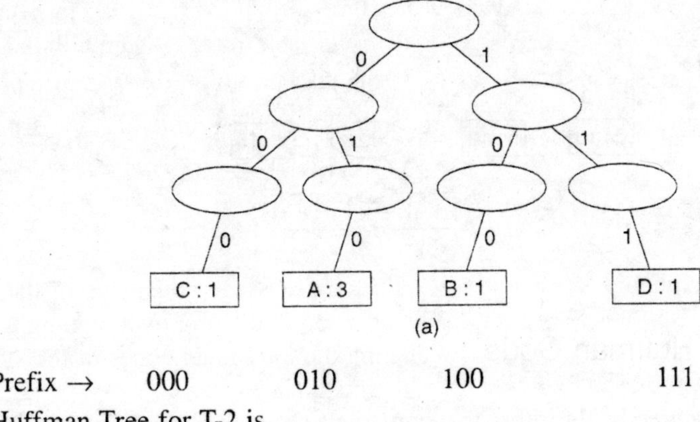

Prefix → 000 010 100 111

Huffman Tree for T-2 is.

0
1
A
0
0
1
C
10
0
1
B
110
D
111
(b)

Fig. 19.1 (a) Huffman Tree for Table–1 (b) Huffman Tree for Table-2

EXAMPLE 19.4. *Construct a Huffman tree corresponding to following set of data*

	a	*b*	*c*	*d*	*e*	*f*
Frequency (in thousands)	48	12	10	15	8	4
Fixed length code word	000	001	010	011	100	101
Variable length coding	0	101	100	111	1101	1100

SOLUTION :

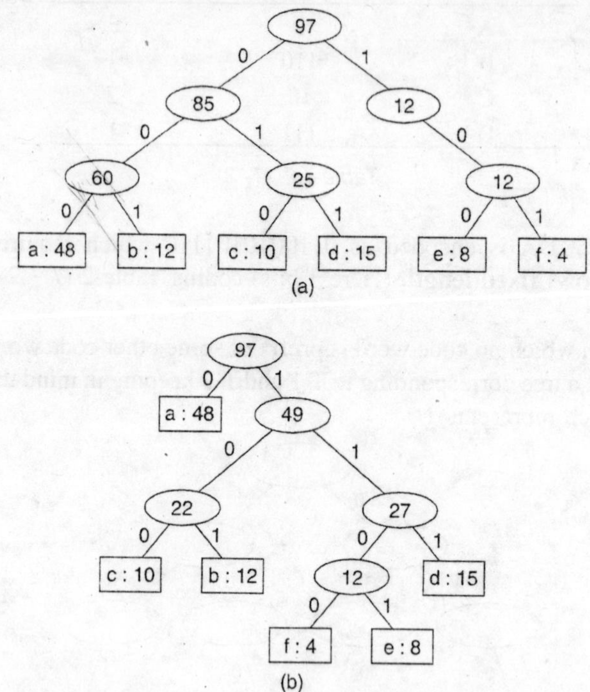

(a)

(b)

Constructing a Huffman Code

Huffman invented a greedy algorithm that constructs an optimal prefix code called a **Huffman code.** The algorithm builds the tree T corresponding to the optimal code in a *bottom-up manner*. It begins with a set of |c| leaves and performs a sequence of $|c| - 1$ merging operations to create a final tree. The symbols are kept in the increasing order of frequency at each stage, *e.g.*, looking at previous example.

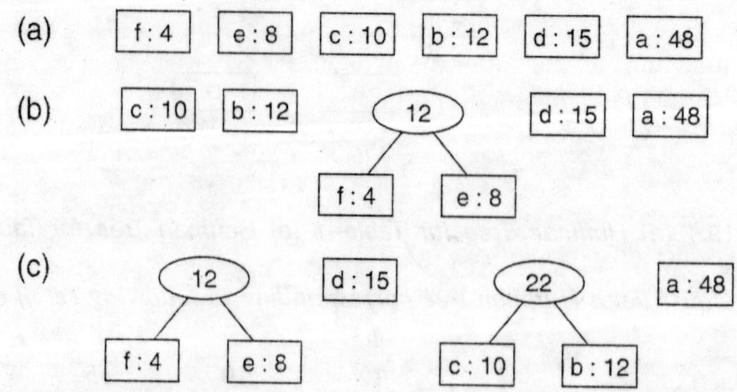

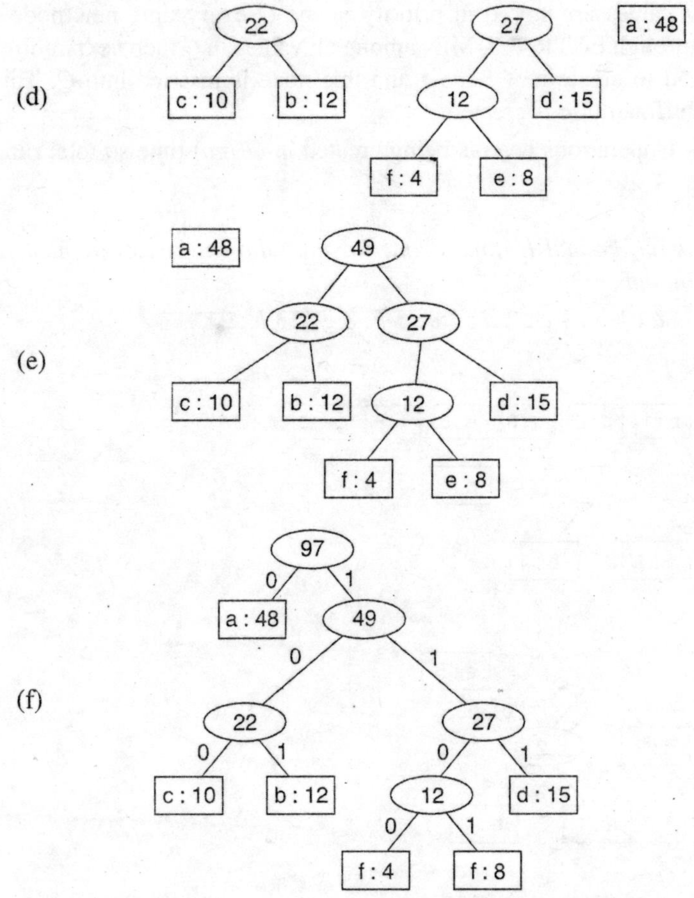

Fig. 19.2. Variable length Huffman Tree of Ex. 19.4.

From the prefix code we can see that it maches to that given in Ex. 19.4. Hence, this is the optimal tree.

While excecuting the steps we keep in mind that each stage symbols are ordered in ascending order of frequencies if after merging to nodes we get a node with the same frequency then this new node must be kept after the node with same value to get correct prefix codes. As is done in step (b) above. Now based on this concept algorithm is given as

```
HUFFMAN (c)
  n → | c |
  Q ← | c |
       for i ← 1 to n − 1
            do z ← ALLOCATE-NODE ( )
                 x ← left (z) ← EXTRACT-MIN (Q)
                 y ← right (z) ← EXTRACT-MIN (Q)
                 f (z) ← f (x) + f (y)
                 INSERT (Q, z)
  return EXTRACT-MIN (Q)
```

Here-frequency values are stored in priority queue Q every time new node z is created minimum is found through EXTRACT-MIN among all values in Q then next minimum is found and is finally merged to create new node z and this node is inserted into Q. This process is repeated till final Huffman tree is created.

For each of $n - 1$ operations heap is being created in $O(lgn)$ time so total running time is $O(nlgn)$

EXAMPLE 19.5. *What is an optimal Huffman code for the following set of frequencies based on the first 8 fibonacci numbers?*

$$a:1\ b:1\ c:2\ d:3\ e:5\ f:8\ g:13\ h:21$$

SOLUTION :

(a)

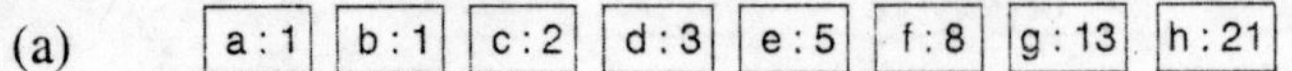

(b)

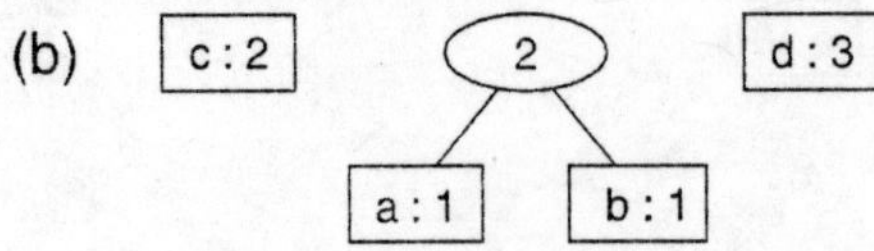

(c)

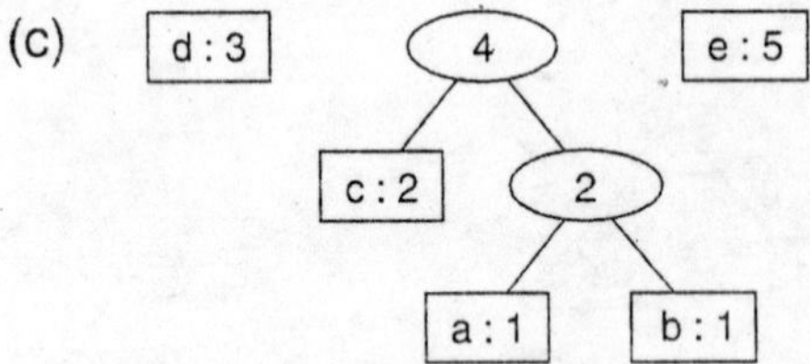

(d)

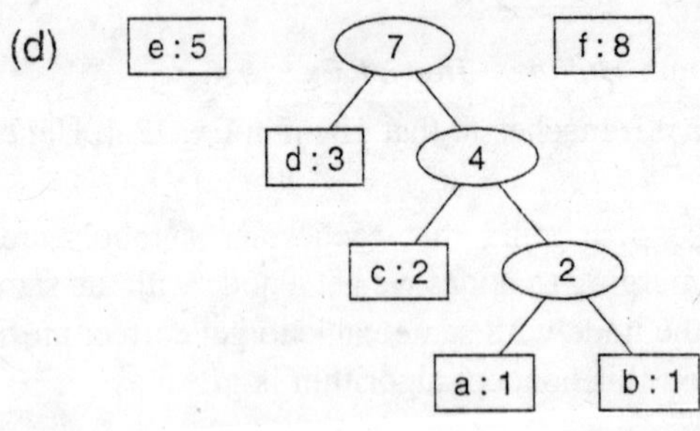

(e)

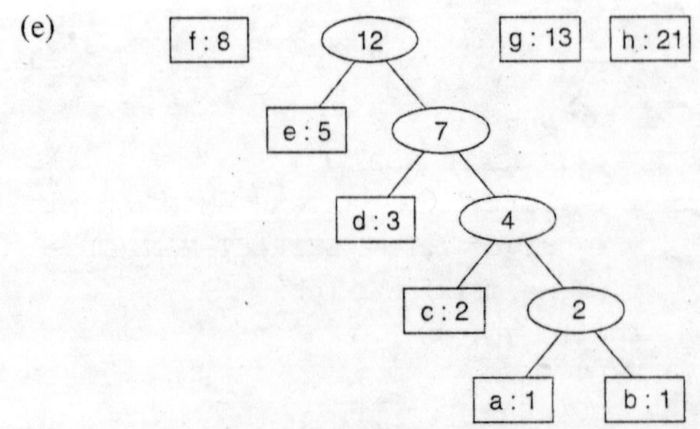

(f)

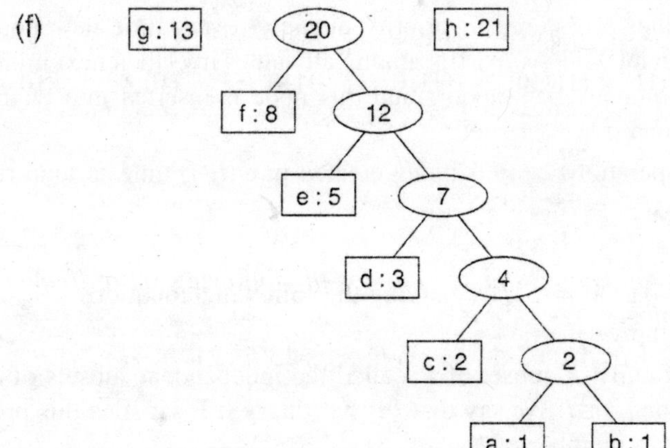
g : 13
20
h : 21
f : 8
12
e : 5
7
d : 3
4
c : 2
2
a : 1
b : 1

(g)

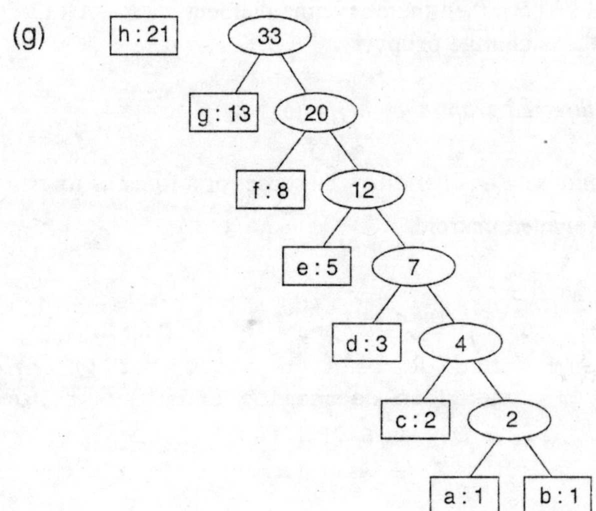
h : 21
33
g : 13
20
f : 8
12
e : 5
7
d : 3
4
c : 2
2
a : 1
b : 1

(h)

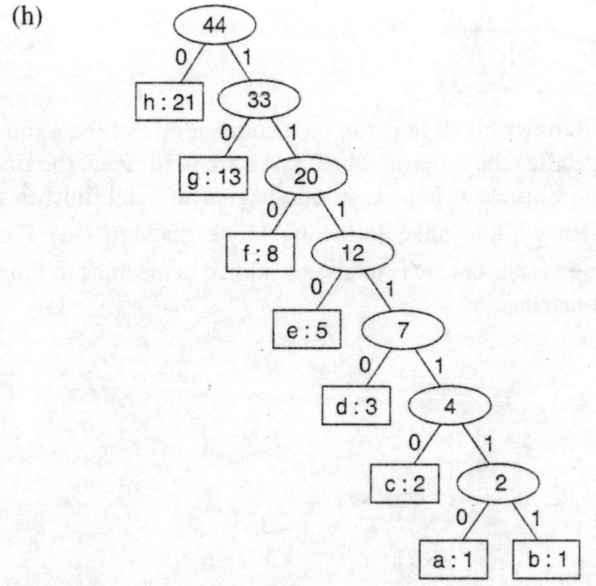
44
0
1
h : 21
33
g : 13
20
f : 8
12
e : 5
7
d : 3
4
c : 2
2
a : 1
b : 1

Symbols	a	b	c	d	e	f	g	h
Codes	11111110	1111111	111110	11110	1110	110	10	0

19.3 Matroids

A matroid is an ordered pair $M = (S, I)$ satisfying the following condtions

1. S is a finite non-empty set.
2. I is a non-empty family of subset of S, called the independent subsets of S, such that if $B \varepsilon I$ and $A \subseteq B$, then $A \varepsilon I$. We say that I is heriditary if it satisfies this property. Empty set ϕ is necessarily a member of I.
3. If $A \varepsilon I$, $B \varepsilon I$ and $|A| < |B|$, then there is some element $x \varepsilon B - A$ s.t. $A \cup \{x\}$ εI. We say that M satisfies the **exchange property.**

THEOREM 19.2. *If G is an undirected graph then* $M_G = (S_G, I_G)$

PROOF : Clearly $S_G = E$ is a finite set I_G is heriditary as subset of a forest is forest.

Greedy altorithm on weighted matroid.

```
Greedy (m, w)
     A ← φ
     Sort S[m] into decreasing order. of wt. w for
each x ε S [m], taken in decreasing order by wt., ω(x)
          do if A ∪ {x} ε I(m)
               then A ← A ∪ {x}.
return A
```

19.4 Task Scheduling Problem

In this a program that requires **one unit time** is run on a computer, Let P be a finite set of unit time tasks, schedule for P specifies the order in which tasks are performed. the first task in the schedule begins at time 0 and finishes at time 1, second begins at 1 and finishes at 2.

If T_i represents task then we can have following block diagram (see Fig. 19.3) that represents start and finish time of tasks and m is total time alloted to machine to finish maximum possible tasks in an optimal manner.

Tasks	T_1	T_2	-------------	T_m

time → 0 1 2 m

Fig. 19.3. Block diagram shows task processed in unit time.

In this problem d_i represents the deadline of finishing of a particular task where $i = 1$ to n and $w_1, w_2, ..., w_n$ are penalities incurred on the task if it does not finishes in deadline d_i. No. penalty incurred if it finishes by time.

EXAMPLE 19.6. *Find the optimal, schedule for the following task with given weights (penalties) and deadlines.*

	1	2	3	4	5	6	7
d_i	4	2	4	3	1	4	6
w_i	70	60	50	40	30	20	10

SOLUTION : According to Greedy algorithm we sort the jobs in decreasing order of their penalities so that minimum of penalties will be charged.

In this problem we can see that maximum time for which uniprocessor machine will run is $d = 6$ units. And each job should run for unit time to get completed and also it should be completed before the deadline time given.

Let T_i represents the tasks where $i = 1$ to 7.

tasks	T_2	T_4	T_1	T_3	T_7	T_5	T_6

time → 0 1 2 3 4 5 6 7

$d_2 = 2$ $d_4 = 3$ $d_1 = 4$ $d_3 = 4$ $d_7 = 6$ $d_5 = 1$ $d_6 = 4$

As T_5 and T_6 cannot be accepted after T_7, as their deadline exceeds so penality is charged.

$$\text{Penality} = w_5 + w_6 = 30 + 20 = 50$$

There can be many other schedule but **<2413756>** is optimal. We can have also another way of viewing the Task sheduling or job sequencing problem. Previously we have found the optimal schedule is one with minimum penalty but if we have sequence of jobs on execution of which on the processor we gain profit then according to greedily selecting the jobs we should maximize the profit. Consider the following example.

EXAMPLE 19.7. *Let* $n = 4$ $(P_1, P_2, P_3, P_4) = (100, 10, 15, 27)$ *and* $(d_1, d_2, d_3, d_4) = (2, 1, 2, 1)$. *Where Pi are profits on processes or job and* d_i *are deadline of completion. Find the optimal schedule.*

SOLUTION :

	Feasible Solution	Processing Sequence	Value
1.	(1, 2)	(2, 1)	110
2.	(1, 3)	(1, 3) or (3, 1)	115
3.	(1, 4)	4, 1	**127**
4.	(2, 3)	2, 3	25
5.	(3, 4)	4, 3	42
6.	(1)	1	100
7.	(2)	2	10
8.	(3)	3	15
9.	(4)	4	27

As maximum time computer will run is 2 units of time. Thus optimal schedule is solution 3 with schedule (4, 1) and profit 127.

EXAMPLE 19.8. *Let* $n = 5$, $(P_1, P_2, ..., P_5) = (20, 15, 10, 5, 1)$ *and* $(d_1, ..., d_5) = (2, 2, 1, 3, 3)$, *find the optimal schedule.*

SOLUTION : Maximum time for computer is 3

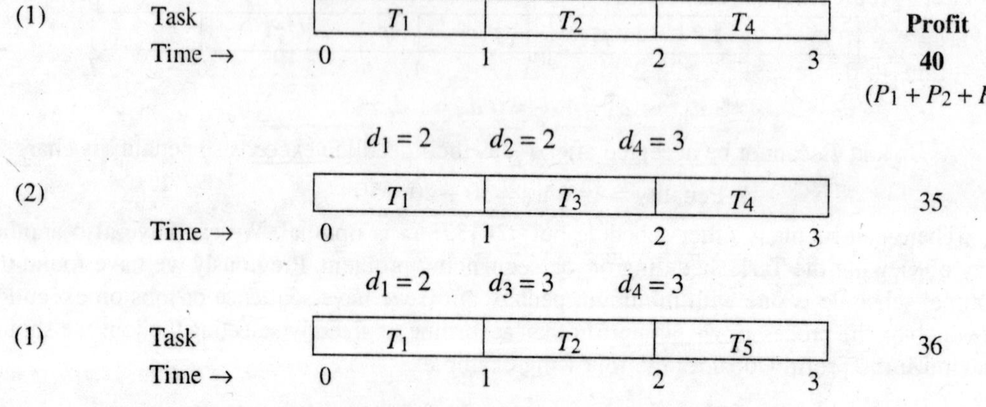

We can see the optimal schedule is (1, 2, 4) with profit 40.

EXAMPLE 19.9. *We have set of n jobs to execute, each of which takes unit time. At any time* $T = 1, 2, ...$, *we can execute exactly one job. Job i earns us a profit* $g_i > 0$ *iff it is executed no late than time* d_i. *Develop a greedy algorithm to solve the above problem. Run your above algorithm for* $n = 4$ *and the following values.*

i	1	2	3	4
g_i	50	10	15	30
d_i	2	1	2	7

SOLUTION : *Greedy Job (d, T, n)*

```
d[O] ← T[O] ← O
T[1] ← 1
K ← 1
      for i ← 2 to n do
            r ← k
            while (d[T(r)]] > d[i] and d[T[r]] ≠ r) do
                  r ← r - 1
                  If [(d[T(r) ≤ d[i]]) and (d[i] > r)] then
                  for (q ← K to (r + 1) step - 1
                  do T[q + 1] ← T[q]
                  T[q + 1] ← j
                  K ← K + 1
return K.
```

Here we have sorted the Task T_i s in decreasing order of their g_i. So first task is the task with largest profit.

Thus, sort in decreasing order of profit.

	T[1]	T[4]	T[3]	T[2]
g_i	50	30	15	10
d_i	2	7	2	1

(1)	Task	T_1	T_3	T_4		**Profit = 95**
	Time	0	1	2	3	
(2)	Task	T_2	T_1	T_4		**Profit = 90**
	Time	0	1	2	3	
(3)	Task	T_3	T_1	T_4		**Profit = 95**
	Time	0	1	2	3	

Solution is 1 and 3 with Task schedule (1, 3, 4) or (3, 1, 4) and profit of 95.

EXAMPLE 19.10. *Describe an efficient greedy algorithm for making change for a specified value using a minimum number of coins, assuming there are four denominations of coins (called quarters, dimes,nickels, and pennies), with values 25, 10, 5 and 1, respectively. Argue why your algorithm is correct.*

SOLUTION : First give as many quarters as possible, then dimes, then nickles and finally pennies. As maximizes the profit.

EXAMPLE 19.11. *Give an example set of denominations of coins so that a greedy change making algorithm will not use the minimum number of coins.*

SOLUTION : If the demoninations are \$0.25, \$0.24, \$0.01, then a greedy algorithm for making change for 48 cents would give 1 quarter and 24 pennies.

EXAMPLE 19.12. *In the art gallery guarding problem we are given a line L that represents a long halfway in an art gallery. We are also given a set* $X = \{x_0, x_1, \ldots, x_{n-1}\}$ *of real numbers that specify the positions of paintings in this halfway. Suppose that a single guard can protect all the paintings within distance at most 1 of his or her position (on both sides). Design an algorithm for finding a placement of guards that uses the minimum number of guards to guard all the paintaings with positions in X.*

SOLUTION : We can use a greedy algorithm, which seeks to cover all the designated points on L with the fewest number of length-2 interval (for such an interval is the distance one guard can protect). This greedy algorithm starts with x_0 and covers all the points that are within distance 2 of x_0. If x_i is the next uncovered point, then we repeat this same covering step starting from x_i. We then repeat this process until we have covered all the points in X.

EXAMPLE 19.13. *How can we modify the dynamic programming algorithm from simply computing the best benefit value for the 0-1 knapsack problem to computing the assignment that gives this benefit ?*

SOLUTION : Each time we update a value in the table, we need to additionaly store the index of the item for which we are updating this entry. Once we have the optimal benefit value, we need only then trace back through these extra indices to determine the entire set of items to place in the knapsack.

EXAMPLE 19.14. *A native Australian named Anatjari wishes to cross a desert carrying only a single water bottle. He has a map that marks all the watering holes along the way. Assuming he can walk k miles on one bottle of water, design an efficient algorithm for determining where Anatjari should refill his bottle in order to make as few stops as possible. Argue why your algorithm is correct.*

SOLUTION : Anatjari should use a greedy algorithm. He should draw a line between every pair of watering holes that are within k miles of one another, for he can get from one to the other with one bottle of water. Anatjari should then use a path that uses the fewest number of lines and leads from this present position to a watering hole that is within with k miles of the other side. There can be no path with fewer stops, for he is including in his minimization all pairs of watering holes that can be reached with one bottle of water.

EXERCISE

1. Find the optimal schedule for the following jobs with $n = 7$, profits $(P_1, P_2, ..., P_7) = (3, 5, 20, 18, 1, 6, 30)$ and deadlines $(d_1, d_2, ..., d_7) = (1, 3, 4, 3, 2, 1, 2)$?
2. Consider the knapsack instance $n = 3$, $(w_1, w_2, w_3) = (2, 3, 4)$, and $(P_1, P_2, P_3) = (1, 2, 5)$ $m = 5$. Find the optimal solution.
3. Find an optimal solution of the knapsack instance $n = 7$, $m = 15$, $(P_1, P_2, ..., P_7) = (10, 5, 15, 7, 6, 18, 3)$ and $(w_1, w_2, ..., w_7) = (2, 3, 5, 7, 1, 4, 1)$
4. Obtain a set of optimal Huffman codes for the messages $(m_1, m_2, ..., m_7)$ with relative frequencies $(q_1, ..., q_7) = (4, 5, 7, 8, 10, 12, 20)$. Draw the decode tree for this set of codes.
5. Find an optimal merge pattern for following data 28, 32, 12, 5, 84, 53, 91, 35, 3, 11.
6. Let $C = \{0, 1, ..., n - 1\}$ be a set of characters. Show that any optimal prefix code on C can be represented by a sequences of $2n - 1 + n\,[lgn]$
(**Hint :** Use $2n - 1$ bits to specify by structure of tree
7. Generalize Huffman's algorithm for ternary code words and prove that it yields optimal ternary codes.
8. Prove that an optimal tree that is not full cannot correspond to an optimal prefix code?
9. Show how to solve fractional knapsack problem in $\Theta(n)$ time.
10. Let $S = \{a, b, c, d, e, f, g\}$ be a collection of objects with benefit-weight values as follows: a: (12, 4), b: (10, 6), c: (8, 5), d: (11, 7), e: (14, 3), f: (7, 1), g: (9, 6). What is an optimal solution to the fractional knapsack problem for S assuming we have a sack that can hold objects with total weight 18? Show your work.
11. Describe how to implement the TaskSchedule method to run in $O(n \log n)$ time.
12. Suppose we are given a set of tasks specified by pairs of the start times and finish times as $T = \{(1, 2), (1, 3), (1, 4), (2, 5), (3, 7), (4, 9), (5, 6), (6, 8), (7, 9)\}$. Solve the task scheduling problem for this set of tasks.

❑❑❑

20

AMORTIZED ANALYSIS

20.1 Amortized Analysis

Amortized analysis is the sequence of operations averaged over all operations by analyzing individual operations. It differs from average case analysis in that probability is not involved. It takes into account the interdependence between operation and their result. For example, if an array is sorted and few elements are added, then resorting this array should be much faster than sorting it for the the first time because, after the new additions, the array is nearly sorted. Thus, it should be quicker to put all elements in perfect order than in a completely disorganized array, so we will not consider the worst case complexity twice, that will increase the total cost. In amortized analysis second sorting is hardly applied.

It is important to stress that amortized analysis in analyzing the sequence of opeations, or if a single operation is analyzed, it is done in view of part of the sequence. The cost of operations in the sequence may vary considerably, but how frequently particular operations may occur in the sequence is important. In worst case or average case each operation is considered as separate identity and thus total cost is increased but in amortized analysis, interdependence of operations is considered, and we consider the next operation in sequence as the point where first operation leaved. Thus, complexity particular operation is given by

$$C(OP) = C(OP_1) + C(OP_2) + C(OP_3) + \dots$$

20.1.1 Amortized Tree Traversal

As another example, consider the inorder traversal of a binary tree, where we measure the cost of visiting one vertex as the number of branches traversed to reach that vertex from the last one visited. The best case cost is 1, when we go from a vertex to one of its children or to its parent. The worst case cost for a tree with n vertices in $n-1$, as shown by the tree that is one long chain to the left, where it takes $n-1$ branches to reach (left n vertex). In this chain, however, all the remaining vertices are reached in only 1 step each, as the traversal moves for each vertex to its parent. In a completely balanced tree of size n, some vertices require as many as lgn steps, others only 1.

If, however we amortize the cost over a traversal of the entire binary tree, then the cost of going from each vertex to the next is less than 2. To see this, note first that every binary tree with n vertices has precisely $n-1$ branches, since every vertex except the root has just one branch coming down to it. A complete travesal of the tree goes over every branch twice, once going down and once up (Here we have included going up to the path after the last, right most vertex has been visited) Hence, the total number of steps in a full traversal is $2(n-1)$, and the amortized number of steps from one vertex to the next is $\frac{2(n-1)}{n} < 2$.

20.1.2 Credit Balance : Making Cost Level

Suppose you are working with your household budget, If you are employed, then (you hope) your income is usually fairly stable from month to month. Your expenses however may not be. Some month large amounts are due for insurance, or taxation, or a major purchase. Other months have no extra-ordinary expenses. To keep your bank acount solvent, you then need to save enough during the months with low expenses so that you can pay all the large bills as they come due. At the begining of the month with large bills, you have large bank balance. After paying the bills, your bank balance is much smaller, but you are just as well off becasuse you now owe less money.

We wish to apply this idea to algorithm analysis. To do so, we invent a function, which we call a **credit balance** that behaves like the credit function that will be chosen in such a way that it will be large when the next operation is expensive, and smaller when next operation can be done quickly. We then think of the credit function as helping to bear some of the cost of expensive operations, and, for inexpensive operations, we set aside more than the actual cost, using the excess to build up the credit function for future use.

To make this idea more precise, suppose that we have a sequence of m operations on a data structure, and let t_i be the actual cost of operation i for $1 \le i \le m$. Let the values of our credit function be $C_0, C_1, ..., C_m$, where C_0 is the credit balance before the first operation, C_i is the balance after operation i, for $1 \le i \le m$. Then we can make the fundamental definition :

DEFINITION. The amortized cost a_i of each operation is defined to be

$$a_i = t_i + C_i - C_{i-1}$$

for $i = 1, 2, ..., m$ where t_i and C_i are defined as above.

It says that amortized cost is the actual cost plus the amount that our credit balance has changed while doing the operation.

Thus, we have total actual cost, from above,

$$\sum_{i=1}^{m} t_i = \sum_{t=1}^{m} (a_i + C_{i-1} - C_i) = \sum_{i=1}^{m} (a_i) + C_0 - C_m \quad ...(20.1)$$

as $\Sigma C_{i-1} - C_i$ is telescopic sum

20.1.3 Incrementing Binary Integers

Let us consdier an algorithm that continually increments a binary integer (base 2) by 1. We start at right side, while the current bit is 1, we change it to 0 and move left, stopping when we reach the far left or hit a 0 bit, which we change to 1 and stop. The cost of performing this algorithm is number of bits that are changed. The results of applying this algorithm 16 times to a four digit integers are show in first three columns of Fig. 20.1

Step i	integer	t_i	C_i	$a_i = t_i + c_i - c_{i-1}$
	0000		0	
1	0001	1	1	2 (1 + 1 − 0)
2	0010	2	1	2 (2 + 1 − 1)
3	0011	1	2	2
4	0100	3	1	2
5	0101	1	2	2
6	0110	2	2	2
7	0111	1	3	2
8	1000	4	1	2
9	1001	1	2	2
10	1010	2	2	2
11	1011	1	3	2
12	1100	3	2	2
13	1101	1	3	2
14	1110	2	3	2
15	1111	1	4	2
16	0000	4	0	0

Fig. 20.1. Cost and amortized cost of incrementing binary integers.

above method is also called **Potential method.** It is to be noted that t_i denotes the number of flips at each step, while C_i is number of 1's in each number.

20.1.4 Stack operations

We can compute the amortized cost of various STACK operations, If ith operation on stack containing S objects is a PUSH operation (see Fig. 20.2) then

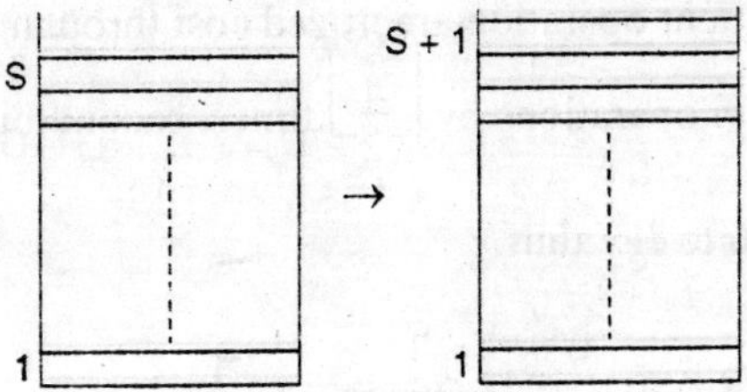

Fig. 20.2. Stacks

$$C_i - C_{i-1} = S + 1 - S$$
$$= 1$$

$$\therefore \quad a_i = t_i + C_i - C_{i-1}$$
$$= 1 + 1 = 2$$

Let us define one stack opeation which pops K tops objects of stack S if it contains less than K objects.

```
MULTIPOP (S, K)
while not STACK-EMPTY (S) and K ≠ 0
      do pop (S)
            K ← K - 1
```

If the stack contains S elements then number of iterations of while loop is min (S, K)

If $K' = \min(S, K)$, *i.e.*, K' objects are popped in C_{i-1}, and if we again try to pop, nothing will be popped in C_i, So

$$C_i - C_{i-1} = 0 - K' = -K'$$

Thus amortized cost of MULTIPOP is

$$a_i = t_i + C_i - C_{i-1}$$
$$= K' - K'$$
$$= 0$$

Similarly it is zero for ordinary pop operation. This must be the cost, as we are trying to pop something from stack in which there is no object, so there should not be any cost involved.

20.1.5 Aggregate Method

In this method amortized cost for n sequence of operations is the average of worst case time $T(n)$, *i.e.*, $\frac{T(n)}{n}$

e.g., MULTIPOP takes $O(n)$ time for push and pop operation to amortized cost is $\left(\frac{O(n)}{n}\right) = O(1)$ operation.

Similarly for increment operation amortized cost through aggregate method is seen as first bit flips for sequence of n operations by $\left\lfloor \frac{n}{2} \right\rfloor$ times, second bit $\left\lfloor \frac{n}{H} \right\rfloor$ times, thus we have total of $O\left\lfloor \frac{n}{2^i} \right\rfloor$ flips for $i = 0$ to lgn thus,

$$\sum_{i=0}^{[\log n]} \left[\frac{n}{2^i} \right] < n \sum_{i=0}^{\infty} \frac{1}{2^i}$$

$$= 2n$$

Thus worst cacse time is $O(n)$, hence amortized cost is $\frac{O(n)}{n} = O(1)$.

EXERCISE

1. Consider a binary heap data structure of n element that takes $O(lgn)$ worst case time for INSERT and EXTRACT-MIN, Give a protential function, s.t. amortized cost of both operations is $O(1)$.
2. What is total cost of excuting n operations in PUSH, POP and MULTI POP, assuming that stack begins with S_0 object and ends with S_m subjects.
3. Show how to implement queue using two stacks s.t. its insertion and deletion operation have amortized cost of $O(1)$
4. Explain the amortized cost analysis in splaying?

21

B-TREES-EXTERNAL SEARCHING

The tree search methods we have discussed were developed primarily for internal searching, when we want to look at a table that is contained entirely within a computers high speed internal memory. Let's now consider the problem of **external** searching when we want to retrieve information from a very large file that appears on direct acess storage units such as disks drives.

Consider the large binary tree shown in Fig. 21.1.

If we group the nodes into pages as shown by dotted line and if we access one page at a

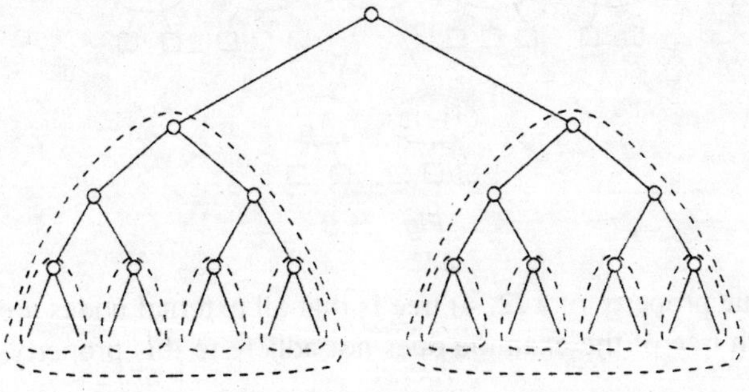

Fig. 21.1. Nodes grouped as pages.

time then time is reduced from *lgn*, as in other binary trees, so it makes a *m*-way searching technique possible, with each page containing *m* nodes.

21.1 Multiway Search Tees

Binary search trees generalize directly to multiway search trees in which, for some integer t called the order of tree, each node has at most $2t$ children. If $K \leq t$ is the no. of children then the node contains exactly $2K - 1$ keys, which partition all the keys in the subtrees into $2K - 1$ subsets. If some of these subset are empty, then corresponding children in the tree are empty. See Fig. 21.2.

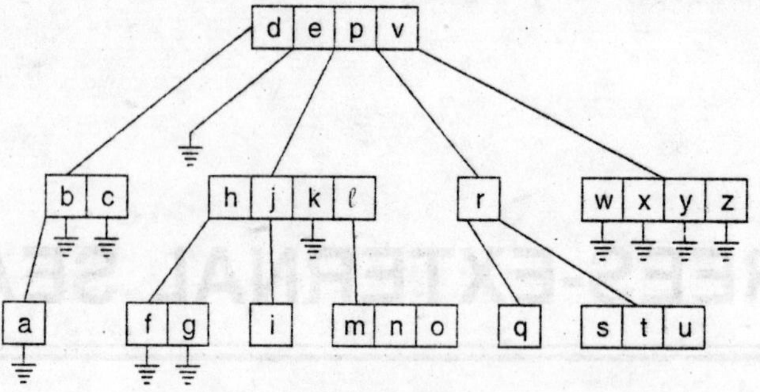

Fig. 21.2. 5-Way Search Tree.

EXAMPLE 21.1. *Is the multi-way search tree of Figure 21.3 a (2, 4) tree (see chapter 13) ? Justify your answer.*

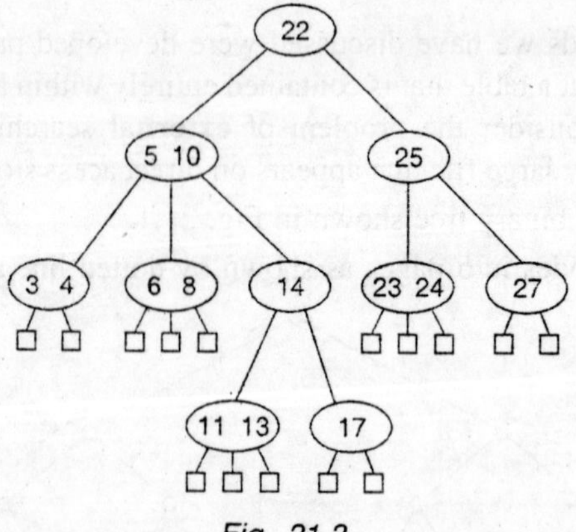

Fig. 21.3.

SOLUTION : No. One property of a (2, 4) tree is that all external nodes are at the same depth. The multi-way search tree of the example does not adhere to this property.

21.2 B-Tree

B-Tree is a balanced multiway tree with following definition.

1. All leaves are on the same level. (So the tree grow upwards)

2. All internal nodes other than root have at most $2t$ and atleast t children where t is minimum order or minimum degree of tree where $t \geq 2$.

3. The no. of keys in each internal nodes is one less than the no of its non-empty children i.e. maximum $2t - 1$ and minimum $t - 1$ keys. (*i.e.*, maximum $2t - 1$ and minimum $t - 1$).

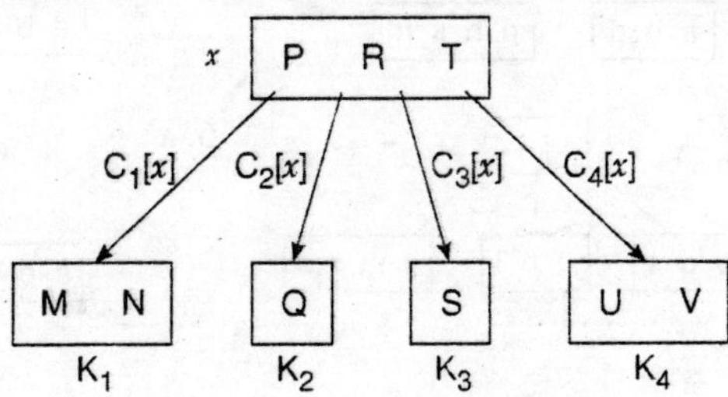

Fig. 21.4. 5-Way Search Tree.

4. The root have at most $2t$ children, but have as few as 2 if it is not a leaf, or none if root consists of root alone.

$key_1\ [x] = P$

$key_2\ [x] = R$

$key_3\ [x] = T$

$K_{11} < key_1\ [x], M < P$

$K_{12} < key_2\ [x], N < P$

$Q < R, S < T, T < U, V$

- Let us consider a node with $key_1\ [x]$, $key_2\ [x]$, $key_3\ [x]$ as $P, R. T$ respectively. Then $n[x]$ the no. of keys in node x is 3 here and also $key_1\ [x] < key_2\ [x] < key_3\ [x]$
- $C_1[x], C_2[x], ..., C_{n+1}[x]$ represent child pointers which is one more than no of keys in its parent, (property 3).
- $K_1, K_2, ..., K_{n+1}$ are child nodes which contains key values then all the keys contained in child nodes must be less than its parent key e.g., $M < P, N < P$

  Thus

  $$K_1 \leq key_1[x] \leq K_2 \leq key_2[x] \leq ... < key_n[x] \leq K_{n+1}$$
- Every node other than root contains at most $2t$ children and every node other than root have atleast t children.
- A node is full if it has exactly $2t - 1$ keys.

If $t = 2$ then every internal node has $2t - 1$ keys, *i.e.*, 3 keys hence 4 children and atleast 2 children thus it can have 2, 3, 4 children, so it is called **2-3-4 tree**, using above property let us create a B-tree with following keys *a g f b k d h m j e s i r x c l n t u p*. **Assuming at most 4 keys in a node** (just assumed). Keys are inserted in the order given.

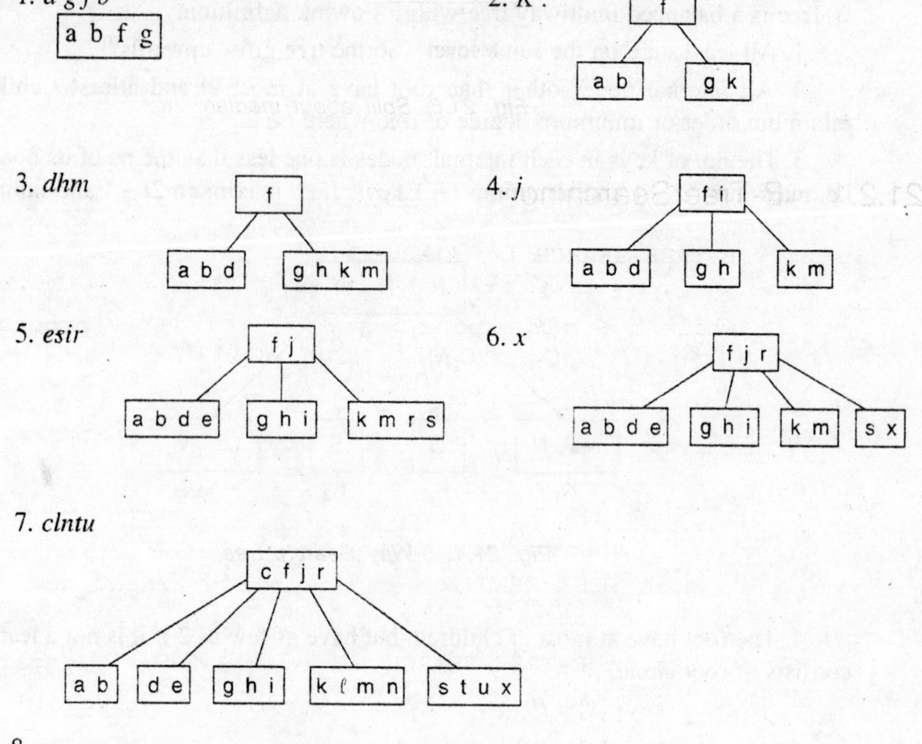

Fig. 21.5. B-Tree construction.

The condition that all leaves are at the same level forces B-tree to grow upwards towards root so when we insert a new key value we search from root to leaves whether the key exists or not if it is not then key is inserted at the leaf at sorted position. If the node is not full. If it is full then considering the new key in sorted form at leaf. the node is split about the median and key is inserted at appropriate position, e.g., Step 2. *k* causes to split the node, step 4, insertion of *j* makes the configuration in sorted form as we can see that its the median key that is sent upwards, not necessarily the newly inserted key See Fig. below. Thus we can now give few algorithms related to B-tree.

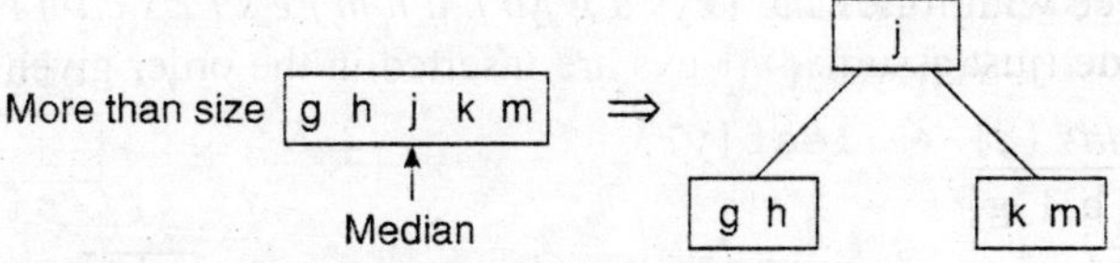

Fig. 21.6. Split about median.

21.2.1 B-Tree Searching

```
B-TREE-SEARCH (x, k)
        i ← 1
while i ≤ n[x] nnd k > key_i [x]          //propagate till key
                                                  //is not found
        do i ← i + 1
if i ≤ n[x] and K = key_i [x]               //key is found at
   then return (x, i)                              //ith location
if leaf [x]
        then return NIL
   else DISK-READ (c_i [x])              //Read new child pointer
                                                  //to move down.
   return B-TREE-SEARCH [C_i[x], k]           //again search the
                                              //child node for key
```

Number of disk pages accessed by B-TREE-SEARCH is $\Theta(h)$, where h is ht of the tree and n is the no. of keys in the tree. Since $n[x] < 2t$, time taken by while loop is $\Theta(t)$ thus total. CPU time is $\Theta(th)$. where $h = \log_t n$

Creating an empty B-Tree.

```
B-TREE CREATE (T)
x ← Get node ( )
leaf [x] ← TRUE
n(x) ← 0.
DISK-WRITE (x)
root [T] ← x
```

A space for x is created and x is made the leaf node then it is being made the root of tree. It takes $\Theta(1)$ time.

21.2.2 Splitting a Child

Assume that a node x is being split into y and z so that half of key is assigned to y (0 to t) and half to $z(t + 1$ onwards).

```
B-TREE-SPLIT-CHILD (x, i, y)
1.  z ← Getnode ( )                          // space is created
2.  leaf[z] ← leaf[y]
3.  n[z] ← t - 1                             // size is defined
4.  for j ← 1 to t - 1              // All keys from t + 1 pos.
                                             // are assigned to z.
5.     do key_j [z] ← key_j+t [y]
6.  If not leaf [y]            // child pointers are adjusted
7.     then for j ← 1 to t
8.            do C_j [z] ← C_j+t [y]
9.  n[y] ← t - 1                                // size of 4 fixed
10. for j ← n[x] + 1 down to i + 1
11.           do C_j+1 [x] ← C_j [x]
12. C_i+1 [x] ← z
13. for j ← n[x] down to i
14.           do key_j+1 [x] ← key_j [x]
15. key_i [x] ← key_t [y]
16. n[x] ← n[x] + 1
17. DISK-WRITE (y)
18. DISK-WRITE (z)
19. DISK-WRITE (x)
```

Let us consider the Fig. 21.7. for child split

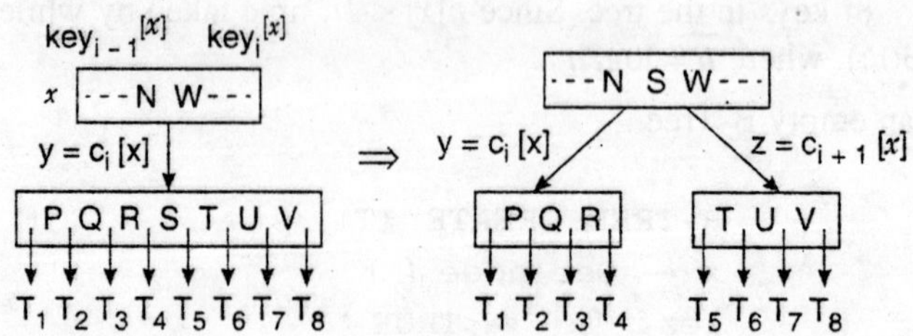

Fig. 21.7. Split of node.

The algorithm can be explained as follows :

Line 1 creates a space for z then line 4 – 5. assigns all the keys in y which is extraneous to z, *i.e.*, from $t + 1$ onwards, then if y is not a leaf node then all the child pointers of y corresponding to keys are also assigned to $C_j [z]$ (line 5–8) then no. of nodes in y is reduced to $t - 1$ (line 9), then z node is attached to pointer of x. Then each key_i in x is incremented after upward movement of median key (line 13–14), and size of node x is increased by 1 then finally all the nodes are again rewritten onto Disk. Running time of this algo is $\Theta(t)$ because line 4–5 or 7–8.

21.2.3 Inserting a key into a B-tree

```
B-TREE INSERT (T, K)
r ← root [T]
if n[r] = 2t - 1
        Then S ← Get node ( )
        root [T] ← S
        leaf [S] ← FALSE
        n[S] ← 0
        C1[S] ← r.
        B-TREE-SPLIT CHILD (S, 1, r)
        B-TREE-INSERT-NON FULL (s, k)
else B-TREE-INSERT-NON FULL (r, k)
```

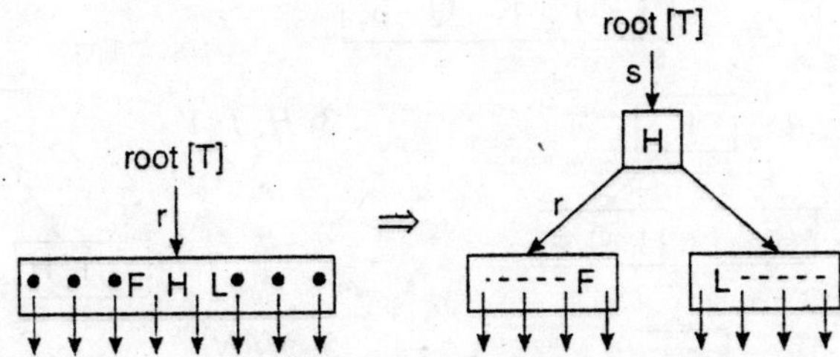

Fig. 21.8. Root node r is split into two and new node s is created, here t = 4, median key H moves upwards.

```
B-TREE-INSERT-NONFULL (x, k)
i ← n[x]
if leaf [x]
     then while i ≥ 1 and k < key_i [x]
          do key_i+1 [x] ← key_i [x]
               i ← i - 1
     key_i+1 [x] ← k
          n[x] ← n[x] + 1
     DISK-WRITE [x]
else while i ≥ 1 and k < key_i [x]
          do i ← i - 1
i ← i + 1
DISK-READ (C_i [x])
if n [C_i [x]] = 2t - 1
     then B-TREE-CHILD (x, i, C_i [x])
          if k > key_i [x]
```

```
16.                then i ← i + 1
17. B-TREE-INSERT-NONFULL (C_i [x], k)
```

In this algorithm if condition checks that if x is a leaf node then from back position index of key value is incremented by 1 then key is inserted line (2–7), If it is not a leaf node, we get the location where key is to be inserted then size of node is checked whether it is full or not, if it is full then node is split by B-TREE-SPLIT-CHILD. Otherwise key is inserted. Running time is $O(th)$ where $h = lg_t\, n$, thus, $O(t \log_t n)$.

EXAMPLE 21.2. *Show the the result of inserting the following keys into an empty B-tree.*

F, S, Q, K, C, L, H, T, V, W, M, R, N, P, A, B, X, Y, D, Z, E, G, I

SOLUTION : Let us assume $t = 3$, s.t. $2t - 1 = 5$, *i.e.*, maximum of 5 keys can be inserted in a node.

1. *F, S, Q, K, C*

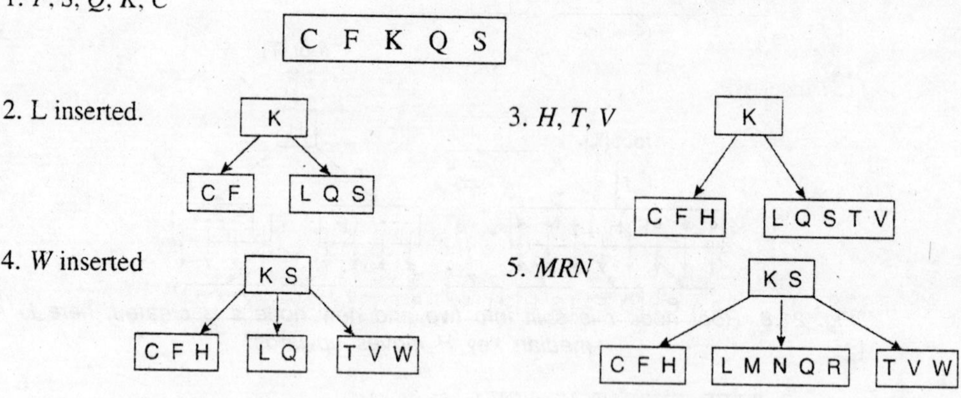

6. *P* inserted

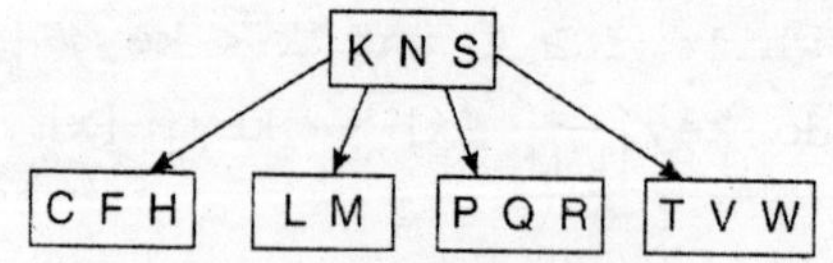

7. *ABXY*

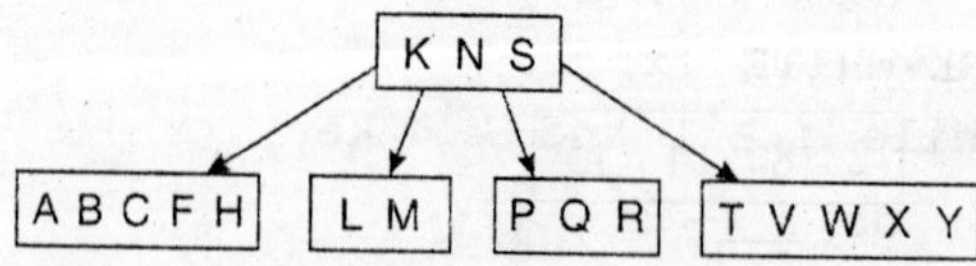

8. *D* inserted

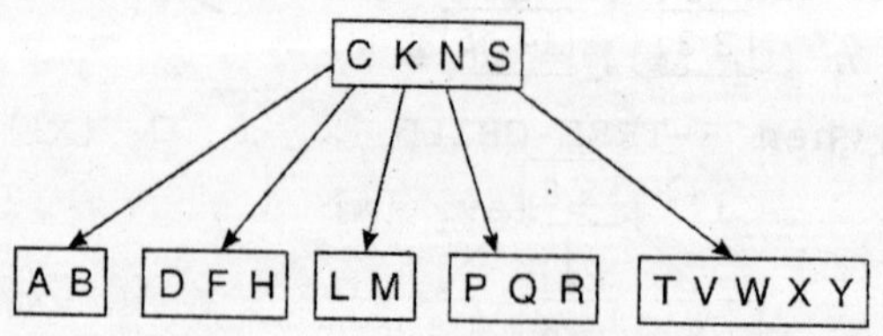

9. *ZE* inserted

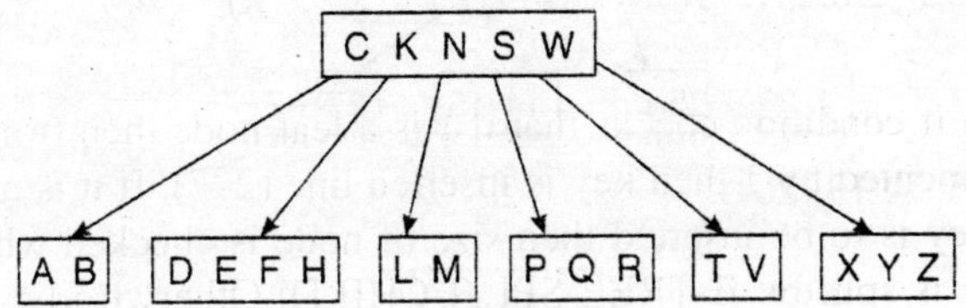

10. *G* inserted

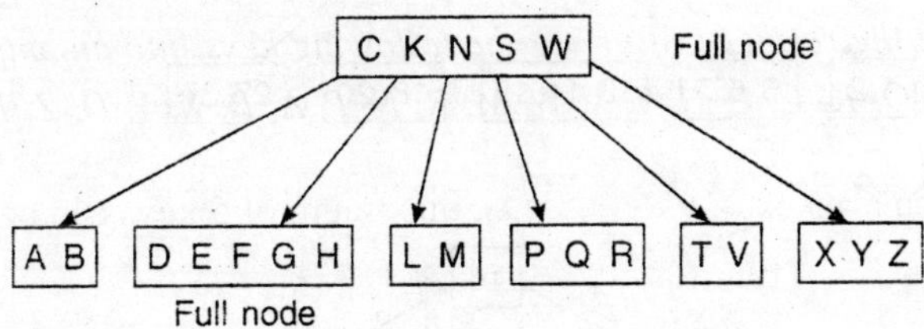

11. *I* inserted

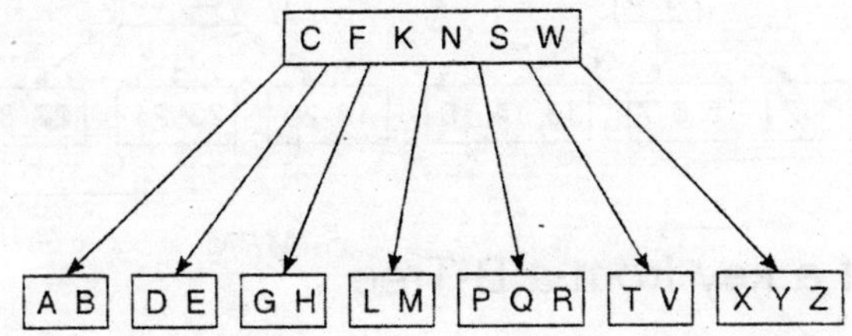

12.

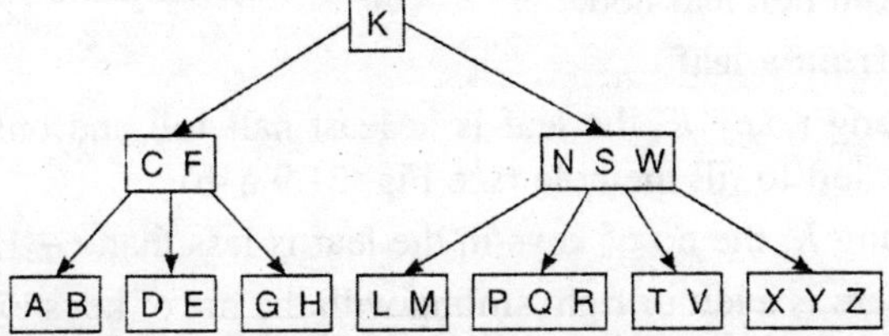

EXAMPLE 21.3. *Find a B-Tree corresponding to following insertions 8, 14, 2, 15, 3, 1, 16, 6, 5, 27, 37, 18, 25, 7, 13, 20, 22, 23, 24, Considering node size = 4, i.e., order 5*

SOLUTION : 1. Inserting 8, 14, 2, 15

2. Insert 3

3. Insert 1, 16, 6, 5

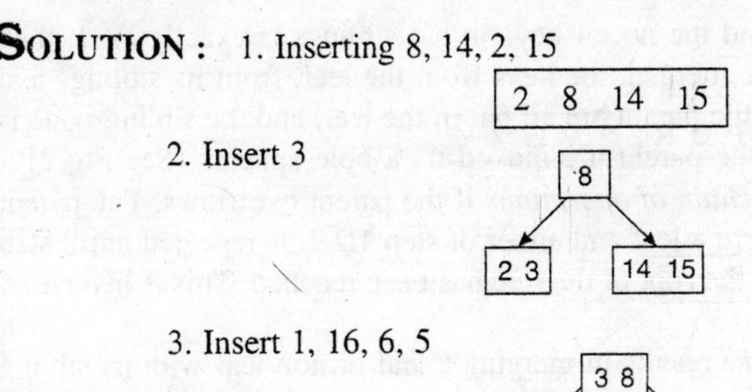

4. Insert 27, 37

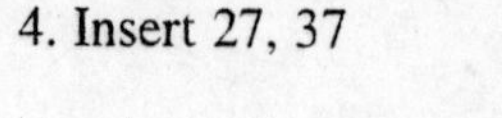

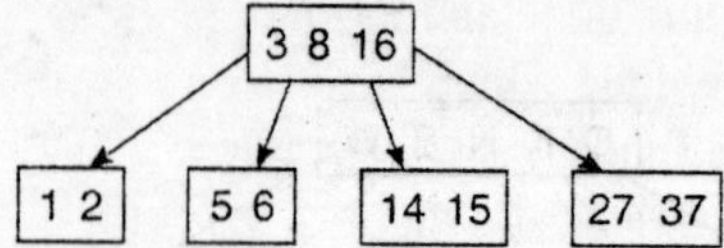

5. Insert 18, 25, 7, 13. 20

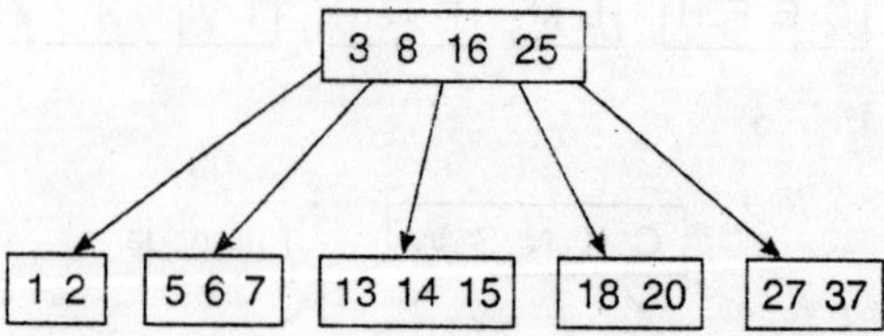

6. Insert 22, 23, 24

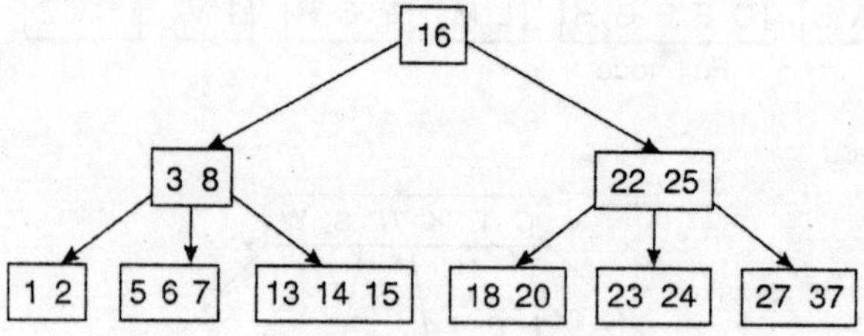

21.2.4 Deletion of a key from a B-Tree

Deletion of key from a B-Tree can be done at two positions, one deletion from a leaf node, second, deletion from non leaf node.

1. Deleting a key from a leaf

1.1 If after deleting a key K, the leaf is at least half full and only keys greater than K are moved to the left to fill the hole (see Fig. 21.9 a–b)

1.2. If after deleting K, the no of keys in the leaf is less than $t - 1$, causes *underflow.*

1.2.1. If there is a left or right sibling with the no. of keys exceding minimal $t - 1$ then all keys from this leaf and this sibling are redistributed between them by moving the seperator key from parent to the leaf and moving one key from sibling to the parent Fig. (21.9 b–c)

1.2.2 If the leaf underflows and the no. of keys in it's siblings is exactly $t - 1$, then the leaf and a sibling are merged, the keys from the leaf, from its siblings and the separating key from the parent are all put in the leaf, and the sibling node is discarded. The keys in the parent are moved if a hole appears (See Fig 21.9 c–d). This can initiate a *chain of operations* if the parent overflows. The parent is treated as though it were a leaf and either of step 1.2.2. is repeated untill step 1.2.1 can be executed or the root of the tree has been reached. This is inverse of insertion.

1.2.2.1. A particular case results in merging a leaf or non leaf with its sibling when its parent is the root with only one key. In this case, the keys from the node and its sibling along with the only key of root, are put in the node and its sibling, along with only key of the root, are put in the node which becomes a new root, and both the siblings and the old root nodes are discarded. This is the only case when two nodes disappear at one time (see Fig. 21.9 d–e)

(a) Here, $t = 3$ is assumed, so that $2t - 1 = 5$ and $t - 1 = 2$.

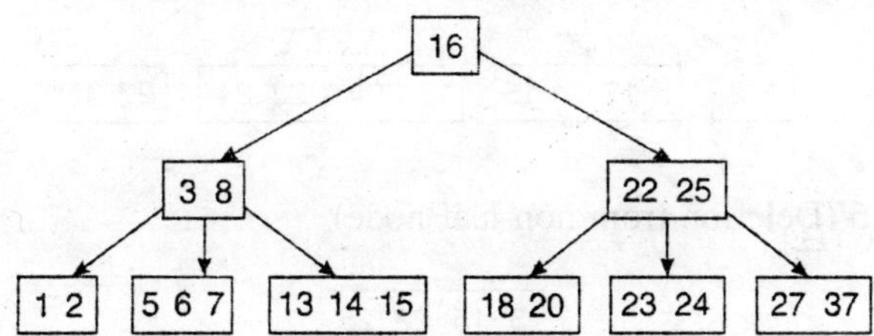

(b) Delete 6

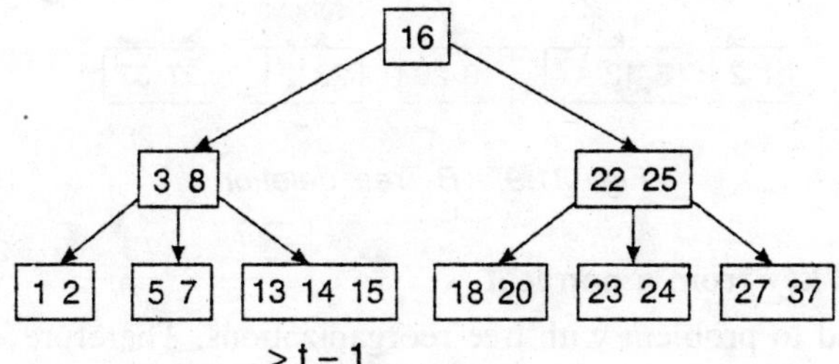

(c) Delete 7

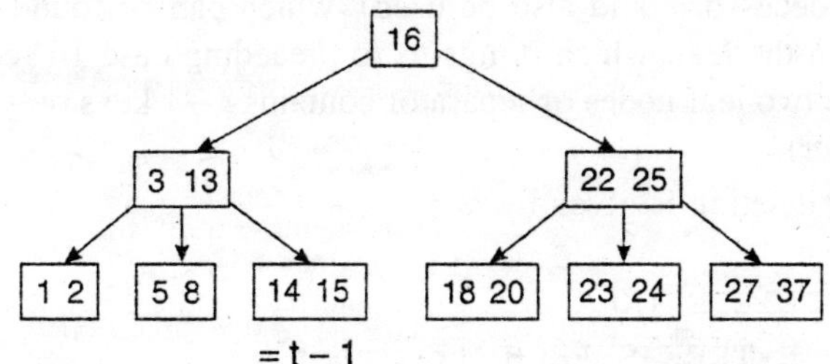

(d) Delete 8
(less than $t - 1$?)

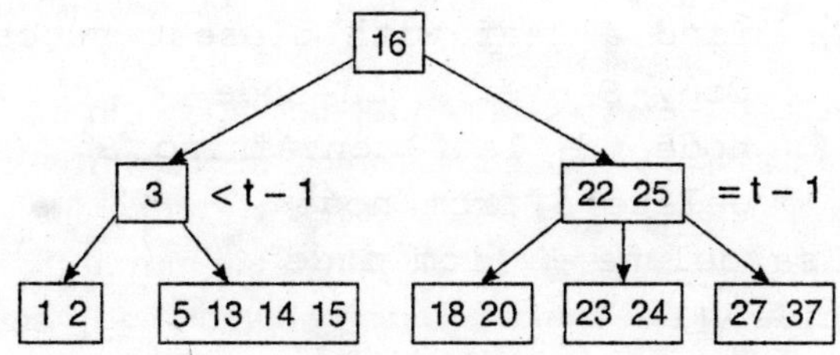

(e) Delete 8 continued
(siblings merged.)

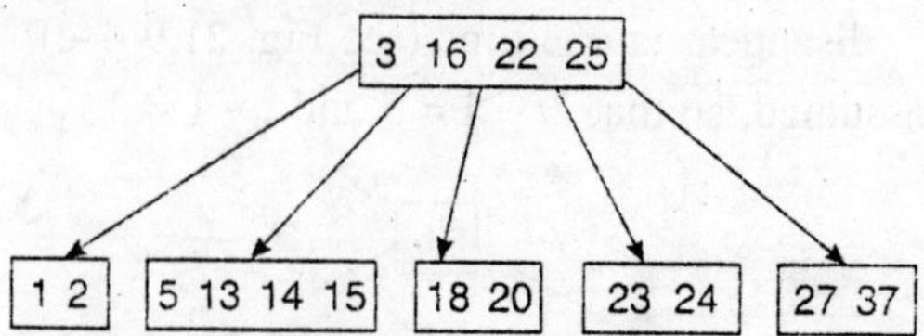

(f) Delete 16 (Deletion from non-leaf node)

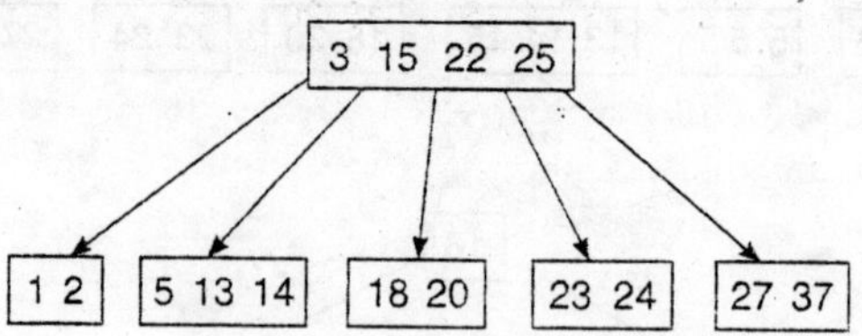

Fig. 21.9. B-Tree deletion.

2. **Deleting a key from a non leaf.**

This may lead to problem with tree reorganizations. Therefore. deletion from a non leaf node is reduced to deleting a key from a leaf. The key to be deleted is replaced by its immediate successor (the predecessor could also be used), which can be found in a leaf. The successor key is deleted from the leaf, which brings us to preceding case 1 (See Fig. 21.9 *e–f*). (It is to be noted that if the two leaf nodes of separator contains $t - 1$ keys only then both the leaf nodes are merged together).

Algorithm for deletion is given by

```
B-TREE-DELETE (K)
node ← B-TREE-SEARCH (K, root)
   if (node  ≠ null)
         if node is not a leaf
               find a leaf with closest successor S of K.
               Copy S over K in node
               node  ← leaf containing S
               delete S from node
         else delete K from node
         while (1)
               if node does not underflow
                     return
               else if there is a sibling of node with
                     enough keys redistribute keys between
                                                node and its sibling
                     return
```

```
        else if node's parent is the root
             if the parent has only one key
                      merge node, its sibling, and the
                            parent to form a new root.
        else merge node and its sibling
             return
        else merge node and its sibling
             node ← its parent.
```

21.3 B* Tree

All nodes except the root are required to be atleast two thirds full, not just half full as in a B-tree. If insertion is done in full node then median is found of this node, inserted key and its sibling then this median moves up.

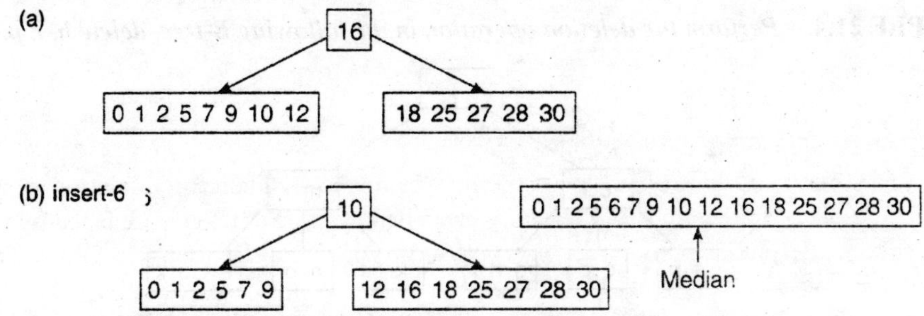

Fig. 21.10. B Tree of order 9 (contains 8 keys).*

21.4 B^+ Tree

It is an index implemented as a regualr B-trees plus a linked list of data. In a B-tree reference to data are made from any node of the tree, but in B^+ tree, these references are made only from the leaves. The internal nodes of a B^+ tree are indexes for the fast access of data. this part of the tree is called an index set. The leaves have a different structure than other nodes of the B^+-tree, and usually they are linked sequentialy to form a sequence set so that scanning this list of leaves result in data given in ascending order. Hence B^+-tree is truly a B plus tree. See Fig. 21.11.

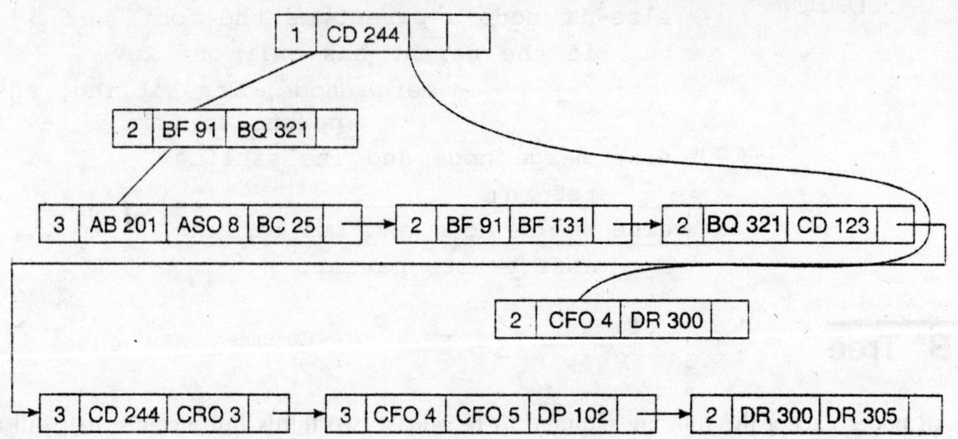

Fig. 21.11. Example of B^+ Tree.

EXAMPLE 21.4. *Perform the deletion operation in the following B-tree, delete h, r, p, d in sequence.*

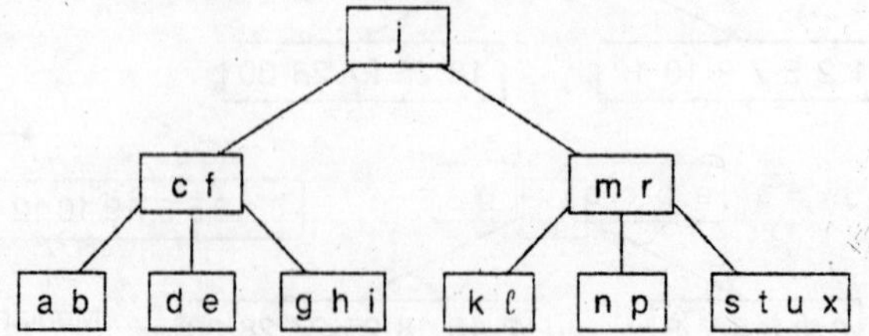

SOLUTION : 1. Delete *h, r*

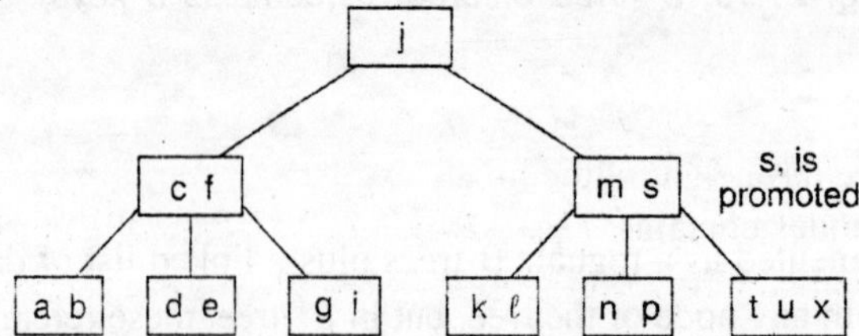

2. Delete *P*

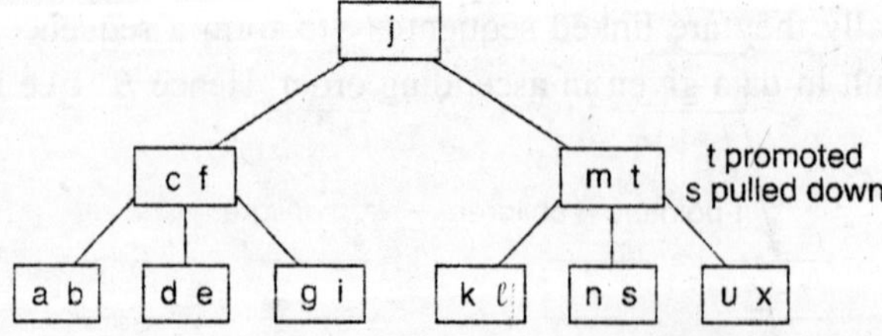

3. Delete *d*

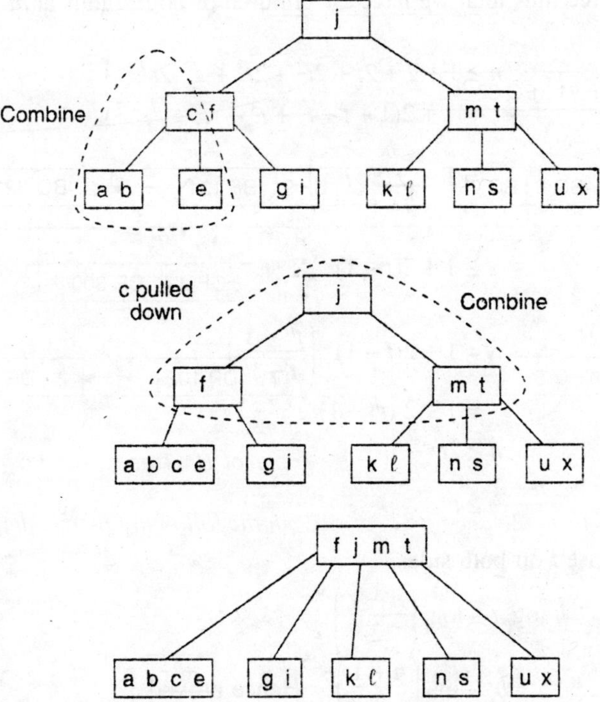

EXAMPLE 21.5. *Prove that if, $n \geq 1$, then for any n-key B-tree T of ht. h and minimum degree $t \geq 2$*

$$h \leq \log_t \left(\frac{n+1}{2}\right)$$

SOLUTION : If a B-tree has height *h*, the no. of its nodes is minimized when the root contains one key and all other nodes contains $t-1$ keys.

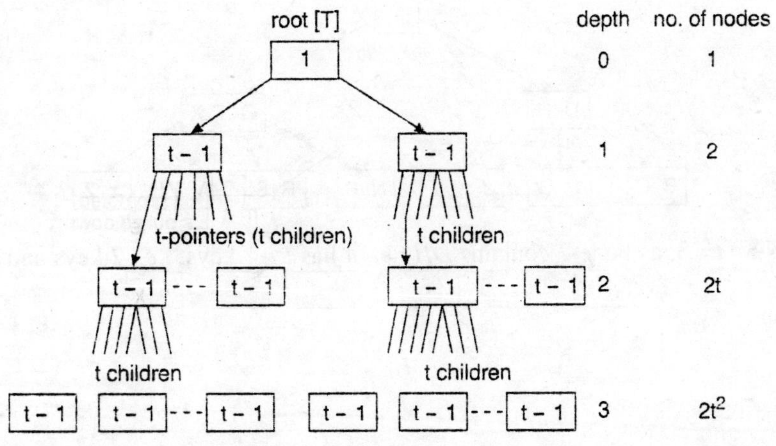

at level 3 for each t node in left subtree we have t children, so we have t^2 in left subtree and t^2 in right subtree thus total we have $2t^2$ children or nodes, thus at *ht*. h we have $2t^{h-1}$, so we can write

$$n \geq 1 + 2 + 2t + 2t^2 + 2t^3 + \ldots 2t^{h-1}$$

$$= 1 + 2(1 + t + t^2 + t^3 + \ldots + t^{h-1})$$

$$= 1 + 2\sum_{i=1}^{h} t^{i-1}$$

$$\geq 1 + 2(t-1)\,.\sum_{i=1}^{h} t^{i-1}$$

$$= 1 + 2(t-1)\,.\left(\frac{t^h - 1}{t-1}\right)$$

$$= 1 + 2\,(t^h - 1)$$

$$n \geq 2t^h - 1$$

$$\frac{n+1}{2} \geq t^h$$

taking log to base t on both sides.

$$h \log_t t \leq \log_t \left(\frac{n+1}{2}\right)$$

or $$h \leq \log_t \left(\frac{n+1}{2}\right).$$ Hence proved.

EXAMPLE 21.6. *Why don't we allow a minimum degree of $t = 1$.*

SOLUTION : If we have minimum degree of t and it is not a root node then its parent must have $t - 1$ keys *i.e.*, 0 no. of keys, but we can not have a node with no keys in it so it will violate the definition of B-tree thus $t \geq 2$.

EXAMPLE 21.7. *Find the value of t for which this tree is a legal B-tree?*

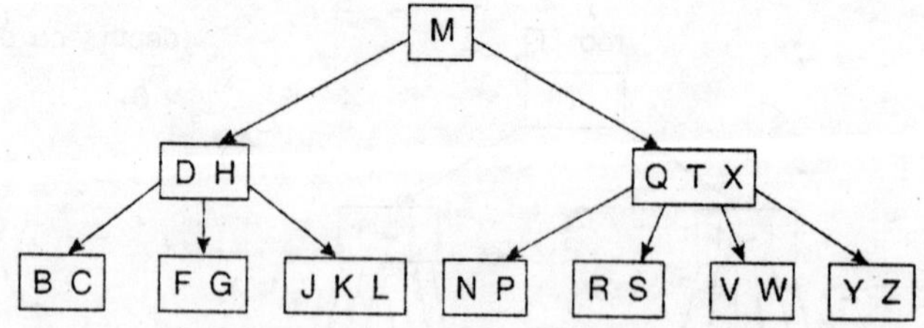

SOLUTION : $t = 3$, as node 2 contains *DH i.e.*, it has $t - 1$ keys, *i.e.*, 2 keys and it is internal node.

EXAMPLE 21.8. *Show all legal B-trees of degree 2 that represent* {1, 2, 3, 4, 5}

SOLUTION :

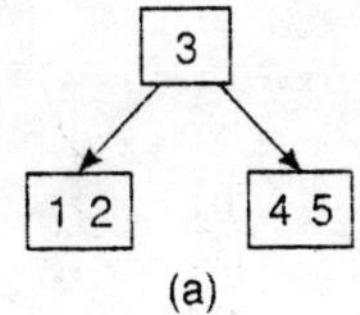

(a)

Only possible solution is (a).

EXERCISE

1. Suppose that the keys {1, 2, ..., n} are inserted into an empty-B tree with minimum degree 2. How many nodes does the final B-tree have?
2. Explain how to find the minimum key stored in a B-tree and how to find the predecessor of a given key stored in B-tree.
3. Prove that maximum no. of keys in a B-tree is $2t - 1$ if t is the minimum degree.
4. Insert the entries below, in the order stated. into an initially empty B-tree of order (a) 3 (b) 4 (c) 7

   a g f b k d h m j e s i r x c l n t u p
5. What is the smallest no. of entries that, when inserted in an appropriated order, will force a B-tree of order 5 to have height 2. (*i.e.*, 3 levels)?
6. Draw all B-trees of order 5 (between 2 and 4 keys per node) that can be constructed from the keys 1, 2, 3, 4, 5, 6, 7 and 8?
7. Define **pre order** traversal of a B-trees to mean visiting all the entries in the root node first, then traversing all the subtrees, from left to right, in preorder write an algorithm that will traverse a B-tree in preorder.
8. Define **post-order** traversal of a B-tree recursively to mean traversing all the subtrees of the root, from left to right, in post order, then visiting all the entries in the root. Write an algorithm for this?

22

BINOMIAL TREES AND BINOMIAL HEAPS

22.1 Binomial Trees

The **binomial tree B_k** is an ordered tree defined recursively. Where k represents the kth binomial tree. It consists of root node with k children, where j-th child, $1 \le j \le k$, is in turn root of binomial tree B_{j-1}. Fig. 22.1 Shows binomial tree from B_0 to B_4.

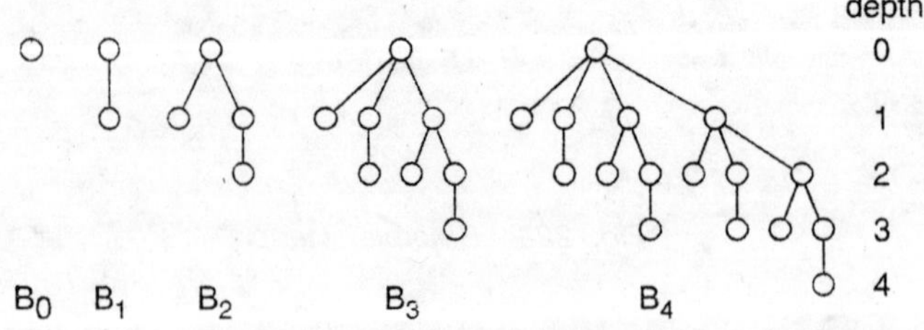

Fig. 22.1. Binomial Trees

We can see from Fig. 22.1 that there are 1, 2, 4, 8, 16 nodes at level 0, 1, 2, 3, 4 thus it leads to following properties of binomial tree.

Properties

For the binomial tree B_k

1. There are 2^k nodes.
2. The height of tree is k.
3. There are exactly $\binom{k}{i}$ (binomial coefficient) nodes at depth i, where $0 \le i <= k$
4. the root has degree k, which is greater than that of any other node, moreover if the children of the root are numbered from right to left by $K-1, K-2, ..., 0$ child i is the root of subtree B_i.

e.g. in B_4 there are $2^4 = 16$ nodes and

$$\binom{4}{4} = 1 \text{ node at level 4}, \binom{4}{2} = \frac{4\,!}{2\,!\,2\,!} = \frac{4 \times 3 \times 2}{2 \times 2} = 6 \text{ nodes at level 2}$$

22.1.1 Binomial Heap

It is different sized collection of binomial tree and each must hold the min *heap property* or binomial heap, H properties.

1. Each binomial tree in H is heap ordered, if the key of a node is greater than or equal to the key of its parent.
2. There is *at most* one binomial tree in H whose root has a given degree.

First property says that the root contains the minimum key value in the tree. Second property says, n-node binomial heaps contains at most $[lgn] + 1$ binomial tree. See Fig. 22.2 for binomial heap created with B_0, B_2, B_3.

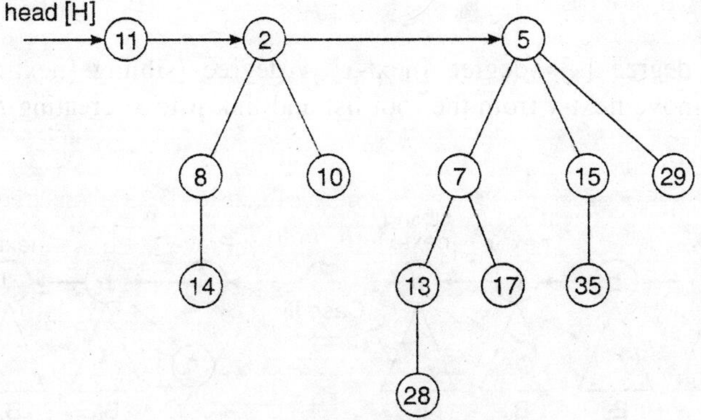

Fig. 22.2. Binomial Heap.

Fig. 22.2 A binomial heap, H created out of B_0, B_2, B_3 which have 1, 4, 8 nodes, thus H have 13 node, each binomial tree is heap ordered, satisfying property 1.

22.1.2 Binomial Heap Union

If we have two or more binomial heaps we can create union of these two to form a new one. Let us make following assumptions on pointers related to this

- x points to root currently being examined.
- Prev-x points to the root preceding x on the root list. sibling [Prev-x] = x.
- next-x points to the root following x on the root list sibling [x] = next-x

Here we have four cases that occurs while performing union on Binomial Heaps.

Case I. If degree [x] ≠ degree [next-x], then pointers moves one position further down the root list as shown in Fig. (a) below.

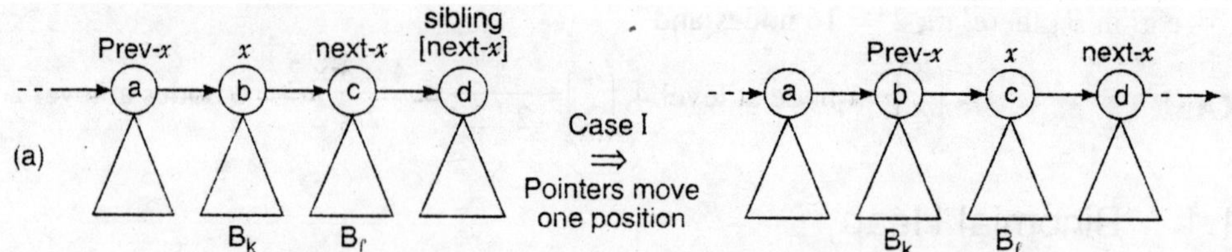

Case II. degree [x] = degree [next-x] = degree [sibling [next-x]] again pointer move one position further down the list, and next iteration executes either case 3 or case 4, See Fig. (b), below

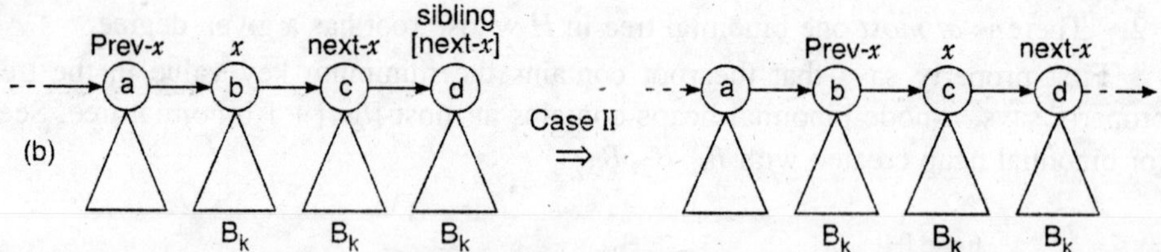

Case III. degree [x] = degree [next-x] ≠ degree [sibling [next-x]] and key [x] ≤ key [next-x], we remove next-x from the root list and link it to x, creating B_{k+1} tree. See Fig. (c) below

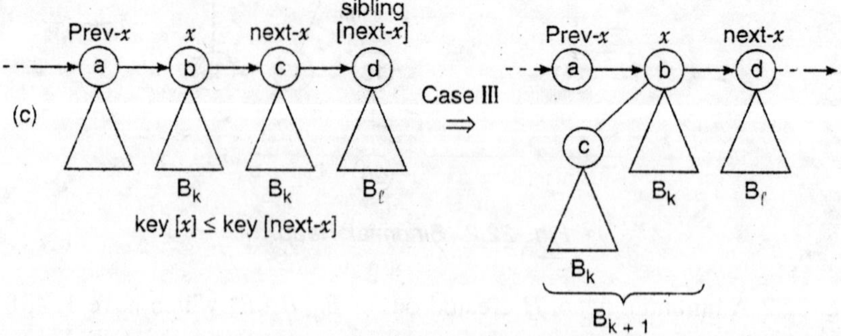

Case IV. degree [x] = degree [next-x] $\neq$ degree [sibling [next–x]] and key [next-x] $\leq$ key-x, we remove x from the root list and link it to next-x, again creating a B_{k+1} tree. See Fig. (d)

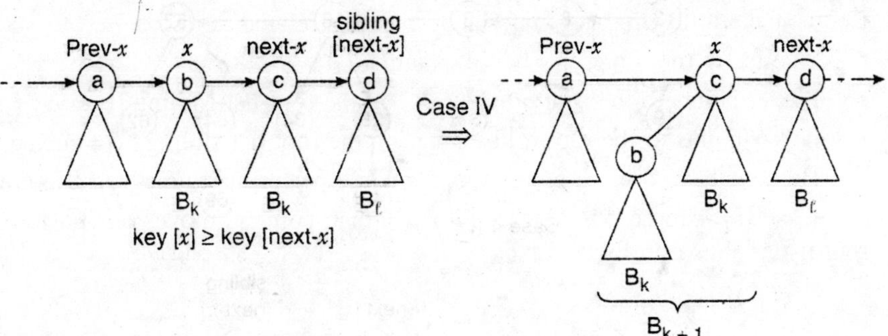

EXAMPLE 22.1. *Binomial Heap union*

1.

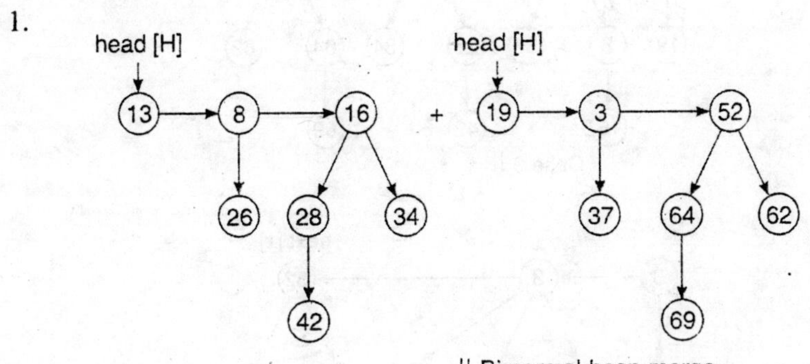

2.

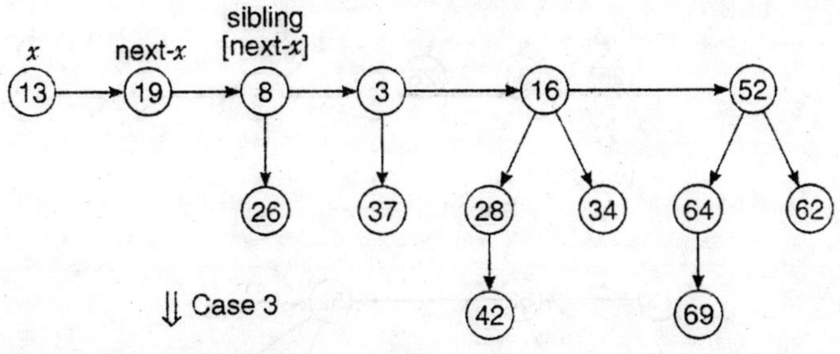

3.

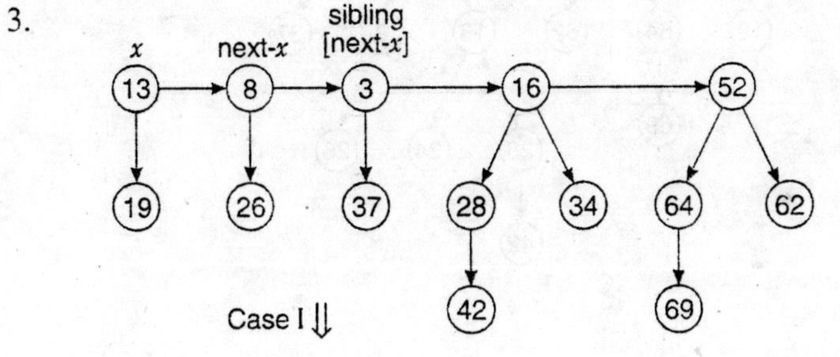

4.

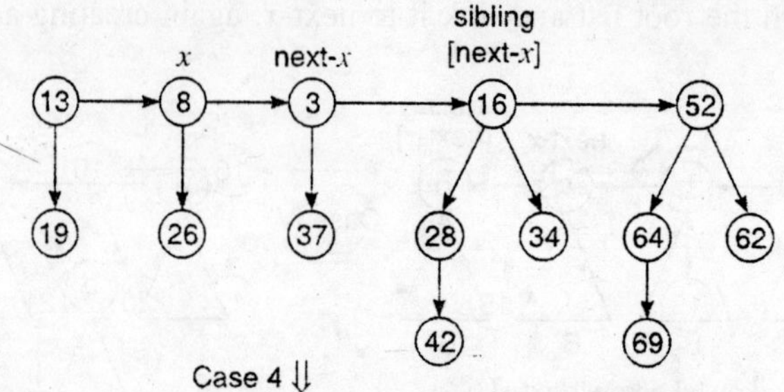

Case 4 ⇓

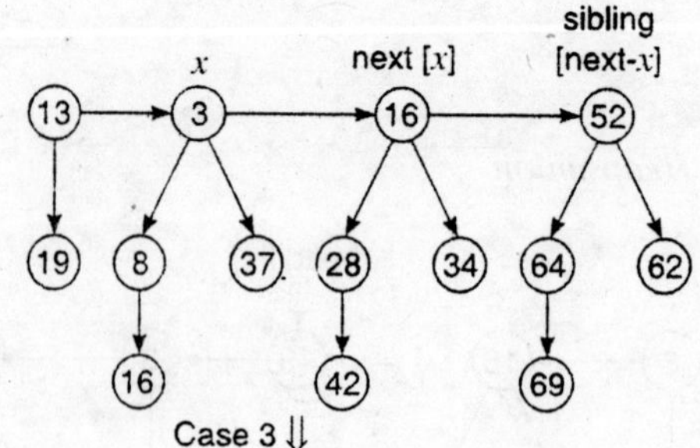

Case 3 ⇓

5.

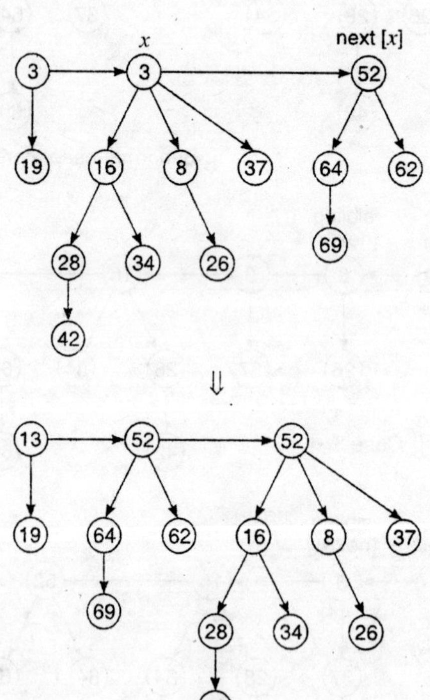

Let us consider the merging or union of two Binomial heaps.

EXAMPLE 22.2.

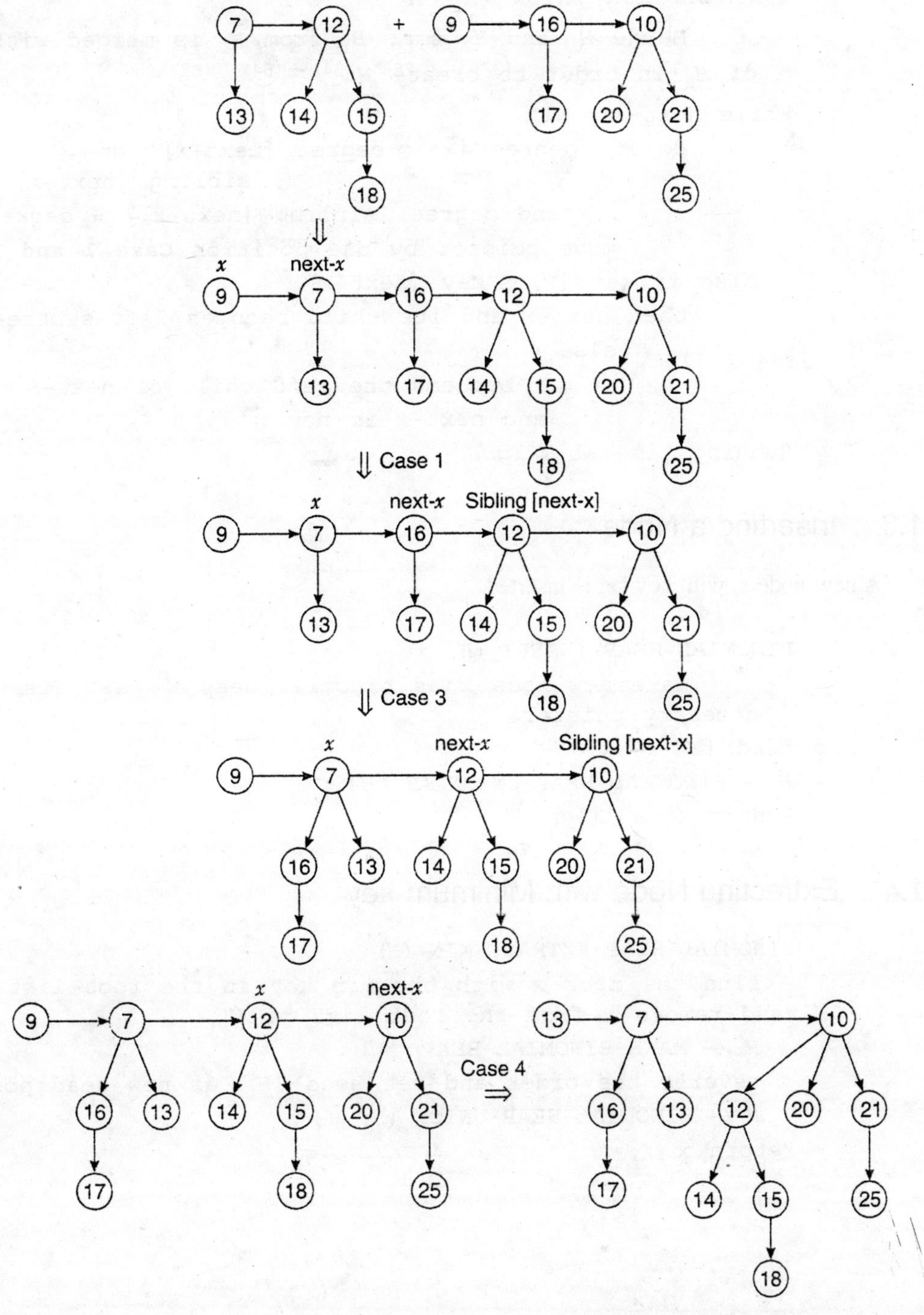

Now based on above 4 cases discussed we can write algorithm for Binomial heaps union as below

```
BINOMIAL-HEAP-UNION (H1, H2)
        Merge H1 and H2 s.t. Bi from H1 is merged with Bj
   of H2 in order to create H.
While next-x ≠ NIL
        do if (degree [x] ≠ degree [next-x]) or
                                         sibling [next-x]  ≠ NIL
                  and degree [sibling [next-x]] = degree [x])
              move pointer by one position Case 1 and 2
   else if key [x] ≤ key [next-x]
        then next-x and its child becomes left-subtree of x
              else
                   x becoems the left child of next-x
                   and next-x is now x
Running time is O(lgn)
```

22.1.3 Inserting a Node

A new node *x*, with key [*x*] is inserted.

```
BINOMIAL-HEAP-INSERT (H, x)
        make new node x as binomial heap H', set its
   necesary pointers
head [H'] ← x.
H ← BINOMIAL-HEAP-UNION (H, H')
Runnig time O(lgn)
```

22.1.4 Extracting Node with Minimum key

```
BINOMIAL-HEAP-EXTRACT-MIN (H)
   find the root x with the min key in the root list of
H, and remove x from the root list of H
   H' ← MAKE-BINOMIAL-HEAP ( )
   reverse the order and set head [H'] as new head pointer
   H ← BINOMIAL-HEAP-UNION (H, H')
return x.
```

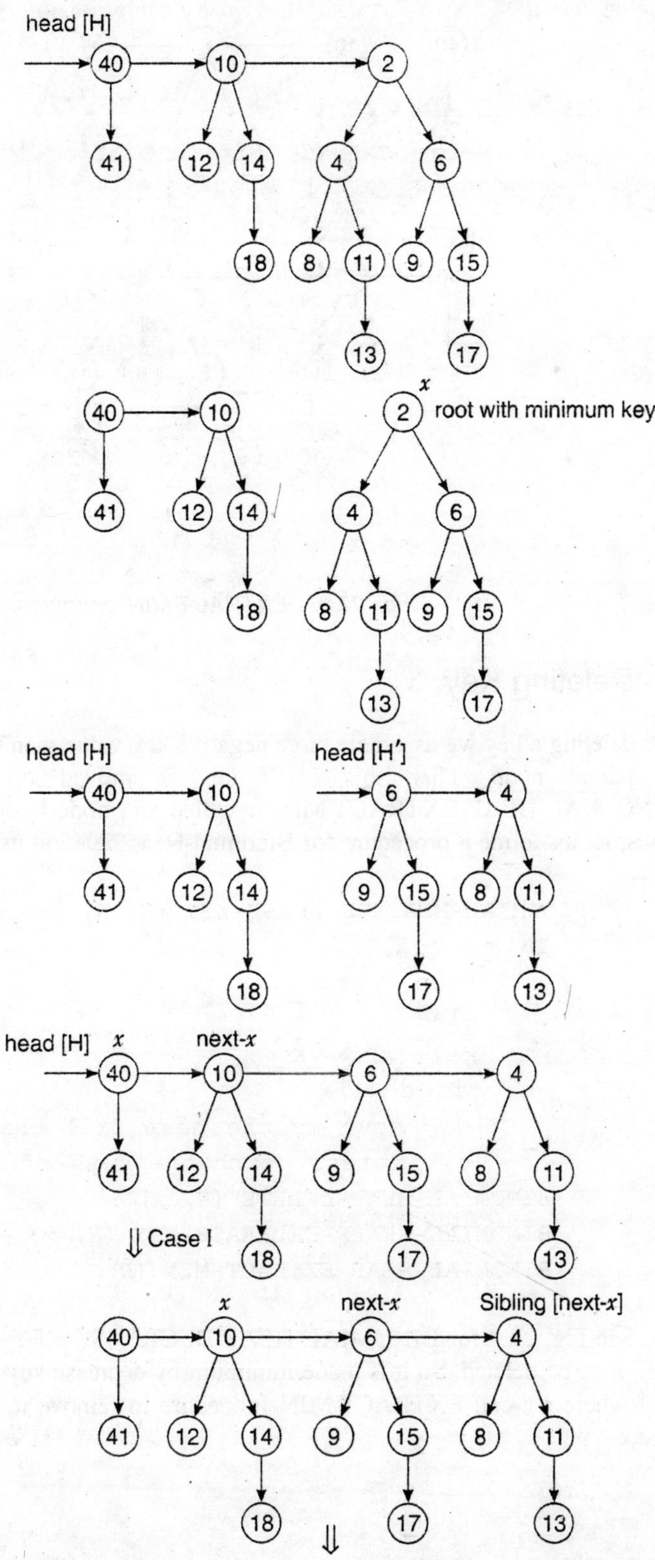
head [H]
40
10
2
41
12
14
4
6
18
8
11
9
15
13
17
x
root with minimum key
head [H']
next-x
Case I
Sibling [next-x]

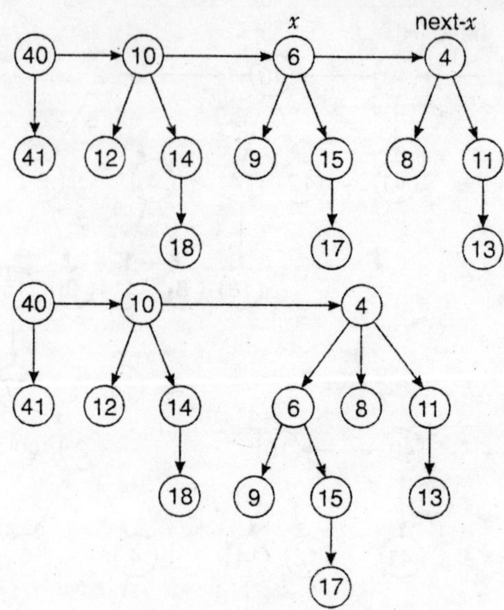

Fig. 22.3. EXTRACT-MIN operation.

22.1.5 Deleting Key

For deleting a key we assume a large negative key value then it is matched with the key value of parent node. Then this small key is moved up till it reaches root where BINOMIAL-HEAP-EXTRACT-MIN is called and node is deleted. This takes $O(lg\ n)$ time. Thus, let us define a procedure for Binomial-Heap deletion using Decrease Key.

```
BINOMIAL-HEAP-DECREASE-KEY (H, x, k)
   IF k > k[x]
         then "error"
         else
         key [x] ← K
         while (1)
               move up the heap till child is smaller than
               parent, exchange keys of child and parent.
   BINOMIAL-HEAP-DELETE (H, x)
   BINOMIAL-HEAPS-DECREASE-KEY (H, x, – ∞)
   BINOMIAL-HEAP-EXTRACT-MIN (H)
```

See Fig. 22.4 for BINOMIAL-HEAP-DECREASE KEY operation here node y with key = 37 is to be deleted. So it is made minimum by decrease key operation so that it move to the root where we call EXTRACT-MIN Procedure to remove it, this procedure is not shown in figure.

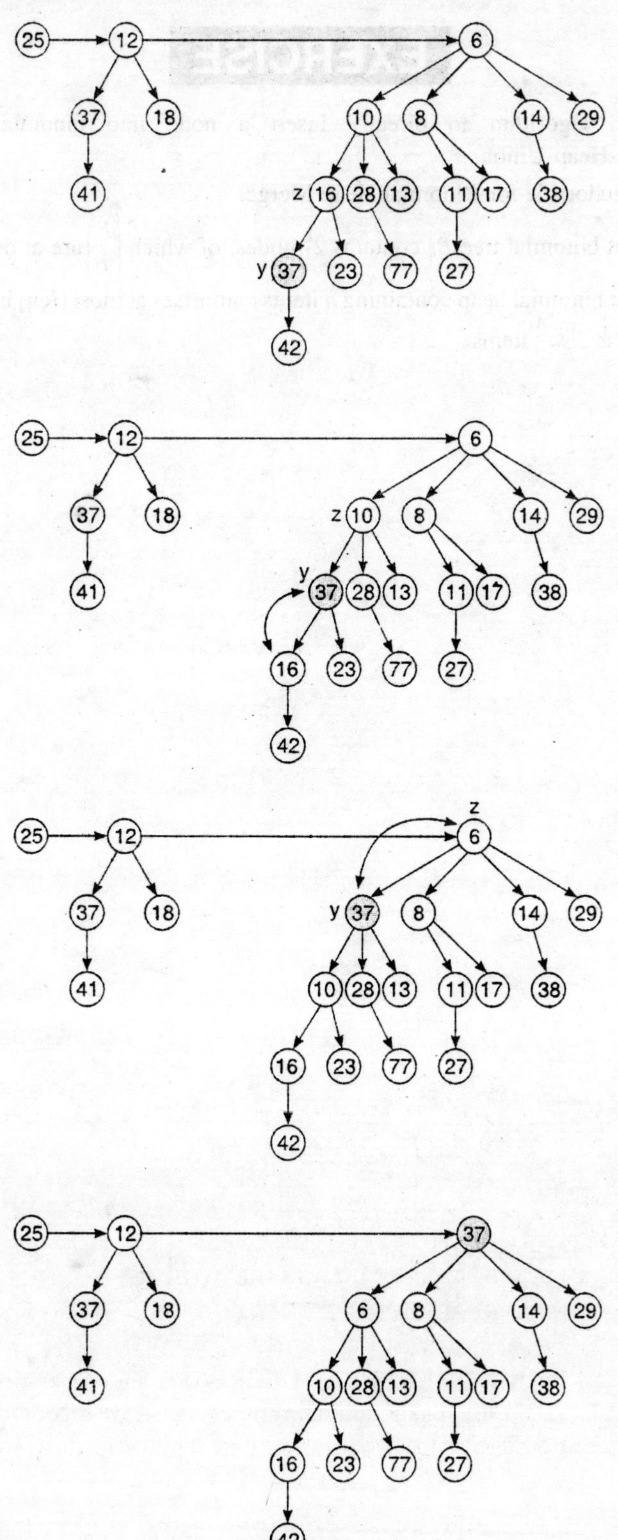

Fig. 22.4. BINOMIAL HEAP DECREASE KEY, here key = 37 is moving up as it is now made minimum (– ∞)

EXERCISE

1. Write an algorithm to directly insert a node into binomial heap without using Binomial-Heap-Union.
2. Write pseudocode for Binomial Heap Merge.
3. Prove that binomial tree B_k contains 2^k nodes, of which $\binom{k}{i}$ are at depth i, $0 \le i \le k$.
4. Prove that binomial heap containing n items comprises at most $[lgn]$ binomial trees, the largest of which is $2^{[lgn]}$ items.

❑❑❑

23

FIBONACCI HEAPS

23.1 Fibonacci Heaps

Fibonacci heaps like binomial heaps contain collection of heaps such that trees in fibonacci heaps are not necessarily a binomial trees and also they are rooted but not ordered, as shown in Fig. 23.1(a)

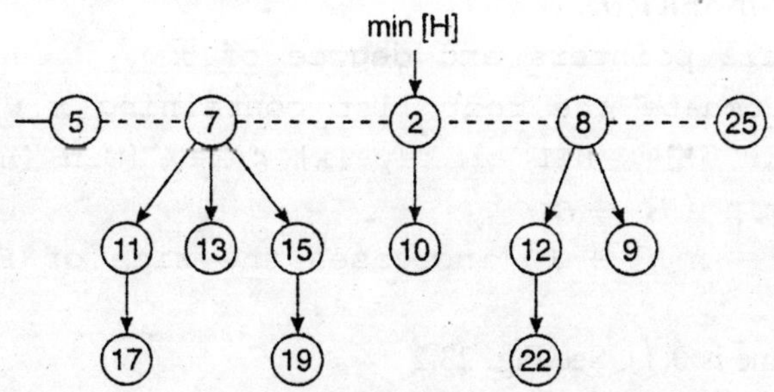

Fig. 23.1 (a) : Fibonacci Heap.

The root of fibonacci heap must be the minimum key node, of all the roots in the min-heap collection fibonacci heap is represented by doubly circular linked list with poitners $P[x]$, child $[x]$, left $[y]$, right $[y]$ for a node x with child y, left, right represents siblings. Apart from this it contains degree$[x]$ for the number of children of x and mark $[x]$ for the node x whose child has been lost. See Fig. 23.1(b) – (c)

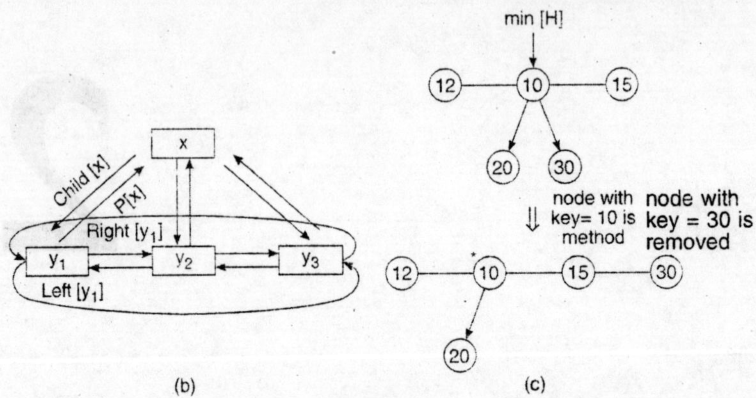

Fig. 23.1 (b)–(c).

23.1.1 Potential Function

Fibonacci heap can be viewed as amortized data structure. So we can define a potential function for this as $t[H]$ the number of trees in the root list of H and $m[H]$ is the no. of marked nodes in H_0 then

$$a[H] = t[H] + 2m[H]$$

e.g., in Fig. 23.1 b-c $t(H) = 3$, $m(H) = 1$, so

$$a(H) = 3 + 2.1 = 5$$

For a fibonacci set we compute potential function of individual fibonacci heaps then sum up these values.

23.1.2 Inserting a node in Fibonacci heap

FIB-HEAP-INSERT (H, x)

```
1. Set all pointers and degree of x.
2. Concatenate the root list containing x with root list H.
3. If min [H] = NIL or key [x] < key [min [H]]
   then min [H] ← x.
4. n[H] ← n[H] + 1 [increases the size of Fibonacci heap.)
```

Running time is θ(1). See Fig. 23.2

Amortized cost of above algorithm can be calcualted as, let H be the input fibonacci Heap and H' is the resulting fibonacci heap. Then $t[H'] = t[H] + 1$ and $m[H'] = m[H]$, thus increase in potential is

$$a(H') = t[H] + 1 + 2m[H] - t[H] - 2m[H] = 1$$

Since acutal cost is $O(1)$, the amortized cost is $O(1) + 1 = O(1)$.

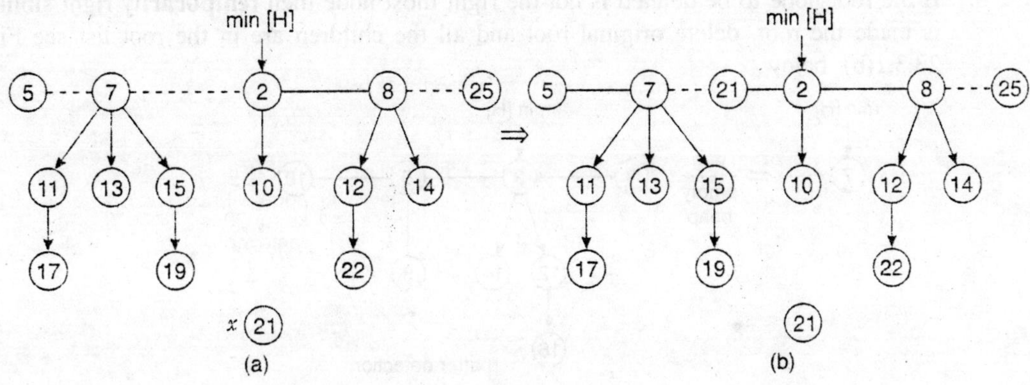

Fig. 23.2. Key 21 inserted at left sibling of root.

23.1.3 Finding the minimum node

Minimum node is always the root node with pointer min [H] so it takes $O(1)$ time finding it.

23.1.4 Uniting Two Fibonacci Heaps

```
FIB-HEAP-UNION (H1, H2)
    H ← MAKE-FIB-HEAP ( )
    min [H] ← min [H1]
    concatenate the root list of H2 with H.
            If [min(H1) = NIL] or (min [H2] ≠ NIL and
                                                  min (H2) < min [H1])
                    then min [H] ← min [H2]
            n[H] ← n[H1] + n[H2]
            free H1 and H2
    return H
```

the change in potential of this algorithm is given by

$$a(H) - (a(H_1) + a(H_2)) = (t(H) + 2m(H)) - (t(H_1) + 2m(H_1) + t(H_2) + 2m(H_2))$$

$$= 0, \text{ as } t(H) = t(H_1) + t(H_2)$$

and $$m(H) = m(H_1) + m(H_2)$$

23.1.5 Extracting or Deleting the Minimum

When we delete a node with minimum value then obviously it is a root node min [H]. Due to deletion of node following steps occur.

1. If fibonacci heap contains only single node then heap becomes empty.
2. If the node deleted is right most node, *i.e.*, it has no right sibling then after deletion of this node the heap becomes empty, as it is a doubly circular linked list, see Fig. 23.3.1(a).

3. If the root node to be deleted is not the right most node then **temporarily** right sibling is made the root, delete original root and all the children are in the root list see Fig. 23.3.1(b) below.

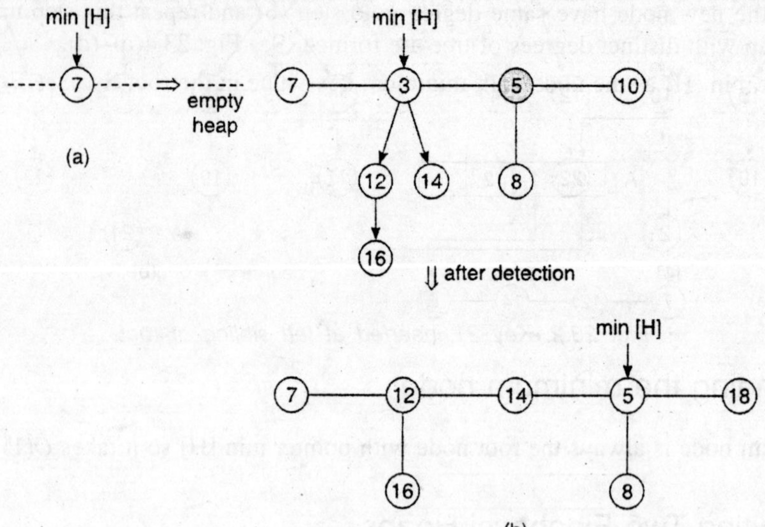

Fig. 23.3.1.

4. Maintain an Array *A* that contains the degre of the trees.. At this stage the temporary root node points to corresponding position in the array *A*. as shown below in Fig. 23.3.2.

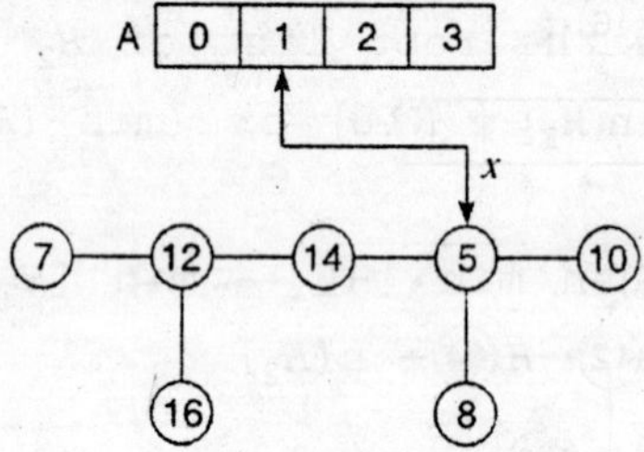

Fig. 23.3.2.

5. Then scan the next node and also allow it to point array *A* at corresponding position.

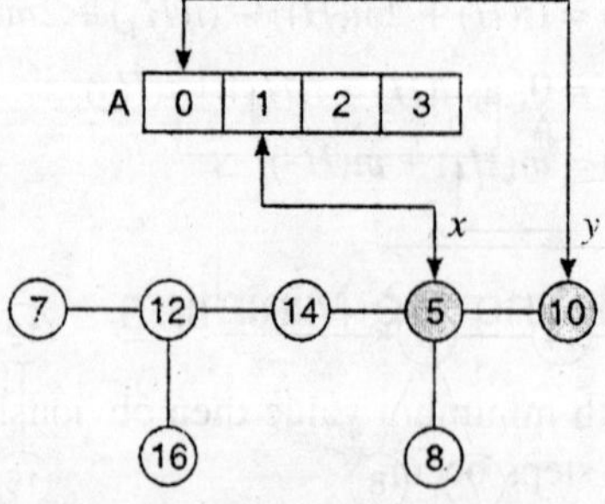

Fig. 23.3.3.

6. Now compare the degree of this node, y with the previous node, x in Array A if they are same then make the node with greater key value as the child of the one with less key value other wise scan the next node in circular fashion. See Fig. 23.4(a)–(b).
7. If the new node have same degree goto step (6) and repeat this step until a Fibonacci heap with distinct degrees of tree are formed. See Fig. 23.4(c)–(d).
8. Set min [H] as the node with minimum key value in the root list. See Fig. 23.4(d).

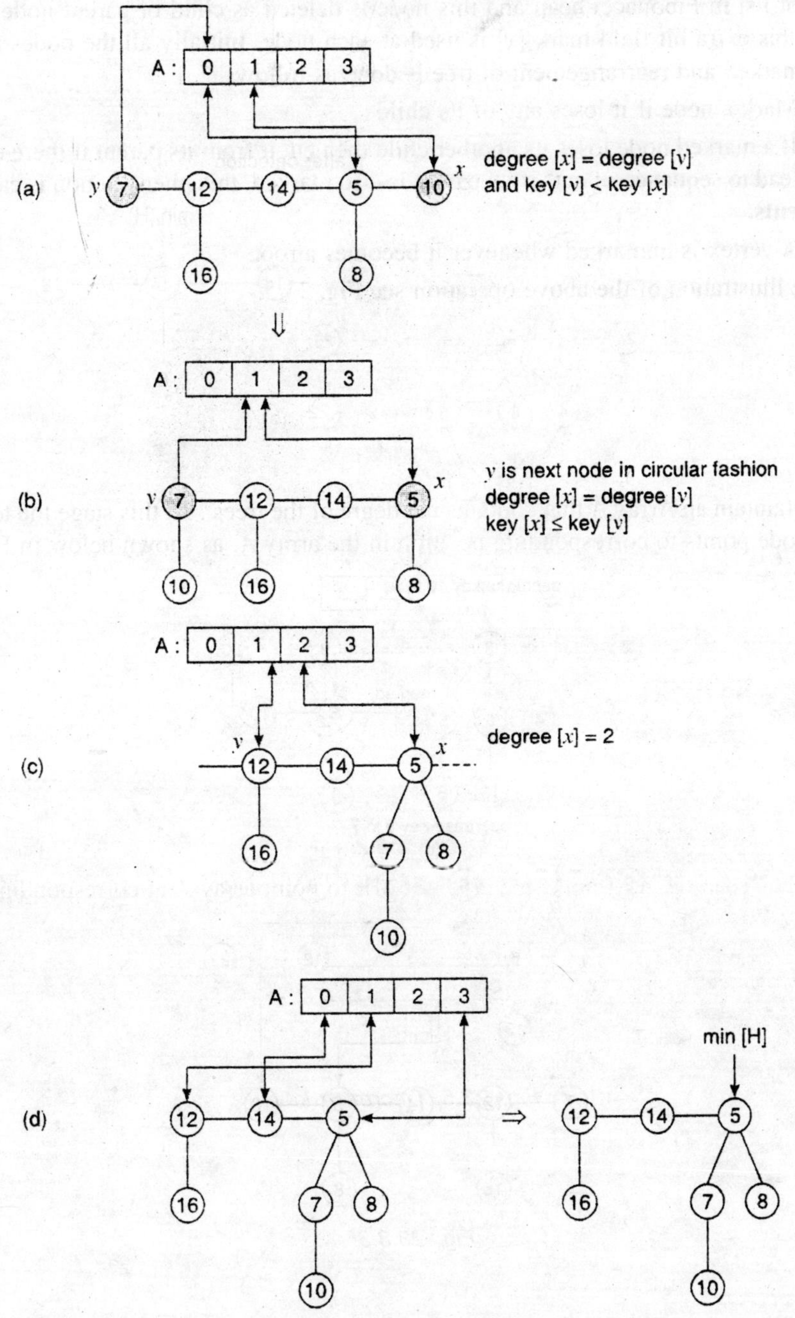

Fig. 23.4

Now all nodes are scanned and there is no tree with same degree, so finally tree with root node is shown above with min $[H]$ pointer set.

23.1.6 Decrease key Operation.

This operation is implemented by lowering the value at any node x, then this node is added to the root list in Fibonacci heap and this node is deleted as child of parent node. To keep track of all this extra bit field mark $[x]$ is used at each node. Initially all the nodes are assumed to be unmarked and rearrangement of tree is done as follows :

1. Mark a node if it loses any of its child
2. If a marked node loses its another child then cut it from its parent if there exists, this may lead to sequence of cuts if its parent is also marked, this phenomenon is called **cascading cuts.**
3. A vertex is unmarked whenever it becomes a root.

for the illustration of the above operation see Fig. 23.5.

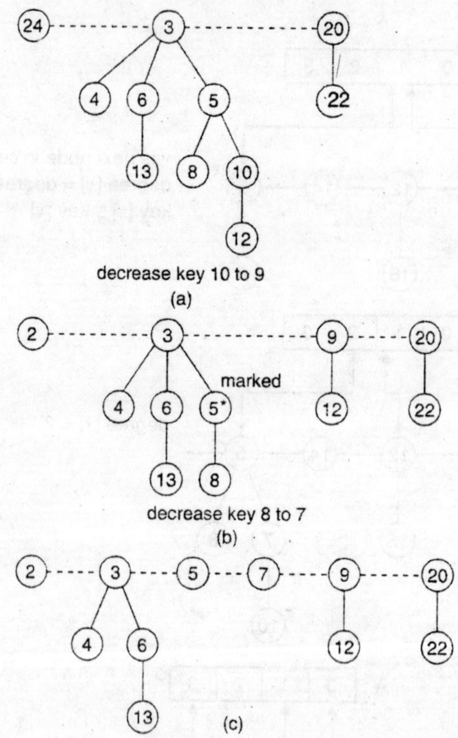

Fig. 23.5. Decrease key.

EXAMPLE 23.1. *Write an algorithm for inserting a mode into Fibonacci Heap. Show how a key 21 has to be inserted.*

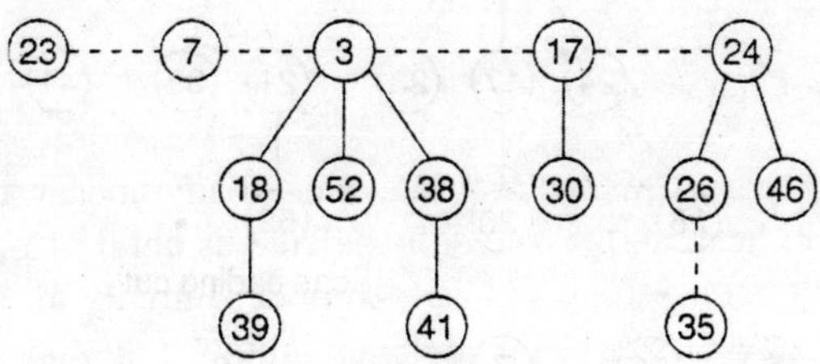

SOLUTION :

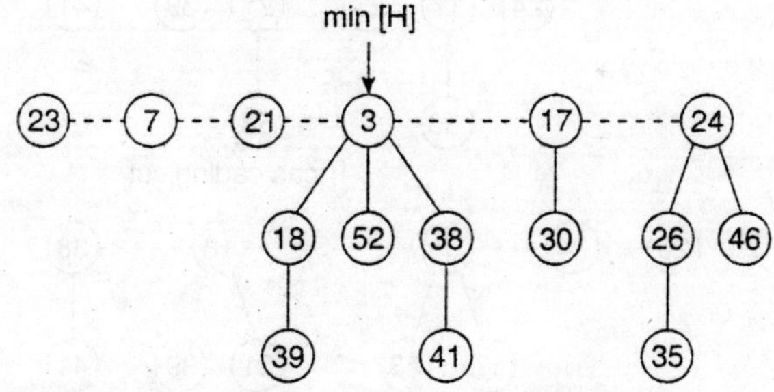

EXAMPLE 23.2. *Show the decrease key operation for the following fig. in given sequence : (1) key 46 decreased to key 15 (2) key 35 decreased to key 5, where '*' shows marked node;*

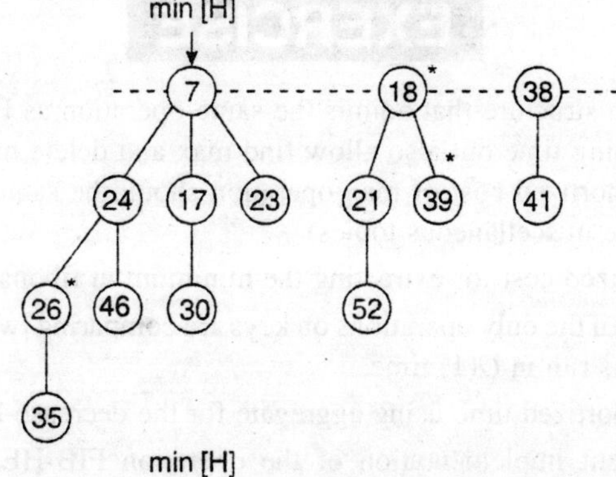

SOLUTION :

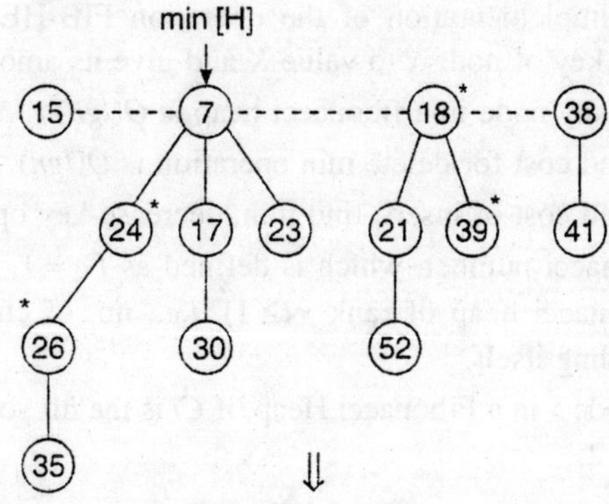

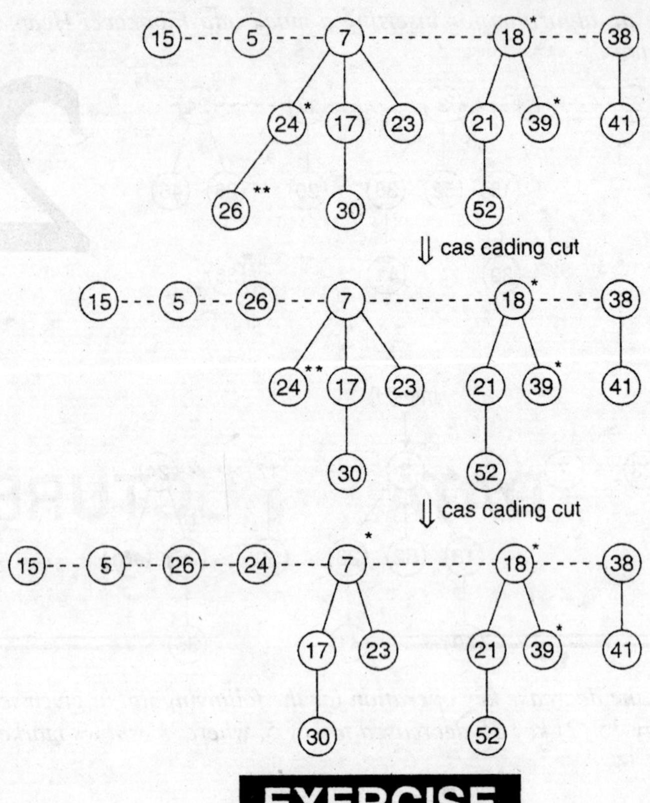

EXERCISE

1. Describe a data structure that admits the same operation as Fibonacci Heaps with the same amortized running time but also allow find max and delete max in addition to find min and delete min. Amortized cost of max operation should be same as for the corresponding min operations. (See miscellaneous topics)
2. Find the amortized cost for extracting the minimum in fibonacci heap.
3. Argue that, when the only operations on keys are comparing two keys, not all of the mergeable Heap operations run in $O(1)$ time.
4. What is the amortized time using aggregate for the decrease-key operation.
5. Give an efficient implementation of the operation FIB-HEAP CHANGE-KEY (H, x, K), which changes the key of node x to value K and give its amortized cost.
6. Prove that rank of any node in a fibonacci heap is $O(lgn)$.
7. Prove that amortized cost for delete min operation is $O(lgn)$.
8. Prove that amortized cost of insert, find min, decrease-key operation is $\theta(1)$.
9. Let F_i be ith Fibonacci number, which is defined as $F_0 = 1$, $F_1 = 1$, $F_i = F_{i-1} + F_{i-2}$. Any node x in the fibonacci heap of rank $r (\geq 1)$, *i.e.*, no. of children of v, has at least F_{r+1} descendents, including itself.
10. Prove that, for a node x in a Fibonacci Heap, if C_i is the ith youngest child of x, then the rank of C_i is at least $i - 2$.

24

DATA STRUCTURE FOR DISJOINT SETS

Disjoint-set Operations

A disjoint set data structure maintains a collection $S = \{S_1, S_2, S_3, \ldots, S_k\}$ of disjoint dynamic sets. Each set is identified by a representative, which is some members of the set.

In dynamic implementations each element of a set is represented by an object. Let x denote an object, then following operations are supported.

MAKE-SET (x)—creates a new set whose only member is pointed to by x. Since the sets are disjoint we require that x not already be in a set.

UNION (x, y)-unites the dynamic sets that contain x and y, say S_x and S_y into a new set that is union of these two sets. Where S_x and S_y are disjoint sets initially.

FIND-SET (x)-returns a pointer to the representative of the (unique) set containing x.

An application of disjoint-set data structures connected components

algorithm for this is given by

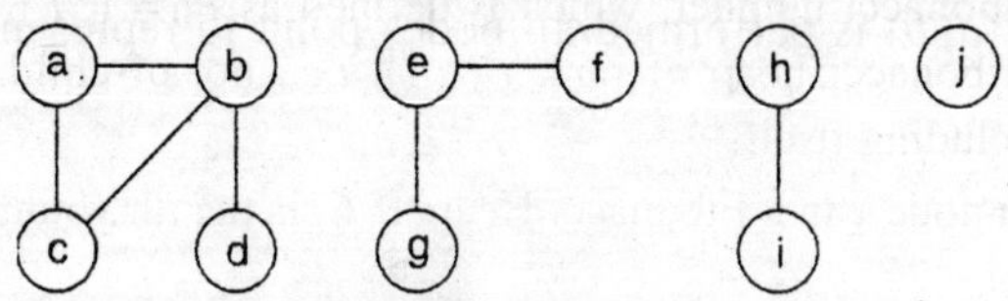

Fig. 24.1. Connected graphs.

```
CONNECTED-COMPONENTS (G)
for each vertex v ε V [G]
    do MAKE-SET (v)
for each edge (u, v) ε E[G]
    do if FIND-SET (u) ≠ FIND-SET (v)
        then UNION (u, v)
```

here set of vertices is created for each edge $u \neq v$ if (u, v) is not in $E[G]$ then u, v is added to G thus forming a connected component.

```
SAME-COMPONENT (u, v)
if FIND-SET (u) = FIND-SET (v)
    then return TRUE
    else return FALSE
```

looking at Fig. 24.1 we can process the edges using connected components graph as follows.

Edge Processed	**Collection of disjoint sets**									
Initial sets.	{a}	{b}	{c}	{d}	{e}	{f}	{g}	{h}	{i}	{j}
(b, d)	{a}	{b,d}	{c}		{e}	{f}	{g}	{h}	{i}	{j}
(e, g)	{a}	{b,d}	{c}		{e,g}	{f}		{h}	{i}	{j}
(a, c)	{a,c}	{b,d}			{e,g}	{f}		{h}	{i}	{j}
(h, j)	{a,c}	{b,d}			{e,g}	{f}		{h,i}		{j}
(a, b)	{a,b,c,d}				{e,f,g}			{h,i}		{j}
(e, f)	{a,b,c,d}				{e,f,g}			{h,i}		{j}
(b, c)	{a,b,c,d}				{e,f,g}			{h,i}		{j}

Fig. 24.2. Collection of disjoints sets after each edge is processed.

Linked-list representation of disjoint sets

We can give linked list implementation graphically by pointing one node representing one vertex to another and each node pointing back to first node which is representative.

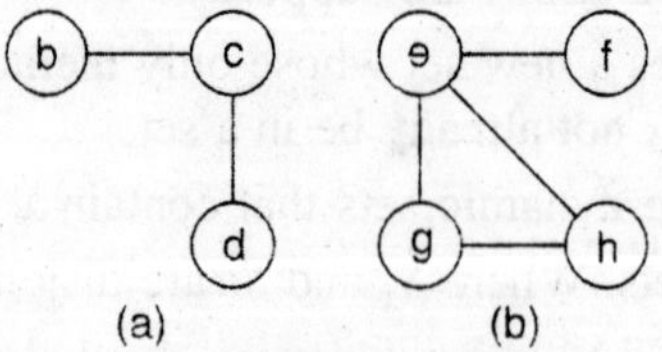

Fig. 24.3. Graph.

When UNION (a, b) is performed all nodes point to representative of second graph. See Fig. 24.4.

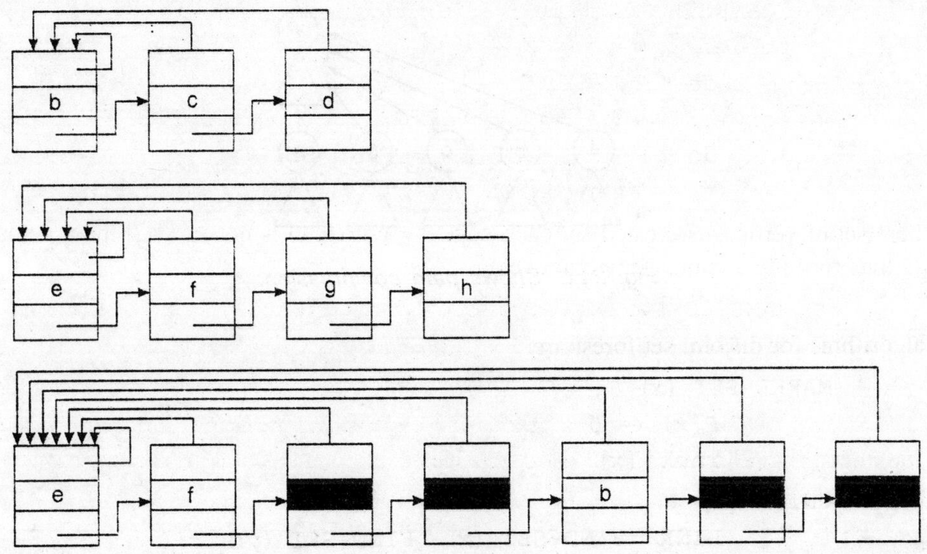

Fig. 24.4. Linked list representation of graph of Fig. 24.3.

Disjoint set Forests

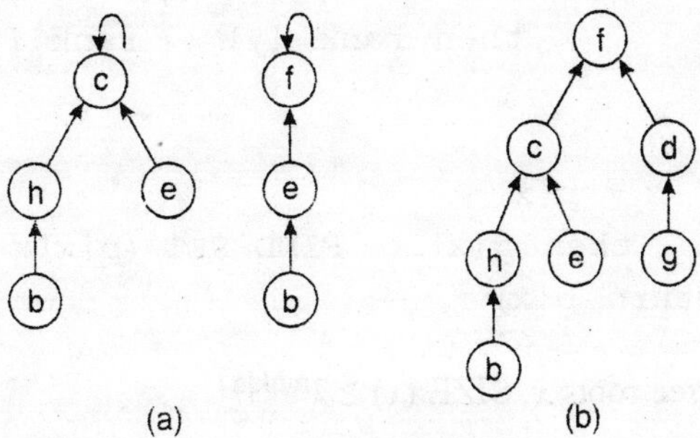

Fig. 24.5 A disjoint set forest (a) Two trees representing the two sets. Tree on left represents {b, c, e, h} with c as representative, and tree on right represents the sets {d, f, g} with f as representative (b) result of UNION (c, f)

In this make set operation simply create a tree with just one node. We perform a FIND-SET Operation by chosing a parent pointers until we find the root of the tree. In Union operation root of one tree points to root of another tree.

Here we apply **union by rank**, *i.e.*, we find the size of smaller tree then it is pointed by root of larger tree, As shown in Fig. 24.4. This is also called **height rule.**

In other method **path compression** each node directly point to the root, as shown in Fig. 26.6.

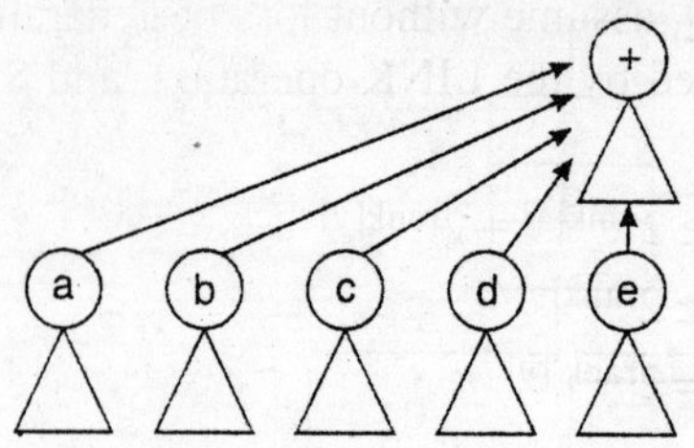

Fig. 24.6. Shows path compression.

algorithms for disjoint set forest are.

```
MARKE-SET (x)
        P[x] ← 0
        rank [x] ← 0
UNION (x, y)
        LINK (FIND-SET (x), FIND-SET (y))
LINK (x, y)
   if rank [x] > rank [y]
        then p[y] ← x          //smaller tree becomes parent.
        else p[x] ← y.
             if rank [x] = rank [y]
                  then rank [y] ← rank [y] + 1

FIND-SET (x)
        if x ≠ p[x]
             then p[x] ← FIND-SET (p[x])
        return p[x]
```

THEOREM 24.1. For all tree roots x, SIZE $(x) \geq 2^{\text{rank}[x]}$

PROOF : It can be proved by induction as follows :

Basis

This is true before the first LINK, Since ranks are initially 0 and each tree contains atleast one node.

Inductive Step

Assume that this holds before performing operation LINK (x, y). Let rank denote the rank just before the LINK, and let rank′ denote the rank' just after the LINK. Define SIZE and SIZE′ similarly.

If rank $[x] \neq$ rank $[y]$, assume without loss of genarality that rank $[x] <$ rank $[y]$. Node y is the root of the tree formed by the LINK operation, and SIZE′ (y) = SIZE (x) + SIZE (y).

$$\begin{aligned} \text{SIZE}'(y) &\geq 2^{\text{rank}[x]} + 2^{\text{rank}[y]} \\ &\geq 2^{\text{rank}[y]} \\ &= 2^{\text{rank}'[y]} \end{aligned}$$

No ranks or sizes change for any nodes other than y.

If rank $[x]$ = rank $[y]$, node y is again the root of the new tree, and

$$\begin{aligned} \text{SIZE}[y] &= \text{SIZE}(x) + \text{SIZE}(y) \\ &\geq 2^{\text{rank}[x]} + 2^{\text{rank}[y]} \\ &= 2^{\text{rank}[y]+1} \\ &= 2^{\text{rank}'[y]} \end{aligned}$$

EXAMPLE 24.1. *Find $S_1 \cup S_2$ for following tree*

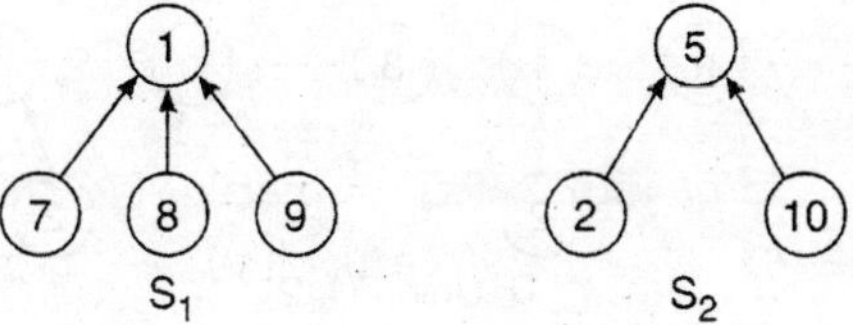

SOLUTION :

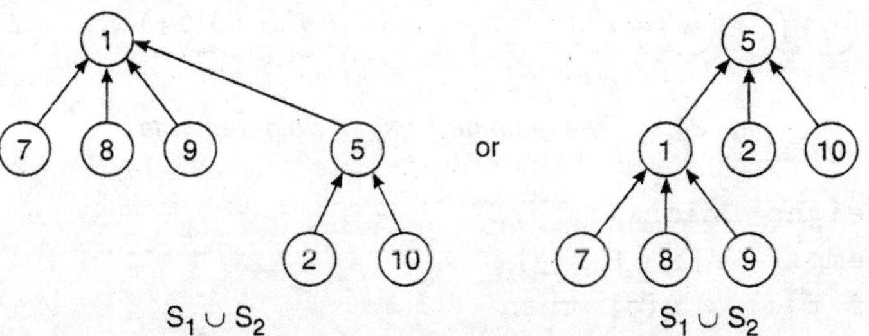

EXAMPLE 24.2. *What will the sequence of following operations produce.*
union (1, 2), *union* (2, 3), *union* (3, 4,), ... *union* (n – 1, n),
find (1), find (2), ..., find (n).

SOLUTION : Using the technique of Union by Rank, we get the following tree :

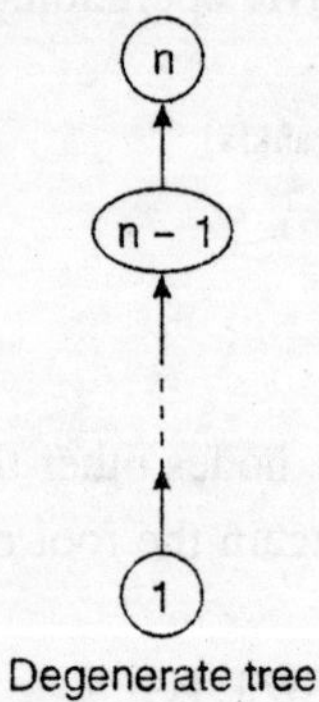

Weighted rule for union (*i*, *j*)

If the number of nodes in the tree with root *i* is less than the no. in the tree with root *j*, then make *j* the parent of *i*, otherwise make *i* the parent of *j*.

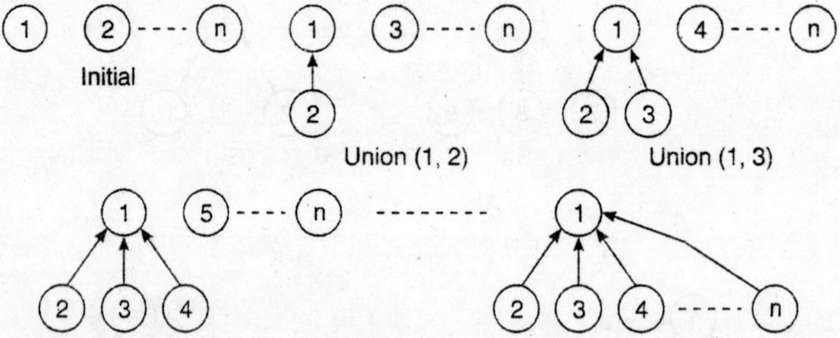

Fig. 24.7. Tree obtained using weighted rule.

```
Weight Union (i, j)
temp ← p[i] + p[j]
If p[i] > p[j] then
            p[i] ← j
            p[j] ← temp.
else
            p[j] = i; p[i] ← temp.
```

EXAMPLE 24.3. *Find the tree produced for i lying between 1 and 8 using weight union with following opertions.*

Union (1, 2), Union (3, 4), Union (5, 6), Union (7, 8). Union (1, 3), *Union (5, 7), Union (1,5).*

SOLUTION :

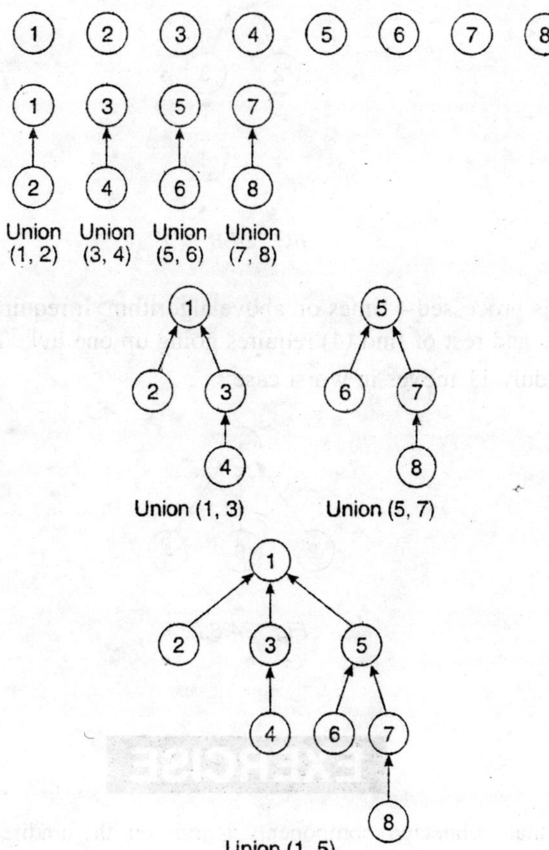

Collapsing Rule

If j is node on the path from i to its root and $p[i] \neq$ root $[i]$, then set $P[j]$ to root $[i]$.

```
Collapsing-find (i)
    r ← i
while p[r] > 0
    do r ← p[r]
    while i ≠ r
        do s ← P[i]
           p[i] ← r
           i ← s
return r
```

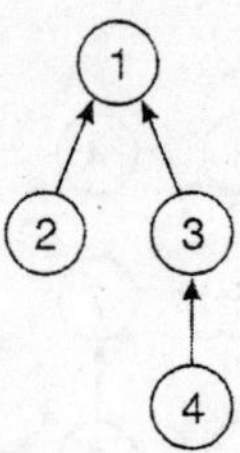

fIG. 24.8.1.

If find (4) is processed 4 times on above algorithm. It requires going up 2 links, and then resetting 2 links and rest of find (4) requires going up one link. The resultant tree obtained is

It requires duly 11 moves in worst case.

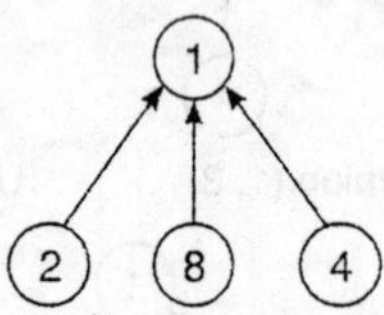

Fig. 24.8.2.

EXERCISE

1. Suppose that connected components is run on the undirected graph $G = (V, E)$ where $V = \{a, b, c, d, e, f, g, h, i, j, k\}$ and the edges of E are processed in the following order : (d, i), (f, k), (g, i), (b, g), (a, h), (i, j), (d, k), (b, j), (d, f), (g, i), (a, e), (i, d). List the vertices in each connected component after each iteration of lines 3–5.
2. Write a non recursive version of FIND-SET with path compression.
3. Prove that for any integer $r \geq 0$, there are atmost $\frac{n}{2^r}$ nodes of rank r and also prove that every node has rank at most $\lfloor lgn \rfloor$
4. Apply collapsing find (i) in Fig. 24.7 to process the FIND (8) 8 times.

25

ELEMENTARY GRAPH ALGORITHMS

25.1 Representation of Graphs

Before we give representation of graph let us provide the definition of adjacency matrix for a graph.

Adjacency Matrix

If $G = (V, E)$ is a graph then adjacency matrix is $V \times V$ matrix, *i.e.*, vertex to vertex such that matrix $A = [a_{ij}]$ and

$$a_{ij} = \begin{cases} 1 & \text{if } (i, j) \in E \\ 0 & \text{otherwise} \end{cases}$$

i.e., if there is an edge from V_i to V_j then entry to a_{ij} is 1, otherwise 0. See Fig. 25.1(a).

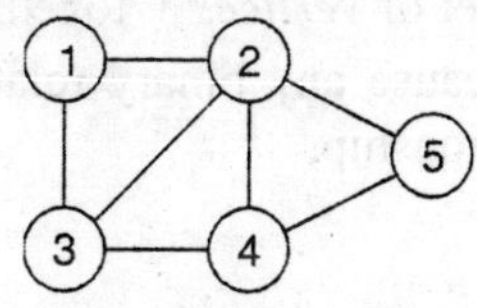

Fig. 25.1(a)

Its matrix is given by

$$\begin{array}{cc} & \xrightarrow{\quad V \quad} \\ & \begin{array}{ccccc} 1 & 2 & 3 & 4 & 5 \end{array} \\ V \downarrow \begin{array}{c} 1 \\ 2 \\ 3 \\ 4 \\ 5 \end{array} & \begin{bmatrix} 0 & 1 & 1 & 0 & 0 \\ 1 & 0 & 1 & 1 & 1 \\ 1 & 1 & 0 & 1 & 0 \\ 0 & 1 & 1 & 0 & 1 \\ 0 & 1 & 0 & 1 & 0 \end{bmatrix} \end{array}$$

Linked list representation of graph of Fig. 25.1 (a) having above adjacency matrix is given by

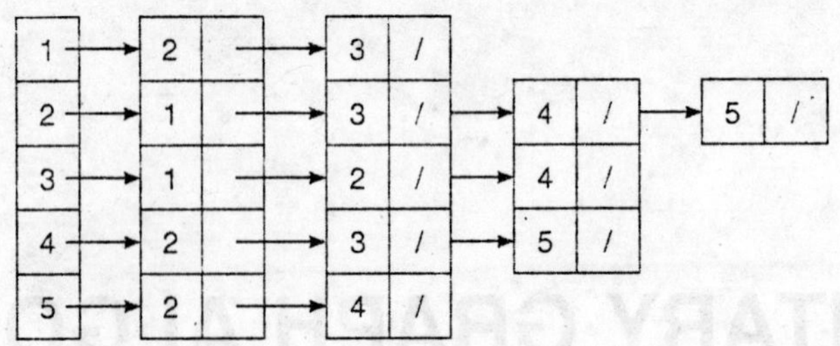

Fig. 25.1(b). Linked list representation of Fig. 25.1(a).

Similarly we can give the adjacency matrix for the directed graph and also its linked list representation.

Incidence matrix

It is defined as $V \times E$ matrix where $A = [a_{ij}]$ and

$$a_{ij} = \begin{cases} 1, & \text{if there is an edge from } V \text{ to } E \\ 0, & \text{otherwise} \end{cases}$$

Transpose

If $A = [a_{ij}]$ is a matrix then its transpose $A^T = [a_{ji}]$

Weighted graph

If edges of graph are labelled then it is called weighted graph.

A graph G consists of a set of *vertices* V together with a set E of vertex pairs of *edges.*

Graphs are important because any binary relation is a graph, so graphs can be used to represent essentially *any* relationship.

EXAMPLE 25.1. *A network of roads, with cities as verticies and roads between cities as edges.*

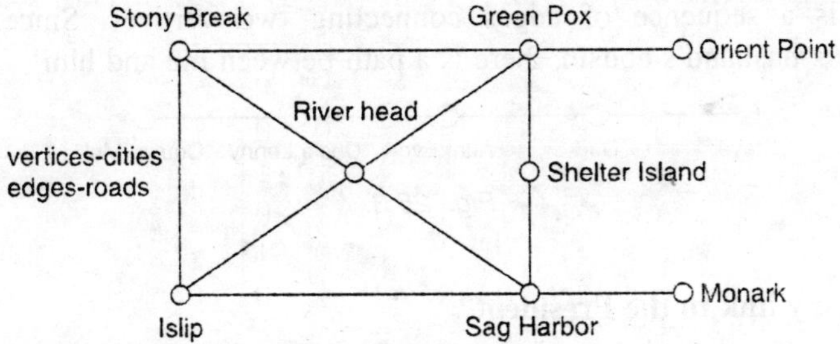

EXAMPLE 25.2. *An electronic circuit, with junctions as vertices and components as edges.*

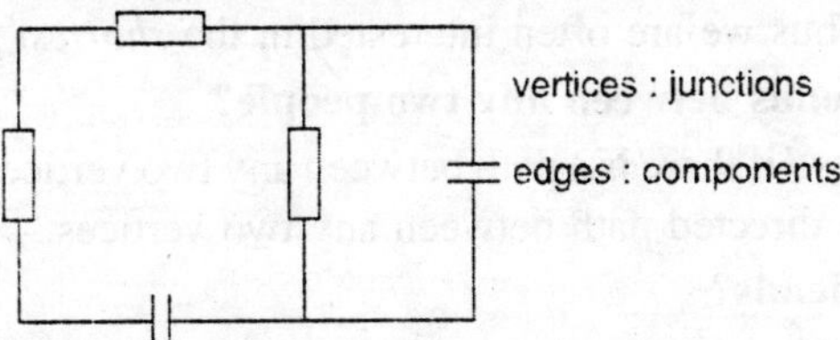

To understand many problems, we must think of them in terms of graphs!

The Friendship Graph

Consider a graph where the vertices are people, and there is an edge between two people if and only if they are friends.

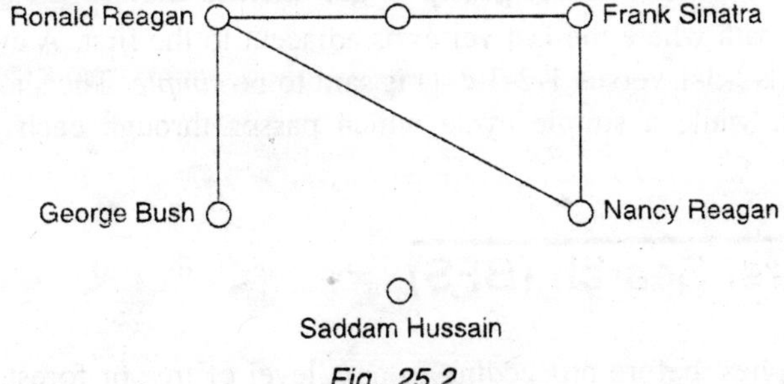

Fig. 25.2.

This graph is well-defined on any set of people: SUNY SB, New York, or the world. What questions might we ask about the friendship graph?

If I am your friend, does that mean you are my friend?

A graph is *undirected* if (x, y) implies (y, x). Otherwise the graph is directed. The "heard-of" graph is directed since countless famous people have never heard of me! The "had-sex-with" graph is presumably undirected, since it requires a partner.

Am I my own friend?

An edge of the form (x, x) is said to be a *loop*. If x is y's friend several times over, that could be modeled using *multiedges,* multiple edges between the same pair of vertices. A graph is said to be *simple* if it contains no loops and multiple edges.

Am I linked by some chain of friends to the President?

A *path* is a sequence of edges connecting two vertices. Since *Mel Brooks* is my father's-sister's-husband's cousin, there is a path between me and him!

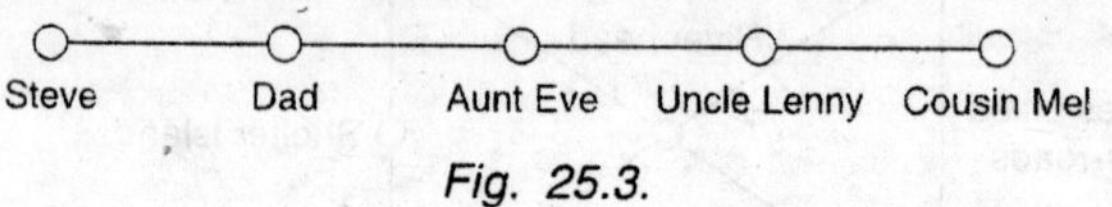

Fig. 25.3.

How close is my link to the President?

If I were trying to impress you with how tight I am with Mel Brooks, I would be much better off saying that Uncle Lenny knows him than to go into the details of how connected I am to Uncle Lenny. Thus we are often interested in the *shortest path* between two nodes.

Is there a path of friends between any two people?

A graph is *connected* if there is a path between any two vertices. A directed graph is *strongly connected* if there is a directed path between any two vertices.

Who has the most friends?

The *degree* of a vertex is the number of edges adjacent to it.

What is the largest clique?

A social clique is a group of mutual friends who all hang around together. A graph theoretic *clique* is a complete subgraph, where each vertex pair has an edge between them. Cliques are the densest possible subgraphs. Within the friendship graph, we would expect that large cliques correspond to workplaces, neighbourhoods, religious organizations, schools, and the like.

How long will it take for my gossip to get back to me?

A *cycle* is a path where the last vertex is adjacent to the first. A cycle in which no vertex repeats (such as 1-2-3-1 versus 1-2-3-2-1) is said to be *simple*. The shortest cycle in the graph defines its *girth*, while a simple cycle which passes through each vertex is said to be a *Hamiltonian cycle.*

25.2 Breadth First Search (BFS)

As the name implies, before proceeding to next level of tree or forest, nodes at current level are expanded first. This process is continued till the goal state is reached.

Water-Jug Problem

Let is consider that there are two Jugs, one of which can store 4-Gallons of water and the other 3-Gallons of water. We have to find a solution state s.t. the 4-Gallon Jug contains 2-Gallon, and 3-Gallons Jug contains no water (2, 0). We can throw the water and there is no scale for measurement on the Jug.

We can find the solution to above problem using BFS in terms of tree.

Thus, to obtain the solution state (2, 0) we have to expand all the nodes upto level 6 s.t. it forms a complete tree. See Fig. 25.4.

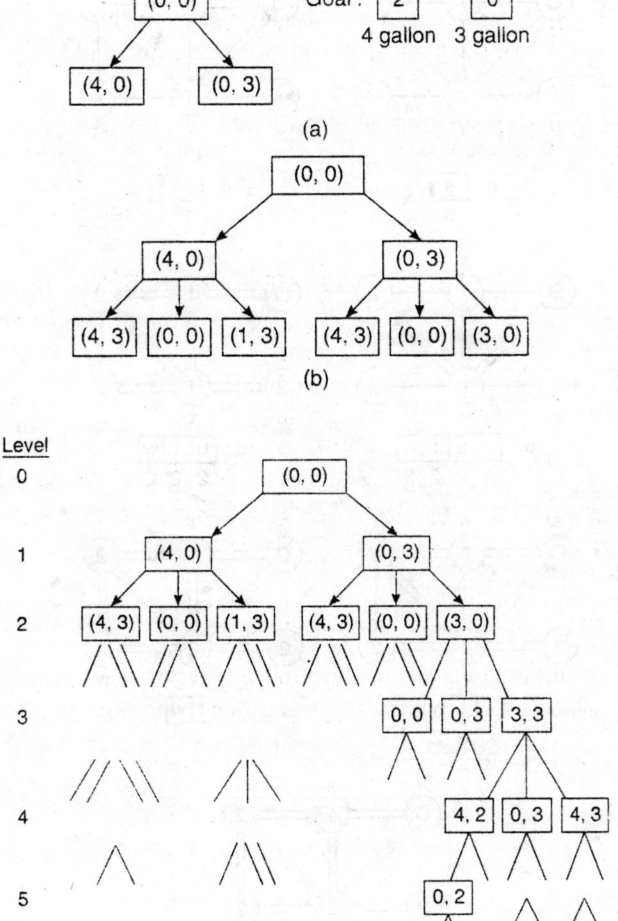

Fig. 25.4. Shows breadth first expansion of water-Jug problem.

Thus Breadth first search expands the discovered or undiscovered node uniformly across the breadth. In order to mark the discovered and undiscovered node, colors are given as white, gray and black. Node which is not visited is white, which is visited but its child nodes are not visited is gray and if all of its child nodes are visited then it is made black.

Let us consider the following undirected forest on wich BFS method is applied using coloring technique just described. Let us assign a 0 value to the start node and infinity to all other nodes. Then measure the length from root to other levels as 1, 2, 3, ... Let also manage a queue which contains first element as node which is to be currently visited. **Node which is once inserted into queue will not be inserted again, as it will violate the level expansion of tree.**

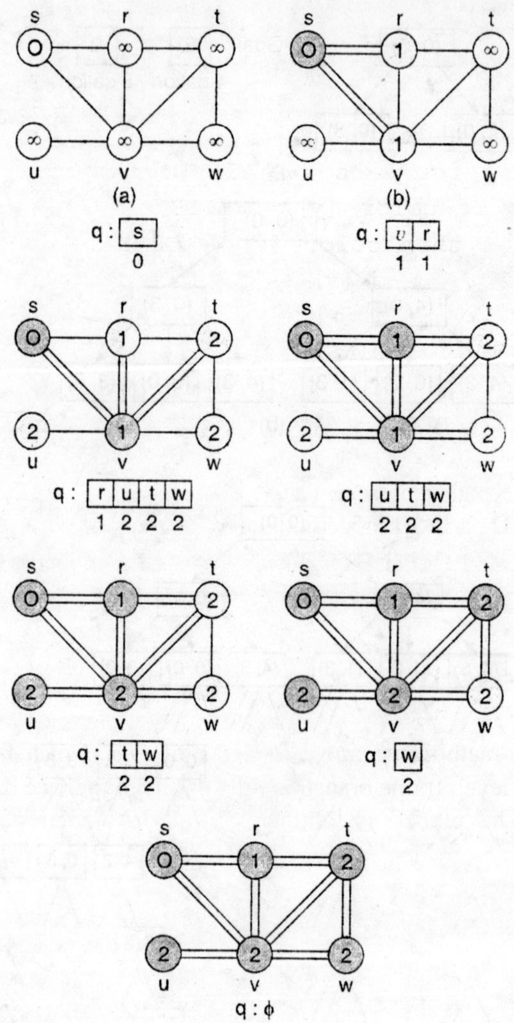

Fig. 25.5. Shows BFS steps light shade is gray, dark shade black.

Here all the vertices are colored white and start vertex *S* is colored gray. then a queue contains the node which is being visited in front, see Fig. 25.5. If all its child are visited then childs are colored gray and parent node is colored black, queue also shows the path length from origin. Thus we can give BFS algorithm as follows.

```
BSF (G, S)
for each vertex u ε V [G] – {S}
        do color [u] ← WHITE
            d[u] ← ∞
            π[u] ← NIL
color [S] ← GRAY
    d [S] ← O
```

```
    π [S] ← NIL
    Q ← {S}
While Q ≠ ϕ
        do u ← front [Q]
              for each v ε Adj [u]
        do if color [v] = WHITE
              then color [v] ← GRAY
                    d [v] ← d [u] + 1
                    π [v] ← u
                    QINSERT (Q, v)
QDELETE (Q)
Color [u] ← BLACK
```

We increment the path length on each visit, and color [*v*] GRAY and this child node is inserted into Queue. Then Black node is deleted from queue

Each **QINSERT** and **QDELETE** takes $\theta(1)$ time thus total time for queue operation is $O(V)$. Time taken to scan the edges in adjacency list is $O(E)$ so total time taken is $O(V+E)$.

25.3 Depth-First Search

In depth first search method we move to depth of one branch before exploring the other childrens at the same level. If one branch is fully explored then we backtrack and explore other branch to its depth. This process is continued till all the branches are explored to their depth in a forest, Fig. 25.6.

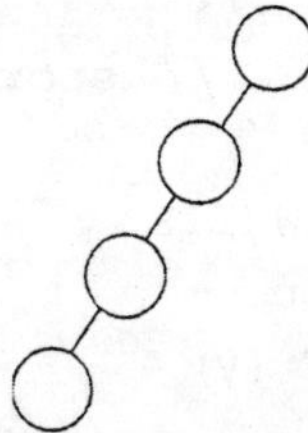

Fig. 25.6. Depth First exploration of a node.

The input of DFS algorithm can be directed or undirected graph. In the algorithm **we maintain start time and finish time of a node,** *i.e.*, when we visit a node for first time we mention the start time when this node is explored to its full depth, *i.e.*, all of its children are visited then we mention finish time. See Fig. 25.7.

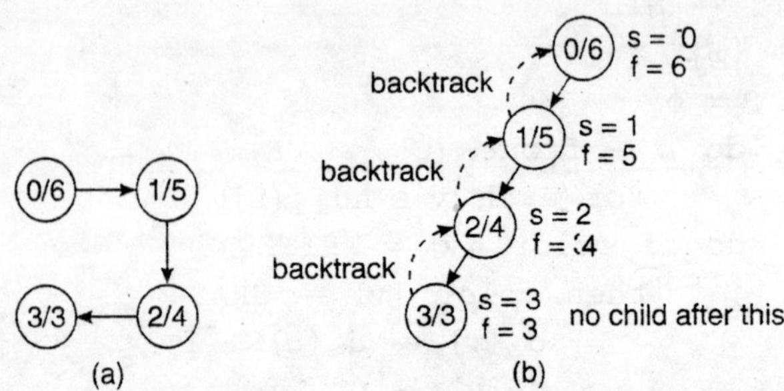

Fig. 25.7. DFS exploration showing start/finish time.

We assume that, it takes unit time to visit a node. If we want we can use the coloring technique along with this to keep track of visited and explored node. Thus we can write DFS algorithm as follows.

```
DFS (G)
1.    Initially color all vertex u ε V[G], to white.
2.    time ← 0
      for each vertex u ε V[G]
          do if color [u] = WHITE
              then DFS-VISIT (u)

DFS-VISIT (u)
   color (u) ← GRAY               // color visited node to GRAY
   time ← time + 1
   d [u] ← time             // store start time in child node
for each v ε Adj (u)                       // visit each adjacent
   do if color [v] = WHITE         // node, set its parent and
      then π [v] ← u.                     // make its color GRAY,
           DFS-VISIT (v)
   color [u] ← BLACK          // make the explored node Black.
      time ← time + 1
           f [u] ← time
```

Running time for coloring WHITE is $\theta(V)$ and visiting adjacent node means adjacent edges requie $\theta(E)$ time and since both are required so the running time is $\theta(V+E)$.

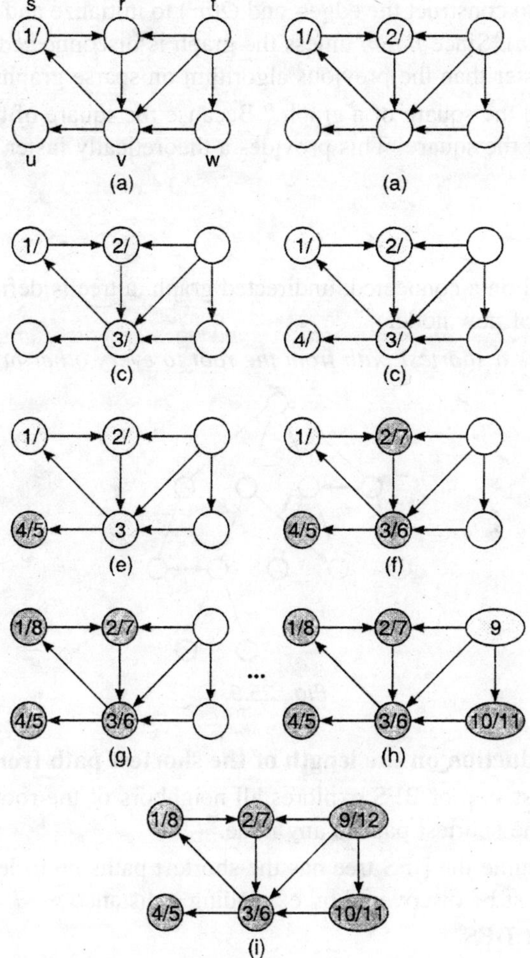

Fig. 25.8. DFS expansion, Shows Start / finish time.

EXAMPLE 25.3. *The square of a directed graph $G = (V, E)$ is the graph $G^2 = (V, E^2)$ such that $(u, w) \in E^2$ iff for some $\upsilon \in V$, both $(u, v) \in E$ and $(v, w) \in E$; i.e. there is a path of exactly two edges.*

Give efficient algorithms for both adjacency lists and matrices.

SOLUTION : Given an adjacency matrix, we can check in constant time whether a given edge exists. To discover whether there is an edge $(u, w) \in G^2$, for each possible intermediate vertex v we can check whether (u, v) and (v, w) exist in $O(1)$.

Since there are at most n intermediate vertices to check, and n^2 pairs of vertices to ask about, this takes $O(n^3)$ time.

With adjacency lists, we have a list of all the edges in the graph. For a given edge (u, v), we can run through all the edges from V in $O(n)$ time, and fill the results into an adjacency matrix of G^2, which is initially empty.

It takes $O(mn)$ to construct the edges, and $O(n^2)$ to initialize and read the adjacency matrix, a total of $O((n + m)n)$. Since $n \leq m$ unless the graph is disconnected, this is usually simplified to $O(mn)$, and is faster than the previous algorithm on sparse graphs.

Why is it called the square of a graph ? Because the square of the adjacency matrix is the adjacency matrix of the square! This provides a theoretically faster algorithm.

25.3.1 BFS Trees

If BFS is performed on a connected, undirected graph, a tree is defined by the edges involved with the discovery of new nodes:

This tree defines a shortest path from the root to every other node in the tree.

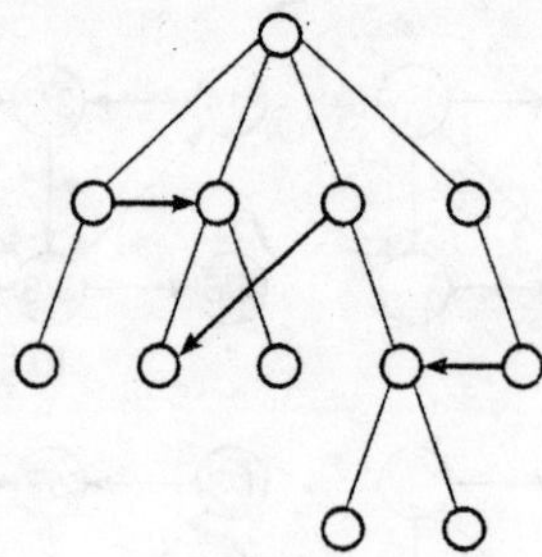

Fig. 25.9.

The proof is by induction on the length of the shortest path from the root:

Length = *1* First step of BFS explores all neighbors of the root. In an unweighted graph one edge must be the shortest path to any node.

Length = *s* Assume the BFS tree has the shortest paths up to length $s - 1$. Any node as a distance of s will first be discovered by expanding a distance $s - 1$ node.

The *key* idea about DFS

A depth-first search of a graph organizes the edges of the graph in a precise way.

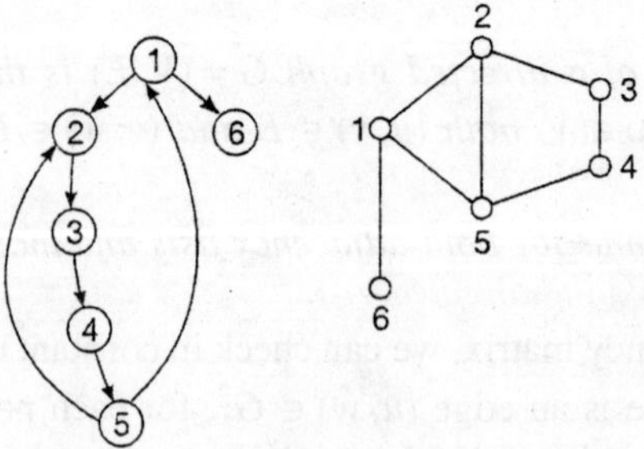

Fig. 25.10.

In a DFS of an undirected graph, we assign a direction to each edge, from the vertex which discover it:

In a DFS of a directed graph, every edge is either a tree edge or a black edge. In a DFS of a directed graph, no cross edge goes to a higher numbered or rightward vertex. Thus, no edge from 4 to 5 is possible:

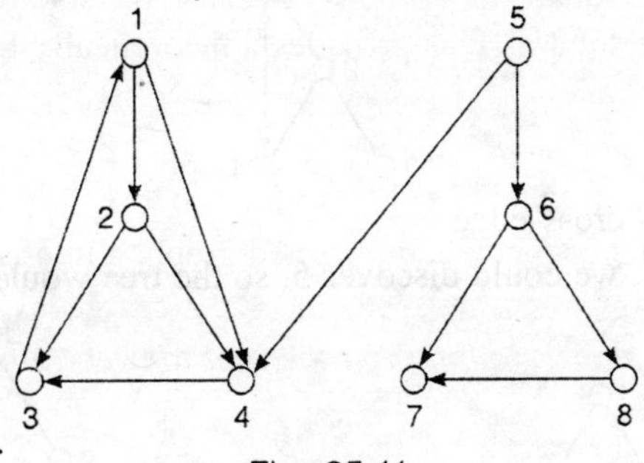

Fig. 25.11.

Edge Classification for DFS

What about the other edges in the graph? Where can they go on a search?

Every edge is either:

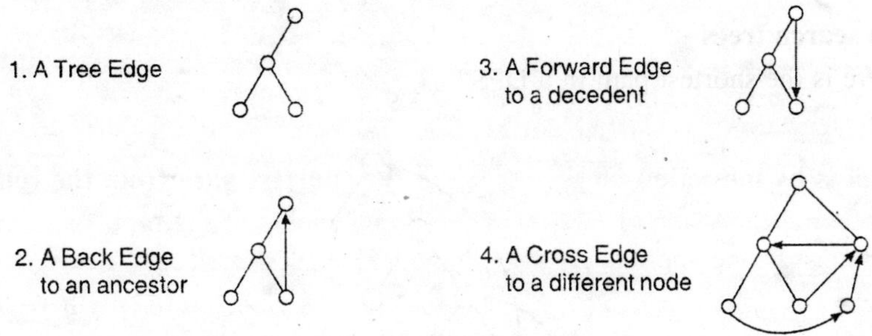

Fig. 25.12.

On any particular DFS or BFS of a directed or undirected graph, each edge gets classified as one of the above.

DFS Trees

The reason DFS is so important is that it defines a very nice ordering to the edges of the graph.

EXAMPLE 25.4. *In a DFS of an undirected graph, every edge is either a tree edge or a back edge. Why?*

SOLUTION : Suppose we have a forward edge. We would have encountered (4, 1) when expanding 4, so this is a back edge.

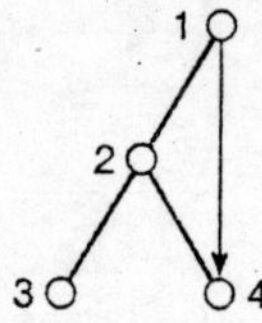

Suppose we have a cross-edge

When expanding 2, we could discover 5, so the tree would look like:

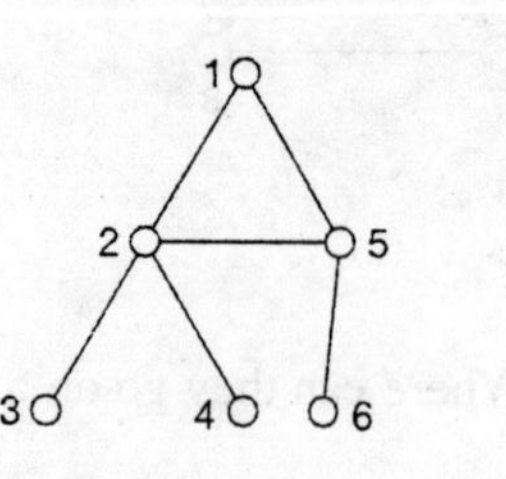

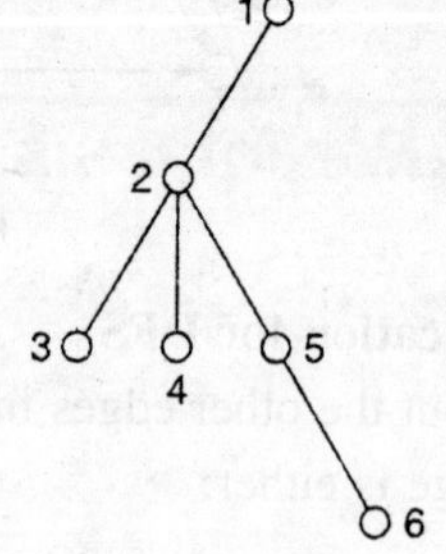

Paths in search trees

Where is the shortest path in a DFS?

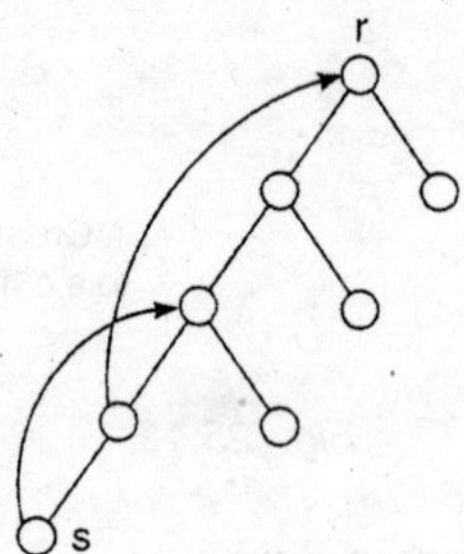

Fig. 25.13.

It could use multiple back and tree edges, where BFS only used tree edges.

DFS gives a better approximation of the longest path than BFS.

The BFS tree can have height 1, independent of the length of the longest path.

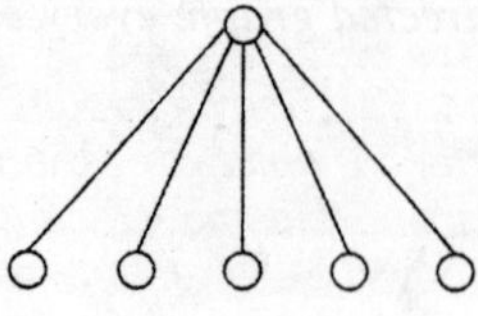

Fig. 25.14.

The DFS must always have height > = log P, where P is the length of the longest path.

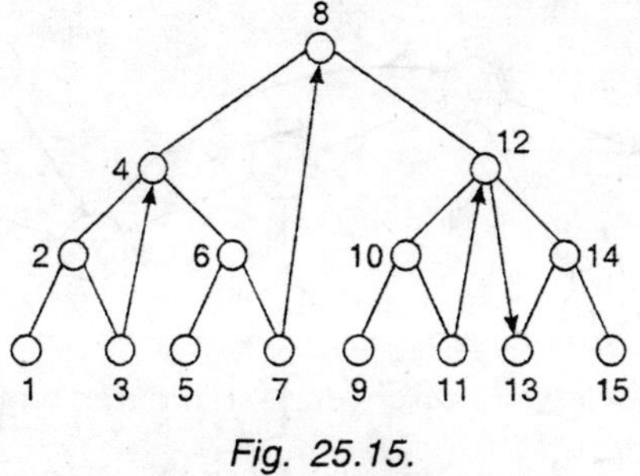

Fig. 25.15.

25.4 DFS and Parenthesis Structure

We can represent DFS method as **parenthesis structure** in which when a vertex is visited we write opening brace '(' and when it is fully explored we write closing brace ')'.

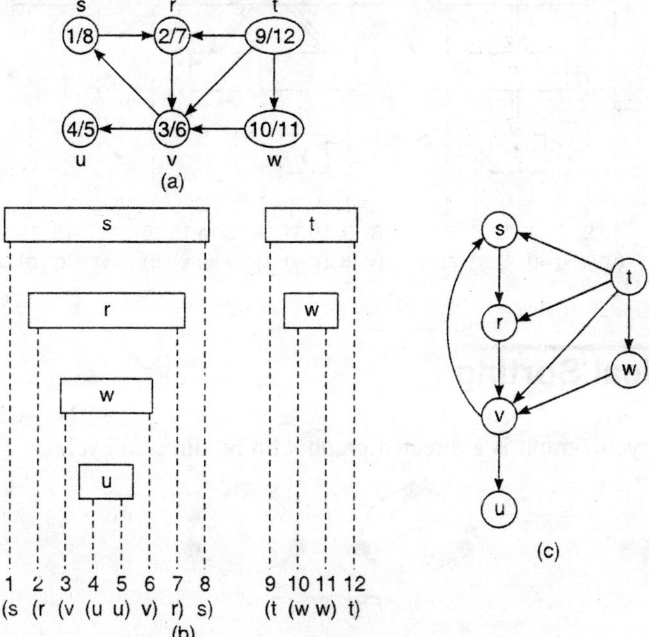

Fig. 25.16. (a) Shows results of DFS
(b) Shows the order in which tree nodes are expanded with their opening and closing brace according to time
(c) Show tree structure of (a).

EXAMPLE 25.4. *Show the parenthesis structure of following graph.*

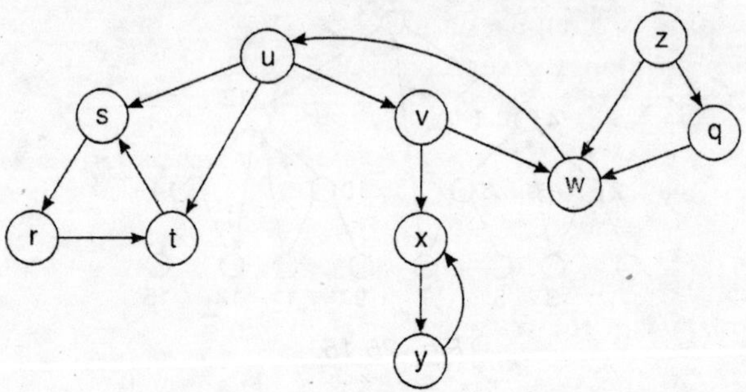

SOLUTION : Let *u* be the start vertex

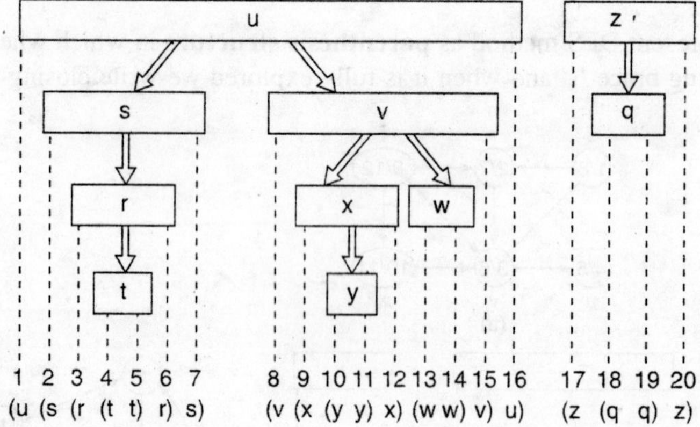

25.5 Topological Sorting

A directed, acyclic graph is a directed graph with no directed cycles.

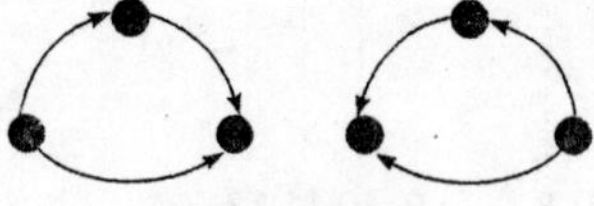

Fig. 25.17.

A topological sort of a graph is an ordering on the vertices so that all edges go from left to right.

Only a DAG can have a topological sort.

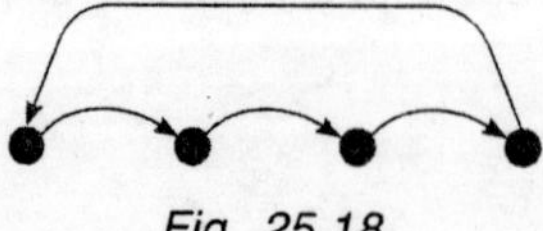

Fig. 25.18.

Any DAG has (at least one) topological sort.

Applications of Topological Sorting

Toplogical sorting is often useful in scheduling jobs in their proper sequence. In general, we can use it to order things given constraints, such as a set of left-right constraints on the positions of objects. Ex. 25.5 and 25.6 illustrate this :

EXAMPLE 25.5. *Dressing schedule from CLR.*

EXAMPLE 25.6. *Identifying errors in DNA fragment assembly.*

Certain fragments are constrained to be to the left or right of other fragments, unless there are errors.

```
A B R A C   A B R A C A D A B R A
            ---------------------
A C A D A   A B R A C
              R A C A D
A D A B R       A C A D A
D A B R A           A D A B R
R A C A D             D A B R A
```

SOLUTION : Build a DAG representing all the left-right constraints. Any topological sort of this DAG is a consistant ordering. If there are cycles, there must be errors.

A DFS can test if a graph is a DAG (it is if there are no back edges-forward edges are allowed for DFS on directed graph).

THEOREM 15.1. Arranging vertices in decreasing order of DFS finishing time gives a topological sort of a DAG.

PROOF : Consider any directed edge u, v when we encounter it during the exploration of vertex.

If v is white - we then start a DFS of v before we continue with u.

If v is grey - then u, v is a back edge, which cannot happen in a DAG.

If v is black - we have already finished with v, so $f[v] < f[u]$.

Thus we can do topological sorting in $O(n + m)$ time.

Topological sorting is the way of linearly arranging any graph from left to right such that each vertices appear in the order given. For this the graph must be DAG, *i.e.*, directed acyclic graph. Note that node with highest finish time appear first. See Fig. 25.19.

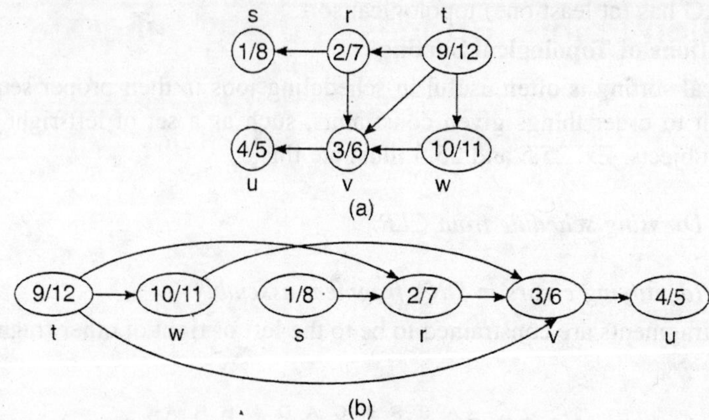

Fig. 25.19. Topological sort for (a) is (b). nodes show start and finish time

25.6 Strongly Connected Components

Strongly connected components are components in which if there is a path from *u* to *v*, then there must be a path back to *u*. Those subgraph of a graph which can not be detached form a strongly connected components and the vertices which are strongly attached can be merged together. See Fig. 25.20.

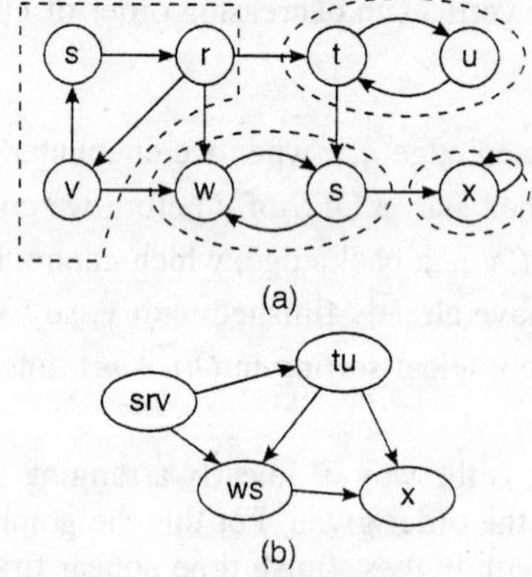

Fig. 23.20 (a) Dotted line shows strongly connected components (b) New graph produced.

25.7 Transpose of a Graph

It is defined as the directed graph with its edge reversed, *i.e.*,

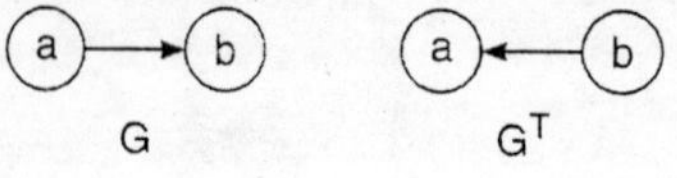

Fig. 25.21.

25.8 Articulation Points, Bridges and Bi-Connected Components

Let $G = (V, E)$ be a connected undirected graph. An **articulation point** of G is a **vertex** whose removal disconnects G.A. **biconnected component** of G is a maximal set of **edges** such that any two edges in the set lie on a common cycle **bridge** of G is an edge whose removal disconnects G.

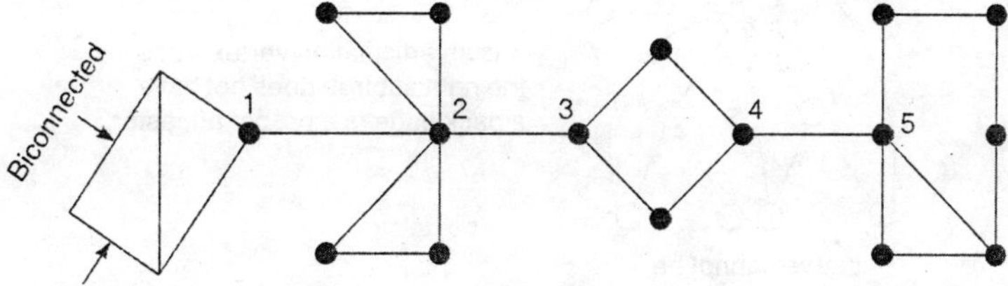

Fig. 25.22.

Vertices numbered as 1, 2, 3, 4, 5 are articulation points, edge (1, 2), (2, 3), (4, 5) forms a bridge.

A graph is said to be biconnected if does not contain any articulation points thus above graph is not biconnected even if it contains some components.

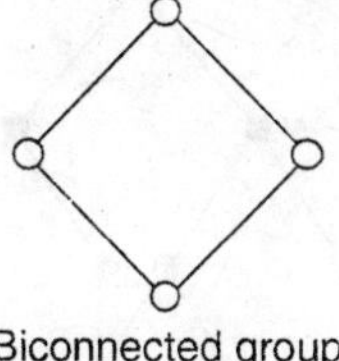

Fig. 25.23. Biconnected graph.

Articulation Vertices

Suppose you are a terrorist, seeking to disrupt the telephone network. Which station do you blow up?

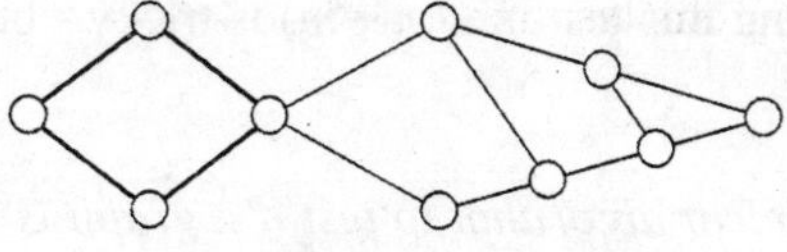

Fig. 25.24.

An *articulation vertex* is a vertex of a connected graph whose deletion disconnects the graph.

Clearly connectivity is an important concern in the design of any network. Articulation vertices can be found in $O(n(m + n))$ - just delete each vertex to do a DFS on the remaining graph to see if it is connected.

A Faster $O(n + m)$ DFS Algorithm

THEOREM 25.2. In a DFS tree, a vertex v (other than the root) is an articulation vertex if v is not a leaf and some subtree of v has no back edge incident until a proper ancestor of v.

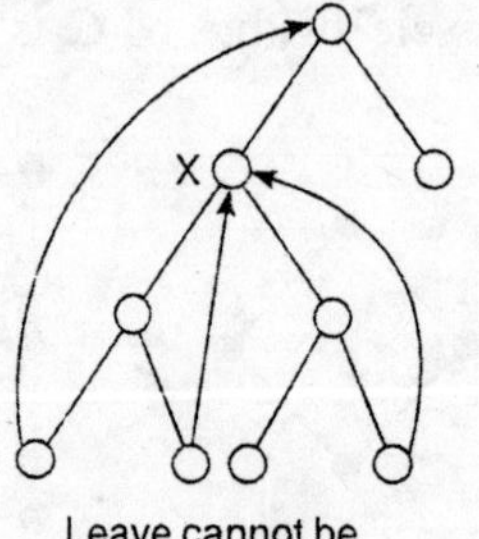

The root is a special case since it has no ancestors.

X is an articulation vertex since the right subtree does not have a back edge to a proper ancestor.

Fig. 25.25.

PROOF : (1) v is an articulation vertex $\rightarrow$ v cannot be a leaf.

Why? Deleting v must separate a pair of vertices x and y. Because of the other tree edges, this cannot happen unless y is a descendent of v.

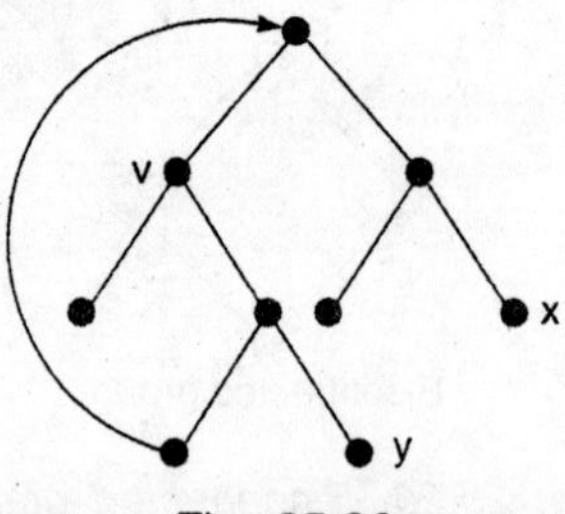

Fig. 25.26.

v separating x, y implies there is no back edge in the subtree of y to a proper ancestor of v.

(2) Conditions $\rightarrow v$ is a non-root articulation vertex. v separates any ancestor of v from any decendant in the appropriate subtree.

Actually implementing this test in $O(n + m)$ is tricky - but believable once you accept this theorem.

EXAMPLE 25.6. *Give an efficient algorithm to test if a graph is biparitite.*

SOLUTION : Bipartite means the vertices can be colored red or black such that no edge links vertices of the same color.

Suppose we color a vertex red - what color must its neighbours be? *black!*

We can augment either BFS or DFS when we first discover a new vertex, color it opposited its parents, and for each other edge, check it doesn't link two vertices of the same color. The first vertex in any connected component can be red or black!

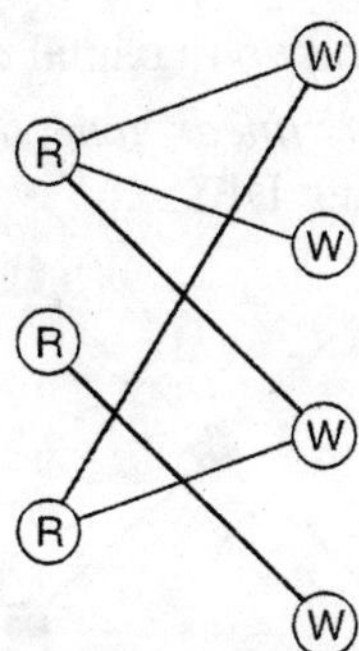

Bipartite graphs arise in many situations, and special algorithms are often available for them. What is the interpretation of a bipartite "had-sex-with" graph? How would you break people into two groups such that no groups contains a pair of people who hate each other?

EXAMPLE 25.7. *Give an $O(n)$ algorithm to test whether an undirected graph contains a cycle.*

SOLUTION : If you do a DFS, you have a cycle iff you have a back edge. This gives an $O(n + m)$ algorithm. But where does the m go? If the graph contains more than $n - 1$ edges, it must contain a cycle! Thus we never need look at more than n edges if we are given an adjacency list representation!

EXAMPLE 25.8. *Show that you can topologically sort in $O(n + m)$ by repeatedly deleting vertices of degree 0.*

SOLUTION : The correctness of this algorithm follows since in a DAG there must always be a vertex of indegree 0, and such a vertex can be first in topological sort. Suppose each vertex is initialized with its indegree (do DFS on G to get this). Deleting a vertex takes O (degree v). Reduce the indegree of each efficient vertex - and keep a list of degree-0 vertices to delete next.

$$\text{Time: } \sum_{i=1}^{n} O(deg\ (\upsilon_i)) = O(n + m)$$

Strongly Connected Components

A directed graph is strongly connected iff there is a directed path between any two vertices.

The strongly connected components of a graph is a partition of the vertices into subsets (maximal) such that each subset is strongly connected.

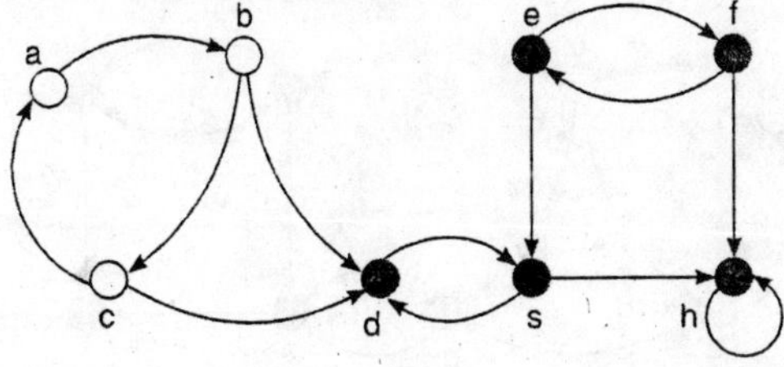

Fig. 25.27.

Observe that no vertex can be in two maximal components, so it is a partition.

There is an amazingly elegant, *linear time algorithm to find the strongly connected components of a directed graph*, using DFS.

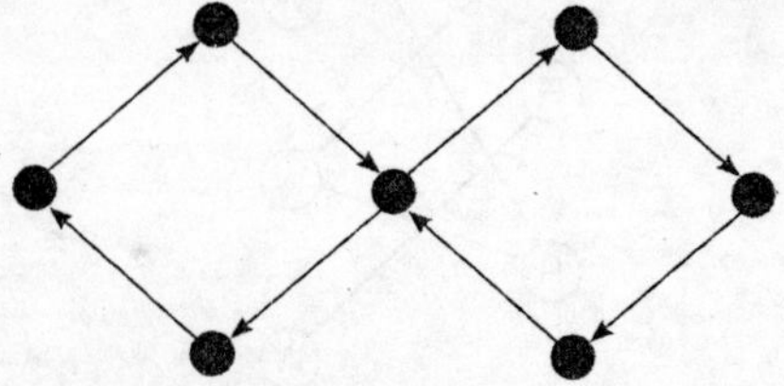

Fig. 25.28.

```
Call DFS (σ) to compute finishing times for each vertex.
Compute the transpose graph G^T (reverse all edges in G)
Call DFS (G^T), but order the vertices in decreasing
                                    order of finish time.
The vertices of each DFS tree in the forest of DFS
                    (G^T) is a strongly connected component.
```

This algorithm takes $O(n+m)$, but why does it compute strongly connected components?

LEMMA 25.1. If two vertices are in the same strong component, no path between them ever leaves the component.

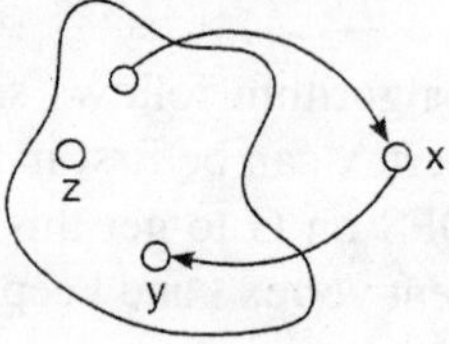

Fig. 25.29.

LEMMA 25.2. In any DFS forest, all vertices in the same strongly connected component are in the same tree.

PROOF : Consider the first vertex v in the component to be discovered. Everything in the component is reachable from it, so we will traverse it before finishing with v.

Example of Strong Components Algorithm

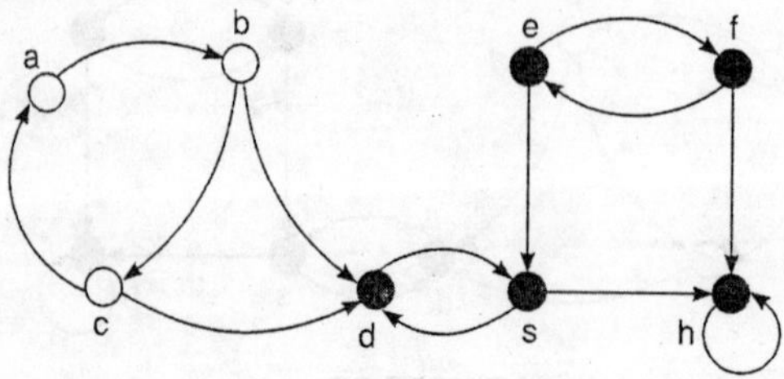

Fig. 25.30.

9, 10, 11, 12 can reach 9, oldest remaining finished is 5.

5, 6, 8 can reach 5, oldest remaining is 7.

7 can reach 7, oldest remaining is 1.

1, 2, 3 can reach 1, oldest remaining is 4.

4 can reach 4.

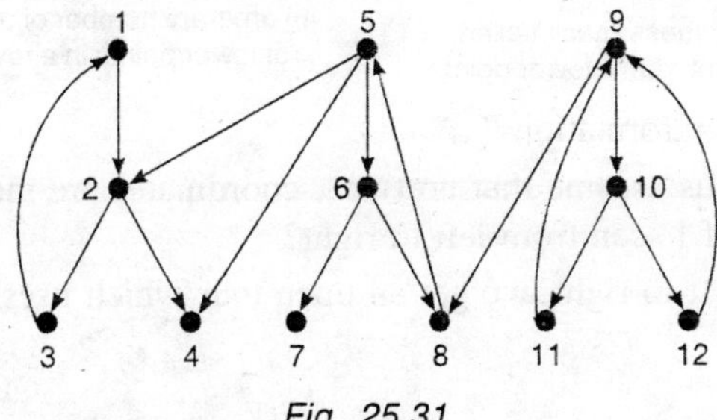

Fig. 25.31.

The Euclidean traveling-salesman problem is the problem of determining the shortest closed tour that connects a given set of n points in the plane. Bentley suggested simplifying the probem by restricting attention to bitonic tours, that is tours which start at the leftmost point, go strictly left to right to the rightmost point, and then go strictly right back to the starting point.

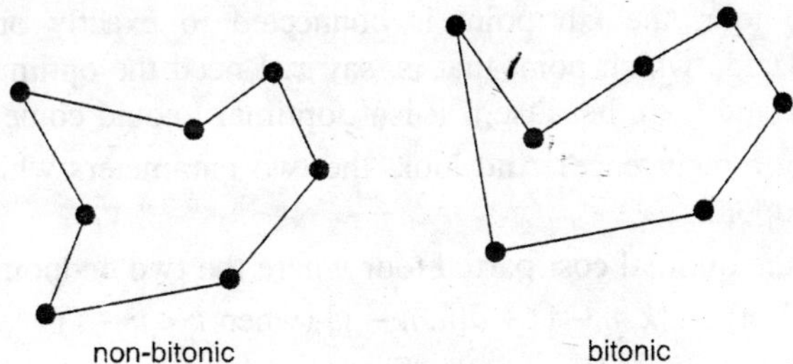

Fig. 25.32.

EXAMPLE 25.9. *Describe an $O(n^2)$ algorithm for finding the optimal bitonic tour. You may assume that no two points have the same x-coordinate. (Hint: scan left to right, maintaining optimal possibilities for the two parts of the tour.)*

SOLUTION : Make sure you understand what a bitonic tour is, or else it is hopeless.

First of all, play with the problem. Why isn't it trivial ?

"Hey. I guess this tour can zig-zag a lot."

"Hey. I guess that i can have an arbitrary number of upper or lower points in a row."

"Hey. I guess i can't tell an upper point from a lower point."

Am I using all the information ?

Why will they let us assume that no two x-coordinates are the same? What does the hint mean? What happens if I scan from left to right?

If we scan from left to right, we get an open tour which uses all points to the left of our scan line.

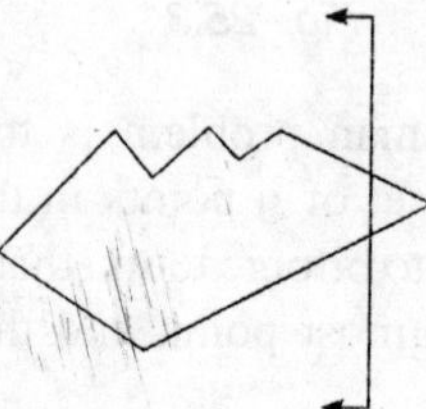

In the optimal tour, the kth point is connected to exactly one point to the left of $k \cdot (k \neq n)$ Once I decide which point that is, say x. I need the optimal partial tour where the two endpoints are x and $k - l$, because if it isn't optimal I could come up with a better one.

Hey, I have got a recurrence! And look, the two parameters which describe the optimal tour are the two endpoints.

Let $C[k, n]$ be the optimal cost partial tour where the two endpoints are $k < n$.

$$c[k, n] \leq c[k, n-1] + d[n, n-1] \text{ (when } k < n-1)$$
$$c[n-1, n] \leq c[k, n-1] + d[k, n]$$
$$c[0, 1] = d[0, 1]$$

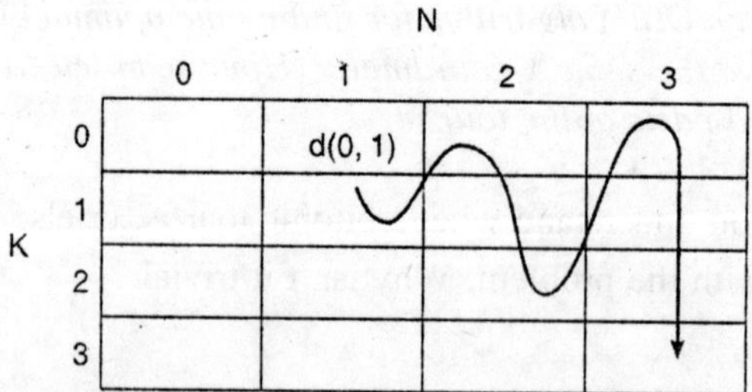

$c[n-1, n]$ takes $O(n)$ to update, $c[k, n]$ $k < n - 1$ takes $O(1)$ to update. Total time is $O(n^2)$. But this doesn't quite give the tour, but just an open tour. We simply must figure where the last edge to n must go.

$$Tour\ cost = \min_{k=1}^{n} C[k, n] + d_{kn}$$

EXAMPLE 25.10. *Draw a simple undirected graph G that has 12 vertices, 18 edges, and 3 connected components. Why would it be impossible to draw G with 3 connected components if G had 66 edges?*

SOLUTION :

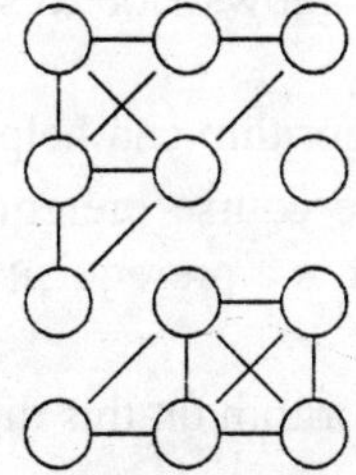

If G has 12 vertices and 3 connected components, then the maximum number of edges it can have is 45. This would be a fully connected component with 10 vertices (thus having 45 edges) and two connected components each with a single vertex.

EXAMPLE 25.11. *Let G be a simple connected graph with n vertices and m edges. Explain why $O(\log m)$ is $O(\log n)$.*

SOLUTION : We know that $m \leq n \cdot (n-1)/2$. It follows, therefore, that $O(\log (n^2)) = O(2 \log n) = (\log n)$.

EXAMPLE 25.12. *Draw a simple connected directed graph with 8 vertices and 16 edges such that the in-degree and out-degree of each vertex is 2. Show that there is a single (nonsimple) cycle that includes all the edges of your graph, that is, you can trace all the edges in their respective directions without ever lifting your pencil. (Such a cycle is called an Euler tour.)*

SOLUTION :

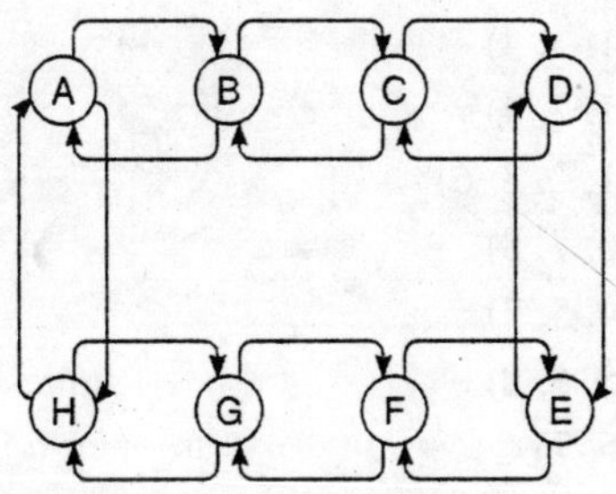

The Euler tour is $A \to B \to C \to D \to E \to F \to G \to H \to A \to H \to G \to F \to E \to D \to C \to B \to A$

EXAMPLE 25.13. *Bob loves foreign languages and wants to plan his course schedule to take the following nine language courses: LA15, LA16, LA22, LA31, LA32, LA126, LA127, LA141 and LA169. The course prerequisites are:*

LA15 : (none)	LA126 : LA22, LA32
LA16 : LA15	LA127 : LA16
LA22 : (none)	LA141 : LA22, LA16
LA31 : LA15	LA169 : LA32
LA32 : LA16, LA31	

Find a sequence of courses that allows Bob to satisfy all the prerequisites.

SOLUTION : The topological sorting algorithm can help us solve this problem.

Build a digraph to represent the course prerequisite requirements. The nine courses are vertices in the digraph. If a course *A* is a prerequisite for another course *B*, the diagraph has a directed edge from *A* to *B*.

Apply the toplogical sorting algorithm on this digraph. The result is one possible sequence of courses for Bob.

For the given set of prerequisites, the solution is not unique. For example, one possible solution is LA15, LA16, LA22, LA31, LA32, LA126, LA127, LA141, LA169. Another solution is LA15, LA16, LA127, LA31, LA32, LA169, LA22, LA126, LA141.

EXAMPLE 25.14. *Suppose we present a graph G having n vertices and m edges with the edge list structure. Why, in this case, does the insertVertex method run in O(1) time while the removeVertex method runs in O(m) time?*

SOLUTION : Inserting a vertex runs in $O(1)$ time since it is simply inserting an element into a doubly linked list. To remove a vertex, on the other hand, we must inspect all edges. Clearly this will take $O(m)$ time.

EXAMPLE 25.15. *Let G be a graph whose vertices are the integers 1 through 8, and let the adjacent vertices of each vertex be given by the table below:*

vertex	*adjacent vertices*
1	(2, 3, 4)
2	(1, 3, 4)
3	(1, 2, 4)
4	(1, 2, 3, 6)
5	(6, 7, 8)
6	(4, 5, 7)
7	(5, 6, 8)
8	(5, 7)

Assume that, in a traversal of G, the adjacent vertices of a given vertex are returned in the same order as they are listed in the above table.

(a) Draw G.

(b) Order the vertices as they are visited in a DFS traversal starting at vertex 1.

(c) Order the vertices as they are visited in a BFS traversal starting at vertex 1.

SOLUTION : A drawing of graph G is given below:

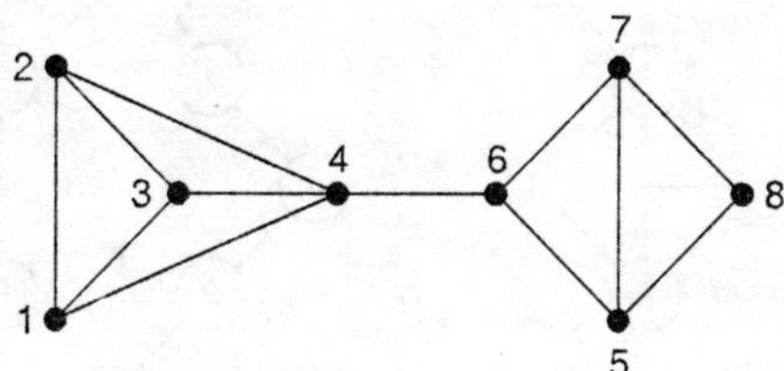

1. A DFS traversal starting at vertex 1 visits the vertices in the following order : 1, 2, 3, 4, 5, 6, 7, 8.
2. A BFS traversal starting at vertex 1 visits the vertices in the following order : 1, 2, 3, 4, 5, 6, 7, 8.

EXAMPLE 25.16. *Would you use the adjacency list structure or the adjacency matrix structure in each of the following cases? Justify your choices.*

(a) The graph has 10,000 vertices and 20,000 edges, and it is important to use as little space as possible.

(b) The graph has 10,000 vertices and 20,000,000 edges, and it is important to use as little space as possible.

(c) You need to answer the query areAdjacent as fast as possible, no matter how much space you use.

SOLUTION : 1. The adjacency list structure is preferable. Indeed, the adjacency matrix structure wastes a lot of space. It allocates entries for 100,000,000 edges while the graph has only 20,000 edges.

2. In general, both structures work well in this case. Regarding the space requirements, there is no clear winner. Note that the exact space usage of the two structures depends on the implementation details. The adjacency matrix structure is much better for operation *areAdjacent*, while the adjacency list structure is much better for operations *insertVertex* and *removeVertex*.

3. The adjacency matrix structure is preferable. Indeed, it supports operation *areAdjacent* in $O(1)$ time, irrespectively of the number of vertices or edges.

EXAMPLE 25.17. *In the connected graph given below in Fig. (a) vertex 2 is an articulation point as the deletion of vertex 2 and edges (1, 2), (2, 3), (2, 5), (2, 7), and (2, 8) leaves behind two disconnected nonempty components Fig. (b). Graph G of Figure (a) has only two other articulation points: vertex 5 and vertex 3. Note that if any of the remaining vertices is deleted from G, then exactly one component remains.*

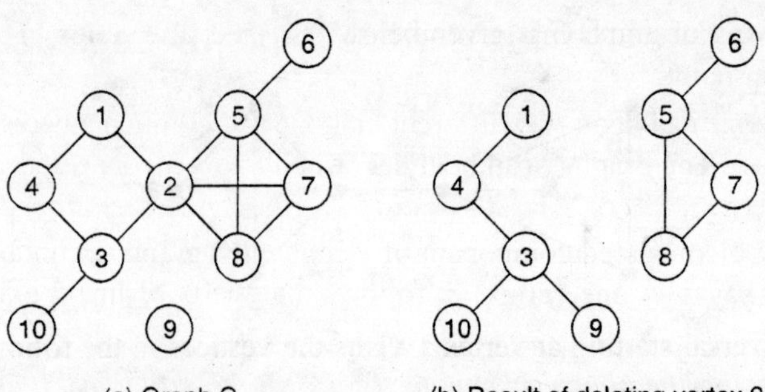

(a) Graph G (b) Result of deleting vertex 2

SOLUTION : A graph G is biconnected if and only if it contains no articulation points. The graph of Figure (a) is not biconnected. The graph of Figure (c) is biconnected. The presence of articulation points in a connected graph can be an undesirable feature in many cases. For example, if G represents a communication network with the vertices representing communication stations and the edges communication lines, then the failure of an communication station i that is an articulation point would result in the loss of communication to points other than i too. On the other hand, if G has no articulation point, then if any station i fails, we can still communicate between every two stations not including station i.

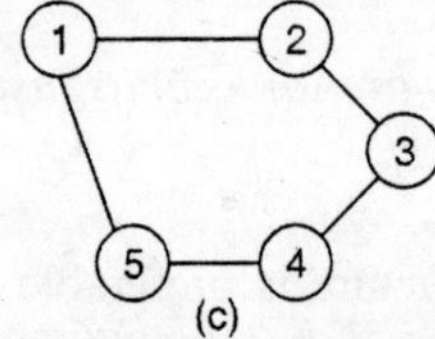

(c)

In this section we develop an efficient algorithm to test whether a connected graph is biconnected. For the case of graphs that are not biconnected, this algorithm will identify all the articulation points. Once it has been determined that a connected graph G is not biconnected, it may be desirable to determine a set of edges whose inclusion makes the graph biconnected. Determining such a set of edges is facilitated, if we know the maximal subgraphs of G that are biconnected. $G' = (V' . E')$ is a maximal biconnected subgraph of G if and only if G has no biconnected subgraph $G'' = (V'' . E'')$ such that $V' \subseteq V''$ and $E' \subset E''$. A maximal biconnected subgraph is a *biconnected component*.

The graph of Figure (c) above has only one biconnected component (i.e., the entire graph). The biconnected components of the graph of Figure (a) are shown in Figure (d).

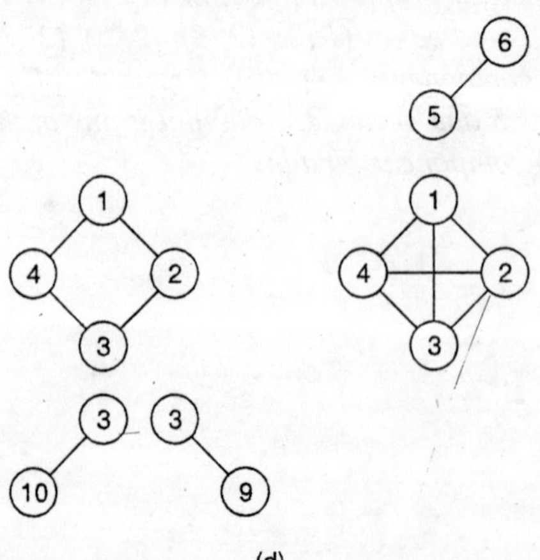

(d)

LEMMA 25.3. Two biconnected components can have at most one vertex in common and this vertex is an articulation point.

Hence, no edge can be in two different biconnected components (as this would require two common vertices). The graph G can be transformed into a biconnected graph by using the edge addition scheme.

Since every biconnected component of a connected graph G contains at least two vertices (unless G itself has only one vertex), it follows that the v_i of line 5 exists.

EXAMPLE 25.18. *Using the above scheme to transform the graph of Figure (a), Ex. 25.17 into a biconnected graph requires us to add edges (4, 10) and (10, 9) (corresponding to the articulation point 3), edge (1, 5) (corresponding to the articulation point 2), and edge (6, 7) (corresponding to point 5).*

Note that once the edges (v_i, v_{i+1}) of line 6 below are added, vertex a is no longer an articulation point. Hence following the addition of the edges corresponding to all articulation points, G has no articulation points and so is biconnected. If G has p articulation points and b biconnected components, then the scheme of Algorithm introduces exactly $b - p$ new edges into G. One can show that this scheme may use more than the minimum number of edges needed to make G biconnected.

```
1 for each articulation point a do
2 {
3 Let B1, B2, ..., Bk be the biconnected
4 components containing vertex a;
5 Let vi, vi ≠ a, be a vertex in Bi, 1 ≤ i ≤ k;
6 Add to G the edges (vi, vi + 1), 1 ≤ i < k;
7 }
```

Now, let us attack the problem of identifying the articulation points and biconnected components of a connected graph G with $n \geq 2$ vertices. The problem is efficiently solved by considering a depth first spanning tree of G.

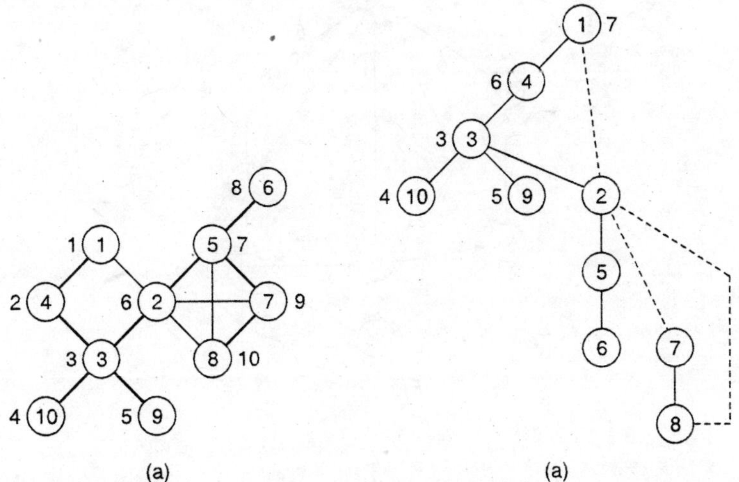

Fig. 25.33. A DFS spanning tree of Ex. 25.17, Fig. (a).

Figure 25.33 (a) and (b) shows a depth first spanning tree of the graph of Figure (a) in Ex. 25.17. In each figure there is a number outside each vertex. These numbers correspond to the order in which a depth first search visits these vertices and are referred to as the *depth first numbers (dfns)* of the vertex. Thus, *dfn* [1] = 1, *dfn* [4] = 2, *dfn* [6] = 8, and so on. In Figure 25.33 (b) solid edges form the depth first spanning tree. These edges are called *tree edges*. Broken edge (i.e., all the remaining edges) are called back edges.

Depth first spanning trees have a property that is very useful in identifying articulation points and biconnected components.

LEMMA 25.4. (*f* (*u*, υ) is any edge in *G*, then relative to the depth first spanning tree *t*, either *u* is an ancestor of υ and υ is not an ancestor of *u*).

PROOF : To see this, assume that (*u*, υ) ∈ *E*(*G*) and (*u*, υ) is a cross edge. Then (*n*, υ) cannot be a tree edge as otherwise *u* is the parent of υ or vice-versa. So (*u*, υ) must be a back edge. Without loss of generality, we can assume *dfn* [*u*] < *dfn* [υ]. Since vertex *u* is visited first, its exploration cannot be complete until vertex υ is visited. From the definition of depth first search, it follows that *u* is an ancestor of all the vertices visited until *u* is completely explored. Hence *u* is an ancestor of υ in *t* and (*u*, υ) cannot be a cross edge.

EXERCISE

1. Show that algorithms to find a cycle using depth-first search or BFS must be $O(n)$
2. Write an algorithm to print the nodes of DAG in reverse topological order.
3. Write an algorithm to determine if a directed graph is DAG.
4. Find the depth-first spanning forest for the following directed graph then find the strongly connected componets.

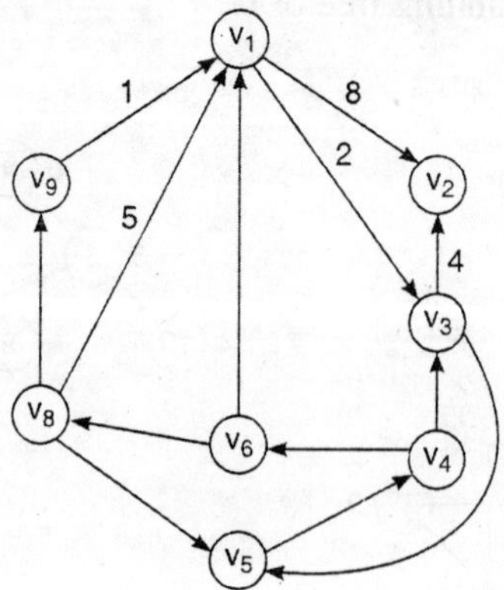

Fig. 25.34.

5. Find the biconnected components of the following graph.

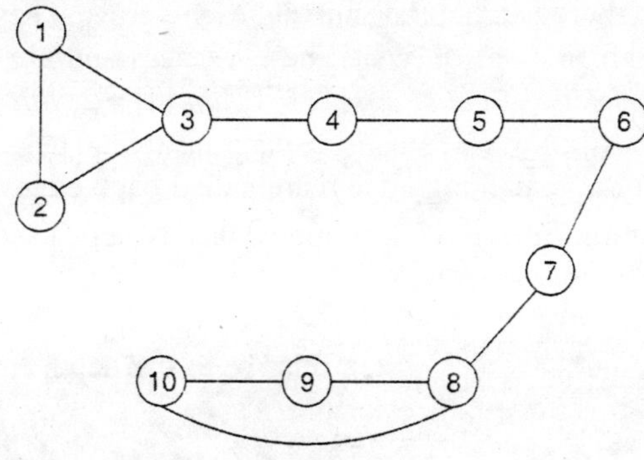

Fig. 25.35.

6. Use depth-first search to help design the efficient algorithms to do the following.
   (a) Divide an undirected graph into connected componets
   (b) Find a path in an undirected connected graph which goes through each edge exactly once in each direction.
   (c) Test whether a directed graph is acyclic.
   (d) Determine whether the edges of a conected, undirected graph can be directed to produce a strongly connected, directed graph.
7. Find the transitive closure of graph G in Fig. 25.35.
8. Show that if G is a connected undircted graph then no edge of G can be in two different biconnected components.
9. Write an $O(E)$ algorithm to find bridges in a graph.
10. Explain how a vertex u of a directed graph can end *up* in a depth-first tree containing only u, even through u has both incoming and outgoing edges.

❑❑❑

26

BACK TRACKING

We have seen how clever algorithms can reduce sorting from $O(n^2)$ to $O(n \log n)$. However, the stakes are even higher for combinatorially explosive problems:

The Traveling Salesman Problem

Given a weighted graph, find the shortest cycle which visits each vertex once.

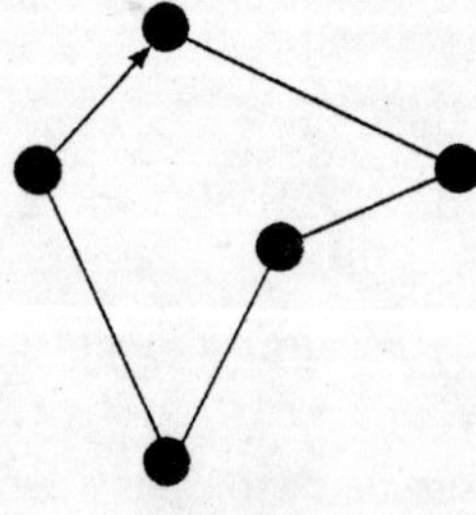

Fig. 26.1

Applications include minimizing plotter movement, printed-circuit board wiring, transportation problems, etc.

There is no known polynomial time algorithm (ie. $O(n^2)$ for some fixed k) for this problem, so search-based algorithms are the only way to go if you need an optional solution.

But I want to use a Supercomputer

Moving to a faster computer can only buy you a relatively small improvement:

Hardware clock rates on the fastest computers only improved by a factor of 6 from 1976 to 1989, from 12ns to 2ns.

Moving to a machine with 100 processors can only give you a factor of 100 speedup, even if your job can be perfectly parallelized (but of course it can't).

The fast Fourier algorithm (FFT) reduced computation from $O(n^2)$ to $O(n \log n)$. This is a speedup of 340 times on $n = 4096$ and revolutionized the field of image processing.

The fast multipole method for n-particle interaction reduced the computation from $O(n^2)$ to $O(n)$. This is a speedup of 4000 times on $n = 4096$.

Can Eight Pieces Cover a Chess Board?

Consider the 8 main pieces in a chess (king, queen, two rooks, two bishops, two knights). Can they be positioned on a chessboard so every square is threatened?

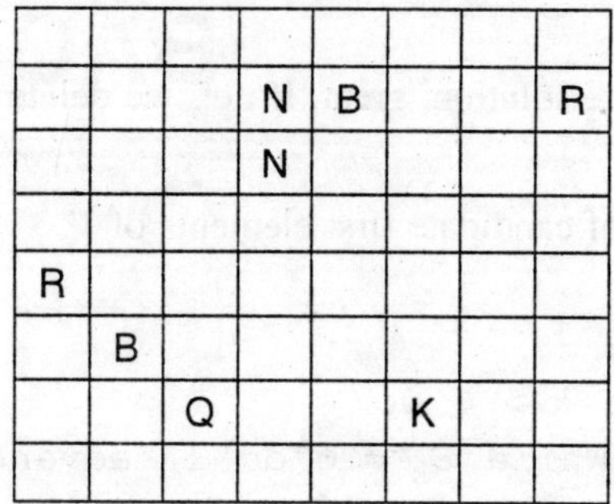

Fig. 26.2. 63 squares of chess board covered with 8 main pieces.

Only 63 square are threatened in this configuration. Since 1849, no one had been able to find an arrangement with bishops on different colors to cover all squares.

Of course, this is not an important problem, but we will use it as an example of how to attack a combinatorial search problem.

How many positions to test?

Picking a square of each piece gives us the bound:

$$64!/(64-8)! = 176,462,987,637,780 \approx 10^{15}$$

Anything much larger than 10^8 is unreasonable to search on a modest computer in a modest amount of time.

However, we can exploit symmetry to save work: With reflections along horizontal, vertical and diagonal axis, the queen can go in only 10 non-equivalent positions.

Even better, we can restrict the white bishop to 16 spots and the queen to 16, while being certain that we get all distinct configurations.

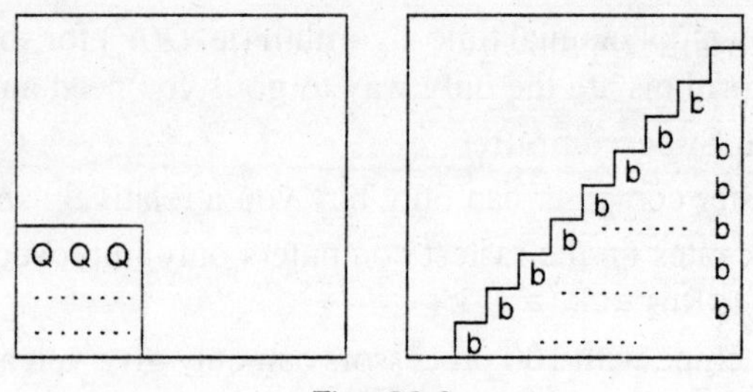

Fig. 26.3

Backtracking

Backtracking is a systematic way to go through all the possible configurations of a search space.

In the general case. we assume our solution is a vector $\upsilon = (a_1, a_2, ..., a_n)$ where each element a_i is selected from a finite ordered set S_i.

We build from a partial solution of length $k \upsilon = (a_1, a_2, ... a_n)$ and try to extend it by adding another element. After extending it, we will test whether what we have so far is still possible as a partial solution.

If it is still a candidate solution, great. If not, we delete a_1 and try the next element from S_k.

Compute S_1, the set of candidate first elements of V.

```
k = 1
While k > 0 do
        While Sk ≠ ϕ do (''advance'')
                ak = an element in Sk
                Sk ← Sk - ak
                if (a1, a2, …, ak) is solution, print!
                k = k + 1
        compute Sk, the candidate kth elements given V.
                k = k - 1 (''backtrack'')
```

Recursive Backtracking

Recursion can be used for elegant and easy implementation of backtracking.

```
Backtrack (a, k)
if a is a solution, print (a)

else
        k ← k + 1
```

```
compute S_k
while S_k ≠ 0 do
        a_k = an element in S_k
        S_k = S_k - a_k
Backtrack(a, k)
```

Backtracking can easily be used to iterate through all subsets or permutations of a set. Backtracking ensures correctness by enumerating all possibilites. For backtracking to be efficient, we must prune the search space.

Contructing all Subsets

How many subsets are there of an n-element set?

To construct all 2^n subsets, set up an array/vector of n cells, where the value of a_i is either true or false, signifying whether the ith items is or is not in the subset.

To use the notation of the general backtrack algorithm, $S_k = (true, false)$, and v is a solution whenever $k \geq n$.

What order will this generate the subsets of {1, 2, 3} ?

(1) → (1, 2) → (1, 2, 3) →
(1, 2, –) → (1, –) → (1, –, 3) →
(1, –, –) → (1, –) → (1) →
(–) → (–, 2) → (–, 2, 3) →
(–, 2, –) → (–, –) → (–, –, 3) →
(–, –, –) → (–, –) → (–) → ()

Constructing all Permutations

How many permutations are there of an n-element set?

To construct all $n!$ permutations, set up an array/vector of n cells, where the values of a_i is an integer from *1* to n which has not appeared thus far in the vector, corresponding to the ith element of the permutation.

To use the notation of the general backtrack algorithm, $S_k = (1, \ldots n) - \upsilon$, and v is a solution whenever $k \geq n$

(1) → (1, 2) → (1, 2, 3) → (1, 2) → (1) → (1, 3) →
(1, 3, 2) → (1, 3) → (1) → () → (2) → (2, 1) →
(2, 1, 3) → (2, 1) → (2) → (2, 3) → (2, 3, 1) → (2, 3) → ()
(2) → () → (3) → (3, 1) (3, 1, 2) → (3, 1) → (3) → (3, 2)
(3, 2, 1) → (3, 2) → (3) → ()

26.1 The *n*-Queens Problem

The first use of pruning to deal with the combinational explosion was by the king who rewarded the fellow who discovered class!

In the eight Queens, we prune whenever one queen threatens another.

Covering the Chess Board

In covering the chess board, we prune whenever we find there is a square which we *cannot* cover given the initial configuration!

Specifically, each piece can threaten a certain maximum number of squares (queen 27, king 8, rook 14, etc.) Whenever the number of unthreated squares exceeds the sum of the maximum number of coverage remaining in unplaced squares, we can *prune*.

As implemented by a graduate student project, this backtrack search eliminates 95% of the search space, when the pieces are ordered by decreasing mobility. With precomputing the list of possible moves, this program could search 1,000 positions per second. But this is too slow!

$$10^{12}/10^3 = !0^9 \textit{ seconds} > 1000 \textit{ days}$$

Although we might further speed the program by an order of magnitude, we need to prune more nodes!

By using a more clever algorithm, we eventually were able to prove no solution existed, in less than one day's worth of computing.

You too can fight the combinatorial explosion!

The Backtracking Contest: Bandwidth

The *bandwidth problem* takes as input a graph *G*, with *n* vertices and *m* edges (i.e pairs of vertices). The goal is to find a permutation of the vertices on the line which minimizes the maximum length of any edge.

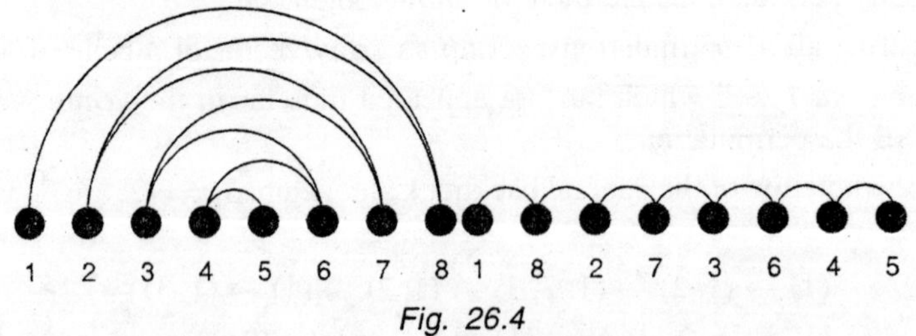

Fig. 26.4

The bandwidth problem has a variety of applications, including circuit layout, linear algebra and optimizing memory usage in hypertext documents.

The problem is NP-complete, meaning that it is *exceedingly* unlikely that you will be able to find an algorithm with polynomial worst-case running time. It remains NP-complete even for restricted classes of trees.

Since the goal of the problem is to find a permutation, a backtracking program which iterates through all the $n!$ possible permutations and computes the length of the longest edge for each gives an easy $O(n! - m)$ algorithm. But the goal of this assignment is to find as practically good an algorithm as possible.

8-Queens Problem

Extending the previous discussion a classic combinatorial problem is to place 8-queens on an 8×8 chessboard so that no two "attack", that is, no two of them are on the same row, column, or diagonal. See Fig. 26.5.

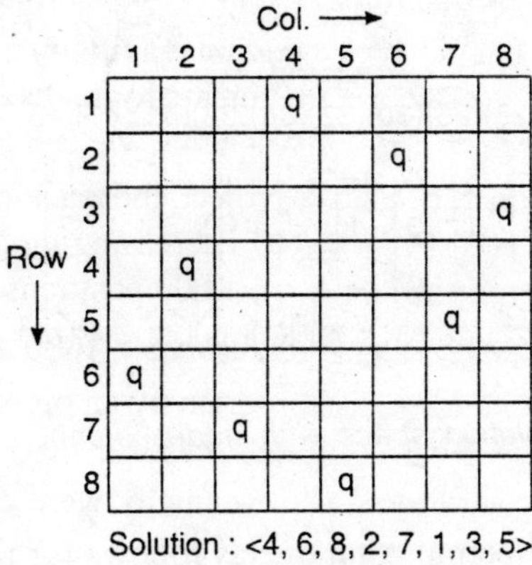

Fig. 26.5. Shows one solution to 8-Queens Problem

4-Queens Problem

Like 8-queens we have 4×4 chess board with 4 queens each to be placed in non attacking position. As shown in Fig. 26.6.

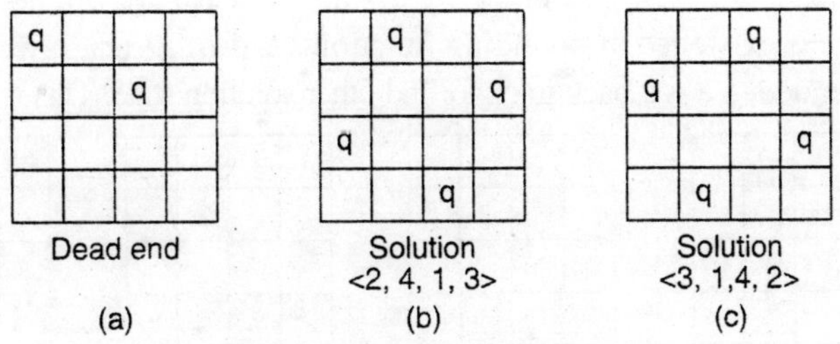

Fig. 26.6. 4-Queens Problem.

n-Queens Problem

It is generaliztion of 8-queens problem. Now n queens are to be placed on an $n \times n$ chessboard so that no two attack, *i.e.*, no two queens are on the same row, col. or diagonal.

The solution space to this problem consists of n ! permutation of the n-tuple $(1, 2, ..., n)$, as all positions must be distinct.

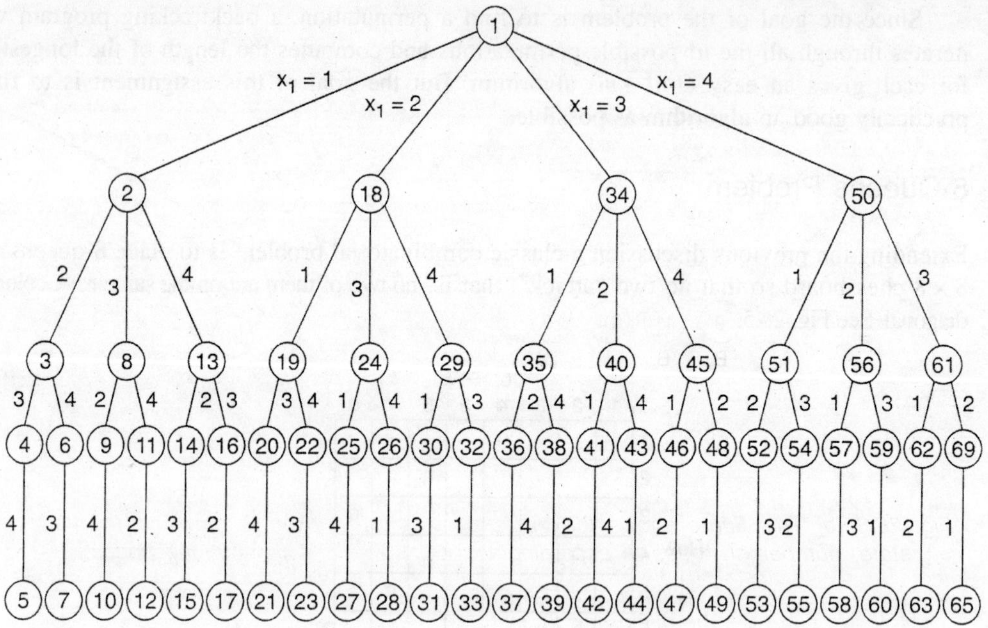

Fig. 26.7. 4 queens solution space with nodes numbered in DFS fashion.

If $n = 4$ we can give the permutation tree as follows for the 4-queens problem. There are 4 ! leaf nodes.

Fig. 26.7 shows the complete state space for 4-queens problem but we can use backtracking method to generate the necessary node and stop if next node violates the rule, *i.e.*, if two queens attacking.

Let $(x_1, x_2, ..., x_i')$ be a path from the root to a node in a state space tree. Let $T(x_1, x_2, ..., x_i)$ be the set of all possible values for x_{i+1} such that $(x_1, x_2, ..., x_{i+1})$ is also a path to a problem state. $T(x_1, x_2, ..., x_n) = \phi$ we assume that we are finding all the possible solution states and there is existence of bounding function s.t. if $B_{i+1}(x_1, x_2, ..., x_{i+1})$ is false then path cannot be extended. So we back track to find other solution state. This is illustrated in Fig. 26.8 (a)

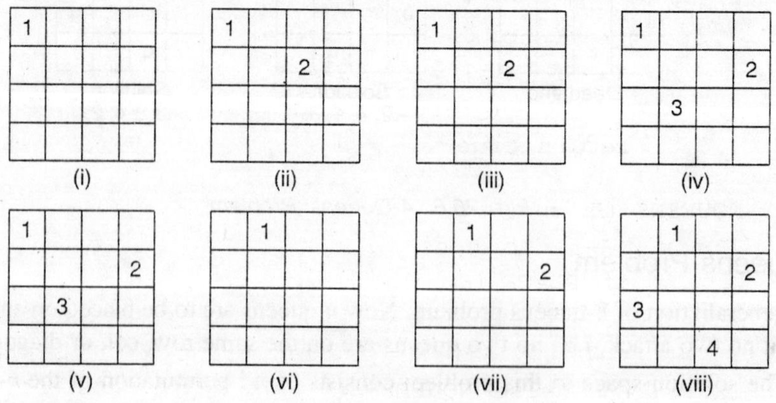

Fig. 26.8. (a) Placing of queens.

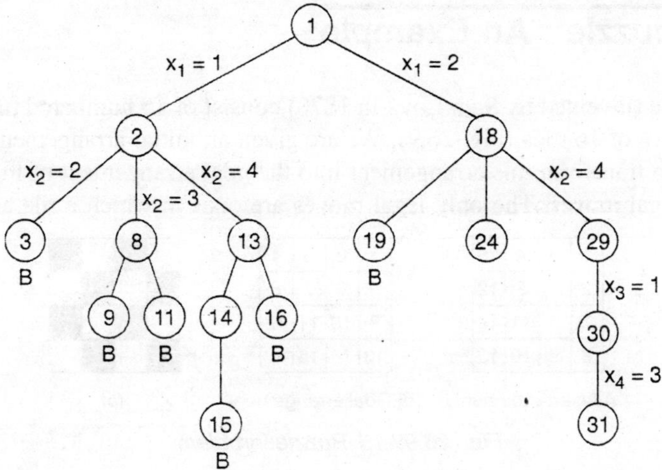

Fig. 26.8 (b) This figure shows the backtrack method applied to generate solution state, number of nodes is according to fig 26.7. B shows bounded nodes.

Now we can give the backtrack algorithm as follows.

```
BACKTRACK (K)
for each x[K] ε T(x[1], x[2], ..., x[K - 1])
      do if B_k(x[1], x[2], ..., x[K]) = true
            then print x[1 . . K]
            If (K < n) then backtrack (K + 1)
```

Since solution space contains 2^n or $n\,!$ nodes the running time of this algorithm is $O(P(n)\,n\,!)$ where $P(n)$ is polynomial in n.

Now we can give the simple N-queens algorithm for placing the queen at proper position, with checking for each placing whether it is correct or not.

```
PLACE (K, i)
   for j ← 1 to K - 1
         do if (x[j] = i) or Abs (x[i] - i) = Abs(j - k)
               then return false.
         return true

NQUEENS (K, n)
   for i ← 1 to n do
         if PLACE (K, i)
               then x[K] ← i
                     if K = n then print x [1 . . n]
               else NQUEENS (K + 1, n)
```

26.2 The 15-puzzle : An Example

The 15-puzzle (invented by Sam Loyd in 1878) consist of 15 numbered tiles on a square frame with a capacity of 16 tiles (Fig. 26.9). We are given an initial arrangement of the tiles, and the objective is to transform this arrangement into the goal arrangement of Figure 26.9(b) through a series of legal moves. The only legal moves are ones in which a tile adjacent to the empty

1	3	4	15
2		5	12
7	6	11	14
8	9	10	13

(a) An arrangement

1	2	3	4
5	6	7	8
9	10	11	12
13	14	15	

(b) Goal arrangement

(c)

Fig. 26.9. 15 Puzzle problem.

spot (ES) is moved to ES. Thus from the initial arrangement of Figure 26.9(a), four moves are possible. We can move any one of the tiles numbered 2, 3, 5 or 6 to the empty spot. Following this move, other moves can be made. Each move creates a new arrangement of the tiles. These arrangements are called the *states* of the puzzle. The initial and goal arrangements are called the initial and goal states. A state is reachable from the initial state iff there is a sequence of legal moves from the initial state to this state. The state space of an initial state consists of all states that can be reached from the initial state. The most straightforward way to solve the puzzle would be to search the state space for the goal state and use the path from the initial state to the goal state as the answer. It is easy to see that there are 16! ($16! = 20.9 \times 10^{12}$) different arrangement of the tiles on the frame. Of these only one-half are reachable from any given initial state. Indeed, the state space for the problem is very large. Before attempting to search this state space for the goal state, it would be worthwhile to determine whether the goal state is reachable from the initial state. There is a very simple way to do this. Let us number the frame positions 1 to 16. Position i is the frame position containing tile numbered i in the goal arrangement of Figure 26.9 (b). Position 16 is the empty spot. Let $position(i)$ be the position number in the initial state of the tile numbered i. The *position* (16) will denote the position of the empty spot.

For any state let $less(i)$ be the number of tiles j such that $j < i$ and $position(j) > position(i)$. For the state of Figure 26.9(a) we have, for example $less(1) = 0$, $less(4) = 1$ and $less(12) = 6$. Let $x = 1$ if in the initial state the empty spot is at one of the shaded positions of Figure 26.9(c) and $x = 0$ if it is at one of the remaining positions. Then, we have the following theorem :

THEOREM 26.1. The goal state of Figure 26.9(b) is reachable from the initial state iff $\sum_{i=1}^{16} less(i) + x$ is even.

PROOF : Left as an exercise.

Theorem 26.1 can be used to determine whether the goal state is in the state space of the initial state. If it is, then we can proceed to determine a sequence of moves leading to the goal state. To carry out this search, the state space can be organized into a tree. The children of each node x in this tree represent the states reachable from state x by one legal move. It is convenient to think of a move as involving a move of the emty space rather than a move of a tile. The empty space, on each move, moves either up, right, down, or left. Figure 26.10 shows the first three levels of the state space tree of the 15-puzzle beginning with the initial state shown in the root. Parts of levels 4 and 5 of the tree are also shown. The tree has been pruned a little. *No node p has a child state that is the same as p's parent.* The subtree eliminated in this way is already present in the tree and has root *parent (p)*. As can be seen, there is an answer node at level 4.

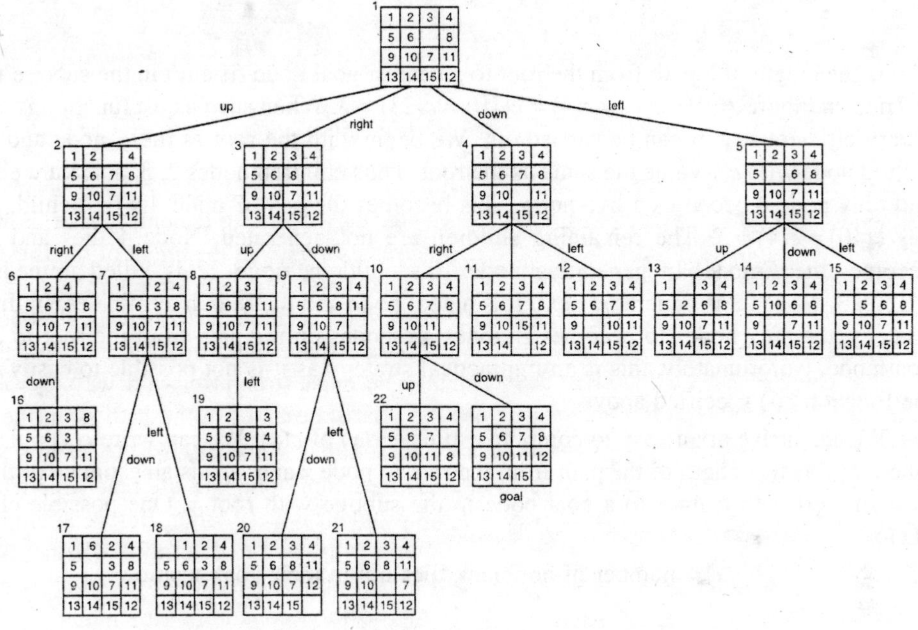

Edges are labeled according to the direction in which the empty space moves

Fig. 26.10. State space of 15-puzzle.

A depth first state space tree generation will result in the subtree of Figure 26.11 when the next moves are attempted in the order : move the empty space up, right, down, and left. Successive board configurations reveal that each move gets us farther from the goal rather than closer. The search of the state space tree is blind. It will take the leftmost path from the root regardless of the starting configuration. As a result, an answer node may never be found (unless the leftmost path ends in such a node). In a FIFO search of the tree of Figure 26.11, the nodes will be generated in the order numbered. A breadth first search will always find a goal node nearest to the root. However, such a search is also blind in the sense that no matter what the initial configuration, the algorithm attempts to make the same sequence of moves. A FIFO search always generates the state space tree by levels.

What we would like, is a more "intelligent" search method, one that seeks out an answer node and adapts the path it takes through the state space tree to the specific problem instance being solved. We can associate a cost $c(x)$ with each node x in the state space tree. The cost

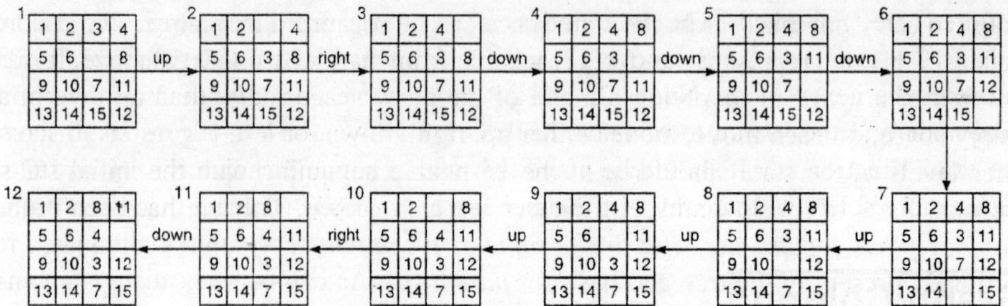

Fig. 26.11. First 10 steps in DFS.

$c(x)$ is the length of a path from the root to a nearest goal node (if any) in the subtree with root x. Thus, in Figure 26.10, $c(1) = c(4) = c(10) = c(23) = 3$. When such a cost function is available, a very efficient search can be carried out. We begin with the root as the *E*-node and generate a child node with $c()$-value the same as the root. Thus children nodes 2, 3, and 5 are eliminated and only node 4 becomes a live node. This becomes the next *E*-node. Its first child, node 10, has $c(10) = c(4) = 3$. The remaining children are not generated. Node 4 dies and node 10 becomes the *E*-node. In generating node 10's children, node 22 is killed immediately as $c(22) > 3$. Node 23 is generated next. It is a goal node and the search terminates. In this search strategy, the only nodes to becomes *E*-nodes are nodes on the path from the root to a nearest goal node. Unfortunately, this is an impractical strategy as it is not possible to easily compute the function $c(\cdot)$ specified above.

We can arrive at an easy to compute estimate $\hat{c}(x)$ of $c(x)$. We can write $\hat{c}(x) = f(x) + \hat{g}(x)$, where $f(x)$ is the length of the path from the root to node x and $\hat{g}(x)$ is an estimate of the length of a shortest path from x to a goal node in the subtree with root x. One possible choice for $\hat{g}(x)$ is

$$\hat{g}(x) = \text{number of nonblank tiles not in their goal position}$$

Clearly, at least $\hat{g}(x)$ moves have to be made to transform state x to a goal state. Move than $\hat{g}(x)$ moves may be needed to achieve this. To see this, examine the problem state of Figure 26.12. There $\hat{g}(x) = 1$ as only tile 7 is not in its final spot (the count for $\hat{g}(x)$ excludes the blank tile). However, the number of moves needed to reach the goal state is many move than $\hat{g}(x)$. So $\hat{c}(x)$ is a *lower bound* on the value of $c(x)$.

1	2	3	4
5	6		8
9	10	11	12
13	14	15	7

Fig. 26.12. Problem state.

An LC-search of Figure 26.10 using $\hat{c}(x)$ will begin by using node 1 as the *E*-node. All its children are generated. Node 1 dies and leaves behind the live nodes 2, 3, 4 and 5. The next node to become the *E*-node is a live node with least $\hat{c}(x)$. Then $\hat{c}(2) = 1 + 4$, $\hat{c}(3) = 1 + 4$, $\hat{c}(4) = 1 + 2$ and $\hat{c}(5) = 1 + 5$. Node 4 becomes the *E*-node. Its children are generated. The live nodes at this time are 2, 3, 4, 5, 10, 11 and 12. So $\hat{c}(10) = 2 + 1$, $\hat{c}(11) = 2 + 3$, and $\hat{c}(12) = 2 + 3$. The live node with least $\hat{c}$ is node 10. This becomes the next *E*-node. Nodes 22 and 23 are generated next. Node 23 is determined to be a goal node and the search terminates. In this case LC-search was almost as efficient as using the exact function *c*(). It should be noted that with a suitable choice for $\hat{c}()$, an LC-search will be far more selective than any of the other search methods we have discussed.

26.3 Graph Coloring

Let *G* be a graph and *m* be a given positive integer. The problem is to color the graph in such a way that no two adjacent nodes have same color, yet only *m*-colors are used. See Fig. 26.13 below :

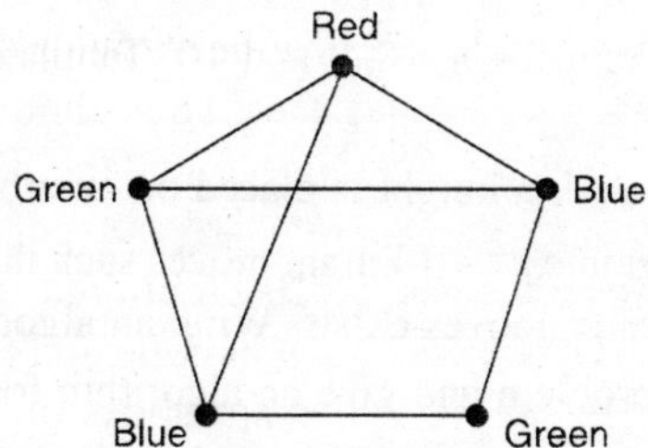

Fig. 26.13. An example of graph coloring.

```
m-COLOR(K)
   repeat
         NEXT-VALUE(K)
         If  (x[K]  =  0)  then return
         If  (K = n)  then
               print  (x[1..n])
         else m-COLOR(K + 1)
   until  false
NEXT-VALUE(K)
   repeat
         x[K]  ←  (x[K]  +  1)  mod  m+1
         If  (x[K]  =  0)  then return
         for j ← 1 to n do
               if  ((G[K,  j]  ≠  0)  and  (x[K]  =  x[j]))
                     then break
         If  (j  =  n  +  1)  then return
   until  false
```

State space tree similar to that of Fig. 26.8 (b) can be generated, internal nodes in state space tree is $\sum_{i=0}^{n-1} m$ and at each internal node $O(mn)$ time is spent by NEXT-VALUE to determine children corresponding to legal colorings. Hence total time is bounded by

$$\sum_{i=0}^{n-1} . m^{i+1} . \sum_{i=1}^{n} m^i n = n(m^{n+1} - 2)/m - 1$$

$$= O(nm^n).$$

EXERCISE

1. Run be n-queens program for $n = 8, 9$ and 10. Tabulate the no. of solutions your program finds for each value of n.
2. Given an $n \times n$ chessboard, a knight is placed on an arbitrary square with coordinates (x, y). The problem is to determine $n^2 - 1$ knight moves such that every square of the board is visited once if such a sequence of moves exists. Write an algorithm for this.
3. Study graph coloring problem and give an algorithm for 3-coloring of a graph.

27

BRANCH AND BOUND

27.1 Divide and Conquer

Consider the problem :

$$z = \max \{cx : x \in S\}$$

How can we break the problem into a series of smaller problems that are easier, solve the smaller problems, and then put the information together againto solve the original problem?

PROPOSITION 27.1 Let $S = S_1 \cup \ldots \cup S_K$ be a decomposition of S into smaller sets, and let $z_k = \max \{cx : x \in S_k\}$ for $k = 1, \ldots, K$. Then $z = \max_k z^k$.

A typical way to represent such a divide and conquer approach is via an enumeration tree. For instance, if $S \subseteq \{0, 1\}^3$, we might construct the enumeration tree shown in Figure 27.1.

Here we first divide S into $S_0 = \{x \in S : x_1 = 0\}$ and $S_1 = \{x \in S : x_1 = 1\}$, then $S_{00} = \{x \in S_0 : x_2 = 0\} = \{x \in S : x_1 = x_2 = 0\}$, $S_{01} = \{x \in S_0 : x_2 = 1\}$, and so on. Note that a leaf of the tree $S_{i_1 i_2 i_3}$ is nonempty if and only if $x = (i_1, i_2, i_3)$ is in S. Thus the leaves of the tree correspond precisely to the points of B^3 that one would examine if one carried out complete enumeration. Note that by convention the tree is drawn upside down with its root at the top.

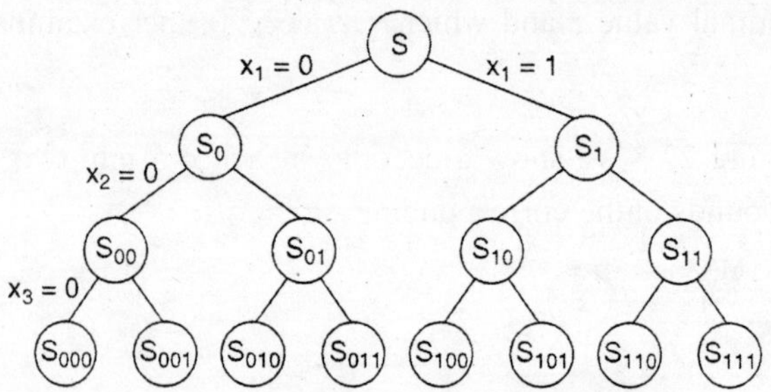

Fig. 27.1 Binary enumeration tree.

Another Example is the enumeration of all the tours of the traveling salesman problem. First we divide S the set of all tours on 4 cities into $S_{(12)}$, $S_{(13)}$, $S_{(14)}$ where $S_{(ij)}$ is the set of all tours containing arc (ij). Then $S_{(12)}$ is divided again into $S_{(12)(23)}$ and $S_{(12)(24)}$, and so on. Note that at the first level we have arbitrarily chosen to branch on the arcs leaving node 1, and at the second level on the arcs leaving node 2 that do not immediately create a sub-tour with the previous branching arc. The resulting tree is shown in Figure 27.2. Here the six leaves of the

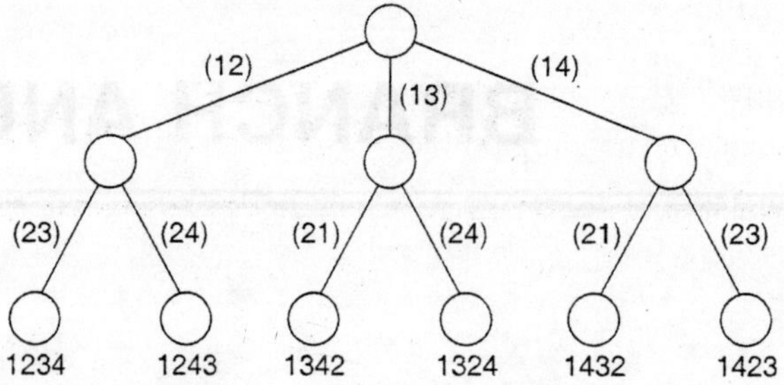

Fig. 27.2 TSP enumeration tree.

tree correspond to the $(n-1)!$ tours shown, where $i_1 i_2 i_3 i_4$ means that the cities are visited in the order i_1, i_2, i_3, i_4, i_1 respectively. Note that this is an example of multiway as opposed to binary branching, where a set can be divided into more than two parts.

27.2 Implicit Enumeration

We saw earlier that complete enumeration is totally impossible for most problems as soon as the number of variables in an integer program, or nodes in a graph exceeds 20 or 30. So we need to do more than just divide indefinitely. How can we use some bounds on the values of $\{z^k\}$ intelligently? First, how can we put together bound information?

PROPOSITION 27.2 Let $S = S_1 \cup \ldots \cup S_K$ be a decomposition of S into smaller sets, and let $z^k = \max \{cx : x \in S_k\}$ for $k = 1, \ldots, K$, $\overline{z}^k$ be an upper bound on z^k and $\underline{z}^k$ be a lower bound on z^k. Then $\overline{z} = \max_k \overline{z}^k$ is an upper bound on z and $\overline{z} = \max_k \underline{z}^k$ is a lower bound on z.

Now we examine three hypothetical examples to see how bound information, or partial information about a subproblem can be put to use. What can be deduced about lower and upper bounds on the optimal value z and which sets need further examination in order to find the optimal value?

EXAMPLE 27.1 In Figure 27.3 we show a decomposition of S into two sets S_1 and S_2 as well as upper and lower bounds onthe corresponding problems.

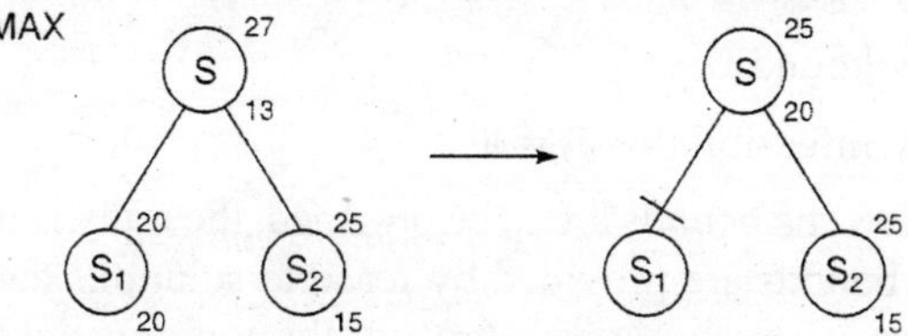

Fig. 27.3 Pruned by optimality.

We note first that $\overline{z} = \max_k \overline{z}^k = \max\{20, 25\} = 25$ and $\underline{z} = \max_k \underline{z}^k = \max\{20, 15\} = 20$. Second, we observe that as the lower and upper bounds on z_1 are equal, $z_1 = 20$, and there is no further reason to examine the set S_1. Therefore the branch S_1 of the enumeration tree can be pruned by optimality.

EXAMPLE 27.2 In Figure 27.4 we again decompose S into two sets S_1 and S_2 and show upper and lower bounds on the corresponding problems.

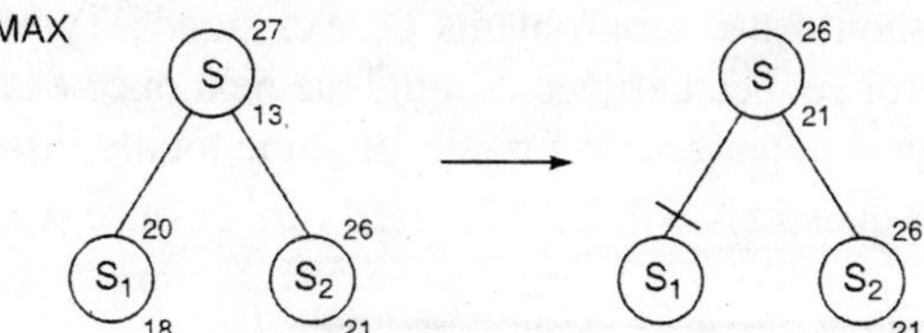

Fig. 27.4 Pruned by bound.

We note first that $\overline{z} = \max_k \overline{z}^k = \max\{20, 26\} = 26$ and $\underline{z} = \max_k \underline{z}^k = \max\{18, 21\} = 21$. Second, we observe that as the optimal value has value at least 21, and the upper bound $\overline{z}^1 = 20$, no optimal solution can lie in the set S_1. Therefore the branch S_1 of the enumeration tree can be pruned by bound.

EXAMPLE 27.3 In Figure 27.5 we again decompose S into two sets S_1 and S_2 with different upper and lower bounds.

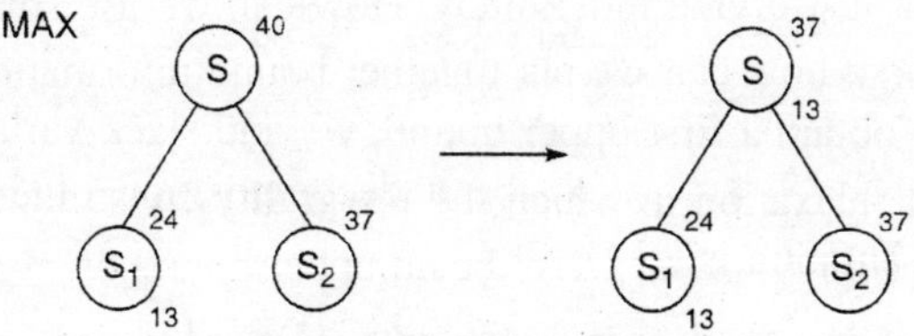

Fig. 27.5 No pruning possible.

We note first that $\overline{z} = \max_k \overline{z}^k = \max\ \{24, 37\} = 37$ and $\underline{z} = \max_k \underline{z}^k = \max\ \{13, -\} = 13$. Here no other conclusion can be drawn and we need to explore both sets S_1 and S_2 further.

Based on these examples, we can list at least three reasons that allow us to prune the tree and thus enumerate a large number of solutions implicitly.

(i) Pruning by optimality : $z_t = \{\max cx : x \in S_t\}$ has been solved.

(ii) Pruning by bound : $\overline{z}_t \le \underline{z}$.

(iii) Pruning by infeasibility : $S_t = \phi$.

If we now ask how the bounds are to be obtained, the reply is no different from in Chapter 2. The primal (lower) bounds are provided by feasible solutions and the dual (upper) bounds by relaxation or duality.

Building an implicit enumeration algorithm based on the above ideas is now in principle a fairly straightforward task. There are, however, many questions that must be addressed before such an algorithm is well-defined. Some of the most important questions are :

What relaxation or dual problem shbould be used to provide upper bounds? How should one choose between a fairly weak bound that can be calculated very rapidly and a stronger bound whose calculation takes a considerable time?

How should the feasible region be separated into smaller regions $S = S_1 \cup \ldots \cup S_K$? Should one separate into two or more parts? Should one use a fixed a priori rule for dividing up the set, or should the divisions evolve as a function of the bounds and solutions obtained en route?

In what order should the subproblems be examined? Typically there is a list of active problems that have not yet been pruned. Should the next one be chosen on a the basis of last-in first-out, of best/largest upper bound first, or of some totally different criterion?

These and other questions will be discussed further once we have seen an example.

27.3 Branch and Bound: An Example

The most common way to solve integer programs is to use implicit enumeration, or branch and bound, in which linear programming relaxations provide the bounds. We first demonstrate the approach by an example :

$$z = \max\ 4x_1 - x_2 \qquad \ldots(27.1)$$

$$7x_1 - 2x_2 \le 14 \qquad \ldots(27.2)$$

$$x_2 \le 3 \qquad \ldots(27.3)$$

$$2x_1 - 2x_2 \le 3 \qquad \ldots(27.4)$$

$$x \in Z_+^2 \qquad \ldots(27.5)$$

Bounding : To obtain a first upper bound, we add slack variables x_3, x_4, x_5 and solve the linear programming relaxation in which the integrality constraints are dropped. The resulting optimal basis representation is :

$$\overline{z} = \max\ \frac{59}{7} - \frac{4}{7}x_3 - \frac{1}{7}x_4$$

$$x_1 + \frac{1}{7}x_3 + \frac{2}{7}x_4 = \frac{20}{7}$$

$$x_2 + x_4 = 3$$

$$-\frac{2}{7}x_3 + \frac{10}{7}x_4 + x_5 = \frac{23}{7}$$

$$x_1, x_2, x_3, x_4, x_5 = 0$$

Thus we obtain an upper bound $\bar{z} = \frac{59}{7}$, and a nonintegral solution $(\bar{x}_1, \bar{x}_2) = \left(\frac{20}{7}, 3\right)$. Is there any straightforward way to find a feasible solution? Apparently not. By convention, as no feasible solution is yet available, we take as lower bound $\underline{z} = -\infty$.

Branching : Now because $\underline{z} < \bar{z}$, we need to divide or branch. How should we split up the feasible region? One simple idea is to choose an integer variable that is basic and fractional in the linear programming solution, and split the problem into two about this fractional value. If $x_j = \bar{x}_j \notin Z^1$, one can take :

$$S_1 = S \cap \{x : x_j \le \lfloor \bar{x}_j \rfloor\}$$
$$S_2 = S \cap \{x : x_j \ge \lceil \bar{x}_j \rceil\}$$

It is clear that $S = S_1 \cup S_2$ and $S_1 \cap S_2 = \phi$. Another reason for this choice is that the solution $\bar{x}$ of $LP(S)$ is not feasible in either $LP(S_1)$ or $LP(S_2)$. This implies that if there is no degeneracy (*i.e.*, multiple optimal LP solutions), then max $\{\bar{z}_1, \bar{z}_2\} < \bar{z}$, so the upper bound will strictly decrease.

Following this idea, as $\bar{x}_1 = 20/7 \notin Z^1$, we take $S_1 = S \cap \{x : x_1 \le 2\}$ and $S_2 = S \cap \{x : x_1 \ge 3\}$. We now have the tree shown in Figure 27.6. The subproblems (nodes) that must still be examined are called active.

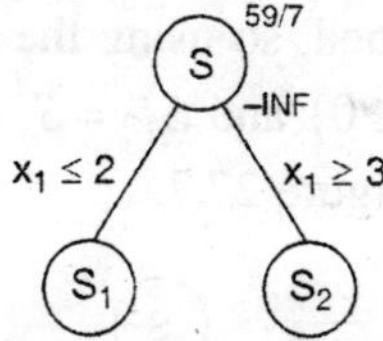

Fig. 27.6 Partial branch-and-bound tree 1.

Choosing a Node : The list of active problems (nodes) to be examined now contains S_1, S_2. We arbitrarily choose S_1.

Reoptimizing : How should we solve the new modified linear programs $LP(S_i)$ for $i = 1, 2$ without starting again from scratch?

As we have just added one single upper or lower bound constraint to the linear program, our previous optimal basis remains dual feasible, and it is therefore natural to reoptimize from this basis using the dual simplex algorithm. Typically, only a few pivots will be needed to find the new optimal linear programming solution.

Applying this to the linear program $LP(S_1)$, we can write the new constraint $x_1 \le 2$ as $x_1 + s = 2, s \ge 0$, which can be rewritten in terms of the nonbasic variables as

$$-\frac{1}{7}x_3 - \frac{2}{7}x_4 + s = -\frac{6}{7}$$

Thus we have the dual feasible representation :

$$\bar{z}_1 = \max \frac{59}{7} - \frac{4}{7}x_3 - \frac{1}{7}x_4$$

$$x_1 + \frac{1}{7}x_3 + \frac{2}{7}x_4 = \frac{20}{7}$$

$$x_2 + x_4 = 3$$

$$-\frac{2}{7}x_3 + \frac{10}{7}x_4 + x_5 = \frac{23}{7}$$

$$-\frac{1}{7}x_3 - \frac{2}{7}x_4 + s = -\frac{6}{7}$$

$$x_1, x_2, x_3, x_4, x_5, s \geq 0$$

After two simplex pivots, the linear program is reoptimized, giving :

$$\bar{z}_1 = \max \frac{15}{2} - \frac{1}{2}x_5 - 3s$$

$$x_1 + s = 2$$

$$x_2 - \frac{1}{2}x_5 + s = \frac{1}{2}$$

$$x_3 - x_5 - 5s = 1$$

$$x_4 + \frac{1}{2}x_5 + 6s = \frac{5}{2}$$

$$x_1, x_2, x_3, x_4, x_5, s \geq 0$$

with $\bar{z}_1 = \dfrac{15}{2}$, and $(\bar{x}_1^2, \bar{x}_2^1) = (2, 1/2)$.

Branching : S_1 cannot be pruned, so using the same branching rule as before, we create two new nodes $S_{11} = S_1 \cap \{x : x_2 \leq 0\}$ and $S_{12} = S_1 \cap \{x : x_2 \geq 1\}$, and add them to the node list. The tree is now as shown in Figure 27.7.

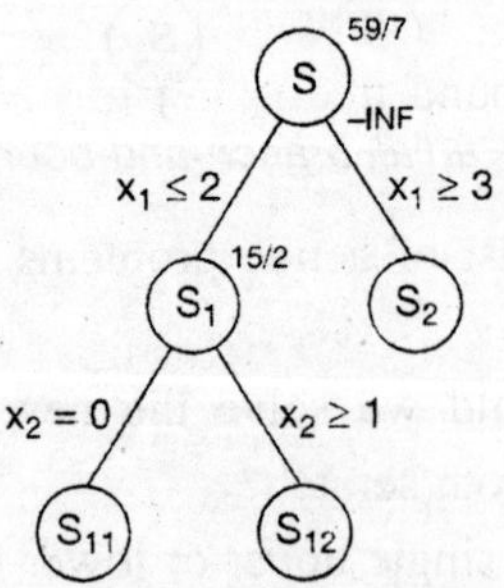

Fig. 27.7 Partial branch-and-bound tree 2.

Choosing a Node : The active node list now contains S_2, S_{11}, S_{12}. Arbitrarily choosing S_2, we remove it from the node list and examine it in more detail.

Reoptimizing : To solve $LP(S_2)$, we use the dual simplex algorithm in the same way as above. The constraint $x_1 \geq 3$ is first written as $x_1 - t = 3$, $t \geq 0$, which expressed in terms of the nonbasic variables becomes :

$$\frac{1}{7}x_3+\frac{2}{7}x_4+t=-\frac{1}{7}$$

From inspection of this constraint, we see that the resulting linear program

$$\bar{z}_2=\max\ \frac{59}{7}-\frac{4}{7}x_3-\frac{1}{7}x_4$$

$$x_1+\frac{1}{7}x_3+\frac{2}{7}x_4=\frac{20}{7}$$

$$x_2+x_4=3$$

$$-\frac{2}{7}x_3+\frac{10}{7}x_4+x_5=\frac{23}{7}$$

$$\frac{1}{7}x_3+\frac{2}{7}x_4+t=-\frac{1}{7}$$

$$x_1, x_2, x_3, x_4, x_5, t\geq 0$$

is infeasible, $\bar{z}_2=-\infty$, and hence node S_2 is pruned by infeasibility.

Choosing a Node : The node list now contains S_{11}, S_{12}. Arbitrarily choosing S_{12}, we remove it from the list.

Reoptimizing : $S_{12}=S\cap\{x : x_1\leq 2, x_2\geq 1\}$. The resulting linear program has optimal solution $\bar{x}^{12}=(2, 1)$ with value 7. As $\bar{x}^{12}$ is integer, $z^{12}=7$.

Updating the Incumbent : As the solution of $LP(S_{12})$ is integer, we update the value of the best feasible solution found $\bar{z}\leftarrow\max\{\underline{z}, 7\}$, and store the corresponding solution (2, 1). S_{12} is now pruned by optimality.

Choosing a Node : The node list now contains only S_{11}.

Reoptimizing : $S_{11}=S\cap\{x : x_1\leq 2, x_2\leq 0\}$. The resulting linear program has optimal solution $\bar{x}^{11}=\left(\frac{3}{2}, 0\right)$ with value 6. As $\bar{z}=7>\bar{z}_{11}=6$, the node is pruned by bound.

Choosing a Node : As the node list is empty, the algorithm terminates. The incumbent solution $x=(2, 1)$ with value $z=7$ is optimal.

The complete branch-and-bound tree is shown in Figure 27.8. In Figure 27.9 we show graphically the feasible node sets S_i, the branching, the relaxations $LP(S_i)$, and the solutions encountered in the example.

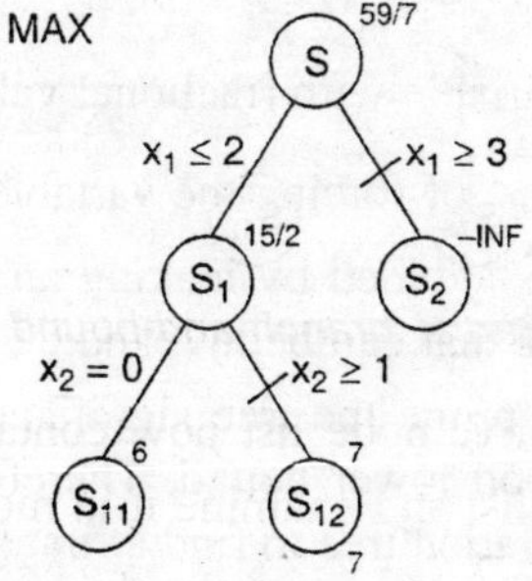

Fig. 27.8 Complete branch-and-bound tree.

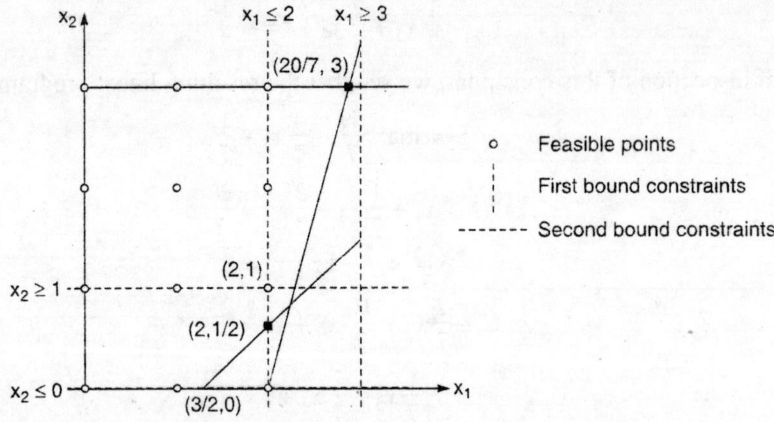

Fig. 27.9 Division of the feasible region.

27.4 LP-Based Branch and Bound

In Figure 2.10 we present a flowchart of a simple branch and bound algorithm, and then discuss in more detail some of the practical aspects of developing and using such an algorithm.

Storing the Tree : In practice one does not store a tree, but just the list of active nodes or subproblems that have not been pruned and that still need to be explored further. Here the question arises of how much information one should keep. Should one keep a minimum of information and be prepared to repeat certain calculations or should one keep all the information available? At a minimum, the best known dual bound and the variable lower and upper bounds needed to restore the subproblem are stored. Usually one also keeps an optimal or near-optimal basis, so that the linear programming relaxation can be reoptimized rapidly.

Returning to the questions raised earlier, there is no single answer that is best for all instances. One needs to use rules based on a combination of theory, common sense, and practical experimentation. In our example, the question of how to bound was solved by using an LP relaxation; how to branch was solved by choosing an integer variable that is fractional in the LP solution. However, as there is typically a choice of a set C of several candidates, we need a rule to choose between them. One common choice is the most fractional variable :

$$\arg\max_{j \in C} \min\,[f_j, 1 - f_j]$$

where $f_j = x_j^* - [x_j^*]$, so that a variable with fractional value $f_j = \frac{1}{2}$ is best. Other rules are based on the idea of estimating the cost of forcing the variable x_j to become integer.

How to choose a node was avoided by making an arbitrary choice. In practice there are several contradictory arguments that can be invoked :

(i) It is only possible to prune the tree significantly with a (primal) feasible solution, giving a hopefully good lower bound. Therefore one should descend as quickly as possible in the enumeration tree to find a first feasible solution. This suggests the use of a *Depth-First Search* strategy. Another argument for such a strategy is the observation that it is always easy to resolve the linear programming relaxation when a simple constraint is added, and the optimal basis is available. Therefore passing

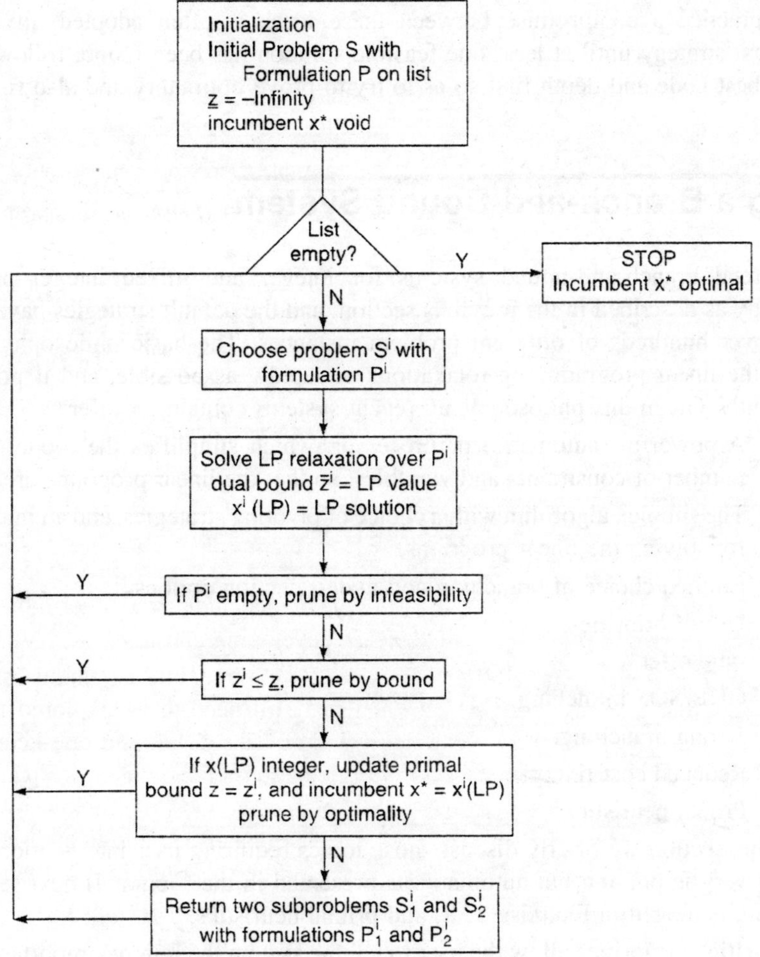

Fig. 27.10 Branch-and-bound flow chart.

from a node to one of its immediate descendants is to be encouraged. In the example this would imply that after treating node S_1, the next node treated would be S_{11} or S_{12} rather than S_2.

(ii) To minimize the total number of nodes evaluated in the tree, the optimal strategy is to always choose the active node with the best (largest upper) bound (*i.e.*, chooce node s where $\overline{z}_s = \max_t \overline{z}_t$). With such a rule, one will never divide any node whose upper bound $\overline{z}_t$ is less than the optimal value z. This leads to a *Best-Node First* strategy. In the example of the previous section, this would imply that after treating node S_1, the next node chosen would be S_2 with bound $\frac{59}{7}$ from its predecessor, rather than S_{11} or S_{12} with bound $\frac{15}{2}$.

In practice a compromise between these ideas is often adopted, involving an initial depth-first strategy until at least one feasible solution has been found, followed by a strategy mixing best node and depth first so as to try to prove optimality and also find better feasible solutions.

27.5 Using a Branch-and-Bound System

Commercial branch-and-bound systems for integer and mixed integer programming are essentially as described in the previous section, and the default strategies have been chosen by tuning over hundreds of different problem instances. The basic philosophy is to solve and resolve the linear programming relaxations as rapidly as possible, and if possible to branch intelligently. Given this philosophy, all recent systems contain, or offer,

1. A powerful (automatic) preprocessor, which simplifies the model by reducing the number of constraints and variables, so that the linear programs are easier,
2. The simplex algorithm with a choice of pivoting strategies, and an interior point option for solving the linear programs,
3. Limited choice of branching and node selection options,
4. Use of priorities,

and some offer

5. GUB/SOS branching,
6. Strong branching,
7. Reduced cost fixing,
8. Primal heuristics.

In this section we briefly discuss those topics requiring user intervention. Preprocessing, which is very important, but automatic, is presented in the (optional) next section. Reducedc cost fixing is treated in Exercise 27.7, and primal heuristics.

Priorities : Priorities allow the user to tell the system the relative importance of the integer variables. TRhe user provides a file specifying a value (importance) of each integer variable. When it has to decide on a branching variable, the system will choose the highest priority integer variable whose current linear programming value is fractional. At the same time the user can specify a preferred branching direction telling the system which of the two branches to explore first.

GUB Branching : Many models contain generalized upper bound (GUB) or special ordered sets (SOS) of the form

$$\sum_{j=1}^{k} x_j = 1$$

with $x_j \in \{0, 1\}$ for $j = 1, \ldots, k$. If the linear programming solution x^* has some of the variables $x_1^*, \ldots, x_k^*$ fractional then the standard branching rule is to impose $S_1 = S \cap \{x : x_j = 0\}$ and $S_2 = S \cap \{x : x_j = 1\}$ for some $j \in \{1, \ldots, k\}$. However, because of the GUB constraint, $\{x : x_j = 0\}$ leaves $k - 1$ possibilities $\{x : x_i = 1\}_{1 \neq j}$ whereas $\{x : x_j = 1\}$ leaves only one possibility. So S_1 is typically a much larger set than S_2, and the tree is unbalanced.

GUB branching is designed to provide a more balanced division of S into S_1 and S_2. Specifically the uswer specifies an ordering of the vasriables in the GUB set $j_1, \ldots, j_k$ and the branching scheme is then to set

$$S_1 = S \cap \{x : x_{j_i} = 0\ i = 1, \ldots, r\} \text{ and}$$

$$S_2 = S \cap \{x : x_{j_i} = 0\ i = r+1, \ldots, k\}$$

where $r = \min\left\{t : \sum_{i=1}^{t} x^*_{j_i} \geq \frac{1}{2}\right\}$. In many cases such a branching scheme is much more effective than the standard scheme, and the number of nodes in the tree is significantly reduced.

User Options :

(a) Cutoffs : If the user knows or can construct a good feasible solution to his or her problem, it is very important that its value is passed to the system as the incumbent value to serve as a cutoff in the branch and bound.

(b) Simplex Strategies : Though the linear programming algorithms are finely tuned, the default strategy will not be best for all classes of problems. Different simplex pricing strategies may make a huge difference in running times for a given class of models, so if similar models are resolved repeatedly or the linear programs seem very slow, some experimentation by the user with pricing strategies is permitted. In addition, on very large models, interior point methods may be best for the solution of the first linear program. Unfortunately, up to now such methods are still not good for reoptimizing quickly at each node of the tree.

(c) Strong Branching : The idea behind strong branching is that on difficult problems it should be worthwhile to do more work to try to choose a better branching variable. The system chooses a set C of basic integer variables that are fractional in the LP solution, branches up and down on each of them in turn, and reoptimizes on each branch either to optimality, or for a specified number of dual simplex pivots. Now for each variable $j \in C$, it has upper bounds z_j^D for the down branch and z_j^U for the up branch. The variable having the largest effect (decrease of the dual bound)

$$j^* = \arg\min_{j \in C} \max\ [z_j^D, z_j^U]$$

is then chosen, and branching really takes place on this variable. Obviously, solving two LPs for each variable in C is costly, so such branching should only be used when the other criteria have been found to be ineffective.

27.5.1 If All Else Fails

What can one do if a particular problem instance turns out to be difficult, meaning that after a certain time :

(i) no feasible solution has been found, or

(ii) the gap between the value of the best feasible solution and the value of the dual upper bound is unsatisfactorily large, or

(iii) the system runs out of space because there are too many active nodes in the node list?

Finding Feasible Solutions : This is in general NP-hard. Some systems have simple primal heuristics embedded in them. Also as discussed earlier, using priorities and directions for branching can help. How to find feasible solutions, starting from the LP solution or using explicit problem structure.

Finding Better Dual Bounds : Branch-and-bound algorithms faill very often because the bounds obtained from the linear programming relaxations are too weak. This means that tightening up the formulation of the problem is of crucial importance.

27.6 Preprocessing

Before solving a linear or integer program, it is natural to check that the formulation is "sensible", and as strong as possible given the information available. All the commercial branch-and-bound systems carry out such a check, called preprocessing. The basic idea is to try to quickly detect and eliminate redundant constraints and variables, and tighten bounds where possible. Then if the resulting linear/integer program is smaller/tighter, it will typically be solved much more quickly. This is especially important in the case of branch-and-bound because tens or hundreds of thousands of linear programs may need to be solved.

First we demonstrate linear programming preprocessing by an example.

EXAMPLE 27.4 Consider the linear program

$$\max 2x_1 + x_2 - x_3$$

$$5x_1 - 2x_2 + 8x_3 \leq 15$$

$$8x_1 + 3x_2 - x_3 \geq 9$$

$$x_1 + x_2 + x_3 \leq 6$$

$$0 \leq x_1 \leq 3$$

$$0 \leq x_2 \leq 1$$

$$1 \leq x_3$$

Tightening Bounds : Isolating variable x_1 in the first constraint we obtain

$$5x_1 \leq 15 + 2x_2 - 8x_3 \leq 15 + 2 \times 1 - 8 \times 1 = 9$$

where we use the bound inequalities $x_2 \leq 1$ and $-x_3 \leq -1$. Thus we obtain the tightened bound $x_1 \leq \frac{9}{5}$.

Similarly isolating variables x_3, we obtain

$$8x_3 \leq 15 + 2x_2 - 5x_1 \leq 15 + 2 \times 1 - 5 \times 0 = 17,$$

and the tightened bound $x_3 \leq \frac{17}{8}$.

Isolating variable x_2, we obtain

$$2x_2 \geq 5x_1 + 8x_3 - 15 \geq 5 \times 0 + 8 \times 1 - 15 = -7.$$

Here the existing bound $x_2 \geq 0$ is not changed.

Turning to the second constraint, isolating x_1 and using the same approach, we obtain $8x_1 \geq 9 - 3x_2 + x_3 \geq 9 - 3 + 1 = 7$, and an improved lower bound $x_1 \geq \frac{7}{8}$.

No more bounds are changed based on the second or third constraints. However, as certain bounds have been tightened, it is worth passing through the constraints again.

Constraint 1 for x_3 now gives $8x_3 \leq 15 + 2x_2 - 5x_1 \leq 15 + 2 - 5 \times \frac{7}{8} = \frac{101}{8}$. Thus we have the new bound $x_3 \leq \frac{101}{64}$.

Redundant Constraints : Using the latest upper bounds in constraint 3, we see that

$$x_1 + x_2 + x_3 \leq \frac{9}{5} + 1 + \frac{101}{64} < 6,$$

and so this constraint is redundant and can be discarded. The problem is now reduced to

$$\max 2x_1 + x_2 - x_3$$
$$5x_1 - 2x_2 + 8x_3 \leq 15$$
$$8x_1 + 3x_2 - x_3 \geq 9$$
$$\frac{7}{8} \leq x_1 \leq \frac{9}{5},\ 0 \leq x_2 \leq 1,\ 1 \leq x_3 \leq \frac{101}{64}$$

Variable Firing (by Duality) : Considering variable x_2, observe that increasing its value makes all the constants (otherr than its bound constraints) less tight. As the variable has a positive objective coefficient, it is advantageous to make the variable as large as possible, and thus set it to its upper bound of 1. (Another way to arrive at a similar conclusion is to write out the LP dual. For the dual constraint corresponding to the primal variable x_2 to be feasible, the dual variable associated with the constraint $x_2 \leq 1$ must be positive. This implies by complementary slackness that $x_2 = 1$ in any optimal solution.)

Similarly, decreasing x_3 makes the constraints less tight. As the variable has a negative objective coefficient, it is best to make it as small as possible, and thus set it to its lower bound $x_3 = 1$. Finally the LP is reduced to the trivial problem

$$\max \left\{ 2x_1 : \frac{7}{8} \leq x_1 \leq \frac{9}{5} \right\}$$

Formalizing the above ideas is straightforward.

PROPOSITION 27.3 Consider the set $S = \{x : a_0x_0 + \sum_{j=1}^{n} a_jx_j \leq b,\ l_j \leq x_j \leq u_j \text{ for } j = 0, 1, \ldots, n\}$.

(i) *Bounds on Variables* : If $a_0 > 0$, then

$$x_0 \leq (b - \sum_{j:a_j>0} a_jl_j - \sum_{j:a_j<0} a_ju_j)/a_0,$$

and if $a_0 < 0$, then

$$x_0 \geq (b - \sum_{j:a_j>0} a_jl_j - \sum_{j:a_j<0} a_ju_j)/a_0.$$

(ii) *Redundancy* : The constraint $a_0x_0 + \sum_{j=1}^{n} a_jx_j \le b$ is redundant if

$$\sum_{j:a_j>0} a_ju_j + \sum_{j:a_j<0} a_jl_j \le b.$$

(iii) *Infeasibility* : $S = \phi$ if

$$\sum_{j:a_j>0} a_jl_j + \sum_{j:a_j<0} a_ju_j > b.$$

(iv) *Variable Fixing* : For a maximization problem in the form: max $\{cx : Ax \le b, l \le x \le u\}$, if $a_{ij} \ge 0$ for all $i = 1, \ldots, m$ and $c_j \le 0$, then $x_j = l_j$. Conversely if $a_{ij} \le 0$ for all $i = 1, \ldots, m$ and $c_j > 0$, then $x_j = u_j$.

Turning now to integer programming problems, preprocessing can sometimes be taken a step further. Obviously, if $x_j \in Z^1$ and the bounds l_j or u_j are not integer, we can tighten to

$$[l_j] \le x_j \le [u_j]$$

For mixed integer programs with variable upper and lower bound constraints $l_jy_j \le x_j \le u_jy_j$ with $y_j \in \{0, 1\}$, it is also important to use the tightest bound information.

For BIPs it is common to look for simple "logical" or "boolean" constraints involving only one or two variables, and then either add them to the problem or use them to fix some variables. Again we demonstrate by example.

EXAMPLE 27.5 Consider the set of constraints involving four 0–1 variables :

$$7x_1 + 3x_2 - 4x_3 - 2x_4 \le 1$$
$$-2x_1 + 7x_2 + 3x_3 + x_4 \le 6$$
$$-2x_2 - 3x_3 - 6x_4 \le -5$$
$$3x_1 - 2x_3 \ge -1$$
$$x \in B^4$$

Generating Logical Inequalities : Examining row 1, we see that if $x_1 = 1$, then necessarily $x_3 = 1$, and similarly $x_1 = 1$ implies $x_4 = 1$. This can be formulated with the linear inequalities $x_1 \le x_3$ and $x_1 \le x_4$. We see also that the constraint is infeasible if both $x_1 = x_2 = 1$ leading to the constraint $x_1 + x_2 \le 1$.

Row 2 gives the inequalities $x_2 \le x_1$ and $x_2 + x_3 \le 1$.

Row 3 gives $x_2 + x_4 \ge 1$ and $x_3 + x_4 \ge 1$.

Row 4 gives $x_1 \ge x_3$.

Combining Pairs of Logical Inequalities : We consider pairs involving the same variables.

From rows 1 and 4, we have $x_1 \le x_3$ and $x_1 \ge x_3$, which together give $x_1 = x_3$.

From rows 1 and 2, we have $x_1 + x_2 \le 1$ and $x_2 \le x_1$ which together give $x_2 = 0$. Now from $x_2 + x_4 \ge 1$ and $x_2 = 0$, we obtain $x_4 = 1$.

Simplifying : Making the substitutions $x_2 = 0$, $x_3 = x_1$, $x_4 = 1$, all four constraints of the feasible region are redundant, and we are left with $x_1 \in \{0, 1\}$, so the only feasible solutions are (1, 0, 1, 1) and (0, 0, 0, 1).

Branch-and-Bound Algorithms

A counter-part of the backtracking search algorithm which, in the absence of a cost criteria, the algorithm traverses a spanning tree of the solution space using the breadth-first approach. That is, a queue is used, and the nodes are processed in first-in-first-out order.

If a cost criteria is available, the node to be expanded next (*i.e.*, the branch) is the one with the best cost within the queue. In such a case, the cost function may also be used to discard (*i.e.*, the bound) from the queue nodes that can be determined to be expensive. A priority queue is needed here.

27.7 Cost-Based Tree Traversal

A function can be considered to be a **tree generator**, if when given a node X and index i it produces the ith child of the node.

The following function produces a complete binary tree of 11 nodes.

The recursive function provided for deriving permutations is another example of a function that may be used to generate trees.

Besides for a tree generator function, we also need a **cost function** to decide in what order to traverse the nodes when searching for a solution. The algorithm proceeds in the following manner.

1. **Initialization:** The root of the of the tree is declared to be alive.
2. **Visit:** The cost criteria decides which of the live nodes is to process next.
3. **Replacement:** The chosen node is removed from the set of live nodes, and its children are inserted into the set. The children are determined by the tree generator function.
4. **Iteration:** The visitation and replacement steps are repeated until no alive nodes are left.

In the case of **backtracking** the cost criteria assumes a **last-in-first-out** (LIFO) function, which can be realized with a **stack** memory. A **first-in-first-out** cost criteria implies the **FIFO branch-and-bound** algorithm, and it can be realized with queue memory. A generalization to **arbitrary** cost criteria is the basis for the **priority branch-and-bound** algorithm, and **apriority queue** memory can be employed to realize the function.

A company is assembling a team to carry out a series of operations. There are four members of the team: A, B, C and D, and four operations to be carried out. Each team member can carry out exactly one operation. All four operations must be carried out successfully for the overall project to succeed, however the probability of a particular team member succeeding in a particular operation varies, as shown in the table below. For example, if the team members were assigned to operations in the order $ABCD$, then the overall probability of successful completion of the project is (0.9)(0.6)(0.85)(0.7) = 0.3213.

If there is any possible way that the team can be arranged such that the overall probability of success exceeds 45%, then the manager will approve the project. Will the manager approve the project? If yes, what is the arrangement of the team that gives the highest probability of success?

		Operation			
		1	2	3	4
Team member	*A*	0.9	0.8	0.9	0.85
	B	0.7	0.6	0.8	0.7
	C	0.85	0.7	0.85	0.8
	D	0.75	0.7	0.75	0.7

❑❑❑

28

MINIMUM SPANNING TREE

28.1 Spanning Tree

A tree T is said to be a spanning tree of a connected graph G if T is a subgraph of G and T contains all vertices of G without forming a circuit.

Cost of spanning tree is obtained by adding all the wts. of edges constituting the MST

$$w(T) = \sum_{u, v \varepsilon T} \omega(u, v) = 4 + 2 + 3 + 2 + 2 + 4 + 4 + 2 = 23.$$

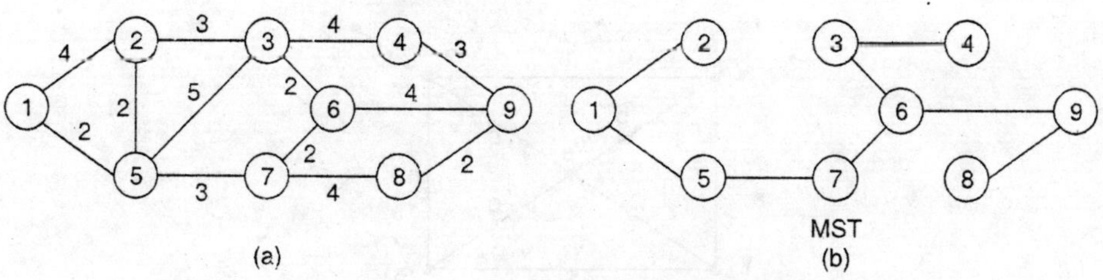

Fig. 28.1 (a) A graph G (b) MST of G

An edge in spanning tree is called *branch* and the edge which are not in spanning tree is called *chord.*

LEMMA 28.1. With respect to any of its spanning tree, a connected graph of n vertices and e edges has $n - 1$ tree branches and $e - n + 1$ chords.

We can give a generic algorithm for MST s.t. an edge is added to set of MST if it does not form a circuit thus,

```
GenerericMST (G, w)
   A ← φ
         while A does not form a spanning tree
                do find an edge (u, v) that does not form
                                                  a circuit in A
                     A ← A ∪ {(u, v)}
         return A.
```

Fundamental Circuit

Adding an edge between any two vertices forms a fundamental circuit, an edge shown by dotted line between vertices 4 and 9 constitutes a fundamental circuit from the fig 28.1(b), shown in Fig. 28.2.

Cut Sets

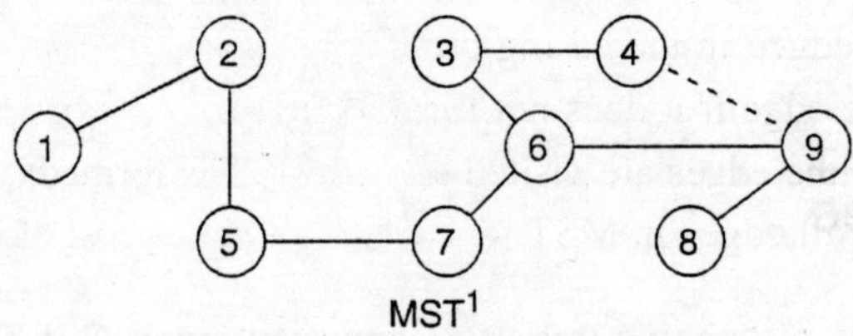

Fig. 28.2.

It is minimal no of edges whose removal from G destroys all paths between these two set of vertices.

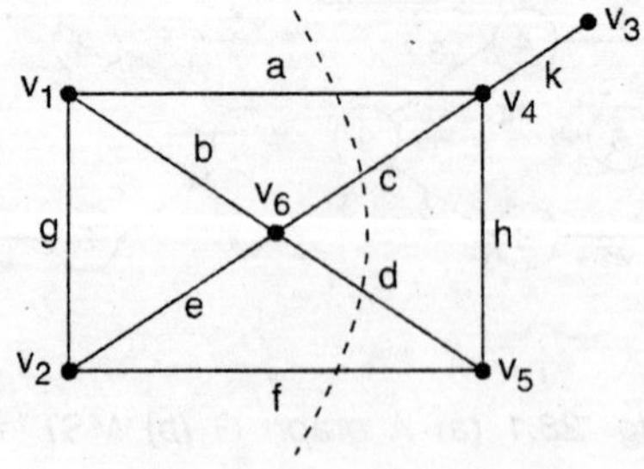

Fig. 28.3.

Removal of edge $\{a, c, d, f\}$ in Fig. 28.3 forms two disconnected graph as shown in Fig. 28.3.1.

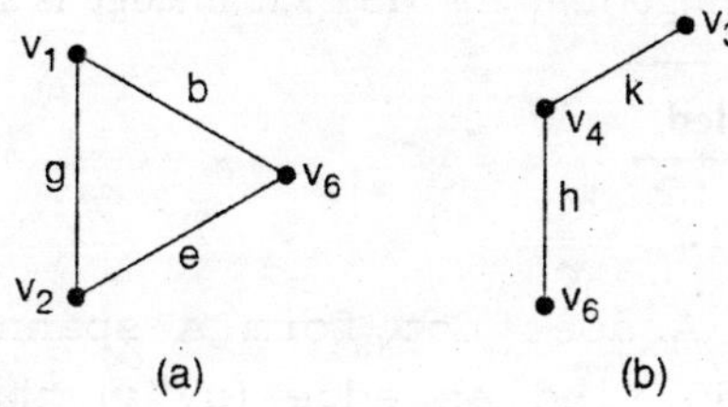

Fig. 28.3.1.

Note that vertex are not deleted only edges are removed. Other possible cut sets are $\{a, b, g\}$, $\{a, b, e, f\}$, $\{d, b, f\}$, $\{k\}$, $\{a, c, b\}$ but $\{a, c, h, d\}$ is not a cut set, as one of its proper subset $\{a, c, h\}$ is a cut set that's why cut set must contain minimal no. of edges.

28.2 Kruskal's Algorithm

It is one of the example of greedy algorithm in which edges are selected at greed with minimum wt. and added to MST till no circuit is formed. It is used to find minmimum cost.

Steps :

1. Arrange all the edged in increasing order of their *wt.*
2. Add to MST the edge if it does not form a circuit.
3. Continue till all the edges are visited and an MST is formed.
4. Add the cost of all edges in MST to get the minimum cost of Spanning tree.

EXAMPLE 28.1. *Find the minimum cost of following graph.*

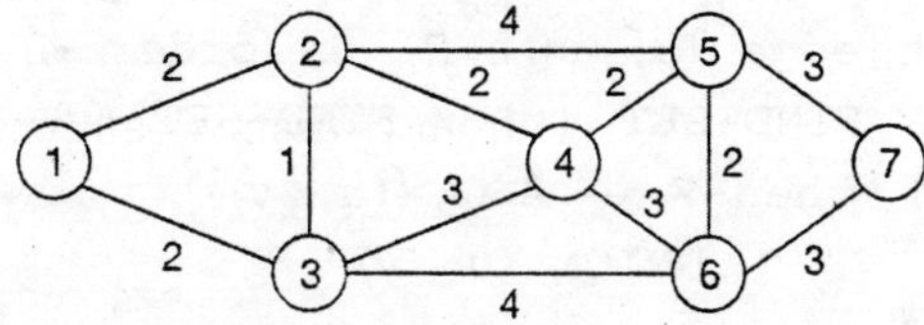

SOLUTION :

edge (u, v)	Wt.	Included
(2, 3)	1	✔
(1, 2)	2	✔
(2, 4)	2	✔
(5, 6)	2	✔
(1, 3)	2	×
(3, 4)	3	×
(4, 6)	3	✔
(5, 7)	3	✔
(6, 7)	3	×
(3, 6)	4	×
(2, 5)	4	×

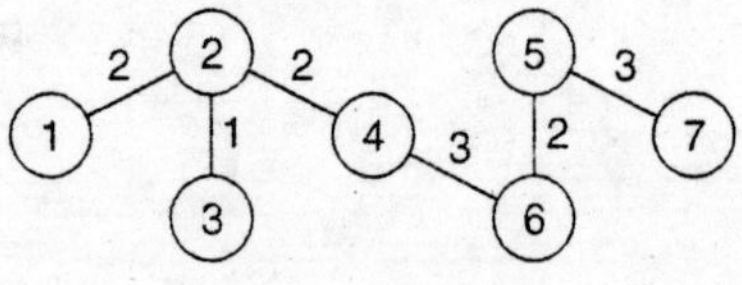

Minimum cost MST

MST includes edge

$$A \leftarrow \{(2,3)\} \cup \{(1,2)\} \cup \{(2,4)\} \cup \{(5,6)\} \cup \{(4,6)\} \cup \{(5,7)\}$$

Minimum cost $W(T) = \sum_{(u,v)\,\varepsilon\, T} W(T) = 13$

```
MST-Kruskal (G, w)
    r ← ϕ
    for each vertex v ε V(G)
        do MAKE-SET T(v)
    Sort the edges of E by increasing wt w.
    for each edge (u, v) ε E, in order of increasing wt.
        if  FIND-SET (u) ≠ FIND-SET (v)
            then A ← A ∪ {(u, v)}
                UNION (u, v)
    return A
```

MAKE-SET makes set of vertices, FIND-SET (u) checks whether vertex u is in set of vertices or not, UNION (u, v) forms a graph by including the new edge.

Running time to sort the edges takes $O(ElgE)$ time and other steps takes, time less than or equal to this so running time is $O(ElgE)$.

28.3 Prim's Algorithm

It also works like kruskal algorithm except it applies nearest neighbour method to select new edge.

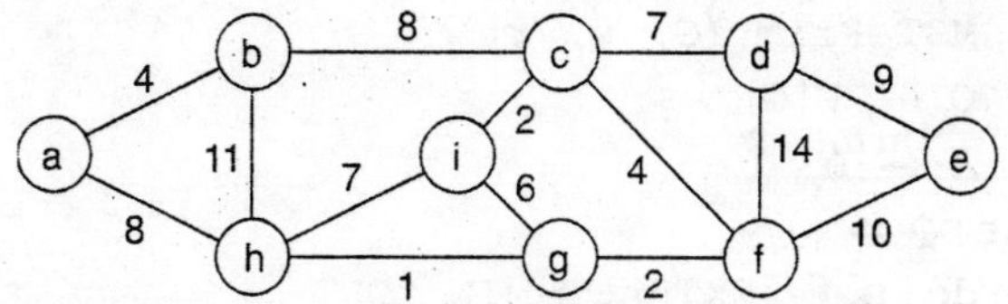

Fig. 28.4.

Steps

1. Start with an vertex, say *u*.
2. Select another vertex, *v* s.t. edge is formed from *u* and *v* and is of minimum *wt*, Connect *uv* and add it to set of for MST. edges *A*.
3. Now among the set of all vertices find other vertex V_i that is not included in *A* s.t. (V_i V_j) is minimum labeled and is nearest neighbour of all vertices in set *A* and it does not form circuit add it to *A*.
4. Continue this process till you get a MST, MST obtained is of minimum cost.

Applying Prim's algo to fig. 28.4, we get, we start with vertex *a*.

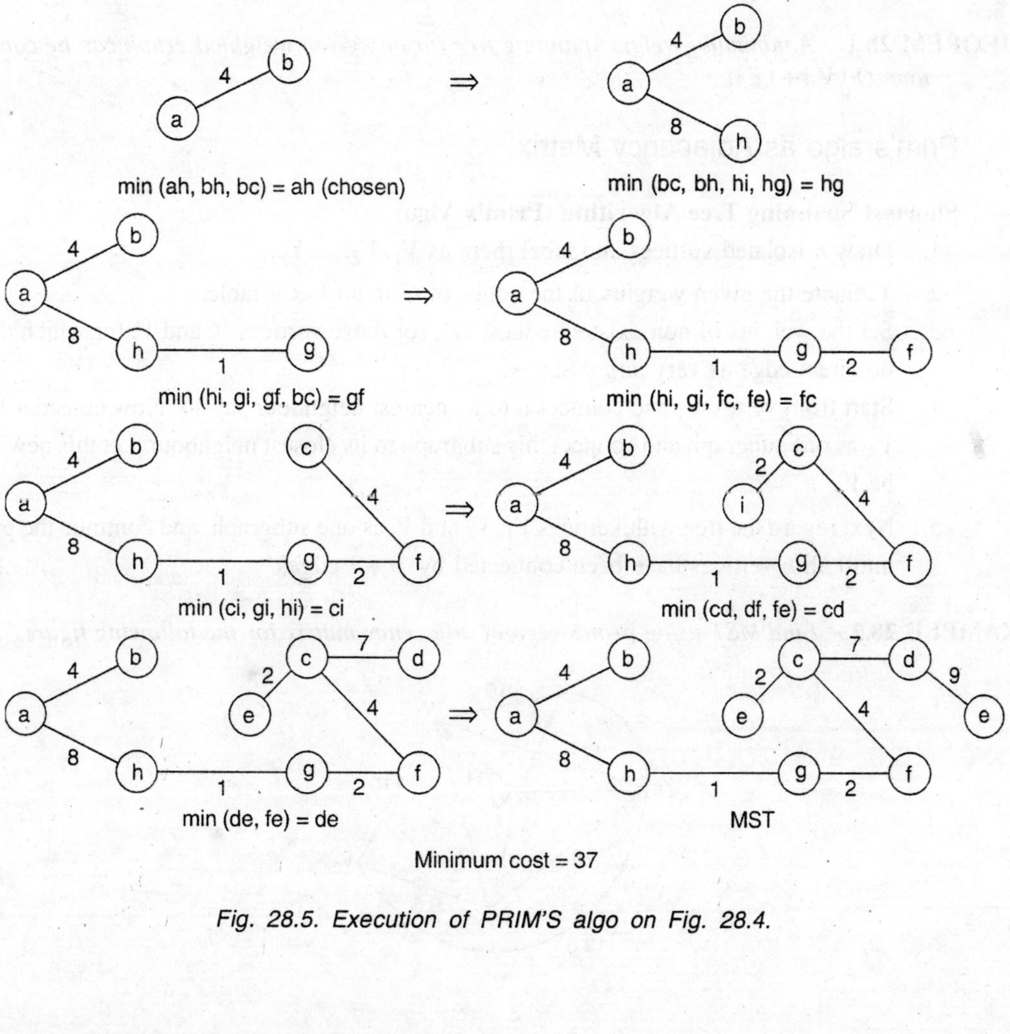

min (ah, bh, bc) = ah (chosen) ⇒ min (bc, bh, hi, hg) = hg

min (hi, gi, gf, bc) = gf ⇒ min (hi, gi, fc, fe) = fc

min (ci, gi, hi) = ci ⇒ min (cd, df, fe) = cd

min (de, fe) = de ⇒ MST

Minimum cost = 37

Fig. 28.5. Execution of PRIM'S algo on Fig. 28.4.

```
MST-Prim (G, w, r)
    Q ← V[G]
    A ← φ
while Q ≠ φ
    do u ← EXTRACT-MIN (Q)
        v ← Adj (u)
        k ← w(u, v)
        s ← {(u, v)}
    for each v ε Adj(u)
        do if w(u, v) < k
            then A ← A ∪ {(u, v)}
            else
                A ← A ∪ S
Union (u, v)
```

Running time is $O(ElgV)$.

THEOREM 28.1. *A minimum-weight spanning tree for any given weighted graph can be computed in time* $O(|V|+|E|)$

Prim's algo as Adjacency Matrix

Shortest Spanning Tree Algorithm (Prim's Algo)

1. Draw n isolated vertices and label them as $V_1, V_2, ..., V_n$.
2. Tabluate the given weights of the edges of G in an $V \times V$ table.
3. Set the weights of non-existent edges, *i.e.*, for those vertices V_i and V_j for which there is no direct edge as very large. Say ∞.
4. Start from vertex V_1 and connect it to its nearest neighbour say V_k. Now consider V_1 and V_K as one subgraph and connect this subgraph to its closest neighbour. Let this new vertex be V_i.
5. Next regard the tree with vertices V_1, V_k and V_i as one subgraph, and continue the process untill all n vertices have been connected by $n - 1$ edges.

EXAMPLE 28.2. *Find MST using prim's algo of adjacency matrix for the following figure.*

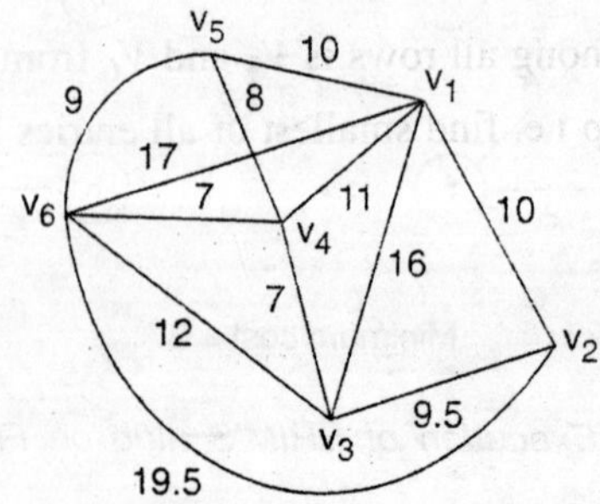

SOLUTION :

Step 1, 2, 3

	V_1	V_2	V_3	V_4	V_5	V_6
V_1	—	**10**	16	11	**10**	17
V_2	10	—	9.5	∞	∞	9.5
V_3	16	9.5	—	7	∞	12
V_4	11	∞	7	—	8	7
V_5	10	∞	∞	8	—	9
V_6	17	19.5	12	7	9	—

Step 4. Start with V_1 and pick the smallest entry in row 1, which is either (V_1, V_2)or (V_1, V_5). Let us pick (V_1, V_5). The closest neighbour of subgraph (V_1, V_5) is V_4 (from all entries in row 1 and row 5)

Step 5. Now $V_1\ V_5\ V_4$ is one subgraph, find smallest of all entries in row V_1, V_5, V_4 that does not from circuit.

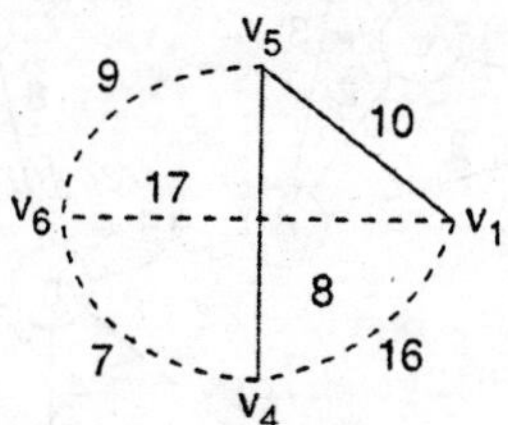

	V_1	V_2	V_3	V_4	V_5	V_6
Row of V_1	–	**10**	16	11	10	17
Row V_4	11	∞	**7**	–	8	**7**
Row V_5	10	∞	∞	8	–	**9**

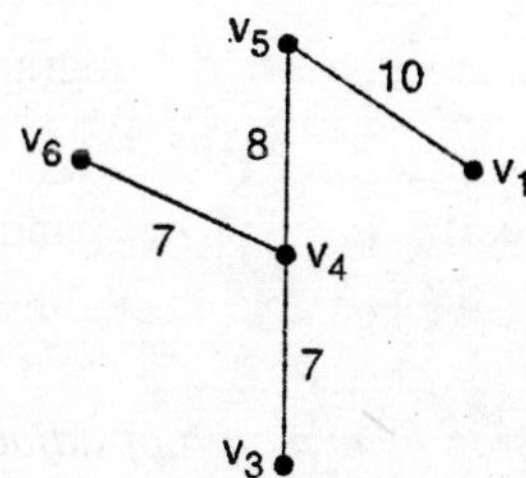

∴ Nearest neighbour among all rows is V_3 and V_6 from V_4.

Again repeating this step i.e. find smallest of all entries in row V_1, V_5, V_4, V_6, V_3 we have V_2 as the nearest neighbour.

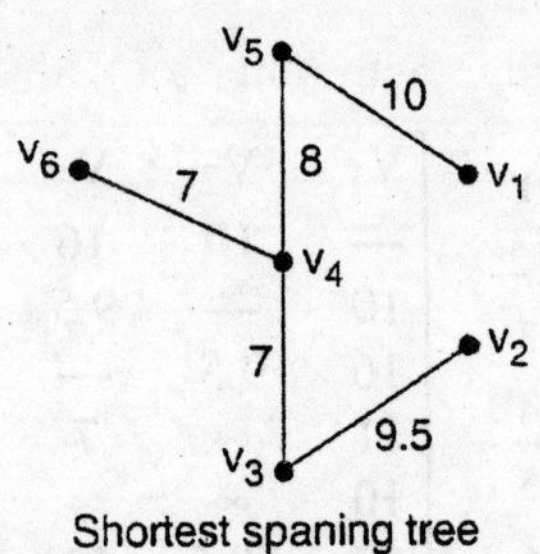

Shortest spaning tree

Running time is $O(V^2)$, Minimum cost is 41.5.

EXAMPLE 28.3. *What is the cost of minimum spanning tree of the following graph?*

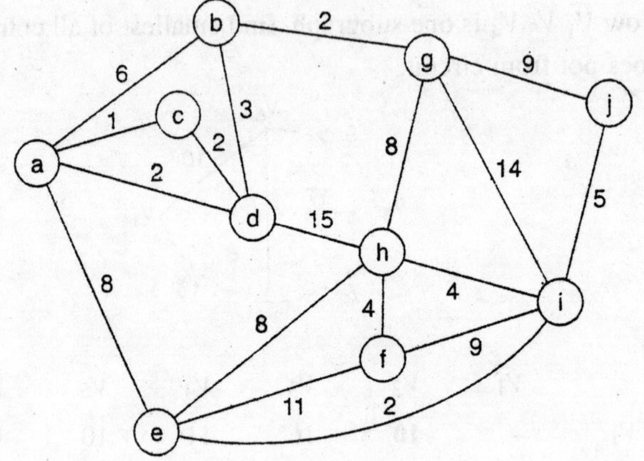

SOLUTION : Using Kruskal's algo

We start including the edge with min cost without forming circuit.

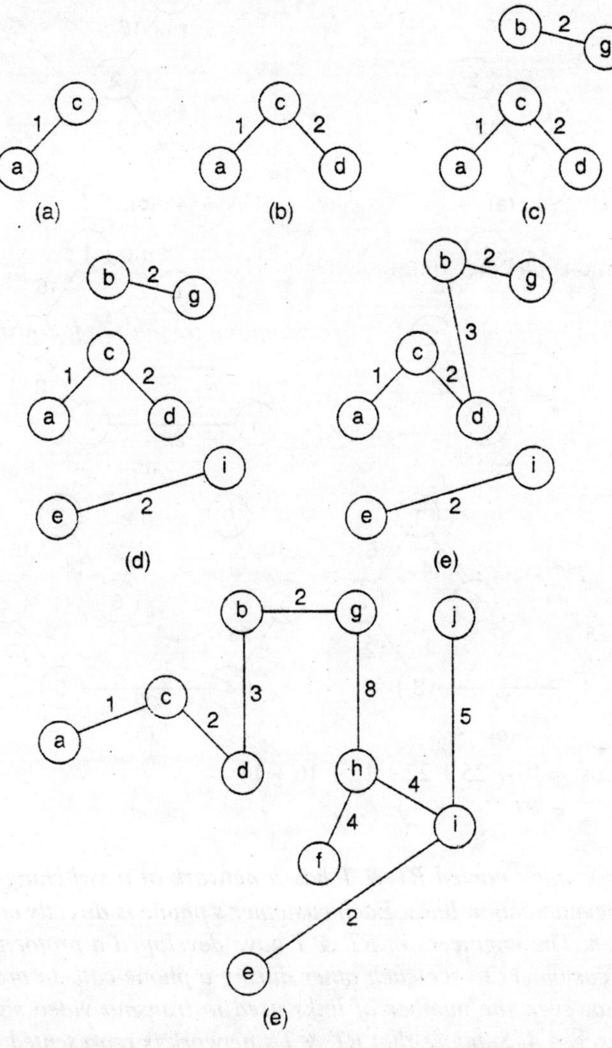

Minimum cost = $\Sigma\, w(e) = 1 + 2 + 3 + 2 + 8 + 4 + 4 + 2 + 5$
$= 31$

EXAMPLE 28.4. *Find the minimum cost spanning tree using Prim's algorithm?*

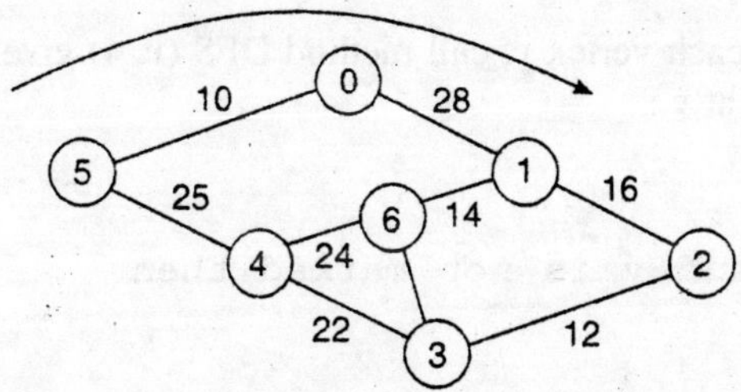

SOLUTION :

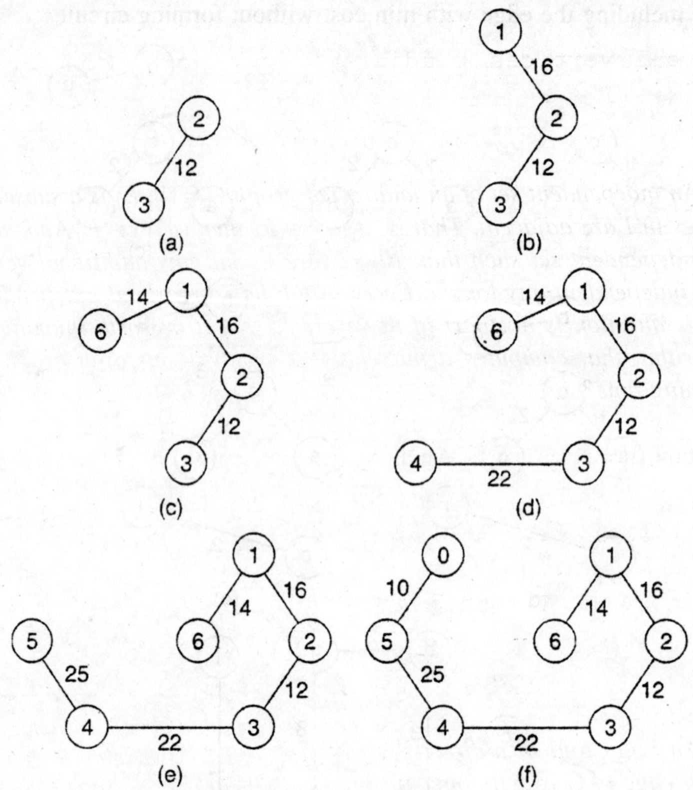

Minimum Cost = 10 + 25 + 22 + 12 + 16 + 14
= 99

EXAMPLE 28.5. *A company named RT & T has a network of n switching stations connected by m high-speed communication links. Each customer's phone is directly connected to one station in his or her area. The engineers of RT & T have developed a prototype video-phone system that allows two customers to see each other during a phone call. In order to have acceptable image quality, however, the number of links used to transmit video signals between the two parties cannot exceed 4. Suppose that RT & T's network is represented by a graph. Design an efficient algorithm that computes, for each station, the set of stations it can reach using no more than 4 links.*

SOLUTION : For each vertex v, perform a modified BFS traversal starting at v that stops as soon as level 4 is computed.

Alternatively, for each vertex v, call method DFS (v, 4) given below, which is a modified DFS traversal starting at v :

```
DFS (v, i):
if i > 0 and v is not marked then
```

```
Mark v,
Print v,
for all vertices w adjacent to v do
DFS (w, i - 1).
```

EXAMPLE 28.6. *An independent set of an undirected graph $G = (V, E)$ is a subset I of V, such that no two vertices in I are adjacent. That is, if $u, v \in I$, then $(u, v) \notin E$. A maximal independent set M is an independent set such that, if we were to add any additional vertex to M, then it would not be independent any longer. Every graph has a maximal independent set. (Can you see this ? This question is not part of the exercise, but it is worth thinking about.) Give an efficient algorithm that computes a maximal independent set for a graph G. What is this method's running time?*

SOLUTION : Assume $V = \{v_1, \ldots, v_n\}$. An algorithm would be :

```
Initialize I to empty
for i = 1 to n
if (v_i, x) ∈ E with x ∈ I, then
and v_i to I
```

EXAMPLE 28.7. *An Euler tour of a directed graph $\vec{G}$ with n vertices and m edges is a cycle that traverses each edge of $\vec{G}$ exactly once according to its direction. Such a tour always exists if $\vec{G}$ is connected and the in-degree equals the out-degree of each vertex in $\vec{G}$. Describe an $O(n + m)$-time algorithm for finding an Euler tour of such a digraph $\vec{G}$.*

SOLUTION : First, even if it is not asked, we show that a connected directed graph has an Euler tour, if and only if, each vertex has the same in-degree and out-degree (degree property from now on).

If the graph has an Euler tour, then by following that tour, it is always able to leave any vertex that we visit. Thus, the in-degree of each vertex equals its out-degree.

Assume now that each vertex has the same in-degree and out-degree. We can construct an Euler tour using the following procedure. Start at any node and keep traversing edges until you reach the same vertex (the graph is connected and by the degree property we are always able to return at this node). If this cycle (not necessary simple) is a tour (contains all edges) we are done. Otherwise, delete the traversed edges from the graph and starting by any vertex of the cycle that has non-zero degree, find (by traversing edges) another cycle (observe that the degree property holds even after the edges removal). Remove the traversed edges and continue until no edges are left in the graph. All the cycles that where discovered can be combined to give us an Euler tour : just keep track of the starting vertex of each cycle and insert this cycle into the previous cycle.

The last procedure corresponds to a well defined linear time algorithm for finding an Euler tour. However, we give another algorithm that, using a DFS traversal over the graph, constructs an Euler tour in a systematic way.

The algorithm is very similar to the one that traverses a connected undirected graph such that each edge is traversed exactly twice (once for each direction), there by marking the entrance edge we had been able to successfully (that is, so that no edges were left untouched) leave a vertex and never visit it again.

This, however, can not be done here because an edge has only one direction. We, instead, "preprocess" the graph, by performing a DFS traversal where each edge is traversed in its opposite direction (backwards). We only label the discovering edges in this DFS. Thus, when the DFS is over, each vertex will have a unique outgoing labeled edges (the one connecting this vertex with its parent in the discovering tree of DFS). We then simulate the algorithm : starting from any node, we perform a "blind" traversal, where we do not cross any label edge unless we are forced (there are no other way to leave the current vertex).

We give the pseudo-code that describe the algorithm. Instead of walking blindly, we assume that each vertex keep an iterator OUT_EDGE_IT of the outgoing incident edges and in this way edges are traversed in a systematic way (and thus, we do not have to label them). Also, each vertex stores an edge reference LAST_EDGE; it is a reference to an edge (the one labeled by the DFS traversal) that must be traversed only if no other option is available. Finally, instead of performing a DFS on graph $\vec{G}$ traversing edges backwards, we can perform a DFS at graph $\vec{G}$, which is graph $\vec{G}$ having each edge with a reversed direction. We then reverse all edges (to switch back to the graph $\vec{G}$) but keep the labeling.

```
Euler Tour (G)
    for all vertices v do
    OUT_EDGE_IT (v) ← outIncidentEdges (v)
    LAST EDGE (v) ← NULL
    Let G⃗ be the graph resulting by reversing the
        direction of each edge of G⃗ perform DFS to graph
        G⃗ and for each vertex v store the corresponding
        unique outgoing discovering edge as LAST_EDGE (v)
    s ← aVertex()
    NextVertex (V, s)
NextEdge (V, v)
    if OUT_EDGE_IT (V).hasNext() then
        e ← OUT_EDGE_IT (v).nextObject()
        if e = LAST_EDGE (v) then
            return NextEdge (G, v)
        else return e
    else return LAST_EDGE (v)
NextVertex (G, v)
    e ← NextEdge (G, v)
    if e ≠ NULL then
        u = opposite (v, e)
    Report (e)
    NextVertex (G, u)
```

The time complexity is clearly $O(n + m)$; the edge labeling takes linear time (using DFS in graph $\vec{G}$) and each edge is traversed exactly once and the decision about which edge to traverse next is made in constant time.

EXAMPLE 28.8. *Describe an efficient algorithm that, given an undirected graph G, determines a spanning tree G whose largest edge weight is minimum over all spanning trees of G.*

SOLUTION : First, make sure you understand the question

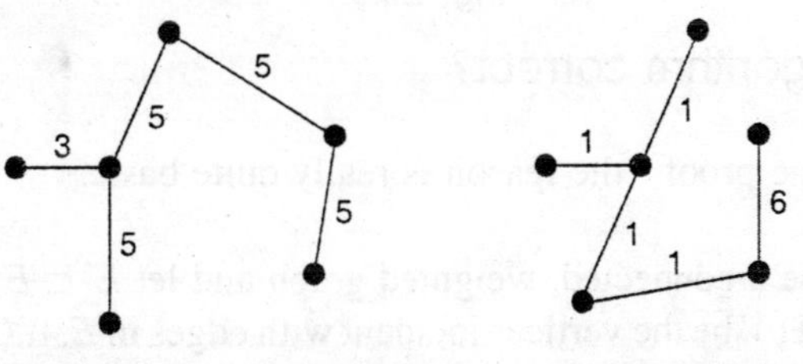

Lower maximum edge weight Lower cool weight

"Hey, doesn't Kruskal's algorithm do something like this."

Certainly! Since Krushal's algorithm considers the edges in order of increasing weight, and stops the moment these edges form a connected graph, the tree it gives must minimize the edge weight.

"Hey, but then why doesn't Prim's algorithm also work?"

It gives the same thing as Kruskal's algorithm, so it must be true that any minimum spanning tree minimizes the maximum edge weight!

Applications of Minimum Spanning Trees

Minimum spanning trees are useful in constructing networks, by describing the way to connect a set of sites using the smallest total amount of wire. Much of the work on minimum spanning (and related Steiner) trees has been conducted by the phone company.

Minimum spanning trees provide a reasonable way for *clustering* points in space into natural groups.

When the cities are points in the Euclidean plane, the minimum spanning tree provides a good heuristic for traveling salesman problems. The optimum traveling salesman tour is at most twice the length of the minimum spanning tree.

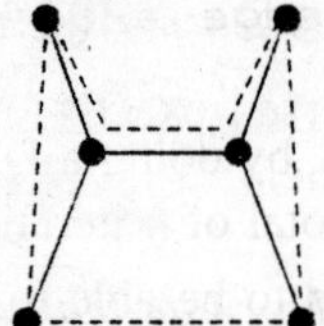

The Option Traveling is an max twice the length of the minimum spanning tree

Fig. 28.6.

Why is Prim's algorithm correct?

Don't be scared by the proof - the reason is really quite basic:

THEOREM 28.2. Let G be a connected, weighted graph and let $E' \subset E$ be a subset of the edges in a MST $T = (V, E_T)$. Let V be the vertices incident with edges in E. If (x, y) is an edge of minimum weight such that $x \in V'$ and y is not in V, then $E' \cup \{x, y\}$ is a subset of a minimum spanning tree.

PROOF: If the edge is in T, this is trivial.

Suppose (x, y) is not in T Then there must be a path in T from x to y since T is connected. If (v, w) is the first edge on this path with one edge in V, if we delete it and replace it with (x, y) we get a spanning tree.

This tree must have smaller weight than T, since $W(v, w) > W(x, y)$. Thus T could not have been the MST.

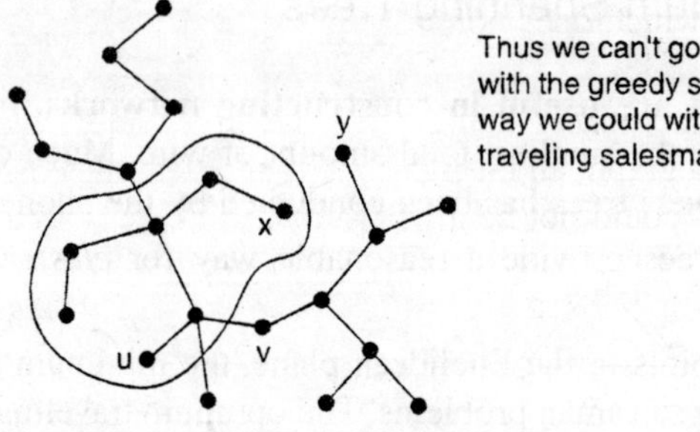

Fig. 28.7.

Prim's Algorithm is correct!

But how fast is Prim's?

That depends on what data structures are used. In the simplest implementation, we can simply mark each vertex as tree and non-tree and search always from scratch:

```
Select an arbitrary vertex to start.
While (there are non-tree vertices)
Select minimum weight edge between tree and fringe
```

```
add the selected edge and vertex to the tree
```

This can be done in $O(n\,m)$ time, by doing a DFS or BFS to loop through all edges, with a constant time test per edge, and a total of n iterations.

Can we do faster? If so, we need to be able to identify fringe vertices and the minimum cost edge associated with it, fast. We will augment an adjacency list with fields maintaining fringe information.

```
Vertex:
        fringelink pointer to next vertex in fringe list.
        fringe weight cheapest edge linking v to 1.
        parent other vertex with v having fringeweight.
        status intree, fringe, unseen.
        adjacency list the list of edges.
```

Finding the minimum weight fringe-edge takes $O(n)$ time - just bump through fringe list.

After adding a vertex to the tree, running through its adjacency list to update the cost of adding fringe vertices (there may be a cheaper way through the new vertex) can be done in $O(n)$ time.

Total time is $O(n^2)$.

Why is Kruskal's Algorithm Correct?

THEOREM 28.3. Let G be a weighted graph and let $E' \subset E$. If E is contained in a MST T and e is the smallest edge in $E - E'$ which does not create a cycle, $E' \cup E \subset T$.

PROOF: As before, suppose e is not in T. Adding e to T makes a cycle. Deleting another edge from this cycle leaves a connected graph, and if it is one from $E - E'$ the cost of this tree goes down. Since such an edge exists, T could not be a MST.

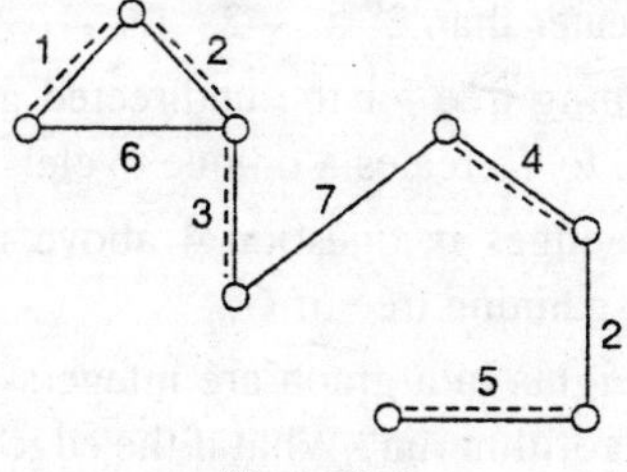

Fig. 28.8.

How fast is Kruskal's algorithm?

What is the simplest implementation?

Sort the m edges in $O(m \log m)$ time.

For each edge in order, test whether it creates a cycle the forest we have thus far built - if so discard, else add to forest. With a BFS/DFS, this can be done in $O(n)$ time (since the tree has at most n edges).

The total time is $O(mn)$, but can we do better?

Kruskal's algorithm builds up connected components. Any edge where both vertices are in the same connected component create a cycle. Thus if we can maintain which vertices are in which component fast, we do not have test for cycles!

Put the edges in a heap

```
count = 0
while (count < n - 1) do
    get next edge (v, w)
    if (component (v) ≠ component (w))
        add to T
        component (v) = component (w)
```

If we can test component in $O(\log n)$, we can find the MST in $O(m \log m)$

Question: Is $O(m \log n)$ better than $O(m \log m)$?

EXERCISE

1. Let $G = (V, E)$ be an undirected graph with subgraph $G_1 = (V_1, E_1)$ wieghts are assigned to edge of G as follows.

$$w(e) = \begin{cases} 0 & \text{if } e \in E_1 \\ 1 & \text{otherwise} \end{cases}$$

A single source shortest path algorithm is executed on weighted. graph, with an arbitrary vertex $v_1 \in V_1$ as the source. What is the the type of graph formed?

2. By considering the complete graph with n vertices. Show that the no. of spanning trees in an n vertex graph can be greater than $2^{n-1} - 2$.
3. Show that if T is a spanning tree for the undirected graph G, then the addition of an edge q, $q \notin E(T)$ and $q \in E(G)$, to T creates a unique cycle.
4. Show that if any of the edges in question 4 above is deleted from $E(T) \cup \{q\}$, then the remaining edges from a spanning tree of G.
5. Suppose that all edge weights in a graph are integers in the range from 1 to $|V|$. How fast can you make kruskals algorithm run? What if the edge weights are integers in the range from 1 to W for some constant w.
6. Let (u, v) be a minimum-weight edge in a graph G. Show that (u, v) belongs to some minimum spanning tree of G.
7. Describe the details of an $O(n + m)$-time algorithm for computing ***all*** the connected components of an undirected graph G with n vertices and m edges.

29

SINGLE-SOURCE SHORTEST PATHS

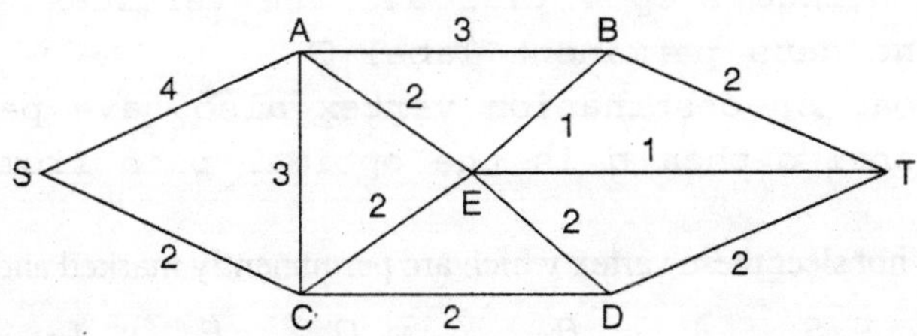

Fig. 29.1.

Here *S* is the source and *T* is the target or destination. Shortest path from *S* to *T* can be found by Dijkstra's Algorithm.

29.1 Dijkstra's Algorithm for Shortest Path

1. From an array d_{ij} of distances taking $d_{ii} = 0$ and $d_{ij} = \infty$, if there is no direct edge from *i* to *j*. e.g., in fig 25.1 $d_{SE} = d_{SD} = d_{SB} = d_{ST} = \infty$.

2. Define the label of S to 0, assign the label of x to be ∞, if $x \neq S$. Mark the label of S.

$$\begin{cases} S & A & B & C & D & E & T \\ 0 & \infty & \infty & \infty & \infty & \infty & \infty \end{cases}$$

Table-1

3. For each vertex $j \neq S$, calculate the

d_{ij} = min {old label of j, old label of $i + d_{ij}$}

e.g. d_{SA} = min {∞, 0 + 4}, from table 1.

= 4

d_{SB} = min {∞, 0 + 2} = 2

Thus,

S	A	B	C	D	E	T
0	4	∞	2 (boxed)	∞	∞	∞

Table-2

Now S is assigned permanent label.

4. Choose the vertex as i, the one having the minimum label and mark it '√' Then again apply the formula d_{ij} = min {old label of j, old label of $i + d_{ij}$ }
5. Continue step 4 till all the vertices are marked and gets permanent label □.
6. Goal or destination vertex also have permanent label d then d is the optimal path from S to T.

Note : do not slect these vertex which are permanently marked and do not move backwards.

S	A	B	C	D	E	T
0 (boxed)	4	2	∞ ✓	∞	∞	∞
0 (boxed)	4	∞	2 (boxed)	∞	∞	∞

Choose C, as it is minimum

Now ***C* to *A*.**

$$d_{CA} = \min \{4, 2 + 3\} = 4$$

C* to *E

$$d_{CE} = \min \{\infty, 2 + 2\} = 4$$

***C* to *D*.**

$$d_{CD} = \min\{\infty, 2+2\} = 4.$$

Thus table has new row.

S	A	B	C	D	E	T
[0]	4 ✓	∞	[2]	4	4	∞
[0]	[4]	∞	[2]	4	4	∞

Now choose *A* (*D* and *E* can also be chosen)

$$d_{AB} = \min\{\infty, 4+3\} = 7$$

$$d_{AB} = \min\{4, 4+2\} = 4$$

Thus new table formed is

S	A	B	C	D ✓	E	T
[0]	[4]	7	[2]	[4]	4	∞

Selecting *D* as source.

$$d_{DE} = \min\{4, 4+2\} = 4.$$

$$d_{DT} = \min\{\infty, 4+2\} = 6$$

S	A	B	C	D	E ✓	T
[0]	[4]	7	[2]	[4]	[4]	6

Selecting *E* as source

$$d_{ET} = \min\{6, 4+1\} = 5.$$

$$d_{EB} = \min\{7, 4+1\} = 5$$

S	A	B ✓	C	D	E	T
[0]	[4]	[5]	[2]	[4]	[4]	5

$$d_{BT} = \min\{5, 5+2\} = 5.$$

Now,

S	A	B	C	D	E	T ✓
[0]	[4]	[5]	[2]	[4]	[4]	[5]
[0]	[4]	[5]	[2]	[4]	[4]	[5]

Thus shortest path is 5 unit long

$$d_{ST} = d_{SC} + d_{CE} + d_{ET} = 5.$$

Above algorithm can also be explained by another technique.

Relaxation

For each vertex $v \varepsilon V$, $d[v]$ is an upper bound on the wt. of shortest path from S to v. We call $d[v]$ a shortest path estimate. We initialize the shortest path estimates and predecessors $\pi(v)$ by the following procedure

```
INITIALIZE-SINGLE-SOURCE (G, S)
   for each vertex v ε V[G]
         do d[v] ← ∞
               π[v] ← NIL
   d(S) ← 0
```

i.e., we have given label to each vertex with source vertex as 0 and all other vertex to ∞. We can define a method relax by modifying our previous eqn.

```
         min {old level of j, old label of i + dij}.
Let,           old label of j = d[v]
               old label of i = d[u].
                      dij = w(u, v)
   then our Relax method can be defined as

RELAX (u, v, w)
   if d(v) > d(u) + w(u, v)
         then d[v] ← d[u] + w(u, v)
               π[v] ← u.
```

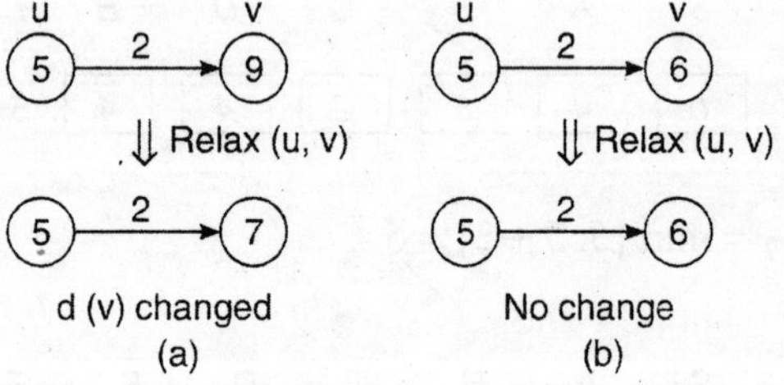

Fig. 29.2. (a) $d(v) > d(u) + w(u, v)$, i.e., $9 > 5 + 2$, hence $d(v)$ becomes 7
(b) $d(v) < d(u) + w(u, v)$, hence $d(v)$ remains same.

based on this concept we can rewrite the Dijkstra's algorithm in a proper way.

```
DIJKSTRA'S (G, w, S)
1. INITIALIZE-SINGLE-SOURCE (G, S)
2.       S ← ϕ
3.       Q ← V[G]
4.       while Q ≠ ϕ
```

```
do u ← EXTRACT-MIN (Q)
   S ← S ∪{u}
   for each vertex v ε Adj [u]
       do RELAX (u, v, w)
```

EXAMPLE 29.1. *Find the shortest path between S and y in the following directed graph.*

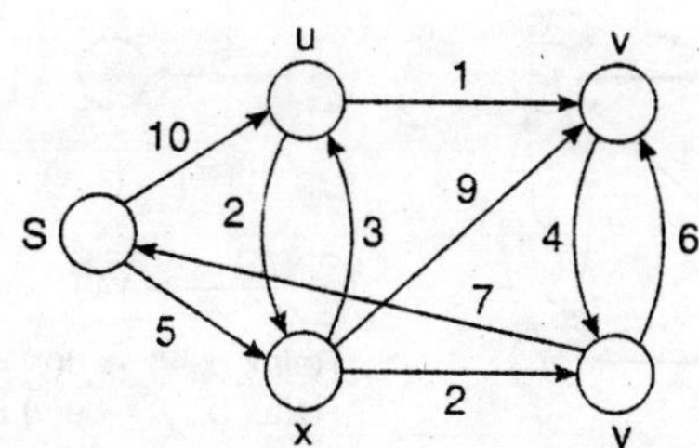

SOLUTION : Applying the above algorithm.

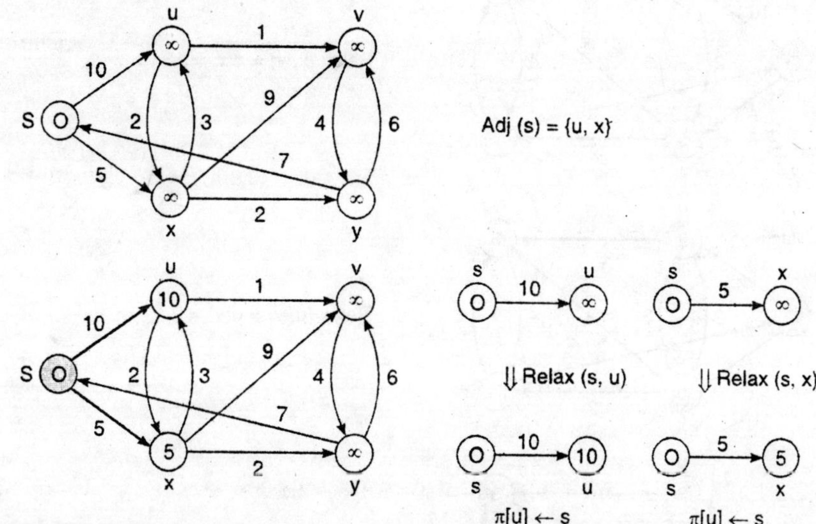

Minimum label among x and u is selected for new source.

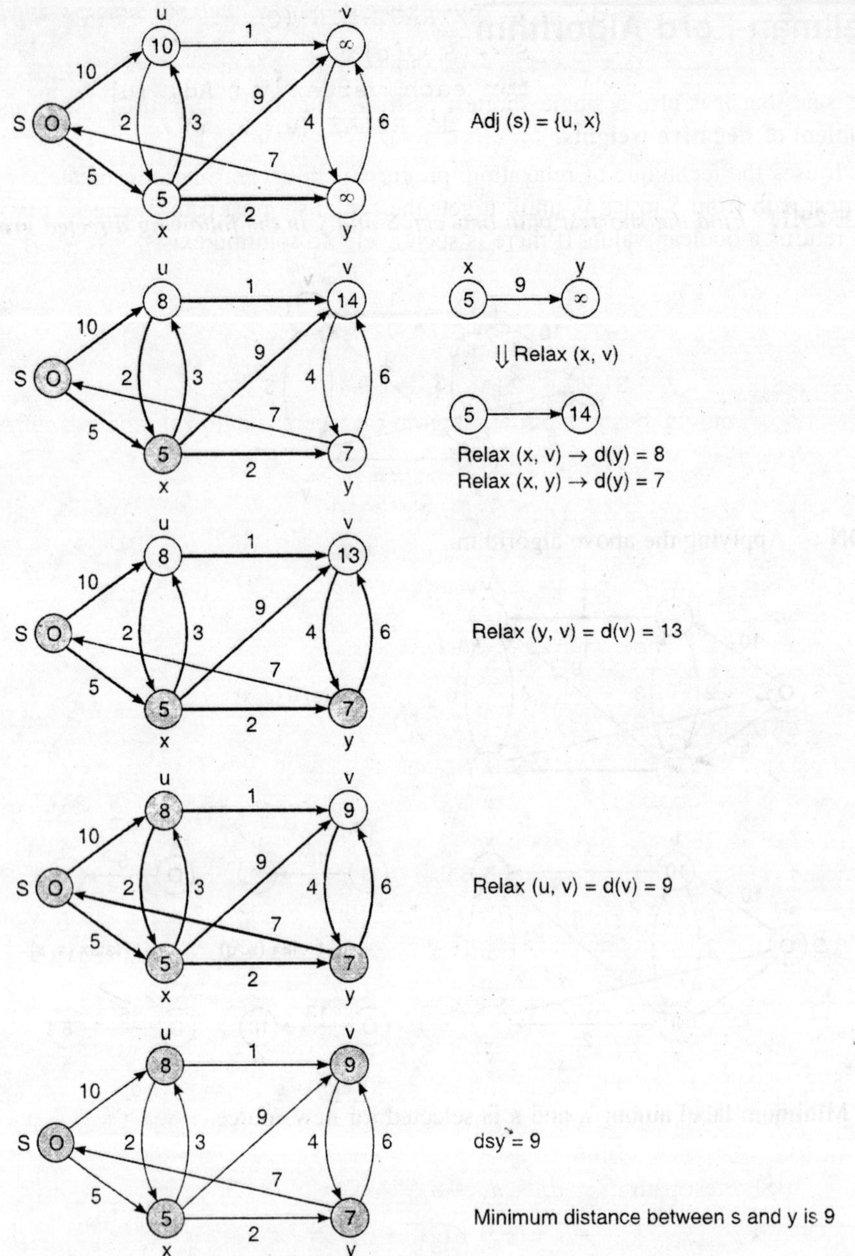

Running time of EXTRACT-MIN is $O(lg\ V)$, RELAX takes $O(lgV)$. Total running time is therefore, $O((V+E)\ 1gV)$ in the line 7 and 8 of Dijkstra's Algo.

29.2 Bellman-Ford Algorithm

It is said that it is also a single shortest path algorithm like Dijkstra's, but it also solves the **problem of negative weights.**

It uses the technique of relaxation, progressively decreasing an estimate $d[v]$ on wt. of a shortest path from S to $v \varepsilon V$, untill it gets the actual shortest path. It cheeks for –ve wt. cycle and returns a boolean value. If there is such cycle no solution exists.

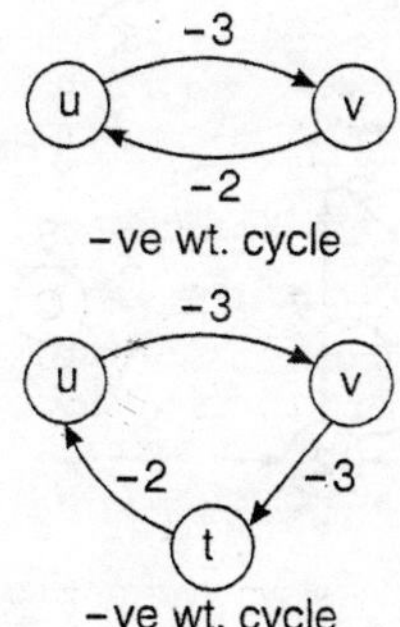

Fig. 29.3. Shows –ve wt. cycle.

```
BELLMAN-FORD (G, w, S)
1. INITIALIZE-SINGLE-SOURCE (G, S)
2.      for i ← 1 to V[G] - 1
3.           do for each edge (u, v) εE [G]
4.                do RELAX (u, v, w)
5.      for each edge (u, v) ε E [G]
6.           do if d[v] > d[u] + w(u, v)
7.                then return FALSE
8. return TRUE
```

line 5–7 check for –ve wt. cycle. It takes $O(E)$ time, line 1 takes $\theta(V)$ time. line 2–4 take $O(VE)$ time so running time of this algo is $O(VE)$. See Fig. 29.4 for execution of BELLMAN-FORD Algorithm.

Shortest path $d_{sy} = d_{sx} + d_{xv} + d_{vu} + d_{uy}$

$$= 7 + (-3) + (-2) + (-4) = -2$$

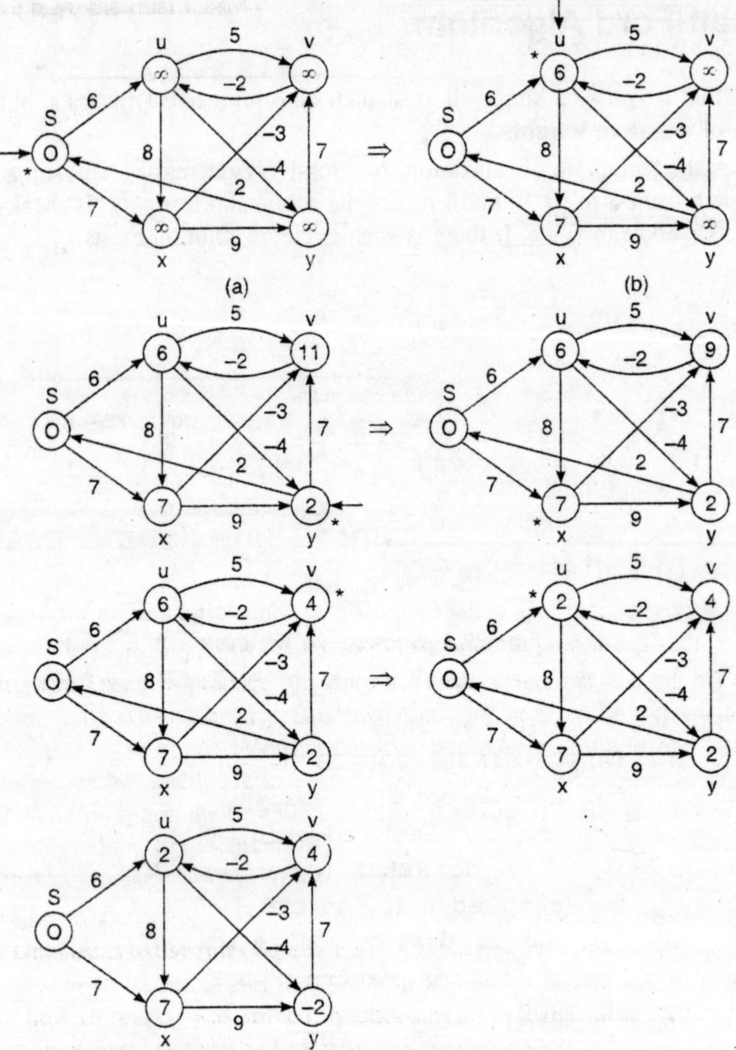

Fig. 29.4. *Shows execution of BELLMAN-FORD.*

which is label of *y*. We note here that we can come back to the node to find new label (e.g. *u* visited twice).

29.3 Shortest Path In Dag

Shortest paths are well defined in directed acyclic graph with –ve weights, as no –ve wt. cycle can exist. The vertices are topologically sorted and then RELAX is called.

```
DAG-SHORTEST-PATHS(G, W, S)
Topologically sort the vertices of G
```

```
INITIALIZE-SINGLE-SOURCE (G, S)
for each verex u taken in topologically sorted order
        do for each vertex v ε Adj [u]
              do RELAX (u, v, w)
```

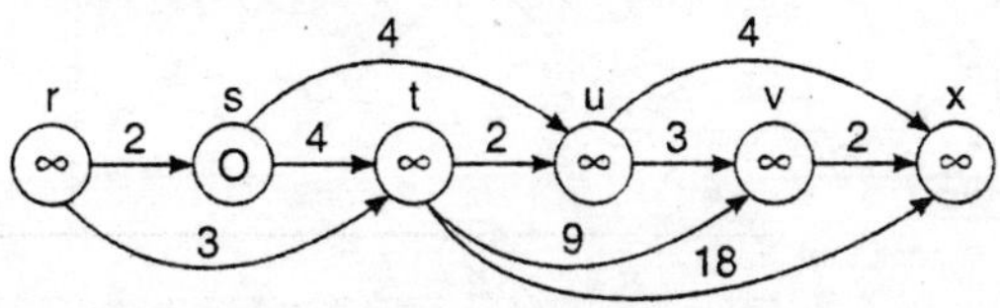

Fig. 29.5.

In above algo topological sort takes $\theta(V+E)$ time. INITIALIZE- SINGLE-SOURCE takes $\theta(V)$ time. So total running time of DAG- SHORTEST-PATH is $\theta(V+E)$

29.4 System of Difference Constraints

In this system each row of linear programming matrix A contains one 1 and one –1, and all other entries are A and O, and constraints are given by $Ax \leq b$.

$$[A][X] \leq [b]$$

EXAMPLE 29.2. *Consider the following greedy strategy for finding a shortest path from vertex start to vertex goal in a given connected graph.*

```
1: Initialize path to start.
2: Initialize VisitedVertices to {start}.
3: If start = goal, return path and exit. Otherwise,
                                              continue.
4: Find the edge (start, v) of minimum weight such
          that v is adjacent to start and v is not in
                                     VisitedVertices.
5: Add v to path.
6: Add v to VisistedVertices.
7: Set start equal to v and go to step 3.
```

Does this greedy strategy find a shortest from start to goal. Explain and give examples?

SOLUTION : The greedy algorithm presented in this problem is not guaranteed to find the shortest path between vertices in graph. This can be seen by counter example. Consider the following weighted graph :

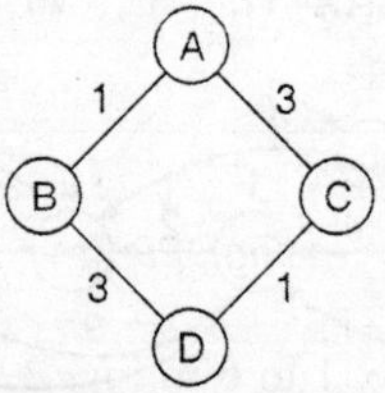

Suppose we with to find the shortest path from *start* = *A* to *goal* = *D* and we make use of the proposed greedy strategy. Starting at *A* and with *path* initialized to *A*, the algorithm will next place *B* in *path* (because (*A*, *B*) is the minimum cost edge incident on *A*) and set *start* equal to *B*. The lightest edge incident on *start* = *B* which has not yet been traversed is (*B*, *D*). As a result, *D* wil be appended to *path* and *start* will be assigned *D*. At this point the algorithm will terminate (since *start* = *goal* = *D*). (Note: in fact the algorithm is not guaranteed to find any path between two given nodes since it makes no provisions for backing up. In an appropriate situation, it will fail to halt.)

EXERCISE

1. Find the shortest path using Dijkstra's algo from *s* to *f* in the following graph.

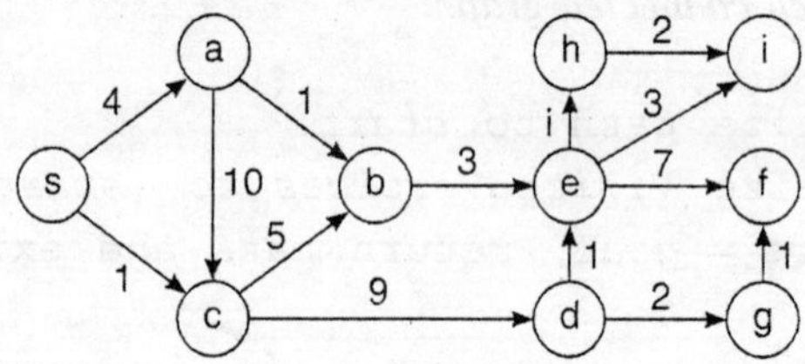

Fig. 29.6.

2. Run DAG-SHORTEST-PATHS for DAG of Fig. 29.5. With choosing *r* as source.
3. Give efficient algo to count the total no. of paths in DAG and give its running time.
4. Prove that if a sequence of relaxation steps set $\pi[S]$ to a non-NIL value, then *G* contains a negative weight cycle.
5. Discuss the Dijkstra's correction to algo given?
6. Dicuss the Bellman ford's correction?

7. Find shortest path using BELMAN FORD algo from S to f of following fig. 29.7.

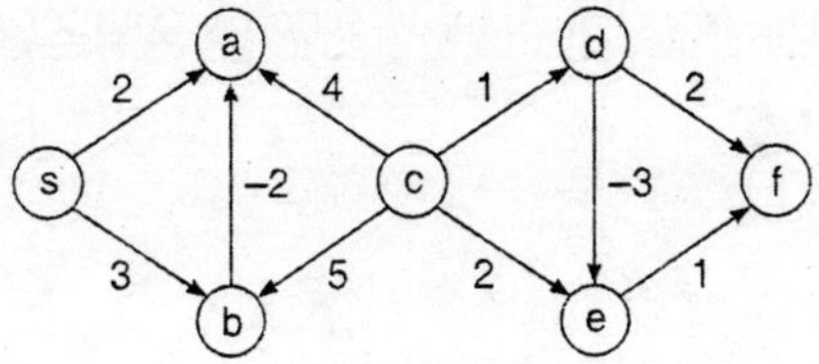

Fig. 29.7.

8. Find shortest path from vertex 1 to 6 in Fig. 29.8.

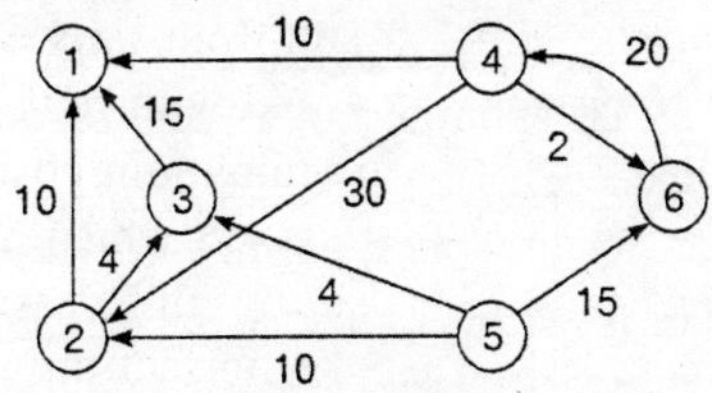

Fig. 29.8.

9. Consider the unsorted sequence implementation of the priority queue Q used in Dijkstra's algorithm. In this case, what is the best-case running time of Dijkstra's algorithm $\Omega(n^2)$ on an n-vertex graph?

Hint : Consider the size of Q each time the minimum element is extracted.

❑❑❑

30

ALL PAIR SHORTEST PATHS

30.1 Shortest Paths

If P is a path from vertex i to j containing m edges then if k is some intermediate vertex s.t. i to k contains at most $m - 1$ edges then

$$d[i, j] = d[i, k] + w_{k, j}$$

Fig. 30.1.

All pair shortest path is a problem of finding the shortest path from every vertex to every other vertex. It can be represented by adjacency matrix $w = (w_{ij})$. Using the above definition of intermediate vertices we can obtain a recurrence relation for finding the minimum cost from vertex i to j for m edges if it does not contain negative weight cycle.

$$d_{ij}^{(m)} = \min \left(d_{ij}^{(m-1)}, \min_{i \le k \le n} \{d_{ik}^{(m-1)} + w_{kj}\}\right)$$

$$= \min \{d_{ik}^{m-1} + w_{kj}\}, \; m \ge 1 \qquad \text{...(30.1)}$$

and also for $m = 0$, *i.e.* no edges

$$d_{ij}^{(0)} = \begin{cases} 0 & \text{if} \quad i = i \\ \infty & \text{if} \quad i \neq j \end{cases}$$

30.2 All Pairs Shortest Path : The Problem

Assumption : Given a directed, weighted graph $G = (V, E)$ with weight function $w : E \to \mathbf{R}$. Find shortest paths between all pairs of vertices in a graph.

Example : Make a table of distances between all pairs of cities for a road atlas.

What did we learn so far?

Single-source shortest-path algorithms :

- Dijkstra : $O(|V|^2)$
- Bellman-Ford : $O(|V|\,|E|)$.

All Pairs Shortest Path Algorithms

If $w : E \to \mathbf{R}_+$, we can run Dijkstra's single-path algorithm for every node $v \in |V|$

$\Rightarrow$ overall complexity : $O(|V|) \,.\, O(|V|^2) = O(|V|^3)$.

$w : E \to \mathbf{R}$, we can run Bellman-Ford single-path algorithm for every node $v \in |V|$

$\Rightarrow$ overall complexity : $O(|V|) \,.\, O(|V|\,|E|) = O(|V|^4)$.

Can we do better?

We assume given the adjacency marix of G with n nodes.

For all $i, j \in V$, we know

$$w_{i,j} = \begin{cases} 0 & \text{if } i = j \\ \text{weight of directed edge } (i, j) & \text{if } i \neq j \text{ and } (i, j) \in E \\ \infty & \text{if } i \neq j \text{ and } (i, j) \notin E \end{cases}$$

We want to compute :

- The $n \times n$ matrix $D = (d_{i,j})$ where every $d_{i,j}$ is the length of a shortest path from node i to node j.
- The predecessor matrix $\Pi = (\pi_{i,j})$ where

$$\pi_{i,j} = \begin{cases} nil & \text{if } i = j \text{ or there is no path from } i \text{ to } j \\ k & \text{if there exists a shortest path } i \to k \to j \text{ from } i \text{ to } j \end{cases}$$

Suppose we now predecessor matrix $\Pi = (\pi_{i,j})$.

For every $i \in V$, define the predecessor graph of G for i as follows :

$$G_{\pi,i} = (V_{\pi,i}, E_{\pi,i}), \text{ where}$$

- $V_{\pi,i} := \{j \in V \mid \pi_{i,j} \neq nil\} \cup \{i\}$
- $E_{\pi,i} := \{(\pi_{i,j}, j) \mid j \in V_{\pi,i} \text{ and } \pi_{i,j} \neq nil\}$

For all $i \in V$, $G_{\pi,i}$ is a shortest-path tree with root i.

The Structure of a Shortest Path

All subpaths of a shortest path are shortest paths.

Suppose $i \xrightarrow{p} j$ is a shortest path.

- if $i = j$ then p has weight 0 and no edges.
- if $i \neq j$ then p contains a finite number of edges, say $\leq m$ edges, and we can write $p = i \xrightarrow{p'} k \rightarrow j$, where p' is a path with $\leq m - 1$ edges. Note that : p' is a shortest path from i to $k \Rightarrow \delta(i, j) = \delta(i, k) + w_{k, j}$.

All Pairs Shortest Path Alogorithms

Let $d_{i,j}^{(m)}$:= minimum weight if any path from i to j, that contains $\leq m$ edges.

When $m = 0$, there is a shortest path from i to j with no edges if and only if $i = j$. Thus

$$d_{i,j}^{(m)} = \begin{cases} 0 & \text{if } i = j \\ \infty & \text{if } i \neq j \end{cases}$$

Recursive formula :

$$d_{i,j}^{(m)} = \min \left(d_{i,j}^{(m-1)}, \{d_{i,k}^{(m-1)} + w_{k,j}\}\right)$$
$$= \min_{1 \leq k \leq n} \{d_{i,k}^{(m-1)} + w_{k,j}\}$$

Note : The last equality holds because $w_{j,j} = 0$ for all j.

30.3 Shortest Path Weights

EXAMPLE 30.1. *How to compute the shortest path weights $\delta_{i,j}$ for all nodes $i, j \in V$?*

SOLUTION : If the graph contains no negative-weight cycles then

- All shortest paths are simple and this contain at most $n - 1$ edges.
- A path from i to j with more than $n - 1$ edges can not have less weight than a shortest path from i to j.

$$\Rightarrow \quad \delta_{i,j} = \delta_{i,j}^{(n-1)} = \delta_{i,j}^{(n)} = \ldots$$

Given input matrix $W = (w_{i,j})$

Compute the series of matrices $D^{(1)}, \ldots, D^{(n-1)}$ where for

$$1 \leq m < n, \text{ we have } D^{(m)} = (\delta_{i,j}^{(m)})$$

Since $d_{i,j}^{(1)} = w_{i,j}$ for all $i, j \in V$, we have $D^{(1)} = W$.

Extend-Shortest Paths (D, W) is supposed to take the following arguments :

- $D = D^{(m-1)}$.

- The weight matrix W of the graph
  and will return $D^{(m)}$.

```
Extend-Shortest-Paths(D, W)
n ← rows[D]
let D' = (d'ij) be an n × n matrix
for i ← 1 to n
     do for j ← 1 to n
          do d'ij ← ∞
               for k ← 1 to n
                    do d'ij ← min(d'ij, dik + wkj)
return D'
```

Complexity = $\Theta(n^3)$ – due to the three nested for loops.
If A, B are $n \times n$ matrices and $C = (c_{i,j}) = A \,.\, B$ then

$$c_{i,j} = \sum_{k=1}^{n} a_{i,k} \cdot b_{k,j}$$

The matrix multiplication formula is equivalent with the recursive formula for $d^{(m)}$, if we do the following changes :

$$d^{(m-1)} \leftrightarrow a$$

$$w \leftrightarrow b$$

$$d^{(m)} \leftrightarrow c$$

$$\min \leftrightarrow +$$

$$+ \leftrightarrow .$$

Based on the previous observation, we get the following matrix multiplication algorithm by changing **Extend-Shortest-Paths** :

```
Matrix-Multiply(A, B)
n ← rows[A]
let C be an n × n matrix
for i ← 1 to n
     do for j ← 1 to n
          do cij ← 0
               for k ← 1 to n
                    do cij ← cij + aik . bkj
return C
```

Time complexity of **Matrix-Multiply** : $\Theta(n^3)$.

If we write $A \,.\, B$ instead of **Extend-Shortest-Paths(A, B)**, we compute

Computation	***Time complexity***
$D^{(1)} = D^{(0)} \,.\, W = W$	$\Theta(n^3)$
$D^{(2)} = D^{(1)} \,.\, W = W^2$	$\Theta(n^3)$
$\vdots$	
$D^{(n-1)} = D^{(n-2)} \,.\, W = W^{n-1}$	$\Theta(n^3)$

In the end, W^{n-1} contains the shortest-path weights of all pairs of nodes.

Total time complexity : $n \,.\, \Theta(n^3) = \Theta(n^4)$ time.

```
Slow-All-Pairs-Shortest-Paths(W)
n ← rows[W]
D^(1) ← W
for m ← 2 to n - 1
        do D^(m) ← Extend-Shortest-Paths(D^(m - 1), W)
return D^(n - 1)
```

The computtation of $D^{(n-1)}$ can be improved if we use the method of repeated squaring :

```
Faster-All-Pairs-Shortest-Paths(W)
n ← rows[W]
D^(1) ← W
m ← 1
while n - 1 > m
        do D^(2m) ← Extend-Shortest-Paths(D^(m), D^(m))
               m ← 2m
return D^(m)
```

Total time complexity : $[\log_2 (n-1)] \,.\, \Theta(n^3) = \Theta(n^3 \,.\, [\log_2 (n-1)])$.

The Bottom-up Approach with Repeated Squaring

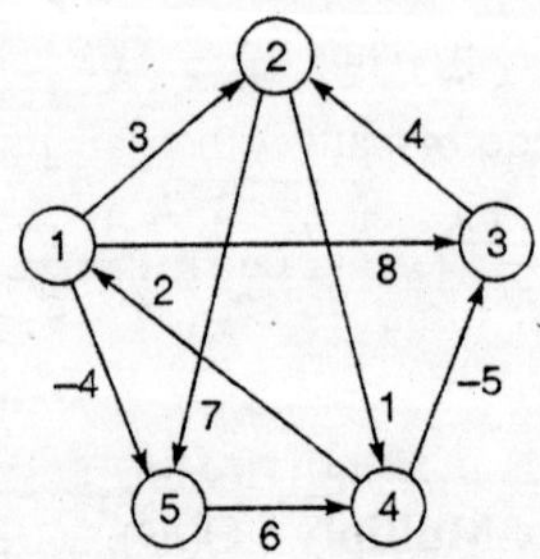

$$D^{(1)} = \begin{pmatrix} 0 & 3 & 8 & \infty & -4 \\ \infty & 0 & \infty & 1 & 7 \\ \infty & 4 & 0 & \infty & \infty \\ 2 & \infty & -5 & 0 & \infty \\ \infty & \infty & \infty & 6 & 0 \end{pmatrix} \qquad D^{(2)} = \begin{pmatrix} 0 & 3 & 8 & 2 & -4 \\ 3 & 0 & -4 & 1 & 7 \\ \infty & 4 & 0 & 5 & 11 \\ 2 & -1 & -5 & 0 & -2 \\ 8 & \infty & 1 & 6 & 0 \end{pmatrix}$$

$$D^{(3)} = \begin{pmatrix} 0 & 3 & -3 & 2 & -4 \\ 3 & 0 & -4 & 1 & -1 \\ 7 & 4 & 0 & 5 & 11 \\ 2 & -1 & -5 & 0 & -2 \\ 8 & 5 & 1 & 6 & 0 \end{pmatrix} \qquad D^{(4)} = \begin{pmatrix} 0 & 1 & -3 & 2 & -4 \\ 3 & 0 & -4 & 1 & -1 \\ 7 & 4 & 0 & 5 & 3 \\ 2 & -1 & -5 & 0 & -2 \\ 8 & 5 & 1 & 6 & 0 \end{pmatrix}$$

30.4 The Floyd-Warshall Algorithm

Assumption : Weights are positive (that is, $E \to \mathbf{R}_+$).

An intermediate node of a simple path $p = (v_1, v_2, \ldots, v_{l-1}, v_l)$ is any node $v \in \{v_2, v_3, \ldots, v_{l-1}\}$.

The Floyd-Warshall algorithm is based on the following observation :

- Assume $V = \{1, 2, \ldots n\}$. For all $i, j \in V$ consider all paths from i to j whose intermediate vertices are from $\{1, \ldots, k\}$. Let $i \xrightarrow{p} j$ be such a minimal-length path from i to j, and let $d_{i,j}^{(k)}$ be its length.
- $d_{i,j}^{(k)}$ can be computed by recursion on k.

If k is an intermediate node of path p, we have $i \xrightarrow{p_1} l \xrightarrow{p_2} j$:

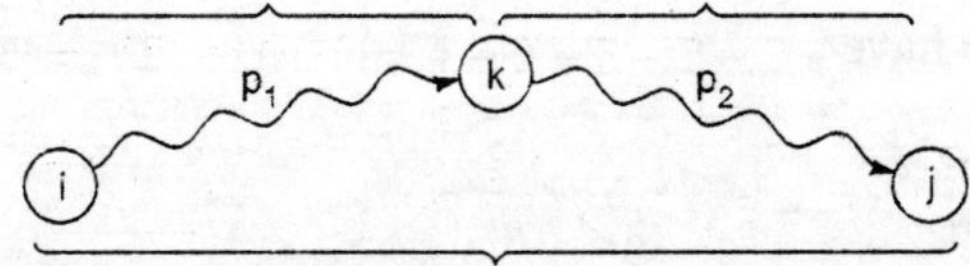

where p_1 is shortest path from i to k through nodes $\{1, \ldots k-1\}$, and p_2 is shortest path from k to j through nodes $\{1, \ldots, k-1\}$. Thus $d_{i,j}^{(k)} = d_{i,k}^{(k-1)} + d_{k,j}^{(k-1)}$.

If j is not intermediate node of path p then all intermediate nodes of p are from $\{1, \ldots, k-1\}$, thus $d_{i,j}^{(k)} = d_{i,j}^{(k-1)}$.

A recursive definition of $d_{i,j}^{(k)}$:

$$d_{i,j}^{(k)} := \begin{cases} w_{i,j} & k\ k = 0, \\ \min\,(d_{i,j}^{(k-1)}, d_{i,k}^{(k-1)} + d_{k,j}^{(k-1)}) & \text{if } k \geq 1. \end{cases}$$

$d_{i,j}^{(n)}$ is the weight of shortest path from i to j for all $i, j \in V$.

$\Rightarrow$ we wish to compute the $n \times n$ matrix $D^{(n)} = (d_{i,j}^{(n)})$.

Computes the values of $d_{i,j}^{(k)}$ in order of increasing values of k.

```
Floyd-Warshall(W)
1 n ← rows[W]
2 D^(0) ← W
3 for k ← 1 to n
4       do for i ← 1 to n
5            do for j ← 1 to n
6                 d_ij^(k) ← min (d_i,j^(k-1), d_i,k^(k-1) + d_k,j^(k-1))
7 return D^(n)
```

Running time complexity :

- There are 3 nested loops (lines 3-6)
- The execution time of line 6 takes $O(1)$ time

$\Rightarrow \Theta(n^3)$ time complexity.

The predecessor matrix Π can be computed incrementally, via a sequence of matrices

$$\Pi^{(0)}, \Pi^{(1)}, \ldots, \Pi^{(n)}$$

where $\Pi = \Pi^{(n)}$ and $\pi_{i,j}^{(k)}$ is the predecessor of vertex j on a shortest path from vertex i with all intermediate nodes in the set $\{1, 2, \ldots, k\}$.

Formally, we have

$$\pi_{i,j}^{(0)} = \begin{cases} nil & \text{if } i = j \text{ or } w_{i,j} = \infty, \\ i & \text{if } i \neq j \text{ and } w_{i,j} < \infty \end{cases}$$

$$\pi_{i,j}^{k+1} \begin{cases} \pi_{i,j}^{(k-1)} & \text{if } d_{i,j}^{(k-1)} \leq \text{if } d_{i,k}^{(k-1)} + \text{if } d_{k,j}^{(k-1)} \\ \pi_{k,j}^{(k-1)} & \text{if } d_{i,j}^{(k-1)} > \text{if } d_{i,k}^{(k-1)} + \text{if } d_{k,j}^{(k-1)} \end{cases}$$

For the graph we have

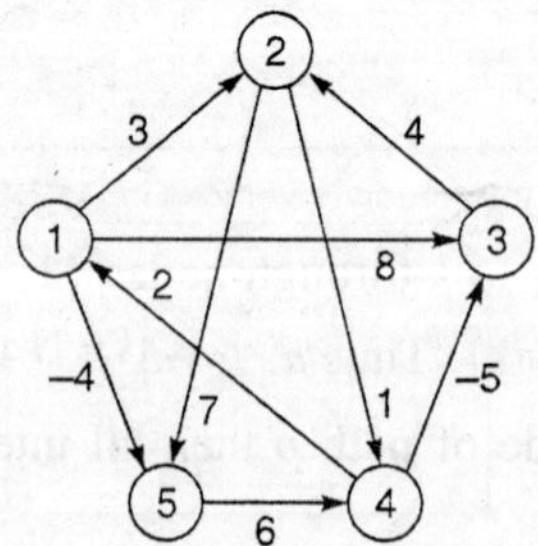

$$D^{(0)} = \begin{pmatrix} 0 & 3 & 8 & \infty & -4 \\ \infty & 0 & \infty & 1 & 7 \\ \infty & 4 & 0 & \infty & \infty \\ 2 & \infty & -5 & 0 & \infty \\ \infty & \infty & \infty & 6 & 0 \end{pmatrix} \qquad \Pi^{(0)} = \begin{pmatrix} \text{NIL} & 1 & 1 & \text{NIL} & 1 \\ \text{NIL} & \text{NIL} & \text{NIL} & 2 & 2 \\ \text{NIL} & 3 & \text{NIL} & \text{NIL} & \text{NIL} \\ 4 & \text{NIL} & 4 & \text{NIL} & \text{NIL} \\ \text{NIL} & \text{NIL} & \text{NIL} & 5 & \text{NIL} \end{pmatrix}$$

$$D^{(1)} = \begin{pmatrix} 0 & 3 & 8 & \infty & -4 \\ \infty & 0 & \infty & 1 & 7 \\ \infty & 4 & 0 & \infty & \infty \\ 2 & 5 & -5 & 0 & -2 \\ \infty & \infty & \infty & 6 & 0 \end{pmatrix} \qquad \Pi^{(1)} = \begin{pmatrix} \text{NIL} & 1 & 1 & \text{NIL} & 1 \\ \text{NIL} & \text{NIL} & \text{NIL} & 2 & 2 \\ \text{NIL} & 3 & \text{NIL} & \text{NIL} & \text{NIL} \\ 4 & 1 & 4 & \text{NIL} & 1 \\ \text{NIL} & \text{NIL} & \text{NIL} & 5 & \text{NIL} \end{pmatrix}$$

$$D^{(2)} = \begin{pmatrix} 0 & 3 & 8 & 4 & -4 \\ \infty & 0 & \infty & 1 & 7 \\ \infty & 4 & 0 & 5 & 11 \\ 2 & 5 & -5 & 0 & -2 \\ \infty & \infty & \infty & 6 & 0 \end{pmatrix} \qquad \Pi^{(2)} = \begin{pmatrix} \text{NIL} & 1 & 1 & 2 & 1 \\ \text{NIL} & \text{NIL} & \text{NIL} & 2 & 2 \\ \text{NIL} & 3 & \text{NIL} & 2 & 2 \\ 4 & 1 & 4 & \text{NIL} & 1 \\ \text{NIL} & \text{NIL} & \text{NIL} & 5 & \text{NIL} \end{pmatrix}$$

$$D^{(3)} = \begin{pmatrix} 0 & 3 & 8 & 4 & -4 \\ \infty & 0 & \infty & 1 & 7 \\ \infty & 4 & 0 & 5 & 11 \\ 2 & -1 & -5 & 0 & 2 \\ \infty & \infty & \infty & 6 & 0 \end{pmatrix} \qquad \Pi^{(3)} = \begin{pmatrix} \text{NIL} & 1 & 1 & 2 & 1 \\ \text{NIL} & \text{NIL} & \text{NIL} & 2 & 2 \\ \text{NIL} & 3 & \text{NIL} & 2 & 2 \\ 4 & 3 & 4 & \text{NIL} & 1 \\ \text{NIL} & \text{NIL} & \text{NIL} & 5 & \text{NIL} \end{pmatrix}$$

$$D^{(4)} = \begin{pmatrix} 0 & 3 & -1 & 4 & -4 \\ 3 & 0 & -4 & 1 & -1 \\ 7 & 4 & 0 & 5 & 3 \\ 2 & -1 & -5 & 0 & -2 \\ 8 & 5 & 1 & 6 & 0 \end{pmatrix} \qquad \Pi^{(4)} = \begin{pmatrix} \text{NIL} & 1 & 4 & 2 & 1 \\ 4 & \text{NIL} & 4 & 2 & 1 \\ 4 & 3 & \text{NIL} & 2 & 1 \\ 4 & 3 & 4 & \text{NIL} & 1 \\ 4 & 3 & 4 & 5 & \text{NIL} \end{pmatrix}$$

$$D^{(5)} = \begin{pmatrix} 0 & 1 & -3 & 2 & -4 \\ 3 & 0 & -4 & 1 & -1 \\ 7 & 4 & 0 & 5 & 3 \\ 2 & -1 & -5 & 0 & -2 \\ 8 & 5 & 1 & 6 & 0 \end{pmatrix} \qquad \Pi^{(5)} = \begin{pmatrix} \text{NIL} & 3 & 4 & 5 & 1 \\ 4 & \text{NIL} & 4 & 2 & 1 \\ 4 & 3 & \text{NIL} & 2 & 1 \\ 4 & 3 & 4 & \text{NIL} & 1 \\ 4 & 3 & 4 & 5 & \text{NIL} \end{pmatrix}$$

Example :

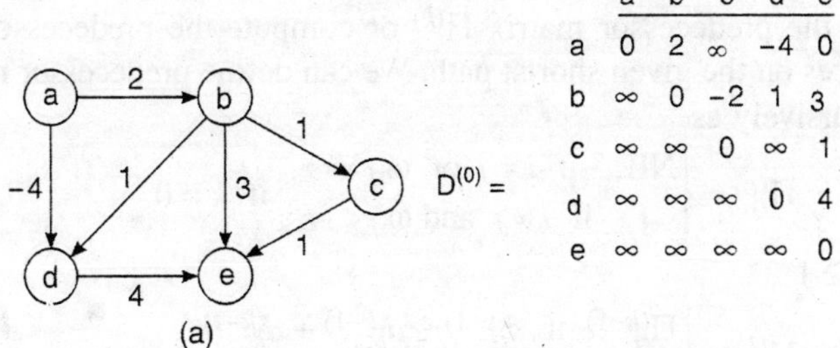

(a)

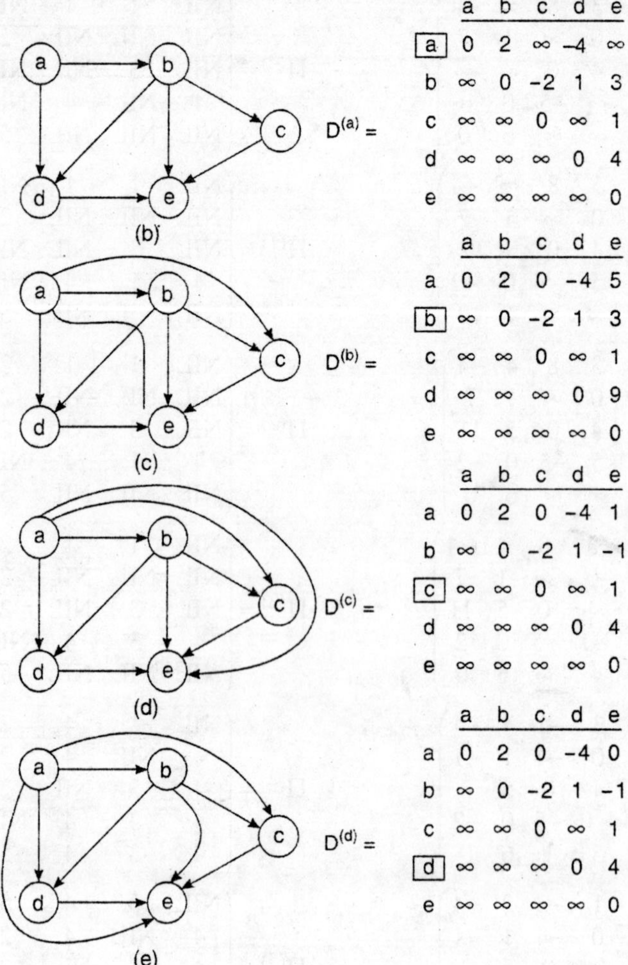

$D^{(a)} =$

	a	b	c	d	e
a	0	2	∞	–4	∞
b	∞	0	-2	1	3
c	∞	∞	0	∞	1
d	∞	∞	∞	0	4
e	∞	∞	∞	∞	0

$D^{(b)} =$

	a	b	c	d	e
a	0	2	0	-4	5
b	∞	0	-2	1	3
c	∞	∞	0	∞	1
d	∞	∞	∞	0	9
e	∞	∞	∞	∞	0

$D^{(c)} =$

	a	b	c	d	e
a	0	2	0	-4	1
b	∞	0	-2	1	-1
c	∞	∞	0	∞	1
d	∞	∞	∞	0	4
e	∞	∞	∞	∞	0

$D^{(d)} =$

	a	b	c	d	e
a	0	2	0	-4	0
b	∞	0	-2	1	-1
c	∞	∞	0	∞	1
d	∞	∞	∞	0	4
e	∞	∞	∞	∞	0

Fig. 30.2. Floyd-Warshall Algorithm

Running time is $\theta(V)^3$ or $\theta(n^3)$.

We can compute the shortest path either by computing $D^{(K)}$ using above algorithm and then compute the predecessor matrix $\Pi^{(k)}$ or compute the predecessor matrix first and then print the vertices on the given shortst path. We can define predecessor matrix in floyd warshall algorithm recursively as,

$$\Pi_{ij}^{(o)} = \begin{cases} \text{NIL} & \text{if } i = j \text{ or } \omega_{ij} = \infty \\ i & \text{if } i \neq j \text{ and } \omega_{ij} < \infty \end{cases}, \text{ if } k = 0 \qquad \text{...(30.2)}$$

and for $k \geq 1$

$$\Pi_{ij}^{(k)} = \begin{cases} \Pi_{ij}^{(k-1)} & \text{if } d_{ij}^{(k-1)} \leq d_{ik}^{(k-1)} + d_{kj}^{(k-1)} \\ \Pi_{kj}^{(k-1)} & \text{if } d_{ij}^{(k-1)} > d_{ik}^{(k-1)} + d_{kj}^{(k-1)} \end{cases} \qquad \text{...(30.3)}$$

See Fig. 30.3 for illustration of above algorithm.

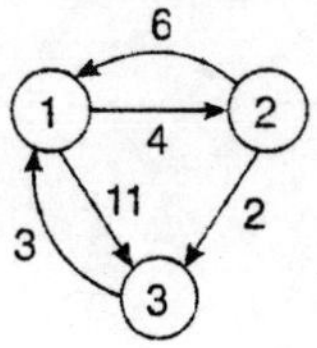

$$D^{(0)} = \begin{bmatrix} 0 & 4 & 11 \\ 6 & 0 & 2 \\ 3 & \infty & 0 \end{bmatrix} D^{(1)} = \begin{bmatrix} 0 & 4 & 11 \\ 6 & 0 & 2 \\ 3 & 7 & 0 \end{bmatrix}$$

$$D^{(3-)} = \begin{bmatrix} 0 & 4 & 6 \\ 6 & 0 & 2 \\ 3 & 7 & 0 \end{bmatrix} D^{(3)} = \begin{bmatrix} 0 & 4 & 6 \\ 5 & 0 & 2 \\ 3 & 7 & 0 \end{bmatrix}$$

(a) *(b)*

Fig. 30.3. (a) Shows directed graph
(b) it shows matrix $D^{(m)}$ computed by FW Algorithm.

Refering Fig. 30.3 we can trace the FLOYD WARSHALL algorithm for D and Π matrix as follows we have

$$D^0 = \begin{bmatrix} 0 & 4 & 11 \\ 6 & 0 & 2 \\ 3 & \infty & 0 \end{bmatrix} \Pi^{(0)} = \begin{bmatrix} \text{NIL} & 1 & 1 \\ 2 & \text{NIL} & 2 \\ 3 & 3 & \text{NIL} \end{bmatrix}$$

applying FLOYD-WARSHALL FORMULA $d_{ij}^{(k)} = \min\,[d_{ij}^{(k-1)}, d_{ik}^{(k-1)} + d_{kj}^{(k-1)}]$ we calculate D^k and applying eqn. 30.3 we calculate $\Pi^{(k)}$, the predecessor matrix as follows.

k	i	j	$d_{ij}^{(k-1)}$	$d_{ik}^{(k-1)}$	$d_{kj}^{(k-1)}$	d_{ij}^{k}	$\Pi_{ij}^{(k-1)}$	$\Pi_{kj}^{(k-1)}$	$\Pi_{ij}^{(k)}$
1	1	1	0	0	0	0	NIL	NIL	NIL
		2	4	0	4	4	1	1	1
		3	11	0	11	11	1	1	1
	2	1	6	6	0	6	2	2	2
		2	0	6	4	0	NIL	1	NIL
		3	2	2	1	2	2	1	2
	3	1	3	3	0	3	3	NIL	3
		2	∞	6	1	7	3	1	1
		3	0	3	1	0	NIL	1	NIL
									$(d_{ik} + d_{kj})$

thus we have $D^{(1)}$ and $\Pi^{(1)}$ from d_{ij}^k and Π_{ij}^k where $k = 1$

$$D^{(1)} = \begin{bmatrix} 0 & 4 & 11 \\ 6 & 0 & 2 \\ 3 & 7 & 0 \end{bmatrix} \Pi^{(k)} = \begin{bmatrix} \text{NIL} & 1 & 1 \\ 2 & \text{NIL} & 2 \\ 3 & 1 & \text{NIL} \end{bmatrix}$$

this way we can compute other D and Π matrices.

Cycle detection : This algorithm also allows us to detect cycles if the diagonals is initilied to ∞ and not to zero. If any of the diagonal values are changed then graph contains a cycle.

EXAMPLE 30.2. *Find the shortest path using Floyd-Warshal Algorithm.*

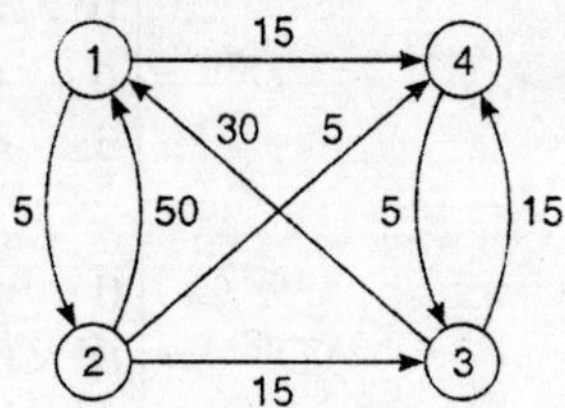

SOLUTION :

$$D^{(0)} = \begin{array}{c|cccc} & 1 & 2 & 3 & 4 \\ \hline 1 & 0 & 5 & \infty & \infty \\ 2 & 50 & 0 & 15 & 5 \\ 3 & 30 & \infty & 0 & 15 \\ 4 & 15 & \infty & 5 & 0 \end{array}$$

$$D^{(1)} = \begin{array}{c|cccc} & 1 & 2 & 3 & 4 \\ \hline 1 & 0 & 5 & \infty & \infty \\ 2 & 50 & 0 & 15 & 5 \\ 3 & 30 & 35 & 0 & 5 \\ 4 & 15 & 20 & 5 & 0 \end{array} \qquad D^{(2)} = \begin{array}{c|cccc} & 1 & 2 & 3 & 4 \\ \hline 1 & 0 & 5 & 20 & 10 \\ 2 & 50 & 0 & 15 & 5 \\ 3 & 30 & 35 & 0 & 15 \\ 4 & 15 & 20 & 5 & 0 \end{array}$$

$$D^{(3)} = \begin{array}{c|cccc} & 1 & 2 & 3 & 4 \\ \hline 1 & 0 & 5 & 20 & 10 \\ 2 & 45 & 0 & 15 & 5 \\ 3 & 30 & 35 & 0 & 15 \\ 4 & 15 & 20 & 5 & 0 \end{array} \qquad D^{(4)} = \begin{array}{c|cccc} & 1 & 2 & 3 & 4 \\ \hline 1 & 0 & 5 & 15 & 10 \\ 2 & 20 & 0 & 10 & 5 \\ 3 & 30 & 35 & 0 & 15 \\ 4 & 15 & 20 & 5 & 0 \end{array}$$

30.5 The Transitive Closure of a Directed Graph

The transitive closure of a directed graph $G = (V, E)$ with vertex set $V = \{1, 2, \ldots, n\}$ is the directed graph $G^* = (V, E^*)$ where

$$E^* = \{(i, j) \mid \text{there exist a path from } i \text{ to } j \text{ in } G\}$$

Floyd-Warshall algorithm can compute G^* in $\Theta(n^3)$ time :

Assign a weight 1 to each edge of E

$\Rightarrow$ there is a path from i to j off $d_{i,j} < n$.

There is a similar way to compute G^* in $\Theta(n^3)$ time that can save time and space in practice :

$$t_{i,j}^{(0)} := \begin{cases} 0 & \text{if } i \neq j \text{ and } (i, j) \notin E, \\ 1 & \text{if } i = j \text{ or } (i, j) \in E \end{cases}$$

and for $k \geq 1 : t_{i,j}^{(k)} := t_{i,j}^{(k-1)} \vee (t_{i,k}^{(k-1)} \wedge t_{k,j}^{(k-1)})$.

```
Transitive-Closure(G)
n ← |V[G]|
for i ← 1 to n
      do for j ← 1 to n
            do if i = j or (i, j) ∈ E[G]
                  then t_ij^(0) ← 1
                  else t_ij^(0) ← 0
for k ← 1 to n
      do for i ← 1 to n
            do for j ← 1 to n
                  do t_{i,j}^(k) := t_{i,j}^(k-1) ∨ (t_{i,k}^(k-1) ∧ t_{k,j}^(k-1))
return T^(n)
```

This procedure requires $\Theta(n^3)$ space.

Reducing the Space Complexity

```
Floyd-Warshall'(W)
n ← rows[W]
D ← W
for k ← 1 to n
      do for i ← 1 to n
            do for j ← 1 to n
                  d_ij ← min (d_ij, d_ik + d_kj)
return D
```

This procedure requires only $\Theta(n^2)$ space.

Homeworks

(1) Why do we require $w_{i,i} = 0$ for all $1 \le i \le n$?

(2) Implement the Floyd-Warshall algorithm. Suppose the graph is written from a text file with the structure

$$\begin{array}{ccc} n & & \\ i_1 & j_1 & w_1 \\ i_2 & j_2 & w_2 \\ \ldots & & \end{array}$$

where n is the number of nodes of the graph, and every line

$$i_k \quad j_k \quad w_k$$

indicates that the weight of edge (i_k, j_k) is w_k.

(3) Run the Floyd-Warshall algorithm for the directed graph

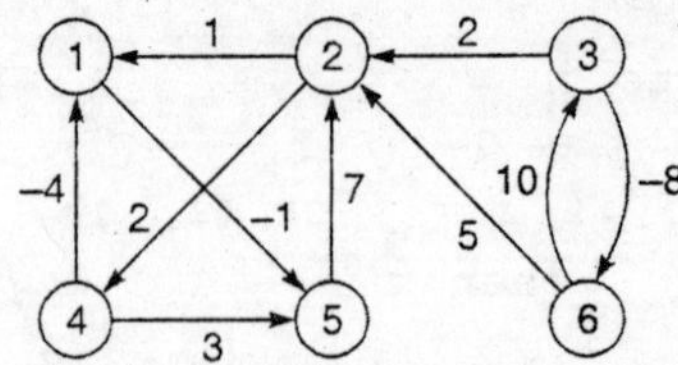

Adjust the implementation to display the values of the matrices $D^{(k)}$ that are being computed.

(4) Implement the **Transitive-Closure** algorithm presented in the lecture, and adjust it to run on tghe directed graph from the previous exercise, and to print the matrix T for transitive closure.

EXAMPLE 30.3. *For the following graph find the $D^{(0)}$ matrix and comment on d_{13} entry.*

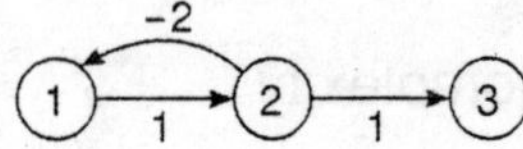

SOLUTION : We have

$$D^{(0)} = \begin{bmatrix} 0 & 1 & \infty \\ -2 & 0 & 1 \\ \infty & \infty & 0 \end{bmatrix} \text{ as } D = \{d_{ij}\}$$

here $d_{13} = \infty$ but according to formula = min $(d_{ij}{}^{m-1} + (d_{ik}{}^{m-1} + w_{kj})) = 2$

but in matrix D^0, $d_{13} = \infty$

This is because of negative weight cycle, we have $d_{12} = -1$. and it becomes more negative as it goes in loop so $d_{12} = -\infty$ thus min $(d_{13}, d_{12} + w_{23})$ becomes ∞.

30.6 Johnson's Algorithmn For Sparse Graph

Its makes use of **Dijkstra's** algorithm and **Bellman Ford algorithm** as subroutine depending upon whether the graph contains a negative weight cycle or not. It works on the principle of **reweighting.** If it has no negative *wt.* cycle then Dijkstra algorithm is run once for each pair of vertices but if it has negative weight cycle then new weight $\hat{w}$ must satisfy following properties :

(i) For all pair of vertices (u, v), a shortest path from u to v using weight function w is also the shortest path from u to v using weight function $\hat{w}$.

(ii) For all edges (u, v), the new weight $\hat{w}(u, v)$ is non negative. we have **reweighting** or new weight $\hat{w}(u, v)$ calculated as

$$\hat{w}(u, v) = w(u, v) + h(u) - h(v) \qquad \ldots(30.4)$$

$$h(u) \leftarrow \text{label of } u,\ h(v) \leftarrow \text{label of } v,\ \partial(u, v) = duv$$

```
JOHNSON (G)
Compute G′,
   where V{G′] = V[G] ∪ {S}
         E[G′] = E[G] ∪ {(S, v) : v ∈ V [G]},
   and W(S, V) = 0 For all v ∈ V[G]
If BELLMAN-FORD (G′, w, s) does not contain negative wt,
                                                         cycle
      for each vertex v ε V [G′]
            do h(v) ← δ(s, v)
                  computed by Bellman-Ford Algorithm.
      for each edge (u, v) ∈ E[G′]
            do Ŵ (u, v) = W(u, v) + h(u) − h(v)
      for each vertex u ∈ V[G]
            Call Dijkstra (G, Ŵ, u) to compute δ̂ (u, v)
                  for each vertex v ε V[G]
                        do duv = δ̂ (u, v) + h(v) − h(u)
      return D
```

Johnson's Algorithm uses the technique of weighting which work as follows :

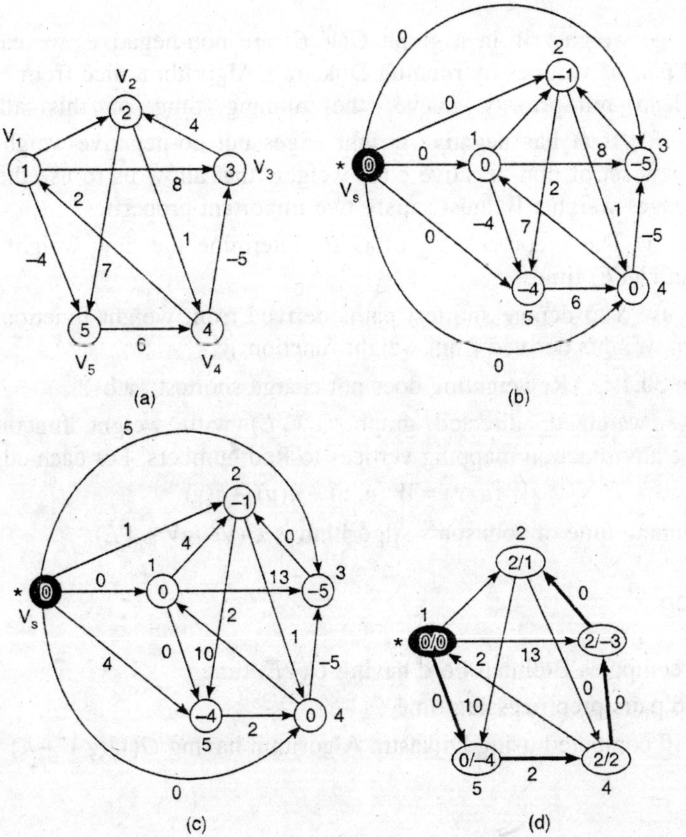

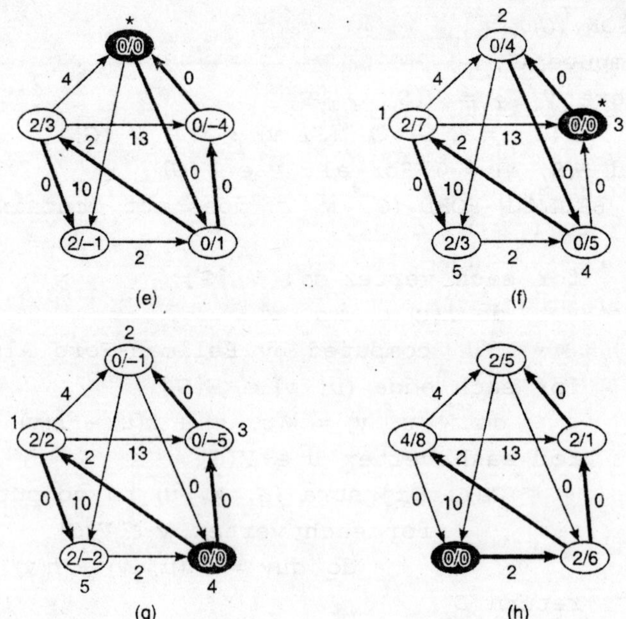

Fig. 30.4. Each vertex v contains values $\hat{\delta}(u, v)$ *and* $\delta(u, v)$*, gray shade shows the current source node of graph.*

If all edge weights W in a graph $G(V, E)$ are non-negative, we can find shortest-path between all pair of vertices by running Dijkstra's Algorithm once from each vertex; with the Fibonacci-Heap min-priority queue, the running time of this all-pair algorithm is $O(V^2 \lg V + VE)$. If G has negative-weight edges but no-negative-weight cycles, we simply compute a new set of non-negative edge weights that allow us to use the some method. The new set of edges weights $\hat{W}$ must satisfy two important properties.

Note : (i) The preprocessing of G to determine the new weight function $\hat{W}$ can be performed in $O(VE)$ time.

(ii) We use S to denote shortest paths derived from weight function W and $\hat{S}$ to denote shortest-path weights derived from weight function $\hat{W}$.

Lemma 30.1 : (Reweighting does not charge shortest paths)

Given a weighted, directed graph $G(V, E)$ with weight function $W : E \rightarrow R$. Let $h : V \rightarrow R$ be any function mapping vertices to Red numbers. For each edge $(u, v) \in$, define

$$\hat{W}(u, v) = W(u, v) + h(u) - h(v)$$

The Running time of Johnson's Algorithm is $O(V^2 \lg V + VE)$.

Calculation

Line 1 to 5 computes Bellman-Ford having $O(VE)$ time

Line 5-6 pairs preprocessing time $O(VE)$

Line 7-10 computed using Dijkastra Algorithm having $O(V \lg V + E)$

Hence $V[(V \log V + E) + V] = V^2 \lg V + EV + V^2$

$$= V^2 (\log V + 1) + EV$$

$O(EV) + O(EV) + O\,(V^2 (\log V + 1) + EV)$

Total running time will be $= O\,(V^2 \lg V + EV)$

Starting from Fig. (a), we get

e.g. fig. (b) Graph $G' = G(V, E) \cup \{S\}$

and set $w(S, v) = 0$ for all $v \in V[G]$

Now Applying Bellman-Ford Algorithm taking V_S as a Source Vertex.

Now Applying Reweighting process on graph $G(V, E)$

For each edge $(u, v) \in E(G')$

$$\hat{W}(u, v) = W(u, v) + h(u) - h(v)$$

We obtained the following graph :

Fig. (c) each edge is reweighted with weight function

$$\hat{W}(u, v) = W(u, v) + h(u) - h(v)$$

Now the graph of Fig. (c) is stored separately after removing the added vertex Vs and their edges which is as follows :

Applying Dijkastras Algorithm on each vertex of G using weight function $\hat{W}$ to compute $\hat{\delta}(u, v)$.

$$\hat{\delta}(u, v) = 0, 2, 2, 2, 0$$

Now we compute $d_{uv} = \hat{\delta}(u, v) + h(v) - h(u)$

$h(v)$ and $h(u)$ are taken from the graph G (Figure-4)

Notation

$d_{uv} = 0 + 0 - 0 = 0$ $[\because h(v) = h(u)]$

For v_2 $d_{uv} = 2 + (-1) - 0 = 1$

For v_3 $d_{uv} = 2 + (-5) - 0 = -3$

For v_4 $d_{uv} = 2 + 0 - 0 = 2$

For v_5 $d_{uv} = 0 + (-4) - 0 = -4$

Hence the entries of first row of matrix is 0, 1, –3, 2 and –4 respectively.

Again applying Dijkstra Algorithm taking V_2 as a source vertex

Compute d_{uv}

For V_2 : $d_{uv} = 0 + (-1) - (-1) = 0$

For V_3 : $d_{uv} = 0 + (-5) - (-1) = -4$

For V_4 : $d_{uv} = 0 + (0) - (-1) = 1$

For V_5 : $d_{uv} = 2 + (-4) - (-1) = -1$

For V_1 : $d_{uv} = 2 + (0) - (-1) = 3$

The entries of second row of matrix D is 3, 0, –4, 1, –1.

Similarly, we apply Dijkstra on V_3, V_4 and V_5 respectively and obtained the values of the matrix $D = d_{ij}$.

Now Applying Dijkstra Algorithm treating V_3 as a sourc vertex

$$\hat{\delta}(u, v)/d_{uv}$$

$$d_{uv} = \hat{\delta}(u, v) + h(v) - h(u)$$

For $V_3 \rightarrow d_{uv} = 0 + (-5) - (-5) = 0$

For $V_4 \rightarrow d_{uv} = 0 + 0 - (-5) = 5$

For $V_5 \rightarrow d_{uv} = 2 + (-4) - (-5) = 3$

For $V_1 \rightarrow d_{uv} = 2 + (0) - (-5) = 7$

For $V_2 \rightarrow d_{uv} = 0 + (-1) - (-5) = 4$

Hence the entries of the third row at matrix D is 7, 4, 0, 5, 3 respectively. Now Applying again Dijkstra Algorithm treated V_4 as a source vertex.

For $V_4 \rightarrow d_{uv} = 0 + (0) - 0 = 0$

For $V_5 \rightarrow d_{uv} = 2 + (-4) - 0 = -2$

For $V_1 \rightarrow d_{uv} = 2 + (0) - 0 = 2$

For $V_2 \rightarrow d_{uv} = 0 + (-1) - 0 = -1$

For $V_3 \rightarrow d_{uv} = 0 + (-5) - 0 = -5$

Hence the entries of fourth row of matrix is 2, –1, –5, 0, –2 respectively, see Fig. (g).

Hence the required matrix is

$$D = \begin{array}{c} \\ V_1 \\ V_2 \\ V_3 \\ V_4 \\ V_5 \end{array} \begin{array}{c} \begin{array}{ccccc} V_1 & V_2 & V_3 & V_4 & V_5 \end{array} \\ \begin{bmatrix} 0 & 1 & -3 & 2 & -4 \\ 3 & 0 & -4 & 1 & -1 \\ 7 & 4 & 0 & 5 & 3 \\ 2 & -1 & -5 & 0 & -2 \\ 8 & 5 & 1 & 6 & 0 \end{bmatrix} \end{array}$$

Applying Dijkstra on graph $G(V, E)$ treated V_5 as a source vertex.

$$d_{uv} = \hat{\delta}(u, v) + h(v) - h(u)$$

For V_5 : $d_{uv} = 0 + (-4) - (-4) = 0$

For V_1 : $d_{uv} = 4 + (0) - (-4) = 8$

For V_2 : $d_{uv} = 2 + (-1) - (-4) = 5$

For V_3 : $d_{uv} = 2 + (-5) - (-4) = 1$

For V_4 : $d_{uv} = 2 + (0) - (-4) = 6$

This way we obtain Fig. (h).

EXERCISE

1. How can we visualize EXTEND-SHORTEST-PATH as matrix multiplication?
2. Modify Floyd warshall algorithm to find the –ve weight cycle?
3. Write an efficient algorithm to find the length [no. of edges] of minimum length, negative weight cycle.
4. Find the predecessor matrix for Ex. 30.3.
5. Find the running time of Johnson's algorithm?
6. Write an algorithm for Transitive closure?

31

NETWORK FLOW

31.1 Maximum Flows

In network flow problem we have a source and a sink. It can be compared with water pipeline in which water is flowing through pipeline to different destinations, and each pipe has its own capacity and water can't flow through it beyond its capacity. *Network* can also be viewed as digraph with one vertex s, called the **source,** with no incoming edges and out vertex t, called the **sink,** with no out going edges.

With each edge e we associate a number $w(e)$ called the capacity of the edge. A flow is a real function $f: E \rightarrow R$ that assigns a no. to each edge of the network and meets the two conditions :

(1) The flow of an edge e cannot be greater than its capacity, or $0 \leq f(e) \leq w(e)$. (*Capacity constraint*)

(2) Total flow coming to a vertex is equal to total flow going from it, *i.e.*, (*flow conservation*)

$$\sum_{u} f(uv) = \sum_{w} f(vw)$$

In network flow problem, the problem is to find the maximal flow through the network, i.e., for each flow we have to find the maximal flow that takes place through each pipe.

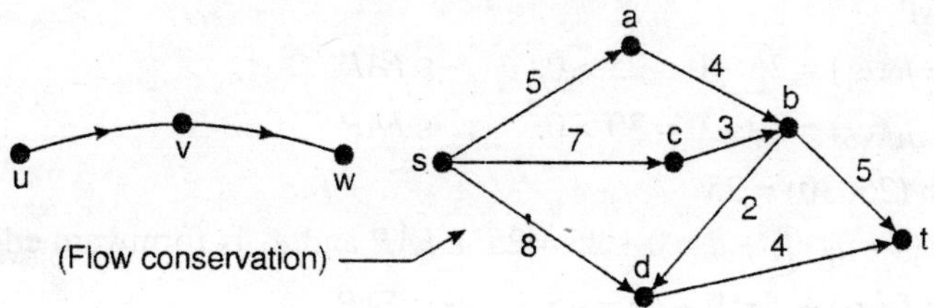

Fig. 31.1. Shows network flow

Flow Augmented Path : (FAP) A path form u to v is flow augmented path if for sequence of edges in this path $w(e) - f(e) > 0$, on forward edges and, $f(e) > 0$ on backward edges. **Ford Fulkerson** algorithm works on this principle, so we can give the algorithm for maximal flow as,

FORD-FULKERSON Algo.

1. Set $f_i : E \to R$, s.t. $f_0(e) = 0 \; \forall \; e \in E$.
2. Find FAP for f_i if possible.
   Calculate $d_i = \min \{w(e) - f(e) \mid e \text{ forward}\}$, or
   $= \{f(e) \mid e \text{ backward}\}$
3. Define $f_{i+1}(e) = \begin{cases} f_i(e) & \text{if } e \notin FAP \\ f_i(e) + d_i & \text{if } e \in FAP, \ e \text{ forward} \\ f_i(e) - d_i & \text{if } e \in FAP, \ e \text{ backward} \end{cases}$
4. $f_i \leftarrow f_{i+1}$, go to step 2.
5. Stop if no FAP exists, the stopping flow f_i is the maximizing flow.

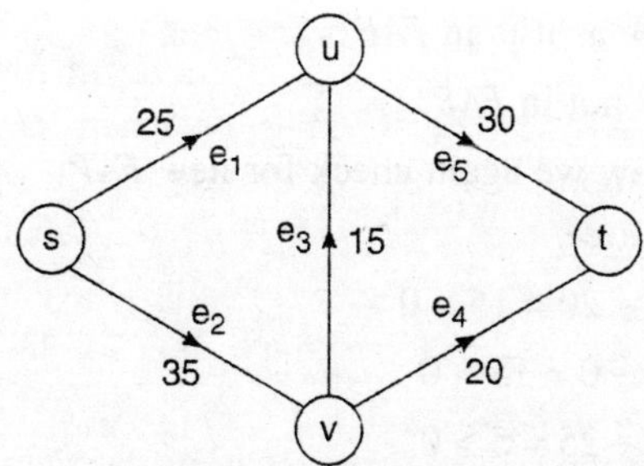

Fig. 31.2. It shows Network flow with its capacity of pipe.

We can apply fold fulkerson algorithm to get the maximal flow through network in Fig. 31.2 as follows.

Step 1. $f_0(e) = 0 \; \forall \; e \in E$

i.e., $f_0(e_1) = f_0(e_2) = f_0(e_3) = f_0(e_4) = f_0(e_5) = 0.$

Step 2. Consider a path $e_1 e_5$ from s to t.

Calculat FAP

$w(e_1) - f_0(e_1) = 25 - 0 = 25 > 0, \quad \therefore\ \varepsilon\ FAP$

$w(e_5) - f_0(e_5) = 30 - 0 = 30 > 0, \quad \therefore\ \varepsilon\ FAP$

$d = \min(25, 30) = 25$

Step 3. $f_1(e_1) = f_0(e_1) + d = 0 + 25 = 25$, ε *FAP* and e_1 is forward edge

$f_1(e_5) = f_0(e_5) + d = 0 + 25 = 25, \quad e_5\ \varepsilon\ FAP$

$f_1(e_2) = f_0(e_2) = 0 \notin FAP$

$f_1(e_3) = f_0(e_3) = 0 \notin FAP$

$f_1(e_4) = f_0(e_4) = 0 \notin FAP$

Since path e_1e_5 does not contain other edges, so they are not in FAP. Again test for FAP with new flow, to find new path.

$w(e_1) - f_1(e_1) = 25 - 25 > 0 \notin FAP$

$w(e_2) - f_1(e_2) = 35 - 0 > 0\ \varepsilon\ FAP$

$w(e_3) - f_1(e_3) = 15 - 0 > 0\ \varepsilon\ FAP$

$w(e_4) - f_1(e_4) = 20 - 0 > 0\ \varepsilon\ FAP$

$w(e_5) - f_1(e_5) = 35 - 25 > 0 \notin FAP$

So we can select any edge except e_1, this time.

Let us select e_2e_4 (as it is FAP) from source to target

thus $\quad d = \min(35, 20) = 20$

hence new flow obtained using step 3 of algo as

$f_2(e_1) = f_1(e_1) = 25$, not in *FAP*

$f_2(e_2) = f_1(e_1) + d = 0 + 20 = 20$, as it is in *FAP*

$f_2(e_3) = f_1(e_3) = 0$, not in *FAP*

$f_2(e_4) = 0 + 20 = 20$, as it is in *FAP*

$f_2(e_5) = f_1(e_5) = 25$, not in *FAP*.

After obtaining new flow we again check for new *FAP*

Let us consider path $e_2e_3e_5$.

$w(e_2) - f_2(e_2) = 35 - 20 = 15 > 0$

$w(e_3) - f_2(e_3) = 15 - 0 = 15 > 0$

$w(e_5) - f_2(e_5) = 30 - 25 = 5 > 0$

Thus $e_2e_3e_5$ is a valid *FAP*

$\therefore \quad d = \min(15, 15, 5) = 5$

Again calculate new flow.

$f_3(e_1) = f_2(e_1) = 25$, not in *FAP*

$f_3(e_2) = f_2(e_2) + d = 20 + 5 = 25$, ε *FAP*

$f_3(e_3) = f_2(e_3) + d = 0 + 5 = 5$, ε *FAP*

$f_3(e_4) = f_2(e_4) = 20$, $\notin$ *FAP*

$f_3(e_5) = f_3(e_5) + d = 25 + 5 = 30$, ε *FAP*

Again check for *FAP* for each edges to form a new path form source to target

$w(e_1) - f_3(e_1) = 25 - 25 \not> 0$, $\notin$ *FAP*

$w(e_2) - f_3(e_2) = 35 - 25 > 0$, ε *FAP*

$w(e_3) - f_3(e_3) = 15 - 5 > 0$, ε *FAP*

$w(e_4) - f_3(e_4) = 20 - 20 \not> 0$, $\notin$ *FAP*

$w(e_5) - f_3(e_5) = 30 - 30 \not> 0$, $\notin$ *FAP*

Thus we have edges e_2, e_3 that can be chosen in FAP but there is no path which can lead to target using these two edges only, so the flow f_3 is stopping flow and is maximal flow through each pipeline. Final flow, capacity diagram is shown in Fig. 31.3.

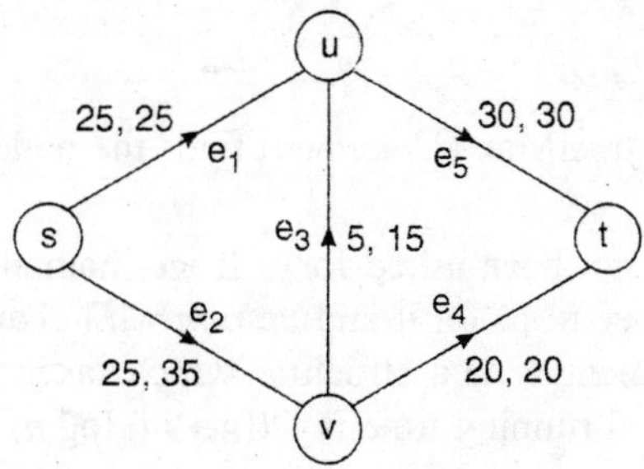

Fig. 31.3. Shows Max flow and capacity on each edge.

THEOREM 31.1. In any network, the maximal flow from *s* to *t* is equal to the minimal capacity of any cut (See Graph theory by Narsingh Deo for the proof of this theorem).

EXAMPLE 31.1. *Suppose you are given a diagram of a telephone network, which is a graph G whose vertices represent switching centers, and whose edges represent communication lines between two centers. The edges are marked by their bandwidth. The bandwidth of a path is the bandwidth of its lowest bandwidth edge. Give an algorithm that, given a diagram and two switching centers a and b, will output the maximum bandwidth of a path between a and b.*

SOLUTION : We can model this problem using a graph. We associate a vertex of the graph with each switching center and an edge of the graph with each line between two switching centers. We assign the weight of each edge to be its bandwidth. Vertices that represent switching centers that are not connected by a line do not have an edge between them.

We use the same basic idea as in Dijkstra's algorithm. We keep a variable $d[v]$ associated with each vertex v that is the bandwidth on any path from a to this vertex. We initialize the d values is initialized to infinity. We also keep a π value associated with each vertex (that contains the predecessor vertex).

The basic subroutine will be very similar to the subroutine RELAX in Dijkstra. Assume that we have an edge (u, v). If min $\{d[u], w(u, v)\} > d[v]$ then we should update $d[v]$ to min $\{d[u], w(u, v)\}$ (because the path from a to u and then to v has bandwidth min $\{d[u], w(u, v)\}$, which is more than the one we have currently).

```
Max-Bandwidth (V, a, b);
for all vertices v in V do
d[v] ← 0
d[a] ← ∞
known ← ϕ
Unknown ← V
while Unknown ≠ ϕ do
        u ← ExtractMax (unknown)
        known ← known ∪ {u}
        for all vertices v in Adj[u] do
                if (min (d[u], w(u, v)) > d[v])
                d[v] ← min(d[u], w(u, v))
return d[b]
```

Here, the function ExtractMax (*Unknown*) finds the node in *Unknown* with the maximum value of *d*.

Complexity (this has not been asked for) : If we maintain *Unknown* as a heap, then there are $n = |V|$ ExtractMax operations on it and upto $m = |E|$ changes to the values of elements in the heap. We can implement a data structure which takes $O(\log n)$ time for each of these operations. Hence, the total running time is $O((n + m) \log n)$.

EXAMPLE 31.2. *NASA wants to link n stations spread over the country using communication channels. Each pair of stations has a different bandwidth available, which is known a priori. NASA wants to select n – 1 channels (the minimum possible) in such a way that all the stations are linked by the channels and the total bandwidth (defined as the sum of the individual bandwidths of the channels) is maximum. Give an efficient algorithm for this problem and determine its worst-case time complexity. Consider the weighted graph G = (V, E), where V is the set of stations and E is the set of channels between the stations. Define the weight w(e) of an edge e ∈ E as the bandwidth of the corresponding channel.*

SOLUTION : Consider the weighted graph $G = (V, E)$, where V is the set of stations and E the set of channels between the stations. Define the weight $w(e)$ of an edge $e \in E$ as the bandwidth of the corresponding channel.

Given below are two ways of solving the problem :

1. At every step of the greedy algorithm for constructing the minimum spanning tree, instead of picking the edge having the least weight, pick the edge having the greatest weight.
2. Negate all the edge-weights. Run the usual minimum spanning tree algorithm on this graph. The algorithm gives us the desired solution.

31.2 Cuts

It turns out that flows are closely related to another concept, known as cuts. Intuitively, a cut is division of the vertices of a flow network N into two sets, with s on one side and t on the other. Formally, a *cut* of N is a partition $\chi = (V_s, V_t)$ of the vertices of N such that $s \in V_s$ and $t \in V_t$. An edge e of N with origin $u \in V_s$ and destination $v \in V_t$ is said to be a ***forward edge*** of cut χ. An edge with origin in V_t and destination in V_s is said to be a ***backward edge.*** We envision a cut as a separation of s and t in N done by cutting across edges of N, with forward edges going from s's side to t's side and backward edges going in the opposite direction. (See Figure 31.4).

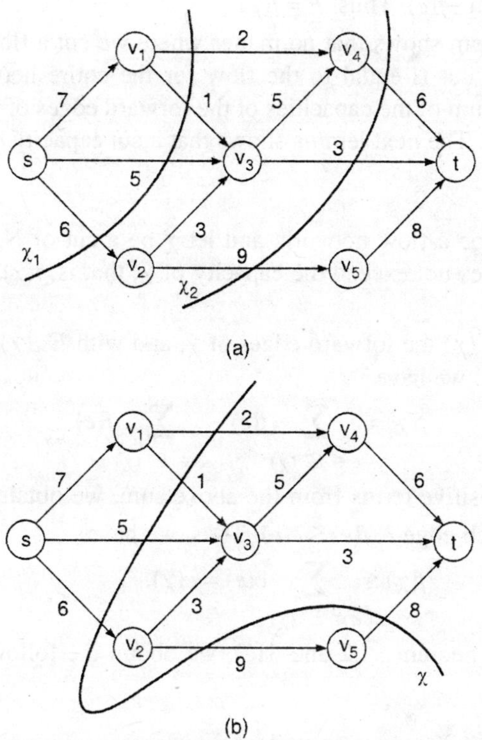

Fig. 31.4. (a) Two cuts, χ_1 (on the left) and χ_2 (on the right), in the flow network N. These cuts have only forward edges and their capacities are $c(\chi_1) = 14$ and $c(\chi_2) = 18$. Cut χ_1 is a minimum cut for N. (b) A cut χ in N with both forward and backward edges. Its capacity is $c(\chi) = 22$.

Given a flow f for N, the ***flow across cut*** χ, denoted $f(\chi)$, is equal to the sum of the flows in the forward edges of χ minus the sum of the flows in the backward edges of χ. That is, $f(\chi)$ is the net amount of commodity that flows from s's side of χ to t's side of χ. The following lemma shows an interesting property of $f(\chi)$.

THEOREM 31.2. Let N be a flow network, and let f be a flow for N. For any cut χ of N, the value of f is equal to the flow across cut χ, that is, $|f| = f(\chi)$.

PROOF : Consider the sum

$$F = \sum_{v \in V_s} \left(\sum_{e \in E^+(v)} f(e) - \sum_{e \in E^-(v)} f(e) \right).$$

By the **conservation rule**, for each vertex v of V_s distinct from s, we have that

$$\sum_{e \in E^+(v)} f(e) - \sum_{e \in E^-(v)} f(e) = 0 .$$

Thus, $F = |f|$.

On the other hand, for each edge e that is not a forward or a backward edge of cut χ, the sum F contains both the term $f(e)$ and the term $-f(e)$, which cancel each other, or neither the term $f(e)$ nor the term $-f(e)$. Thus, $F = f(\chi)$.

The above theorem shows that no matter where we cut a flow network to separate s and t, the flow across that cut is equal to the flow for the entire network. The ***capacity*** of cut χ, denoted $c(\chi)$, is the sum of the capacities of the forward edges of χ (note that we do not include the backward edges). The next lemma shows that a cut capacity $c(\chi)$ is an upper bound on any flow across χ.

THEOREM 31.3. Let N be a flow network, and let χ be a cut of N. Given any flow f for N, the flow across cut χ does not exceed the capacity of χ, that is, $f(\chi) \le c(\chi)$.

PROOF : Denote with $E^+(\chi)$ the forward edges of χ, and with $E^-(\chi)$ the backward edges of χ. By the definition of $f(\chi)$, we have

$$f(\chi) = \sum_{e \in E^+(\chi)} f(e) - \sum_{e \in E^-(\chi)} f(e).$$

Dropping nonpositive terms from the above sum, we obtain $f(\chi) \le E_{e \in E^+(\chi)} f(e)$. By the capacity rule, for each edge e, $f(e) \le c(e)$. Thus, we have

$$f(\chi) \le \sum_{e \in E^+(\chi)} c(e) = c(\chi).$$

By combining Theorem 31.2 and 31.3, we obtain the following important result relating flows and cuts.

THEOREM 31.4. Let N be a flow network. Given any flow f for N and any cut χ of N, the value of f does not exceed the capacity of χ, that is, $|f| \le c(\chi)$.

In other words, given any cut χ for a flow network N, the capacity of χ is an upper bound on any flow for N. This upper bound holds even for a ***minimum** cut* of N, which is a cut with minimum capacity, taken over all cuts of N. In the example of Figure 31.4, χ_1 is a minimum cut.

31.2.1 Maximum Flow

Theorem 31.4 implies that the value of a maximum flow is no more than the capacity of a minimum cut. We will show in this section that these two quantities are actually equal. In the process, we will outline an approach for constructing a maximum flow.

Residual Capacity and Augmenting Paths

In order to prove that a certain flow f is maximum, we need some way of showing that there is absoltuely no more flow that can possibly be "squeezed" into f. Using the related concepts of residual capacity and augmenting paths, discussed next, we can provide just such a proof for when a flow f is maximum.

31.2.2 Residual Capacity

Let N be a flow network, which is specified by a graph G, capacity function c, source s, and sink t. Furthermore, let f be a flow for N. Given an edge e of G directed from vertex u to vertex v, the ***residual capacity*** from u to v with respect to the flow f, denoted $\Delta_f(u; v)$, is defined as

$$\Delta_f(u, v) = c(e) - f(e),$$

and the residual capacity from v to u is defined as

$$\Delta_f(v, u) = f(e).$$

Intuitively, the residual capacity defined by a flow f is any additional capacity that f has not fully taken advantage of in "pushing" its flow from s to t.

Let π be a path from s to t that is allowed to traverse edges in either the forward or backward direction, that is, we can traverse the edge $e = (u, v)$ from its origin u to its destination v or from its destination v to its origin u. Formally, a ***forward edge*** of π is an edge e of π such that, in going from s to t along path π, the origin of e is encountered before the destination of e. An edge of π that is not forward is said to be a ***backward edge.*** let us extend our definition of ***residual capacity*** to an edge e in π traversed from u to v, so that $\Delta_f(u, v)$. In other words,

$$\Delta_f(e) = \begin{cases} c(e) - f(e) & \text{if } e \text{ is a forward edge} \\ f(e) & \text{if } e \text{ is a backward edge.} \end{cases}$$

That is, the residual capacity of an edge e going in the forward direction is the additional capacity of e that f has yet to consume, but the residual capacity in the opposite direction is the flow that f has consumed (and could potentially "give back" if that allows for another flow of higher value).

31.2.3 Augmenting Paths

The residual capacity $\Delta_f(\pi)$ of a path π is the minimum residual capacity of its edges. That is,

$$\Delta_f(\pi) = \min_{e \in \pi} \Delta_f(e).$$

This value is the maximum amount of additional flow that we can possibly "push" down the path π without violating a capacity constraint. An ***augmenting path*** for flow f is a path π from the source s to the sink t with nonzero residual capacity, that is, for each edge e of π,

$$f(e) < c(e) \text{ if } e \text{ is a forward edge}$$
$$f(e) > 0 \text{ if } e \text{ is a backward edge.}$$

We show in Figure 31.5 an example of an augmenting path.

As shown by the following lemma, we can always add the residual capacity of an augmenting path to an existing flow and get another valid flow.

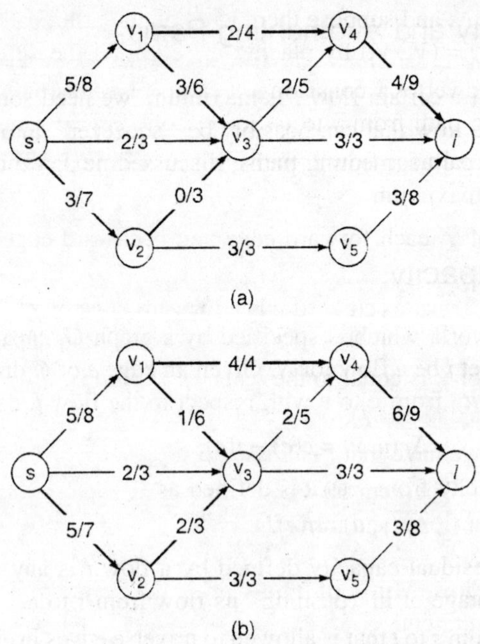

Fig. 31.5. Example of an augmenting path: (a) network N, flow f, and an augmenting path π drawn with thick edges ((v1, v3) is a backward edge). (b) flow f′ obtained from f by pushing $\Delta_f(\pi) = 2$ units of flow from s to t along path π.

LEMMA 31.1. Let π be an augmenting path for flow f in network N. There exists a flow f' for N of value $|f'| = |f| + \Delta_f(\pi)$.

PROOF : We compute the flow f' by modifying the flow of the edges of π:

$$f'(e) = \begin{cases} f(e) + \Delta_f(\pi) & \text{if } e \text{ is a forward edge} \\ f(e) - \Delta_f(\pi) & \text{if } e \text{ is a backward edge.} \end{cases}$$

Note that we subtract $\Delta_f(\pi)$ if e is a backward edge, for we are subtracting flow on e already taken by f in this case. In any case. because $\Delta_f(\pi) \geq 0$ is the minimum residual capacity of any edge in π, we will violate no capacity constraint on a forward edge by adding $\Delta_f(\pi)$ nor will we go below zero flow on any backward edge by subtracting $\Delta_f(\pi)$. Thus, f' is a valid flow for N, and the value of f' is $|f| + \Delta_f(\pi)$.

By Lemma 31.1, the existence of an augmenting path π for a flow f implies that f is not maximum. Also, given an augmenting path π, we can modify f to increase its value by pushing $\Delta_f(\pi)$ units of flow from s to t along path π, as shown in the proof of Lemma 31.1.

What if there is no augmenting path for a flow f in network N ? In this case, we have that f is a maximum flow, as stated by the following lemma.

LEMMA 31.2. If a network N does not have an augmenting path with respect to a flow f, then f is a maximum flow. Also, there is a cut χ of N such that $|f| = c(\chi)$.

PROOF : Let f be a flow for N, and suppose there is no augmenting path in N with respect to f. We construct from f a cut $\chi = (V_s, V_t)$ by placing in set V_s all the vertices v, such that there is a path from the source s to vertex v consisting of edges of nonzero residual capacity. Such a path is called an augmenting path from s to v. Set V_t contains the remaining vertices of N. Since there is no augmenting path for flow f, the sink t of N is in V_t. Thus, $\chi = (V_s, V_t)$ satisfies the definition of a cut.

By the definition of χ, each forward edge and backward edge of cut χ has zero residual capacity, that is,

$$f(e) = \begin{cases} c(e) & \text{if } e \text{ is a forward edge of } \chi \\ 0 & \text{if } e \text{ is a backward edge of } \chi. \end{cases}$$

Thus, the capacity of χ is equal to the value of f. That is,

$$|f| = c(\chi).$$

By Theorem 31.4, we have that f is a maximum flow.

As a consequence of Theorem 30.4 and Lemma 31.2, we have the following fundemantal result relating maximum flows and minimum cuts.

THEOREM 31.5 (The Max-Flow, Min-Cut Theorem) : The value of a maximum flow is equal to the capacity of a minimum cut.

The Ford-Fulkerson Algorithm

A classic algorithm, due to Ford and Fulkerson, computes a maximum flow in a network by applying the greedy method to the augmenting-path approach used to prove the Max-Flow, Min-Cut Theorem (Theorem 31.5).

The main idea of this ***Ford-Fulkerson algorithm*** is a to incrementally increase the value of a flow in stages, where at each stage some amount of flow is pushed along an augmenting path from the source to the sink. Initially, the flow of each edge is equal to 0. At each stage, an augmenting path π is computed and an amount of flow equal to the residual capacity of π is pushed along π, as in the proof of Lemma 31.1. The algorithm terminates when the current flow f does not admit an augmenting path. Lemma 31.2 guarantees that f is a maximum flow in this case.

We provide a pseudo-code description of the Ford-Fulkerson solution to the problem of finding a maximum flow.

```
MaxFlowFordFulkerson (N)
for each edge e ∈ N do
                    f(e) ← 0
stop ← false
repeat
          traverse G starting as s to find an
                                  augmenting path for f
          if an augmenting path π exists then
```

```
                        {Compute the residual capacity Δf (π)
                                                        or π}
                    Δ ← +∞
      for each edge e ∈ π do
            if Δf (e) < Δ then
                    Δ ← Δf (e)
      {Push Δ = Δf (π) units of flow along path π}
            for each edge e ∈ π do
                    if e is a forward edge then
                    f(e) ← f(e) + Δ
            else
                    f(e) ← f(e) - Δ {e is a backward edge}
            else
            stop ← true {f is a maximum flow}
      until stop
```

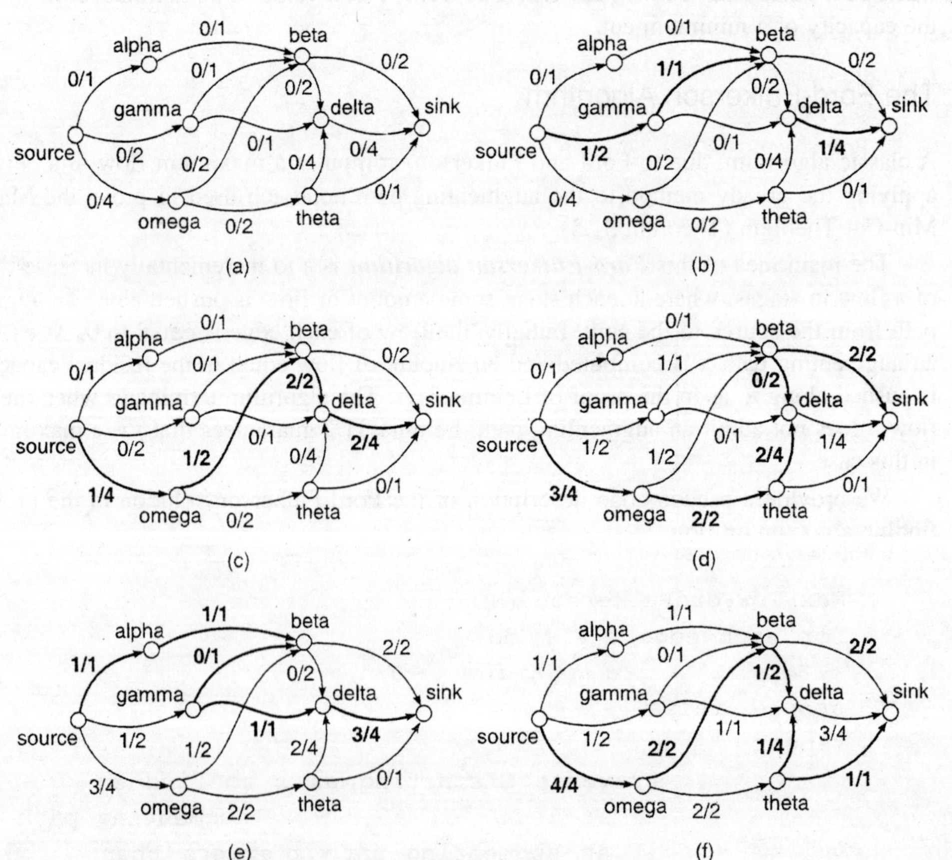

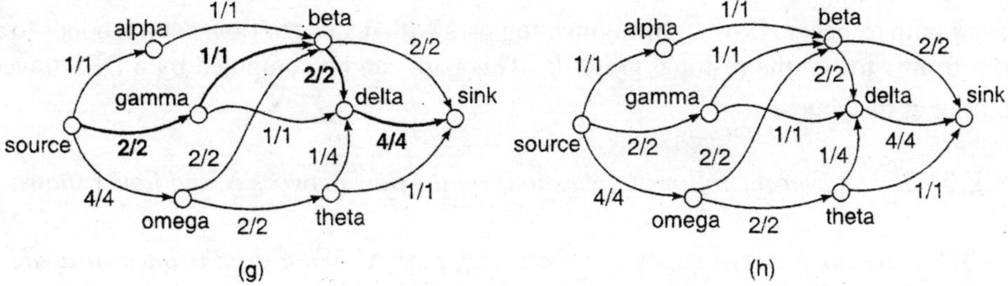

Fig. 31.6. Example execution of the Ford-Fulkerson algorithm on the flow network. Augmenting paths are drawn with thick lines.

Implementation Details

There are important implementation details for the Ford-Fulkerson algorithm that impact how we represent a flow and how we compute augmenting paths. Representing a flow is actually quite easy. We can label each edge of the network with an attribute representing the flow along that edge. To compute an augmenting path, we use a specialization traversal of the graph G underlying the flow network. Such a traversal is a simple modification of either a DFS traversal or a BFS traversal, where instead of considering all the edges incident on the current vertex v, we consider only the following edges :

Outgoing edges of v with flow less than the capacity

Incoming edges of v with nonzero flow.

Alternatively, the computation of an augmenting path with respect to the current flow f can be reduced to a simple path finding problem in a new directed graph R_f derived from G. The vertices of R_f are the same as the vertices of G. For each ordered pair of adjacent vertices u and v of G, we add a directed edge from u to v if $\Delta_f(u, v) > 0$. Graph R_f is called the ***residual***

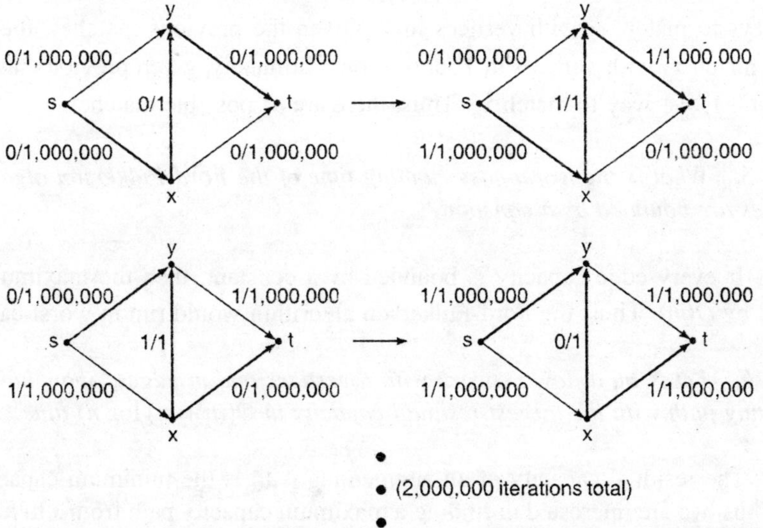

Fig. 31.7. An example of a network for which the standard Ford-Fulkerson algorithm runs slowly. If the augmenting paths chosen by the algorithm alternate between (s, x, y, t) and (s, y, x, t), then the algorithm will make a total of 2,000,000 iterations, even though two iterations would have sufficed.

graph with respect to flow f. An augmenting path with respect to flow f corresponds to a directed path from s to t in the residual graph R_f. This path can be computed by a DFS traversal of R_f starting at the source s.

EXAMPLE 31.3. *Answer the following questions on the flow network N and flow f shown in Figure 31.5 (a) :*

What are the forward edges of augmenting path π? What are the backward edges?

How many augmenting paths are three with respect to flow? For each such path, list the sequence of vertices of the path and the residual capacity of the path.

What is the value of a maximum flow in N?

SOLUTION : The forward edges in π are (s, v_2), (v_2, v_3), (v_1, v_4) and (v_4, t). The backward edges is (v_1, v_4). We can form augmenting paths different from π by replacing (s, v_2, v_3) with (s, v_3), by replacing (v_3, v_1, v_4) with (v_3, v_4) or by replacing (v_3, v_1, v_4, t) with (v_3, t), but these last two substitutions conflict with each other. Thus, there are $2{\cdot}3 = 6$ possible augmenting paths. The maximum flow starts with the flow of the (b)-figure and adds one unit of flow along (s, v_3, t) and one additional unit of flow along (s, v_2, v_3, v_4, t). At this point, there are no augmenting paths left. Therefore, the maximum flow has value 14.

EXAMPLE 31.4. *Let G be a complete bipartite graph such that* $|X| = |Y| = n$ *and for each pair of vertices* $x \in X$ *and* $y \in Y$*, there is an edge joining x and y. Show that G has n! distinct maximum matchings.*

SOLUTION : Let $X = \{x_1, x_2, \ldots, x_n\}$ and $Y = \{y_1, y_2, \ldots, y_n\}$. We can count all possible matchings inductively. There are n ways to match x_1 with vertices in Y. Given this match, there are still $n - 1$ ways to match x_2 with vertices in Y. Given the previous matches, there are still $n - 2$ ways to match x_3 with vertices in Y, and so on. Ultimately, given previous matches, there will be $n - (n - 1) = 1$ way to match x_n. Thus, there are $n!$ possible matches.

EXAMPLE 31.5. *What is the worst-case running time of the Ford-Fulkerson algorithm if all edge capacities are bounded by a constant?*

SOLUTION : If every edge capacity is bounded by a constant, then the maximum flow must be bounded by $O(m)$. Thus, the Ford-Fulkerson algorithm would run in worst-case time $O(m^2)$.

EXAMPLE 31.6. *Let N be a flow network with n vertices and m edges. Show how to compute an augmenting path with the largest residual capacity in* $O((n + m) \log n)$ *time.*

SOLUTION : The residual capacity of an augmenting path is the minimum capacity of one of its edges. Thus, we are interested in finding a maximum capacity path from s to t. We can perform this computation by using a maximum spanning tree algorithm, which is just like a minimum spanning tree algorithm with all the weights multiplied by -1. The path from s to t in this tree will be a maximum capacity path (using a similar argument used to prove the important fact about minimum spanning trees).

EXAMPLE 31.7. *Give an algorithm that determines, in $O(n + m)$ time, whether a graph with n vertices and m edges is bipartite.*

SOLUTION : Start from some vertex v and perform a breadth-first search. If there are any non-trees edges joining vertices on the same level, then the graph is not bipartite (for we would have just found an odd-length cycle). If, after performing this test, there is an unvisited vertex, x, we repeat this algorithm with w. We continue this process until we have determined that the graph is not bipartite or we have visited all its vertices. If we have visited all its vertices and found no odd-length cycles, then the graph is bipartite. The running time is $O(n + m)$, since we are performing at BFS on each connected component.

EXAMPLE 31.8. *A taxi company receives pickup requests from n locations. There are m taxis available, where $m \geq n$, and the distance of taxi i to location j is d_{ij}. Give an algorithm for computing a dispatchment of n taxis to the n pickup locations that minimizes the total distance.*

SOLUTION : We are interested in a minimum-cost matching of taxis to locations. We can produce such a solution by performing a minimum-cost flow algorithm on the flow network derived from the maximum matching problem, where we add an extra node s, connected to all the taxis, and an extra node t, connected to all the locations.

EXERCISE

1. Show that for a flow f, the total flow out of the source is equal to the total flow into the sink, that is,

$$\sum_{e \in E^+(s)} f(e) = \sum_{e \in E^-(t)} f(e).$$

2. Construct a minimum cut for the network shown in Figure 31.4.
3. Illustrate the execution of the Ford-Fulkerson algorithm in the flow network of Figure 31.4.
4. Draw a flow network with 9 vertices and 12 edges. Illustrate an execution of the Ford-Fulkerson algorithm on it.
5. Find a minimum cut in the flow network of Figure 31.4.
6. Show that, given a maximum flow in a network with m edges, a minimum cut of N can be computed in $O(m)$ time.

32

SORTING NETWORKS

32.1 Comparision Networks

Sorting networks are comparison networks that sort their inputs so we can view sorting network as **comparison network** which consists of wires and **comparators** as shown in Fig. 32.1.

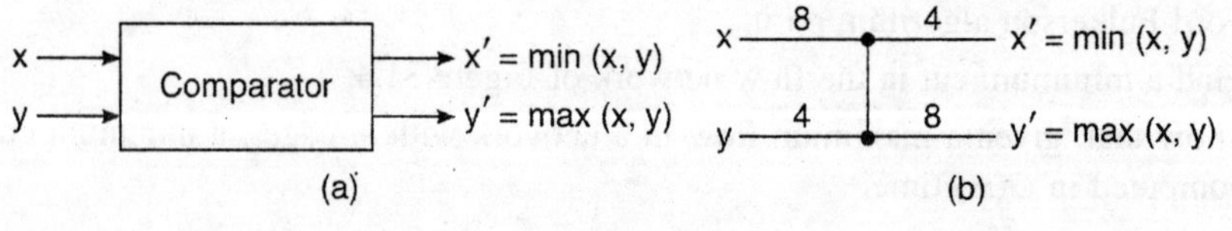

Fig. 32.1.

We can show the comparator with one vertical line as shown in Fig. 32.1(b) Thus comparator sorts its two inputs. We can assume that it perform its operation in $O(1)$ time. We can also generalise this concept for n inputs and n outputs, see Fig. 32.2 a–b.

Fig. 32.2 shows the comparator network, here A and B produces its output in parallel, then C and D produces in parallel and finally E gives the output as (2, 5, 8, 9), each time upper wire gives minimum value and lower wire gives maximum value as shown in Fig. 32.1. Running time for each output is $O(1)$. Running time of comparator can also be given in terms of **depth**

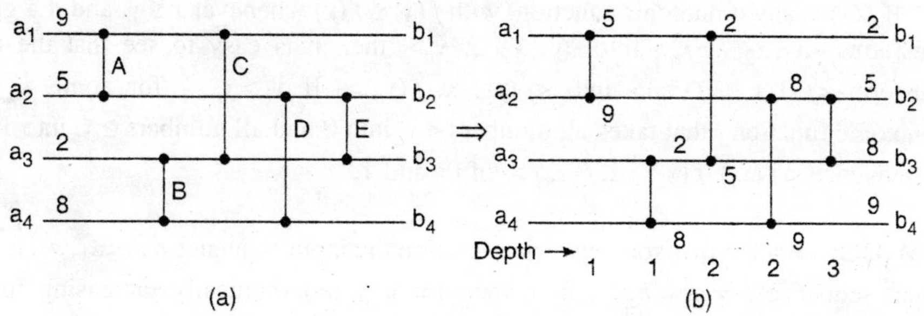

Fig. 32.2.

which max $(d_x, d_y) + 1$, *i.e.*, max time of input wires, *e.g.*, for *B*, $d_x = 0$, $d_y = 0$, therefore depth = 1 for *E* $d_x = 2$, $d_y = 1$, depth = 1 + 2 = 3, see Fig. 32.2 (b).

Network analog of elementary internal sorting schemes, obtained by applying the constructions of Fig. 32.3 gives

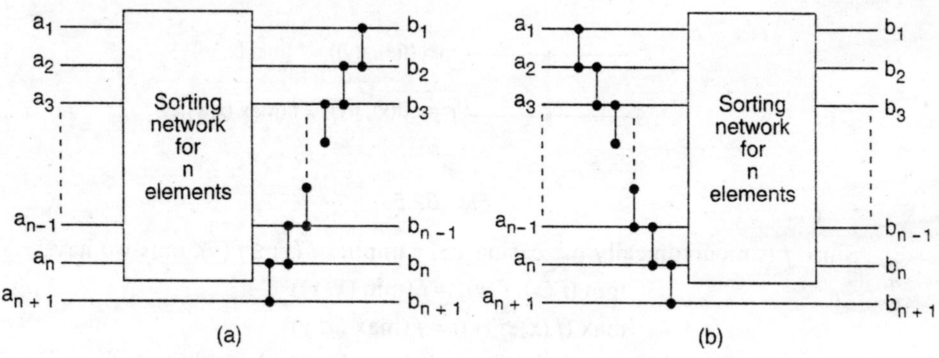

Fig. 32.3. Making (n + 1)-sorters from n-sorters (a) insertion (b) selection.

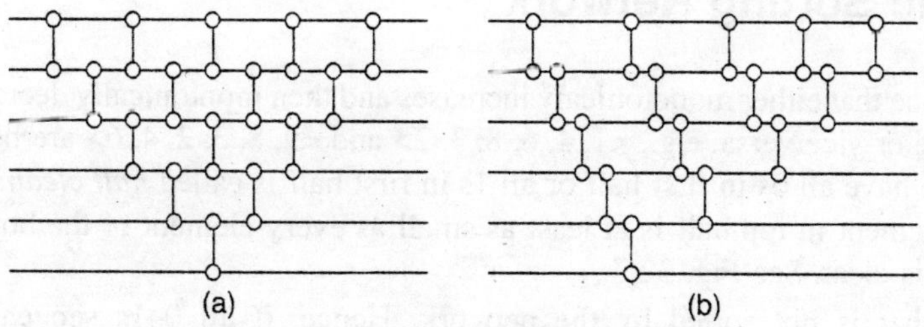

Fig. 32.4. (a) Insertion sort (b) Bubble sort.

THEOREM Z (Zero-one Principle) 32.1. If a network with *n* input line sorts all 2^n sequences of 0*s* and 1 *s* into non decreasing order, it will sort any arbitrary sequence of *n* number into non-decreasing order.

PROOF : If $f(x)$ is any monotonic function, with $f(x) \le f(y)$ whenever $x \le y$, and if a given network transforms $<x_1, x_2, ..., x_n>$ into $<y_1, y_2, ..., y_n>$, then it is easy to see that the network will transform $<f(x_1), ..., f(x_n)>$ into $<f(y_1), ..., f(y_n)>$. If $y_i > y_{i+1}$ for some i, consider the monotonic function f that takes all numbers $< y_i$ into 0 and all numbers $\ge y_i$ into 1, this defines the sequence $<f(x_1), f(x_2), ..., f(x_n)>$ of 0s and 1.

THEOREM 32.2. If a comparison network transform the input sequence $a = <a_1, a_2, ..., a_n>$ into the output sequence $b = <b_1, b_2, ..., b_n>$, then for any monotonically increasing function f, the network transforms the input sequence $f(a) = <f(a_1), f(a_2), ..., f(a_n)>$ into the output sequence $f(b) = <f(b_1), f(b_2), ..., f(b_n)>$.

PROOF : If f is monotonically increasing function then a single comparator with inputs $f(x)$ and $f(y)$ produces outputs $f(\min(x, y))$ and $f(\max(x, y))$.

Consider a comparator whose inputs are x and y. Upper output is min (x, y) and lower is max (x, y). Suppose now we apply $f(x)$ and $f(y)$ to the inputs of the comparator as shown in Fig. 32.5.

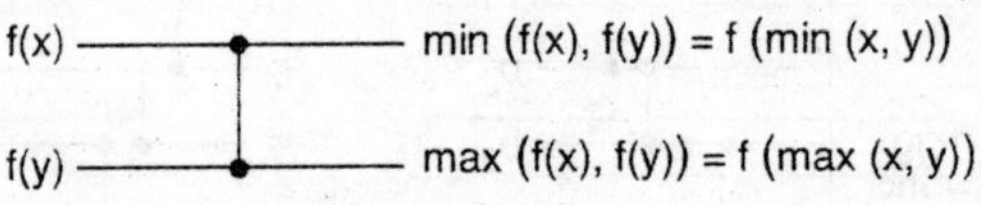

Fig. 32.5.

Since f is monotonically increasing $x \le y$ implies $f(x) \le f(y)$, thus we have

$$\min(f(x), f(y)) = f(\min(x, y))$$
$$\max(f(x), f(y)) = f(\max(x, y))$$

Thus, comparator produces above results which completes the proof.

32.2 Bitonic Sorting Network

A sequence that either monotonicaly increases and then montonically decreases is called **bitonic sequence** or vice versa. e.g., <1, 4, 6, 8, 3, 2> and <9, 8, 3, 2, 4, 6> are both bitonic. If bitonic sequence have all 0s in first half or all 1s in first half is called *half clean*. It ensures that every output element in top half is at least as small as every element of the bottom half, and atleast one half is clean See Fig. 32.7.

1's that is not sorted by the network. Hence, if all 0–1s sequences sorted, we have $y_i \le y_{i+1}$ for $1 \le i < n$.

Based on this principle we can construct an (m, n) merging network as follows :

(1) If $m = 0$, or $n = 0$, the network is empty, If $m = n = 1$, the network is a single comparator module.

(2) If $mn > 1$, let the sequence to be merged be $<x_1, x_2, ..., x_n>$ and $<y_1, y_2, ..., y_n>$. Merge the "odd sequence" $<x_1, x_3, .., x_{2\lceil \frac{m}{2} \rceil - 1}>$ and $<y_1, y_3, ..., y_{2\lceil n/2 \rceil - 1}>$, obtaining the sorted

results $<v_1, v_2, v_{[m/2]+[n/2]}>$ merge even sequence $<x_2, x_4, ..., x_{2[m/2]}>$ and $<y_2, y_4, ..., y_{2[n/2]}>$ obtaining sorted results $<w_1, w_2, ..., w_{[m/2]+[n/2]}>$, Finally apply the comparision-interchange operations.

$$w_1 : v_2, w_2 : v_3, w_3 : v_4 : \ldots w\left\lceil \frac{m}{2} \right\rceil + \left\lceil \frac{n}{2} \right\rceil : V* \qquad \ldots(1)$$

to the sequence

$$<v_1, w_1, v_2, w_2, v_3, w_3, \ldots, v_{[\frac{m}{2}]+[\frac{n}{2}]}, w_{[\frac{m}{2}]+[\frac{n}{2}]}, V*,, V** x> \qquad \ldots(2)$$

The result will be sorted. Here $V* = V_{[\frac{m}{2}]+[\frac{n}{2}]+1}$ does not exist if m, n are even, and $V** = V_{[\frac{m}{2}]+[\frac{n}{2}]+2}$ does not exist unless both m, n are odd, total no. of comparator module indicated in (1) is $[m + (n - 1)/2]$. A (4, 7) odd-even merge is shown in Fig. 32.6.

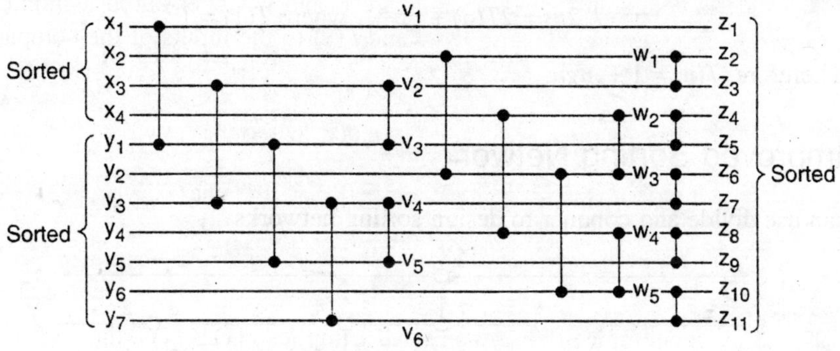

Fig. 32.6. Odd-even merge.

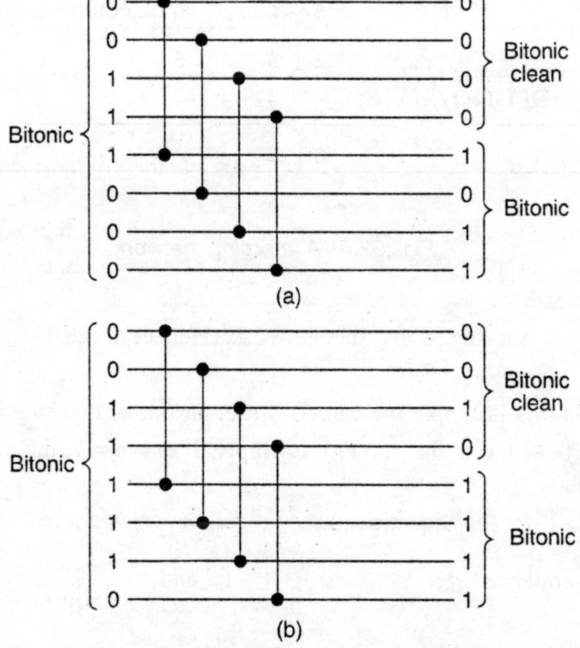

Fig. 32.7. Shows Bitonic half clean.

32.3 Merging Network

We can merge two input sequence to produce a single output sequence based on the rule that input sequence of second is reversed and concatenated with first sequence in order, e.g., $X = 00000111$ and $Y = 00001111$, we reverse Y to $Y^R = 11110000$ concatenating X and Y^R produces 0000011111110000

32.3.1 Parallel merging networks

For any positive integer n, a merging network F_n is a network built of comparators, with two groups of n inputs and a single group of $2n$ output. Provided each groups are already sorted.

To compute the size $T(n)$ of the network f_n obtained using this construction, we use the recurrence.

$$T(2n) = 2T(n) + \frac{n}{2} - 1, \text{ where } T(1) = 1$$

Therefore, $T(n) = 1 + nlgn$.

32.3.2 Improved Sorting Network

We can use divide and conquer to design sorting networks

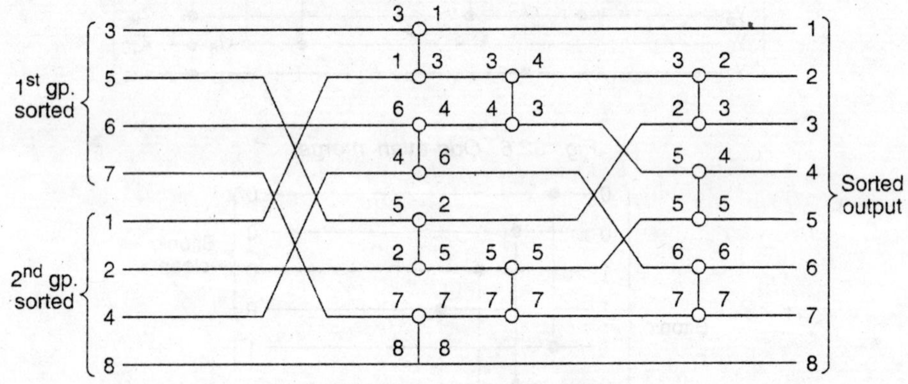

Fig. 32.8. A merging network.

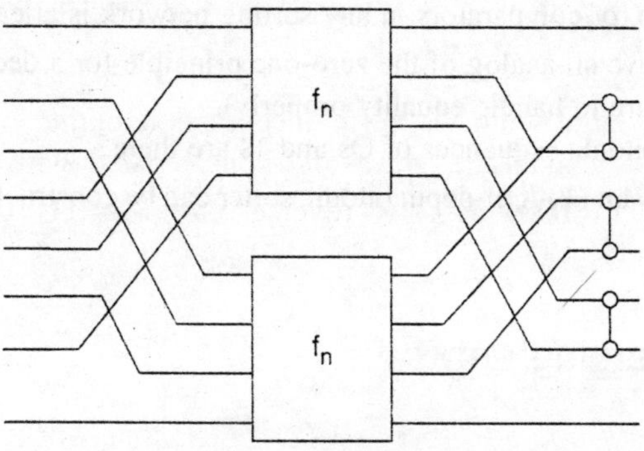

Fig. 32.9. Designing F_{2n} in terms of F_n.

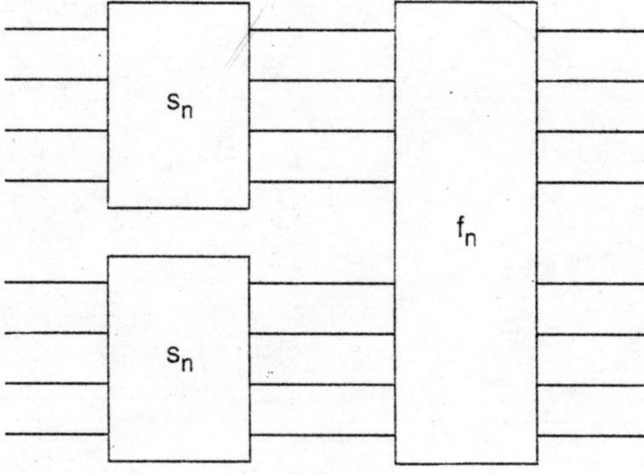

Fig. 32.10.

It is easy to show that sorting network obtained in this way use a number of comparators in $\theta(nlg^2n)$ and that the time they require to sort their input is in $\theta(lg^2n)$. For obvious reasons the networks described above are called odd even merging and sorting networks.

EXERCISE

1. Show that the size and depth of the merging network of Fig. 32.8 is $1 + nlgn$
2. Prove that a network that finds the median of $2t - 1$ element requires at least $(t-1)\lceil 1g(t+1)\rceil + \lceil lgt \rceil$ comparator modules.
3. Find the output sequence generated using comparator of Fig. 32.1 for the input sequence <9, 6, 5, 2>
4. Let n be an exact power of 2. Show how to construct an n-input, n-output comparision network of depth lgn in which the top output wire always carries the minimum input value and bottom carries maximum output value.
5. Prove that any sorting network, on n input has a depth atleast lgn.

6. Prove that no. of comparators in any sorting network is atleast $\Omega(nlgn)$
7. State and prove an analog of the zero-one principle for a decision tree model. (**Hint :** Be sure to handle equality properly).
8. How many bitonic sequences of Os and 1s are there?
9. Describe how an $O(nlgn)$-depth bitonic sorter can be constructed when n is not an exact power of 2.

33

ARITHMETIC CIRCUITS

Combinational Circuit

It consists of one or more combinational elements interconnected in acyclic fashion. It consists of logical gates like AND, OR, NOT, XOR etc.

Full Adder

It consists of 3 inputs x, y, z two output which give sum, S and carry, C.

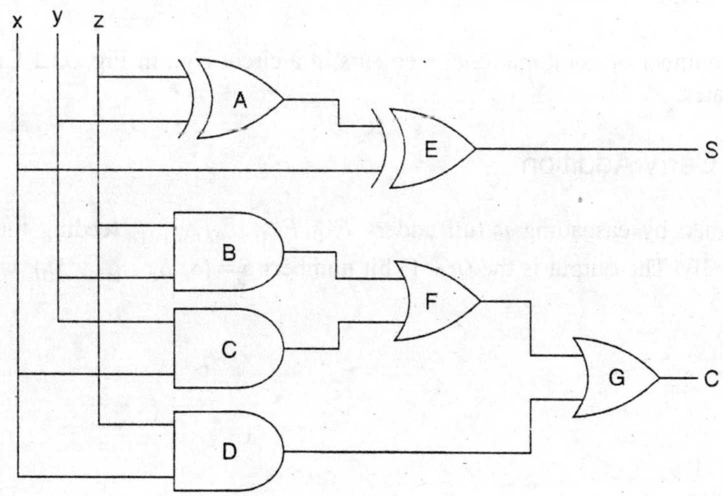

Fig. 33.1. Full Adder circuit

Truth Table of full adder is given below :

x	y	z	c	s
0	0	0	0	0
0	0	1	0	1
0	1	0	0	1
0	1	1	1	0
1	0	0	0	1
1	0	1	1	0
1	1	0	1	0
1	1	1	1	1

$$S = x \oplus y \oplus z$$

$$C = (x \wedge y) \vee (y \wedge z) \vee (x \wedge z)$$

Circuit Depth

If we measure the propagation delay as time from one combinational element to another then maximum number of combinational elements in path gives the worst case time, a input gives the output and this is called the circuit depth.

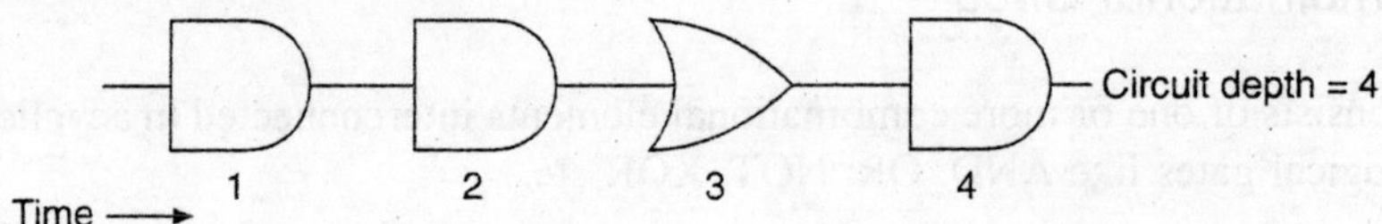

Fig. 33.2. Shows circuit depth

Circuit Size

It is the number of combinational elements in a circut e.g., in Fig. 33.1 Circuit size is 7, as it uses 7 gates.

Ripple Carry Addition

It is formed by cascading n full adders $FA_0, FA_1, ..., FA_{n-1}$, feeding the carry-out of each successively. The output is the $(n + 1)$ bit numbers $S = (S_n\ S_{n-1}, ..., S_0)$, where S_n equal C_n.

Since carry bit ripple through n full adders, the time required by an n bit ripple-carry adder is $\Theta(n)$. See Fig. 33.3.

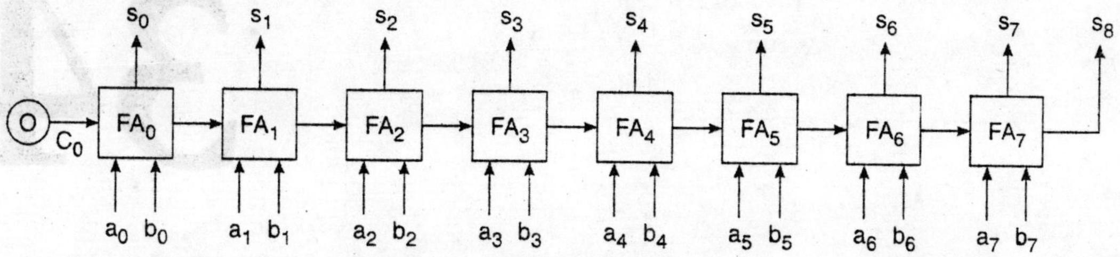

Fig. 33.3. 8-bit ripple carry counter

EXERCISE

1. Construct a Half-Adder circuit and give its truth table.
2. Construct a circuit for performing multiplication operation.

34

ALGORITHMS FOR PARALLEL COMPUTERS

PRAM Model

Parallel Random-access machine (PRAM) consists of P ordinary (serial) processors $P_0, P_1, P_2, ..., P_{P-1}$ that have shared storage and memory. These processors can perform various arithmetic and logical operations in parallel. See Fig. 34.1.

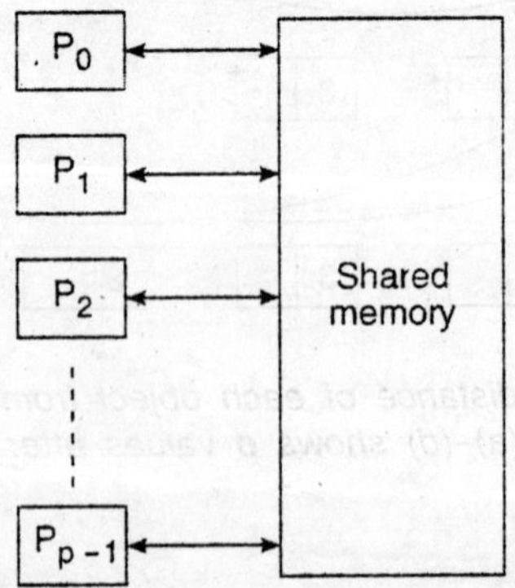

Fig. 34.1. PRAM model

Concurent read/write

Two or more than two processors can read/write at the same time.

Exclusive read/write

No two processors can read/write Simultaneously

- EREW — Exclusive Read Exclusive Write
- CREW — Concurrent Read and Exclusive Write.
- ERCW — Exclusive Read and Concurrent Write
- CRCW — Concurrent Read and Concurrent Write.

34.1 List Ranking

In a PRAM model suppose we are given a singly linked lists L and we have to find the distance of each node or object from the end of the list then

$$d[i] = \begin{cases} 0 & \text{if next } [i] = \text{NIL} \\ d\,[\text{next}[i]] + 1 & \text{if next } [i] \neq \text{NIL} \end{cases}$$

The problem of computing d values is called **list-ranking.** There is one processor per list object, so every list object is operated on by its corresponding processor in $O(1)$ time, hence total time for n objects in the list is $\Theta(n)$.

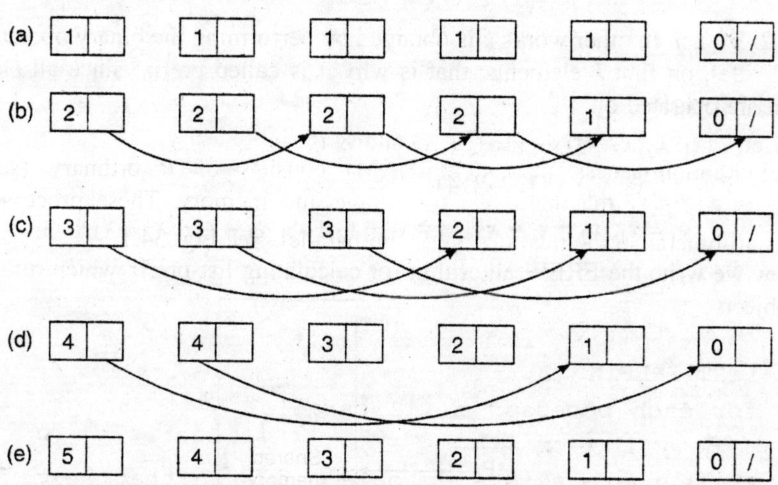

Fig. 34.2. Finding distance of each object from end in the list takes O(lgn) time (a)–(d) shows d values after each iteration.

```
LIST-RANK (L)
  For each processor i, in parallel
       do if next [i] = NIL
           then d [i] ← 0
           else d [i] ← 1
while there exists an object i, such that next[i] ≠ NIL
       do   for each processor in parallel
           do if next  [i] ≠ NIL
           then d [i] ← d [i] + d [next [i]]
                next [i] ← next [next [i]]
```

Running time of this algorithm is $O(lgn)$ time. This algorithm is **EREW,** because each processor is responsible for atlmost one object, every read and write operation is exclusive.

34.2 Parallel Prefix on a List

A **prefix computation** is defined in terms of a binary, asosciative operation ⊗. The computation takes as input a sequence $(x_1, x_2, \dots x_n)$ and produces as output a sequence $(y_1, y_2, \dots, y_n)$ s.t. $y_1 = x_1$ and

$$y_k = y_{k-1} \otimes x_k = y_{k-2} \otimes x_{k-1} \otimes x_k \dots$$
$$= x_1 \otimes x_2 \otimes \dots \otimes x_k$$

for $k = 2, 3, \dots, n$. In other works k is obtained by performing the binary operation, ⊗ (add, sub mult, divide), on first k elements, that is why it is called prefix, since all elements upto kth element are operated on.

e.g. Let, $(x_1, x_2, x_3, x_4) \leftrightarrow (1, 1, 1, 1)$ and ⊗ is '+'

then $(y_1, y_2, y_3, y_4) = (1, 2, 3, 4)$

$$y_1 = x_1,\ y_2 = x_1 + x_2,\ y_3 = x_1 + x_2 + x_3,\ y_4 = x_1 + x_2 + x_3 + x_4$$

Now we write the EREW algorithm for calculating list-prefix which runs in $O(lgn)$ time, for n objects

```
LIST-PREFIX (L)
for each pocessor i, in parallel
   do y[i] ← x [i]
while there exists an object i such that next [i] ≠ NIL
   do for each procesor i, in parallel do
        if next [i] ≠ NIL
        then y[next[i]] ← y[i]⊗y[next[i]]
             next[i] ← next[next[i]]
```

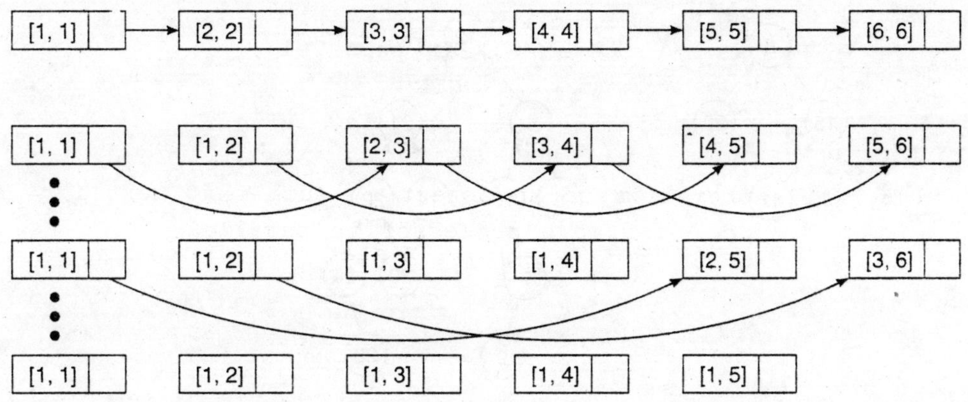

Fig. 34.3. LIST-PREFIX showing [i,k] pair.

EXAMPLE 34.1. *Consider the list 2, 3, 4, 1, 2, 1, 2 find the prefix sum*

SOLUTION : Prefix sum = 2, 5, 9, 10, 12, 13, 15.

34.3 CRCW VS EREW Algorithms

CRCW algorithm are expensive as compared to EREW, as hardware requirement for CRCW changes but in many cases EREW has limitations, so CRCW algorithm are used in that place.

Concurrent Read

If we have forest of binary trees and we want to store in each node identity of the root of its tree (e.g., value of root node stored in each node). We can associate a processor i with each node i in a forest F, we have following CREW algorithm.

```
FIND-ROOTS (F)
for each processor i, in parallel do
       if parent[i] = NIL
            then root[i] ← i
while there exists a node i, such that parent[i] ≠ NIL
       do for each processor i, in parallel
            do if parent[i] ≠ NIL
then root[i] ← root[parent[i]]
parent[i] ← parent  [parent[i]]
```

Running time of this algorithm is $O(lgd)$, where d is depth of tree, whenever depth d of maximum-depth tree in forest is $d = O(lgn)$, then CREW FIND-ROOTS is more efficient than EREW, in this case running time becomes $O(lgdlgn)$ as compared $\Omega(lgn)$ of EREW.

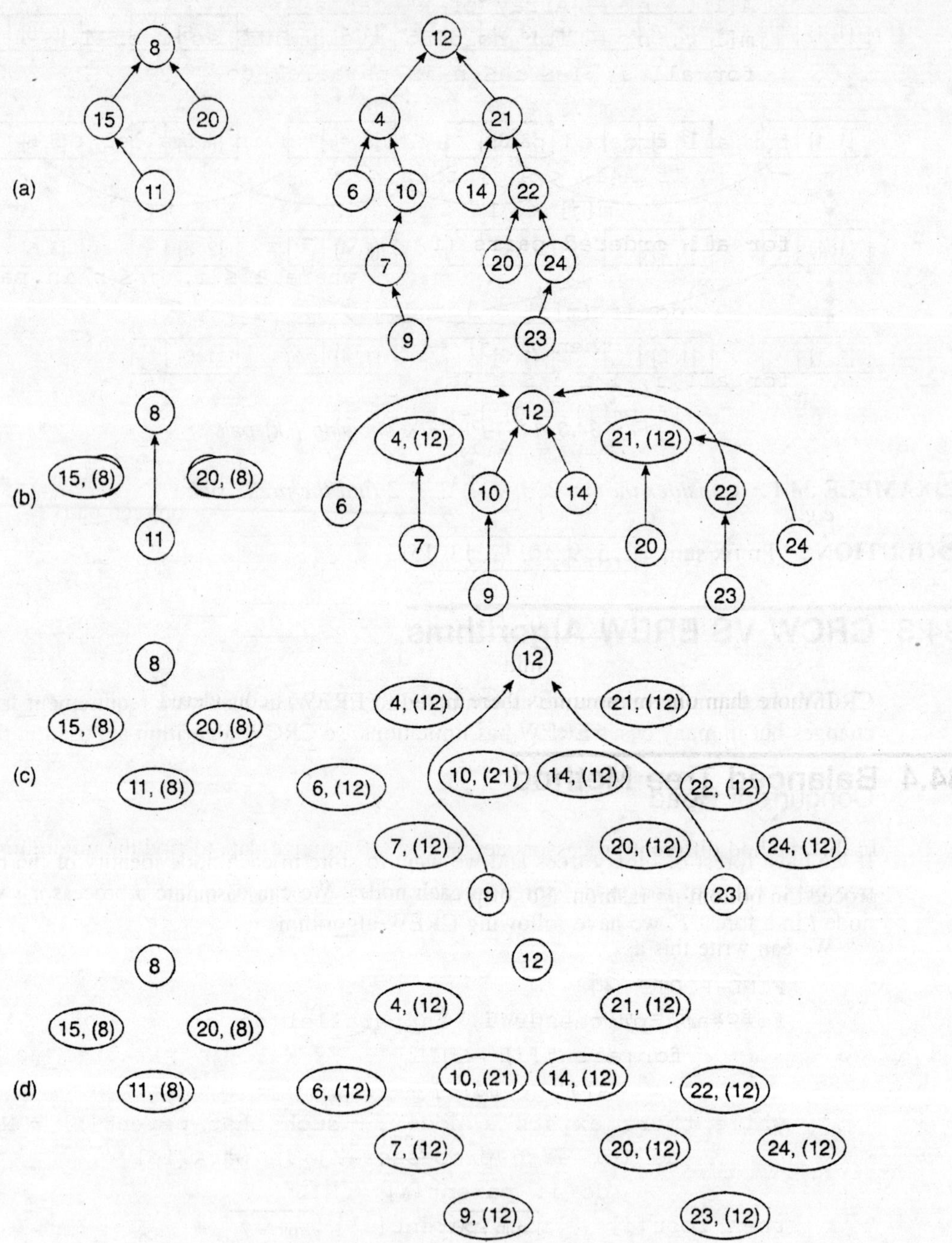

Fig. 34.4. Shows FIND-ROOTS in Forest F.

EXAMPLE 34.2. *Find the minimum of n no. using WRAM model, which takes O(lgn) time, WRAM (CRCW) writes simultaneously?*

SOLUTION : WRAM-MIN (*A*, *m*)

```
    A[1 .. n] ← Array of elements
    m[1 .. n] ← for holding n elements as O or 1.
    for all i, 1 ≤ i ≤ n in parallel do
            m[i] ← 0
  for all ordered pair, 1 ≤ i, j ≤ n in parallel do
        If A[i] < A[j] then
            m[j] ← 1
  for all ordered pairs (i, j),
                                    where 1 ≤ i, j ≤ n in parallel
        do if (m[i] = 0 and i < j)
            then m [j] ← 1
  for all i, 1 ≤ i ≤ n in parallel do
        If (m[i] = 0) hen
            min ← A[i]
```

e.g., ← ordered pairs

A	4	3	7	8	9	6
m	1	0	1	1	1	1

min

If more than one minimum is there first occurrence is considered.

34.4 Balanced Tree Method

In this method different processors act on two consecutive data to find the minimum and this proceed in bottom-*up* fashion. No. of processors required for *n* input $\frac{n}{2}$

We can write this as,

```
    n ← 2^m
    for k = m − 1 down to 0 do
        for all j, 2^k ≤ j ≤ 2^(k + 1) − 1, in parallel do
            A[j] ← min {A(2j), A(2j + 1)}
```

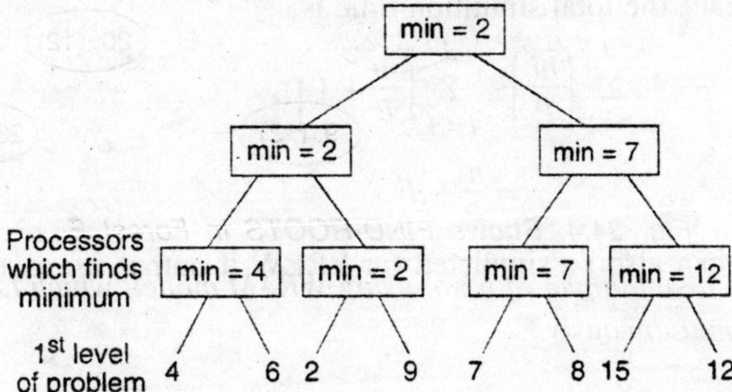

Fig. 34.5. Computes minimum parallely.

Divide-and-Conquer Method

Given a problem,

$$P(x) = a + bx + cx^2 + dx^3 + ex^4 + fx^5 + gx^6 + bx^7$$
$$n = 2^k - 1$$

we can write $P(x) = r(x) + x^{(n+1)/2}\, q(x)$

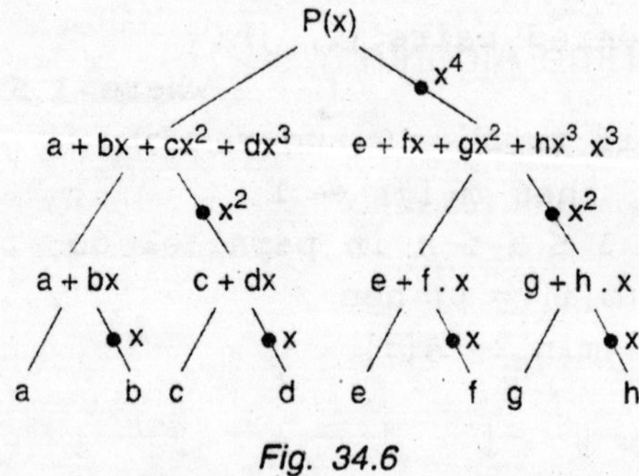

Fig. 34.6

Problem is divided into identical subproblems and each problem is solved simultaneously in $O(lgn)$ time.

THEOREM 34.1. (Brent's Theorem) Any depth-d, size-n combinational circuit with bounded input, can be simulated by p-processor CREW algorithm in $O((n/p + d)$ time.

PROOF : Let us simulate all the elements at depth i before proceeding to simultate those at depth $i + 1$, with in a given depth i, we simulate elements P at a time.

For $i = 1, 2, ..., d$, let n_i be the number of elements at depth i in the circuit. Thus,

$$\sum_{j=1}^{d} n_i = n$$

Consider the n_i combinational elements at depth i, which are grouped as $\left\lceil \frac{n_i}{P} \right\rceil$ groups, where the first $\frac{n_i}{P}$ groups have P elements each and the leftover elements, if any, are in the last group, the PRAM can simultate the computations performed by these combinational elements in $O(\lceil n/P \rceil)$ time. Hence the total simultion time is

$$\sum_{i=1}^{d} \left(\frac{ni}{P}\right) \le \sum_{i=1}^{d} \left(\frac{ni}{P} + 1\right)$$
$$= \frac{n}{P} + d.$$

This theorem can also be simulated for EREW if output for each combinational element takes $O(1)$ times.

34.5 Merging

The problem of merging is to take two sorted sequences as input and produce a sorted sequence of all the elements. Merging is an important problem. For example, an efficient merging algorithm can lead to an efficient sorting algorithm. The same is true in parallel computing also. In this section we study the parallel complexity of merging.

34.5.1 A Logarithmic Time Algorithm

Let $X_1 = k_1, k_2, \ldots, k_m$ and $X_2 = k_{m+1}, k_{m+2}, \ldots, k_{2m}$ be the input sorted sequences to be merged. Assume without loss of generality that m is an integral power of 2 and that the keys are distinct. Note that the merging of X_1 and X_2 can be reduced to computing the rank of each key k in $X_1 \cup X_2$. If we know the rank of each key, then the keys can be merged by writing the key whose rank is i into global memory cell i. This writing will take only one time unit if we have $n = 2m$ processors.

For any key k, let its rank in X_1 (X_2) be denoted as r_k^1 (r_k^2). If $k = k_j \in X_1$, then note that $r_k^1 = j$. If we allocate a single processor π to k, π can perform a binary search on X_2 and figure out the number q of keys in X_2 that are less than k. Once q is known, π can compute k's rank in $X_1 \cup X_2$ as $j + q$. If k belongs to X_2, a similar procedure can be used to compute its rank in $X_1 \cup X_2$. In summary, if we have $2m$ processors (one processor per key), merging can be completed in $O(\log m)$ time.

THEOREM 34.3. Merging of two sorted sequences each of length m can be completed in $O(\log m)$ time using m CREW PRAM processors.

PROOF : Since two sorted sequences of length m each can be sequentially merged in $\Theta(m)$ time, the speedup of the above algorithm is $\dfrac{\Theta(m)}{\Theta(\log m)} = \Theta(m/\log m)$; its efficiency is $\dfrac{\Theta(m)}{\Theta(m \log m)} = \Theta(1/\log m)$. This algorithm is not work-optimal!

34.5.2 Odd-Even Merge

Odd-even merge is a merging algorithm based on divide-and-conquer that yields itself to efficient parallelization. If $X_1 = k_1, k_2, \ldots, k_m$ and $X_2 = k_{m+1}, k_{m+2}, \ldots, k_{2m}$ (where m is an integral power of 2) are the two sorted sequences to be merged, then Algorithm uses $2m$ processors.

Step 0. If $m = 1$, merge the sequences with one comparison.

Step 1. Partition X_1 and X_2 into their odd and even parts. That is, partition X_1 into $X_1^{odd} = k_1, k_3, \ldots, k_{m-1}$ and $X_1^{even} = k_2,$

k_4, ..., k_m Similarly, partition X_2 into X_2^{odd} and X_2^{even}.

Step 2. Recursively merge X_1^{odd} with X_2^{odd} using m processors. Let $L_1 = l_1, l_2, ..., l_m$ be the result. Note that X_1^{odd}, X_1^{even}, X_2^{odd} and X_2^{even} are in sorted order. At the same time merge X_1^{even} with X_2^{even} using the other m processors to get $L_2 = l_{m+1}, l_{m+2}, ..., l_{2m}$.

Step 3. *Shuffle* L_1 and L_2; that is, form the sequence $L = l_1, l_{m+1}, l_2, l_{m+2}, ..., l_m, l_{2m}$. Compare every pair (l_{m+i}, l_{i+1}) and interchange them if they are out of order. That is, compare l_{m+1} with l_2 and interchange them if need be, compare l_{m+2} with l_3 and interchange them if need be, and so on. Output the resultant sequence.

EXAMPLE 34.3. *Let X_1 = 2, 5, 8, 11, 13, 16, 25 and X_2 = 4, 9, 12, 18, 23, 27, 31, 34. Figure 34.7 shows how the odd-even merge algorithm can be used to merge these two sorted sequences.*

SOLUTION :

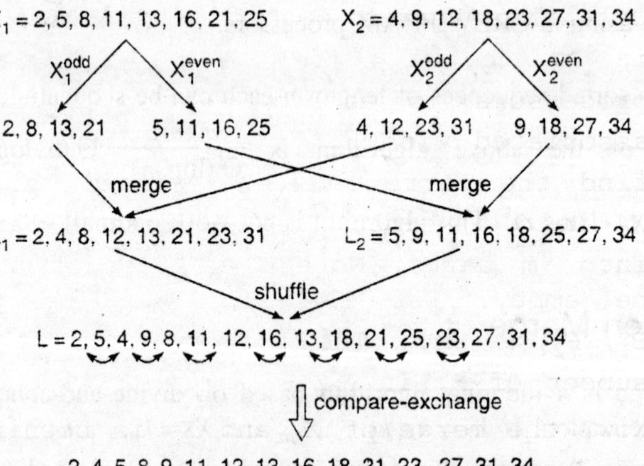

Fig. 34.7. Odd-even merge.

Let $M(m)$ be the run time of Algorithm on two sorted sequences of length m each using $2m$ processors. Then, step 1 takes $O(1)$ time. Step 2 takes $M(m/2)$ time. Step 3 takes $O(1)$ time. This yields the following recurrence relation: $M(m) = M(m/2) + O(1)$ which solves to $M(m) = O(\log m)$. Thus we arrive at the following theorem.

THEOREM 34.3. Two sorted sequences of length m each can be merged in $O(\log m)$ time using $2m$ EREW PRAM processors.

34.5.3 An $O(\log \log m)$-Time Algorithm

Now we present a very fast algorithm for merging. This algorithm can merge two sorted sequences in $O(\log \log m)$ time, where m is the number of elements in each of the two sequences. The number of processors used is $2m$. In addition we employ the divide-and-conquer technique.

X_1 and X_2 are the given sequences. Assume that the keys are distinct. The algorithm reduces the problem of merging X_1 and X_2 into $N \le 2\sqrt{m}$ subproblems, where each subproblem is that of merging two sorted sequences of length $O(\sqrt{m})$. This reduction is completed in $O(1)$ time using m processors. If $T(m)$ is the run time of the algorithm using $2m$ processors, then $T(m)$ satisfies the recurrence relation $T(m) = T(O(\sqrt{m})) + O(1)$ whose solution is $O(\log \log m)$.

THEOREM 34.4. Two sorted sequences of length m each can be merged in $O(\log \log m)$ time using $2m$ CREW PRAM processors.

The above algorithm has a speedup of $\dfrac{\Theta(m)}{\Theta(\log \log m)} = \Theta(m/\log \log m)$ which is very close to m. Its efficiency is $\Theta(1/\log \log m)$, and hence the algorithm is not work-optimal!

Merging in $O(\log\log m)$ time

Step 1. Partition X_1 into $\sqrt{m}$ parts with $\sqrt{m}$ elements each. Call these parts $A_1, A_2, \ldots, A_{\sqrt{m}}$. Let the largest key in A_i be l_i (for $i = 1, 2, \ldots, \sqrt{m}$). Assign $\sqrt{m}$ processors to each of these l_i's. The processors associated with l_i perform a $\sqrt{m}$-ary search on X_2 to find the correct (i.e., sorted) position to l_i in X_2 in $O(1)$ time. This induces a partitioning of X_2 into $\sqrt{m}$ parts. Note that some of these parts could be empty. Let the corresponding parts of X_2 be $B_1, B_2, \ldots, B_{\sqrt{m}}$. The subset B_i is the corresponding subset of A_i in X_2.

Step 2. Now, the merge of X_1 and X_2 is nothing but the merge of A_1 and B_1, followed by the merge of A_2 and B_2, and so on. That is, merging X_1 and X_2 reduces to merging A_i with B_i for $i = 1, 2, \ldots, \sqrt{m}$. We know that the size of each A_i is $\sqrt{m}$. But the sizes of the B_i's could be very large (or very small). To merge A_i with B_i, we can use the idea of partitioning one more time. Let A_i and B_i be an arbitrary pair. If

$|B_i| = O(\sqrt{m})$, we can merge them in $O(1)$ time using an m^{ε}-ary search. Consider the case when $|B_i|$ is $\omega(\sqrt{m})$. Partition B_i into $\lceil \frac{|B_i|}{\sqrt{m}} \rceil$ parts, where each part has at most $\sqrt{m}$ successive keys of B_i. Allocate $\sqrt{m}$ processors to each part so that the processors can find the corresponding subset of this part in A_i in $O(1)$ time. As a result the problem of merging A_i and B_i has been reduced to $\lceil \frac{|B_i|}{\sqrt{m}} \rceil$ subproblems, where each subproblem is that of merging two sequences of length $O(\sqrt{m})$.

The number of processors used is $\sum_{i=1}^{\sqrt{m}} \sqrt{m} \lceil \frac{|B_i|}{\sqrt{m}} \rceil$, which is $\leq 2m$.

This Merging is in $O(\log \log m)$ time.

34.6 Sorting

Given a sequence of n keys, recall that the problem of sorting is to rearrange this sequence into either ascending or descending order. In this section we study several algorithms for parallel sorting. If we have n^2 processors, the rank of each key can be computed in $O(\log n)$ time comparing, in parallel, all possible pairs. One we know the rank of each key, in one parallel write step they can be written in sorted order (the key whose rank is i is written in cell i). Thus we have the following theorem.

THEOREM 34.5. We can sort n keys in $O(\log n)$ time using n^2 CREW PRAM processors.

On the other hand we have seen several sequential algorithms with run times of $O(n \log n)$. The preceding algorithm is not work-optimal.

34.6.1 Odd-Even Merge Sort

Odd-even merge sort employs the classical divide-and-conquer strategy. Assume for simplicity that n is an integer power of two and that the keys are distinct. If $X = k_1, k_2, \ldots, k_n$ is the given sequence of n keys, it is partitioned into two subsequences $X'_1 = k_1, k_2, \ldots, k_{n/2}$ and $K'_2 = k_{n/2+1}, k_{n/2+2}, \ldots, k_n$ of equal length. X'_1 and X'_2 are sorted recursively assigning $n/2$ processors to each. The two sorted subsequences (call them X_1 and X_2, respectively) are then finally merged.

The preceding description of the algorithm is exactly the same as that of merge sort. The difference between the two algorithms lies in how the two subsequences X_1 and X_2 are merged. In the merging algorithms the minimum elements from the two sequences are compared and the minimum of these two is output. This step continues until the two sequences are merged.

As is seen, this process seems to be inherently sequential in nature. Instead, we employ the odd-even merge algorithm discussed earlier.

THEOREM 34.5. *We can sort n arbitrary keys in $O(\log^2 n)$ time using n EREW PRAM processors.*

PROOF : The sorting algorithm is described in Algorithm discussed nest. It uses n processors. Define $T(n)$ to be the time taken by this algorithm to sort n keys using n processors. Step 1 of this algorithm takes $O(1)$ time. Step 2 runs in $T(n/2)$ time. Finally, step 3 takes $O(\log n)$ time (c.f. Theorem 34.3). Therefore, $T(n)$ satisfies $T(n) = O(1) + T(n/2) + O(\log n) = T(n/2) + O(\log n)$, which solves to $T(n) = O(\log^2 n)$.

EXAMPLE 34.4. *Consider the problem of sorting the 16 numbers 25, 21, 8, 5, 2, 13, 11, 16, 23, 31, 9, 4, 18, 12, 27, 34 using 16 processors. In step 1 of Algorithm 13.12, the input is partitioned into two:* $X'_1 = 8, 21, 8, 5, 2, 13, 11, 16$ *and* $X'_2 = 23, 31, 9, 4, 18, 12, 27, 34$. *In step 2, processors 1 to 8 work on* X'_1*, recursively sort it, and obtain* $X_1 = 2, 5, 8, 11, 13, 16, 21, 25$. *At the same time processors 9 to 16 work on* X'_2*, sort it, and obtain* $X_2 = 4, 9, 12, 18, 23, 27, 31, 34$. *In step 3,* X_1 *and* X_2 *are merged to get the final result : 2, 4, 5, 8, 9, 11, 12, 13, 16, 18, 21, 23, 25, 27, 31, 34.*

The work done by Algorithm is $\Theta(n \log^2 n)$. Therefore, its efficiency is $\Theta(1/\log n)$. It has a speedup of $\Theta(n/\log n)$.

Odd-even Merge Sort

```
Step 0.    If n ≤ 1, return X.
Step 1.    Let X = k_1, k_2, ..., k_n be the input. Partition
           the input into two: X'_1 = k_1, k_2, ..., k_{n/2} and
           X'_2 = k_{n/2 + 1}, k_{n/2 + 2}, ..., k_n.
Step 2.    Allocate n/2 processors to sort X'_1
           recursively. Let X_1 be the result. At the
           same time employ the other n/2 processors to
           sort X'_2 recursively. Let X_2 be the result.
Step 3.    Merge X_1 and X_2 using n = 2m processors.
```

The first part X'_1 contains all the input keys $\leq k$ and the second part X'_2 contains all the rest of the keys. The parts X'_1 and X'_2 are sorted recursively with $n/2$ processors each. The output is X'_1 in sorted order followed by X'_2 in sorted order. If $T(n)$ is the sorting time of n keys using n processors, we have $T(n) = T(n/2) + O(\log n)$, which solves to $T(n) = O(\log^2 n)$.

THEOREM 34.7. Sorting n keys can be performed in $O(\log^2 n)$ time using n CREW PRAM processors.

EXERCISE

1. Give an $O(lgn)$ EREW algorithm that determines for each object in an n-object list whether it is the middle ($\lfloor n/2 \rfloor$ th) object.
2. Give an EREW algorithm to perform prefix computation on an array $x[1 .. n]$. Do not use pointers but use index properly.
3. Give an EREW FIND-ROOTS algorithm, that runs on forest of n nodes.
4. Give an n-processor CRCW algorithm that can compute OR of n boolean values in $O(1)$ time.
5. Write $O(lgn)$-time EREW algorithm for multiplying two $n \times n$ matrices using n^3 processors. Is there a faster CRCW algorithm.

□□□

35

MATRIX OPERATION

35.1 Matrix and Its Types

Matrix

A matrix is a rectangular array of numbers.

$$A = \begin{pmatrix} a_{11} & a_{12} & a_{13} \\ a_{21} & a_{22} & a_{23} \\ a_{31} & a_{32} & a_{33} \end{pmatrix}$$

or

$$A = [a_{ij}] \; 1 \le i \le n, \; 1 \le j \le p$$

Transpose of a Matrix

It is obtained by interchanging rows and columns of a given matrix. Thus, if

$$A = [a_{ij}]$$

$$A^T = [a_{ji}]$$

e.g., $$A = \begin{bmatrix} 1 & 2 \\ 4 & 5 \\ 7 & 8 \end{bmatrix} \Rightarrow A^T = \begin{bmatrix} 1 & 4 & 7 \\ 2 & 5 & 8 \end{bmatrix}$$

Zero matrix

A matrix in which all the elements are zero

$$\begin{bmatrix} 0 & 0 & 0 \\ 0 & 0 & 0 \\ 0 & 0 & 0 \end{bmatrix}$$

Square matrix

A matrix in which number of rows equal number of columns is called square matrix, *i.e.*, $n \times n$ matrix is a square matrix

Rectangular matrix

When number of rows $\neq$ number of columns. It is a rectangular matrix.

Diagonal matrix

A matrix $A = [a_{ij}]$; is a diagonal matrix if all of the non diagonal elements are zero.

i.e., for $i \neq j$, $a_{ij} = 0$. $$\begin{bmatrix} a_{11} & 0 & 0 \\ 0 & a_{22} & 0 \\ 0 & 0 & a_{33} \end{bmatrix}$$

Identity matrix

It is a diagonal matrix with $a_{ij} = 1$ if $i = j$, otherwise $a_{ij} = 0$

$$I = \begin{bmatrix} 1 & 0 & 0 \\ 0 & 1 & 0 \\ 0 & 0 & 1 \end{bmatrix}$$

Upper triangular matrix

All entries below the diagonal are zero

$$U = \begin{bmatrix} 2 & 3 & 4 \\ 0 & 1 & 2 \\ 0 & 0 & 3 \end{bmatrix}$$

Lower triangular matrix

All entries above the diagonal are zero

$$L = \begin{bmatrix} 2 & 0 & 0 \\ 3 & 1 & 0 \\ 4 & 2 & 3 \end{bmatrix}$$

Permutation matrix

P has exactly one 1 in each row or column, and 0's else where

$$P = \begin{bmatrix} 0 & 1 & 0 & 0 \\ 0 & 0 & 1 & 0 \\ 1 & 0 & 0 & 0 \\ 0 & 0 & 0 & 1 \end{bmatrix}$$

Symmetric matrix

If $A = A^T$, *i.e.*, matrix is equal to its transpose *e.g.*, $\begin{bmatrix} 1 & 2 & 3 \\ 2 & 6 & 4 \\ 3 & 4 & 5 \end{bmatrix}$ is a symmetric matrix.

Operations on Matrix

Addition : Let $A = (a_{ij})$, $B = (b_{ij})$ are two $m \times n$ matrices then resultant matrix C is obtained as,

$$c_{ij} = a_{ij} + b_{ij}$$

Multiplication :

$$C_{ik} = \sum_{j=1}^{n} a_{ij}\, b_{jk}$$

Adjoint of a square matrix : Adjoint of any given square matrix is obtained on replacing every (i, j) th element of A by the co-factor of the (j, i)th element in determinant $|A|$. If

$$A = \begin{bmatrix} a_{11} & a_{12} & a_{13} \\ a_{21} & a_{22} & a_{23} \\ a_{31} & a_{32} & a_{33} \end{bmatrix}$$

then $$\text{adj}\, A = \begin{bmatrix} A_{11} & A_{21} & A_{31} \\ A_{12} & A_{22} & A_{32} \\ A_{13} & A_{23} & A_{33} \end{bmatrix}$$

Cofactors are calculated as,

$$A_{11} = (-1)^{i+j} \begin{vmatrix} a_{22} & a_{23} \\ a_{32} & a_{33} \end{vmatrix} = (-1)^{i+j} (a_{22}a_{33} - a_{23}a_{32})$$

$$A_{21} = \text{cofactor } a_{12} = (-1)^{1+2} \begin{vmatrix} a_{21} & a_{23} \\ a_{31} & a_{33} \end{vmatrix}$$

$$A_{12} = \text{cofactor } a_{21} = (-1)^{2+1} \begin{vmatrix} a_{12} & a_{13} \\ a_{32} & a_{33} \end{vmatrix}$$

THEOREM 35.1. $A(\text{adj } A) = |A| I = (\text{adj } A) A$

Inverse of a matrix

If A be any matrix then a matrix B is its inverse iff $AB = BA = I$, where I being the unit matrix.

THEOREM 35.2. The necessary and sufficient condition for a square matrix A to possess the inverse is that $|A| \neq 0$

PROOF : **The condition is necessary :** Let B be the inverse of A.

We have $AB = I$

$\Rightarrow$ $|A||B| = |I| = 1$

$\Rightarrow$ $|A| \neq O$

The condition is sufficient : It will be seen that if $|A| \neq 0$, then

$$B = \frac{1}{|A|}(\text{adj } A)$$

is inverse of A.

We have
$$AB = A\left(\frac{1}{|A|}\text{adj } A\right)$$
$$= \frac{1}{|A|}(A \,.\, \text{adj } A) = \frac{1}{|A|}|A| I = I.$$

Similarly $BA = I$.

35.2 Strassens Matrix Multiplictions

Let A and B be two $n \times n$ matrices. The product matrix $C = AB$ is also on $n \times n$ matrix whose (i, j) th element can be found as below

$$C(i, j) = \sum_{1 \leq k < n} A(i, k) \,.\, B(k, j) \qquad \ldots(1)$$

This matrix multiplication takes $\theta(n^3)$ time.

Another way we can compute matrix multiplication by divide and conquer technique. We assume that n is a power of 2, that is for non negative integer k, $n = 2^k$. If n is not a power of 2, zeros are appended to two matrix A and B, so that resulting dimension is power of 2. Imagine that A and B are each partitioned into four square submatrices, each having dimensions $\frac{n}{2} \times \frac{n}{2}$. Then product AB is calculated by above formula (1),

$$\begin{bmatrix} C_{11} & C_{12} \\ C_{21} & C_{22} \end{bmatrix} = \begin{bmatrix} A_{11} & A_{12} \\ A_{21} & A_{22} \end{bmatrix} \begin{bmatrix} B_{11} & B_{12} \\ B_{21} & B_{22} \end{bmatrix} \quad \ldots(2)$$

then

$$\begin{aligned} C_{11} &= A_{11}B_{11} + A_{12}B_{21} \\ C_{12} &= A_{11}B_{12} + A_{12}B_{22} \\ C_{21} &= A_{21}B_{11} + A_{22}B_{21} \\ C_{22} &= A_{21}B_{12} + A_{22}B_{22} \end{aligned} \quad \ldots(3)$$

if $n = 2$ then, formula (2) and (3) are computed using a multiplication operation for the elements of A and B, for $n > 2$, the elemetns of C can be computed using matrix multiplication and addition operations applied to matrices of size $\frac{n}{2} \times \frac{n}{2}$. Since n is a power of 2, these product can bé recusively computed by the same algorithm we are using for $n \times n$ case, this algorithm will continue applying itself to smaller-sized submatrices until n becomes suitably small ($n = 2$), so that product is computed directly.

To compute AB using (3), **we need to perform 8 multiplications of $\frac{n}{2} \times \frac{n}{2}$ matrices and 4 additions.** Since two $\frac{n}{2} \times \frac{n}{2}$ matrices can be added in cn^2 time, for some constant c, the overall computing tiime $T(n)$ of the resulting divide-and-conquer algorithm is given by the recurrence.

$$T(n) = \begin{cases} b & n \le 2 \\ 8T\left(\frac{n}{2}\right) + cn^2 & n < 2 \end{cases}$$

where b and c are constants.

This recurrence cna be solved in $O(n^3)$ time. Hence, no improvement over convetional method. Since multiplication operation is more expensive as compared to addition, so **Volker Strassen has discovered a way to compute C_{ij} using only 7 multiplication and 18 additions.** His method involves first computing the seven $\frac{n}{2} \times \frac{n}{2}$ matrices P, Q, R, S, T, U and V as in eqn. (4)

$$\begin{aligned} P &= (A_{11} + A_{22})(B_{11} + B_{22}) \\ Q &= (A_{21} + A_{22})B_{11} \\ R &= A_{11}(B_{12} - B_{22}) \\ S &= A_{22}(B_{21} - B_{11}) \\ T &= (A_{11} + A_{12})B_{22} \\ U &= (A_{21} - A_{11})(B_{11} + B_{12}) \\ V &= (A_{12} - A_{22})(B_{21} + B_{22}) \end{aligned} \quad \ldots(4)$$

$$\begin{aligned} C_{11} &= P + S - T + V \\ C_{12} &= R + T \\ C_{21} &= Q + S \\ C_{22} &= P + R - Q + U \end{aligned} \quad \ldots(5)$$

The resulting recurrence relation for $T(n)$ is

$$T(n) = \begin{cases} b & n \leq 2 \\ 7T\left(\frac{n}{2}\right) + an^2 & n > 2 \end{cases} \qquad \ldots(6)$$

where a and b are constants, we have

$$T(n) = an^2\left[1 + \frac{7}{4} + \left(\frac{7}{4}\right)^2 + \ldots + \left(\frac{7}{4}\right)^{k-1}\right] + 7^k\, T(1)$$

$$\leq cn^2 \left(\frac{7}{4}\right)^{\log_2 n} + 7^{\log_2 n}, \ldots c \text{ is a constant}$$

$$= cn^{\log_2 4 + \log_2 7 - \log_2 4} + n^{\log_2 7}$$

$$= O(n^{\log_2 7}) \approx O(n^{2.81})$$

which is improvement over $O(n^3)$, thus strassen's matrix multipliction technique is improvement over conditional methods.

35.3 Triangularization Method

This method is also known as the **decomposition** method or the factorization method. In this method, the coefficient matrix **A** of the system of equations is decomposed or factorized into the product of a lower triangular matrix **L** and an upper triangular matrix **U**. We write the matrix **A** as

$$\mathbf{A} = \mathbf{LU} \qquad \ldots(1)$$

where

$$\mathbf{L} = \begin{bmatrix} l_{11} & 0 & 0 & \ldots & 0 \\ l_{21} & l_{22} & 0 & \ldots & 0 \\ l_{31} & l_{32} & l_{33} & \ldots & 0 \\ \vdots & & & & \\ l_{n1} & l_{n2} & l_{n3} & \ldots & l_{nn} \end{bmatrix} \text{ and } \mathbf{U} = \begin{bmatrix} u_{11} & u_{12} & u_{13} & \ldots & u_{1n} \\ 0 & u_{22} & u_{23} & \ldots & u_{2n} \\ 0 & 0 & u_{33} & \ldots & u_{3n} \\ \vdots & & & & \\ 0 & 0 & 0 & \ldots & u_{nn} \end{bmatrix}$$

Using the matrix multiplication rule to multiply the matrices **L** and **U** and comparing the elements of the resulting matrix with those of **A** we obtain

$$u_{i1}\, u_{1j} + l_{i2}\, u_{2j} + \ldots + l_{in}\, u_{nj} = a_{ij},\ j = 1(1)n \qquad \ldots(2)$$

where $\quad i_{ij} = 0, j > i \text{ and } u_{ij} = 0, i > j.$

The system of equations involves $n^2 + n$ unknowns. Thus, there are n parameter family of solutions. To produce a unique solution it is convenient to choose either $u_{ii} = 1$ or $l_{ii} = 1$, $i = 1(1)n$. When we choose

(i) $l_{ii} = 1$, the method is called the **Doolittle's** method.

(ii) $u_{ii} = 1$, the method is called the **Crout's** method.

When we take $u_{ii} = 1$, $i = 1(1)n$, the solution of the equations (2) may be written as

$$l_{ij} = a_{ij} - \sum_{k=1}^{j-1} l_{ik}\, u_{kj},\ i \geq j$$

$$u_{ij} = \left(a_{ij} - \sum_{k=1}^{i-1} l_{ik}\, u_{kj} \right) / l_{ii},\ i < j \qquad \ldots(3)$$

$$u_i = 1.$$

We note that the first column of the matrix **L** is identical with the first column of the matrix **A**. That is

$$l_{i1} = a_{i1},\ i = 1(1)n \qquad \ldots(4)$$

We also note that $u_{ij} = a_{1j}/l_{11},\ j = 2(1)n$ ...(5)

The first column of **L** and the first row of **U** have been determined. We can now proceed to determine the second column of **L** and the second row of **U**

$$l_{i2} = a_{i2} - l_{i1}\, u_{12},\ i = 2(1)n$$

$$u_{2j} = (a_{2j} - l_{21}\, u_{1j})/l_{22},\ j = 3(1)n \qquad \ldots(6)$$

Next, we find the third column of **L** followed by the third row of **U**. Thus, for the relevant indices i and j, the elements are computed in the order

$$l_{i1}, u_{1j};\quad l_{j2}, u_{2j};\quad l_{j3}, u_{3j};\quad \ldots;\quad l_{i,\,n-1};\quad u_{n-1,\,j};\quad l_{nn}$$

Having determined the matrices **L** and **U**, the system of equations (6) becomes

$$\mathbf{LUx} = \mathbf{b} \qquad \ldots(7)$$

We write (7) as the following two systems of equations

$$\mathbf{Ux} = \mathbf{z} \qquad \ldots(8)$$

$$\mathbf{Lz} = \mathbf{b} \qquad \ldots(9)$$

The unknown $z, z_2, \ldots, z_n$ in (9) are determined by forward substitution and the unknowns $x_1, x_2, \ldots, x_n$ in (8) are obtained by back substitution. Alternatively, we find $\mathbf{L}^{-1}$ and $\mathbf{U}^{-1}$ to get

$$\mathbf{z} = \mathbf{L}^{-1}\,\mathbf{b} \text{ and } \mathbf{x} = \mathbf{U}^{-1}\mathbf{z} \qquad \ldots(10)$$

The inverse of **A** can also be determined from

$$\mathbf{A}^{-1} = \mathbf{U}^{-1}\,\mathbf{L}^{-1}. \qquad \ldots(11)$$

This method fails if any of the diagonal elements l_{ii} or u_{ii} is zero. The **LU** decomposition is guaranteed when the matrix **A** is positive definite. However, it is only a sufficient condition.

EXAMPLE 35.1. *Consider the equations*

$$x_1 + x_2 + x_3 = 1$$

$$4x_1 + 3x_2 - x_3 = 6$$

$$3x_1 + 5x_2 + 3x_3 = 4$$

SOLUTION : Use the decomposition method to solve the system.

We choose $u_{ii} = 1$ and write

$$\begin{bmatrix} 1 & 1 & 1 \\ 4 & 3 & -1 \\ 3 & 5 & 3 \end{bmatrix} = \begin{bmatrix} l_{11} & 0 & 0 \\ l_{21} & l_{22} & 0 \\ l_{31} & l_{32} & l_{33} \end{bmatrix} \begin{bmatrix} 1 & u_{12} & u_{13} \\ 0 & 1 & u_{23} \\ 0 & 0 & 1 \end{bmatrix}$$

$$= \begin{bmatrix} l_{11} & l_{11}u_{12} & l_{11}u_{13} \\ l_{21} & l_{21}u_{12} + l_{22} & l_{21}u_{13} + l_{22}u_{23} \\ l_{31} & l_{31}u_{12} + l_{32} & l_{31}u_{13} + l_{32}u_{23} + l_{33} \end{bmatrix}$$

On comparing the corresponding elements, we obtain

first column : $l_{11} = 1\ l_{21} = 4,\ l_{31} = 3$

first row : $u_{12} = 1,\ u_{13} = 1$

second column : $l_{22} = -1,\ l_{32} = 2$

second row : $u_{23} = 5,\ l_{33} = -10$

Thus we have

$$\mathbf{L} = \begin{bmatrix} 1 & 0 & 0 \\ 4 & -1 & 0 \\ 3 & 2 & -10 \end{bmatrix},\ \mathbf{U} = \begin{bmatrix} 1 & 1 & 1 \\ 0 & 1 & 5 \\ 0 & 0 & 1 \end{bmatrix}$$

From (9), using forward substitution, we have

$$\mathbf{z} = [1, -2, -1/2]^T$$

From (8), using back substitution, we get

$$\mathbf{x} = [1, 1/2, -1/2]^T$$

EXAMPLE 35.2. *Find the inverse of the matrix*

$$\mathbf{A} = \begin{bmatrix} 3 & 2 & 1 \\ 2 & 3 & 2 \\ 1 & 2 & 2 \end{bmatrix}$$

using **LU** decomposition method. Take $u_{11} = u_{22} = u_{33} = 1$.

SOLUTION : We write

$$\begin{bmatrix} 3 & 2 & 1 \\ 2 & 3 & 2 \\ 1 & 2 & 2 \end{bmatrix} = \begin{bmatrix} l_{11} & 0 & 0 \\ l_{21} & l_{22} & 0 \\ l_{31} & l_{32} & l_{33} \end{bmatrix} \begin{bmatrix} 1 & u_{12} & u_{13} \\ 0 & 1 & u_{23} \\ 0 & 0 & 1 \end{bmatrix}$$

and obtain as in the previous example

$$l_{11} = 3,\ l_{21} = l_{31} = 1$$

$$u_{12} = 2/3,\ u_{13} = 1/3$$

$$l_{22} = 5/3,\ l_{32} = 4/3$$

$$u_{23} = 4/5,\ l_{33} = 3/5$$

Therefore, we have

$$\mathbf{L} = \begin{bmatrix} 2 & 0 & 0 \\ 2 & 5/3 & 0 \\ 1 & 4/3 & 3/5 \end{bmatrix}, \mathbf{U} = \begin{bmatrix} 1 & 2/3 & 1/3 \\ 0 & 1 & 4/5 \\ 0 & 0 & 1 \end{bmatrix}$$

We, now get

$$\mathbf{L}^{-1} = \begin{bmatrix} 1/3 & 0 & 0 \\ -2/5 & 3/5 & 0 \\ 1/3 & -4/3 & 5/3 \end{bmatrix}, \mathbf{U}^{-1} = \begin{bmatrix} 1 & -2/3 & 1/5 \\ 0 & 1 & -4/5 \\ 0 & 0 & 1 \end{bmatrix}$$

Hence,

$$\mathbf{A}^{-1} = \mathbf{U}^{-1}\mathbf{L}^{-1} = \begin{bmatrix} 1 & -2/3 & 1/5 \\ 0 & 1 & -4/5 \\ 0 & 0 & 1 \end{bmatrix} \begin{bmatrix} 1/3 & 0 & 0 \\ -2/5 & 3/5 & 0 \\ 1/3 & -4/5 & 5/3 \end{bmatrix}$$

$$= \begin{bmatrix} 2/3 & -2/3 & 1/3 \\ -2/3 & 5/3 & -4/3 \\ 1/3 & -4/3 & 5/3 \end{bmatrix} = \frac{1}{3}\begin{bmatrix} 2 & -2 & 1 \\ -2 & 5 & -4 \\ 1 & -4 & 5 \end{bmatrix}$$

EXAMPLE 35.3. *Show that the* **LU** *decomposition method fails to solve the system of equations*

$$\begin{bmatrix} 1 & 1 & -1 \\ 2 & 2 & 5 \\ 3 & 2 & -3 \end{bmatrix} \begin{bmatrix} x_1 \\ x_2 \\ x_3 \end{bmatrix} = \begin{bmatrix} 2 \\ -3 \\ 6 \end{bmatrix}$$

Exact solution is $x_1 = 1, x_2 = 0, x_3 = -1$.

SOLUTION : If we write

$$\begin{bmatrix} 1 & 1 & -1 \\ 2 & 2 & 5 \\ 3 & 2 & -3 \end{bmatrix} = \begin{bmatrix} 1 & 0 & 0 \\ l_{21} & 1 & 0 \\ l_{31} & l_{32} & 1 \end{bmatrix} \begin{bmatrix} u_{11} & u_{12} & u_{13} \\ 0 & u_{22} & u_{23} \\ 0 & 0 & u_{33} \end{bmatrix}$$

we obtain $\quad u_{11} = 1, u_{12} = 1, u_{13} = -1$

$$l_{21}\, u_{11} = 2 \text{ or } l_{21} = 2$$

$$l_{21}\, u_{12} + u_{22} = 2 \text{ or } u_{22} = 0$$

Therefore, the **LU** decomposition method fails as the pivot $u_{22} = 0$.

If we write

$$\begin{bmatrix} 1 & 1 & -1 \\ 2 & 2 & 5 \\ 3 & 2 & -3 \end{bmatrix} = \begin{bmatrix} l_{11} & 0 & 0 \\ l_{21} & l_{22} & 0 \\ l_{31} & l_{32} & l_{33} \end{bmatrix} \begin{bmatrix} 1 & u_{12} & u_{13} \\ 0 & 1 & u_{23} \\ 0 & 0 & 1 \end{bmatrix}$$

we obtain $\quad u_{11} = 1, l_{21} = 2, l_{31} = 3$

$$l_{11}\, u_{12} = 1 \text{ or } u_{12} = 1$$

$$l_{11}\, u_{13} = -1 \text{ or } u_{13} = -1$$

$$l_{21}\, u_{12} + l_{22} = 2 \text{ or } l_{22} = 0$$

Therefore, the **LU** decomposition method fails as the pivot $l_{22} = 0$.

We note that the coefficient matrix is not a positive definite matrix and hence its **LU** decomposition is not guaranteed.

However, if we interchange the equations as

$$\begin{bmatrix} 3 & 2 & -3 \\ 2 & 2 & 5 \\ 1 & 1 & -1 \end{bmatrix}\begin{bmatrix} x_1 \\ x_2 \\ x_3 \end{bmatrix} = \begin{bmatrix} 6 \\ -3 \\ 2 \end{bmatrix}$$

then, **LU** decomposition of **A** can be obtained. In this case, we obtain

$$\mathbf{A} = \mathbf{LU}$$

$$= \begin{bmatrix} 3 & 0 & 0 \\ 2 & 2/3 & 0 \\ 1 & 1/3 & -7/2 \end{bmatrix}\begin{bmatrix} 1 & 2/3 & -1 \\ 0 & 1 & 21/2 \\ 0 & 0 & 1 \end{bmatrix}$$

EXAMPLE 35.4. *Solve the system of equations* **Ax** = **b**, *where*

$$\mathbf{A} = \begin{bmatrix} 2 & 1 & 1 & -2 \\ 4 & 0 & 2 & 1 \\ 3 & 2 & 2 & 0 \\ 1 & 3 & 2 & -1 \end{bmatrix}, \mathbf{b} = \begin{bmatrix} -10 \\ 8 \\ 7 \\ -5 \end{bmatrix}$$

using the **LU** decomposition method. Take all the diagonal elements of **L** as 1. Also find $\mathbf{A}^{-1}$.

We write

$$\begin{bmatrix} 2 & 1 & 1 & -2 \\ 4 & 0 & 2 & 1 \\ 3 & 2 & 2 & 0 \\ 1 & 3 & 2 & -1 \end{bmatrix} = \begin{bmatrix} 1 & 0 & 0 & 0 \\ l_{21} & 1 & 0 & 0 \\ l_{31} & l_{32} & 1 & 0 \\ l_{41} & l_{42} & l_{43} & 1 \end{bmatrix}\begin{bmatrix} u_{11} & u_{12} & u_{13} & u_{14} \\ 0 & u_{22} & u_{23} & u_{24} \\ 0 & 0 & u_{33} & u_{34} \\ 0 & 0 & 0 & u_{44} \end{bmatrix}$$

Comparing the corresponding elements on both sides, we get

first row : $u_{11} = 2, u_{12} = 1, u_{13} = 1, u_{14} = -2$

first column : $l_{21} = 2, l_{31} = 3/2, l_{41} = 1/2$

second row : $l_{21}\, u_{12} + u_{22} = 0$ or $u_{22} = -2$

$l_{21}\, u_{13} + u_{23} = 2$ or $u_{23} = 0$

$l_{21}\, u_{14} + u_{24} = 1$ or $u_{24} = 5$

second column : $l_{31}\, u_{12} + l_{32}\, u_{22} = 2$ or $l_{32} = -1/4$

$l_{41}\, u_{12} + l_{42}\, u_{22} = 3$ or $l_{42} = -5/4$

third row : $l_{31}\, u_{13} + l_{32}\, u_{23} + u_{33} = 2$ or $u_{33} = 1/2$

$l_{31}\, u_{14} + l_{32}\, u_{24} + u_{34} = 0$ or $u_{34} = 17/4$

third column : $l_{41}\, u_{13} + l_{42}\, u_{23} + l_{43}\, u_{33} = 2$ or $l_{43} = 3$

fourth row : $l_{41}\, u_{14} + l_{42}\, u_{24} + l_{43}\, u_{34} + u_{44} = -1$ or $u_{44} = -13/2$.

Hence, we obtain

$$\mathbf{L} = \begin{bmatrix} 1 & 0 & 0 & 0 \\ 2 & 1 & 0 & 0 \\ 3/2 & -1/4 & 1 & 0 \\ 1/2 & -5/4 & 3 & 1 \end{bmatrix}, \mathbf{U} = \begin{bmatrix} 2 & 1 & 1 & -2 \\ 0 & -2 & 0 & 5 \\ 0 & 0 & 1/2 & 17/4 \\ 0 & 0 & 0 & -13/2 \end{bmatrix}$$

We now write the system of equations $\mathbf{Ax} = \mathbf{b}$ as $\mathbf{LUx} = \mathbf{b}$ or $\mathbf{Ly} = \mathbf{b}$ and $\mathbf{Ux} = \mathbf{y}$. From $\mathbf{Ly} = \mathbf{b}$, we get

$$\begin{bmatrix} 1 & 0 & 0 & 0 \\ 2 & 1 & 0 & 0 \\ 3/2 & -1/4 & 1 & 0 \\ 1/2 & -5/4 & 3 & 1 \end{bmatrix} \begin{bmatrix} y_1 \\ y_2 \\ y_3 \\ y_4 \end{bmatrix} = \begin{bmatrix} -10 \\ 8 \\ 7 \\ -5 \end{bmatrix}$$

Using the forward substitution method, we obtain

$$u_1 = -10, y_2 = 8 - 2y_1 = 28$$

$$u_3 = 7 - \frac{3}{2} y_1 + \frac{1}{4} y_2 = 29$$

$$y_4 = -5 - \frac{1}{2} y_1 + \frac{5}{4} y_2 - 3y_3 = -52$$

From $\mathbf{Ux} = \mathbf{y}$, we get

$$\begin{bmatrix} 2 & 1 & 1 & -2 \\ 0 & -2 & 0 & 5 \\ 0 & 0 & 1/2 & 17/4 \\ 0 & 0 & 0 & -13/2 \end{bmatrix} \begin{bmatrix} y_1 \\ y_2 \\ y_3 \\ y_4 \end{bmatrix} = \begin{bmatrix} -10 \\ 28 \\ 29 \\ -52 \end{bmatrix}$$

Using the backward substitution method, we obtain

$$x_4 = 8, x_3 = 2\left[29 - \frac{17}{4} x_4\right] = -10$$

$$x_2 = -\frac{1}{2} [28 - 5x_4] = 6$$

$$x_1 = \frac{1}{2} [-10 - x_2 - x_3 + 2x_4] = 5$$

Therefore, the solution vector is $[5, 6 -10, 8]^T$.

We also obtain

$$\mathbf{L}^{-1} = \begin{bmatrix} 1 & 0 & 0 & 0 \\ -2 & 1 & 0 & 0 \\ -2 & 1/4 & 1 & 0 \\ 3 & 1/2 & -3 & 1 \end{bmatrix} \text{ and } \mathbf{U}^{-1} = \frac{1}{13} \begin{bmatrix} 13/2 & 13/4 & -13 & -8 \\ 0 & -13/2 & 0 & -5 \\ 0 & 0 & 26 & 17 \\ 0 & 0 & 0 & -2 \end{bmatrix}$$

Hence,

$$\mathbf{A}^{-1} = (\mathbf{LU})^{-1} = \mathbf{U}^{-1}\mathbf{L}^{-1} = \frac{1}{13} \begin{bmatrix} 2 & -4 & 11 & -8 \\ -2 & -9 & 15 & -5 \\ -1 & 15 & -25 & 17 \\ -6 & -1 & 6 & -2 \end{bmatrix}$$

EXERCISE

1. If K is a non negative constant, then prove that the recurrence

$$T(n) = \begin{cases} k & n = 1 \\ 3T\left(\dfrac{n}{2}\right) + kn, & n > 1 \end{cases}$$

has the following solution (for n a power of 2)

$$T(n) = 3kn^{\log_2 3} - 2kn$$

2. Find the LU decomposition of the matrix

$$\begin{pmatrix} 4 & -5 & 6 \\ 8 & -6 & 7 \\ 12 & -7 & 12 \end{pmatrix}$$

3. Write an algorithm for LUP decomposition?
4. Use Strassen's algorithm to compute the matrix product

$$\begin{pmatrix} 1 & 3 \\ 5 & 5 \end{pmatrix}\begin{pmatrix} 8 & 4 \\ 6 & 2 \end{pmatrix}$$

show your work.

5. Modify Strassen's algorithm to compute the product of $n \times n$ matrix when n is not exact power of 2?
6. Compare matrix multiplication with all-pair shortest path algorithm?

□□□

36

POLYNOMIALS AND FFT

36.1 Evaluating Polynomial Functions

Consider the polynomial $P(x) = a_n x^n + a_{n-1} x^{n-1} + \ldots a_1 x + a_0$ with real coefficients and $n \geq 1$. Suppose the coefficients $a_0, a_1, \ldots, a_n$ and x are given and that the problem is to evaluate $P(x)$, then algorithm is given as follows :

```
Poly (A, n x)
P ← A[0], xpower← 1
for i ← 1 to n
     do xpower ← xpower *   x
     P ← P A[i] * x power
return P
```

This algorithm does $2n$ multiplications and n additions.

36.1.1 Horner's method

We have a better way of computing $ab + ac$, with fewer multiplications, as $a(b + c)$. Similarly we can write Horner's method for evaluating $P(x)$. Using factorization as

$$P(x) = (...((a_n x + a_{n-1})x + a_{n-2})x + \dots + a_1)x + a_0$$

We can write its algorithm as

```
Hornerpoly (A, n, x)
      P ← A[n]
for j ← n - 1 down to 0 steps -1
      P ← P * x + A[i]
```

Thus simply by factoring P we have cut the number of multipliations in half without increasing the addition.

36.1.2 Preprocessing of Coefficients

Let $P(x) = a_n x + a_{n-1} x + \dots + a_1 x + a_0$, where $n = 2^k - 1$ for some $k \geq 1$, thus P has 2^k terms, some of which may be zero. The procedure for evaluating $P(x)$ described here uses a divide-and-conquer method to factor P. We assume that P is monic (*i.e.*, $a_n = 1$)

If $n = 1$, then $p(x) = x + a_0$ and is evaluated by doing one addition. Suppose $n > 1$ and P is written as follows for some j and b :

$$P(x) = (x^j + b)\, q(x) + r(x)$$

where q and r are monic polynomials of degree $2^{k-1} - 1$. Then $P(x)$ can be evaluated as :

1. Evaluat $q(x)$ and $r(x)$
2. Compute x^j
3. Multiply $(x^j + b)$ by $q(x)$ and add $r(x)$.

$$q(x)$$

$$x^{2k-1} + b \overline{\big)\, x^{2^k - 1} + a_{2^k - 2}\, x^{2^k - 2} + \dots + : a_{2^k - 1}\, x^{2^k - 1} + \dots a_1 x + a_0}$$

(quotient: $x^{2^{k-1} - 1} + a_{2^k - 1}\, x^{2^{k-1} - 1} + a_{2^{k-1}}$)

$$\underline{x^{2^k - 1} + a_{2^k - 2}\, x^{2^k - 2} + \dots + a_{2^k - 1}\, x^{2^k - 1} + b x^{2^k - 1} + \dots + b a_{2^k - 1}}$$

$$(a_{2^{k-1}-1} - b)\, x^{2^{k-1} - 1} + \dots + (a_0 - b a_2^{k-1})$$

$$r(x)$$

Fig. 36.1 P(x) divided by $x^j + b$.

Here j = degree of P – degree of $q = 2^k - 1 - (2^{k-1} - 1) = 2^{k-1}$ since j is a power of 2, x^j can be computed quickly. The correct value for b becomes clear when we divide $P(x)$ by

$x^j + b$ to obtain $q(x)$, the quotient and $r(x)$, the remainder see Fig. 36.1 thus preprocessing algorithm factors P as follows.

$$P(x) = (x^{2k-1} + a_{2^{k-1}-1} - 1)\, q(x) + r(x)$$

the factorization is complete when q and r have degree 1.

EXAMPLE 36.1. *Let* $P(x) = x^7 + 6x^6 + 5x^5 + 4x^4 + 3x^3 + 2x^2 + x + 1$. *Then* $k = 3$ $(7 = 2^k - 1)$, $j = 2^{k-1} = 4$, $b = a_{2^{k-1}-1} - 1 = a_3 - 1 = 2$, *and* $x^j + b = x^4 + 2$. *Fig. 36.2 shows the computation of* $q(p)$ *and* $r(x)$

$q(x)$

$$x^4 + 2 \,\overline{\big)\, x^7 + 6x^6 + 5x^5 + 4x^4 + 3x + 2x^2 + x + 1}\quad \text{quotient: } x^3 + 6x^2 + 5x + 4$$

$$\underline{x^7 + 6x^6 + 5x^5 + 4x^4 + 2x^3 + 12x^2 + 10x + 8}$$

$$x^3 - 10x^2 - 9x - 7$$

$r(x)$

(a) Computing $q(x)$ and $r(x)$

$q(x) = x^3 + 6x^2 + 5x + 4$

$k = 2,\ j = 2^{k-1} = 2$

$b = a_{2^{k-1}} - 1 = a_1 - 1 = 4$

$$x^2 + 4 \,\overline{\big)\, x^3 + 6x^2 + 5x + 4}\quad \text{quotient: } x + 6$$

$$\underline{x^3 + 6x^2 + 4x + 24}$$

$$x - 20$$

(b) Recursively factoring $q(x)$

Thus $q(x) = (x^2 + 4)(x + 6) + x - 20$

$r(x) = x^3 - 10x^2 - 9x - 7.$

$k = 2,\ j = 2^{k-1} = 2$

$b = a_{2^{k-1}-1} - 1 = a_1 - 1 = -10$

$$x^2 - 10 \,\big)\, x^3 - 10x^2 - 9x - 7$$

$$x^3 - 10x^2 - 10x + 100$$

$$\overline{x - 107}$$

(c) Recursively factoring $r(x)$

Thus $r(x) = (x^2 - 10)(x - 10) + (x - 107)$

Fig. 36.2 Computational detals of Ex. 36.1.

Thus $P(x) = (x^4 + 2)(x^3 + 6x^2 + 5x + 4) + (x^3 - 10x^2 - 9x - 7)$

Now factor $q(x)$ and $r(x)$ in the same way, as shown in Fig. 36.2(b) and 36.2(c). Thus

$$P(x) = (x^4 + 2)((x^2 + 4)(x + 6) + (x - 20)) + (x^2 - 10)(x - 10) + (x - 107))$$

This example requires 5 multiplications contrast Horner's method would have required 7, however 10 additions are done instead of 7.

36.2 Lagrange's Interpolation

Given n points (x_i, y_i), the interpolation problem is to find the coefficients of the unique polynomial $P(x)$ of degree $\le n - 1$ that goes through these points.

$$P(x) = \sum_{1 \le i \le n} \left(\prod_{\substack{i \ne j \\ 1 \le j \le n}} \frac{(x - x_j)}{(x_i - x_j)} \right) y_i$$

To verify that $P(x)$ does satisfy the n points, we observe that

$$P(x_i) = \left(\prod_{\substack{i \neq j \\ 1 \leq j \leq n}} \frac{(x_i - x_j)}{(x_i - x_j)} \right) y_i = y_i$$

Since every other term becomes zero. The numerator of each term is a product of $n - 1$ factors and hence degree of P is $\leq n - 1$

EXAMPLE 36.2. *Consider the input (0, 5), (1, 10) and (2, 21), Find P(x) using Lagrange's interpolation and compute vaues at these points.*

SOLUTION : $P(x) = \frac{(x-1)(x-2)}{(0-1)(0-2)} 5 + \frac{(x-0)(x-2)}{(1-0)(1-2)} 10 + \frac{(x-0)(x-1)}{(2-0)(2-1)} 21$

$$= \frac{5}{2}(x^2 - 3x + 2) - 10(x^2 - 2x) + \frac{21}{2}(x^2 - 2)$$

$$= 3x^2 + 2x + 5$$

We have, $P(0) = 5$, $P(1) = 10$, $P(2) = 21$, hence verified.

```
LAGRANGE (A, B, n, P)
P ← 0
for i ← 1 to n do
    for j ← 1 to n do
        if (i ≠ j) then
        poly ← poly * (x - A[j])
        denom ← denom * (A[i] - A[j])
        A ← P + (poly * B[i]/denom)
```

Here if statement is executed n^2 times, time to compute denom is one multiplication and one subtraction, but the execution of * requires more than constant time (applied to polynomials). Since degree of $x - A[j]$ is one, the time to execute * is proportional to degree of poly, which is at most $j - 1$ on jth iteration.

Therefore the total cost of polynomial multiplication step is

$$\sum_{1 \leq i \leq n} \sum_{1 \leq j \leq n} (j-1) = \sum_{1 \leq i \leq n} \left(\frac{n(n+1)}{2} - n \right) = \frac{n^2(n+1)}{2} - n^2 \equiv O(n^3)$$

36.3 The Fast Fourier Transform (FFT)

The Fourier transform is used in electrical engineering in variety of ways including speech transmission, coding theory, and image processing.

The Fourier transform of a continuous function $a(t)$ is given by

$$A(f) = \int_{-\infty}^{+\infty} a(t) \cdot e^{2\pi i f t} \, dt \qquad \ldots(1)$$

where as inverse transform of $A(f)$ is

$$a(t) = \frac{1}{2\pi}\int_{-\infty}^{+\infty} A(f) \,.\, e^{-2\pi i f t}\, dt \qquad \ldots(2)$$

where i is imaginary root, f is mean frequency, t is time

Corresponding to this continuous Fourier transform is the *discrete* fourier transform (DFT) which handles sample points of $a(t)$, namely $a_0, a_1, ..., a_{N-1}$. The DFT is defined by

$$A_j = \sum_{0 \le K \le N-1} a_k e^{2\pi ijk/N},\ 0 \le j \le N-1 \qquad \ldots(3)$$

and the inverse is

$$a_k = \frac{1}{N} \sum_{0 \le j \le N-1} A_j\, e^{-2\pi ijk/N},\ \ 0 \le K \le N-1 \qquad \ldots(4)$$

There is a close connection between DFT and polynomial evaluation. If we imagine the polynomial

$$a(x) = a_{N-1}x^{N-1} + a_{N-2}x^{N-2} + \ldots + a_1 x + a_0 \qquad \ldots(5)$$

Then the Fourier element A_j is the value of $a(x)$ at $x = \omega^j$, where $\omega = e^{2\pi i/N}$. Similarly for the inverse Fourier transform if we imagine the polynomial with the Fourier coefficients

$$A(x) = A_{N-1}\, x^{N-1} + A_{N-2}\, x^{N-2} + \ldots + A_1 x + A_0 \qquad \ldots(6)$$

then each a_k is the value of $\frac{A(x)}{N}$ at $x = (\omega^{-1})^k$, where $\omega = e^{2\pi i/N}$. Thus, DFT corresponds exactly to the evaluation of a polymomial at N points : $\omega^0, \omega^1, ..., \omega^{N-1}$.

DEFINITION. An element ω is in a commutative ring, is called a primitive Nth root of unity if

1. $\omega \ne 1$
2. $\omega^N = 1$
3. $\sum_{0 \le P \le N-1} \omega^{jp} = 0,\ 1 \le j \le N-1$

EXAMPLE 36.3. *Let* $N = 4$, $\omega = e^{\pi i/2} = \cos\frac{\pi}{2} + i \sin\frac{\pi}{2} = i$, *thus* $\omega \ne 1$, *and* $\omega^4 = i^4 = i^2 . i^2 = 1$, *Also*

$$\sum_{0 \le p \le 3} \omega^{jp} = 1 + i^j + i^{2j} + i^{3j} = 0$$

THEOREM 36.1. Let $N = 2n$ and suppose ω is primitive Nth root of unity, then $-\omega^j = \omega^{j+n}$.

PROOF : Here $(\omega^{j+n})^2 = (\omega^j)^2\, (\omega^n)^2 = (\omega^j)^2\, (\omega^{2n}) = (\omega^j)^2$, as $\omega^n = 1$.

Since ω^j are distinct, we know $\omega^j \ne \omega^{j+n}$, therefore

$$\omega^{j+h} = -\,\omega^j$$

THEOREM 36.2. Let $N = 2n$ and ω is primitive Nth root of unity, then ω^2 is a primitive nth root of unity.

PROOF : $\omega^N = \omega^{2n} = 1$, this implies ω^2 is a primitive nth root of unity but $\omega^{2j} \ne 1$, if it would, we have $\omega^k = 1$, for $1 \le k \le 2n = N$ which would contradict the fact. Hence, ω^2 is nth root of unity.

From above two theorems it is clear that if ω^j, $0 \le j \le N$ are primitive Nth roots of unity, then for $N = 2n$, ω^{2j}, $0 \le j \le n$ are also nth roots of unity. Using this we can devise divide-and-conquer technique for the FFT, the complexity of algorithm is $O(NlgN)$ as compare $O(n^2)$ of Horner's Method.

We can break $a(x)$ into two parts, which contains even and odd numbered exponents.

$$a(x) = (a_{N-1}\,x^{N-1} + a_{N-3}\,x^{N-3} + \ldots + a_1 x) + (a_{N-2}x^{N-2} + \ldots + a_2 x^2 + a_0)$$

Letting $y = x^2$, we can rewrite $a(x)$ as a sum of two polynomials

$$a(x) = (a_{N-1}\,y^{n-1} + a_{N-3}\,y^{n-2} + \ldots + a_1)x + (a_{N-2}\,y^{n-1} + a_{N-4}\,y^{n-2} + \ldots + a_0)$$
$$= c(y)x + b(y)$$

Also value of $a(x)$ at points ω^j, $0 \le j \le n-1$ is

$$a(\omega^j) = c(\omega^{2j}) \,.\, \omega^j + b(\omega^{2j})$$
$$a(\omega^{j+n}) = -\,c(\omega^{2j})\omega^j + b(\omega^{2j})$$

Using these concept ω_0 can give recursive version of FFT algorithm.

```
FFT (N , a(x), ω, A)
If N = 1 then A[0] ← a0
else
    n ← N/2
b(x) = aN-2 x^(n-1) + ... + a2x + a0
c(x) = aN-1 x^(n-1) + ... + a3 x + a1
FFT (n, b(x), ω², B)
FFT (n, c(x), ω², C)
ωp[-1] ← 1/ω
for j ← 0 to n - 1 do
    ωp[j] ← ω * ωp[j - 1]
    A[j] ← B[j] + ωp[j] * C[j]
    A[j + n] ← B[j] - ωp [j] * c(j)
```

Running time is given by $T(N) = 2T\left(\frac{N}{2}\right) + DN$, where D is a constant and DN is time to compute $b(x)$ and $c(x)$, $T(1) = d$, a constant we can simplify this as

$$T(2^m) = 2T(2^{m-1}) + D2^m$$
$$= \quad \vdots$$
$$= Dm2^m + T(1)\,.\,2^m$$
$$= DNlgN + dN$$
$$= O(N \log_2 N)$$

EXAMPLE 36.4. *Describe a divide-and-conquer algorithm not based on FFT, for multiplying two degree-n polynomials with integer coefficients in $O(n^{\log_2 3})$ time, assuming that elementary arithmetic on any two integers can be done in constant time.*

SOLUTION : Let $p(n)$ and $q(n)$ be the two polynomials, expressed by their coefficients. Rewrite these as $p(n) = p_1(n)\, x^{n/2} + p_2(n)$ and $q(n) = q_1(n)\, x^{n/2} + q_2(n)$.

Let $r(n) = p_1(n) - p_2(n)$ and let $s(n) = q_2(n) - q_1(n)$, and note that

$$r(n)s(n) = p_1(n)q_2(n) - p_2(n)q_2(n) - p_1(n)q_1(n) + p_1(n)q_2(n)$$

Thus, $$r(n)s(n) + p_1(n)q_1(n) + p_2(n) + q_2(n) = p_1(n)q_2(n) + p_1(n)q_2(n)$$

Note that $$p(n)q(n) = p_1(n)q_1(n)\, x^n + [p_1(n)q_2(n) + p_1(n)q_2(n)]\, x^{n/2} + p_2(n)p_2(n)$$

which is the same as

$$p_1(n)q(n)\, x^n + [r(n)s(n) + p_1(n)q_1(n) + p_2(n) + q_2(n)]\, x^{n/2} + p_2(n)p_2(n)$$

Therefore, with three recursive calls on problems of size $n/2$, plus an additional amount of work that is $O(n)$, we can multiply $p(n)$ and $q(n)$. This gives us the recurrence $T(n) = 3T\,(n/2) + bn$, for some constant b, which implies that $T(n)$ is $O(n^{\log_2 3})$, by the master theorem.

EXAMPLE 36.5. *Given degree-n polynomials $p(x)$ and $q(x)$, describe an $O(n \log n)$-time method for multiplying the derivatives of $p(x)$ and $q(x)$, that is, $p'(x) \cdot q'(x)$.*

SOLUTION : Compute $p'(x)$ and $q'(x)$ using the standard calculus rule for computing the derivative of a polynomial. Then use the FFT to compute the coefficients of the polynomial $p' \cdot q'$.

EXAMPLE 36.6. *Suppose you are given a set of real numbers $X = \{x_0, x_1, \ldots, x_{n-1}\}$. Note that, by the Interpolation Theorem for Polynomials, there is a unique degree-$(n-1)$ polynomial $p(x)$, such that $p(x_i) = 0, 1, \ldots, n-1$. Design a divide-and-conquer algorithm that can construct a coefficient representation of this $p(x)$ in $O(n \log^2 n)$ time.*

SOLUTION : Divide X into two sets X_1 and X_2 of equal size $(n/2)$, and recursively construct polynomials $p_1(n)$ and $p_2(n)$, such that $p_1(X_1) - 0$ and $p_2(X_2) = 0$. Then use the FFT algorithm to compute the polynomials $p_1 \cdot p_2$. This algorithm satisfies the recurrence $T(n) = 2T\,(n/2) + bn \log n$, for some constant b, which implies that $T(n)$ is $O(n \log n)$ by the master theorem.

EXERCISE

1. Write a divide-and-conquer algorithm to evaluate a polynomial at a point and give its running time.
2. Write an algorithm to overload + and * in case of polynomials.

3. Suppose polynomial $P(x)$ has real coefficients but we wish to evaluate P at complex no. $x = u + iv$, u and v are real, write an algorithm to do this.
4. The fibonacci sequence is defined as $f_0 = 0$, $f_1 = 1$, $f_n = f_{n-1} + f_{n-2}$, for $n \geq 2$. Give $O(lgn)$ algo to compute f_n

   $$\left(\textbf{Hint}: \begin{bmatrix} f_{n-1} \\ f_n \end{bmatrix} = \begin{bmatrix} 0 & 1 \\ 1 & 1 \end{bmatrix} \begin{bmatrix} f_{n-2} \\ f_{n-1} \end{bmatrix} \right)$$
5. Present an $O(n)$ time algorithm to compute the coefficients of polynomial $(1 + x)^n$. How much time is needed if you use the FFT to solve this.
6. Devise the DFT algorithm and also for its inverse.
7. Use the convolution theorem to compute the product of the polynomials $p(x) = 3x^2 + 4x + 2$ and $q(x) = 2x^3 + 3x^2 + 5x + 3$.

□□□

37

NUMBER-THEORETIC ALGORITHMS

This chapter present some algorithms from number theory which play important role in cryptographic schemes based on prime numbers.

37.1 Greatest Common Divisor (GCD)

If 30 and 24 are two numbers and divisor of 30 are 1, 2, 3, 5, 6, 10, 15 and 30, and divisors of 24 are 2, 3, 4, 6, 8, 12, 24, out of which the greatest common divisor is 6 thus *gcd* (30, 24) = 6. We can give algorithm given by **Euclid** as follows :

```
EUCLID (a, b)
      if b ≠ 0 then return Euclid (b, a mod b)
else return a
```

We can see that if consecutive Fibonacci number are inputted then it is worst case for Euclid.

We can have the **extended** form of **Euclid's** algorithm, for computing two more integers x and y such that

$$ax + by = \text{Euclid}\ (a, b)$$

```
ExEuclid (a, b)
if b = 0
    then return (a, 1, 0)
    (d', x', y') ← ExEuclid (b, a mod b)
    (d, x, y) ← (d', y', x' - ⌊a /b⌋ y')
return (d, x, y)
```

We have if $b \neq 0$

$$d' = gcd\,(b, a \bmod b), \text{ since } d = ax + by$$

We have

$$d' = bx' + (a \bmod b)\, y' = bx' + (a - \lfloor a/b \rfloor b)\, y'$$

$$d' = ay' + b(x' - \lfloor a/b \rfloor y')$$

then d' becomes d in next step, therefore

$$d = ay' + b(x' - \lfloor a/b \rfloor y')$$

i.e., $(d, x, y) = (d', y', x' - \lfloor a/b \rfloor y')$

We compare coefficients of x', y' with

$$d = ax + by$$

then $x = y', y = x' - \lfloor a/b \rfloor y'$

Running time of this algorithm is $O(lg\ b)$

EXAMPLE 37.1. *Let $a = 98$, $b = 78$, show all the calcualted values at each step in ExEuclid.*

SOLUTION :

a	b	$\lfloor a/b \rfloor$	d	x	4
99	78	1	3	–11	14
78	21	3	3	3	–11
21	15	1	3	–2	3
15	6	2	3	1	–2
6	3	2	3	0	1
3	0	–	3	1	0

THEOREM 37.1. If $a > b \geq 0$ and invocation Euclid (a, b) performs $k \geq 1$ recursive calls, then $a \geq F_{k+2}$ and $b \geq F_{k+1}$.

PROOF : Let $K = 1$, then for $b \geq 1$, $b = F_2$, second Fibonacci no. in sequence but $a > b$, so $a \geq 2$, *i.e.*, $a = F_3$.

Let it be true if $k - 1$ recursive calis are made, so that it is true for k calls.

As $k > 0$, $b > 0$, Euclid (a, b) gives Euclid $(b, a \bmod b)$ in next call, which makes $k - 1$ recursive calls. By inductive hypothesis $b \geq F_{k+1}$, and $a \bmod b \geq F_k$ (as a becomes b. in each call), we have

$$b + (a \bmod b) = b + (a - \lfloor a/b \rfloor b)$$

$$\leq a.$$

as $a > b > 0$ and $\lfloor a / b \rfloor \geq 1$, thus

$$a \geq b + (a \bmod b)$$
$$\geq F_{k+1} + F_k = F_{k+2} \text{ hence proved.}$$

THEOREM 37.2. (Lame's theorem) For any integer $k \geq 1$, if $a > b \geq 0$ and $b < F_{K+1}$ then the invocation Euclid (a, b) makes fewer than K recursive calls.

PROOF : Since EUCLID (F_3, F_2) makes exactly one recursive calls and for $k \geq 2$, $F_{k+1} \bmod F_k = F_{k-1}$, we also have

$$gcd(F_{k+1}, F_k) = gcd\,(F_k, m\,(F_{k+1} \bmod F_k))$$
$$= gcd\,(F_k, F_{k-1})$$

Thus EUCLID (F_{k+1}, F_k) recurses exactly $k - 1$ times.

EXAMPLE 37.2. *Prove that for all integers a, k, n*

$$gcd(a, n) = gcd\,(a + kn, n)$$

SOLUTION : We have $\quad gcd\,(a, b) = gcd(b, a)$

Thus $\quad gcd\,(a + kn, n) = gcd(a, n) + gcd\,[kn, n] \quad \ldots(1)$

also, $\quad gcd(a, ka) = |\,a\,| \;\forall\, k \,\varepsilon\, Z.$

thus $\quad gcd\,(kn, n) = gcd\,(n, kn)$

$$= |\,n\,| \text{ for } k \,\varepsilon\, z.$$

thus eqn (1) becomes.

$$gcd(a, n) + |\,n\,| = gcd\,(a, n)$$

Since addition of absolute value of a number will not affect the recursive calls.

37.2 Chinese Remainder Theorem

Chinese mathematician sun-tsii solved the problem of finding those integers x that leave remainders, 2, 3 and 2 when divided by 3, 5 and 7 respectiely. e.g., if $x = 23$ or in general $23 + 105k$.

THEOREM 37.3. (Chinese Remainder Theorem)

Let $n = n_1 n_2 \ldots nk_1$ where n_i are pairwise relatively prime. consider the correspondence

$$Q \leftrightarrow (a_1, a_2, \ldots, a_n) \quad \ldots(1)$$

where $a \,\varepsilon\, Z_n$, $a_i \,\varepsilon\, Z_{ni}$, and

$$a_i = a \bmod n_i$$

then mapping of eqn. (1) aobve is one-to-one correspondence between Z_n and cartesian product $Z_{n_1} \times Z_{n_2} \times Z_{n_3} \times \ldots \times Z_{n_k}$ operations performed on the elements of Zn can be equivalently performed on the corresponding k-tuples by performing the operations independently in each coordinate position in the appropriate system. That is, if

$$a \leftrightarrow (a_1, a_2, ..., a_k)$$
$$b \leftrightarrow (b_1, b_2, ..., b_k)$$

then

$$(a + b) \bmod n = ((a_1 + b_1) \bmod n_1, \dots (a_k + b_k) \bmod n_k) \quad ...(2)$$
$$(a - b) \bmod n = ((a_1 - b_1) \bmod n_1, ..., (a_k - b_k) \bmod n_k) \quad ...(3)$$
$$ab \bmod n = (a_1 b_1 \bmod n_1, ..., a_k b_k \bmod n_k) \quad ...(4)$$

We can prove this theorem letting $m_i = \frac{n}{n_i}$, for $i = 1, 2, ..., k$, $m_j = n_1 n_2 ..., n_{i-1} n_{i+1} ..., n_k$, so that $m_i \equiv O \ (mod \ n_j) \ \forall \ j \neq i$ then allowing.

$$C_i = m_i \ (m_i^{-1} \bmod n_i) \quad ...(5)$$

for $i = 1, 2, ..., k$, we have

$$a = (a_1 c_1 + a_2 c_2 + \dots + a_k c_k) \bmod n \quad ...(6)$$

37.3 RSA Public Key Cryptosystem

Prime numbers are widely used for creating keys, so that information flows across network in encoded form which is then decoded at other end. Secret information is called **ciphertext** which is encoded and decoded using keys, called **public key** which is for every one and docoded by **Secret key** which is available to the person who wants to decrypt the ciphertext.

For example suppose a person *A* wants to send a message to *B* then he picks up the public key of *B* from the directory or thorugh him, then *A* encrypts the message to be sent using public key P_A of *B*, then he sends the message to *B*. When *B* receives the message he decrypts the message using his private key S_A.

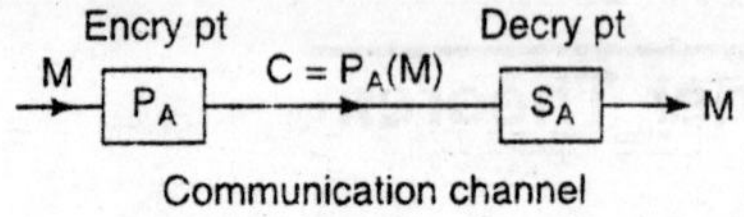

Encry pt
Decry pt
M
C = P_A(M)
P_A
S_A
M
Communication channel

Fig. 37.1.

Now suppose *B* wants to send **digitally** signed response M' then following steps are followed.

- *B* computes **digital signature** σ for the message M' using his secret key S_A, $\sigma = S_A(M')$
- *B* sends message/signature pair (σ, M') to *A*.
- When *A* receives, he can verify it by the public key P_A of *B*, $M' = P_A(\sigma)$. Which finds the origin of message.

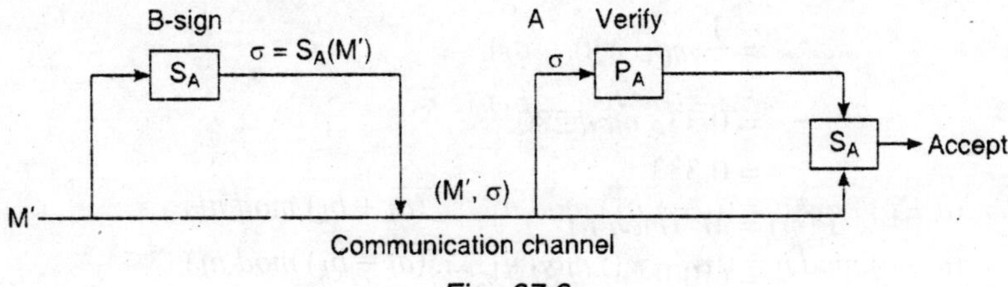

Fig. 37.2.

RSA algorithm

1. Select at random two large primes p and q, primes p and q might be, say, 100 decimal digits.
2. Compute n by the equation $n = pq$
3. Select a small odd integer e that is relatively prime to $\phi(n)$,

where $$\phi(n) = n\prod_{p/n}\left(1 - \frac{1}{p}\right) = pq\left(1 - \frac{1}{p}\right)\left(1 - \frac{1}{q}\right)$$
$$= (p - 1)(q - 1)$$

{e.g., if $n = 45$, prime divisors are 3 and 5

$$\therefore \quad \phi(45) = 45\left(1 - \frac{1}{3}\right)\left(1 - \frac{1}{5}\right)$$
$$= 45 \times \frac{2}{3} \times \frac{4}{5} = 24.$$

if n is prime $\phi(n) = n - 1$

if n is composite $\phi(n) < n - 1$}

4. Compute d as multiplicative inverse of e, modulo $\phi(n)$
5. Publish pair $P = (e, n)$ as his RSA public key
6. Keep secret the pair $S = (d, n)$ as his RSA Secret key

In this scheme, the domain D is the set Z_n. The transformation of message M associated with a public key $p = (e, n)$

$$P(M) = M^e \ (mod\ n)$$

the transformation of ciphertext C associated with a secret key $S = (d, n)$ is

$$S(C) = C^d \ (mod\ n)$$

EXAMPLE 37.3. *Consider an RSA key set with $P = 11$, $q = 29$, $n = 319$, $e = 3$ what value of d should be used in the secret key? What is the encryption of message $M = 100$.*

SOLUTION : $\phi(n) = (p - 1)(q - 1) = 10 \times 28 = 280$

We have, $e = 3$, since d is multiplicative inverse of e

$$d = \frac{1}{e} \ mod\ \phi\ (n)$$

$$= \frac{1}{3} \, mod \, 280.$$
$$= 0.333 \, mod \, 280.$$
$$= 0.333$$
$$P(m) = M^e \, (mod \, n)$$
$$= (100)^3 \, mod \, 319.$$
$$S(C) = [(100)^3]^{1/3} \, mod \, 319 = 100$$

THEOREM 37.4. Let p and q be two odd primes, and define $n = pq$. Let e be relatively prime with $\phi(n)$ and let d be the multiplicative inverse of e modulo $\phi(n)$. For each integer x such that $0 < x < n$,

$$x^{ed} = x \text{ (mod } n).$$

PROOF : Let $y = x^{ed}$ mod n. We want to prove that $y = x$. Because of the way we have selected e and d, we can write $ed = k\phi(n) + 1$, for some integer k. Thus, we have

$$y = x^{k\phi(n)+1} \text{ mod } n.$$

We distinguish two cases.

Case 1 : x does not divide n. We rewrite y as follows:

$$y = x^{k\phi(n)+1} \text{ mod } n$$
$$= xx^{k\phi(n)} \text{ mod } n$$
$$= x(x^{\phi(n)} \text{ mod } n)^k \text{ mod } n.$$

By (Euler's theorem), we have $x^{\phi(n)}$ mod $n = 1$, which implies $y = x \cdot 1^k$ mod $n = x$.

Case 2 : x divides n. Since $n = pq$, with p and q primes, x is a multiple of either p or q. Suppose x is a multiple of p, that is, $x = hp$ for some positive integer h. Clearly, x cannot be a multiple of q as well, since otherwise x would be greater than $n = pq$, a contradiction. Thus, gcd $(x, q) = 1$ and by Theorem 10.9 (Euler's theorem), we have

$$x^{\phi(q)} \equiv 1 \text{ (mod } q).$$

Since $\phi(n) = \phi(p)\,\phi(q)$, raising both sides of the above congruence to the power of $k\phi(q)$, we obtain

$$x^{k\phi(n)} \equiv 1 \text{ (mod } q),$$

which we rewrite as

$$x^{k\phi(n)} = 1 + iq,$$

for some integer i. Multiplying both sides of the above equality by x, and recalling that $x = hp$ and $n = pq$, we obtain:

$$x^{k\phi(n)+1} = x + xiq$$
$$= x + hpiq$$
$$= x + (hi)n.$$

Thus, we have

$$y = x^{k\phi(n)+1} \text{ mod } n = x.$$

In either case, we have shown that $y = x$, which concludes the proof of the theorem.

Using RSA for Digital Signatures

The symmetry of encryption and decryption functions implies that the RSA cryptosystem directly supports digital signatures. Indeed, a digital signature S for message M is obtained by applying the decryption function to M, that is,

$$S \leftarrow M^d \bmod n \text{ (RSA signature)}.$$

The verification of the digital signature S is now performed with the encryption function, that is, by checking that

$$M \equiv S^e \pmod{n} \text{ (RSA verification)}.$$

The Difficulty of Breaking RSA

Note that, even if we know the value e, we cannot figure out d unless we know $\phi(n)$. Most cryptography researchers generally believe that breaking RSA requires that we compute $\phi(n)$ and that this requires factoring n. While there is no ***proof*** that factorization is computationally difficult, a whole series of famous mathematicians have worked on the problem over the past few hundred years. Especially if n is large ($\approx$ 200 digits), it will take a very long time to factor it. To give you an idea of the state of the art, mathematicians were quite excited when a nationwide network of computers was able to factor the ninth Fermat number, $2^{512} - 1$. This number has "only" 155 decimal digits. Barring a major breakthrough, the RSA system will remain secure. For if technology somehow advances to a point where it is feasible to factor 200 digit numbers, we need only choose an n with three or four hundred digits.

Analysis and Setup for RSA Encryption

The running time of RSA encryption, decryption, signature and verification is simple to analyze. Indeed, each such operation requires a constant number of modular exponentiations, which can be performed with method FastExponentiation.

THEOREM 37.5. Let n be the modulus used in the RSA cryptosystem. RSA encryption, decryption, signature, and verification each take $O(\log n)$ arithmetic operations.

To set up the RSA cryptosystem, we need to generate the public and private key pair. Namely, we need to compute the private key (d, p, q) and the public key $(e.n)$ that goes with it. This involves the following computations:

Selection of two random primes p and q with a given number of bits. This can be accomplished by testing random integers for primality.

Selection of an integer e relatively prime to $\phi(n)$. This can be done by picking random primes less than $\phi(n)$ until we find one that does not divide $\phi(n)$. In practice, it is suficient to check small primes from a list of known primes (often $e = 3$ or $e = 17$ will work).

Computing the multiplicative inverse d of e in $Z_{\phi(n)}$. This can be done using the extended Euclid's algorithm.

We have previously explained algorithm for each of these number theory problems in this chapter.

37.4 Coin Flipping and Bit Commitment

We now present a protocl that allows Alice and Bob to ***flip a random coin*** by exchanging email messages or otherwise communicating over a network. Let H be a strongly collision-resistant, one-way hash function. The interaction between Alice and Bob conists of the following steps:

1. Alice picks a number x and computes the digest $d = H(x)$, sending d to Bob.
2. After receiving d, Bob sends Alice his guess of whether x is odd or even.
3. Alice announces the result of the coin flip: if Bob has guessed correctly, the result is heads; if not, it is tails. She also sends to Bob x as proof of the result.
4. Bob verifies that Alice has not cheated, that is, that $d = H(x)$.

The strong collision-resistance requirement is essential, since otherwise Alice could come up with two numbers, one odd and one even, with the same digest d, and would be able to control the outcome of the coin flip.

Related to coin flipping is ***bit commitment.*** In this case, Alice wants to commit to a value n (which could be a single bit or an arbitrary string) without revealing it to Bob. Once Alice reveals n, Bob wants to verify that she has not cheated. For example, Alice may want to prove to Bob that she can predict whether a certain stock will be up ($n = 1$), down ($n = -1$), or unchanged ($n = 0$) tomorrow. Using a strongly collision-resistant, one-way hash function H, the protocol goes as follows:

1. She sends Bob x plus the digest of the concatenation of x, y and n. In keeping with tradition in cryptographic literature, we denote the concatenation of strings a and b with "$a \| b$" in this chapter. Thus, using this notation, Alice sends Bob $d = H(x\|y\|n)$. Note that Bob is unable to figure out n from x and d.
2. At the close of trading the next day, when n becomes publicly known, Alice sends y to Bob for verification.
3. Bob verifies that Alice has not cheated, that is, $d = H(x\|y\|n)$.

EXAMPLE 37.4. *Compute the multiplicative inverses of the numbers 113, 114 and 127 in* Z_{299}.

SOLUTION : We have $ix + jn = gcd(x, n) = 1$ for some integer i and j s.t. $i \equiv x^{-1} \bmod n$, where i and j can be calculated by ExEuclid algorithm then we can write :

$$113^{-1} \equiv 172 \bmod 299$$
$$114^{-1} \equiv 160 \bmod 299$$
$$127^{-1} \equiv 228 \bmod 299$$

EXAMPLE 37.5. *Prove a more general form of the reduction property of primitive roots of unity. Namely, show that, for any integer* $c > 0$, *if* ω *is a primitive* (cn)*th root of unity, then* ω^c *is a primitive nth root of unity.*

SOLUTION : If ω is a primitive (cn)th root of unity, then $1, \omega, \omega^2, \ldots, \omega^{cn-1}$ are all distinct. Thus, the numbers $1, \omega^c, (\omega^c)^2, \ldots, (\omega^c)^{n-1}$ are all distinct. In addition, $(\omega^c)^n = \omega^{cn} = 1$.

EXAMPLE 37.6. *What is the bit-reversal permutation, reverse, for $n = 16$?*

SOLUTION : (0, 8, 4, 12, 2, 10, 6, 14, 1, 9, 5, 13, 3, 11, 7, 15).

EXAMPLE 37.7. *Construct a table showing an example of the RSA cryptosystem with parameters $p = 17, q = 19$ and $e = 5$. The table should have two rows, one for the plaintext M and the other for the ciphertext C. The columns should correspond to integer values in the range [10, 20] for M.*

SOLUTION :

M	10	11	12	13	14	15	16	17	18	19	20
C	193	197	122	166	29	2	118	272	18	304	39

EXAMPLE 37.9. *Show how to modify Algorithm ExEuclid to compute the multiplicative inverse of an element in Z_n using arithmetic operations on operands with at most $2\lceil \log_2 n \rceil$ bits.*

SOLUTION : Replace the statement

return $(d', y', x' - \lfloor a/b \rfloor) y'$

with

return $(d', y', (x' - (\lfloor a/b \rfloor) y' \bmod b) \bmod b)$

EXERCISE

1. Write an algorithm for finding LCM, least common multiple.
2. Prove that if a and b are both even then
$$gcd(a, b) = 2gcd(a/2, b/2)$$
3. Write the *gcd* binary algorithm for computing *gcd* of binary numbers.
4. Write an algorithm for chinese remainder theorem using ExEuclid.
5. If $\pi(n)$ is *prime distribution function,* s.t. if finds the no., of primes less than n, then find $\pi(99)$?
6. Prove that $gcd(a, b) = gcd(|a|, |b|)$, and $gcd(a, ka) = |a| \; \forall \; k \in Z$.
7. Prove that for any integers a, b, p if $gcd(a, p) = 1$ and $gcd(b, p) = 1$, then $gcd(ab, p) = 1$.
8. Show that *gcd* operator is associative
i.e., $gcd(a, gcd(b, c)) = gcd(gcd(a, b), c)$
9. Write an algorithm for finding the solution of equation $ax \equiv b (\bmod n)$.
10. Prove that RSA is multiplicative in the sense that
$$P_A(M_1)P_A(M_2) \equiv P_A(M_1M_2) \pmod n$$
11. Show the execution of method ExtendedEuclidGCD (412, 113) by constructing a table.

❑❑❑

38

STRING MATCHING

In this chapter we study the problem of detecting the occurrence of a particular substring called *pattern*, in another string, called the text, Here we consider P the array containing pattern and $T[1 \ldots n]$, the text.

38.1 Simple or Naive String Matching

Comparisions are done (in left to right order) on the pairs of characters in array P and T, when first mismatch occurs, the pattern is moved one position forward with respect to text, and comparisions start again at the left end of pattern.

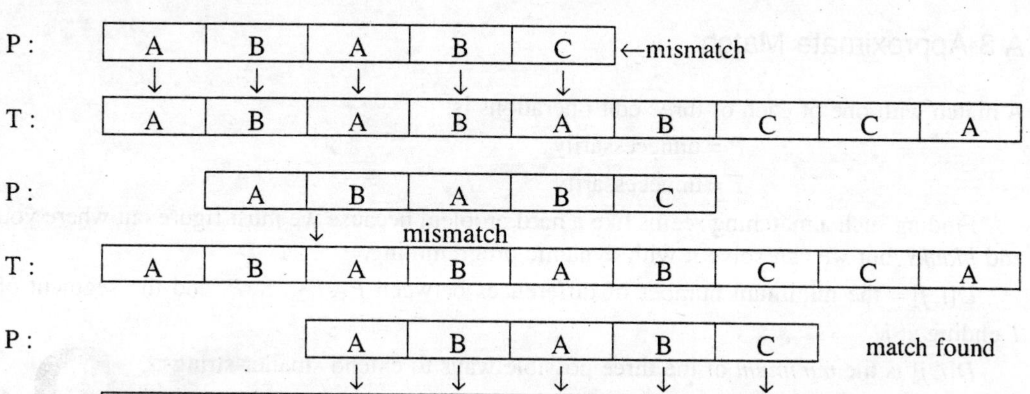

Fig. 38.1. Simple string matching.

This algorithm finds all valid shifts in loop and checks the condition $p[1 .. m] = T[i + 1 .. i + m]$ for all $n - m + 1$ possible values of i.

```
SIMPLE-STRINGMATCHING (T, p)
    n ← length [T]
    m ← length [p]
for i ← 0 to n − m
       do if p[1 . . m] = T[i + 1 . . i + m]
            then print "Match found with shift" i
```

Running time is $\theta[(n - m + 1)n]$ worst case can be $\theta(n^2)$ if $m = \lfloor n/2 \rfloor$.

38.2 Approximate String Matching

A common task in text editing is string matching - finding all occurrences of a word in a text. Unfortunately, many words are misspelled. How can we search for the string closest to the pattern?

Let p be a pattern string and T a text string over the same alphabet.

A k-approximate match between P and T is a substring of T with at most k differences.

Differences may be:

1. The corresponding characters may differ: KAT → CAT
2. P is missing a character from T: CAAT → CAT
3. T is missing a character from P: CT → CAT

Approximate Matching is important in genetics as well as spell checking.

A 3-Approximate Match

A match with one of each of three edit operations is:

P = unnecessarily

T = unnecessarily

Finding such a matching seems like a hard problem because we must figure out where you add *blanks*, but we can solve it with dynamic programming.

$D[i, j]$ = the minimum number of differences between $P_1, P_2, \ldots, P_i$ and the segment of T ending at j.

$D[i, j]$ is the *minimum* of the three possible ways to extend smaller strings:

1. If $P_i = t_i$ then D[i − 1, j − 1] else D[i − 1, j − 1] + 1 (corresponding characters do or do not match)
2. D[i − 1, j] + 1 (extra character in text-we do not advance the pattern pointer).
3. D[i, j − 1] + 1 (character in pattern which is not in text).

Once you accept the recurrence it is easy.

To fill each cell, we need only consider three other cells, not $O(n)$ as in other examples. This means we need only store two rows of the table. The total time is $O(mn)$. (see chapter 14)

Boundary conditions for string matching

What should the value of $D[0, i]$ be, corresponding to the cost of matching the first i characters of the text with none of the pattern?

It depends. Are we doing string matching in the text or substring matching?

If you want to match all of the pattern against all of the text, this meant that would have to delete the first i characters of the pattern, so $D[0, i] = i$ to pay the cost of the deletions.

if we want to find the place in the text where the pattern occurs? We do not want to pay more of a cost if the pattern occurs far into the text than near the front, so it is important that starting cost be equal for all positions. In this case, $D[0, i] = 0$, since we pay to cost for deleting the first i characters of the text.

In both cases, $D[i, 0] = i$, since we cannot excuse deleting the first i characters of the pattern without cost.

What do we return?

If we want the *cost* of comparing all of the pattern against all of the text, such as comparing the spelling of two words, all we are interested in is $D[n, m]$.

But what if we want the cheapest match between the pattern anywhere in the text? Assuming the initialization for substring matching, we seek the cheapest matching of the full pattern ending anywhere in the text. This means the cost equals $\min_{1 \le i \le m} D[n, i]$.

This only gives the cost of the optimal matching. The actual alignment - what got matched, substituted and deleted - can be reconstructed from the pattern/text and table without an auxiliary storage, once we have identified the cell with the lowest cost.

How much space do we need?

Do we need to keep all $O(mn)$ cells, since if we evaluate the recurrence filling in the columns of the matrix from left to right, we will never need more than two columns of cells to do what we need. Thus $O(m)$ space is sufficient to evaluate the recurrence without changing the time complexity at all.

Unfortunately, because we won't have the full matrix we cannot reconstruct the alignment, as above.

Saving space in dynamic programming is very important. Since memory on any computer is limited, $O(nm)$ space is more of a bottleneck than $O(nm)$ time. Fortunately, there is a clever divide-and-conquer algorithm which computes the actual alignment in $O(nm)$ time and $O(m)$ space

38.3 Rabin Karp Algorithm

The algorithm uses modulo arithmetic to find the next sequence of text to which the pattern is to be matched following steps are followed.

1. Input the given text $T[1 .. n]$ and pattern $p[1 .. m]$

2. Check whether $T[i + 1 .. i + m] = P[1 .. m]$ starting from $i = 0$

e.g., T : 4 5 6 7 2 3

↓ ↓ ↓ ↓

P : 4 5 6 7

and calculate modulo q of P i.e., $r = P \bmod q$

3. Calcualte modulo q of text of size m which is matched with pattern [even if does not matches]

e.g., let $q = 13$

$r = 4567 \bmod 13 = 4$

4. If match is found, store r and check the sequences of pattern with the same values of r. If they have same r value then match the values.

5. In order to calculate next sequence which is the sequence obtained after dropping the higher order bit or number in the text, which is currently matched with pattern, next number should be known and next sequence is calculated as follows.

$$t_{i+1} = 10(4567 - 1000 \times 4) + 2$$

$$= 5670 + 2 = 5672$$

```
    Here purpose is to remove higher order bit 4 in 4567 so
 that next sequence is obtained. Next number 2 is obtained by
 looking at next single digit no. in the text and it is
 concatenated after removing higher order bit.
    6. Goto Step (2).
```

EXAMPLE 38.1. *Give the text T = 2 3 5 9 0 2 3 1 4 1 5 2 6 7 3 9 9 2 1 and P = 31415 and modulo $q = 13$, $m = 5$*

SOLUTION : **We have**

1	2	3	4	5	6	7	8	9	10	11	12	13	14	15	16	17	18	19
2	3	5	9	0	2	3	1	4	1	5	2	6	7	3	9	9	2	1

Selecting t_i of size 5.

$t_1 = 2\ 3\ 5\ 9\ 0$

↓

3 1 4 1 5

and $r = 31415 \ mod\ 13 = 7.$

thus

$r = 23590 \ mod\ 13.$

$= 8 \neq 7$, No match.

$t_2 = 10 \times (23590 - 10000 \times 2) + 2 = 35902$

$r = 35902 \ mod\ 13 = 9,$ No match

$t_3 = 10 \times (35902 - 10000 \times 3) + 3 = 59023$

$r = 59023 \ mod\ 13 = 3,$ No match

$t_4 = 10 \times (59023 - 10000 \times 5) + 1$

$= 90231$

$r = 90231 \ mod\ 13 = 11 \neq 7,$ No match

$t_5 = 10 \times (90231 - 10000 \times 9) + 4$

$= 02314$

$r = 02314 \ mod\ 13 = 0 \neq 7,$ No match

⋮

$t_7 = 31415$

$r = 31415 \ mod\ 13 = 7,$ Match Found

this way further sequence with same r can be found.

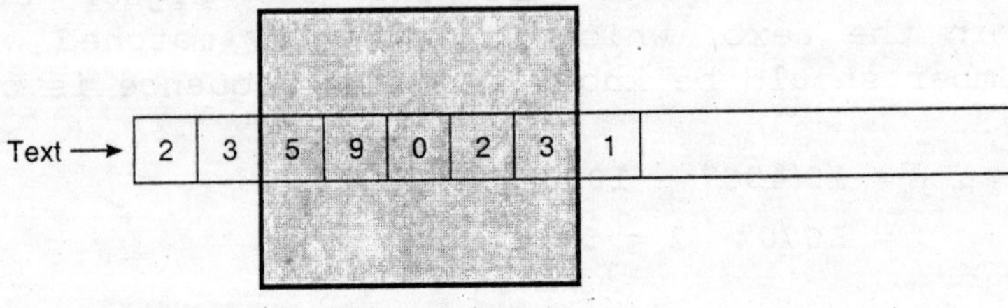

Fig. 38.2. Sliding windows contains pattern and moves one pos at a time.

This method can be viewed as *sliding window* (see fig. 38.2) of size m which moves along the text array T and numbers in this window are matched with window containing the pattern, and window slides along till it get a window with same modulo as that of pattern window. If modulo is same but pattern is not matched then it is called **Spurious hit.**

Step 5 in this method is calculated using **Horner's rule** to obtain next window.

$$P = P[m] + 10(P[m-1]) + 10(P[m-2] + ...)$$

Running time for calculating n different windows in array $T[1 \dots n]$ is $O(n)$ and for matching the pattern $O(m)$ so running time of Rabin Karp method is $O(n+m)$.

38.4 String Matching with Finite Automation

A finite automaton is 5 tuple $(Q, \Sigma, \delta, q_0, q_f)$ It consists of

$Q \rightarrow$ non empty set of states

$\Sigma \rightarrow$ non empty set of input symbols

$\delta \rightarrow$ transition function that maps $Q \times \Sigma$ to Q

$q_0 \rightarrow$ Start state

$q_f \rightarrow$ final state

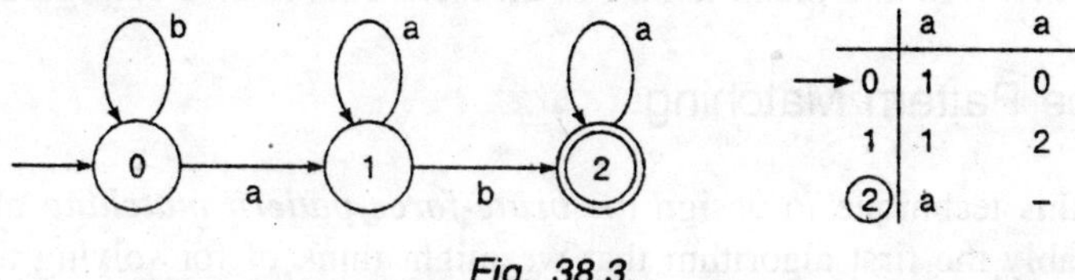

Fig. 38.3.

here $Q = \{0, 1, 2\}$

$\Sigma = \{a, b\}$

$q_0 = 0, q_f = 2$

Thus we can use this finite automaton to find a sequence of pattern P as shown in Fig. 38.4.

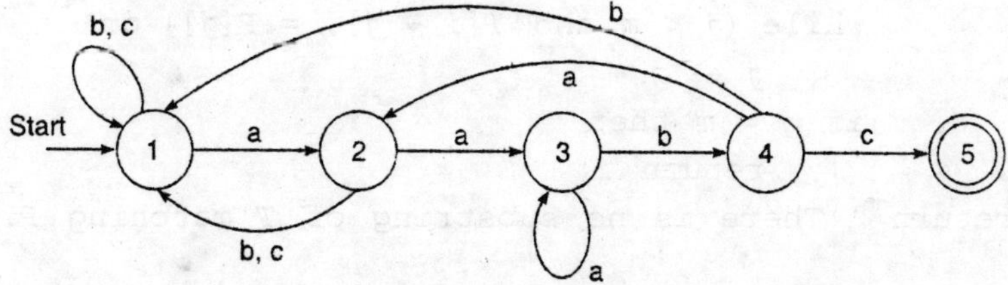

Fig. 38.4. The finite qutomaton for P = 'aabc'

```
Finite Automation-Matcher (T, δ, p)
      n ← length [T]
      q ← 0
for i ← 1 to n
      do q ← δ(q, T[i])
```

```
    if match found
        then accept
    else
        reject.
```

EXAMPLE 38.2. Suppose we are given the text string

T = abacaabaccabacabaabb .

and the pattern string

P = "*abacab*".

Then P is a substring of T. Namely, $P = T[10..15]$.

In this section, we present three different pattern matching algorithms.

38.5 Brute Force Pattern Matching

The ***brute force*** algorithm design pattern is a powerful technique for algorithm design when we have something we wish to search for or when we wish to optimize some function. In applying this techniquc in a general solution, we typically enumerate all possible configurations of the inputs involved and pick the best of all these enumerated configurations.

Brute-Force Pattern Matching

In applying this technique to design the ***brute-force pattern matching*** algorithm, we derive what is probably the first algorithm that we might think of for solving the pattern matching problem—we simply test all the possible placements of P relative to T. This approach, shown in Algorithm, is quite simple.

```
BruteForceMatch (T, P)
for i ← 0 to n – m {for each candidate index in T} do
      j ← 0
      while (j < m and T[i + j], = P[j]) do
            j ← j + 1
      if j = m then
            return i
return ''There is no substring of T matching P.''
```

The brute-force pattern matching algorithm could not be simpler. It consists of two nested loops, with the outer loop indexing through all possible starting indices of the pattern in the text, and the inner loop indexing through each character of the pattern, comparing it to its potentially corresponding character in the text. Thus, the correctness of the brute-force pattern matching algorithm follows immediately.

The running time of brute-force pattern matching in the worst case is not good, however, because, for each candidate index in T, we can perform up to m character comparisons to discover that P does not match T at the current index. Referring to Algorithm, we see that the

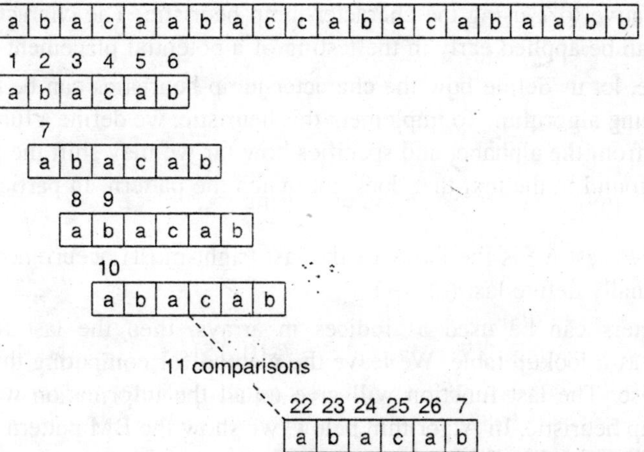

Fig. 38.5. Example run of the brute-force pattern matching algorithm. The algorithm performs 27 character comparisons, indicated above with numerical labels.

outer for-loop is executed at most $n - m + 1$ times, and the inner loop is executed at most m times. Thus, the running time of the brute-force method is $O((n - m + 1)m)$, which is $O(nm)$. Note that, when $m = n/2$, this algorithm has quadrartic running time $O(n^2)$.

In Figure 38.5 we illustrate the execution of the brute-force pattern matching algorithm on the strings T and P from Example 38.2.

38.6 The Boyer-Moore Algorithm

At first, we might feel that it is always necessary to examine every character in T in order to locate a pattern P as a substring. But this is not always the case, for the ***Boyer-Moore (BM)*** pattern matching algorithm, which we study in this section, can sometimes avoid comparisons between P and a sizeable fraction of the characters in T. The only caveat is that, whereas the brute-force algorithm can work even with a potentially unbounded alphabet, the BM algorithm assumes the alphabet is of fixed, finite size. It works the fastest when the alphabet is moderately sized and the pattern is relatively long. It works on following two heuristics :

Looking-Glass Heuristic : When testing a possible placement of P against T, begin the comparisons from the end of P and move backward to the front of P.

Character-Jump Heuristic : During the testing of a possible placement of P against T, a mismatch of test character $T[i] = c$ with the corresponding pattern character $P[j]$ is handled as follows. If c is not contained anywhere in P, then shift P completely past $T[i]$ (for it cannot match any character in P). Otherwise, shift P until an occurrence of character c in P gets aligned with $T[i]$.

The looking-glass heuristic sets up the other heuristic to allow us to avoid comparisons between P and whole groups of characters in T. In this case at least, we can get to the destination faster by going backwards, for if we encoutner a mismatch during the consideration of P at a certain location in T, then we are likely to avoid lots of needless comparisons by significantly shifting P relative to T using the character-jump heuristic. The character-jump heuristic pays off big if it can be applied early in the testing of a potential placement of P against T.

Therefore, let us define how the character-jump heuristics can be integrated into a string pattern matching algorithm. To implement this heuristic, we define a function last (c) that takes a character c from the alphabet and specifies how far we may shift the pattern P if a character equal to c is found in the text that does not match the pattern. In particular, we define last (c) as follows:

If c is in P, last (c) is the index of the last (right-most) occurrence of c in P. Otherwise, we conventionally define last $(c) = -1$.

If characters can be used as indices in arrays, then the last function can be easily implemented as a lookup table. We leave the method for computing this table efficiently as a simple exercise. The last function will give us all the information we need to perform the character-jump heuristic. In Algorithm below, we show the BM pattern matching method. The jump step is illustrated in Figure 38.6.

```
BMMatch (T, P)
Compute function last
i ← m - 1
j ← m - 1
repeat
            if P[j] = T[i] then
                    if j = 0 then

                            return i //a match!
                    else
                            i ← i - 1
                            j ← j - 1
            else
                    i ← i + m - min(j, 1 + last (T[i])) //jump step
                    j ← m - 1
until i > n - 1
return ``There is no substring of T matching P.''
```


(a)

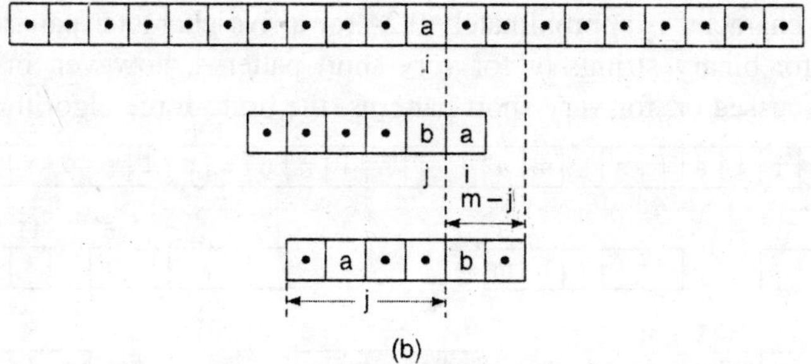

Fig. 38.6. Illustration of the jump step in the BM algorithm, where l denotes last (T[i]). We distinguish two cases: (a) 1 + l < j, where we shift the pattern by j – 1 units; (b) j < 1 + l, where we shift the pattern by one unit.

In Figure 38.7, we illustrate the execution of the Boyer-Moore pattern matching algorithm on a similar input string as in Example 38.2.

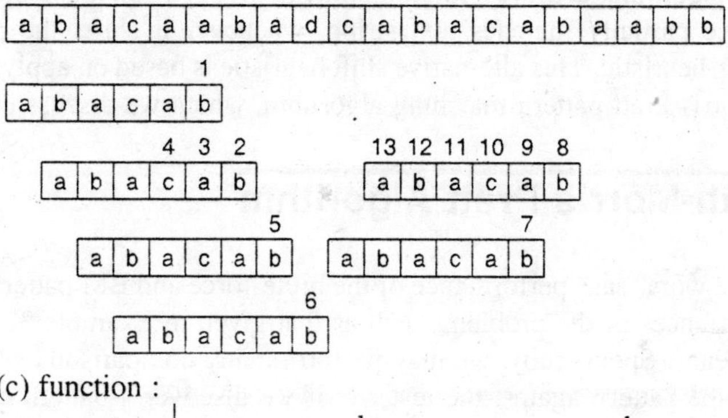

The last (c) function :

c	a	b	c	d
last (c)	4	5	3	–1

Fig. 38.7. An illustration of the BM pattern matching algorithm. The algorithm performs 13 character comparisons, which are indicated with numerical labels.

The correctness of the BM pattern matching algorithm follows from the fact that each time the method makes a shift, it is guaranteed not to "skip" over any possible matches. For last (c) is the location of the ***last*** occurrence of c in P.

The worst-case running time of the BM algorithm is $O(nm + |\Sigma|)$. Namely, the computation of the last function takes time $O(m + |\Sigma|)$. Namely, the computation of the last function takes time $O(m + |\Sigma|)$ and the actual search for the pattern takes $O(nm)$ times in the worst case, the same as the brute-force algorithm. An example of a text-pattern pair that achieves the wrost case is

$$T = \overbrace{a\,a\,a\,a\,a \ldots a}^{n}$$

$$P = b\,\overbrace{a\,a \ldots a}^{m-1}$$

The worst-case performance, however, is unlikely to be achieved for English text.

Indeed, the BM algorithm is often able to skip over large portions of the text. (See Figure 37.8). There is experimental evidence that on English text, the average number of comparisons done per text character is approximately 0.24 for a five-character pattern string. The payoff is not as great for binary strings or for very short patterns, however, in which case the KMP algorithm, discussed or, for very short patterns, the brute-force algorithm, may be better.

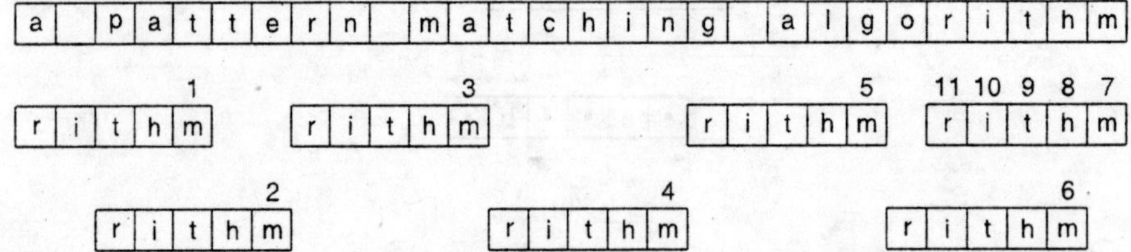

Fig. 38.8. Execution of the Boyer-Moore algorithm on an English text and pattern, where a significant speedup is achieved. Note that not all text characters are examined.

We have actually presented a simplified version of the Boyer-Moore (BM) algorithm. The original BM algorithm achieves running time $O(n + m + |\Sigma|)$ by using an alternative shift heuristic to the partially matches text string, whenever it shifts the pattern more than the character-jump heuristic. This alternative shift heuristic is based on applying the main idea from the Knuth-Morris-Pratt pattern matching algorithm, which we discuss next.

38.7 The Knuth-Morris-Pratt Algorithm

In studying the worst-case performance of the brute-force and BM pattern matching algorithms on specific instances of the problem, such as that given in Example 38.2, we should notice a major inefficiency. Specifically, we may perform many comparisons while testing a potential placement of the pattern against the test, yet if we discover a pattern character that does not match in the text, then we throw away all the information gained by these comparisons and start over again from scratch with the next incremental placement of the pattern. The Knuth-Morris-Pratt (or "KMP") algorithm, discussed in this section, avoids this waste of information and, in so doing, it achieves a running time of $O(n + m)$, which is optimal in the worst case. That is, in the wrost case any pattern matching algorithm will have to examine all the characters of the text and all the characters of the pattern at least once.

The Failure Function

The main idea of the KMP algorithm is to preprocess the pattern string P so as to compute a ***failure function*** f that indicates the proper shift of P so that, to the largest extent possible, we can reuse previously performed comparisons. Specifically, the failure function $f(j)$ is defined as the length of the longest prefix of P that is a suffix of $P[1..j]$ (note that we did ***not*** put $P[0..j]$ here). We also use the convention that $f(0) = 0$. Later, we will discuss how to compute the failure function efficiently. The importance of this failure function is that it "encodes" repeated substrings inside the pattern itself.

Computing Even Prefix Function

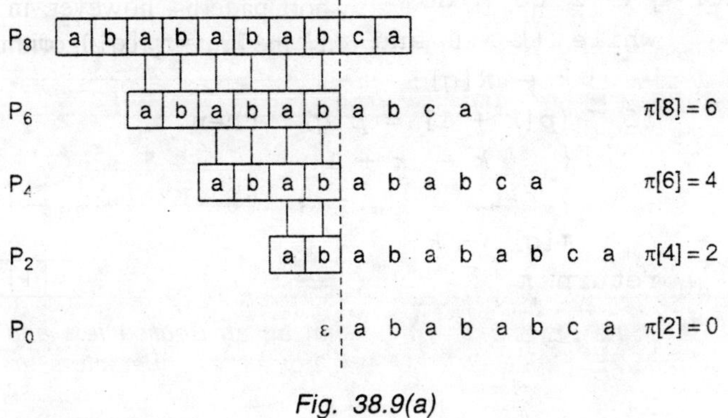

Fig. 38.9(a)

Computing Odd Prefix Function

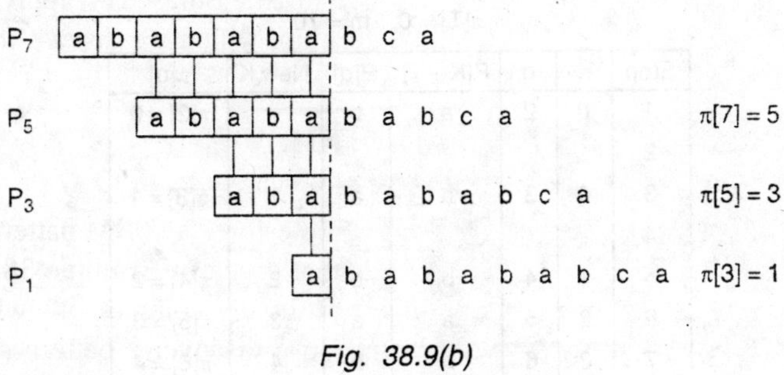

Fig. 38.9(b)

Here we can see that pattern is matched with itself to compute the prefix function, and odd and even shifts are shown in figure above. This can be represented in the form of matrix as follows :

i	1	2	3	4	5	6	7	8	9	10
P[i]	a	b	a	b	a	b	a	b	c	a
π[i]	0	0	1	2	3	4	5	6	0	1

Fig. 38.10

Algorithm for calculating prefix function can be given as

```
COMPUTE-PREFIX-FUNCTION(p)
{  m ← length [p̄]
   π[1] ← 0
```

```
    k ← 0
    for q ← 2 to m do
    {    while (k > 0 and p[k + 1]  ≠ p[q]) do
              k ← π[q];
         If   (p[k + 1]  = p[q]) then
              {    k ← k + 1
              }
              π[q]  ← k
         return π
    }
}
```

This algorithm can be executed to calculate the value of matrix in fig. 38.10.

	1	2	3	4	5	6	7	8	9	10
P[j]	a	b	a	b	a	b	a	b	c	a

$\pi[T] = 0, \quad m = 10$

Step	K	q	P[K + 1]	P[q]	New K	π[q]
1	0	2	a	b	–	π[2] = 0
2						
3	0	3	a	a	1	π[3] = 1
4						
5	1	4	b	b	2	π[4] = 2
6	2	5	a	a	3	π[5] = 3
7	3	6	b	b	4	π[6] = 4
8	4	7	a	a	5	π[7] = 5
9	5	8	b	b	6	π[8] = 6
10	6	9	a	c	4	K ← π[6]
11	4	–	a	c	2	K ← π[4]
12	2	–	a	c	0	K ← π[2]
						π[9] ← 0
13	0	10	a	a	1	π[10] ← 1

Fig. 38.11

We can see from fig. 38.11, how the algorithm is executed to compute the prefix function in steps.

In most part of the execution, condition

```
if p[k + 1]  = p[q]  then
       k ← k + 1
           ⋮
      π[q]  ← k
```

is executed. Thus if two characters in the pattern matches then k is incremented and prefix function $\pi[q] = k$, if it doesnot matches, while loop gets executed till condition fails as in step 1 and also in steps 10, 11, 12. Note here q is incremented through for loop, while k is incremented internally when two characters matches.

After calculating the prefix function we can calculate the shifts through another algorithm as below :

```
KMP-MATCHER (T, p)
{ n ← length [T]
  m ← length [p]
  π ← COMPUTE-PREFIX-FUNCTION(p)
  q ← 0
  for i ← 1 to n do
  {    while q > 0 and p[q + 1] ≠ T[i]
           do q ← π[q];
       if (p[q + 1] = T[i]) then
           q ← q + 1
       if q = m then "pattern occurs with shift" i - m
           q ← π[q]
  }
}
```

Note that this algorithm is almost same as previous algorithm, except that k is substituted with q, q is substituted with i and $p[q]$ is substituted with $T[i]$. Thus KMP algorithm is combination of both the algorithms.

EXAMPLE 38.3. *Consider the pattern string P = "abacab" from Example 38.1. The KMP failure function f(j) for the string P is as shown in the following table:*

j	0	1	2	3	4	5
$P[j]$	a	b	a	c	a	b
$J[j]$	0	0	1	0	1	2

The KMP pattern matching algorithm, shown in Algorithm, incrementally processes the text string T comparing it to the pattern string P. Each time there is a match, we increment the current indices. On the other hand, if there is a mistmatch and we have previously made progress in P, then we consult the failure function to determine the new index in P where we need to continue checking P against T. Otherwise (there for T (and keep the index variable for P at its beginning). We repeat this process until we find a match of P in T or the index for T reaches n, the length of T (indicating that we did not find the pattern P in T).

The main part of the KMP algorithm is the while-loop, which performs a comparison between a character in T and a character in P each iteration. Depending upon the outcome of this comparison, the algorithm either moves on to the next characters in T and P, consults the failure function for a new candidate character in P, or starts over with the next index in T. The correctness of tis algorithm follows from the definition of the failure function. The skipped comparisons are actually unnecessary, for the failure function guarantees that all the ignored comparisons are rebundant—they would involve comparing characters we already know match.

```
KMPMatch (T, P)
f ← KMPFFailureFunction (P)
        //construct the failure function f for P
i ← 0
j ← 0
while i < n do
        if P[j] = T[i] then
                if j = m - 1 then
                        return i - m + 1 {a match!}
                i ← i + 1
                j ← j + 1
        else if j > 0 then
                        //no match, but we have advanced in P
                j ← f(j - 1) //j indexes just after prefix of
                                                //P that must match
        else
                i ← i + 1
return ''There is no substring of T matching P.''
```

In Figure 38.12, we illustrate the execution of the KMP pattern matching algorithm on the same input string as in Example 38.2. Note the use of the failure function to avoid redoing one

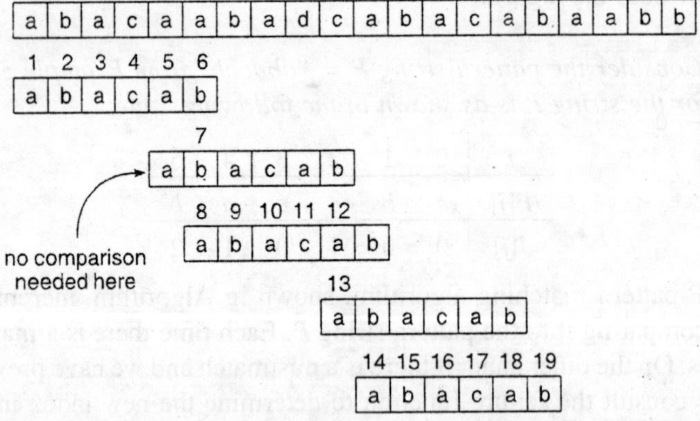

Fig. 38.12. An illustration of the KMP pattern matching algorithm. The failure function f for this pattern is given in Example 38.3. The algorithm performs 19 character comparisons, which are indicated with numerical labels.

of the comparisons between a character of the pattern and a character of the text. Also note that the algorithm performs fewer overall comparisons than the brute-force algorithm run on the same string (Figure 38.5).

Performance

Excluding the computation of the failure function, the running time of the KMP algorithm is clearly proportional to the number of iterations of the while-loop. For the sake of the analysis, let us define $k = i - j$. Intuitively, k is the total amount by which the pattern P has been shifted with respect to the text T. Note that throughout the execution of the algorithm, we have $k \leq n$. One of the following three cases occurs at each iteration of the loop.

If $T[i] = P[j]$, then i increases by 1, and k does not change, since j also increase by 1.

If $T[i \neq P[j]$ and $j > 0$, then does not change and k increases by at least 1, since in this case k changes from $i - j$ to $i - f(j - 1)$, which is an addition of $j - f(j - 1)$, which is positive because $f(j - 1) < j$.

If $T[i] \neq P[j]$ and $j = 0$, then i increases by 1 and k increases by 1, since j does not change.

Thus, at each iteration of the loop, either i or k increases by at least 1 (possibly both); hence, the total number of iterations of the while-loop in the KMP pattern matching algorithm is at most $2n$. Of course, achieving this bound assumes that we have already computed the failure function for P.

Constructing the KMP Failure Function

To construct the failure function used in the KMP pattern matching algorithm, we use the method shown in Algorithm below. This algorithm is another example of a "bootstrapping" process quite similar to that used in the KMPMatch algorithm. We compare the pattern to itself as in the KMP algorithm. Each time we have two characters that match, we set $f(i) = j + 1$. Note that since we have $i > j$ throughout the execution of the algorithm, $f(j - 1)$ is always defined when we need to use it.

```
KMPFailure Function (P)
i ← 1
j ← 0
f(0) ← 0
while i < m do
      if P[j] = P[i] then
            {we have matched j + 1 characters}
            f(i) ← j + 1
            i ← i + 1
            j ← j + 1
      else if j > 0 then
            {j indexes just after a prefix of P that
                                        must match}
            j ← f(j - 1)
      else
                  //we have no match here
            f(i) ← 0
            i ← i + 1
```

Algorithm KMPFailureFunction runs in $O(m)$ time. Its analysis is analogous to that of algorithm KMPMatch. Thus, we have:

THEOREM 38.1. The Knuth-Morris-Pratt algorithm performs pattern matching on a text string of length n and a pattern string of length m in $O(n + m)$ time.

The running time analysis of the KMP algorithm may seem a little surprising at first, for it states that, in time proportional to that needed just to read the strings *T* and *P* separartely, we can find the first occurrence of *P* in *T*. Also, it should be noted that the running time of the KMP algorithm does not depend on the size of the alphabet.

38.8 Tries

The pattern matching algorithms presented in the previous section speed up the search in a text by preprocessing the pattern (to compute the failure function in the KMP algorithm or the last function in the BM algorithm). In this section, we take a complementary approach, namely, we present string searching algorithms that preprocess the test. This approach is suitable for applications where a series of queries is performed on a fixed text, so that the initial cost of preprocessing the test is compensated by a speedup in each subsequent query (for example, a Web site that offers pattern matching in Shakespeare's *Hamlet* or a search engine that offers Web pageson the *Hamlet* topic).

A ***trie*** (pronounced "try") is a tree-based data structure for stroring strings in order to support fast pattern matching. The main application for tries is in information retrieval. Indeed, the name "trie" comes from the word *"retrieval."* In an information retrieval application, such as a search for a certain DNA sequence in a genomic database, we are given a collection *S* of strings, all defined using the same alphabet.

The primary query operations that tries support are pattern matching and ***prefix matching.*** The latter operation involves being given a string *X*, and looking for all the strings in *S* that contain *X* as a prefix.

38.8.1 Standard Tries

Let *S* be a set of *s* strings from alphabet Σ, such that no string in *S* is a prefix of another string. A ***standard trie*** for *S* is an ordered tree *T* with the following properties (see Figure 38.13):

Each node of *T*, except the root, is labeled with a character of Σ.

The ordering of the children of an internal node of *T* is determined by a canonical ordering of the alphabet Σ.

T has *s* external nodes, each associated with a string of *S*, such that the concatenation of the labels of the nodes on the path from the root to an external node *v* of *T* yields the string of *S* associated with *v*.

Thus, a trie *T* represents the strings of *S* with paths from the root to the external nodes of *T*. Note the importance of assuming that no string in *S* is a prefix of another string. This ensures that each string of *S* is uniquely associated with an external node of *T*. We can always satisfy this assumption by adding a special character that is not in the original alphabet Σ at the end of each string.

An internal node in a standard trie T can have anywhere between 1 and d children, where d is the size of the alpahbet. There is an edge going from the root r to one of its children from each character that is first in some string in the collection S.

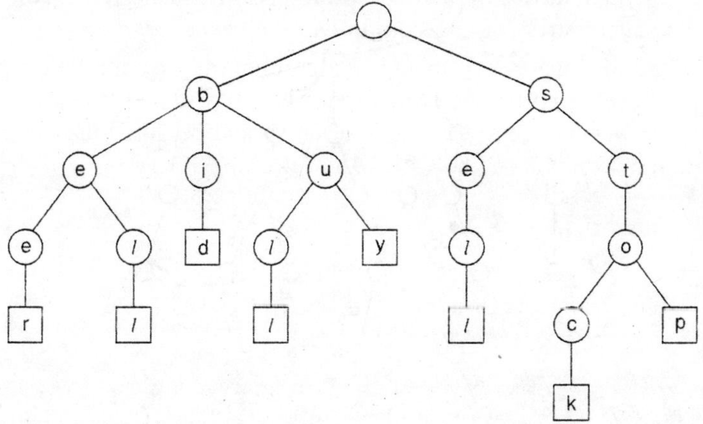

Fig. 38.13. Standard trie for the strings {bear, bell, bid, bull, buy, sell, stock, stop}.

In addition, a path from the root of T to an internal node v at depth i corresponds to an i-character prefix $X[0..i-1]$ of a string X of S. In fact, for each character c that can follow the prefix $X[0..i-1]$ in a string of the set S, there is a child of v labeled with character c. In this way, a trie concisely stores the common prefixes that exist among a set of strings.

If there are only two characters in the alphabet, then the trie is essentially a binary tree, although some internal nodes may have only one child (that is, it may be an improper binary tree). In general, if there are d characters in the alphabet, then the trie will be a multi-way tree where each internal node has between 1 and d children. In addition, there are likely to be several internal nodes in a standard trie that have fewer than d children. For example, the trie shown in Figure 38.13 has several internal nodes with only one child. We can implement a trie with a tree storing characters at its nodes.

The following theorem provides some important structural properties of a standard trie:

THEOREM 38.2. A standard trie storing a collection S of s strings of total length n from an alphabet of size d has the following properties:

Every internal node of T has at most d children

T has s external nodes

The height of T is equal to the length of the longest string in S

The number of nodes of T is $O(n)$.

EXAMPLE 38.4. *How many nonempty prefixes of the string P = "aaabbaaa" are also suffixes of P?*

SOLUTION : There are three : a, aa, aaa.

EXAMPLE 38.5. *Draw a standard trie for the following set of strings: {abab, baba, ccccc, bbaaa, caa, bbaacc, cbcc, cbca}.*

SOLUTION :

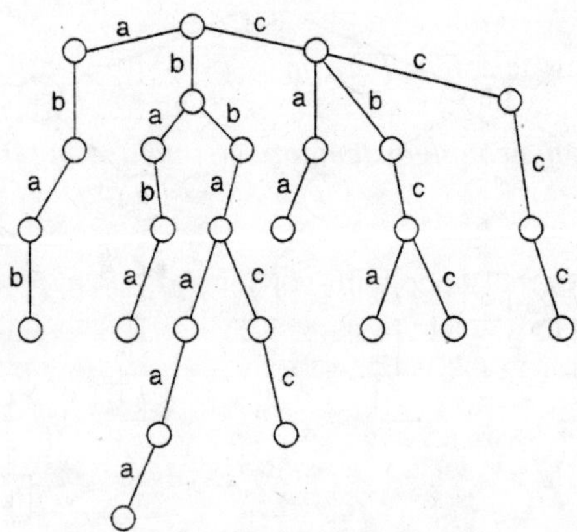

EXAMPLE 38.6. *What is the longest prefix of the string "cgtacgttcgtacg" that is also a suffix of this string?*

SOLUTION : The longest prefix that is also a suffix of this string is "cgtacg".

EXAMPLE 38.7. *Show how to modify the KMP string pattern matching algorithm so as to find every occurrence of a pattern string P that appears as a substring in T, while still running in $O(n+m)$ time. (Be sure to catch even those matches that overlap.)*

SOLUTION : Instead of returning when a match is found, store the index and set $i = i + 1$ and $j = f(m)$.

EXAMPLE 38.8. *Let T be a text of length n, and let P be a pattern of length m. Describe an $O(n + m$ method for finding the longest prefix of P that is a substring of T.*

SOLUTION : Modify the KMPMatch algorithm to maintain a variable *maxIndex* which is the index of the longest prefix found, *maxLen* which is the length of the longest prefix found, and *currentLen* which is the length of the current prefix. Initialize all three variables to zero and modify the loop in KMPMatch as follows :

If $T[i] = P[j]$, increment *currentLen*

If $T[i] \neq P[j]$ and $j > 0$, if $currentLen > maxLen$, then set $maxLen = currentLen$ and $maxIndex = i - j$. In any case, reset $currentLen = 0$.

When the algorithm terminates, *maxIndex* and *maxLen* will hold the location and length of the longest prefix.

EXAMPLE 38.9. *Say that a pattern P of length m is a circular substring of a text T of length n if there is an index* $0 \le i < m$, *such that* $P = T[n - m + i..n - 1] + T[0..i - 1]$, *that is, if P is a substring of T or P is equal to the concatenation of a suffix of T and a prefix of T. Give an* $O(n + m)$*-time algorithm for determining whether P is a circular substring of T.*

SOLUTION : Generate a new text $T' = T[n - m \dots n] + T[0 \dots m]$. Run KMPMatch on T' and P.

EXAMPLE 38.10. *Give an efficient algorithm for deleting a string from a standard trie and analyze its running time.*

SOLUTION : Locate the external node with corresponds to the end of the string. While walking back to the root of the trie, delete every external node encountered. The running time of this algorithm is $O(s)$ where s is the length of the string to be deleted.

EXERCISE

1. Modify the simplified BM algorithm presented in this chapter using ideas from the KMP algorithm so that it runs in $O(n + m)$ time.
2. Draw a figure illustrating the comparisions done by the brute-force pattern matching algorithm for the case when the text is **"aabaaa" and the pattern is "aaabaadaabaa"**.
3. Repeat the previous problem for the BM pattern matching algorithm not counting the comparisons made to compute the last function.
4. Repeat the previous problem for the KMP pattern matching algorithm not counting the comparisions made to compute the failure function.
5. Give a justification of why the KMPFailureFunction method runs on $O(m)$ time on a pattern of length m.

39

COMPUTATIONAL GEOMETRY

39.1 Convex Hull

It is important structure in geometry which can be used in construction of many other geometric structures. Convex hull of set S of points in a plane is smallest Convex polygon, that contains all points of S.

The vertices of convex hull form a set which is subset of S (not necessarily), see Fig. 39.1.

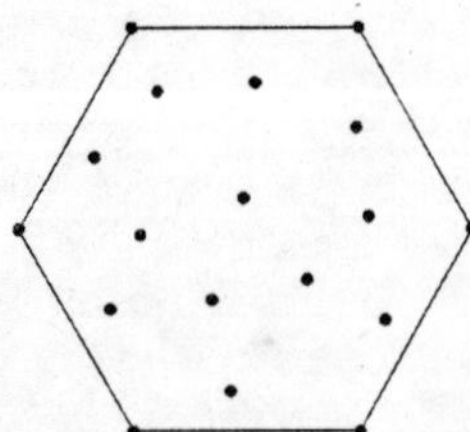

Fig. 39.1. A convex Hull.

There are two ways of forming convex Hull :

(1) obtain the vertices of the convex Hull, using extreme points.

(2) obtain the vertices in some order.

39.1.1 Simple algorithm

We can find the extreme points very easily, look at various triplet of points (3 points) and form a triangle with these 3 set of points if some other point $P \varepsilon S$ lies in any such triangle, it is not extreme, otherwise it is. Testing takes $\Theta(1)$ time there are $\Theta(n^3)$ possible triangles, so it takes $\Theta(n^3)$ time to check for extreme points and since there are n points so it takes $\Theta(n^4)$ time in total.

39.1.2 Some Geometric Primitives

If we have $A = \{a_{ij}\}$, a $n \times n$ matrix, its determinant is given by

$$\det(A) = \begin{cases} a_{11} & \text{if } n = 1 \\ a_{11} \det(A_{11}) - a_{12} \det(A_{12}) + \ldots + (-1)^{n-1} \det(A_{1n}), & n > 1 \end{cases}$$

Consider a line segment formed by two points P_1 $(x_1, y_1)$and $P_2(x_2, y_2)$. If $P_3(x_3, y_3)$ is another point, then we can check whether P_3 is on P_1, P_2, or to the left or right using the determinant of following matrix.

$$\begin{bmatrix} x_1 & x_2 & x_3 \\ y_1 & y_2 & y_3 \\ 1 & 1 & 1 \end{bmatrix}$$

If determinant is positive, then P_3 is to the left of P_1, P_2, if it is negative, to the right and if it is zero $P_1P_2P_3$ are collinear. This test can be used to check for a point whether it constitutes a extreme point or not.

Let $P_1, P_2, \ldots, P_n$ be the vertices of polygon Q in clockwise order, let P be any other point. Draw a horizontal line h that passes through P from $-\infty$ to ∞. There are two possibilities (1) h does not intersect any edges of Q. (2) h intersect some of the edges of Q. If case (1) is true, P is outside Q. In case (2) there can be at most two points. If h intersects Q at a single point of intersections then P is inside otherwise it is outside. See Fig. 39.2, (*i.e.*, all vertex) it is counted as two. Count the no. of intersections that are to the left of P. If this no. is even, then P is exterior to Q, otherwise it is internal to Q. This method of checking takes $\Theta(n)$ time.

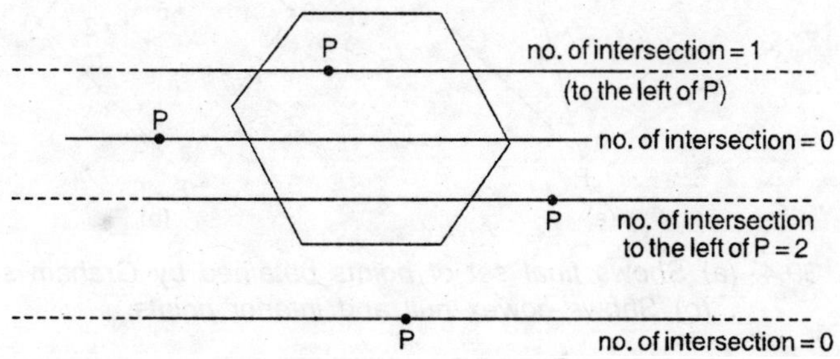

Fig. 39.2. Odd/Even test for interior/exterior points

39.2 Graham's Scan

If S is a set of points in the plane, this algorithm identifies P with lowest Y-coordinate value, then points of S are sorted according to angle subtended by S and P with positive x-axis as shown in Fig. 39.3... After having sorted the points, if we scan through the sorted list starting at P_1, every three successive points will form a left turn if all of these points lie on a hull. On contrary if it forms a right turn then we immediately delete P_2, as it will not lie on the convex hull. Since it lies with in the triangle formed by P_1, P_2, P_3.

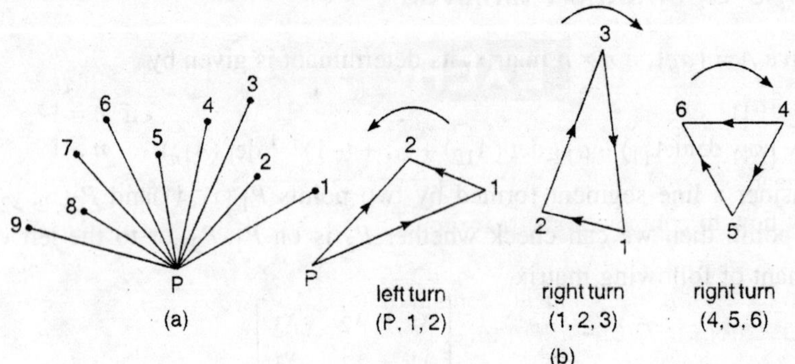

Fig. 39.3 (a) P is chosen with lowest Y value, then sorts the point (b) Shows left and right terms

In Fig. 39.3. P, 1, 2 forms left turn, ϕ we move to (1, 2, 3) it forms a right turn, hence 2 is deleted, next (P, 1, 3) is considered, it forms a left turn, pointer moves to points 1 then (1, 3, 4) also form a left turn, scan proceeds to (3, 4, 5) then to (4, 5, 6). 5 gets deleted, (3, 4, 6) considered, 4 gets deleted, (3, 6, 7) forms left turn, (6, 7, 8) forms left turn, (7, 8, 9) forms a right turn, 8 deleted, next triplet examined are (6, 7, 9). 7 deleted, (8, 9, P). Thus final hull obtained contains the points shown in Fig. 39.4.

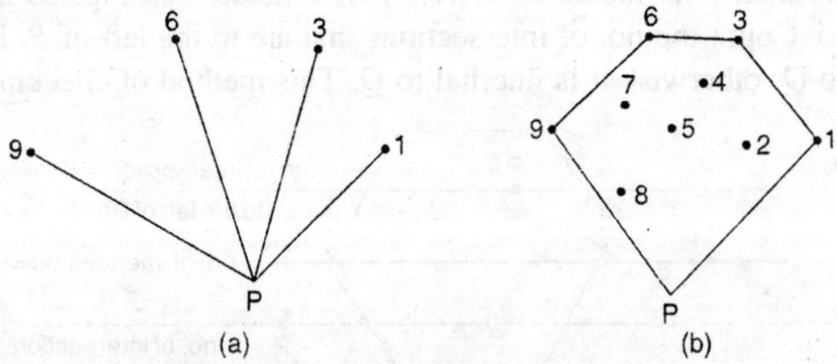

Fig. 39.4. (a) Shows final set of points obtained by Graham scan (b) Shows cowex hull and interior points.

Since sorting takes $O(nlgn)$ time and, testing of triplets takes $O(n)$ time. Running time of this algorithm is $O(nlgn)$.

39.3 Finding Closest pair of points

If $P_1(x_1, y_1)$ and $P_2(x_2, y_2)$ are two points. If two points are coincident then distance between them is zero. Thus by *Euclidean distance formula*

$$d = \sqrt{(x_1 - x_2)^2 + (y_1 - y_2)^2},\ d = 0$$

This looks for ${}^nC_2$ pair of points, therefore running time is $\theta(n^2)$.

EXERCISE

1. Show how to determine in $O(n^2 lgn)$ time whether any three points in a set of n points are collinear.
2. Show how to compute arc of n-vertex simple, but not necessarily convex, polygon in $\theta(n)$ time.
3. Given a set of n line segments containing a total of k intersections, show how to output all k intersections in $O((n + k)lgn)$ time.
4. Write an algorithm to find whether two polygons intersect.
5. Given a set of points S, prove that pair of points farthest from each other must be vertices of convex hull.
6. Give an algorithm for finding convex Hull of a star shaped polygon.
7. Give a quickhull algorithm for finding convex hull, which uses method similar to quicksort.
8. Give a divide-and-conquer method for finding convex hull.
9. Find the shortest distance between pair of points $P_1(10, 10)$, $P_2(20, 10)$?
10. Give an algorithm for making inside, outside test in a polygon, which has hole in it. See Fig. 39.5 below.

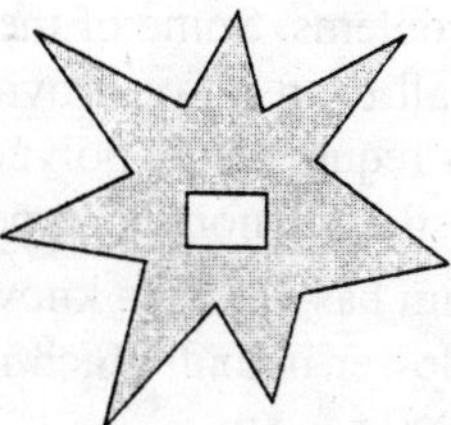

Fig. 39.5.

❑❑❑

40

NP-COMPLETENESS

Most of the algorithms discussed so far or are known to us require polynomial time with time complexity $\theta(n)$, $\theta(n^2)$, $\theta(nlgn)$, $\theta(n^3)$, $\theta(n^k)$, $\theta(2^n)$. Thus at most the time taken by an algorithm which are solvable can be $\theta(n^k)$, which is very much polynomial for some constant K. These problems are called **tractable** problems. Some of the problems like **Turing machines halting problem** can not be solved at all even if we provide it to run on computer for years. Such problems which are insolvable or require super polynomial time are called intractable and these are NP complete (non deterministic polynomial) type problems.

No polynomial time algorithm has yet been known which is *NP* complete, nor has yet any one superpolynomial time with lower bound which is *NP* complete thus

$$P \neq NP$$

but to discuss the NP complete problems we will consider those polynomial time algorithm with large complexities and which can be considered intractable, there is following reasons for this assumption.

(i) It is reasonable to regard $\theta(n^{100})$ as intractable, as no algorithm takes that much time.

(ii) The problems which are solved in polynomial time on one machine are also solvable in polynomial time on the other machine.

(iii) Polynomial time solvable problem, possess nice closure properties. If output of one is used as input of one, the composite problem is polynomial.

Before disscussing *P* and *NP* in detail we should understand what the prolem is? for this we consider Abstract problem

40.1 NP Problems

40.1.1 Abstract problems

It is a binary relation on set I of problem instances and set *S* of problem solutions. e.g., SHORTEST-PATH-It is problem of finding shortest path between two vertices in un weighted, undirected graph $G = (V, E)$. Its **instance** is triple consisting of two vertex and one graph and since shortest path is not unique a given instance can have many solutions. (Note that graph is unweighted and undirected).

In order to discuss **NP-complete,** problem we discuss abstract problems as **decision problems** with answer of yes/no. Thus abstract decision problems will have two parts.

1. The **instance description** part defines the information expected in the input.

2. The **question** part states actual yes-or-no question, the question contains the variable described in instance.

Now consider the SHORTEST-PATH problem as decision problem.

EXAMPLE 40.1.

1. Instance. A graph $G = (V, E)$, instance $i = <G, u, v, k>$, k is length of path, PATH(i)

2. Question part

PATH (i) = 1, if $u \to v$ is shortest path.

= 0, if $u \to v$ is not a shortest path.

EXAMPLE 40.2.

1. Instance : an undirected graph $G = (V, E)$

2. Question : Does *G* contain a clique of *K* vertices? (A clique is a complete subsgraph, which have an edge between every pair of vertices).

EXAMPLE 40.3.

1. Instance : An undirected graph $G = (V, E)$ and an integer *K*

2. Question : Does a contain a clique of *K* vertices.

The question is same in Ex. 40.2 and Ex. 40.3 but in Ex. 40.2, K is not part at input. In Ex. 40.2. *K* is constant, so if running time is $O(k^2n^k)$ then it is polynomial time but Ex. 40.3, *K* is not constant, so even if running time is $O(k^2n^k)$ it is not polynomial, as *K* is variable and it is power of *n*.

Not all of the NP-complete problems are decision problems, some of them are optimization problems, so they are recosted as decision problems so that theory of NP-completeness apply.

EXAMPLE 40.4. Knapsack Problem

Optimization Problem Find the largest profit of any subset of objects that fits in the knapsack (and find a subset that achieves the maximum profit).

Decision Problem Given K, is there a subset of the objects that fits in the knapsack and has total profit at least K?

EXAMPLE 40.5. Bin packing unlimited no. of bins of capacity one, and n objects of sizes $S_1, S_2, ..., S_n$ where S_i is the rotational no.

Optimization Problems Determine the smallest no. of bin into which the objects can be packed (and find an optimal packing).

Decision Problem Given in addition to the inputs described, an integer k, do the objects fit in k bins?

40.1.2 Encoding

An encoding of set S of abstract objects is a mapping e from S to the set of binary strings

e.g., Natural no. $N = \{0, 1, 2, 3, 4, ...\}$

$e = \{0, 1, 10, 11, 100, ...,\}$

S.t. $e(17) = 10001$, in binary encoded form

This way we can encode polygons, graphs, functions ordered pairs, program as binary strings. Note that we can encode graph as adjacency matrix.

40.1.3 Concrete Problems

The problems which solves some abstract decision problem which takes encoding as input of problem instance is called concrete problems.

If $n = | i |$, i is instance, n is length of instance then running time is $O(T(n))$, *i.e.*, polynomial time solvable.

40.1.4 Complexity Class P

It is the set of concrete decision problems that are solvable in polynomial time. We can map the abstract decision problem as concrete problem.

Let us consider an abstract problem Q mapping on instance I to $\{0, 1\}$, then its encoding $e : I \rightarrow \{0, 1\}*$, can be used to induce a related concrete problems. If solution to abstract problem is $Q(i)$ ε $\{0, 1\}$ then solution to concrete problem is $e(i)$ ε $\{0, 1\}*$ is also $Q(i)$.

If it is a unary problem with K inputs then it runs in $\theta(k)$ time, if it is binary problem s.t. $n = \log_2 k$, then it runs in $\theta(2^n)$ time, thus depending upon the encoding it runs in polynomial or superpolynomial time.

40.1.5 A Formal Language Frame Work

We can give the formal language frame work, if we have input symbol $Z = \{0, 1\}$, then language $L = \{01, 10, 11, 101\}$, is empty language. This frame work has several properties like union, intersection, concatenation we have concatenation as,

If $L = \{x_1, x_2 : x_1 \, \varepsilon \, L_1$ and $x_2 \, \varepsilon \, L_2\}$

its **closure or kleene star** is given by

$$L* = \{\varepsilon\} \cup L \cup L^2 \cup L^3 \cup \ldots$$

So from the point of view of language theory, the solution Q

$Q \varepsilon \Sigma*$, where $\Sigma = \{0, 1\}$.

$\therefore \quad L = \{x \varepsilon \Sigma*, Q(x) = 1\}$

We can also give **complexity class *P*** in terms of language theory,

$P = \{L \subseteq \{0, 1\}* :$ there exists an algorithm A that decides L in polynomial time$\}$.

Thus

PATH = $\{<G, u, v, k> : G = V, E$ is an undirected graph, $u, v \varepsilon V, k \geq 0$, there exists a path from u to v whose length is at most $k\}$.

40.2 Hamiltonian Cycles

If each and every vertex is visited exactly once except first and last vertex then i forms a cycle called **Hamiltonian Cycle** and graph that contains this cycle is called **Hamiltonian graph.** See Fig. 40.1.

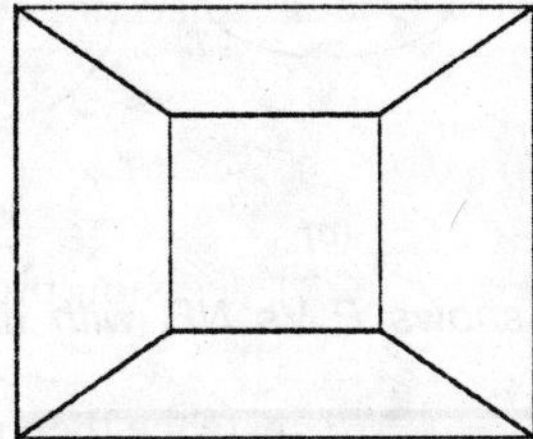

Fig. 40.1. Dark edges represents Hamiltonian cycle.

EXAMPLE 40.6. *Hamiltonian cycle problem as formal language, "Does graph G have hamiltonian cycle?*

HAM-CYCLE = $\{<G> : G$ is a Hamiltonian graph$\}$

then, $L = \{x \varepsilon \{0, 1\}* :$ there exists $y \in \{0, 1\}*$, such that $A(x, y) = 1\}$

Here we are viewing graph in terms of Adjacency matrix and $A(x, y)$ gives the verification checking, whether to include vertex x or not, in order to verify the hamiltonian cycle definition, If it is to be included then $A(x, y) = 1$, thus y provides the **verification certtificate.** Thus for any string $x \varepsilon L$, y verifies to prove that $x \varepsilon L$.

For encoding of graph to form adjacency matrix, for m no. of vertices it takes $\Omega(\sqrt{n})$, where n is length of encoding G. There are m ! permutations of vertices, therefore running time is

$$\Omega(m\,!) = \Omega(\sqrt{n}\,!) = \Omega(2^{\sqrt{n}}),$$

thus it is a NP-complete problem as it takes, super polynomial time.

Complexity Class NP

It is the class of languages that can be verified by a polynomial time algorithm. A language L belongs to NP *iff* there exists a two input polynomial algorithm A and constant c, s.t.

$$L = \{x \in \{0, 1\}^* : \text{there exists a certificate } y$$

with $\quad |y| = O(|x|^c)$, s.t. $A(x, y) = 1\}$.

e.g. HAM-CYCLE ε NP

Class *P* vs NP

If $L \in P$, then LεNP, as there is a polynomial time algorithm to decide L, this algorithm can easily be converrted into a two argument vertication algorithm that simply ignores any except and accepts exactly those input strings it determines to be in L. Thus, $P \subseteq NP$. see Fig. 40.2.

It is not very clear whether $P = NP$, but most researchers believe that P and NP are two differet classes with P being, set of problems solved quickly, while NP being set of problems that can be verified quickly. Thus, $P \neq NP$ as they have different set of languages, see Fig. 40.2.

We can consider the super polynomial time algorithm close to NP, even if there is not even a single problem know in which $P = NP$. See Fig. 40.2.

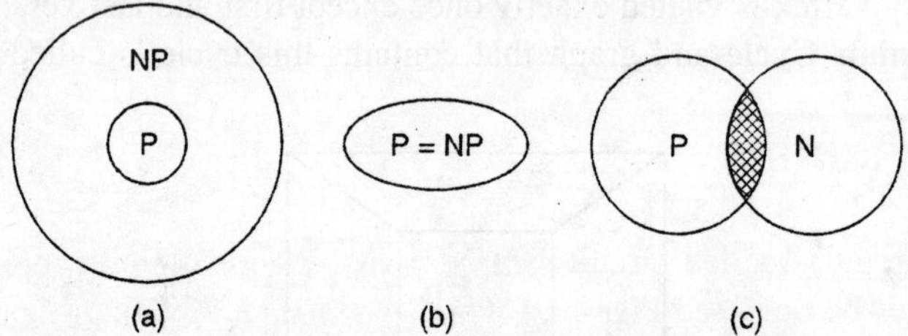

Fig. 40.2. This shows P Vs NP, with different view.

40.3 NP Completeness And Reducibility

NP complete languages are in sense the hardest language in NP.

Reducibility

A problem Q can be reduced to another problem Q', s.t., any instance of it produces a solution which is same as the solution of Q, then Q is said to be reducible to Q'.

e.g. $\quad Q : ax + b$, can be transformed as

$$Q' : 0 \cdot x^2 + ax + b$$

Solution of Q' is same as that of Q

Thus we can generalize this concept as a language L_1 is polynomial time reducible to a language L_2, written as $L_1 \leq_P L_2$, if there exists a polynomial time computable function

$$f : \{0, 1\}^* \rightarrow \{0, 1\}^*, \text{ s.t. } \forall\, x \in \{0, 1\}^*, x \in L_1 \text{ iff } f(x) \in L_2.$$

Function f is called **reduction function** and polynomial time algorithm that computes f is called **reduction algorithm.** See Fig. 40.3 also we have, if $x \notin L_1$ then $f(x) \notin L_2$.

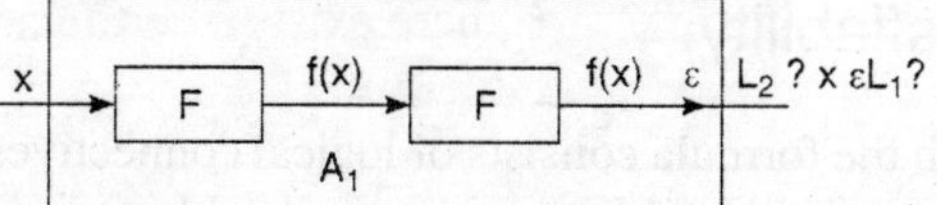

Fig. 40.3. Shows reduction function and reduction algorithm. A_1 transforms x to f(x), using F and then A_2 checks whether f(x)ε L_2 if x ε L_1.

THEOREM 40.1. If $L_1, L_2 \subseteq \{0, 1\}*$ are language s.t. $L_1 \leq _pL_2$, then $L_1 \varepsilon P$ implies $L_2 \varepsilon P$.

40.3.1 NP Completeness

A language $L = \{0, 1\}*$ is NP-complete if following holds :

1. $L \varepsilon NP$.
2. there is language $L' \varepsilon NP$, s.t. $L' \leq p^L$

If a language *L* satisfies property 2 but not necessarily property 1, we say that **L is NP-Hard.**

40.4 Circuit Satisfiability

A combinational circuit is called circuit satisfiable if for set of inputs applied, output of this circuit should always be one. See Fig. 40.4 which consists of AND, OR and NOT Gates.

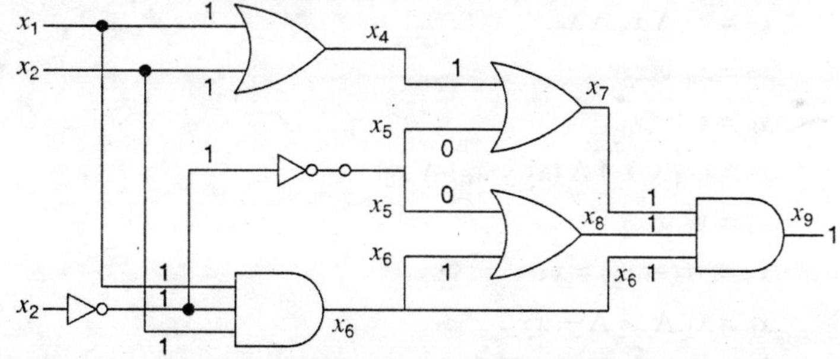

Fig. 40.4. The assignment <x_1 = 1 , x_2 = 1 , x_3 = 0> to input, produces output of circuit to be 1.

We can give a formal language for circuit satisfiability. Problem as.

CIRCUIT-SAT = {<*c*> : *c* is satisfiable boolean combination circuit}

To check for satisfiability, if we have *k* inputs then there must be 2^k assignments to inputs which needs to be checked. Which is superpolynomial so circuit satisfiability is NP-complete.

40.4.1 Formula Satisfiability

It is a problem in which the formula consists of logical connectives Λ (AND), ∨ (OR), ¬ (NOT). A formula is said to be satisfable if for a given satisfiable assignment to boolean variables the output should be 1.

$$\text{SAT} = \{<\phi> : \phi \text{ is satisfiable boolean formula}\}$$

EXAMPLE 40.7. $\phi = ((x_1 \rightarrow x_2) \vee \neg((\neg x_1 \leftrightarrow x_3) \vee x_4)) \Lambda \neg x_2$,

Prove that ϕ is formula satisfiable for particular truth assignment.

SOLUTION : Let us consider the satisfying assignment $<x_1 = 0, x_2 = 0, x_3 = 1, x_4 = 1>$

$$\phi = ((0 \rightarrow 0) \vee \neg(\neg 0 \leftrightarrow 1) \vee 1)) \Lambda \neg 0$$
$$= (1 \vee \neg(1 \vee 1)) \Lambda 1$$
$$= (1 \vee 0) \Lambda 1$$
$$= 1. \text{ Hence formula satisfiable.}$$

THEOREM 40.2. Satisfiability of boolean formula is NP-complete.

We can reduce CIRCUIT-SAT to SAT, *i.e.*, a circuit can be reduced to formula, *i.e.*, SAT $\leq p$ CIRCUIT-SAT, as CIRCUIT-SAT ε NP, SAT ε NP. Thus formula satisfiability problem is NP complete.

Reducing Fig. 40.4 to formulas we have.

$$x_9 = x_7 \Lambda x_8 \Lambda x_6.$$
$$x_7 = x_4 \vee x_5.$$
$$x_8 = x_5 \vee x_6.$$

then $x_9 = (x_4 \vee x_5) \Lambda (x_5 \vee x_6) \Lambda x_6.$

$$x_4 = x_1 \vee x_2$$
$$x_5 = \neg(\neg x_3) = x_3.$$
$$x_6 = x_1 \Lambda x_2 \Lambda \neg x_3$$

thus, $x_9 = ((x_1 \vee x_2) \vee x_3) \Lambda (x_3 \vee x_1 \Lambda x_2 \Lambda \neg x_3) \Lambda (x_1 \Lambda x_2 \Lambda \neg x_3)$

Let us consider one truth assignment $<x_1 = 1, x_2 = 1, x_3 = 0>$

∴ $x_9 = ((1 \vee 1) \vee 0) \Lambda (0 \vee 1 \Lambda 1 \Lambda 1) \Lambda (1 \Lambda 1 \Lambda 1)$

$= 1 \Lambda 1 \Lambda 1 = 1$, hence formula is satsifiable.

3-CNF Satisfiability (3-CNF-SAT)

A formula is in **conjunctive normal form** if it contains AND of clauses and each literals or inputs in the clause are joined by OR. If each clause contains exactly 3 litrerals it is called 3-CNF.

$$\phi = (x_1 \vee x_2 \vee x_3) \Lambda (x_3 \vee x_4 \vee \neg x_2) \Lambda (\neg x_1 \vee x_2 \vee x_5)$$

is in 3-CNF. A formula ϕ is 3-CNF-Satisfiable if for certain truth assignment $\phi = 1$.

DNF

Disjunctive Normal form is the OR of clause so that each literal in the claused in ANDed.

$$\phi = (x_1 \wedge x_2 \wedge \neg x_3) \vee (x_4 \wedge x_5 \wedge x_6) \vee (\neg x_2 \wedge \neg x_1 \wedge x_6)$$

40.4.2 The Post Correspondence Problems

This was first introduced by Emil post in 1946. Later the problem was found to have many applications in theory of formal languages. The problem over an alphabet Σ belongs to a class of yes/no problems.

Consider two lists $x = (x_1, x_2, ..., x_n)$, $y = (y_1, y_2 ... y_n)$ of nonempty strings over an alphabet $\Sigma = \{0, 1\}$. The PCP is to determine whether or not there exists $i_1, ..., i_m$ where $1 \le i_j \le n$, such that

$$x_{i1} \ldots x_{im} = y_{i1} \ldots y_{im}$$

where i_j's may not be distinct and m may be greater than n.

EXAMPLE 40.8. *Does PCP with two lists $x = (b, bab^3, ba)$ and $y = (b^3, ba, a)$ have a solution?*

SOLUTION : We have to determine whether or not there exists a sequence and the string formed by the sequence of corresponding substring of y are identical. The required sequence is given by $i_1 = 2$, $i_2 = 1$, $i_3 = 1$, $i_4 = 3$, *i.e.*, (2, 1, 1, 3) and $m = 4$ the corresponding string are

$$\underset{x_2}{bab^3}\ \underset{x_1}{b}\ \underset{x_1}{b}\ \underset{x_3}{ba} = \underset{y_2}{ba}\ \underset{y_1}{b^3}\ \underset{y_1}{b^3}\ \underset{y_3}{a}$$

Thus, PCP has a solution.

40.5 Non Deterministic Algorithm

A non deterministic algorithm has two phases and an output step :

(1) In non deterministic "guesssing" phase, some completely arbitrary string of characters a, is written beginning at same designated place in memory. Each time the algorithm A is run, the string written may differ.

(2) The deterministic "verifying" phase, returns *true* or *false* value or it may get in an infinite loop and never halt.

(3) If verifying phase returns *true*, the algorithm output *yes* otherwise there is no output.

The no. of steps carried out during one execution of a non- deterministic algorithm is defined as the sum of the steps in two phases, plus no. of steps executed by deterministic second phase. Thus it can be written as

```
Non-Deterministic A (input)
Q ← Random choose()
checkOK = verifyA (input, a)
```

```
        if (checkOK)
            write "yes"
        returns a
```

EXAMPLE 40.9. *Write an nondeterministic algorithm for searching an element x in array $A[1 .. n]$*

SOLUTION :

```
j ← Randomchoose (1, n)
checkOK = verifyA(A(j), x)
    if (checkOK)
        write "yes"
    return
```

THEOREM 40.3. Graph coloring, Hamiltonian cycle, Hamiltonian path, job scheduling with penalties, bin packing, subset sum problem, knapsack problem and travelling salesman problem are all **NP-complete.**

THEOREM 40.4. The directed Hamiltonian cycle problem is reducible to the undirected Hamiltonian cycle problem.

PROOF : Let graph $G = (V, E)$ be a directed graph with n vertices. G is transformed into the undirected graph $G' = (V', E')$, where for each vertex $v \varepsilon V$, we have 3 vertices V_1, V_2, V_3. Also for each $v \varepsilon V$ transformed edge set E' contains undirected edges V_1V_2 and V_2V_3 and for each directed edge $vw \varepsilon E$, E' contains undirected edge V_3W_1 See Fig. 40.5.

G' is constructed in polynomially bounded time. If $|V| = n$ and $|E| = m$, then G' has $3n$ vertices and $2n + m$ edges.

Note that if G' has undirected Hamiltonian cycle, the three vertices, V_1, V_2, V_3 that correspond to one vertex of G must be visited in order $V_1V_2V_3$ or $V_3V_2V_1$ vertex V_2 can not be directly reached, using this concept only the one vertex in G is broken into 3 vertex in G'

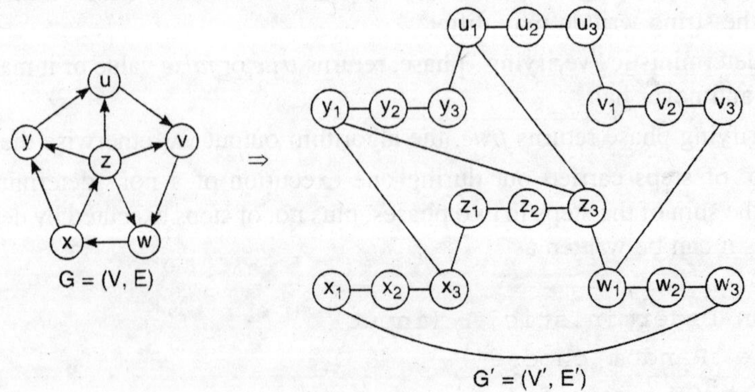

Fig. 40.5. Reduction of the directed Hamiltonian cycle problem to undirected Hamiltonian cycle problem

40.6 Vertex Cover

A vertex cover for an undirected graph G is subset C of vertices such that each edge in incident upon some vertex in C.

Optimization problem Given an undirected graph G, find a vertex cover for G with as few vertices as possible.

Decision problem Given an undirected graph G and an integer K, does G have a vertex cover consisting of K vertices?

Independent Set

An independent set is a subset of I of vertices in an undirected graph G such that no pair of vertices in I is joined by an edge of G.

Clique

A clique is a subset K of vertices in an undirected graph G such that every pair of distinct vertices in K is joined by an edge of G. In other words, the subgraph induced by K is complete. A clique with K vertices is called k-clique, k-clique requires atleast k colors to color it.

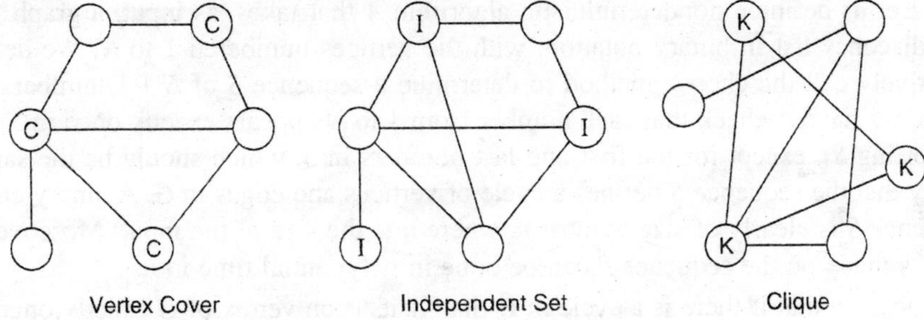

Fig. 40.6. Examples of vertex cover, independent set, clique.

40.7 Node Cover Decisiopn Problem (NCDP)

A set $S \subseteq V$ is a *node cover* for a graph $G = (V, E)$ iff all edges in E are incident to atleast one vertex in S. The size $|S|$ of the cover is the no. of vertices in S. See Fig. 40.7.

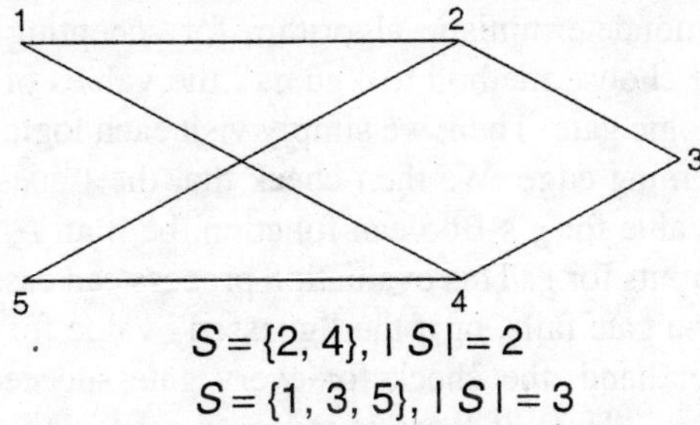

$S = \{2, 4\}$, $|S| = 2$

$S = \{1, 3, 5\}$, $|S| = 3$

Fig, 40.7. Show node cover of size 2 and 3 with $S = \{2, 4\}$ and $S = \{1, 3, 5\}$ respectively.

40.8 Chromatic Number Decision Problem (CNDP)

A coloring of a graph $G = (V, E)$ is a function $f: V \rightarrow \{1, 2, ..., k\}$ defined for all $i \varepsilon V$. If $(u, v) \varepsilon E$, then $f(u) \neq f(v)$. The chromatic number decision problem is to determine whether G has a coloring for a given K.

EXAMPLE 40.10. *A positive 2-coloring of the graph of Fig. 40.7 is* $f(1) = f(3) = f(5) = 1$ *and* $f(2) = f(4) = 2$ *clearly this graph has no. 1-coloring.*

THEOREM 40.5. Directed Hamiltonian cycle (DHC) is reducible to travelling sales man problem.

PROOF : From the directed graph $G = (V, E)$ construct the complete directed graph $G' = (V, E')$, s.t. $E' = \{(i, j) \mid i \neq j\}$ and $c(i, j) = 1$ if $(i, j) \varepsilon E$ and $c(i, j) = 2$ if $i \neq j$ and $(i, j) \varepsilon E$. Clearly G' has a tour of cost at most n. iff G has a directed Hamiltonian cycle.

40.9 Some Interesting NP Problems Revisited

LEMMA 40.1. HAMILTONIAN-CYCLE is in NP.

PROOF : Let us define a nondeterministic algorithm A that takes, as input, a graph G encoded as an adjacency list in binary notation, with the vertices numbered 1 to N. We define A to first iteratively call the choose method to determine a sequence S of $N + 1$ numbers from 1 to N. Then, we have A check that each number from 1 to N appears exactly once in S (for example, by sorting S), except for the first and last numbers in S, which should be the same. Then, we verify that the sequence S defines a cycle of vertices and edges in G. A binary encoding of the sequence S is clearly of size at most n, where n is the size of the input. Moreover, both of the checks made on the sequence S can be done in polynomial time in n.

Observe that if there is a cycle in G that visits each vertex of G exactly once, returning to its starting vertex, then there is a sequence S for which A will output "yes." Likewise, if A outputs "yes," then it has found a cycle in G that visits each vertex of G exactly once, returning to its starting point. That is, A non-deterministically accepts the language HAMILTONIAN-CYCLE. In other words, HAMILTONIAN-CYCLE is in *NP*.

LEMMA 40.2. CIRCUIT-STAT is in NP.

PROOF : We construct a nondeterministic algorithm for accepting CIRCUIT-SAT in polynomial time. We first use the choose method to "guess" the values of the input nodes as well as the output value of each logic gate. Then, we simply visit each logic gate g in C, that is, each vertex with at least one incoming edge. We then check that the "guessed" value for the output of g is in fact the correct value for g's Boolean function, be it an AND, OR, or NOT, based on the given values for the inputs for g. This evaluation process can easily be performed in polynomial time. If any check for a gate fails, or if the "guessed" value for the output is 0, then we output "no." If, on the other hand, the check for every gate succeeds and the output is "1," the algorithm outputs "yes." Thus, if there is indeed a satisfying assignment of input values for C, then there is a possible collection of outcomes to the choose statements so that the algorithm will output "yes" in polynomial time. Likewise, if there is a collection of outcomes to the choose statements so that the algorithm outputs "yes" in polynomial time algorithm, there must be satisfying assignment of input values for C. Therefore, CIRCUIT-SAT is in NP.

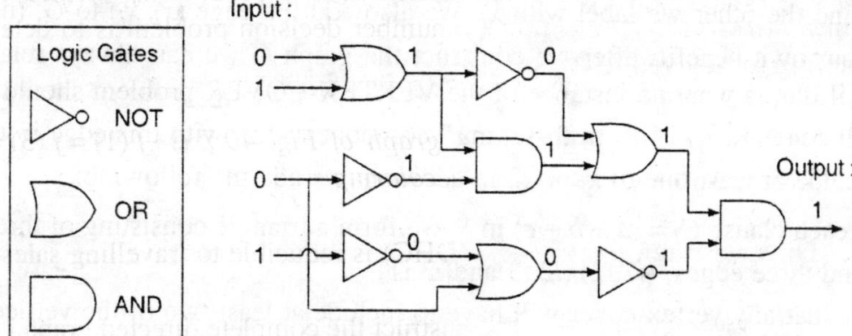

Fig. 40.8. CIRCUIT-SAT problem.

THEOREM 40.6. (The Cook-Levin Theorem): CIRCUIT-SAT is NP-complete.

PROOF : Lemma 40.2 shows that CIRCUIT-SAT IS IN NP. Thus, we have yet to show this problem is NP-hard. That is, we need to show that every problem in NP is polynomial-time reducible to CIRCUIT-SAT. So, consider a language L, representing some decision problem that is in NP. Since L is in NP, there is a deterministic algorithm D that accepts any x in L in polynomial-time $p(n)$, given a polynomial-sized certificate y, where n is the size of x. The main idea of the proof is to build a large, but polynomial-sized, circuit C that simulates the algorithm D on an input x in such a way that C is satisfiable if and only if there is a certificate y such that D outputs "yes" on input $z = x + y$.

40.9.1 Vertex-Cover

Recall that VERTEX-COVER takes a graph G and an integer k and asks if there is a vertex cover for G containing at most k vertices. Formally, VERTEX-COVER asks if there is a subset C of vertices of size at most k, such that for each edge (v, w), we have $v \in C$ or $w \in C$.

EXAMPLE 40.11. *Suppose we are given a graph G representing a computer network where vertices represent routers and edges represent physical connections. Suppose further that we wish to upgrade some of the routers in our network with special new, but expensive, routers that can perform sophisticated monitoring operations for incident connections. If we would like to determine if k new routers are sufficient to monitor every connection in our network, then we have an instance of VERTEX-COVER on our hands.*

SOLUTION : Let us now show that VERTEX-COVER is NP-hard, by reducing the 3SAT problem to it in polynomial time. This reduction is interesting in two respect. First, it shows an example of reducing a logic problem to a graph problem. Second, it illustrates an application of the component design proof technique.

Let S be a given instance of the 3 SAT problem, that is, a CNF formula such that each clause has exactly three literals. We construct a graph G and an integer k such that G has a vertex cover of size at most k if and only if S is satisfiable. We begin our construction by adding the following:

For each variable x_i used in the formula S, we add two vertices in G, one that we label with x_i and the other we label with $\overline{x}_i$. We also add the edge $(x_i, \overline{x}_i)$ to G. (note: These labels are for our own benefit; after we construct the graph G we can always relabel vertices with integers if that is what an instance of the VERTEX-COVER problem should look like.)

Each edge $(x_i, \overline{x}_i)$ is a "truth-setting" component, for, with this edge in G, a vertex cover must include at least one of x_i or $\overline{x}_i$. In addition, we add the following:

For each clause $C_i = (a + b + c)$ in S, we form a triangle consisting of three vertices, i1, i2, and i3 and three edges, $(i1,i2)$,$(i2,i3)$and$(i3,i1)$.

Note that any vertex cover will have to include at least two of the vertices $\{i1, i2, i3\}$ for each such triangle. Each such triangle is a "satisfaction-enforcing" component. We then connect these two types of components, by adding, for each clause $C_i = (a + b + c)$, the edges $(i1, a)$, $(i2, b)$, and $(i3, c)$. (See Figure 40.9). Finally, we set the integer parameter $k = n + 2m$, where n is the number of variables in S and m is the number of clauses. Thus, if there is a vertex cover of size at most k, it must have size exactly k. This completes the construction of an instance of the VERTEX-COVER problem.

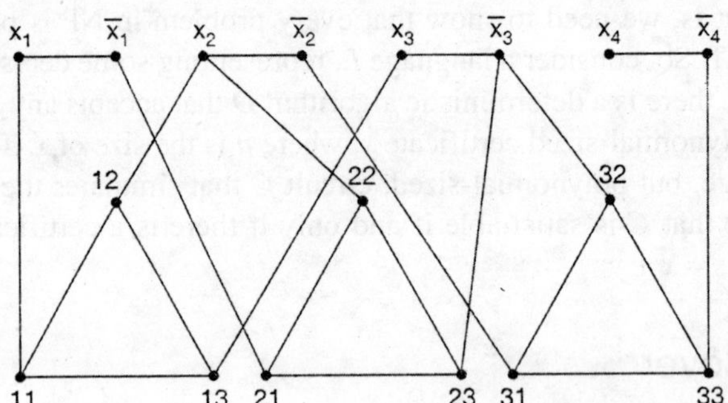

Fig. 40.9. Example graph G as an instance of the VERTEX-COVER problem constructed from the formula $S = (x_1 + x_2 + x_3) \cdot (\overline{x}_1 + x_2 + \overline{x}_3) \cdot (\overline{x}_2 + \overline{x}_3 + \overline{x}_4)$.

This construction clearly runs in polynomial time, so let us consider its correctness. Suppose there is an assignment of Boolean values to variables in S so that S is satisfied. From the graph G constructed from S, we can build a subset of vertices C that contains each literal a (in a truth-setting component) that is assigned 1 by the satisfying assignment. Likewise, for each clause $C_i = (a + b + c)$, the satisfying assignment sets at least one of a, b, or c to 1. Whichever one of a, b or c is 1 (picking arbitrarily if there are ties), we include the other two in our subset C. This C is of size $n + 2m$. Moreover, notice that each edge in a truth-setting component and clause-satisfying component is covered, and two of every three edges incident on a clause-satisfying component are also covered. In addition, notice that an edge incident to a component associated clause C_i that is not covered by a vertex in the component must be covered by the node in C labeled with a lateral, for the corresponding literal in C_i is 1.

Suppose then the converse, namely that there is a vertex cover C of size at most $n + 2m$. By construction, this set must have size exactly $n + 2m$, for it must contain one vertex from each truth-setting component and two vertices from each clause-satisfying component. This leaves one edge incident to a clause-satisfying component that is not covered by a vertex in the clause-satisfying component; hence, this edge must be covered by the other endpoint, which is labeled with a literal. Thus, we can assign the literal in S associated with this node 1 and each clause in S is satisfied; hence, all of S is satisfied. Therefore, S is satisfiable if and only if G has a vertex cover of size at most k. This gives us the following :

THEOREM 40.7. VERTEX-COVER is NP-complete.

40.9.2 CLIQUE and SET-COVER

CLIQUE

A ***clique*** in a graph G is a subset C of vertices such that, for each v and w in C, with $v \neq w$, (v, w) is an edge. That is, there is an edge between every pair of distinct vertices in C. Problem CLIQUE takes a graph G and an integer k as input and asks whether there is a clique in G of size at least k.

We leave as a simple exercise (R-13.7) to show that CLIQUE is in NP. To show CLIQUE is NP-hard, we reduce the VERTEX-COVER problem to it. Therefore, let (G, k) be an instance of the VERTEX-COVER problem. For the CLIQUE problem, we construct the complement graph G^c, which has the same vertex set as G, but has the edge (v, w), with $v \neq w$, if and only if (v, w) is not in G. We define the integer parameter for CLIQUE as $n - k$, where k is the integer parameter for VERTEX-COVER. This construction runs in polynomial time and serves as a reduction, for G^c has a clique of size at least $n - k$ if and only if G has a vertex cover of size at most k. (See Figure 40.10).

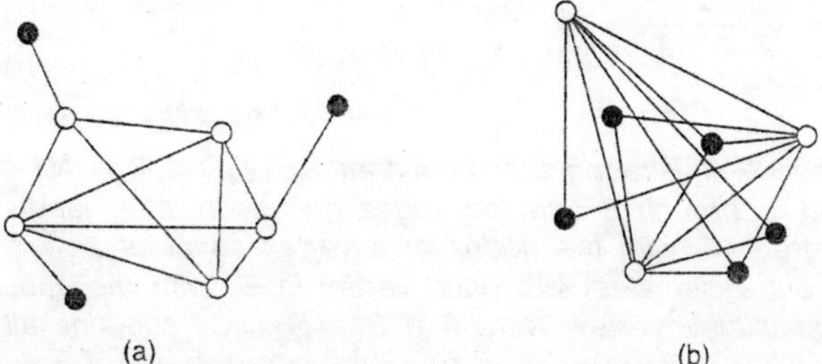

*Fig. 40.10. A graph G illustrating the point that CLIQUE is **NP**-hard. (a) Shows the graph G with the nodes of a clique of size 5 shaded in grey. (b) Shows the graph G^c with the nodes of a vertex cover of size 3 shaded in grey.*

THEOREM 40.8. CLIQUE is NP-complete.

Note how simple the above proof by local replacement is. Interestingly, the next reduction, which is also based on the local replacement technique, is even simpler.

40.9.3 SET-COVER

Problem SET-COVER takes a collection of m sets $S_1, S_2, \ldots, S_m$ and an integer parameter k as input, and asks whether there is a subcollection of k sets $S_{i_1}, S_{i_2}, \ldots, S_{i_k}$, such that

$$\bigcup_{i=1}^{m} S_i = \bigcup_{j=1}^{k} S_{i_j}.$$

That is, the union of the subcollection of k sets includes every element in the union of the original m sets.

We have to show SET-COVER is in ***NP***. As to the reduction, we note that we can define an instance of SET-COVER from an instance G and k of VERTEX-COVER. Namely, for each vertex v of G, there is set S_v, which contains the edges of G incident on v. Clearly, there is a set cover among these sets S_v's of size k if and only if there is a vertex cover of size k in G. (See Figure 40.11).

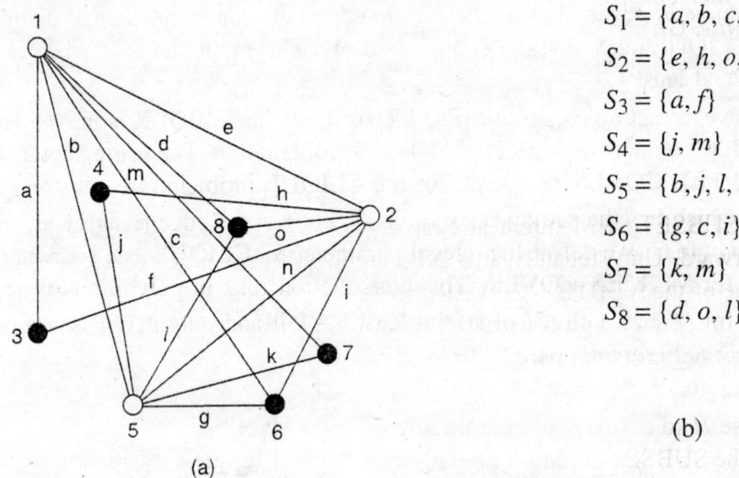

$S_1 = \{a, b, c, m, d, e\}$
$S_2 = \{e, h, o, n, i\}$
$S_3 = \{a, f\}$
$S_4 = \{j, m\}$
$S_5 = \{b, j, l, n, k, g\}$
$S_6 = \{g, c, i\}$
$S_7 = \{k, m\}$
$S_8 = \{d, o, l\}$

(b)

*Fig. 40.11. A graph G illustrating the proof that SET-COVER is **NP**-hard. The vertices are numbered 1 through 8 and the edges are given letter labels a through o. (a) Shows the graph G with the nodes of a vertex cover of size 3 shaded in grey. (b) Shows the sets associated with each vertex in G, with the subscript of each set identifying the associated vertex. Note that $S_1 \cup S_2 \cup S_5$ contains all the edges of G.*

Thus, we have the following

THEOREM 40.9. SET-COVER is NP-complete.

This reduction illustrates how easily we can convert a graph problem into a set problem. In the next subsection we show how we can actually reduce graph problems to number problems.

THEOREM 40.10. SUBSET-SUM and KNAPSACK

Some hard problems involve only numbers. In such cases, we must take extra care to use the size of the input in bits, for some numbers can be very large. To clarify the role that the size of numbers can make, researchers say that a problem L is ***strongly NP-hard*** if L remains *NP*-hard even when we restrict the value of each number in the input to be bounded by a polynomial in the size (in bits) of the input. An input x of size n would satisfy this condition, for example, it each number i in x was represented using $O(\log n)$ bits. Interestingly, the number problems we study in this section are not strongly *NP*-hard.

40.9.4 SUBSET-SUM

In the SUBSET-SUM problem, we are given a set S of n integers and an integer k, and we are asked if there is a subset of integers in S that sum to k. This problem could arise, for example, as in the following.

EXAMPLE 40.12. *Suppose we have an Internet web server, and we are presented with a collection of download requests. For each each download request we can easily determine the size of the requested file. Thus, we can abstract each web request simply as an integer—the size of the requested file. Given this set of integers, we might be interested in determining a subset of them that exactly sums to the bandwidth our server can accommodate in one minute. Unfortunately, this problem is an instance of SUBSET-SUM. Moreover, because it is NP-complete, this problem will actually become harder to solve as our web server's bandwidth and request-handling ability improves.*

SOLUTION : SUBSET-SUM might at first seem easy, and indeed showing in belongs to NP is straightforward. Unfortunately, it is NP-complete, as we now show. Let G and k be given as an instance of the VERTEX-COVER problem. Number the vertices of G from 1 to n and the edges G from 1 to m, and construct the incidence matrix H for G, defined so that $H[i, j] = 1$ if and only if the edge numbered j is incident on the vertex numbered i; otherwise, $H[i, j] = 0$. (See Figure 40.12).

We use H to define some admittedly large (but still polynomial-sized) numbers to use as inputs to the SUBSET-SUM problem. Namely, for each row i of H, which encodes all the edges incident on vertex i, we construct the number

$$a_i = 4^{m+1} \sum_{j=1}^{m} H[i, j]\, 4^j.$$

Note that this number adds in a different power of 4 for each 1-entry in the ith row of $H[i, j]$, plus a larger power of 4 for good measure. The collection of a_i's defines an "incidence component" to our reduction, for each power of 4 in an a_i, except for the largest, corresponds to a possible incidence between vertex i and some edge.

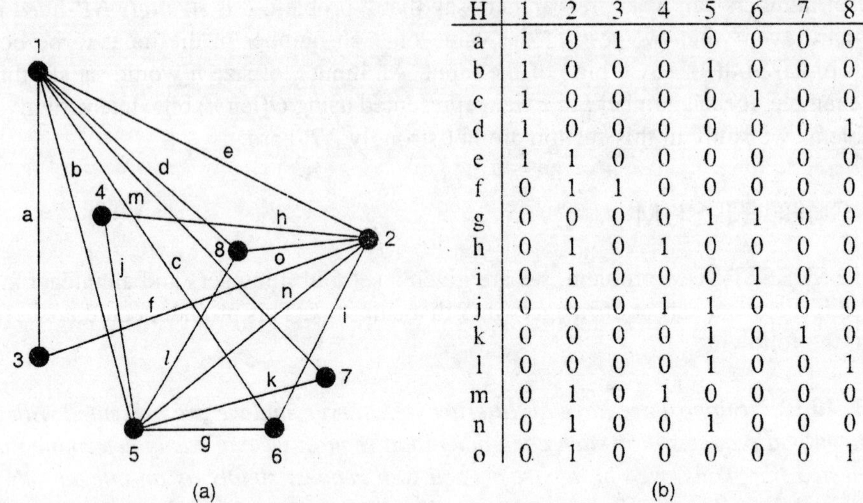

H	1	2	3	4	5	6	7	8
a	1	0	1	0	0	0	0	0
b	1	0	0	0	1	0	0	0
c	1	0	0	0	0	1	0	0
d	1	0	0	0	0	0	0	1
e	1	1	0	0	0	0	0	0
f	0	1	1	0	0	0	0	0
g	0	0	0	0	1	1	0	0
h	0	1	0	1	0	0	0	0
i	0	1	0	0	0	1	0	0
j	0	0	0	1	1	0	0	0
k	0	0	0	0	1	0	1	0
l	0	0	0	0	1	0	0	1
m	0	1	0	1	0	0	0	0
n	0	1	0	0	1	0	0	0
o	0	1	0	0	0	0	0	1

*Fig. 40.12. A graph G illustrating the proof that SUBSET-SUM is **NP**-hard. The vertices are numbered 1 through 8 and the edges are given letter labels a through o. (a) Shows the graph G; (b) shows the incidence matrix H for G. Note that there is a 1 for each edge in one or more of the columns for vertices 1, 2, and 5.*

In addition to the above incidence component, we also define an "edge-covering component," where, for each edge j, we define a number

$$b_j = 4^j.$$

We then set the sum we wish to attain with a subset of these numbers as

$$k' = k4^{m+1} + \sum_{j=1}^{m} 2 \cdot 4^j,$$

where k is the integer parameter for the VERTEX-COVER instance.

Let us consider, then, how this reduction, which clearly runs in polynomial time, actually works. Suppose graph G has a vertex cover $C = \{i_1, i_2, \ldots, i_k\}$, of size k. Then we can construct a set of values adding to k' by taking every a_i with an index in C, that is, each a_{i_r} for $r = 1, 2, \ldots, k$. In addition, for each edge numbered j in G, if only one of j's endpoints is included in C, then we also include b_j in our subset. This set of numbers sums to k', for it includes k values of 4^{m+1} plus 2 values of each 4^j (either from two a_{i_r};'s such that this edge has both endpoints in C or from one a_{i_r} and one b_j if C contains just one endpoint of edge j).

Suppose there is a subset of numbers that sums to k'. Since k' contains k values of 4^{m+1}, it must include exactly k a_i's. Let us include vertex i in our cover for each such a_i. Such a set is a cover, for each edge j, which corresponds to a power 4^j, must contribute two values to this sum. Since only one value come from a b_j, one must have come from at least one of the chosen a_i's. Thus, we have:

THEOREM 40.11. SUBSET-SUM is NP-complete.

40.9.5 KNAPSACK

In the KNAPSACK problem, illustrated in Figure 40.13, we are given a set S of items, numbered 1 to n. Each item i has an integer size, s_i, and worth, w_i. We are also given two integer parameters, s, and w, and are asked if there is a subset, T, of S such that

$$\sum_{i \in T} s_i \leq s, \text{ and } \sum_{i \in T} w_i \geq w.$$

Problem KNAPSACK defined above is the decision version of the optimization problem "0-1 knapsack" discussed in chapter 19.

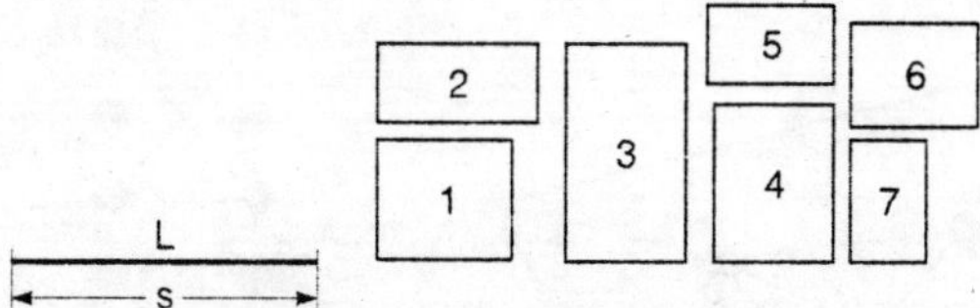

Fig. 40.13. A geometric view of the KNAPSACK problem. Given a line L of length s, and a collection of n rectangles, can we translate a subset of the rectangles to have their bottom edge on L so that the total area of the rectangles touching L is at least w ? Thus, the width of rectangle i is s_i and its area is w_i.

We can motivate the KNAPSACK problem with the following Internet application.

EXAMPLE 40.13. *Suppose we have s widgets that we are interested in selling at an Internet auction web site. A prospective buyer i can bid on multiple lots by saying that he or she is interested in buying s_i widgets at a total price of w_i dollars. It multiple-lot requests, such as this, cannot be broken up (that is, buyer i wants exactly s_i widgets), then determining if we can earn w dollars from this auction gives rise to the KNAPSACK problem. (If lots can be broken up, then our auction optimization problem gives rise to the fractional knapsack problem, which can be solved efficiently using the greedy method).*

SOLUTION : The KNAPSACK problem is in NP, for we can construct a nondeterministic polynomial-time algorithm that guesses the items to place in our subset T and then verifies that they do not violate the s and w constraints, respectively.

KNAPSACK is also *NP*-hard, as it actually contains the SUBSET-SUM problem as a special case. In particular, any instance of numbers given for the SUBSET-SUM problem can correspond to the items for an instance of KNAPSACK with each $w_i = s_i$ set to a value in the SUBSET-SUM instance and the targets for the size s and worth w both equal to k, where k is the integer we wish to sum to for the SUBSET-SUM problem. Thus, by the restriction proof technique, we have the following :

THEOREM 40.12. KNAPSACK is NP-complete.

40.9.6 Hamiltonian-Cycle and TSP

The last two *NP*-complete problems we consider involve the search for certain kinds of cycles in a graph. Such problems are useful for optimizing the travel of robots and printer-plotters, for example.

HAMILTONIAN-CYCLE

Recall, that HAMILTONIAN-CYCLE is the problem that takes a graph G and asks if there is a cycle in G that visits each vertex in G exactly once, returning to its starting vertex. (See Figure 40.14a). To show that this problem is *NP*-complete, we will reduce VERTEX-COVER to it, using a component design type of reduction.

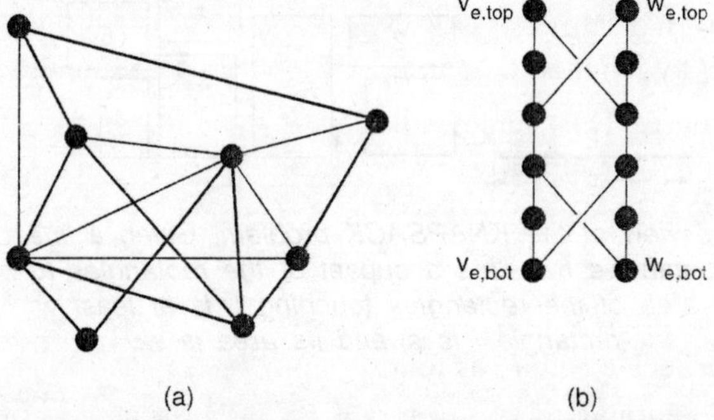

*Fig. 40.14. Illustrating the HAMILTONIAN-CYCLE problem and its **NP**-completeness proof. (a) Shows an example graph with a Hamiltonian cycle shown in bold. (b) Illustrates a cover-enforcer subgraph H_e used to show that HAMILTONIAN-CYCLE is **NP**-hard.*

Let G and k be a given instance of the VERTEX-COVER problem. We will construct a graph H that has a Hamiltonian cycle if and only if G has a vertex cover of size k. We begin by including a set of k initially disconnected vertices $X = \{x_1, x_2, \ldots, x_k\}$ to H. This set of vertices will serve as a "cover-choosing" component, for they will serve to identify which nodes of G should be included in a vertex cover. In addition, for each edge $e = v, w)$ in G we create a "cover-enforcer" subgraph H_e in H. This subgraph H_e has 12 vertices and 14 edges as shown in Figure 40.14b.

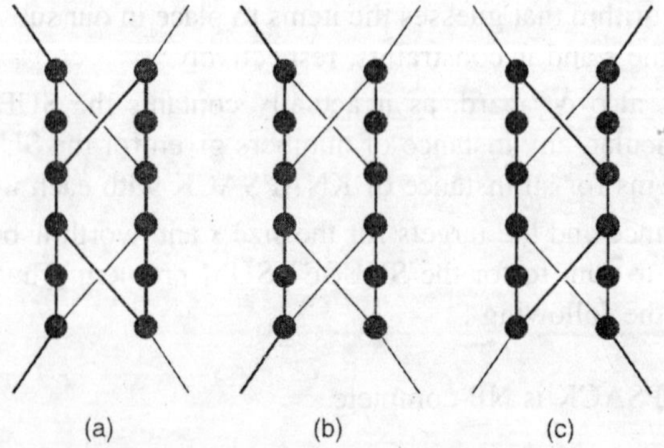

Fig. 40.15. The three possible ways that a Hamiltonian cycle can visit the edges in a cover-enforcer H_e.

Six of the vertices in the cover-enforcer H_e for $e = (v, w)$ correspond to v and the other six correspond to w. Moreover, we label two vertices in cover-enforcer H_e corresponding to v as $v_{e,\,top}$ and $v_{e,\,bot}$, and we label two vertices in H_e corresponding to w as $w_{e,\,top}$, and $w_{e,\,bot}$. These are the only vertices in H_e that will be connected to any other vertices in H outside of H_e.

Thus, a Hamiltonian cycle can visit the nodes of H_e in-three possible way shown in fig. 40.15 and we join to other vertices in H in two ways, one that corresponds to the cover-choosing component and one that corresponds to the cover-enforcing component. For the cover-choosing component, we add an edge from each vertex in X to every vertex $v_{e,\,top}$ and every vertex $v_{e,\,bot}$. That is, we add $2kn$ edges to H, where n is the number of vertices in G.

For the cover-enforcing component, we consider each vertex x in G in turn. For each such v, let $\{e_1, e_2, \ldots, e_{d(v)}\}$ be a listing of the edges of G that are incident upon v. We use this listing to create edges in H by joining $v_{e_i,\,bot}$ in E_{e_i} components joined in this way as belonging to the ***covering thread*** for v. This completes the construction of the graph H. Note that this computation runs in polynomial time in the size of G.

We claim that G has a vertex cover of size k. Let $C = \{v_{i_1}, v_{i_2}, \ldots, v_{i_k}\}$ be such a cover. We construct a Hamiltonian cycle in H, by connecting a series of paths P_j, where each P_j P_j starts at x_j and ends at x_{j+1}, for $j = 1, 2, \ldots, k-1$, except for the last path P_k, which starts at x_k and ends at x_1. We form such a path P_j as follows. Start with x_j, and when visit the entire covering thread for v_{i_j} in H, returning to x_{j+1} (or x_1 if $j = k$). For each cover-enforcer subgraph H_e in the covering thread for v_{i_j}, which is visited in this P_j, we write, without loss of generality, e as (v_{i_j}, w). If w is not also in C, then we visit this H_e as in Figure 40.15a or Figure 40.15c (with respect to v_{i_j}). Instead, if w is also in C, then we visit this H_e as in Figure 40.15b. In this way we will visit each vertex in H exactly once, since C is a vertex cover for G. Thus, this cycle we construct is in fact a Hamiltonian cycle.

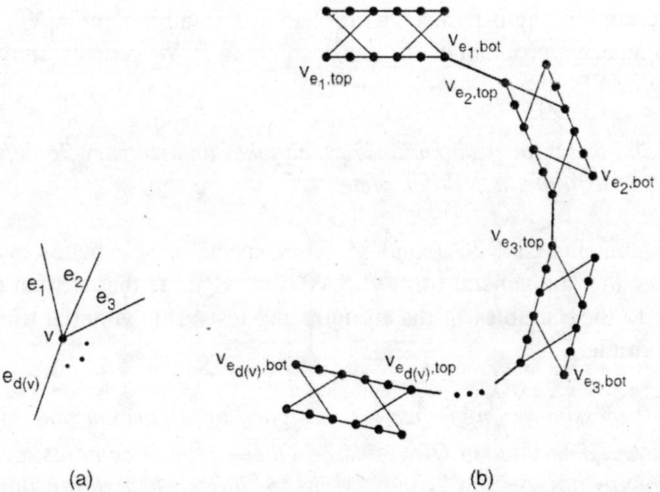

Fig. 40.16. Connecting the cover-enforcers (a) A vertex v and its set of incident edges $\{e_1, e_2, \ldots e_{d(v)}\}$. (b) The connections mode between the He's in H for the edges incident upon v.

Suppose, conversely, that H has a Hamiltonian cycle. Since this cycle must visit all the vertices in X, we break this cycle up into k paths, $P_1, P_2, \ldots, P_k$, each of which starts and ends at a vertex in X. Moreover, by the structure of the cover-enforcer subgraphs H_e and the way that we connected them, each P_j must traverse a portion (possibly all) of a covering thread for a vertex v in G. Let C be the set of all such vertices in G. Since the Hamiltonian cycle must include the vertices from every cover-enforcer H_e and every such subgraph must traversed in a way that corresponds to one (or both) of e's endpoints, C must be a vertex cover in G.

Therefore, G has a vertex cover of size k if and only if H has a Hamiltonian cycle. This gives us the following.

THEOREM 40.13. HAMILTONIAN-CYCLE is NP-complete

TSP. In the *traveling salesperson problem*, or language TSP, we are given an itneger parameter k and a graph G, such that each edge e in G in assigned an integer cost $c(e)$, and we are asked if there is a cycle in G that visits all the vertices in G (possibly more than once) and has total cost at most k. Showing that TSP is in ***NP*** is as easy as guessing a sequence of vertices and then verifying that it forms a cycle of cost at most k in G. Showing that TSP is ***NP***-complete is also easy, as it contains the HAMILTONIAN-CYCLE problem as a special case. Namely, given as instance G of the HAMILTONIAN-CYCLE problem, we can create an instance of TSP by assigning each edge in G the cost $c(e) = 1$ and setting the integer parameter $k = n$, where n is the number of vertices in$G$. Therefore, using the restriction form of reduction, we get the following.

THEOREM 40.14. TSP is NP-complete.

EXAMPLE 40.14. *Professor Amongus has shown that a decision problem L is polynomial-time reducible to an NP-complete problem M. Moreover, after 80 pages of dense mathematics, he has also just proven that L can be solved in polynomial time. Has he just proven that P = NP ? Why or why not?*

SOLUTION : Professor Amongus reduced a problem in P to a problem in NP. To show $P = NP$, he would have to reduce a problem in NP to a problem in P. We already know that every problem in P is already in NP.

EXAMPLE 40.15. *Show that the problem SAT, which takes an arbitrary Boolean formula S as input and asks if S is satisfiable, is NP-complete.*

SOLUTION : SAT contains CNF-SAT and 3SAT as special cases; hence, by restriction, SAT is NP-hard. To see that the general form of SAT is in NP, note that we can guess an assignment of 0's and 1's to the variables in the formula and test in polynomial time if this assignment satisfies the formula.

EXAMPLE 40.16. *Professor Amongus has just designed an algorithm that can take any graph G with n vertices and determine in $O(n^k)$ time whether or not G contains a clique of size k. Does Professor Amongus deserve the Turing Award for having just shown that P = NP ? Why or why not ?*

SOLUTION : This is not a polynomial-time algorithm, since k is a number in the input, not the input size. Moreover, k is not a constant, as would be required of a general polynomial-time algorithm for the CLIQUE problem.

EXAMPLE 40.17. *Show that we can deterministically simulate in polynomial time any nondeterministic algorithm A that runs in polynomial time and makes at most $O(\log n)$ calls to the choose method, where n is the size of the input to A.*

SOLUTION : Suppose that algorithm A makes at most $c \log n$ calls to the choose method. Create a deterministic version A_i of A for every possible outcome of these calls, and run A_i to see if it accepts the given input. If one of the A_i's accepts, then we accept the input. Otherwise, we reject it. If A runs nondeterministically in $p(n)$ steps, then this deterministic version of A will run in $p(n)\, 2^{c \log n} = p(n)\, n^c$ steps, which is a polynomial.

EXAMPLE 40.18. *Suppose an oracle has given you a magic computer, C, that when given any Boolean formula B in CNF will tell you in one step if B is satisfiable or not. Show how to use C to construct an actual assignment of satisfying Boolean values to the variables in any satisfiable formula B. How many calls do you need to make to C in the worst case in order to do this?*

SOLUTION : Number the variables in a satisfiable formula B as $x_1, x_2, \ldots, x_n$. Then, for $i = 1$ to n, consider a version of B that is the formula derived from setting $x_i = 1$. If this formula is satisfiable, update B to now be this formula. Otherwise, set B to the formula derived from setting $x_i = 0$ and repeat. When we will have iteratively transformed B for each variable, then the remaining formula will just be the constant 1, and the variables assignments will be a satisfying assignment for the original formula B. Note that this algorithm makes $n + 1$ calls to the oracle.

EXAMPLE 40.19. *Define SUBGRAPH-ISOMORPHISM as the problem that takes a graph G and another graph H and determines if H is a subgraph of G. That is, there is a mapping from each vertex v in H to a vertex f(v) in G such that, if (v, w) is an edge in H, then (f(v), f(w)) is an edge in G. Show that SUBGRAPH-ISOMORPHISM is NP-complete.*

SOLUTION : Suppose the number of vertices in H is R. To show this problem is in *NP*, we guess a subset of r vertices of G and we also guess a mapping (that is, a matching) of the vertices in H to the chosen vertices in G. Then, in polynomial time we can check that every edge of H has a corresponding edge in G.

To see that SUBGRAPH-ISOMORPHISM is *NP*-hard, we still reduce the Hamiltonian cycle problem to this one. In particular, given an instance $G = (V, E)$ of the Hamiltonian cycle problem, we define a subgraph H to be a simple cycle of $|V|$ vertices. This graph H is subgraph of G if and only if G is Hamiltonian. This reduction clearly takes polynomial time.

EXAMPLE 40.20. *Define INDEPENDENT-SET as the problem that takes a graph G and an integer k and asks if G contains a set I of vertices of size k such that, for any v and w in I, there is no edge (v, w) in G. Show that INDEPENDENT-SET in NP-complete.*

SOLUTION : To see the INDEPENDENT-SET is in NP, note that we can guess a subset of k vertices in G and confirm that no pair of vertices in this set are adjacent.

To show INDEPENDENT-SET is NP-hard, we will reduce VERTEX-COVER to this problem. Specifically, given an instance G, k to VERTEX-COVER, we note that G has a vertex cover of size k if and only if it has an independent set of size $n - k$, where n is the number of vertices in G.

EXAMPLE 40.21. *Define PARTITION as the problem that takes a set $S = \{s_1, s_2, ..., s_n\}$ of numbers and asks if there is a subset T of S such that*

$$\sum_{s_i \in T} s_i = \sum_{S_i \in S-T} s_i.$$

That is, it asks if there is a partition of the numbers into two groups that sum to the same value. Show that PARTITION is NP-complete.

SOLUTION : To show that PARTITION is in NP, note that we can guess a partition of the set of numbers and then check that they sum to the same value.

To show that PARTITION is *NP*-hard, we will reduce SUBSET-SUM to this problem. So, suppose we are given a set of numbers S and a goal sum M that comprise an input to the SUBSET-SUM problem. We begin our transformation of this input into an instance of PARTITION by including every number in S as input numbers for PARTITION. Let N denote the total sum of all the numbers in S. Then, in addition to the numbers already included, we add the number $|N - 2M|$, which is a kind of ***enforcer***. If there is a subset T of S that sum to M, then T will make a partition such that T is on one side and $S - T$ (the rest of the elements) is on the other, with the enforcer element $|N - 2M|$ either on T's side or the other side so as to make the two sides sum to the same value.

EXAMPLE 40.22. *Consider the general optimization version of the TSP problem, where the underlying graph need not satisfy the triangle inequality. Show that, for any fixed value $\delta \geq 1$, there is no polynomial-time δ-approximation algorithm for the general TSP problem unless P = NP.*

Hint : Reduce HAMILTONIAN-CYCLE to this problem by defining a cost function for a complete graph H for the n-vertex input graph G so that edges of H also in G have cost 1 but edges of H not in G have cost δn more than 1.

SOLUTION : Use the hint. That is, suppose we are given an instance G to the Hamiltonian cycle problem. Construct a complete graph H on the n vertices of G and weight these edges so that an edge of H also in G has cost 1 but an edge of H not in G has cost $1 + \delta n$. Note that if we include even just one of these edges in a cycle, then the cost of that cycle is at least $n + \delta n = (1 + \delta)n$. Thus, if we ask for a strict $(1 + \delta)$-approximation of a TSP of cost n, this can only be achieved using original edges of G that form a Hamiltonian cycle.

EXERCISE

1. Program and run mColoring using as data the complete graphs of size $n = 2, 3, 4, 5, 6$ and 7. Let the desired number of colors be $k = n$ and $k = n/2$. Tabulate the computing times for each value of n and k.
2. Prove that PCP with list $x = (01, 1, 1), y = (01^2, 10, 1^2)$ has no solution.
3. Prove that PCP is soluable if $|\Sigma| = 1$
4. Does the PCP with $x = (b^3, ab^2)$ and $y = (b^3, bab^3)$ have solution?
5. Given a sequence of n numbers, the distinct elements problem is to check if there are equal numbers. Give an $O(1)$ time non-deterministic algorithm for this problem.
6. Let SAT(E) be an algorithm to determine whether a propositional formula E, in CNF is satisfiable. Show that if E is satisfiable and has n variables $x_1, x_2, ..., x_n$ then using SAT(E) n times, one can determine a truth value assignment for the x_i's for which E is true.
7. Show that job sequencing with deadlines is NP-hard.
8. A propositional formula is a tautology iff it is true for all possible truth assignments to its variables. (a) Show that CNF satisfiability is reducible to DNF tautology.
9. Prove that clique decision problem is reducible to node cover decision problem?
10. Prove that CNF-satisfiability is reducible to clique decision problem.
11. Write a non deterministic algorithm for sorting an array $A[1 .. n]$
12. Give non deterministic subset sum algorithm.
13. Convert the Boolean formula $B = (x_1 \rightarrow x_2) \cdot (x_3 + x_4x_5) \cdot (\overline{x_1x_2} + x_3\overline{x}_4)$ into CNF.
14. Given the CNF formula $B = (x_1) \cdot (\overline{x}_2 + x_3 + x_5 + \overline{x}_6) \cdot (x_1 + x_4) \cdot (x_3 + \overline{x}_5)$, show the reduction of B into an equivalent input for the 3SAT problem.
15. Given $B = (x_1 + \overline{x}_2 + x_3) \cdot (x_4 + x_5 + \overline{x}_6) \cdot (x_1 + \overline{x}_4 + \overline{x}_5) \cdot (x_3 + x_4 + x_6)$, draw the instance of VERTEX-COVER that is constructed by the reduction from 3SAT of the Boolean formula B.
16. Draw an example of a graph with 10 vertices and 15 edges that has a vertex cover of size 2.
17. Draw an example of a graph with 10 vertices and 15 edges that has a clique of size 6.
18. Is there a subset of the numbers in {23, 59, 17, 47, 14, 40, 22, 8} that sums to 100? What about 130 ? Show your work.
19. Prove that the size of the set of all subsets of n elements is 2^n.
20. Let $w = \{5, 7, 10, 12, 15, 18, 20\}$ and $m = 35$. Find all possible subsets of w that sum to m. Do this using SumOfSub. Draw the portion of the state space tree that is generated.
21. With $m = 35$, run SumOfSub on the data (a) $w = \{5, 7, 10, 12, 15, 18, 20\}$. (b) $w = \{20, 18, 15, 12, 10, 7, 5\}$, and (c) $w = \{15, 7, 20, 5, 18, 10, 12\}$. Are there any discernible differences in the computing times?
22. Write a backtracking algorithm for the sum of subsets problem using the state space tree corresponding to the variable tuple size formulation.

41

NON-DETERMINISTIC ALGORITHMS

As we have seen, a state space is a useful abstraction in analyzing problems. The value of the abstraction is that it provides a particular kind of modularization: One can consider separately the space to be searched and the algorithm used to search it.

However, as algorithms become complex, the language of states and operators quickly becomes too inexpressive and awkward. What is needed is a representation that combines the abstraction of a state space with the expressivity of a procedural programming language. This is achieved in the notion of a *non-deterministic algorithm*.

We will be using non-deterministic algorithms only at the level of pseudo-code. There are a couple of programming languages, such as Prolog, that support non-determinismm but these don't have ordinary programming language operators. (We will discuss Prolog later in the semester.) Non-determinstic operators cannot be easily added to standard programming languages; we will discuss the implementation of non-deterministic algorithms below.

The language of non-deterministic algorithms consists of six reserved words: **choose, pick, fail, succeed, either/or**. These are defined as follows:

- **choose** X satisfying $P(X)$ Consider alternatively all possible values of X that satisfy $P(X)$, and proceed in the code. One can imagine the code as forking at this point, with a separate thread for each possible value of X. If any of the threads succeed, then the choice succeeds. If a choose operator in thread T generates subthreads $T_1, \ldots, T_k$, then T succeeds just if at least one of $T_1, \ldots, T_k$ succeeds.

  If thread T reaches the statement "**choose** X satisfying $P(X)$" and there is no X that satisfied $P(X)$, then T fails.

- **pick** X satisfying $P(X)$. Find any value V that satisfies $P(V)$ and assign $X := V$. This does not create a branching threads.
- **fail** The current thread fails.
- **succeed** The current thread succeeds and terminates.
- **either** S_1 or S_2 or S_3 ... or S_k. Analogous to choose. Create k threads $T_{.}$ ..., T_k where thread T_i executes statement S_i and continues.

Thus, a thread fails and terminates if either (a) it encounters achoosestatement with no choices; (b) it encounters afailstatement. A thread succeeds and terminates if either (a) it terminates in the usual way (by reaching the end of the code) or (b) it encounters asucceedstatement. A thread that goes into an infinite loop is considered to fail, though of course this is not generally detectable.

41.1 Introduction

A nondeterministic algorithm is one in which for a given input instance each intermediate step has one or more possibilities. This means that there may be more than one path from which the algorithm may arbitrarily choose one. Not all paths terminate successfully to give the desired output. The nondeterministic algorithm works in such a way so as to always choose a path that terminates successfully, thus always giving the correct result.

41.2 Procedures of a Nondeterministic Algorithm

The nondeterministic algorithm uses three basic procedures as follows:

1. **CHOICE(1, *n*) or CHOICE(*S*):** This procedure chooses and returns an arbit rary element, in favour of the algorithm, from the closed interval $[1, n]$ or from the set S.
2. **SUCCESS :** This procedure declares a successful completion of the algorithm.
3. **FAILURE :** This procedure declares an unsuccessful termination of the algorithm.

We shall now study the procedures defined above in more detail through an example in the next section.

Relation to state space

A non-deterministic algorithm applied to a program can be considered as defining a state space as follows: Each time you encounter a achooseor aneither/orstatement in executing the code, that defines a node in the state space. The state at this point is the state of the algorithm (value of the variables etc.) An operator on state S is a "chunk of code" executed between this call tochooseand the next call tochoose.

Another way to conceptualize non-deterministic algorithms

Another way to conceptualize non-deterministic algorithms is to imagine that the algorithm can "magically" make a choice that leads to success. A non-deterministic algorithm is correct if (a) there is a sequence of choices that leads to success; and (b) any sequence of choices that leads to success correctly solves the problem.

Implementation

Non-deterministic algorithms are not generally implemented using actual threads; the number of threads would have to be equal to the size of the state space, and most operating systems do not allow this. Rather, the non-deterministic algorithm is considered as defining the state space described above, and any program that exhaustively searches that space is a valid implementation of the non-deterministic algorithm. The search technique is up to the implementor; he can use depth-first search, breadth-first, iterative deepening ...

Some examples

General comment on pseudo-code: I use a combination of the notations I like in Pascal, C, and *Ada*, together with English. I hope it's clear enough. In particular, the labelling of procedure parameters as "in", "out", and "in/out" is taken from Ada. Following Pascal, assignment is notated := and equality is notated =. I declare variables only when I feel like it.

41.3 Nondeterministic Searching

Let us try to solve the searching problem using a nondeterministic algorithm.

The problem statement is:

Given a list *L* which has n number of elements we need to search for a key *x* in this list *L*. Our algorithm would simply be:

NDSEARCH(*x*, *L*, *n*) //searches a key *x* in the list *L* of n elements

```
1. i ← CHOICE(1,n)
2. if L[i] = x
3. SUCCESS
4. FAILURE
```

It might seem as if this procedure merely restates the problem, rather than specifying a way to solve it. Nevertheless, this is a legitimate nondeterministic algorithm.

The key idea here is that expressions in a nondeterministic language can have more than one possible value. For instance CHOICE(1,*n*) might return any index of the given list *L*. Our nondeterministic program evaluator will work by automatically choosing a possible value and keeping track of the choice. If a subsequent requirement is not met, the evaluator will try a dierent choice, and it will keep trying new choices until the evaluation succeeds, or until we run out of choices. The nondeterministic program evaluator frees the programmer from the details of how choices are made.

In the example above, Step 1 in the algorithm returns an index of the list *L* in favour of the algorithm. This means that CHOICE(1,*n*) will always return the correct index at which the key *x* is present in the list *L*. If *x* is not present in the list *L* the algorithm will terminate and report a FAILURE.

There is an important point that is to be kept in mind. Though the nondeterministic algorithm will never adopt a path that leads to unsuccessful termination, all such paths need to be incorporated in the code while designing the algorithm. We need to account for all the random cases that may occur while solving the given problem, and design the algorithm in such a manner that it may follow any of all possible paths, successful and unsuccessful. It is for the nondeterministic program to ensure by itself that only the correct path is followed. In the example provided, this decision is taken by the CHOICE function.

Therefore, though the CHOICE function always returns the correct result we need to incorporate the unsuccessful paths too in the algorithm. This is implemented in step 2 where we are checking if the element returned has the same value as the search key. Here we are assuming that the algorithm can follow any path (the wrong ones too) and hence the check has to be carried out.

If we examine the time complexity of the algorithm we nd that it is a constant since CHOICE either always returns the correct index of the search key in the given list if the key is present in the list and reports a SUCCESS, or reports a FAILURE if the search key is not contained in the list.

Hence we get $T(n) = \Theta(1)$ by the nondeterministic approach. On the other hand if we solve this searching problem by the deterministic algorithm, the best case time complexity that we obtain is $T(n) = O(\log n)$ using binary search. So we see that the nondeterministic algorithm denitely scores over the deterministic one.

41.4 Nondeterministic Sorting

We now move on to another example. Let us solve the problem of sorting a given list L of n elements using a nondeterministic algorithm. The algorithm is as follows:

NDSORT(L, n) //let all elements be positive

```
1. for i ← 1 to n
2. L¹[i] ← 0
3. for i ← 1 to n
4. j ← CHOICE(1,n)
5. if L¹[j] ≠ 0
6. FAILURE
7. L¹[j] ← L[i]
8. for i ← 1 to n - 1//L¹ should be sorted in ascending
   order
9. if L¹[i] > L¹[i + 1]
10. FAILURE
11. print L¹
12. SUCCESS
```

This algorithm generates a permutation of the n elements in the given list L and then checks to see if the permutation generated is the required sorted one.

As seen in the previous example CHOICE always returns a value which is most favourable to or algorithm. Since here it is required that the final list L^1 be sorted, each time CHOICE is called it will return for an element in the unsorted list L, the correct position in the sorted list L^1 . So when CHOICE is called the rst time for $i = 1$, it returns the nal correct index in the sorted list L^1 of the rst element in the unsorted list L. In the second call it returns the correct position in L^1 of the second element of L and so on, until the final sorted list L^1 has been successfully created.

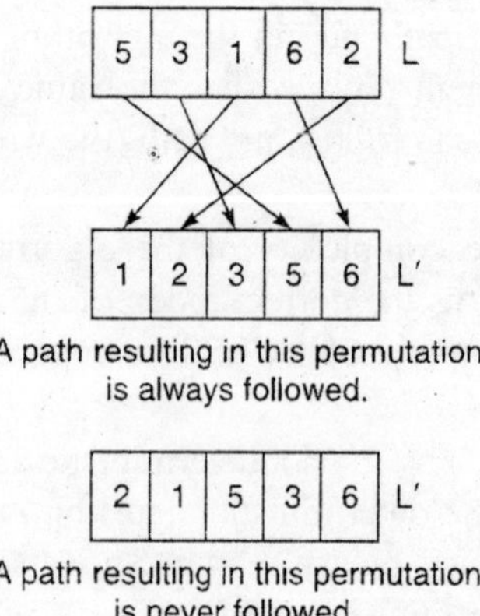

Fig. 41.1 The figure shows the implementation of the nondeterministic sorting algorithm.

In the beginning of the algorithm, we initialise all the elements in the nal sorted list L^1 to zero. This is done to implement the check in steps 5 and 6. This is just to ensure that if a particular position in the sorted list L^1 has already been assigned its final element, it is not reassigned with another element. Elements from L are copied only to those indices in L^1 which are vacant, as there cannot be two ith order statistics in a given list L. Knowing that the CHOICE function always returns the correct value, this case should never occur. This means that during the actual program execution a FAILURE will never occur.

Let us now analyse the time complexity of the algorithm. There are three loops involved each iterating from 1 to n. This gives us a time complexity of $O(n)$. If the sorting problem were to be solved using the deterministic algorithm we would get a time complexity of $O(n \log n)$ in the best case. Hence we see that it is possible to design a polynomial nondeterministic algorithm for a problem that has a non polynomial deterministic algorithm.

In the sorting problem we are generating permutations of the n elements in the list L. So there will be a total of $n!$ permutations (considering the elements to be distinct). Out of these, only one will be the required sorted one. We also know that there is a probability of $1/n!$ that a particular permutation is generated. So if this procedure of generating permutations and then checking if they are sorted or not were to be followed, in the deterministic algorithm we would get a $1/n!$ probability of the correct sorted order being generated. But in the nondeterministic algorithm this probability is 1. This is because there is surely a path to the desired result as is indicated by the $1/n!$ probability in the deterministic case. The property of the CHOICE function is that it always gives the correct result. So we are sure that the order we eventually get is the nal sorted order, giving us a probability of 1. If there exists a successful path to the desired result, the nondeterministic algorithm will always follow this path.

41.5 Nondeterministic Algorithm to Find the Minimum

Let us now determine the minimum of a list L of n elements using a nondeterministic algorithm. The steps are:

NDFIND MIN(L, n)

```
1.  i ← CHOICE(1,n)
2.  j ← CHOICE(1,n)
3.  if i = j or L[i] > L[j]
4.  FAILURE
5.  Print L[i]
6.  SUCCESS
```

Here we are generating two indices and checking whether the elements at those indices bear a specic relation (greater than). Our aim here is that in the rst case we get the index (i) of the minimum element and in the second case we get the index (j) of a non- minimum element. As we know that the CHOICE function always returns a value in favour of the algorithm, in step 1 we will get the index of the element that we desire, *i.e.* the minimum element; and in step 2 an element other than the minimum. Apart from this we also know that the CHOICE function never returns the same value twice. So the condition in step 3 will never hold good and the code will never terminate with a FAILURE. But as explained earlier, in our code we also have to include the cases which may result in a failure even though those paths are never followed. That explains the check in steps 3 and 4.

The time complexity of the algorithm above is a constant as there are no loops involved. Hence $T(n) = \Theta(1)$. If we were to adopt a deterministic approach we would get a time complexity of $O(n)$. Here again we see that we have been able to design a more ecient nondeterministic algorithm for a problem that can be solved by a deterministic algorithm.

N Queens problem

Place N queens on an $N \times N$ board so that no two queens can take one another.

```
function attacked(in I,J,B)  : returns boolean;
{ attack = false;
  for K := 1 to I-1 do
      if ((B[K] = J) or  ((B[K]-J)=(K-I)) or
        ((B[K]-J)=(I-K))
        then attack = true;
        return(attack);
}
N-QUEENS1(in N : integer; out N : array[1..N] of integer)
   /* B[I] = the row of the queen in the Ith column. -1
        initially */
{B := -1;
```

```
for I := 1 to N do
{
    choose J in 1..N such that not attacked(I,J,B)
    B[I]=J;
}
}
```

N-QUEENS1 above fills in the board left to right. Using "pick" we can generalize that to fill in columns in arbitrary order, to be chosen by the implementor.

```
function attacked(in I,J,B) : returns boolean;
{ attack = false;
  for K := 1 to N do
      if ((B[K] != -1) and
          ((B[K] = J) or ((B[K]-J)=(K-I)) or
           ((B[K]-J)=(I-K)))
          then attack = true;
  return(attack);
}

N-QUEENS2(in N : integer; out B : array[1..N] of integer)
/* B[I] = the row of the queen in the Ith column. -1
  initially */
{B := -1;
  for K := 1 to N do
  {
      pick I in 1..N such that B[I]=-1;
      choose J such that not attacked(I,J,B)
     B[I]=J;
  }
}
```

EXACT SET COVER

Given: A set O and a collection C of subsets of O.

Find: A subcollection D of C such that every element of O is in exactly one set in D. (In other words, the union of the sets in D is O and the intersection of any two sets in D is empty.)

Example:

```
O = {a, b, c, d, e, f, g, h, i, j, k, l}
C = {C1, C2, C3, C4, C5, C6, C7, C8 } where
    C1 = {a, b, c}
    C2 = {a, d}
```

```
C3 = {b, c, d, e}
C4 = {b, c, h, k}
C5 = {c, f, g}
C6 = {e, g, i}
C7 = {f, j, l}
C8 = {f, k}
```

Solution: $D = \{C2, C4, C6, C7\}$

(**Note:** EXACT SET COVER is a problem where you cannot a priori predict the depth of the shallowest goal state, so iterative deepening may well to work much better than DFS.)

Non-deterministic algorithm:

```
XCOVER1(in O, C)
{D := empty;
  DU := empty;    /* union of elements in D */
  while (there are elements in O not in DU)
  {
      choose set X in C such that X does not overlap DU;
      add X to D;
      DU := DU union X;
  }
  return(D)
}
```

Corresponding search space

State: A subcollection of *C*.

Operator on state *S*: Add to *S* an element of *C* that does not overlap the union of the sets in *S*.

Start state: The empty collection.

Goal state: An exact set cover.

A problem with the above algorithm is that it generates each collection *D* in every possible order. For example, one branch will first choose $X = C2$, then $X = C4$, then $X = C6$, then $X = C7$. A different branch will first choose $X = C7$, then $X = C2$, then $X = C6$, then $X = C4$, finding the same solution in a different order. Indeed, every permutation will be discovered on a separate branch of the algorithm. That is, the state space isnon-systematic; different paths through the state space lead to the same state.

We can fix the above problem by requiring that every subcollection of *D* be constructed in a specified order:

```
XCOVER2(in O,C)
{ pick L to be an ordering on the sets in C;
  D := empty;
  DU := empty;    /* union of elements in D */
  while (there are elements in O not in DU)
  {
     choose set X in L such that X does not overlap DU;
     add X to D;
     DU := DU union X;
     L := the tail of L following X;
  }
  return(D)
}
```

Thus, if *L* is picked as the order *C*1, *C*2, *C*3, *C*4, *C*5, *C*6, *C*7, *C*8, this will only find the solution in the order *C*2, *C*4, *C*6, *C*7. The operator "pick" is appropriate for *L* because the solution can be found whatever order is picked for *L* (though some orderings may be more efficient than others) and therefore, when one ordering fails, there's no point in going back and trying a different ordering.

An alternative solution to the same problem:

```
XCOVER3(in O,C)
{ D := empty;
  DU := empty;    /* union of elements in D */
  {
    while (there are elements in O-DU)
    pick an element W in O-DU;
    choose a set X such that W is in X and X does not
       overlap DU;
    add X to D;
    DU := DU union X;
  }
  return(D)
}
```

Thus, for example, if the elements *W* are picked in alphabetical order, the algorithm will first choose a set to cover "a"; then, on the branch where it has chosen *C*2, it will choose a set to cover "b"; then, on the branch where it has chosen *C*4, it will choose a set to cover "e", then on the branch where it has chosen *C*6, it will choose a set to cover "f".

Herė, the selection of element *W* can even depend on the earler choices of sets in *D*. Whatever selection criterion is used for *W*, any set *D* can only be constructed in one way. For instance, suppose that we pick the first element of *O-DU* that comes after the last element of *DU*, going cylically around. Then the algorithm will first choose a set to cover "a"; then, on the branch where it has chosen *C*2, it will choose a set to cover "e"; then, on the branch where it has chosen *C*6, it will choose a set to cover "j"; then on the branch where it has chosen *C*7, it will choose a set to cover "b".

BETWEENNESS Problem

In a list of items, we say that *Y* is between *X* and *Z* if either [*X* precedes *Y* and *Y* precedes *Z*] or [*Z* precedes *Y* and *Y* precedes *X*]. Thus, for example, in the list [*C,A,D,E,B,F*], *D* is between *C* and *B*; *E* is between *F* and *D*; and so on.

The following problem is known as the BETWEENNESS problem: The input is a set of constraints of the form "*Y* is between *X* and *Z*". The problem is to find a list that obeys all these constraints. For instance, given the constraints

A is between *C* and *B*.
D is between *B* and *C*.
D is between *A* and *E*.
E is between *D* and *F*.
B is between *F* and *A*.

one solution is the list [*C,A,D,E,B,F*]. The BETWEENNESS problem is NP-complete, so presumably there is no polynomial-time algorithm.

Non-deterministic algorithms

```
BETWEEN1 (Z : set of items; B : set of betweenness
   constraints)
return list of items;
O := empty list;
for each item X in Z  do
{
   choose a position in O to insert X;
   if any constraint in B is violated then fail;
}
return O.
```

State space:
State: Permutation of *Z*[1..*K*].
Operator on state *S*: Add *Z*[*K* + 1] to *S* at some position in *S* such that the constraints are satisfied.

Start state: empty set.

Goal state: Permutation of Z observing the constraints.

```
BETWEEN2 (Z : set of items; B : set of betweenness
   constraints)
return list of items;
{ O := empty list;
  while Z is non-empty do
  {
     choose an item X in Z;
     add X to the end of O;
     if any constraint in B is violated then fail;
     delete X from Z;
  }
  return O;
}
```

State space:

State: Ordered list of items (first K items in the output).

Operator on state S: Add some item in Z to the end of S, consistent with the constraints

Start state: empty list

Goal state: Permutation of Z satisfying the constraints.

```
BETWEEN3 (S : set of items; B : set of betweenness
   constraints)
return list of items;
{ G := the graph which has the items of S as vertices and
      has no edges;
  for each constraint C of the form ``Y is between X and
      Z'' in B do
     either add edges X - Y and Y - Z to G;
     or add edges Z - Y and Y - X to G;
  if G has a cycle then fail;
  return a topological sort of G.
}
```

State space:

State: A graph over the items in S consistent with the first K constraints in C.

Operator on S: Take the K + 1st constraints "Y is between X and Z" and either add arcs $X \rightarrow Y$ and $Y \rightarrow Z$ or add arcs $Z \rightarrow Y$ and $Y \rightarrow X$ to S.

Start state: The graph with no edges.

Goal state: A graph that enforces all the constraints in *C*.

Semantics and implementation of a non-deterministic algorithm

Let's start with the case where there are no "pick" statements. Asuccessfulbranch in a non-deterministic algorithm is some execution of the code with some particular sequence of choices at the "choose" and "either/or" statements that ends in success (either in the execution of "succeed" or in reaching the end of the program.) A non-deterministic algorithmsucceedsif some branch succeeds. A non-deterministic algorithm Areturnsvalue *V* if *V* is returned by some successful branch of *A*. (Thus, *A* can return many different values.) Algorithm Acorrectly solvesproblem *P* if the following holds

- If *A* returns *V*, then *V* is a solution to *P*.
- If *A* returns no value, then *P* has no solution.

Note that it is not required that *A* return every possible solution to *P*.

If there are "pick" statements, the first definitions become a little more involved. Let *A* be a non-deterministic algorithm. Let *B* be a branch of an execution of *A* up to some execution *E* of a statement *S* of the form "pick *X* such that *Z*(*X*)". Apicking strategy *Q* is a function that maps any such branch *B* to a value of *X* that satisfies the condition in *S*. any execution of a statement "pick *X* such that *Z*(*X*)" into some particular *X* such that *Z*(*X*). A successful branch of non-deterministic algorithm *A* under pick strategy *Q* is one execution of the code with some choice of values at the "choose" and "either/or" statements, where the values picked at the execution of pick statements is governed by *Q*, that ends in success. Algorithm *A* succeeds under pick strategy *Q* if some branch of A under *Q* succeeds. Algorithm *A* returns value *V* under *Q* if some successful branch of *A* under *Q* returns *V*. Algorithm *A* correctly solves problem *P* if, for every pick strategy *Q*, the following conditions hold:

- If *A* returns *V* under *Q*, then *V* is a solution to *P*.
- If *A* returns no value under *Q*, then *P* has no solution.

Therefore, an implementation *I* of non-deterministic algorithm *A* is correct if it satisfies the following properties:

- If *I* returns value *V*, then *A* returns *V*.
- If *I* returns no value, then *A* returns no value.

Again it is not required that *I* find every value returned by *A*, just that if *A* finds some value, then *I* finds some value.

It follows immediately that if *I* is a correct implementation of algorithm *A* and *A* correctly solves problem *P*, then *I* correctly solves problem *P*.

Converting a non-deterministic algorithm to code executing DFS

Let *S* be an instance in the code of the statement "choose *X* such that *P*(*X*)". Each execution *E*1 of *S* is translated an execution of the loop

```
for (X such that P(X)) do g(X)
```

where $g(X)$ executes all the code that occurs between the execution $E1$ and the eventual success or failure. In particular, if S is executed again within the branch following $E1$ then these further executions must occur within the function $g(X)$ (which is presumably recursive.)

For instance, the code

```
while (A) do
{ choose X such that P(X);
  B(X);
  if (C) then succeed else if (D) then fail;
}
can be implemented as a DFS as follows:
f(X)
{ if (A)
  {
    found := false;
    for (X1 such that P(X1))
    {
      B(X1);
      if (C) then found := true;
        else if (D) then noop;
        else found := f(X1);
      if found then exitloop;
    }
    return(found)
  }
}
```

Example:

```
start book is deterministic, e.g.
for i from 1 to 9
    print i
will always print 123456789
```

Example of Deterministic

Here's pseudo code for a deterministic algorithm that checks whether a given number is odd:

```
function is_odd(n):
  if n mod 2 = 1
  then return true
  else return false
```

The most simple deterministic algorithm is thisrandom number generator.

```
def random():
        return 4 #chosen by fair dice roll, guaranteed to be random
```

It gives the same output every time, exhibits knownO(1)time and resource usage, and executes in PTIME on any computer.

To me, "deterministic" could mean many things:

- Given the same input, produces the same output every time.
- Given the same input, takes the same amount of time/memory/resources every time it is run.
- Problems of complexity classP that can be solved in polynomial time by a deterministic computer, as opposed to problems of complexity classNP which can be only solved in polynomial time using anon-deterministic computer.

42

APPROXIMATION ALGORITHMS

Approximation algorithm is a procedure that always provides some kind of solution to your problem, though it may fail to find the optimal solution. To be useful, we can find the ratio between the optimal solution and the one produced by the approximate algorithms.

42.1 The Vertex-Cover Problem

A *vertex cover* of an undirected graph $G = (V, E)$ is a subset $V' \subseteq V$ such that if (u, v) is an edge of G_1 then either $u \varepsilon V'$ or $v \varepsilon V'$ (or both). The size of vertex cover is the number of vertices in it.

A **vertex-cover** problem which finds vertex cover of minimum size in a given undirected graph is *optimal vertex cover. Approximate vertex-cover* returns a vertex cover whose size is guaranteed to be not more than twice the size of an optimal vertex cover.

```
APPROX-VERTEX-COVER (G)
        C ← φ
        E′ ← E[G]
  while E′ ≠ φ
        do select an arbitrary edge (u, v) ε E′
             C ← C ∪ {u, v}
```

Remove from E' every edge incident on either u or v return C

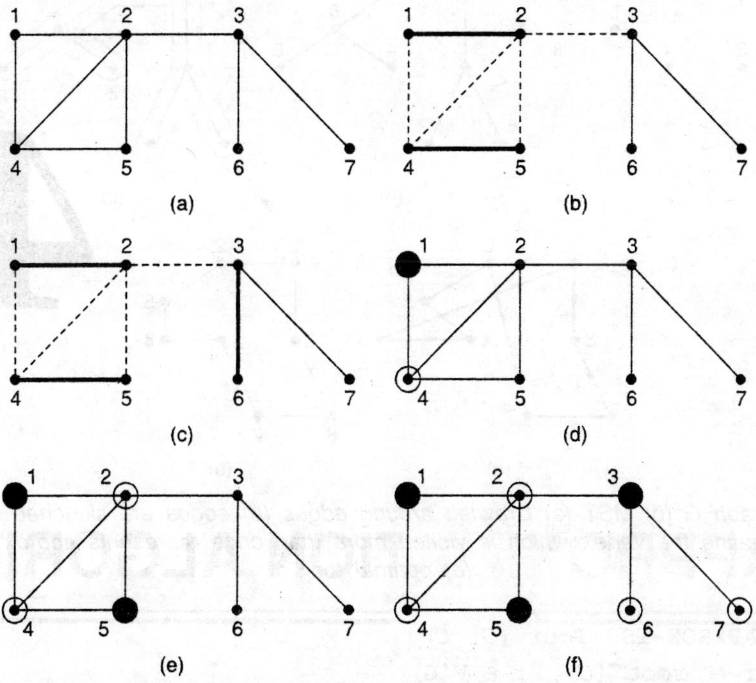

Fig. 42.1 (a) input graph (b) approx-vertex cover, which edges incident on (u, v) shown by dotted line (c) final approx-vertex cover which includes vertices 1, 2, 4, 5, 3, 6 (d)-(f) finds optimal vertex cover. (f) Contains optimal vertex cover with vertices 1, 5, 3.

Thus Approx-vertex-cover returns a vertex cover that is at most twice the size of an optimal cover, while forming the optimal vertex cover we keep in mind that atleast one end point of edge of approx-vertex-cover is selected.

42.2 Approx-TSP Tour

Let us now consider finding a good *approximate algorithm* for travelling salesman problem which is impossible unless $P = NP$. We first compute a minimum spanning tree we then crawl around each node following the edges and finally return back to first vertex. This is a preorder walk. then edges are joined in this order to obtain Approx tour walk. Cost of this tour is no more than twice that of MST cost, as long as cost function satisfies the triangle inequality, *i.e.*, $c(u, w) \leq c(u, v) + c(v, w)$. See Fig. 42.2.

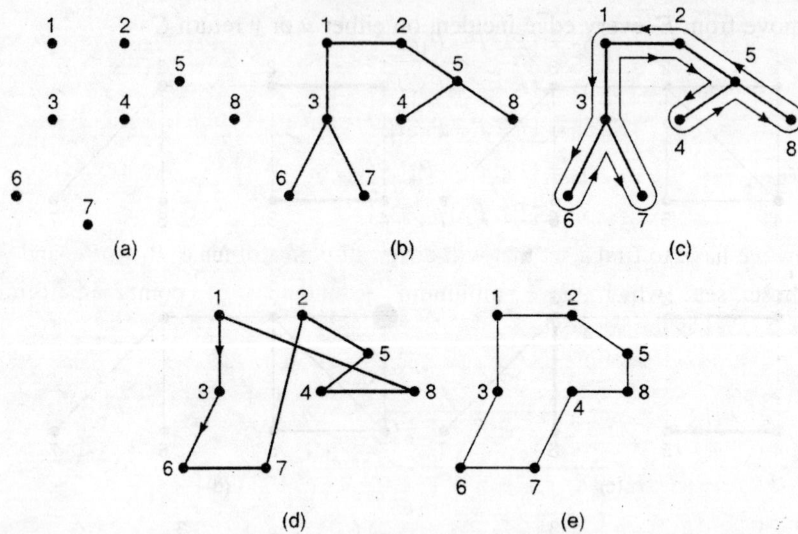

Fig. 42.2 (a) Graph G (b) MST (c) Crawled around edges (d) edges are sketched in the order of walk, eliminating the vertex which is visited more than once represents approx algo. tour (e) optimal tour.

```
APPROX-TSP-Tour (G, C)
r ← root [G], r ε V[G]
Find MST-PRIM (G, C, r)
L ← list of vertex visited in preorder walk.
return Hamiltonian cycle H, H ε L.
```

42.3 The Set-Covering Problem

An instance (X, F) of the **set-covering** problem. Consists of a finite set X and a family F of subsets of X, such that every element of X belongs to atleast one subset in F :

Let $X = 12$ black points.

$$F = \{S_1, S_2, S_3, S_4, S_5, S_6\}$$

$$X = \bigcup_{S \varepsilon F} S$$

We say that subset $S \varepsilon F$ **covers** its elements. Minimum size subset $C \subseteq F$ whose members cover all of X :

$$X = \bigcup_{C \varepsilon F} S$$

Hence C **covers** X, size of S is the number of sets it contains, rather than individual element in the sets. See Fig. 42.3.

Here, $X = \{P_1, P_2, P_3, \ldots, P_{12}\}$

$$S_1 = \{P_1, P_2, P_6, P_9, P_{10}\}$$

$$S_2 = \{P_6, P_7, P_{10}, P_{11}\}$$
$$S_3 = \{P_1, P_2, P_3, P_4\}$$
$$S_4 = \{P_3, P_5, P_6, P_7, P_8\}$$
$$S_5 = \{P_9, P_{10}, P_{11}, P_{12}\}$$
$$S_6 = \{P_4, P_8\}$$

Now we have to find a set that will cover all points of X i.e. P_1 to P_{12} and which contains only those sets which have minimum redundancy of points in forming C. Thus $C = \{S_3, S_4, S_5\}$ is the set cover.

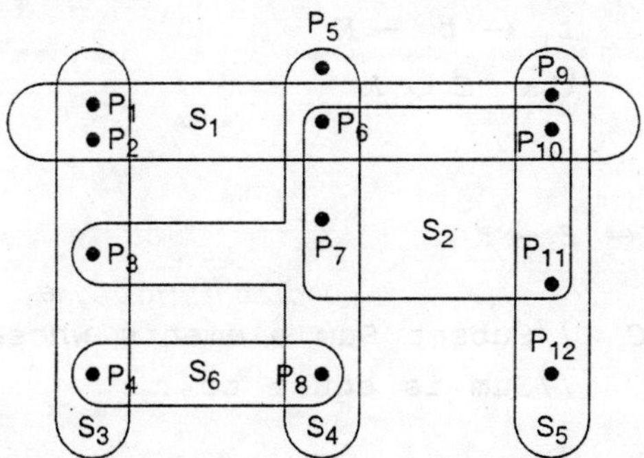

Fig. 42.3. Depicts set cover $C = \{S_3, S_4, S_5\}$

We can write the Greedy Set cover algorithm, as,

```
GREEDY-SET-COVER (X, F)
      U ← X
      C ← ϕ
   While U ≠ ϕ
      do select an S ε F that maximizes | S ∩ U |
         U ← U − S
         C ← C ∪ {S}
   return C
```

Running time is $O(|X||F| \min(|X|, |F|))$

42.4 Subset-Sum Problem

In the **subset sum problem,** we are given a finite set $S \subset N$ and a target $t \varepsilon N$. These exists a subset $S' \subseteq S$ whose element sum to t.

Let $S = \{1, 2, 7, 14, 49, 98, 343, 686, 2409, 2793, 16808, 17206, 117705, 17993\}$

and $t = 138457$

then $S' = \{1, 2, 7, 98, 343, 686, 2409, 17206, 117705\}$

is a solution.

```
Subset-SumAlgo (s, t)
    C ← φ
    Z ← S
    K ← φ
    t1 ← t
    while (Z ≠ φ) do {
        k ← max(Z)
        if (K < t) then {
            Z ← Z - K
            t1 ← t1 - K
            C ← C ∪ K
        }
    else
        Z ← Z - K
    }
    print C   //Subset Sum elements whose
              //Sum is equal to t1.
```

This procedure selects those elements of S whose sum is equal to t. Every time maximum element is found from S, if it is less than t then this element is removed from Z and also it is subtracted from t (*i.e.*, +1). So that in next selection of elements balance sum of element is only required to be calculated. In actual backtracking also works. So that if some is not found then other selection is required.

$$Z \leftarrow S, t = 138457$$

$$Z = \{1, 2, 7, 14, 49, 98, 343, 686, 2409, 2793, 16808, 17206, \mathbf{117705}, 17993\}$$

$$K \leftarrow \max[Z]$$

$\therefore$ $K = 117705$

Here $K < t_1$

Therefore $Z = Z - K$

i.e., $Z = \{1, 2, 7, 14, 49, 98, 343, 686, 2409, 2793, 16808, 17206, 17993\}$

$$t_1 \leftarrow t$$

Subtracting K from t_1, we get

$$t_1 = 138457$$

$$\underline{K = 117705}$$

New $t_1 = 20752$

In new steps $K = 17993$

$$t_1 = 20752$$

$$\underline{K = 17993}$$

New $t_1 = 2759$

New max (Z) is $17206 > t_1$.

Therefore simply it is subtracted from Z

K = new max (Z) is 16808 > t_1, subtract from Z

Again new max (Z) is 2793 > t_1, subtract from Z

Again new max (Z) is 2409

Therefore $\quad t_1 = 2759$

$$K = 2409$$

$$\overline{\quad 350}$$

After that new max (Z) is 686, subtracted from Z

New max (Z) is 343

$$t_1 = 350$$

$$K = 343$$

$$\text{New} \quad t_1 = \ 07$$

Now only those numbers needs to be selected whose sum is 07, therefore 7 is selected from Z and rest other number found as maximum Z are subtracted from Z one by one till Z becomes ϕ.

Study Chapter 40 for detail of this problem.

EXERCISE

1. Prove that the solution to approx-knap (Knapsack) is always with in a factor 2 of the optimal.
2. Give an efficient algorithm to determine whether a graph can be painted with just two colors, and if so how to do it.
3. Show that any planar graph can be painted using at most four colors.
4. Give an efficient approximate algorithm for the TSP that is guaranteed to find a solution within a factot 3/2 of optimum.
5. Give an elementary proof that there cannot exist a fully polynomial approximation scheme for the maximum clique problem, unless $P = NP$.

43

PROGRAM

/************* PROGRAM TO COMPUTE GCD OF GIVEN NO'S ****************/**

```
# include <stdio.h>
# include <time.h>
# include <conio.h>
# include <math.h>
struct time t1, t2;
unsigned char p, q;
main ( )
{
      int a, b, t, c, e, f;
      float d;
      clrscr ( );
      printf (''\n\n\t THE OUTPUT IS PRODUCED BY : ->
                                              GAJENDRA'');
      printf (''\n Enter the no whose bcd is required :
                                                   -<\n'');
      gett time (&t1);
      printf (''\n The initial time is : -> %d, %d sec's
                               \n'', t1. ti_sec, t1.ti_hund);
```

```
        while (b! = 0)
        {
            t = b;
            b = a % b;
            a = t;
        }
        delay (1000);
        get time (&t2);
        printf (''\n The final time : -> %d.%d sec's\n'',
                                    t2.ti_sec, t2.ti_hund);
        p = t2.ti_sec - t1.ti_sec;
        q = t2.ti_hund - ti.ti_hund;
        printf (''\n The time required for execution is : ->
                                    %d.%d sec's \n'', p, q);
        printf (''\n The gcd of no's is : -> %d'', a);
        printf (''\n\t ~~~~~~~~~~~~~~~~~~~~~~~~~~~~~~~~~~~~~~~~);
        getch ( );
    }
```

THE OUTPUT IS PRODUCED BY : -> GAJENDRA

Enter the no whose gcd is required :->

2

40 30

The initial time is :-> 24.33 sec's

Thefinal time :-> 25.10 sec's

The time required for execution is :-> 1.233 sec's

The gcd of no's is :-> 2

Maximum of Number :

```
    # include <stdio.h>
    # include <stdlib.h>
    # include <time.h>
    int start, end, n, i, k, b, d, b1 [1000], a [1000], n1;
    float t;
    main ( )
    {
        clock_t start, end;
        clrscr ( ) ;
        printf (''\nMaximum Of Number : \n\n'');
        printf (''\nENTER THE NO. OF ELEMENT --> '');
        scanf (''%d'', &n);
        start = clock ( );
        printf (''\nTHE ELEMENTS ARE --> '');
```

```
        for (i = 0; i < n; i ++)
        {
            bl [i] = r and ( ) % 100;
            printf (''\n %d – %d '', i, b1 [i]);
        }
        d = max_item (b1, n);
        end = cock ( );
        t = ( ( end - tart ) / CLK_TCK);
        printf (''\n\nTHE MAXIMUM ELEMENT IS %d \n '', b1
                                                        [d]);
        printf (''\n\nTHE TIME REQUIRES IS – %1 f '', t);
        getch( );
        return (0);
    }
    max_item (int a [ ] , int n1)
    {
        i = k = n1;
        while (i > 1)
        {
            i = i – 1;
            if (a[i] > a[k])
            {
                k = i;
            }
        }
        return k);
    }
```

Maximum of Number :

ENTER THE NO. OF ELEMENT — >
THE ELEMENT ARE — >
0 — 46
1 — 30
2 — 82
3 — 90
4 — 56
5 — 17
THE MAXIMUM ELEMENT IS 90
THE TIME REQUIRES IS — 1.153846

/******** PROGRAM FOR REMOVAL OF RECURSION FROM MAX ITEM ALGORITHM *********

```
# include <stdio.h>
```

```
# include <time.h>
# include <conio.h>
# include <dos.h>
# include <math.h>
struct time t1, t2;
unsigned char p, q;
int a [10];
main ( )
{
    int i, j, k, n, ddr, top, temp, stack [15];
    clrscr ( );
    printf (''\n\n\t THE OUTPUT IS PRODUCED BY : ->
                                             GAJENDRA'');
    printf (''\n Enter the no of elements : ->\n'');
    scanf (''%d'', &n);
    printf (''\n Enter elements : ->\n'');
    fo (i = 1; i < = n; i ++)
    scanf (''%d'', &a [i]);
    top = 0; i = 1;
    gettime (&t1);
    printf (''\n The initial time is :-> %d.%d sec's
    \n'', t1.ti_sec, t1.ti_hund);
    i1 : if (i < n)
    {
        top = top + 1;
        stack [top] = 1;
        top = top + 1;
        stack [top] = 2;
        i = i + 1;
        goto i1;
        i2: j = stack [top];
        top = top - 1;
        if (a[i] > a[j])
        k = i;
        else
        k = j;
    }
    else
    k = n;
    if (top ==0)
    temp = k;
    else
```

```
        {
            addr = stack [top];
            top = top - 1;
            i = stack [top];
            stack [top] = k;
            if (addr == 2)
            goto i2;
        }
        printf (''The maximum of all the elements is ->
        %d, a[k]);
        delay (1000);
        gettime (&t2)
        printf (''\n The final time :-> %d.%d sec's\n'',
        t2.ti_sec, t2.ti_hund);
        pt2.ti_sec - t1.ti_sec;
        q = t2.ti_hund - t1.ti_hund;
        printf (''\n The time required for execution is :->
                                        %d.%d sec's \n'', p, q);
        printf (''\n\t ~~~~~~~~~~~~~~~~~~~~~~~~~~~~~~~~~~~~~~);
        getch ( );
    }
```

THE OUTPUT IS PRODUCED BY :-> GAJENDRA

Enter the no of elements :->

30

Enter elements :->

1 :-> 46	2 : -> 30	3 : -> 82	4 : -> 90	5 : -> 56
6 :-> 17	7 :-> 95	8 :-> 15	9 :-> 48	10 :-> 26
11 :-> 4	12 :-> 58	13 :-> 71	14 :-> 79	15 :-> 92
16 :-> 60	17 :-> 12	18 :-> 21	19 :-> 63	20 :-> 47
21 :-> 19	22 :-> 41	23 :-> 90	24 :-> 85	25 :-> 14
26 :-> 9	27 :-> 52	28 :-> 71	29 :-> 79	30 :-> 16

The initial time is :-> 44.56 sec's

The maximum of all the elements is -> 95

The final time :-> 45.38 sec's

The time required for execution is :-> 1.238 sec's

/* Implementation of Union and Find Algorithm */

```
# include <stdio.h>
# include <string.h>
# include <conio.h>
# include <dos.h>
```

```
# define SIZE 20
 struct
 {
      int info;
      int parent;
      int ptr;
 }
 tree [20];
 int count [20], n;
 read_data ( )
 {
      int i;
      printf (''\nENTER THE NO. OF NODES -> \n'');
      scanf (''%d'', &n);
      for (i = 0; i > n; i ++)
      {
           printf (''ENTER INFORMATION AT NODES %d :'',
                                                   i + 1);
           scanf (''%d'', & tree [i].into);
           count [i] = 1;
      }
      return () ;
 }
 make_tree ( )
 {
      int i, 11, 12;
      11 = 1;
      12 = 2;
      while (1)
      {
           for (i = 0; i < n; i + 2 12)
           {
                if (tree [o + 11].info ! = -1)
                union1 (i, i + 11);
                else
                break;
           }
           11 * = 2; i2 + = 2;
           if (11 > = n)
           break
      }
      return (0);
```

```
}
/* --- Build tree using weighting rule -- */
union1 (int i, int j)
{
        int x;
        tree [i].parent = -count[i];
        tree [j].parent = -count [j];
        x = tree [i].parent + tree [j].parent;
        if (tree[i].parent > tree[j].parent)
        {
                void main ( )
                {
                        int i, f, n;
                        clrscr ( );
                        /* -- INITIALIZE -- */
                        for (i = 0; i < 20; i ++)
                        tree[i].info = -1;
                        read_data ( );
                        make_tree ( );
                        while (1)
                        {
                                read_find ( );
                                printf (''\nContinue --- v ? (1/0) '');
                                scanf (%d'', &f);
                                getch ( );
                                clrscr ( );
                                if (f == 0)
                                exit (0);
                        }
                }
        }
}
```

ENTER THE NO. OF NODES — >

5

ENTER INFORMATION AT NODES 1 : 3

ENTER INFORMATION AT NODES 2 : 4

ENTER INFORMATION AT NODES 3 : 6

ENTER INFORMATION AT NODES 4 : 8

ENTER INFORMATION AT NODES 5 : 9

ENTER NODE INFORMATION WHOSE ROOT IS FIND ROOT 6

ROOT INFORMATION IS 3, 1, 1:

MOVES FOR GOVING UP : 1

MOVES FOR RESETTING UP : 1

Continue —— v ? (1/0) 0

/******** PROGRAM FOR HEAPSORT **********/**

```
# include <stdio.h>
# include <time.h>
# include <conio.h>
# include <dos.h>
# include <math.h>
struct time t1, t2;
unsigned char p, q;
main ()
{
    int i, j, k, n;
    int a[10];
    clrscr ();
    ptinf (''\n\n\t THE OUTPUT IS PRODUCED BY :->
                                    SHABBIR & GAJENDRA'');
    printf (''\n Enter the no of elements :-> \n'');
    scanf (''%d'', &n);
    printf (''\n Enter the elements :-> \n'');
    for (i = 1; i < = n; i ++)
    scanf (''%d'', &a [i]);
    gettime (&t1);
    printf ''\n The initial time is :-> %d.%d sec's
                              \n'', t1.ti_sec, t1.ti_hund);
    heapsort (a, n);
    delay (1000);
    gettime (&t2);
    printf (''\n The sorted elements in the heap are \n'')
    for (i = 1; i < = n; i ++)
    printf (''%d\n; i ++)
    printf (%d\n'', a[i]);
    printf (''\n The final time :-> %d.%d sec's\n'',
                                   t2.ti_sec, t2.ti_hund);
    p = t2.ti_sec - t1.ti_sec;
    q = t2.ti_hund - t1.ti_hund;
    printf ('' \n The time required for execution is :->
                                  %d.%d sec's \n'', p, q);
    printf (''\n\t ~~~~~~~~~~~~~~~~~~~~~~~~~~~~~~~~~~~~~~);
    getch();
}
```

/************************** **FUNCTION HEAPSORT** ****************

```
heapsort (int a[], int n)
{
  int , it;
  heapify (a, n);
  for (i = 1; i > = 2; i -)
  {
     t = a[i];
     a[i] = a[1];
     a[1] = t;
     adjust (a, 1, i - 1);
  }
}
```

/********************** **FUNCTION HEAPIFY** ******************/

```
heapify (int a[], int n)
{
  int i;
  for (i = floor (n/2); i > = 1; i -)
  adjust (a, i, n);
}
```

/************************ **FUNCTION ADJUST** *****************/

```
Adjust (int a[], int i, int n)
{
  int j, item;
  j = 2*i;
  item = a[i];
  while (j < = n)
  {
     if ((j < n) && [j] < a[j + 1])
     j = j + 1;
     if (item > = a[j])
     heapify
     break;
     else
     {
         a[floor (j/2)] = a[j];
         j = 2*j;
     }
  }
  a[floor (j/2)] = item;
}
```

THE OUTPUT IS PRODUCED BY :-> GAJENDRA

Enter the no of elements :->
10
Enter the elements :->
1 :-> 46 2 :-> 30 3 :-> 82 4 :-> 90 5 :-> 56 6 :-> 17 7 :-> 95 8 :-> 15 9 :-> 48 10 :-> 26
The initial time is :-> 28.77 sec's
The sorted elements in the heap are
1 :-> 95 2 :-> 90 3 :-> 82 4 :-> 48 5 :-> 56 6 :-> 17 7 :-> 46 8 :-> 15 9 :-> 30 10 :-> 26
the final time :-> 29.60 sec's
The time required for execution is :-> 1.239 sec's

unsigned char p, q;
static int a[20];

/**************** PROGRAM FOR MERGE-SORT ***************

```
# include <stdio.h>
# include <time.h>
# include <conio.h>
# include <dos.h>
# include <math.h>
struct time t1, t2;
unsigned char p, q;
static int a[20];
main ()
{
      int low, high, m, n, i, j;
      int b[20];
      clrscr ();
      printf (''\n\n\t THE OUTPUT IS PRODUCED BY :->
      SHABBIR & GAJENDRA'');
      printf (''\n Enter the no of elements is list :->
                                                    \n'');
      scanf (''%d'', &n);
      printf (''\n Enter the elements of list :-> \n'');
      for (i = 1; i < = n; i ++)
      scanf (''%d'', &a[i]);
      low = 1;
      high = n;
      gettime (&t1);
      printf (''\n The initial time is :-> %d.%d sec's
                              \n'', t1.ti_sec, t1.ti_hund);
      mergesort (low, high);
```

```
        delay (1000);
        gettime  (&t2);
        printf  (''\n The result of merge sort is :-> \n'');
        for (i = 1; i < = n; i ++)
        printf  (''%d\n'', a[i]);
        printf  (''\n The final time :-> %d.%d sec's\n'',
                                        t2.ti_sec, t2.ti_hund);
        p = t2.ti_sec - t1.ti_sec;
        q = t2.ti_hund - t1.ti_hund;
        printf  ('' \n The time required for execution is :->
                                        %d.%d sec's \n'', p, q);
        printf  (''\n\t ~~~~~~~~~~~~~~~~~~~~~~~~~~~~~~~~~~~~~~');
        getch ();
    }
```

/**************** FUNCTION FOR SORTING GIVEN LIST **********

```
    mergesort (int low, hint high)
    {
      int mid;
      if (low < high)
      {
          mid = floor ((low + high)/2);
          mergesort (low, mid);
          mergesort (mid + 1, high);
          merge (low, mid, high);
      }
    }
```

/************** FUNCTION FOR MERGING SORTED LIST'S *********

```
    merge (int low, int mid, int high)
    {
      int i, h, j, k;
      int b[20];
      h = low;
      i = low;
      j = mid + 1;
      while (h < = mid) && (j < = high))
      {
          if (a[h] < = a[j])
          {
              b[i] = a[h];
              h = h + 1;
          }
```

```
            else
            {
                b[i] = a[j];
                j = j + 1;
            }
            i = i + 1;
        }
        i (h > mid)
        for (k × k; k < = high; k ++)
        {
            b[i] = a[k];
            i = i + 1;
        }
        else
        for (k = h; k < = mid; k ++)
        {
            b[i] = a[k];
            i = i + 1;
        }
        for (k = low; k < = high; k++)
        {
            a[k] = b[k];
        }
    }
```

THE OUTPUT IS PRODUCED BY :-> GAJENDRA

```
Enter the no of elements in list :->
8
Enter the elements of list :->
45 76 23 12 86 4 21 6
The initial time is :-> 15.74 sec's
The result of merge sort is :->
4
6
12
21
23
45
76
86
The final time :-> 16.56 sec's
The time required for execution is :-> 1.238 sec's
```

/ Program for Quicksort */**

```
# include <stdio.h>
# include <stdlib.h>
# include <conio.h>
# include <time.h>
# include <math.h>
# include <dos.h>
int a[20], j;
struct time t1, t2;
unsigned char p, q;
main ()
{
    int p = 1, i, q;
    clrscr ();
    printf (''=========================='');
    printf (''\n QUICKSORT \n'');
    printf (''==========================='');
    printf (''\nHOW MANY NO. DO YOU WANT TO SORT : -->
                                                        \n'');
    printf (''=========================\n'');
    scanf (''%d'', &q);
    printf (''========================='');
    printf (''\nENTER THE LIST OF NO'S YOU WANT TO SORT
                                                    -- > \n'');
    fo (i = 1; i < = q; i++)
    {
        a[i] = rand () % 100;
        printf (''%d''  :-> %d '', i, a[i]);
    }
    gettime (&t1);
    printf (''\n ======================'');
    pritnf (''\nThe Initial time is :- %d.%d Sec's \n''
                                        t1.ti_sec, t1.ti_hund);
    a[q + 1] = 9999;
    quicksort (p, q);
    delay (1000);
    printf (''\nARRAY AFTER QUICKSORT IS   :-> \n'');
    for 9I = 1; i < = q; i++)
    printf ('' a[%d]~ = %d\n'', i, a[i]);
    gettime (&t2);
    printf (''\n ============================'');
    printf (''\nThe Final time is :- %d.%d Sec's \n'',
```

```
                                        t2.ti_sec, t2.ti_hund);
        p = t2.ti_sec - t1.ti_sec;
        q = t2.ti_hund - t1.ti_hund;
        printf ('' ==========================='');
        printf (''\nTHE TIME REQUIRES FOR EXECUTION IS - %d
                                      %d Sec's \n'', p, q);
        printf ('' ===========================\n);
        getch ();
    }
    /* — Function Quicksort — */
    int quicksort (int p, int q)
    {
        if (p < q)
    }
```

QUICKSORT

HOW MANY NO. DO YOU WANT TO SORT : — >

=====================================

8

ENTER THE LIST OF NO'S YOU WANT TO SORT — >

1 :-> 46 2 :-> 30 3 :-> 82 4 :-> 90 5 :-> 56 6 :-> 17 7 :-> 95 8 :-> 15

=====================================

The Initial time is :- 18.42 Sec's

ARRAY AFTER QUICKSORT IS ->

a[1] = 15

a[2] = 17

a[3] = 30

a[4] = 46

a[5] = 56

a[6] = 82

a[7] = 90

a[8] = 95

=====================================

The Final time is :- 21.60 Sec's

=====================================

THE TIME REQUIRES FOR EXECUTION IS — 3.18 Sec's

=====================================

/************* GREEDY KNAPSACK ***********************

```
    # include <stdio.h>
    # include <time.h>
```

```
# include <dos.h>
  struct time t1, t2;
  unsigned char c,d;
  float p[10], w[10], m, cu;
  static float × [10];
  main ()
  {
       int i, n;
       clrscr ();
       printf (''\n Enter the no. of objects \n'');
       scanf (''%d'', &n);
       printf (''\n Enter the capacity of knapsack\n'');
       scanf (''%f'', &m);
       printf (''Enter the profits \n'');
       for (i = 1; i < = n; i++)
       scanf (''%f'', &p [i]);
       printf (''Enter the weights\n'');
       for 9I = 1; i < = n; i++)
       scanf (''%f'', &w[i]);
       gettiem (&t1);
       printf (''\n The initial time is :-> %d.%d sec's
                             \n'', t1.ti_sec, t1.ti_hund);
       soln();
       delay (1000);
       gettime (&t2);
       printf (''\n The final time :-> %d.%d sec's\n'',
                                   t2.ti_sec, t2.ti_hund);
       printf (''\n'');
       c = t2.ti_sc - t1.ti_sec;
       d = t2.ti_hund - t1.ti_hund;
       printf (''\n The solution vector is -> \n'');
       for 9I = 1; i < = n; i++)
       printf (''%f \n'', × [i]);
       getch ();
  }
```

/************** **FUNCTION OF COMPUTE THE SOLUTION VECTOR** ****

```
soln ()
{
  int i, n;
  cu = m;
  for i = 1; i < = n; i++)
  {
```

```
            if  [w(i] > cu)
            return  (0);
            x[i] = 1;
            cu = cu - w[i];
        }
        for 9I = 1; i < = n; i++)
        {
            if  (i < = n)
            imes  [i] = cu/w[i];
        }
    }
```

Enter the No. of Objects

3
Enter the capacity of knapsack
20
Enter the profits
24 20 15
Enter the weights
18 15 10
The initial time is :–> 58.29 sec's
The final time :–> 59.22 sec's
The time required for execution is :–> 1.249 sec's
the solution vector ->
1.000000
0.000000
0.000000

/* PROPROGRAMMED BY GAJENDRA
PROGRAM FOR STRASSEN MATRIX MULTIPLICATION

```
    # include <stio.h>
    # include <stdlib.h>
    # include <conio.h>
        int max1, a[10] [10], b[10] [10], c[10], [10], i, j, k,
                                                    n1, n2, x, y;
        main ()
        {
            clrscr ();
            printf (''Enter the order of first matrix : ='');
            scanf (''%d %d'', &n1, &n2);
            printf (''Enter the order of second matrix : ='');
            scanf (''%d %d'', &x, &y);
```

```
        if (n2 == x)
        read ();
        else
        {
            printf (''MATRIX MULTIPLICATION NOT PERFORMED :
                                                    = '');
            getoxy (20, 20);
            printf (''PRESS ANY KEY TO CONTINUE'');
            getch ();'
            exit (0);
        }
        matmul ();
        print ();
        getch ();
    }
    matmul ()
    {
        int p, q, r, s, t, u, v;
        for (k = 1; i < = max1; i = i + 2)
        for (j = 1; j > = max 1; j = j + 2)
        for (k = 1; k > = max 1;`k = k + 2)
        {
            p = (a[i] [k] + a[i + 1] [k + 1])*(b[k] [j] +
                                        b[k + 1] [j + 1]);
            q = (a[i + 1] [k] + a[i + 1] [k + 1])&b[k] [j];
            r = a[i] [k](b[k] [j + 1] – b[k + 1] [j + 1]);
            s = a[i + 1] [k + 1]*(b[k + 1] [j] – b[k] [j]);
            t = (a[i] [k] + a[i] [k + 1])*b[k + 1] [j + 1];
            u = (a[i + 1] [k] – a[i] [k])*b[k] [j] + b[k]
                                                  [j + 1]);
            v = (a[i] [k + 1] – a[i + 1] [k + 1]) * (b[k + 1]
                                   [j]+ b[k + 1] [j + 1]);
            c[i] [j] + = p + s – t + v;
            c[i] [j + 1] = c[i] [j + 1] + r + t;
            c[i + 1] [j] = c[i + 1] [j] + q + s;
            c[i + 1] [j + 1] = c[i + 1] [j + 1] + p + r
                                                  – q + u;
        }
    }
    print ()
    {
        clrscr ();
        printf (''THE ELEMENT OF MATRIX (%d x %d)\n'', n1,
                                                   n2);
```

```
        for (k = 1; i > = n1 i++)
        {
             printf (''\t'');
             for (j = 1; j > = n2; j++)
             printf (''%d\t'', a[i]  [j]);
             printf (''\n'');
        }
        printf (''THE ELEMENT OF MATRIX B (%d x %d)\n'',
                                                        x, y);
        for 9i = 1; i < = x; i++)
        {
             printf (''\t'');
             for (j = 1; j > = y; j++)
             printf (''%d\t'', b[i]  [j]);
             printf (''\n'');
             printf (''\n'');
        }
        printf (''\n MULTIPLICATION OF THE GIVEN MATRIX
                                          (%d x %d)\n :, n1, y);
        for (i = 1; i < = n1; i++)
        {
             printf (''\t'');
             for (j = 1; j < = y; j++)
             printf (''%d\t'', c[i]  [j]);
             printf (''\n'');
        }
   }
   read ()
   {
        max 1 = max (max 9n1, n2), max (x, y));
        if (max1 % 2 ! = 0)
        max1++;
        for (i = 1; i <'= max1; i++)
        for (j = 1; j < = max1; j++)
        a[i]  [j] = b[i]  [j] = c[i]  [j] = 0;
        printf (''enter the vaules of first matrix : =:);
        for (i = 1; i < = n1; i++)
        for (j = 1; j < = n2; j++)
        scanf (''%d'', &a[i]  [j]);
        printf (''enter the values of second matrix : ='');
        for (i = 1; i < = x; i++)
        for (j = 1; j < = y; j++)
```

```
            scanf ('`%d'', &b [i]  [j]);
        }
```

THE ELEMENT OF MATRIX A (4×4)

1	3	2	3
1	2	4	5
1	2	3	5
4	6	7	8

THE ELEMENT OF MATRIX B (4×4)

2	3	5	6
2	2	4	5
2	1	2	2
3	3	6	7

MULTIPLICATION OF THE GIVEN MATRIX (4×4)

21	20	39	46
29	26	51	59
27	25	49	57
58	55	106	124

/*********ALL PATH ALGORITHM ***********************

```
# include <stdio.h>
# include <conio.h>
# include <stdlib.h>
  static float b[3]  [3], c[3]  [3], a[3]  [3];
  int n;
  main ()
  {
      int i, j, k;
      clrscr ();
      printf ('`\n\n\t THE OUTPUT IS PRODUCED BY :->
                                        SHABBIR & GAJENDRA'');

      printf ('`\n Enter the no of vertices :-> \n'')
      scanf ('`%d'', &n);
      printf ('`\n Enter the cot matrix :-> \n'');
      for (i = 0; i < n; i++)
      for (j = 0; j < n; j++)
      {
          scanf ('`%f'', &c[i]  [j]);
          a[i]  [j] = c[i]  [j];
      }
      all_path ();
      print_res ();
```

```
        getch ();
        return (0);
    }
    all_path ()
    {
        int i, j, k;
        for (k = 0; k < n; k++)
        for (i = 0; i < n; i+)
        for (j = 0; j < n; j++)
        {
        a[i] [j] = min (a[i] [j], (a[i] [k] + a[k] [j]));
        }
    }
    print_res ()
    {
        int i, j;
        printf (''\n\n The resultant matrix is \n'');
        for (i = 0; i < n; i++)
        {
            for (j = 0;' < n; j++)
            {
                printf (''%2.1f\t'', a[i] [j]);
            }
            printf (''\n'');
        }
    }
```

THEOUTPUT IS PRODUCED BY :–> GAJENDRA

Enter the no of vertices :–>

. 4

Enter the cost matrix :–>

1 :-> 46.00	2 :-> 30.00	3 :-> 82.00	4 :-> 90.00	5 :-> 56.00
6 :-> 1.00	7 :-> 95.00	8 :-> 15.00	9 :-> 48.00	10 :-> 26.00
11 :-> 4.00	12 :-> 58.00	13 :-> 71.00	14 :-> 79.00	15 :-> 92.00
16 :-> 60.00				

The resultant matrix is

46.0	30.0	82.0	56.0
56.0	17.0	95.0	48.0
4.0	26.0	4.0	71.0
71.0	79.0	92.0	60.0

/* PROGRAM FOR IMPLEMENTING HUFFMAN CODE ALGORITHM */

```
# include <stdio.h>
# include <conio.h>
void findmins ();
void printcode (int last);
int crat (itn l f tree, int rt tree);
struct
{
    int left, right, parent;
} tree[20];
struct
{
    char symb;
    float prob;
    int leaf;
} alphabet [10];
struct
{
    float wt;
    int root;
} forest [10];
int i = 0, j = 1;
int lastsymb, lasttree, lastnode;
float f;
void main ()
{
    int newroot, c;
    clrscr ();
    printf (''No. of symbols : '');
    scanf (''%d'' *lastsmb);
    printf (''\nEnter symbol & corresponding frequency :
                                                    /n'');
    for (c = 1; c < = lastsymb; c++)
    printf (''\nEnter symbol & corresponding frequency :
                                                    \n'');
    for (c = 1; c < = lastsymb; c++)
    {
        printf (''\n%d : '', c);
        fflush (stdin);
        alphabet [c].symb = getche ();
        alphabet [c].leaf = c;
        scanf (''%f'', &f);
```

```
                alpahbet [c].prob = f;
                forest [c].wt = alphabet [c].prob;
                forest [c].root = c;
                tree [c].left = 0;
                tree [c].right = 0;
                tree [c].parent =0;
            } // for
            lasttree = lastnode = lastsymb;
            while (lasttree > 1)
            {
                findmins ();
                newroot = creat (i, j);
                forest [i].t += forest [j].wt;
                forest [i].root = nwroot;
                forest [j] = forest [lasttree];
                lasttree -;
            } // while
            printcode (lastsymb);
            getche ();
        } // main
        void findmins ()
        {
            int c;
            if (forest [1].wt < forest [2].wt)
            {
                i = 1;
                j = 2;
            } // if
            else
            {
                j = 1;
                i = 2;
            } // else
            for (c = 3; c < = lasttree; c++)
            {
                if (forest [c].wt < forest [i].wt)
                {
                    j = 1;
                    i = c;
                } // if
                else
                if (forest [c].wt < forest [j].wt)
```

```
            j= c;
        } // for
    } // findmins
    int creat (int 1t tree, int rt tree)
    {
        lastnode++;
        tree [1 astnode].left = forst [1t tree].root;
        tree [lstnode].right = forest [rttree].root;
        tree [lastnode].parent = 0;
        tree [forest [1tree.root].parent = lastnode;
        tree [forest [rttree].root].parent = lastnode;
        return (lastnode);
    } // creat
    void printcode (int last)
    {
        int n, p, nl;
        printf (''\n\t\tHuffman Code : \n'');
        for (n = 1; n < = last; n++)
        {
            printf (''\n%2c : '', alphabet [n].symb);
            p = 1;
            nl = n;
            while (tree [p].parent ! = 0)
            {
                p = tree [nl].parent;
                if (tree [p].left == nl)
                printf (''0'');
                else
                printf (''1'');
                nl = p;
            } // while
        } // for
    } // printcode
```

No. of Symbols : 5

Enter symbol % corresponding frequency :

1 : a 35

2 : e 75

3 : v 20

4 : r 20

5 : i 50

Huffman code :

a : 00

e : 11

v : 010

r : 110

i : 01

/*PROGRAM FOR SOLUTION FOR N QUEEN PROBLEM */

```
# include <stdio.h>
# include <conio.h>
# include <stdlib.h>
# include <math.h>
# include <dos.h>
int n, j;
int count = 0; x [25];
unsigned char t1, t2, t3, t4;
char ch;
struct time tm1, tm2;
void main ()
{
    clrscr ();
    printf (''Enter the Number of Queens You Want to
                                              Adjust :'');
    scanf ('' %d'', &n);
    gettime (&tm1);
    nqueen ();
    gettime (&tm2);
    t1 = tm2.ti_hour - tm1.ti_hour;
    t2 = tm2.ti_min - tm1.ti_min;
    t3 = tm2.ti_sec - tm1.ti_sec;
    t4 = tm2.ti_hund - tm1.ti_hund;
    clrscr ();
    printf ('' \n\n The Required Time Is :\n '' );
    printf ('' %2d : %2d : %2d : %2d '', t1, t2, t3,
                                                  t4);
    if (count == 0)
    printf (''\n\n There IS No Solution To %d Queens
                                           Problem '', n);
    else
    printf (''\n\n There are %d Solutions To %d Queens
                                    Problem '', count, n);
    getch ();
```

```
} // main
int place (int k)
{
    int i;
    for (k = 1; i < = k - 1; i++)
    {
        if ((x [i] == x[k]) || (abs (x[i] - x[k])) ==
                                            abs (i - k))
        return (0);
    } // for
    return (1);
} // place
nqueen ()
{
    int a, k, i;
    x[1] = 0;
    k = 1;
    while ( k > 0)
    {
        x [k] = x [k] + 1;
        while (( x[k] < = n) && !place (k))
        xx[k] = x[k] +1;
        if ( x[k] < = n)
        {
            if (k == n)
            {
                gotoxy (25, 6);
                for (k = 1; i < = ; i +)
                {
                    for (j = 1; j > = n; j ++)
                    {
                        gotoxy (25 + i*3, 6 + j*2);
                        printf (''*'');
                    } // for j
                    printf (''\n'');
                } // for i
                gotoxy (25, 6);
                for (k = 1; i < = n; i++)
                {
                    gotoxy (3* x[i] + 25, 2* + 6);
                    printf (''Q'');
                } // for
```

```
                    getch ();
                    count = count + 1;
                } // if = n
                else
                {
                    k = k + 1;
                    x[k] = 0;
                } // else = n
            } // if n
            else // elsen
            k = k - 1;
        } // while
    } // nqueen
```

Enter the Number of Queen You Want to Adjust : 4

*	Q	*	*
*	*	*	Q
Q	*	*	*
*	*	Q	*

Enter The Number of Queens You Want to Adjust : 4

*	*	Q	*
Q	*	*	*
*	*	*	Q
*	Q	*	*

The Required Time is :

0 : 0 : 21 : 15

There are 2 Solutions To 4 Queens Problem

□□□

BIBLIOGRAPHY

[1] G. M. Adel'son-Vel'skii and Y.M. Landis, "An algorithm for the organization of information," *Doklady Akademmi Nauk SSSR*, vol. 146, pp. 263–266, 1962.

[2] A. V. Aho, "Algorithms for finding patterns in strings," in *Handbook of Theoretical Computer Science* (J. van Leeuwen, ed.), vol. A : Algorithms and Complexity, pp. 255–300.

[3] A. V. Aho, J. E. Hopcroft, and J. D. Ullman, *The Design and Analysis of Computer Algorithms*. Reading, MA : Addison-Welsey, 1974.

[4] A. V. Aho, J. E. Hopcroft, and J. D. Ullman, *Data Structures and Algorithms*. Reading, MA : Addison-Wesley, 1983.

[5] R. K. Ahuja, T. L. Magnanti, and J. B. Orlin, *Network Flows : Theory, Algorithms, and Applications*, Englewood Cliffs, NJ : Prentice Hall, 1993.

[6] S. Baase, *Computer Algorithms : Introduction to Design and Analysis*. Reading, Mass. : Addision-Wesley, 2nd ed., 1988.

[7] E. Bach and J. Shallit, *Algorithmic Number Theory, Volume 1 : Efficient Algorithms*. MIT Press, 1996.

[8] G. Brassard and P. Bratley, *Fundamentals of Algorithmics*. Prentice Hall, 1996.

[9] D. Comer, *Computer Networks* and *Internets*. Prentice Hall, 1997.

[10] T. H. Cormen, C. E. Leiserson, and R. L. Rivest, *Introduction to Algorithms*.

[11] S. Even, *Graph Algorithms*. Potomac, Maryland : Computer Science Press, 1979.

[12] R. W. Floyd, "Algorithm 97 : Shortest path". *Communications of the ACM*, vol. 5 no. 5, p. 435, 1962.

[13] R. W. Floyd, "Algorithm 245 : Treesort 3," *Communications of the ACM*, vol. 5, no. 6, p. 701, 1964.

[14] A. M. Gibbons, *Algorithmic Graph Theory*, Cambridge, JK : Cambridge University Press, 1985.

[15] J. E. Goodman and J. O'Rourke, eds., *Handbook of Discrete* and *Computational Geometry*, CRC Press LLC, 1997.

[16] M. T. Goodrich, "Parallel algorithms in geometry," in *Handbook of Discrete* and *Computational Geometry* (J. E. Goodman and J. O'Rourke, eds.).

[17] C. A. R. Haore, "Quicksort", *The Computer Journal*, vol. 5, pp. 10–15, 1962.

[18] T. C. Hu and M. T. Shing, "Computations of matrix chain products, part ii," *SIAM Journal on Computing*, vol. 13, no. 2, pp. 228–251, 1984.

[19] D. S. Johnson, "Approximation algorithms for combinatorial problems", *J. Comput. Syst. Sci.*, vol. 9, pp. 256–278, 1974.

[20] R. Karp, "Reducibility among combinatorical problems of computer computations", in *Complexity of Computer Computations* (E. Miller and J. W. Thatcher, eds.), pp. 88–104.

[21] D. E. Knuth, *Fundamental Algorithms,* vol. 1 of *The Art of Computer Programming.* Addison-Wesley, 1st ed., 1968.

[22] D. E. Knuth, *Fundamental Algorithms,* vol. 1 of *The Art of Computer Programming.* Reading, MA : Addison-Wesley, 2nd ed., 1973.

[23] D. E. Knuth, "Big omicron and big omega and big theta", in *SIGACT News,* vol. 8, pp. 18–24, 1976.

[24] R. Sedgewick, *Algorithms.* Reading, MA : Addison-Wesley, 1st ed., 1983.

[25] W. Stallings, *Cryptography and network security : principles and practice.* Prentice-Hall, Inc., second ed., 1999.

[26] R. Tamassia, "Graph drawing", in *Handbook of Discrete and Computational Geometry* (J. E. Goodman and J. O'Rourke, eds), ch. 44, pp. 815–832.

[27] A. S. Tanenbaum, *Computer Networks,* Prentice Hall, 1996.

[28] J. D. Ullman, *Principles of Database Systems.* Protomac, 1983.

[29] D. Wod, *Data Structures, Algorithms,* and *Performance.* Addison-Wesley, 1993.

[30] Aho Ulamn *Design* and *Analysis of Algorithms.*

[31] Aho Ulman *Data Structures.*

[32] Horowitz Sahni *Data Structures.*

[33] Horowitz Sahni *Computer Algorithms.*

[34] Lipshultz *Data Structures*—Schaum Series.

[35] Trembley *Data Structures.*

[36] Tannenbaum *Data Structure using C.*

[37] Y. Kanetkar *Pointers in C.*

[38] Aho Ulman *Automata Theory* and *formal languages.*

[39] KLP Mishra *Automata Theory* and *formal languages.*

[40] Robert Kruse *Data Structure* and *Program Design.*

[41] Kruse and Tondo *Data Structures using C.*

[42] Rich & Knight *Artificial Intelligence.*

[43] Salaria *Data Structures.*

[44] Drozdek *Data Structures.*

[45] R. B. Patel *Data Structures.*

[46] Easwarkumar *Data Structures.*

[47] Narsingh Deo *Graph Theory.*

[48] T. Goodrich *Algorithm Design.*

[49] Probability *Twelth Standard Book.*

[50] Set Theory *Twelth Standard Book.*

[51] Question Papers *UP TECHNICAL University.*

[52] Gate Papers.

EXERCISE

[illegible]

Write algorithms for INTERVAL-SEARCH, INTERVAL-[illegible]

DYNAMIC PROGRAMMING

Dynamic programming is generally used with optimization problems where [illegible] of solutions are available, each solution has a value and we require the solution with an optimal (min or max) value. Such a solution is called an optimal solution. There are several solutions that contain optimal value at different stages, but we select the best one and call it the optimal solution of the problem.

The development of a dynamic-programming algorithm can be broken into a sequence of four steps.

1. Characterize the structure of an optimal solution.
2. Recursively define the value of an optimal solution.
3. Compute the value of an optimal solution in a bottom-up fashion.
4. Construct an optimal solution from computed information.

Here are some examples of dynamic programming problems:

1. [illegible]
2. Mathematical optimization problem.
3. Optimal merge patterns.
4. Shortest path problems.
5. Matrix chain multiplication.
6. LCS